God for All

God for All

The Biblical Foundation of Universal Grace

ARCH B. TAYLOR JR.

RESOURCE *Publications* · Eugene, Oregon

GOD FOR ALL
The Biblical Foundation of Universal Grace

Copyright © 2013 Arch B. Taylor Jr. All rights reserved. Except for brief quotations in critical publications or reviews, no part of this book may be reproduced in any manner without prior written permission from the publisher. Write: Permissions, Wipf and Stock Publishers, 199 W. 8th Ave., Suite 3, Eugene, OR 97401.

Resource Publications
An Imprint of Wipf and Stock Publishers
199 W. 8th Ave., Suite 3
Eugene, OR 97401
www.wipfandstock.com

ISBN 13: 978-1-62032-939-9
Manufactured in the U.S.A.

Unless otherwise identified, all Scriptural references are from the New Revised Standard Version of the Bible, copyright © 1989, Division of Christian education of the National Council of Churches of Christ in the United States of America. Used by permission. All rights reserved.

To William, John, and Samuel
In memory of Margaret

Contents

List Abbreviations / xv

Introduction / 1
    1. Religions or God? / 2
    2. Competing aspects of God / 3
    3. The Christian Bible, Old and New Testaments / 6
    4. American Christianity / 7
    5. Summary of Contents / 8
        Part 1 The Universal Matrix, chapters 3–7 / 8
        Part 2 From Abraham to the Settlement of Canaan, chapters 8–13 / 9
        Part 3 The Monarchy from Beginning to End, chapters 14–16 / 10
        Part 4 From Exile to the Time of Jesus, chapters 19–21 / 10
        Part 5 Jesus of Nazareth, chapters 22–27 / 11
        Part 6 Paul, Apostle to the Gentiles, chapters 28–32 / 12
        Part 7 After Jesus and Paul, chapters 33–36 / 12

1   My Spiritual Pilgrimage / 15
    1. Benjamin B. Warfield / 15
    2. Catherine and Peter Marshall / 17
    3. The equality of women and men / 18
    4. The Bible's universal texts / 19
    5. My "Aha!" moment / 21

2   The Beginnings of Monotheism / 23
    1. Two worldviews / 23
    2. The polytheistic worldview of Enuma elish and Japanese Shinto / 24
    3. The monotheistic worldview of Genesis 1:1—2:4a / 26
    4. A minority view / 27
    Reflection / 29
    5. Note on the sources of the creation story / 29

Contents

Part One: The Universal Matrix

3 God and the Creation of Humanity / 33
    1. The Creator / 33
    2. The human creature / 35
    Summary and reflection / 36

4 The Creator and Humans in Relationship / 38
    1. YHWH God, the garden, and the first humans / 38
    2. Creatures defy the Creator / 41
    3. Out of the garden into the real world / 42
    Summary and reflection / 43

5 Biblical Creation, Evolution, and Brain Science / 44
    1. The age of the earth / 44
    2. Conservative Christians reject evolution / 45
    3. The human brain / 45
    4. Near-death experience / 46
    5. Recent brain research / 48
    Summary and reflection / 50

6 The Spread of Population and Sin / 53
    1. The spread of sin / 53
    2. The flood / 55
    3. The flood story in Genesis / 55
    4. God's post-flood purpose of grace / 57
    5. The ancestors of Israel / 60
    6. Comparison of three versions of the flood story / 60

7 The Covenant with Abram / 62
    1. Abram the stateless alien / 63
    2. Covenant in the ancient Near East / 64
    3. Abram's covenant with the Amorite brothers / 64
    4. God's covenant with Abram / 65
    5. Abram's son Ishmael / 67
    Summary and Reflection / 69

Part Two: Abraham to the Settlement of Canaan

8 Children of Abraham—Exclusion and Assimilation / 73
    1. A theme of unity / 74
    2. Evidence of diversity / 75
    3. A new name for Jacob and for his God / 77

   4. Jacob/Israel assimilates others / 79
   Summary / 81

9 **Moses, the Name, and the Exodus / 82**
   1. Moses and the Midianites / 82
   2. The origin of the Name / 83
   3. Moses and the Name / 84
   4. The meaning of the Name / 85
   5. YHWH the God of the Hebrews / 88
   6. The meeting at the mountain / 88
   Summary / 90

10 **Moses and the Sinai Covenant / 91**
   1. The divine appearance / 92
   2. The Decalogue / 94
     2a. The first word / 95
     2b. The second word / 96
     2c. The third word / 97
     2d. The fourth word / 97
       The second table of the Decalogue / 98
       The tenth word / 99
   3. Solemnizing the covenant / 99
   Summary / 100

11 **Covenant as Gift and Obligation / 101**
   1. The golden calf / 102
   2. Covenant as gift / 103
   3. Covenant as obligation / 106
   4. The specious covenant with Adam / 106
   Summary and reflection / 107

12 **From Sinai to Canaan / 109**
   1. Israel in the wilderness / 109
   2. Canaan in the Late Bronze Age / 111
   3. The Book of the Covenant as guide for the tribes / 112
   Summary / 116

13 **The Conquest and Settlement of Canaan / 117**
   1. The conquest by Joshua / 117
   2. In the days of the judges / 119
     2a. Gideon, Judges 6–9 / 120
     2b. Deborah, Judges 4–5 / 121
     2c. Jephthah, Judges 11 / 122

Contents

       3. Decline and degradation of tribal Israel, Judges 17–21 / 122
      Summary and reflection / 123

PART THREE: THE MONARCHY FROM BEGINNING TO END

14   Like Other Nations: David's Monarchy / 127
      1. The transition to monarchy / 127
      2. The kingdom established / 128
      3. David and his tribe of Judah / 130
      4. David solidifies the YHWH cult / 131
      5. David, temple, and dynasty / 133
      6. The mystique of David / 134

15   Like Other Nations: Solomon's Shadows / 137
      1. Solomon's wives / 137
      2. Solomon's temples / 138
      3. The kingdom resisted, divided, and plundered / 140
      4. The origin of the J material / 141
      Summary / 142
      Contact points among Genesis 2:4b—3:24, Ezekiel 28:1–19, and 1 Kings 3–11 / 143

16   The People of YHWH Like Other Nations / 145
      1. Nations made for war / 146
      2. The question: Where is YHWH? / 147
      3. David sets the standard / 150
      4. YHWH's concern for non-Israelites / 152
      Summary and reflection / 153

17   The Covenant as Family Relationship / 154
      1. Hosea lives the covenant / 155
      2. Jeremiah confirms Hosea's message / 158
      3. Ezekiel affirms God's total commitment / 160
      4. Isaiah confirms the restoration / 162
      Summary and reflection / 162

18   The Prophets and the End of the State / 164
      1. Amos and the extension of YHWH's sovereignty / 164
      2. The gap between rich and poor / 165
      3. YHWH rejects their cultic sacrifices / 166
      4. Prophets and the rejection of war / 167
      5. The new covenant / 172
      Summary and reflection / 173

Part Four: From Exile to the Time of Jesus

19 Exile: Re-imagining God and Humanity / 177
1. Ezekiel: YHWH's glory and judgment / 177
2. The prophet of the exile: re-imagining servanthood / 180
   - 2a. Israel, servant people / 181
   - 2b. Cyrus, servant emperor / 182
   - 2c. YHWH, servant deity / 183
3. The universal Elohim / 185
   - 3a. Humankind, the image of Elohim / 185
   - 3b. Elohim's universal covenant / 187

Summary / 188

20 Return, Rebuild, Retrench / 189
1. Temple and priesthood restored under Persian rule / 189
2. YHWH's partiality toward Israel / 193
3. Jews under Greek and Roman rule / 194

Summary / 199

21 Roman Palestine in the Time of Jesus / 200
1. Social and political conditions / 200
   - 1a. The successors of Herod / 200
   - 1b. Jewish opposition movements / 202
2. Cosmology and anthropology of the Mediterranean peoples / 203
   - 2a. The great chain of being / 203
   - 2b. Human beings / 204
3. The religious pattern based on altered states of consciousness (ASC) / 205
4. Note on shaman / 206

Part Five: Jesus of Nazareth

22 Introduction to Jesus and the Gospels / 209
1. The stories of Jesus / 210
2. Jesus the Jew / 211

23 The Call of Jesus / 214
1. John the Baptist / 214
2. The baptism of Jesus / 216
3. The temptations of Jesus / 218
   - 3a. The first temptation / 218
   - 3b. The second temptation / 219
   - 3c. The third temptation / 220

Summary / 221

Contents

24 Jesus's Ministry as Healer and Exorcist / 222
   1. Evaluating Jesus's acts of healing and exorcism / 223
   2. Jesus responds to criticism and questions / 228
   Summary / 229

25 Jesus and the Oneness of God / 231
   1. Affirming the goodness of the material world / 231
   2. Affirming human equality / 232
      2a. Women disciples / 233
      2b. Women and divorce / 235
   3. The true value of time: the sabbath controversies / 236
   4. The assault on the Temple: the hierarchy of space / 237

26 Jesus Challenges the Domination System / 241
   1. The Beatitudes / 242
   2. Other sayings from Q / 242
   3. Recovering the social context of Jesus's parables / 244
      3a. The Pharisee and the tax collector, Luke 18:9–14 / 244
      3b. The widow and the unjust judge, Luke 18:1–8 / 245
      3c. The parable of the talents, Matt 25.14–30; Luke 19:11–27 / 246
      3d. The laborers in the vineyard, Matt 20:1–16 / 247
      3e. Other parables briefly / 248
   4. Jesus and Nicodemus, John 2:23–3.12 / 249
   Summary and reflection / 250

27 Who Did Jesus Say That He Was? / 251
   1. The Messiah? / 251
   2. The Son of Man? / 252
   3. Why all this ambiguity? / 255
   4. To err is human, to forgive divine / 256
   Summary and reflection / 258

Part Six: Paul, Apostle to the Gentiles

28 In Quest of Saul/Paul / 263
   1. Pre-Christian Saul of Tarsus / 264
   2. The religious environment of Saul/Paul / 265

29 The Death of Saul and Birth of Paul / 268
   1. The deathly crisis of Saul / 268
   2. The appearance of Jesus to Saul / 270
   3. The birth of Paul / 272

30 Paul's New Understanding of God / 275
   1. Paul's ministry at Corinth / 276
   2. Christ crucified turns the world's power system upside down / 277
   3. The reign of Christ (Phil 2:5–11) / 280

31 Universal Grace in Romans / 282
   1. All are under the power of Sin / 283
   2. Justification for all who believe / 284
   3. Christ restores what Adam lost / 286
   4. God's mercy on all / 287
   Summary and reflection / 289

32 Paul and the Oneness of God / 291
   1. Forgiveness of sin / 291
   2. Desacralizing matter, time, and space / 292
      2a. Meat offered to idols / 292
      2b. Observing special days / 293
      2c. Holy space, God's true dwelling / 294
   3. Paul's egalitarianism / 296
      3a. Equality within the fellowship of believers / 296
      3b. Paul's co-workers / 297
      3c. Paul and women / 298
   Summary and reflection / 301

PART SEVEN: AFTER JESUS AND PAUL

33 The Jesus Movement's Breakout / 305
   1. Diversity and tension in the Jesus Movement in Jerusalem / 306
   2. Opposition, dispersion, and expansion / 307
   3. Questions of policy toward Gentiles / 310
   4. Paul's ongoing ministry / 312
   Summary and reflection / 313

34 Jesus of Nazareth in God's Plan / 315
   1. First Century Judaism not strictly monotheistic / 315
   2. Evidence from Hellenistic Jewish documents / 316
   3. Evidence from the New Testament / 317
   4 Jesus and the worship of God / 320
   5. The Nicene Creed / 321
   Summary and Reflection / 325

35 Humanity in God's Plan—1 / 327

1. Humanity, the image of God / 327
2. The human response to God / 328
3. Priests and prophets in Israel / 330
4. Prophets and priests in the NT / 332
5. Jesus as prophet, priest, and image of God / 333
6. The Constantinople Council proclaims the deity of Jesus / 334
7. The break with Judaism / 335

Reflection / 337

36 Humanity in God's Plan—2 / 338

1. The cosmic time frame / 338
2. The global scope of the Jesus way / 339
3. The Jesus way without Jesus / 342
4. An answer to war / 343
5. The universal golden rule / 344
6. Some grounds of hope / 345
   - 6a. Reduction of war and violence / 345
   - 6b. The International Criminal Court / 346
   - 6c Improvement in the status of women / 347
   - 6d. Brain science and mystical experience / 348

Summary and reflection / 349

Afterword / 351

Appendix A / 357
Appendix B / 360
Bibliography / 363
Scripture Index / 369
Author Index / 393

Abbreviations

ABD	*The Anchor Bible Dictionary,* 6 vols. Edited by David Noel Freedman. New York: Doubleday, 1992
BAR	*Biblical Archaeological Review*
HCSB	*The HarperCollins Study Bible*, New Revised Standard Version. Wayne A. Meeks et al. Editors, 1993
IDB	*Interpreter's Dictionary of the Bible.* George A. Buttrick, ed. Nashville: Abington, 1962
JBL	*Journal of Biblical Literature*
KJV	King James Version, or Authorized Version of the Bible in English, 1611
NIV	New International Version of the Old Testament and the New Testament
NRSV	New Revised Standard Version, Old Testament, New Testament, Apocrypha
NJPS	The New Jewish Publication Society English Translation of the Hebrew Bible, 1999
REB	*The Revised English Bible.* Oxford University Press, Cambridge University Press, 1989
TLOT	*Theological Lexicon of the Old Testament.* Ernst Jenni, Claus Westermann, eds., Mark E. Biddle translator. Peabody MA: Hendrickson, 1997

Introduction

ACCORDING TO A NATIONAL survey by a reputable polling foundation, "A majority of all American Christians (52 percent) think that at least some non-Christian faiths can lead to eternal life. Indeed, among Christians who believe many religions can lead to eternal life, 80 percent name at least one non-Christian faith that can do so.[1] The Survey asked respondents to answer in their own words, "How does one obtain eternal life?" The words in quotation marks appear in the survey's report of their answers:

- Thirty percent of Americans believe eternal life "is determined" by what one believes,
- twenty-nine percent say it "depends on" actions, and
- ten percent say "the key to obtaining eternal life" lies in both belief and actions.
- The remaining one-third say it's something else but they don't know what—some say they don't believe in eternal life anyhow, others that everyone or nearly everyone "achieves" eternal life.

This marks quite a change from the days of my youth in the 1930s. Then, I would say, the typical American Christian thought Christianity was the only true religion by which people could be saved, and among Christian denominations Catholics and Protestants might question whether their opposite numbers were really going to heaven, if not absolutely certain that they weren't. Perhaps I might offer myself as an example of a prejudiced Wasp, i.e., a White Anglo-Saxon Protestant.

I was born, baptized, and brought up in the Presbyterian Church in the United States (the old "Southern Presbyterian" or PCUS[2]). My church nurtured me in the faith of my forebears, but it assumed without question the culture of the South: one hundred percent segregated, white supremacist, male dominant and female subordinate. Southern Presbyterian theologians (who had defended slavery by means of Scripture) strenuously promoted the principle of "the spirituality of the church" to discourage any attempts to apply biblical faith to issues outside the realm of individual salvation. There was no question that Catholics and Jews were not going to heaven, to

---

1. http://pewforum.org/docs/?DocID=380 The Pew Forum on Religion and Public Life/Surveys, Dec 18, 2008.

2. At the outbreak of the Civil War the major Presbyterian Church in the United States split into "Southern" and "Northern" branches. In 1983 the two voted to reunite as the Presbyterian Church (USA).

say nothing of atheists and non-religious people, and adherents of all non-Christian religions.

During the summer after my junior year in high school, I attended a Synod Youth Conference at which I felt a deep call into the ministry. Later, while a student in seminary, I felt similarly moved to volunteer for foreign mission work. In college and seminary I began to work through some of my cultural prejudices, but my conviction concerning the exclusive superiority of Christianity and salvation through faith in Christ alone did not waver. I considered myself conservative with a high view of the inspiration and authority of Scripture. I was not trained in the critical historical approach to studying the Bible, but I certainly did not insist on the literal inerrancy of every word. In seminary, study of Hebrew and Greek, the languages underlying the English translations of the Bible, enabled me to get beyond the simplicity of my immature level of respect for the near absolute authority of Scripture, but I have never abandoned my conviction that I must have a sound biblical basis for whatever position I might take on any major issue.

The Presbyterian Church traces its theology to John Calvin, founder of Reformed Protestantism. A defining motto is *ecclesia reformata, semper reformanda*—church reformed, always to be reformed. We must never think that we have achieved the final word on any issue but must always keep minds and hearts open and prepared to examine new ideas critically and be willing to change when convinced on the grounds of Scripture and a reasonable understanding of reality.

My pilgrimage of faith, now in the ninth decade of my life, has been a steady liberation from presuppositions of my youth, one after another. Personal experience, the influence of significant people, and growing understanding of Scripture have worked a reforming change within me, step by step. I sympathize with those Christians whom the Pew survey numbers as acknowledging that our religion is not the only effective one. After a lifetime of studying and teaching the Bible in the United States and Japan, I have come to believe that the God revealed in Scripture and supremely in Jesus Christ is the Creator of all and the Savior of all.

1. RELIGIONS OR GOD?

As I read the Pew Trust Survey I can't help wondering about the depth of the change of attitude it reports as taking place in the hearts and minds of American Christians. Perhaps my questions stem from the way in which the survey phrased the questions or how the report presents the answers, but I get the unmistakable impression that "eternal life" is a goal that people "achieve" or "obtain" by their beliefs or deeds or both, and that the function of religion is to assist the individual to obtain eternal life. As for me, study and experience lead me to this conclusion: The God who has created us all is the God who by his own will and eternal purpose saves us all.

God far exceeds human comprehension and likewise all religions, which are inescapably finite since they are human enterprises. My struggle to trace the developing concept of the oneness of God in the Bible led me finally to the conviction that the totality of redemption for all humankind was a natural corollary of belief in the oneness of God, what we popularly call "monotheism."

Many people (some of whom I have known personally) have dropped out of the Church or have never been willing to affiliate with the Church precisely because they cannot accept the traditional exclusive Christian view that salvation depends on one's personal faith in Jesus Christ, and that all those, anywhere, who do not believe in Jesus are lost to eternal damnation. I should like to appeal to them by means of my book.

There may be other Christians who have been accustomed to an exclusive view, but who now feel some nagging doubts about it, yet hesitate to face the question. They might be happy to learn that they will not have denied authentic biblical faith if they sincerely and openly declare their own belief that God's reconciling grace embraces everybody. In addition there remains that large number, 48 percent or nearly one-half of Christians in America, who, according to the Pew report, still cling to the belief that Christianity (or perhaps their own *particular brand* of Christianity) is the only true religion and that there is no possibility of salvation or eternal life for anyone outside it. Therefore I am sharing my pilgrimage of faith, sustained by thorough biblical grounding, and I offer a more gracious understanding of God, not only Creator and Judge of all, but also Sustainer of all and ultimately Redeemer and Reconciler of all.

2. COMPETING ASPECTS OF GOD

As the closing sentence of the previous paragraph indicates, our natural, almost unthinking concept of God seems to comprise at least two aspects, God Almighty as righteous Judge of wrongdoers and Merciful Savior of sinners who seek forgiveness. Depending on time, cultural context, and characteristics of individual persons, these two aspects may be described in a variety of ways, but it's possible to see them as a sort of paradoxical contradiction, and there may be an inclination of human response to lay greater emphasis on one or the other of these aspects, but with a notable effort to elevate the aspect of divine mercy. In my study of Scripture and my observation of life, I think humankind seeks as far as possible to assure, somehow, that we receive the divine mercy while also appropriating the divine power to satisfy our own ends.

John B. Carman has described the way that not only Christianity but also Hinduism, Buddhism, Rabbinic Judaism, and Islam deal with the apparent dual aspects of God.[3] I'm not an expert on world religions, but I feel strongly that Carman is correct in demonstrating that they all exhibit this common feature: At the most primitive level, our human ancestors feared the forces of nature as mysterious, threatening

---

3. Carman, *Majesty & Meekness*.

powers. Only through a long evolutionary process have humans come to conceive of a God who shows mercy, but generally only toward the particular God's devotees. As nation-states emerged in history, rulers have tended to use religious faith to encourage national solidarity for self-defense and conquest, and to set boundaries to exclude others. Modern technology and ease of emigration and immigration of peoples make possible a closer contact and more intimate acquaintance with other people, cultures, and religious faiths. Undoubtedly this contributes to the fact that people increasingly embrace the concept of God whose mercy may be bestowed on those we formerly considered exotic foreigners and outsiders.

Carman got his start as a Christian missionary in a predominantly Hindu region of India. He explains how Hinduism, which is well known for the multiplicity of its gods and goddesses and its internal variations according to geographic and ethnic differences, has a particular concept of deity as such. Deity may display the conflicting roles of creator and destroyer not only by means of different deities for different characteristics, but also combined in one and the same deity. Within divinity one finds mercy and compassion toward the God's devotees but merciless destruction to all others. As a break-away from Hinduism, Buddhism that officially denies the existence of God can still, on the popular level, tolerate a panorama depicting the suffering of the damned in various levels of hell, while also praising Amida, the merciful one who achieved the right to enter Nirvana, or Paradise, but who chose to remain outside and to exercise that virtue to save any sinner who simply called on his Name in faithful surrender.

I vividly remember my first encounter at a young age with Hinduism's depiction of Kali or Siva in the role of destroyer, wearing a necklace of skulls and trampling on bloody corpses. Imagine my shock when later I encountered in my Bible these words of the LORD:

> See now that I, even I, am he; there is no god besides me. I kill and I make alive; I wound and I heal; and no one can deliver from my hand. For I lift up my hand to heaven, and swear: As I live forever, when I whet my flashing sword, and my hand takes hold on judgment; I will take vengeance on my adversaries, and will repay those who hate me. I will make my arrows drunk with blood, and my sword shall devour flesh—with the blood of the slain and the captives, from the long-haired enemy. (Deuteronomy 32:39-42 KJV)

If the Old Testament had not forbidden the making of images, it's possible we might have seen the LORD portrayed like Kali/Siva, acting in this blood-curdling manner. In the context of this declaration the LORD takes vengeance on his enemies and on behalf of his own people, the people of Israel. Such favoritism is characteristic in other religions as well, as Carman describes them—utmost mercy and compassion on the deity's own adherents, but merciless destruction of enemies.

Introduction

"Fear of God" and "fear of the LORD" are common expressions in the Bible to designate the proper human attitude toward deity. Over time it came to have a great variety of nuances, but it originated in the human reaction of terror in response to thunderstorm or earthquake, as we see reflected in the account of the LORD's descent on Mount Sinai: "When all the people witnessed the thunder and lightning, the sound of the trumpet, and the mountain smoking, they were afraid and trembled and stood at a distance" (Exod 20:18). Fear of punishment was used to compel Israelites to obey God's commands, and their faithful obedience and loyalty was called "fear of the LORD." Eventually the fear of the LORD was understood principally as the worship of the LORD with particular attention to the concept of faithfulness to him as the covenant God.[4] Thus the people of God could expect divine protection, to fear neither human enemies nor the forces of nature considered to be at least semi-divine—"The sun shall not strike you by day, nor the moon by night" (Ps 121:6; the English words "lunacy" and "lunatic" still reflect the belief that the moon projected evil influence). A quick computer check of the NRSV strings "do not be afraid" and "do not fear" shows a total of seventy-eight examples of divine reassurance given to humans.

There are preachers and television evangelists who routinely play on the fears of hearers by describing in vivid terms the wrath of God. I heard a preacher once use the story of the priest Eli and his two venal sons who ignored God's warnings to amend their ways. The sons accompanied the ark to battle, where the Philistines captured the ark and killed the sons. When aged Eli heard of it he fell backward off his bench and died, as did his pregnant daughter-in-law who gave birth when she heard of her husband's death (1 Sam 4:10–22). *Four funerals in one family!* shouted the preacher. *Our God really knows how to punish!* Without doubt other Bible stories are susceptible of a similar use to scare people out of hell or "to scare the hell out of" people.

Early in the second century CE one Marcion, a native of Sinope in Pontus of Asia Minor, proposed a radical break with Judaism, its Scripture, and its deity, a God of wrath whom he denied could possibly be the Father of Jesus. Marcion greatly reduced the Gospel story of Jesus and emphasized his own revision of Paul's writings. Marcion established a faith community that for nearly two centuries challenged growing catholic Christianity and forced the church councils to determine a Christian canon to include the Old Testament and a New Testament comprising the four Gospels, a longer list of Paul's epistles, and other writings including Revelation.[5] In rejecting Marcion, the Christian Fathers acknowledged polarity in both Testaments. The Roman Emperor Constantine imposed authority not only in producing the Nicene Creed but also in determining the NT Canon.[6] Constantine and his successors exploited Christianity as

---

4. Stähli, *TLOT* II, 575.

5. Clabeaux, "Marcion," *ABD*. The only available material presenting Marcion's teachings is scattered in the writings of his opponents.

6. Rubenstein, *When Jesus Became God*, and Dungan, *Constantine's Bible*.

a tool of imperial policy, broadly adopted thereafter by other nationalist/imperialist regimes, West and East, down to the modern era.

And so I cannot deny that there is textual support for those who wish to portray the God of the Bible as righteous judge of sinners, especially condemning those that do not believe in Jesus as Savior, and showing mercy to those who humbly and penitently seek his forgiveness and faithfully obey him. I have shared some of my draft material with a fundamentalist acquaintance, and for each of my assertions of God's mercy he can riposte with a text of judgment. Clearly, people can treat the Bible as an armory, from which debaters on either side choose texts to hurl against their opponents.

My early upbringing and religious education included the biblical theme that depicted God as judge of the whole sinful human race, and Jesus as the Savior of those who put their trust in him. If one reads the Bible only with those presuppositions, one can find plenty of "ammunition" to defend such a position. My purpose is to tell my own story, how my study of the Bible and interaction with my teachers and with students began to open my eyes to other texts that spoke of God's mercy as triumphing over judgment. My experiences of the realities of human life in the United States, my career as Bible teacher in Japan, as visitor in other foreign countries, such as Taiwan, Korea, China, Pakistan, Nicaragua, and Palestine, and as informed observer of world affairs, have contributed to my understanding and interpretation of Scripture as I present it here. Other strong influences on my mindset and worldview as well as on my interpretation of Scripture are my understanding of evolution and the structure and functioning of the human brain. In the course of this book I shall describe how this knowledge contributes to my belief that God saves all. Certainly there is in the Bible the aspect of God as merciful and compassionate, and I am convinced God bestows compassion on all. While fully acknowledging what Carman calls the Majesty of God, I intend to give proper emphasis to the divine Meekness.

3. THE CHRISTIAN BIBLE, OLD AND NEW TESTAMENTS

Marcion's ancient view that the Old Testament presents a God of judgment and punishment, while the New Testament presents a God of mercy and salvation persists in the minds of many people, but it is dangerously misinformed. The Jesus of the New Testament is certainly the merciful Savior, but his cultural upbringing and worldview were firmly based on teachings of the Hebrew Bible, contents of which, translated into Greek and in a somewhat different order, were later adopted as the Old Testament of the Christians. Within the teachings of Jesus and the New Testament interpretations of his life, ministry, and death we also find the theme of judgment, but the themes of mercy and salvation so prominent in the New Testament find their root in the Old Testament and provide the abundant fruit that has matured and blossomed from that root. Thus the New Testament gives credibility to themes of grace that I present in my chapters on the Old Testament.

In my family upbringing we read the Bible daily, and the unquestioned assumption was that God was its author. Even in seminary in the nineteen forties we never studied the origins of the Bible—by what process were these books collected and joined together to form a single book considered to be the authoritative "word of God"? With a similar background it is easy for fundamentalists to think that the Bible is a special gift, handed down by God from heaven as a finished product. My Bible has been that of the Protestant branch of Christianity, but the Roman Catholics consider authoritative a larger collection of documents, and the Eastern Orthodox yet a different set. Historical and scientific knowledge indicates that the Bible developed over time (an evolutionary process) written by human beings reflecting on their experience of God in particular situations. Others of a later generation, who received those traditions, adapted them to the changed conditions that they faced and added their understanding of how God was at work in them and in their world. At still later times, influenced by political and ethnic conditions as well as controversies over religious issues, high-level consultative bodies determined which documents should be considered authoritative for their particular branch of the church.

This all presupposes that God is, and that humans can receive inspiration from God, can respond to God, and can share their experiences of God by means of written records. Recent scientific research and reporting on the evolutionary development of the human brain and its functioning not only in daily existence but also in spiritual and mystical experience, has produced at least a degree of scientific acknowledgement that the human brain is so constituted as to communicate with the Transcendent Reality that many people call God. I shall refer to all this in detail as occasion arises in the writing of this book.

4. AMERICAN CHRISTIANITY

A blend of Enlightenment rationalism and a particular Western European type of Protestant Christianity had a profound influence on the writing of the Declaration of Independence and the Constitution of the United States of America. There is a vocal minority who claim that America was founded as a Christian nation, and they would like to promote their interpretation of Christian faith as the official religion of the nation. These assumptions and ambitions are based on a mistaken reading of history and the documents themselves. One biblical theme that becomes clear in my presentation is the ultimate failure of the Israelite kingdoms that were inextricably wedded to a particular religious faith. Religion in the service of a nation (or vice versa) is bound to corrupt both.

The United States today is home to the greatest diversity of religions of any nation in the world. Already it is obvious that people of different religions in the lands of their origin find it possible to live here without their religion automatically drawing them into conflict that plagued them at home and may have motivated them to emigrate. Interfaith meetings and joint action programs are increasing in number, especially among students at colleges and universities. They promote not only personal acquaintance and mutual understanding, but also cooperative works that accomplish positive good.

The United States still suffers the malign effects of the attack on the World Trade Center on September 11, 2001. Many U.S. citizens now take a negatively suspicious attitude toward Muslims, whether citizens or visitors or residents of other countries. The attack also spurred attempts of people of good will on both sides to make special efforts at interaction and greater mutual understanding. My book can provide Christian participants in such meetings not only a biblical foundation for understanding our own faith, but also a confidence that they can meet on non-controversial terms with people of other faiths, with hearts and minds open to mutual understanding and to cooperation in the effort to build a national and world society where we can embrace religious diversity in a common life, under the One God who transcends all.

Recently several Christian authors much more conservative than I have published books promoting the theme of universal salvation. This is an encouraging sign, and it confirms the findings of the Pew Trust Survey with which I began this introduction. In Appendix 2 of my book I have listed some of these books with a brief review and summary of their contents.

My approach is different. My personal pilgrimage began precisely with the opening words of the Bible that place the focus on God, where it properly belongs. The Sovereign Creator takes special care in the creation of humanity, equips us with rich gifts and takes us into a partnership that is still in force. Jesus of Nazareth, the Man acknowledged as God's son, is the New Human Being who represents us all and enables us to fulfill our God-given partnership. This is the theme I trace through the Christian Scripture. My approach is different from the authors with whom I am familiar. My contribution is a thorough biblical exposition of God for all.

Following this Introduction the first two chapters offer a fuller narrative of the personal spiritual pilgrimage that led me to believe that God's plan of salvation embraces every human being, and a comparison between the monotheistic and polytheistic worldviews. The rest of the book is divided into seven parts as follows:

SUMMARY OF CONTENTS

Part 1 The Universal Matrix, chapters 3–7

The Christian Old Testament, like the Hebrew Bible, tells the story of God's relation with the world, viewed through the lens of God's special relation with Israel. But before concentrating on that special relationship, the first sixteen chapters of Genesis describe God's creation of the world and relation with humanity in universal terms. Humanity, undifferentiated except as male and female, is in one sense the crown of creation, made in the image of God, appointed as God's co-regents to represent God toward the rest of creation. The first humans' disobedience and selfish ambition to exploit the divine gift infected all humanity and excited divine retribution. God's punishment by a flood was nearly universal. God saved Noah, his family, and representative animals to repopulate the earth. Even though punishment effected no change in sinful human character, God made a universal covenant never to destroy the earth again by flood. God did not cancel the human role as divine agents, but determined on a plan of reconciliation.

God called and blessed Abram and promised to make him a blessing for all the families of the earth. God promised to multiply Abram's descendants even though he was childless. Abram responded in trust to God, who then made a covenant to relate to Abram as Divine Kinsman in a fictive family relationship. In that state Abram, through Hagar, slave girl of his wife Sarai, became the father of Ishmael, progenitor of an innumerable offspring. Here is the limit of what I call the Universal Matrix, the total context *within which* God later narrowed the scope of the covenant with Abram, now called Abraham. Chapters 3 through 7 of this book explicate the Universal Matrix, the basis on which I develop my theme that the one God of Creation and Reconciliation is God for All. Evolution and the science of the human brain support the universality of the Bible's message.

Part 2: From Abraham to the Settlement of Canaan, chapters 8–13

From Genesis 17 the Bible story concentrates on Abraham, Sarah, and their son Isaac as God's covenant partners. This "family story" omits Abraham's son Ishmael by Hagar, six sons by Keturah, and even Isaac's elder son Esau, ancestor of the Edomites, in favor of younger son Jacob. The Bible presents Jacob's sons as ancestors of "the twelve tribes of Israel," shorthand for the special people of God who dominate the rest of the Old Testament.

The family went to Egypt to escape famine, where they later became state slaves. Through Moses God revealed the name YHWH and delivered his people in the exodus. Moses mediated YHWH's covenant with the twelve tribes at Sinai and renewed it after forty years in the wilderness. Joshua led the conquest of Canaan and its apportionment to the twelve tribes.

One receives the impression that this is one people descended from Abraham, related by covenant to the God YHWH. In fact, many other nations sprang from Abraham, and "Israel" actually comprised diverse elements gradually added by assimilation or conquest. Biblical evidence supports the conclusion that the "family story" was devised later, spurred by the need for unity in a small new kingdom facing threats both internal and external. I note the idealistic character of this "family story," but I supplement it by biblical and extrabiblical material to give a realistic picture of tribal Israel before the establishment of that new kingdom.

The book of Judges depicts tribal Israel realistically, comprising diverse groups with syncretistic religious tendencies, lacking political unity, and succumbing to the chaos resulting from excess practice of individual freedom that seemed to call for the authority of a king.

Part 3: The Monarchy from Beginning to End, chapters 14–18

The Israelite monarchy was established around 1050 and survived until 587-6 BCE. The first king Saul never united all the tribes, and his death in battle left the future bleak. David united his tribe of Judah and became their king. The ineptitude of Saul's successors led Israel to make David their king, so he ruled a Federated Kingdom. As a military and organizational genius, David achieved a degree of security and unity and made YHWH the national God. Solomon completed transforming the people of YHWH into a state like other nations by building temples for YHWH and for many foreign wives. His failure to maintain the fragile unity forged by David led in 922 BCE to division of the kingdom into northern Israel and southern Judah.

The two kingdoms kept YHWH faith by different traditions and practices, and they often fought each other disastrously. Still, YHWH treated both as "my people" but also showed mercy to people of other nations. The Bible favors Judah because of David's successes and the Jerusalem Temple where YHWH dwelt. Northern Israel was more vulnerable to international conflicts and fell to Assyria in 721 BCE. Southern Judah was left exposed, and zealous YHWH-only kings doggedly resisted the empires until Babylonia destroyed Judah in 587 BCE.

The Deuteronomistic History is ambivalent about monarchy: YHWH approved it in principle and in the choice of Saul, yet rejected Saul for David. David installed YHWH as Israel's God and extended YHWH's authority to neighboring states, so YHWH overlooked his human failings. Prophets in both kingdoms showed more concern for justice and human rights than for national ambitions, force of arms, and lavish cult. Prophets attributed the kingdoms' fall to egregious injustice, alliances with other nations, and trust in war rather than in YHWH. The prophets promised YHWH would preserve the people even after their deserved punishment.

Part 4: From Exile to the Time of Jesus, chapters 19–21

Destruction of the kingdoms was a tragedy for the people of YHWH, but in hindsight that was not all bad. Monarchy had corrupted the people of YHWH by making them like other nations. Without a state, Israelite people were still objects of divine grace with a role to play to bring blessing to all the nations. In captivity scribes reflected on YHWH's mercies, and much of the Bible from Genesis through Kings shows influence of that introspection, including the Universal Matrix, even though the family story of twelve-tribe Israel predominates from Genesis 17 on.

Introduction

Under Persia's relatively benign rule, Jews returned from Babylon to Judea. The Persian court subsidized building and maintaining the Second Temple. Rebuffing aid from survivors of both former kingdoms still living in Samaria, the dominant returnees excluded foreigners and discriminated against Samaritans, whom they considered illegitimate due to policies of Assyria. Some prophetic texts present a more inclusive point of view that influenced Jesus among others.

After Alexander the Great died, many Jews remained in Babylon under Seleucid rule and other Jews settled in Egypt under the Ptolemies. A Seleucid king Antiochus IV persecuted Jews in Palestine. The Hasmonean priestly family (nicknamed Maccabees) led guerrilla forces successfully against the Seleucids. Rome expanding eastward enabled the Jews to declare a client kingdom like other nations that lasted about a century, but this Jewish kingdom self-destructed in corruption. Rome took control and appointed the Idumean (Edomite) Herod as King of the Jews. He and his successors faced constant resistance.

The elite priestly class centered on the Temple remained subservient to whichever power controlled civil and military authority. They not only abetted the Roman power in exploiting the Jews but also added the burden of tithes and Temple taxes on the poor of the land.

Part 5: Jesus of Nazareth, chapters 22–27

Jesus was born in the waning years of Herod the Great and grew up in Galilee under Herodian royal successors and the Roman Procurator Pilate who ruled Jerusalem and Judea.

As a devout Jew, Jesus responded to the prophet John the Baptizer. When John baptized Jesus he heard a call as God's son with spiritual empowerment. Jesus used this power for others instead of personal advantage. After Herod imprisoned John, Jesus began proclaiming God's reign now as relief for the oppressed, healing the sick, exorcising demons, and forgiving sins. From among his followers Jesus chose a few as assistants later called apostles. Lists of names differ, but they are called "the twelve," implying a new manifestation of the people of God.

The disciples shared the hope of a Messiah (an anointed king like David) to gain national independence. Jesus was consistently nonviolent. He rejected a power-based messiahship and predicted tragic consequences for any who wanted war. Religious leaders objected to Jesus's fellowship with unclean sinners and forgiving sins apart from Temple cult and scribal authority.

Jesus called himself "son of man," ostensibly self-effacing, but it implied a claim to be an apocalyptic figure in Daniel who was to rule a universal kingship for the people of God. Jesus foretold the death of the son of man, to be followed by resurrection.

Opposition solidified when Jesus condemned the religious powers and predicted the end of the Temple in prophetic terms. Jewish authorities accused Jesus as pretender to kingship of the Jews, and Pilate was willing to crucify him on those terms. The disciples, grief-stricken by Jesus's death and fearing a similar fate, were surprised and emboldened by appearances of the risen Christ. They henceforth proclaimed him publicly as the Messiah who was meant to suffer, but whom God had raised, and whose early return in power they anticipated.

Part 6: Paul, Apostle to the Gentiles, chapters 28–32

The pre-Christian Pharisee Paul zealously persecuted the followers of the Jesus Way, though he hadn't known Jesus or the prominent disciples personally. A later account *about* Paul tells that he was downed by a blinding light and heard a voice from heaven that stopped his attempt to arrest believers in Damascus. Paul wrote that God revealed to him the resurrected Jesus, who appointed him apostle to the Gentiles.

I believe Paul had a near-death experience that overcame his objection to a suffering Messiah and his prejudice against Gentiles. Apart from Jerusalem church leaders, Paul itinerated in Greco-Roman cities proclaiming the crucified Jesus Christ as Lord—in the sense of YHWH for Jews and Caesar for Roman subjects. He did works of healing, exorcism, and tongue speaking. Before the Gospels were written, Paul wrote letters to guide and to respond to questions from churches he established.

Jesus Christ crucified reverses worldly ideas of power. In a display of meekness without imposing power, God works within by Christ's self-giving for sinners, reconciling their enmity and fear of God. All that humanity lost because of Adam, God abundantly restored in Christ.

Convinced of the oneness of God, Paul desacralized matter, time, and space. God is creator of all, all is sacred, and God treats all humans impartially. Adoption, covenants, and Messiah, God's gifts to Israel, were meant for all humanity, to fulfill God's promise to Abraham. Paul envisioned Gentiles integrated into the people of God without becoming Jews, and he expected Christ's early return to accomplish that goal. In spite of many problems and continued questions regarding relations between Paul and the original Jesus movement, he remains the chief individual human through whom the Jesus movement became a great worldwide faith.

Part 7: After Jesus and Paul, chapters 33–36

The late book of Acts, sequel to the Gospel of Luke, tells how the Jesus Way spread from Jerusalem to Rome. Peter led in welcoming Gentiles, but he would segregate Jewish and Gentile believers. Paul had established many congregations of Jews and Gentiles, and in his letters, all written before the Gospels, Paul opposed attempts to Judaize or segregate Gentile believers.

Jews exalted the Most High Father of creation as supreme, but also venerated "lesser gods" appointed to act for the High God toward creation. Philo, a Jewish philosopher contemporary with Paul, wrote of figures, such as Wisdom and the Word (Logos) that assisted in creating and maintaining the world. Christians tended to see Jesus in such terms but never proposed to offer him sacrifice, which Jews and Christians offered only to the High God.

Jesus knew himself Son of God and Son of Man, special, yet subordinate to God the Father. The Temple's destruction in 70 CE left no material means to distinguish the ranks of Father and Son by sacrifice. As the church spread in the Roman Empire, one party, assisted by emperors, declared that the Son was of equal substance and being as the Father, along with the Holy Spirit, comprising the Trinity.

The NT highly esteems Jesus, but stops short of making him equal with God. One may honor Jesus as the model of what God intended in creating humanity in the divine image and making humanity his sovereign emblem and co-regent. In this book I have tried to show that God saves everyone and that all people, as human, have a place in God's plan. Those of us who agree on these points are liberated and empowered to share that good news everywhere and to work tirelessly to effect the Jesus Way of compassion and peace. We can meet people of other religions or none at all, without fear or prejudice and welcome and celebrate all the good that any people may accomplish toward God's purpose of total reconciliation.

I offer my personal witness to the One God who created us all, who loves us all, and who reconciles us all. I pray that my presentation will prove persuasive to those who read it and help us all to be reconciled.

1

My Spiritual Pilgrimage

I WAS AMONG THE more conservative students at seminary, for my family upbringing and Southern Presbyterian origins naturally inclined me in that direction. If I had been presented with the idea that salvation was possible outside the Christian faith at that early time I would have dismissed it at once. Not until I was about to close my career as a missionary in Japan and return home for retirement did I finally admit to myself that I had, really, reached the point at which I could no longer equivocate; I had to speak openly of my belief that for me the God revealed in Scripture and supremely in Jesus Christ was the Savior of all people. As I expressed it to myself, finally I "came out of the closet" on that question. Yet as I reflected on my life and experience, I could identify certain people and events that left a deep impression on me even from early days that finally bore fruit in my change of mind.

1. BENJAMIN B. WARFIELD

At Louisville Presbyterian Theological Seminary in 1942 to 1945 I came under influence from my teacher of church history and apologetics, Dr. Andrew K. Rule. Dr. Rule had come to the U.S. from his native New Zealand to study with Dr. Benjamin B. Warfield of Princeton Seminary. Under Dr. Rule's guidance I purchased and read nearly all of Warfield's writings. Yet the first and most impressive was the little book, *The Plan of Salvation*.[1] Through the years I read the book several times, writing comments in the margin. As I reflect on my spiritual pilgrimage, I credit Warfield with giving me a good start, by means of *The Plan of Salvation*.

From the Reformed theological position stemming from John Calvin, Warfield placed utmost emphasis upon the sovereignty and initiative of God, rather than upon anything that humans can do to gain salvation. Starting from the assumption that all humans are lost sinners, Warfield explained his view of how God goes about saving them. Warfield says God deals with humans as individuals, what he calls "particular

---

1. Warfield, *The Plan of Salvation*.

evangelicalism." He notes that there are some theologians who teach that humans must contribute something to their own salvation—that although God *desires* the salvation of all, and Christ died for the sins of *all*, each one must respond to God's offer of salvation by accepting it, by believing the message, by confessing sin, and requesting forgiveness. If a person refuses to respond in this way, he or she can, in effect, frustrate God's *desire*. On the other hand, if the person does respond positively, that act of response is what effectively accomplishes salvation, for without it the person would not have been saved. Warfield brands this doctrine "autosoterism"—saving one's self. He dismisses it as an affront to the sovereignty of God.

According to Warfield, righteousness is the defining characteristic of the divine nature, and the righteousness of God determines salvation or damnation. Only by God's righteous decree can anyone be saved, and since it is obvious (he wrote) that not everybody is saved, it must be because they were not included in God's decree. In short, God really and truly predestines some to be saved and some to be lost. No matter how urgently people, such as Warfield and my professor Dr. Rule, stressed the goodness and love of God and expressed this "double predestination" in as moderate terms as possible, I could not escape the sense of revulsion most people feel at hearing it.

Warfield was only expounding a section of the Westminster Confession of Faith (WCF), a foundational statement of Christian doctrine held by major Presbyterian churches. WCF Chapter III "Of God's Eternal Decrees" speaks of those who "are predestinated unto eternal life and others foreordained to everlasting death." God's dealing with the latter is described in WCF Chapter V paragraph 6 "Of Providence" in part as follows:

> As for those wicked and ungodly men whom God, as a righteous judge, for former sins, doth blind and harden, from them he not only withholdeth his grace, whereby they might have been enlightened in their understandings, and wrought upon in their hearts; ... whereby it cometh to pass that they harden themselves, even under those means which God useth for the softening of others.[2]

In 1903 the General Assembly of the Presbyterian Church (USA)—"Northern"—aiming to ease the consciences of those repelled by this and other similar statements, approved a Declarative Statement that included the following:

> ... concerning those who perish, the doctrine of God's eternal decree is held in harmony with the doctrine that God desires not the death of any sinner, but has provided in Christ a salvation sufficient for all, adapted to all, and freely offered in the gospel to all; that men are fully responsible for their treatment of

---

2. *The Constitution of the Presbyterian Church (USA) Part I Book of Confessions* Assembly) §6.029 p 127.

God's gracious offer; that his decree hinders no man from accepting that offer; and that no man is condemned except on the ground of his sin.[3]

The Declarative Statement allows Presbyterians to be what Warfield called "autosoterists" with a clear conscience and without honestly acknowledging any "affront" to God. In my day the church never made it an issue in ordination, and I was happy not to have to face the question myself. But I could never evade the nagging of those texts that spoke in terms of God's love for the *world*, God's concern for *all*. The first time I read Warfield's book, on a page where he discussed this question of God's righteous decrees I wrote: "Double predestination and universalism can both be supported by scriptural texts. Each position expresses one of the opposite *logical* extremes of supernatural evangelicalism. I reject both as extremes."

Concerning universal salvation, Warfield wrote, "There is no reason why a Calvinist might not be a universalist in the most express meaning of that term, holding that each and every human soul shall be saved; and in point of fact some Calvinists (forgetful of Scripture here) have been universalists in this most express meaning of the term."[4] Resting strongly on these words of Warfield, I join the ranks of those Calvinists who have become universalists. I have done so, not as Warfield would charge by being "forgetful of Scripture," but precisely because I take seriously the universal texts within Scripture itself.

2. CATHERINE AND PETER MARSHALL

During my second and third years in seminary I served as student pastor of the Presbyterian Church in Charlestown, Indiana. The women of the church asked me to lead a study of Ephesians based on a guide titled *The Mystery of the Ages* by Catherine and Peter Marshall. Recalling that experience, I can't be sure how much the women learned, but I received a deep impression of the scope of God's eternal purpose as I followed the Marshalls' leading.

In their introduction, the authors alluded to the ongoing World War Two. They proposed that Ephesians could guide Christians as we anticipated reconstructing world order when peace again prevailed. They offered Ephesians 1:10 as the key to God's purpose to which we Christians should devote ourselves: "That in the dispensation of the fullness of times [God] might gather together in one all things in Christ, both which are in heaven, and which are on earth, even in him" (King James Version). The Marshalls gave three lines of evidence to support this view that God would eventually overcome all divisions by gathering together all things and people in Christ.

1. Death is the greatest force dividing people. God has overcome death by his "mighty power, which he wrought in Christ, when he raised him from the dead"

---

3. *The Book of Confessions* §6.192 p 164.
4. Warfield, *Plan*, 98.

(Ephesians 1:20 KJV). Resurrection, then, is the first ground of the ultimate unity of all things in Christ.

2. Sin is the next divisive power, which separates us from God. By the forgiveness of sins through Christ, God has brought us to new life and reconciliation with God (Ephesians 2:1–10).

3. Divisions among people, most poignantly demonstrated by division between Jews and Gentiles, has been overcome by the cross of Christ, who broke down the wall of partition and made "one new humanity" (Ephesians 2:11–22).

In my sense of call to mission service and my early years in Japan, I followed the Marshalls' concept that this unity of humankind would be accomplished "through the Church"—eventually by God's plan all people would become Christians. I shared the Marshalls' supersessionist view, that God rejected the Jews and that Christians had superseded or replaced them. Henceforth the Church must be the locus for the oneness of humankind. In the course of my pilgrimage I have come to believe that God's universal plan of reconciling all people is broader than the Christian church, though I am committed to the church in which I was born and nurtured, and I continue to witness and serve through and in the church as well as by other means. Nevertheless, Catherine and Peter Marshall gave me the vision of God's eternal plan of total reconciliation, which has now become my universalism.

3. THE EQUALITY OF WOMEN AND MEN

I took an important step toward universalism by acknowledging the equality of women and men. My wife, Margaret Ruth Hopper, was the most important person guiding me on this step. Daughter of a Presbyterian minister, Margaret earned a master's degree in social work to answer her call to ministry, since as a female she was precluded from ordained office in the church at that time. We became missionaries in Japan, where we both taught in a small Christian school, Shikoku Christian College. Margaret demonstrated powers of intellect and ability, combined with a deep commitment to the Christian faith, which clearly marked her as the type of person the church needed for ministry, yet the ages-long cultural straightjacket of patriarchy had controlled the interpretation of select texts of Scripture so as to solidify discrimination against women. In her teaching she addressed the prejudice and discrimination against women in Japan, which were far more severe than those she herself faced. Not only so, but she was able to check my tendencies toward chauvinistic behavior towards her in a firm, but gentle manner, and somehow God gave me grace to pay attention.

Beside the living example of my own wife, I knew other women of superior qualifications. Dr. Rachel Henderlite, of the Presbyterian School of Christian Education in Richmond, Virginia taught the Bible lessons on God's call to Jeremiah at that youth conference that had been an important influence that led to my call to ministry. When the Southern Presbyterian Church eventually approved ordaining women to ministry, Dr. Henderlite was the first woman to be ordained.

Dr. Henderlite's contribution to my personal call into the ministry and the daily evidence of my wife prompted me to question the church's ban on women ministers. Faced with reality, I undertook a serious study of the Bible to try to resolve my doubts. Besides careful attention to the Bible itself, my research included ancient cultural history and extrabiblical mythological material, traditional and more recent biblical interpretations, and writings by modern feminists. Simply put, the conclusion of my essay, "Male–Female–Nature–Scripture," was a strong affirmation of the basic equality of the sexes as is clearly taught in Genesis 1:27–8 and 5:1–2, encouraged by the teaching and example of Jesus, and implied in many places elsewhere in the Bible as a whole.[5]

4. THE BIBLE'S UNIVERSAL TEXTS

It is true that a great many texts in the Bible seem to make a division between "the saved" and "the lost" among humans. Theologians, poets, and graphic artists have expended great effort and ingenuity to describe heaven and hell as the ultimate fate of these two divisions of humanity. The average person has been culturally conditioned to assume that heaven and hell are real, whether figuratively or literally, and everybody is destined to end up in one place or the other. Fewer in number are what I call the Bible's universal texts, but whenever I encountered one it would inevitably challenge my presuppositions. These texts caused me to question Warfield, and they continued to bother me as I tried to present the biblical and Christian monotheistic worldview to my Japanese students:

John. 1:9: The true light, which enlightens everyone, was coming into the world.

1:29b: Here is the Lamb of God who takes away the sin of the world.

3:16–17: For God so loved the world that he gave his only Son, so that everyone who believes in him may not perish but may have eternal life. Indeed, God did not send the Son into the world to condemn the world, but in order that the world might be saved through him.

12:32: [Jesus said] And I, when I am lifted up from the earth, will draw all people [margin: all things] to myself.

Romans 5:18: Therefore just as one man's trespass led to condemnation for all, so one man's act of righteousness leads to justification and life for all.

11:32a: For God has imprisoned all in disobedience so that he may be merciful to all.

14:11: For it is written, "As I live, says the Lord, every knee shall bow to me, and every tongue shall give praise to God."

---

5. Taylor, "Male–Female–Nature–Scripture".

God For All

1 Corinthians 15:22: For as all die in Adam, so all will be made alive in Christ.

2 Corinthians 5:19: In Christ God was reconciling the world to himself, not counting their trespasses against them.

Ephesians 1:9–10: [God] has made known to us the mystery of his will, according to his good pleasure that he set forth in Christ, as a plan for the fullness of time, to gather up all things in him, things in heaven and things on earth.

Philippians 2:9–11: [Because of Jesus' obedience unto death] Therefore God also highly exalted him and gave him the name that is above every name, so that at the name of Jesus every knee should bend, in heaven and on earth and under the earth, and every tongue should confess that Jesus Christ is Lord, to the glory of God the Father.

3:20–21: Our citizenship is in heaven, and it is from there that we are expecting a Savior, the Lord Jesus Christ. He will transform the body of our humiliation that it may be conformed to the body of his glory, by the power that also enables him to make all things subject to himself.

Colossians 1:19–20: For in [Christ] all the fullness of God was pleased to dwell, and through him God was pleased to reconcile to himself all things, whether on earth or in heaven, by making peace through the blood of his cross.

1 Timothy 2:3–4: This is right and is acceptable in the sight of God our Savior, who desires everyone to be saved and to come to the knowledge of the truth.

4:10: For to this end we toil and struggle, because we have our hope set on the living God, who is the Savior of all people, especially of those who believe.

Titus 2:11: For the grace of God has appeared, bringing salvation to all.

Revelation 5:13–14: Then I heard every creature in heaven and on earth and under the earth and in the sea, and all that is in them, singing, "To the one seated on the throne and to the Lamb be blessing and honor and glory and might forever and ever!"

Simply to list individual texts like this does not fully serve my purpose; we need to examine texts more completely in their immediate as well as in their full canonical context. Here I wish only to call attention to the occurrence of words like "the world" and "all" and "every" and to urge that we give them due weight. If we take the texts of ultimate separation of "saved" and "lost" to be the *final* word, then we have to ignore these universal texts. One must bend logic and word usage to make them say something different from what they actually say, or else honestly admit that they do not belong in one's personal canon of Scripture or theology. On the contrary, in my view, we should use these universal texts as the standard by which to interpret the rest of Scripture.

5. MY "AHA!" MOMENT

For some years I had been teaching the required Bible course to first-year students at Shikoku Christian College, starting with Genesis: "In the beginning God created the heaven and the earth." One year, I had finished with the prophet Amos, who began by pronouncing God's judgment on the nations surrounding Israel (Amos 1:3—2.3), and after he had attracted the smug Israelites' attention, he pronounced God's judgment precisely on *them*, leading to this climax: "You only have I known of all the families of the earth; therefore I will punish you for all your iniquities" (2:4—3:2). Before the one Creator God, all sinners equally stand condemned, even, or especially, the chosen people.

Next I took up Amos's contemporary Hosea, a prophet who showed no interest whatsoever in neighboring nations, but who condemned sinful Israel even more vigorously than Amos (Hosea 4–5). Hosea depicted God as a cruel, ravening lion or bear ripping people to pieces (5:14; 13:8). Yet in the end, God declares: "How can I give you up? ... My heart recoils within me; my compassion grows warm and tender . . ." (11:8). "I will heal their disloyalty; I will love them freely, for my anger has turned from them" (14:4).

The juxtaposition of Amos's impartial condemnation and Hosea's unconditional love struck me forcefully and raised a nagging question in my mind: *If God loved* that *Israel like* that, *wouldn't an impartial God love* all people *the same?*

Just at that very time there occurred one of those periodic tragedies in Bangladesh, a terrible typhoon sweeping inland from the Bay of Bengal. Abnormally high tides driven by preternaturally strong winds inundated islands and plains and drowned uncounted thousands of human beings. Bangladeshi life expectancy was little over forty years, and the majority of the people never had enough to eat. Only a tiny minority of Bangladeshis had confessed Jesus Christ as Savior. What about all the rest? Did they suffer oppression, poverty, malnutrition, disease, and the ravages of wind and water during their short and bitter life on earth, only to spend eternity in hell? Must I believe that God destined them to eternal damnation, because of a narrow interpretation of the Bible texts that say there is no other name by which people can be saved; and no one comes to God the Father except through Jesus?

God gave me the answer as Amos, Hosea, and Jesus came together in my mind with those universal texts that speak so clearly of "the world" and "all" and "every." I *must* believe and proclaim that the God revealed by Jesus in Scripture, the God who has blessed me without my deserving, would *never* inflict the cruel fate of eternal hell upon any human being, each of whom has been created by God and who bears the image of God.

This was my "aha!" moment. It confirmed my suspicion that Warfield's argument that God's sovereign decree of reprobation for the majority of humankind was the fatal flaw of his book, *The Plan of Salvation*. It confirmed for me my belief that the Marshalls were unknowingly correct when they wrote in *The Mystery of the Ages* that

God's eternal purpose was to sum up all things in Christ, even though they narrowly expected it all to be accomplished by the Church.

In the next chapter I describe the powerful challenge I faced trying to introduce the biblical monotheistic worldview to Japanese students who had been brought up in a polytheistic culture. The more I tried to convince them that God is One, the more my own conviction of the Oneness of God grew stronger. My belief that there is only one God is the necessary precondition for believing that God saves all people. The One God revealed in the Bible transcends all finite human conceptions of god and the religions that cling to their respective gods. God lovingly embraces the whole creation—everything, everyone. God is love. God is for all.

2

The Beginnings of Monotheism

AS A TEACHER OF Bible at Shikoku Christian College in Japan,[1] I soon became aware of the polytheistic worldview that characterized Japanese culture and the thinking of my students, especially in contrast to the monotheistic worldview of my Christian faith. I observed that many of the features of indigenous Shinto religion in Japan bore striking similarities to the Canaanite practices against which the biblical prophets and priests had struggled so bitterly.

1. TWO WORLDVIEWS

To introduce my Bible course I drew on a lecture, "Two Worldviews," by Prof. Ei-ichirō Ishida, delivered on the occasion of his retirement from the chair of cultural anthropology at the University of Tokyo.[2] Professor Ishida developed the thesis that all the religions of the world may be classified as one of two types, polytheism, or monotheism. Monotheistic religions are Judaism, Christianity, and Islam, while all the rest are polytheistic, he declared. Professor Ishida then proceeded to demonstrate the differences between these two worldviews by means of several points, which I condensed and revised somewhat as follows:

Monotheistic	Polytheistic
1. One transcendent God	1. Universe as a given existence
2. A created universe	2. Gods within the universe
3. Intolerance of other gods	3. Acceptance of numerous gods
4. God transcends sexuality	4. Gods reproduce sexually
5. God exists & rules universally	5. Gods are limited locally
6. Universe is finite & rational	6. Universe is infinite & irrational

1. Our textbook was the 1955 colloquial Japanese translation of the Japan Bible Society, Tokyo.
2. Ishida Ei-ichirō, "Two Worldviews" ["Futatsu no Sekaikan"].

God For All

The clear distinction between these two worldviews can be contrasted so starkly because we have available, on the one hand, the creation story with which the Bible of the Jews and Christians opens, and on the other hand, the more ancient myths of origins cherished by other ancient Near Eastern peoples. Contemporary students of the Bible are fortunate to have available a translation of an ancient liturgical poem, *Enuma elish*, a mythological account of the foundation of Babylon, which offers a clear expression of the contrasting polytheistic worldview. It seems a reasonable conjecture that the author(s) of the biblical creation story must have been familiar with *Enuma elish* and may have had it in mind as a foil against which they told their story. A brief summary of the principal features of *Enuma elish* will provide a basis for comparison.

2. THE POLYTHEISTIC WORLDVIEW OF ENUMA ELISH

In 587 BCE Babylon had destroyed the kingdom of Judah with its capital city Jerusalem, burned the temple of its national God, and deported the total power elite and artisan class to Babylon. Every New Year, the Babylonian priests recited and re-enacted the liturgical drama *Enuma elish* with the aim of persuading the gods to preserve and prosper the ruling order for another year. The poem and its ritual went back to famous King Hammurabi in the eighteenth century BCE when he established his kingdom and proclaimed the supremacy of his god Marduk. Present day knowledge of *Enuma elish* is possible because scholars have pieced it together from clay tablets recovered from various archaeological sites in the Middle East. The poem begins: "When there was no heaven, no earth, / no height, no depth, no name . . . / when there were no gods,/ . . . / then from Apsu and Tiamat / in the waters gods were created. . . ."[3]

The scene is a watery chaos, apparently descriptive of the point where the waters of what we call the Tigris and Euphrates Rivers empty into the Persian Gulf. Apsu is the male principle symbolizing the fresh water and Tiamat the female principle symbolizing salt water. By means of their commingling, they engendered other deities. The lethargic parent gods remained in the deepest abyss, while their offspring ascended to the upper regions. The obstreperous younger gods disturbed the sleep of their elders, which led to a deadly conflict. Ea, the god of wisdom, assassinated Apsu, but Tiamat, enraged, created all sorts of dragons and monsters as allies, and appointed Kingu as her war commander. The frightened gods called a council at which Marduk, god of light, the handsome young son of Ea and Damkina, offered to fight Tiamat, provided that the other gods acknowledge him as their chief if he won. Marduk slew Tiamat and split her body in two like the halves of a seashell. He used one half to form the sky like a solid shield to restrain the waters above the sky. In the sky he placed the heavenly gods, moon and sun, and the stars that determine fates. The other half he used to form the earth and contain the waters of the abyss below the earth. Upon

---

3. Sandars, *Poems of Heaven and Hell*.

the earth he decreed the establishment of Babylon, abode of the gods.[4] They forced the vanquished gods to feed and care for them, but soon Marduk took council with his father Ea, who decided to create humankind to do this work. They killed Kingu, erstwhile enemy chief, and from his blood Ea formed humankind and decreed that they would be slaves to the gods. The gods worshipped Marduk as the Lord of the Universe. They built Marduk a palace, the famous ziggurat, or pyramid-like Babel Tower, called Esagila, which "towered, the earthly temple, the symbol of infinite heaven."[5] In conclusion, the Great Gods Enlil and Anu kissed Marduk's bow and placed it in the heaven "a god among the gods."[6]

The annual liturgical recitation of *Enuma elish* was, of course, the tool of the king and his inner circle, including the chief religious authorities, to assure divine approval of the political and economic status quo. The king was recognized as the image of the god and exercised Marduk's power as his semi-divine agent, and Marduk's temple was adjacent to the royal palace to facilitate the unity of religion and governance. The royal and religious elites enjoyed the favor of the gods and acted as their sub-agents to manage the great wealth and affairs of state, while directing the masses of slaves, serfs, and underclass who actually performed all the hard work and produced the wealth.

Enuma elish is not a creation story, but only a religious myth fabricated to justify the imposition of power by the ruling house to overcome the resistance of all opponents, to bring order out of disorder, and to impose the "peace" of total domination. Walter Wink calls this a version of the myth of redemptive violence. "It enshrines the belief that violence saves, that war brings peace, that might makes right. It is one of the oldest continuously repeated stories in the world."[7]

Of particular interest to me was the fact that Japan had its own myth of origins, *Kojiki*, (*Records of Ancient Matters*)[8] which has some details similar to *Enuma elish*. Out of a watery chaos a male-female couple emerges. They solidify the islands that eventually become known as Japan.[9] They mate and produce other deities, including Amaterasu[10] and her obstreperous brother Susano-o. The siblings engage in heated rivalry until Amaterasu routs Susano-o. Amaterasu sends her august, divine grandson Jimmu to rule on earth, to overcome the forces of evil, and to establish order.

Kojiki reflects the prehistoric rivalry of the Yamato clan in the central region of what is known as Honshu Island, against the older Izumo clan in Kyushu Island in the west. Victorious Yamato overcame the "evil" Izumo and established hegemony over

4. Sandars, *Poems of Heaven and Hell*, 96.
5. Ibid., 99.
6. Ibid., 100.
7. Wink, *The Powers that Be*, 47–48.
8. Phillipi, *Kojiki*.
9. "Japan" is English adaptation from the name given to the islands by the Chinese who first discovered and named them. It means literally, "the source of the sun." Japanese call their land Nippon, their adaptation of the Chinese.
10. Literal meaning, "Heaven Shining."

all the adjacent territories. The victors named the newly established state Yamato after their clan, and Amaterasu their deity became supreme over all the gods. Amaterasu's grandson Jimmu, the first emperor, established a dynasty that zealous Japanese nationalists claim has continued without interruption till today.

After 1856–7 when the U.S. forced Japan to open after two centuries of isolation, the military oligarchy that took control and ruled in the name of the Emperor Meiji revived this nearly forgotten myth. They made it the basis for National Shinto, the religious ideology of an ironclad dictatorship and mobilized the nation to resist the "Western Barbarians" and escape colonization like the rest of Asia and Africa. *Kojiki* was one of the most effective of many myths of redemptive violence. After World War Two, General Douglas MacArthur, Supreme Commander of the Allied Powers, permitted Emperor Hirohito to keep his throne. One of the titles of the Japanese Emperor is Tenno, King of Heaven, borne by the present Emperor Heisei (throne name of former Crown Prince Akihito).

3. THE MONOTHEISTIC WORLDVIEW OF GENESIS 1:1—2:4a

The authors of the creation story were probably priests exiled to Babylon after Judah and Jerusalem were destroyed.[11] In popular thought, the gods of Babylon had defeated the God of Israel. Point by point the Judean priests declared their faith in defiance of their captors:

> In the beginning God created the heavens and the earth. 2 The earth was without form and void, and darkness was upon the face of the deep; and the Spirit of God was moving over the face of the waters. 3 And God said, "Let there be light"; and there was light. 4 And God saw that the light was good; and God separated the light from the darkness. 5 God called the light Day, and the darkness he called Night. And there was evening and there was morning, one day. (Gen 1:1–5 RSV)[12]

Thus the Bible boldly declares the basic principle of the monotheistic worldview: A sole deity, pre-existent, acting alone with transcendent sovereignty and without struggle, creates everything else, making clear distinction between God and not-god. The negative description, "without form and void" and "darkness on the face of the deep" is answered by "the Spirit of God moving over the face of the waters" followed by the terse divine command that brings light into being. The primeval sea became the "soup" in which, according to evolutionary hypothesis, light could give rise to life.

---

11. See the note at the end of this chapter for consensus on the approximate date and source of Gen 1:1—2:4a.

12. More recent English translations render Genesis 1:1 differently: "In the beginning when God created the heavens and the earth . . ." (NRSV); "When God began to create heaven and earth—" (NJPS). I use the RSV version here, for it is by far the most familiar English translation, following the Authorized Version of 1611 (KJV), and it gives the sense of the Japanese translation available to me.

The description proceeds, step by step for the next five stages, or "days." The author(s) of the Genesis story shared with their contemporaries a common view of the observable world: The sky was solid, like a dome,[13] which God made to restrain the waters above, but which had windows that could open to allow rain to fall. God restricted the seawaters below to expose the dry earth, which by divine command put forth vegetation (1:6–13). The author(s) also accepted that the sun and moon were set in the dome of the sky to give light by day and night, but they disdained to use their names *shemesh* and *yareach*, which in Hebrew were names of gods. The account refers to them as greater and lesser "lamps," a word different from "light" itself; then adds, almost as an afterthought, "and the stars," barely mentioning the celestial gods so important for Babylonian astrology (1:14–17). Unlike the many myths, such as *Enuma elish*, that describe battles between gods and monsters, Gen 1:21 simply states: "So God created the great sea monsters . . ."[14] Then God created other sea creatures and birds, then animals of every kind on land in an orderly progression (1:20–25).

The creation of humanity marks the most significant differences between the biblical and the polytheistic worldview, especially that of *Enuma elish*, in which humans were made from blood of an evil god and destined as slaves to the other gods. This point is typical of pagan myths of origin; as one author puts it, "It represents the universal Mesopotamian opinion."[15] By contrast, the God of Genesis created humanity in the divine image and likeness, male and female together, and gave them authority over the rest of creation (Gen 1:6–30). The Hebrew nouns for God and humanity are generic—*'elohim*=God and *'adam*=humanity. The deity has no name; as is proper when this is the only exemplar of the category "god." Humankind has no distinguishing race, nationality, or class, simply male and female named *'adam*=humankind (see also Gen 5:2, part of a related priestly text).

4. GENESIS 1, A MINORITY VIEW

The creation story was a confession of faith on the part of Israelite priests, who belonged to the class of religious professionals who had guarded and transmitted the traditions of their national religion through ups and downs over many centuries. One might say it is a distillation of their faith. On the one hand Genesis 1 is a protest against the arrogance of the victorious Babylonians, and on the other a testimony to the One God who transcends all gods and all nations and is, in fact, the maker and ruler of them all. In my view, this is the beginning of what modern scholars refer to as monotheism. At the time of promulgation, this was a new and distinctly minority view.

---

13. Heb *raqiʿa*. The noun is based on a verb that means to beat or to hammer or to press into a solid. See Num 16:36–40 for a description of the type of material and workmanship that is implied in Genesis 1:6–8. Job 37:18 speaks of "the skies, hard as a molten mirror."

14. Older traditions of the Hebrew Bible refer to similar primeval battles, e.g., Pss 74:12–17; 89:10–11.

15. Lohfink, *Theology of the Pentateuch*, 7.

Some exiles evidently believed that they had left their God behind and they were now in the domain of another god. They lamented their fate in the words of Psalm 137: "By the rivers of Babylon—there we sat down and there we wept when we remembered Zion . . . How could we sing the LORD's song in a foreign land?" (Ps 137:1, 4). Perhaps they thought the LORD was too far away to hear their praises or respond to their cries. They consoled themselves with hope of revenge: "O daughter Babylon, you devastator! Happy shall they be who pay you back what you have done to us! Happy shall they be who take your little ones and dash them against the rock!" (137:8–9). Back home in devastated Jerusalem the poverty-stricken survivors demanded, "O God, why do you cast us off forever?" (Ps 74:1). They described in detail how the enemy had wrecked God's holy dwelling, while God passively let it happen (74:4–11). Was not their God the one who had broken the heads of the dragons in that primeval battle when God imposed order on chaos? (74:12–17). They cried: "Rise up, O God, plead your cause; remember how the impious scoff at you all day long" (74:18–23).

Another psalm describes the cruel slaughter visited on God's servants in Jerusalem (Ps 79:1–5). The psalmist pleads for revenge and forgiveness (79:6–9) and complains, "How long, O LORD? . . . Why should the nations say, 'Where is their God?'" and ends with an eloquent plea for vengeance (79:10–13). The unstated presupposition of these laments is that "the enemies" against whom they rail are not only the armies of the nations but also the gods of the nations. Obviously those who expressed their worship in these terms still conceived of their deity as one who had formerly displayed victorious power, who had imposed redemptive violence on chaos to bring an ordered world into being, and lived in Jerusalem. But now they suspected that perhaps their God was no longer effective in competition with other gods. Their nation and their national religious cult were destroyed; perhaps their God had gone down in defeat too? Genesis 1:1—2:4a expresses a new vision of God, which alone was capable of preventing Israel and Israel's God from going the way of other nations and their gods. The emerging conviction that God is One resists such defeatism.

To open my Bible course I followed the points of Professor Ishida's "Two Worldviews" backed up by the Genesis account and contrasted with Japanese and ancient Near Eastern myths. The Bible's opening chapter exalts the sovereignty of the One Creator God. Before this God, all that is not-god stands on the same level. The Bible itself declares more than once, "God shows no partiality" (Deut 10:17, Job 34:17, Luke 20:21, Acts 10:34, Rom 2:11, Gal 2:6). As a corollary, the monotheistic worldview encourages equality among humans, which I emphasized as precondition for democracy. In those days so soon after their total defeat, the Japanese were striving to understand the newly introduced ideas of "democracy." By contrast, polytheism encourages hierarchy, not only among the many gods of ancient Canaan, but also the Japanese *yaoyorozu no kami*—eight hundred myriad gods—who appear in unmistakable ranks, from earthy *kami* represented by a small pile of rocks in the corners of farmers' fields, all the way up to the Sun Goddess, putative ancestor of the emperor even in modern, technologically advanced Japan. As I went on year after year opening my OT course with this exposition of the oneness of God, the more strongly I came to the conviction that a basic aspect of belief that God is one must be that one God is God for all.

REFLECTION

From the Pew Trust poll with which I introduced this work, I couldn't escape the strong impression that perhaps the average person thinks "eternal life" or "salvation" is a goal of human effort, and that religions are spiritual or cultural means to assist individuals to "attain" their goal. By means of Professor Ishida's description of the monotheistic worldview in contrast to the polytheistic worldview, I wish to emphasize that the teaching that we can derive from the Bible of Jews and Christians lays primary emphasis upon the Sovereign God. God is the Creator, and hence not a mere assistant to help human beings fulfill their desires. Yet, as we better understand the teaching of Genesis 1, we see that God the Creator has made humankind in such a way as to endow us with an extremely high value, which we often find it all too easy to ignore or violate.

5. NOTE ON THE DATE AND SOURCE OF THE CREATION STORY

As noted above, Israelite priests probably composed the Creation Story that opens the Bible in response to their exile in Babylon after 586 BCE. Therefore, rather than being the first and oldest teaching in the Bible, it is the fruit of a long experience of Israelite priests who led worship and taught religious traditions over many generations. Meticulous study of the Hebrew text of Genesis by Jewish and Christian scholars indicates that Gen 1.1—2:4a is part of a longer document, parts of which are distributed in Genesis, Exodus, Leviticus, and Numbers. Scholars call this material P or priestly, because its vocabulary, style, and themes reflect special priestly concerns. In Genesis, P begins the story of heaven and earth, to set the stage for the later emergence of Israel, the Chosen People. The author(s) of P believed that the special Name LORD/YHWH was not revealed until God was preparing to redeem the people from Egypt (Exod 6:2–3). Thus, the Hebrew name for the God of this Creation story is simply Elohim, a generic word; it is a plural form of a noun El, or Eloah. Plural Elohim used with singular verbs and adjectives expresses deity in a singular or comprehensive sense, implying that one god has absorbed the powers and functions of lesser gods. When Elohim is used with plural verbs it means plural gods. In Genesis 1 God/Elohim creates the creation, of which humanity is the crown. The special relationship between God and humanity underlies the entire Bible. In the next chapter I will pay closer attention to the details of what the priestly creation account in Genesis teaches about Elohim.

PART ONE

The Universal Matrix

3

God and the Creation of Humanity

I UNDERTOOK THIS WORK in part to respond to the Pew Trust Survey that indicated that a growing number of American Christians now believe that religions other than Christianity can help people achieve or obtain eternal life by means of their beliefs or deeds or both. As I described my personal pilgrimage of faith, I noted how Dr. Benjamin B. Warfield had convinced me that no person can contribute anything to his or her own salvation, but that it is all a gift of God; and how Catherine and Peter Marshall had convinced me that God's eternal plan as stated in Ephesians 1:10 (and other universal texts) embraces all people. My subsequent life experience and career as Bible teacher led to my conviction that the sovereign God revealed in the Bible not only is the creator of all but also is the savior of all. The One God revealed in the Bible transcends even the Bible that reveals God. God embraces the Jews, Christians, and Muslims who to any degree depend on the Bible for revelation and instruction concerning God, but even beyond them God embraces all people, of whatever religion or none at all. All depends not on humans, but on God for all.

1. THE CREATOR

From ancient times Jews and Christians, and later Muslims, read Genesis 1:1 as a complete sentence: "In the beginning, God created the heaven and the earth."[1] The biblical authors were concerned with "heaven and earth" in terms only of planet Earth as they could observe it. Having created everything ("out of nothing" as expressed by the Latin *ex nihilo*) God proceeded to create new things in sequence and to bring everything into ordered being. God is like a sculptor, creating the raw material separate from himself, and then going to work shaping it to suit a preconceived plan. Unlike other ancient Near Eastern stories of beginnings, here God did everything alone, without a

---

1. The rendering of KJV, the authorized English version of 1611, was also adopted by the Jewish Publication Society's *The Holy Scriptures* 1955, revision of an earlier version of 1916 for English speaking Jews of the United States, who at the time comprised the largest number of Jews in the world. This translation also conformed to that of the Greek (LXX) translation made by Jews in Egypt in the early centuries BCE.

violent battle with monsters, though other Israelite traditions describe God as victorious in such struggles (e.g., Ps 74:13–14; 89:5–10; Isa 27:1). In Genesis sea monsters too are God's creatures (1:21). Whereas in *Enuma elish*, for example, the young god Marduk was the god of light, in Genesis, God creates light by simple command.

Recently some Jewish and Christian linguist-theologians suggest that Gen 1 pictures God at work upon a pre-existent dark and watery chaos (not totally dissimilar from *Enuma elish*): "When God was about to create heaven and earth, the earth was a chaos, unformed, and on the chaotic waters' face there was darkness" (Gen 1.1–2).[2] I am personally disinclined to think that God is not totally responsible for all of creation, even though that raises the problem of God's responsibility for evil.

Whichever version of Gen 1:1–2 we adopt, the raw material is still out there, separate from God, but God's spirit, the divine immanence, is moving over the waters. The priestly account affirms the positive results of God's first acts, overcoming darkness by light, controlling the swirling waters by separating them and fixing firm limits for them above and below by making a solid dome and uncovering the dry land. With God's permission the land produces vegetation (1:11–12). There is no mention of *life*—life is just *there*, inhering in the vegetation that land produces. Afterward God creates living creatures in great variety—animals in the sea, in the air, and on the land, a discernible progression from less to more complex stages (compatible with evolutionary thought).

Humanity is the crown of material creation, but before creating it, God says: "Let us make humankind in our image, according to our likeness; and let them have dominion over the fish of the sea, and over the birds of the air, and over the cattle, and over all the wild animals of the earth, and over every creeping thing that creeps upon the earth" (Gen 1:26). These plural forms—"Let *us* make humankind in *our* image"—have puzzled expositors, but if we read the Hebrew Bible carefully, we see a number of references to "sons of gods" translated sometimes as "celestial beings" (Gen 6:2, 4; Job 1:6; 2:1; 38:7; Ps 89:6). Other spiritual beings of various sorts may also be found in Scripture. "So God created humankind in his image, in the image of God he created them; male and female he created them. God blessed them, and God said to them, "Be fruitful and multiply, and fill the earth and subdue it; and have dominion over the fish of the sea and over the birds of the air and over every living thing that moves upon the earth" (Gen 1:27–28 NRSV).

In the Assyrian and Babylonian empires of ancient times a great king used to place images of himself throughout his realm, to assert his ownership and sovereignty. The language of Genesis implies that the Creator God created humanity, male and female in God's image, and put them in creation to represent God's sole ownership

---

2. *The Torah: A Modern Commentary Revised Edition*, Gen 1:1–3. "Creation out of nothing" emerged in early Jewish and Christian debate with Greek philosophy, which distinguished divine spirit=good from matter=evil. The Jewish philosopher, Philo of Alexandria (d. 50 CE), offered the Logos=Word as agent through which God created the material world and brought life to the primordial chaos. In John 1:1–5 the Word=Logos accomplishes that divine purpose. McGrath, *The Only True God*, 56–58.

and sovereignty. Jon D. Levenson says, God "appoints the entire human race as God's royal stand-in" and speaks of "the coregency of God and humanity."[3] According to Randall Garr, the priestly account implies that in creating humankind in *his own* image, God ignored the lesser gods whom he had previously addressed and thereafter substituted humanity as his proxies instead of the lesser deities: "P's God therefore achieves sole majestic rule over the world and, in the process, establishes monotheism itself."[4] God's image comprises both male and female. "The story is not indifferent to humanity's being composed of two genders . . . Not only is there no subordination of the woman in this account, but she is specifically given a ruling task along with the man," writes Patrick D. Miller.[5] It seems to me the Creator has invested an astounding degree of confidence in the human creature.

2. THE HUMAN CREATURE

The Bible itself is not interested in what moderns think of as "science," or in the details by which God actually accomplished all this; it affirms that God made it, and God owns it. Besides this there are other, disparate biblical texts dealing with the general theme of creation. Yet the present account does not preclude our thinking of it in terms of evolution and the big bang. From that first bang, what experts call the laws of physics and chemistry came into play and evolved the vast cosmos of galaxies, gas, dust, and solar systems, including Earth. In the cosmos Earth is hardly more than a mere speck, yet so far as we know, it is unique in having life.[6] This living Earth is the object of God's creative work in the Bible. When life mysteriously emerged on Earth, a force besides physics and chemistry came into effect: biology. Some modern scientists consider biology to be as rigidly deterministic as physics and chemistry, controlling life just like everything else in the cosmos. Based on the belief that everything has a purely material, hence mechanistic basis, some people declare themselves atheists, and some adopt a stridently anti-religious attitude.

One Christian scholar, Holmes Rolston III, in his Gifford Lectures at Edinburgh University in 1997, contradicted the materialists.[7] Using impeccable scientific evidence, Rolston demonstrates that the emergence of life (the "bio-" of biology), which comprises genes, neurons, and DNA with sexual reproduction, introduces factors of uncertainty and randomness that the material world governed by physics and chemistry cannot permit. As the blurb on the back cover of Rolston's book states: "Especially

---

3. Levenson, *Creation and the Persistence of* Evil, 116–17.
4. Garr, *In His Own Image and Likeness*, 216.
5. Miller, "Man and Woman."
6. Recent advances in cosmic exploration disclose a great number of stars with planets. Scientists accept the possibility (probability?) that somewhere a planet may have conditions similar to those on Earth, in which case life will emerge.
7. Rolston, *Genes, Genesis, and God*, winner of the 2003 Templeton Prize.

remarkable in this narrative is the genesis of human beings with their capacities for science, ethics, and religion." In other words, life as it has emerged and culminated in humankind involves a degree of freedom of will and creative assertiveness impossible in the material determinism that physics and chemistry impose.[8] God, the divine free agent, creator of creation, created the human creature in God's own image and likeness, which turns out to include a degree (impossible to measure) of creaturely freedom of will. This creature can defy, even frustrate the creator. That is the great risk that God took in the creation of humanity, and that is a measure of God's meekness and the majesty and value of humanity when considered from the side of God.

From the side of humanity, as we have only recently learned, all people, male or female, of whatever so-called race or tribe or language or culture, all of us human beings share 99.99 percent of the same DNA. All the differences among us, which seem so many and so obvious to our natural observance, result from one-tenth of one per cent of difference in our genetic makeup! This fact rebukes our typical American propensity to over-emphasize the individual and his or her individual rights. Warfield premised his plan of salvation on what he called "particular evangelicalism," that God deals with "each and every" human strictly as individuals. I acknowledge with gratitude that we all are, that I am, known and loved by God as an individual. I rejoice that, as the Bible teaches, God knows our names. But I wish to remind everyone that on biblical grounds alone we know that God deals with humans not only as individuals but also as families and peoples and nations, *and as a species*. Before we had this exact scientific DNA knowledge, more than three hundred fifty years ago the poet John Donne expressed the truth: "No man is an *Island*, entire of it self . . . Never send to know for whom the *bell* tolls; it tolls for *thee*." This is not just a nice poetic turn of phrase but a profound statement of the truth that all humanity, both singly and in totality, created in the image of God, are threads intertwined in an intricate web. The designer and weaver of the pattern is God.

SUMMARY AND REFLECTION

Some of what I have written here to describe God and the human creature has been borne in on me in new and persuasive ways in relatively recent time, but it all serves to reinforce my previous conviction that the one God, the creator of all, embraces all human beings in the divine plan of reconciliation. By God's personal will and creative decision, we human creatures have been conceived in relation with God in ways deep and mysterious. God does not wield the power of absolute and external control over creation that people have been accustomed to think according to the doctrine of God's total creation of everything out of nothing.[9] Evolutionary science supplies additional

---

8. Poet, essayist, and novelist Wendell Berry has also challenged the materialists with *Life is a Miracle*.

9. The Bible does not support the belief that God personally controls everything that happens in nature and to each individual human being. Rolston (*Genes, Genesis, and God*) has demonstrated to

information that gives us a better way to think about God as moving persuasively within, and not just acting causatively from without. The total picture is humanity in a mutual relationship with God that allows for a degree of give and take on both sides. As I will show, God gives us freedom to go our own way, even when that leads to tragic consequences, but God has created us so that we live in a divine environment from which God does not allow us to be finally lost.

---

my satisfaction that biological life is not subject to the same level of determinism as are other entities determined by physics and chemistry. Clark and Grundstein, *Are We Hardwired?* describe in great detail the interaction of genes, environment, and the complexities of the human neurological system, especially the brain. The result is to introduce such a vast number of possibilities impacting human behavior that it is impossible to prove that human behavior is determined. Clark and Grundstein conclude: "We [humans] can see and understand fully how our behavior affects our own lives, and the lives of those around us. Perhaps therein lies the definition of moral choice, and thus the nature of free will; the ability to choose among personal and social possibilities dictated by neither genes nor experience" (p 270).

4

The Creator and Humans in Relationship

As we have just seen, the first chapter of Genesis, what many refer to as P or the priestly story of creation, discloses God=ʾ*Elohim* creating humankind, male and female together in the divine image, set to rule over the rest of creation as God's agents, thus bestowing on them a high degree of divine approval, but also a truly awesome responsibility as well.

At Gen 2:4b—3:24 a sequel presents Creator and humans in more intimate personal relation including acts and words. The literary connection between the accounts is not smooth. The setting, style, vocabulary, and order of events of the second are quite different. Most important, the name of the divine subject in the second story, translated in English as "the LORD God," renders the Hebrew "*YHWH* ʾ*Elohim*." YHWH is the English of four unpronounced Hebrew consonants, the ineffable Name of Israel's special God first revealed to Moses in Egypt (Exod 3:13-15; 6:2-3).[1] All these differences convinced devout students of Scripture that this sequel came from a tradition source different from that of Genesis 1:1—2:4a. German scholars, who rendered the Name JHVH, called this source J because of its consistent use of this divine name, to distinguish it from P, the priestly source. In my discussion I will use YHWH instead of LORD even when I quote from Scripture. According to the J tradition, people began to call on YHWH in the third generation after Adam (Gen 4:26). The J tradition apparently did not know the revelation of the Name to Moses in Egypt (Exod 3:13-15; 6:2-3).

1. YHWH GOD, THE GARDEN, AND THE FIRST HUMANS

The setting is an arid wasteland, barren like the edge of the Egyptian desert where it never rains, valueless for want of a human (ʾ*adam*) to serve[2] the ground (ʾ*adamah*),

---

1. Devout Jews do not pronounce the Name; they may substitute *Adonai*, an honorific title meaning Lord, or they may read *Hashem*=The Name. Non-Jews proposed Jehovah, but now Yahweh is considered more accurate. Many people simply write YHWH and leave the pronunciation to the reader.

2. The Hebrew word ʿ*abad* most frequently means "to serve" or "to work" in the service of another (the noun ʿ*ebed*=servant or slave). The NIV rendering "to work the ground" is closer to the original

even though wetted by occasional mists or rising floods. Then YHWH God takes some of that reddish[3] ground and forms a human creature, into whose nostrils YHWH God breathes, so that the earthling becomes a living being (*nephesh chayah* 2:7, not a *living soul*, as in the well known KJV).[4] The first human creature was but a common farmer, made in order to serve/work the ground, and to keep the garden that YHWH God prepared for the earthling to live and work in (2:15). This is a stark contrast to the typical mythologies of ancient Near Eastern royal propaganda, e.g., that of Tyre, according to which the king was created first and was considered at least semi-divine (cf. Ezek 28:12b–15a). YHWH God planted the garden with every kind of tree, including the tree of life and the tree of the knowledge of good and evil, in the middle of the garden, and gave the human permission to eat from any tree except the tree of the knowledge of good and evil on pain of death (2:16–17).

YHWH God observed that the human was alone, which was "not good" and declared the intention to make a help suitable for him (2:18). For a solitary male person, life is incomplete; he cannot reproduce! Thereupon YHWH God formed from the same ground all the animals, and each one also was a living being (*nephesh chayah* 2:19) just like the human. As is abundantly demonstrated, humans and animals often enter mutually helpful relationships and enjoy rich companionship. The human gave all the animals names, but still there was no help suitable for him. I must point out subtle nuances in the text that people often overlook or even misinterpret.

1) Using the same Hebrew words, the biblical text states that God *formed* both the human and the animals out of the *ground*, and both human and animals are *living beings* (*nephesh chayah*). Translations may make a distinction by calling the human "a living being" but an animal "a living creature." Whether one chooses "being" or "creature," either term applies equally to both human and animal species (see footnote 4). The biblical vocabulary is more compatible with evolutionary biology than are typical Bible translations.

2) The frequent conception of the woman as the man's "helper" encourages the tendency to think of her as inferior and to enforce female subordination to male, but this is incorrect. The man, being single, needs *help* that is *suitable* or appropriate for him. The KJV translation of this phrase is correct: a "help meet for him." ("meet" being Elizabethan English for "suitable"[5]). Even after God forms all the animals as

---

meaning than "to till" (RSV, NRSV, NJPS).

3. Hebrew ʾ*edom*="red" shows etymological relation to ʾ*adam* and ʾ*adamah*.

4. "Living being" referring to the human in 2:7 (as also "living creature" referring to animals in 2:19) translates the Hebrew *nephesh chayah*. *Nephesh* literally is the throat or gullet, through which air and nourishment enter to maintain life in the body. It came to have the meaning of a living body. Equating *nephesh* with "soul" in the sense of a spiritual component distinct from the material body introduces a dualistic concept foreign to early Hebrew. The centuries-old debate as to when the "soul" enters the physical body, and the fanciful notion that an ovum fertilized by a sperm becomes at once a human person, are without biblical support and result in great controversy and many intractable problems.

5. The unjustifiable combination "helpmeet" to describe a wife as subordinate is a gross distortion.

living creatures from the same ground as the human, they are not the help that is meet=suitable for him. Why? Because a solitary human male can't have babies, and no other animal can supply that help. The Hebrew noun for help is ʾ*ezer*, and almost exclusively it is used of God, who supplies for people a rescue or succor or some form of help that they are incapable of providing for themselves.[6] The Genesis texts are the only ones where ʾ*ezer* specifically declares what one human being can do for another, and it is *woman* who is the help for *man*. Note that the final form of Genesis combines this J account with the P account (1:1—2:4a) in which God created humankind in the image of God, male and female, blessed them, and said, "be fruitful and multiply." A solitary male cannot be fruitful. Depending on context, Hebrew ʾ*adam* may mean one male person, but ʾ*adam* may also mean collective humankind. God alone creates humankind, but it takes both a man and a woman to birth another human.

YHWH God put the man to sleep and from one of his ribs made a woman and brought her to the man, who welcomed her with joy as being truly of his same bone and flesh (not of some other animal). Scripture adds: "Therefore a man leaves his father and his mother and clings to his wife and they become one flesh" (2:24). This is a remarkable note, for in the ancient patriarchal societies, the woman left her family to become a member, more exactly the *property*, of her husband's family. From ancient times even till today, some people cite Genesis texts to demand and to maintain women's subordination to men, but that is a result of ancient male power, male biblical translation, and male biblical interpretation serving male privilege. Actually, humanity as such does not exist without both genders, so that in this J account, the creation of the woman is the completion of the creation of humanity, which is the completion of creation. A forthright reading of the Hebrew text should impress us with the lengths to which God went to establish the origin and to guarantee the propagation of the human race, which, according to the P teaching, God made in the divine image and likeness (1:27), and named ʾ*adam*=humankind (5:1).

Two Jews of a later era showed appreciation for the importance of women. When debaters questioned Jesus about divorce, he said that men's exclusive right of divorce was a concession to men's "hardness of heart." Jesus cited Gen 1:27 and 2:24 to affirm equal rights for women: "But from the beginning of creation, 'God made them male and female.' For this reason 'a man shall leave his father and mother and be joined to his wife, and the two shall become one flesh.' So they are no longer two but one flesh" (Mark 10:5–8). The Apostle Paul reveals his change of attitude in a context in which he reflects earlier male chauvinistic traditions derived from literal reading of Genesis (2:18, 21–23): "Indeed, man was not made from woman, but woman from man. Neither was man created for the sake of woman, but woman for the sake of man... Nevertheless, in the Lord woman is not independent of man or man independent of woman. For just as

---

6. Gen. 2:18, 20; Exod. 18:4; Deut. 33:7, 26, 29; Pss. 20:2; 33:20; 70:5; 89:19; 115:9–11; 121:1f; 124:8; 146:5; Isa. 30:5; Ezek. 12:14; Dan. 11:34; Hos. 13:9.

woman came from man, so man comes through woman; but all things come from God" (2 Cor 11:8–9, 11–12).

2. CREATURES DEFY THE CREATOR

Now the serpent was more crafty than any other wild animal that YHWH God had made. He said to the woman, "Did God say, 'You shall not eat from any tree in the garden?'" (Gen 3:1). Thus begins the familiar story of the serpent's temptation of Eve. The text states that this serpent was a creature of God. It takes the lead to tempt another of God's creatures, the woman. That the woman succumbs to the temptation implies that God, by creative act, endowed these creatures with the capacity to choose against the will of the Creator. God does *not* maintain absolute control of creation, yet in the final analysis, sovereign God has responsibility for a creation that includes evil as well as good. The randomness and uncertainty that inhere in biological life makes possible both desirable and undesirable consequences of creatures' choices. In biblical terms, the malign presence of a mysterious third force complicates the relationship between Creator and creation. Thus quickly develops a consequence of the risk God took in making humanity in the divine image, as stewards to take charge of the earth and all the other animals in creation (Gen 1:27–8) as God's co-regents.

The New Testament identifies the serpent as Satan and the Devil (=*diabolos* a Greek word ordinarily used to translate Hebrew *satan*), acting tirelessly to tempt humans away from God, but ultimately overcome by God (Rev 12:9, 14–15; 20:2).[7] Warfield's argument that God determines the decree of salvation or condemnation for every human individual obviously pictures a deity willing to destroy the vast majority of humanity, the crown of creation that bears the very image of God. A more acceptable understanding of God is that God saves all people. Some wish to exonerate God of the responsibility of double predestination by making each individual responsible for own damnation by failure of personal decision for Christ. That ploy does not increase the number of saved. In consequence, the mysterious enemy of God—whatever its name—enjoys greater success at causing more humans to be lost than God saves to eternal life. In my view, that's a pretty paltry score for God! Both the P creation story and the J story of Adam and Eve in Genesis 1–3 speak to me of God displaying such a high degree of favor and concern for the human creature that when we trace the divine plan of salvation throughout the whole of Scripture, we shall see that God really embraces all humanity in eternal life.

---

7. See articles on Satan and Devil in *ABD*.

3. OUT OF THE GARDEN INTO THE REAL WORLD

The serpent enticed the woman by implying that by partaking of the fruit of the tree of knowledge of good and evil, she would be made wise like God, so she took it and ate, and gave some to her husband who was with her, and he ate (3:5–6). Some expositors condemn the woman as having tempted the man, but the Hebrew text states that he was with her, and if he was not deceived (see 1 Tim 2:14) then he sinned knowingly. The human beings try to exploit their privileges. Dissatisfied with their dependent status, even though well supplied and cared for by God, they grasp for autonomy by eating the forbidden fruit. On their own they have to face the real world. The primitive animal emotion of insecurity causes fear of God and of each other and rouses their instinct for self-preservation and for blaming others, even God (3:7–13). To the serpent YHWH God announces enmity with the woman and with her offspring: "he will strike your head, and you will strike his heel" (3:15). Traditionally Christians interpret this text to assure humanity's final defeat of Satan, with God's aid, of course.

The woman has desire for her husband (some expositors may specify this as sexual desire, though the text does not specify it), but beyond that she certainly desires his help, for she must undergo the pain and physical disadvantages inherent in the female role—menstruation, pregnancy, childbirth, lactation, and nurturance. She desires her husband to help her fulfill her role, but in his sinful state he exploits her dependent condition to rule over her. When seen in light of Darwinian evolution, this word is all the more realistic, as testified by abundant evidence of conditions of almost total male domination in all animal species including human, which is prevalent even today in many societies. For the man, God cursed the ground. Weeds make painful the man's toil to till/serve the ground to get food to sustain life. The story has suddenly become very complicated, yet the author(s) have pretty accurately described the way things were for men and women in their time and place. The Genesis account of the consequences of disobedience is *descriptive* of life as the biblical authors observed it, not *prescriptive* as though imposed by God.

YHWH God continued to show favor to the humans, first by providing more substantial clothing for their nakedness than the flimsy aprons of leaves they had devised (3:7, 21). In their changed condition, it would be no favor for them to eat of the tree of life and live forever, as YHWH God remarked to the other celestial beings, so YHWH God sent the humans out of the garden and blocked their access to the tree of life (3:22–24). Biological mortality is a fact of creaturely life.

This J account, like the P one before it, clearly reveals its superiority in comparison with pagan myths. Here again Scripture affirms the high dignity of human beings. They are not slaves to the gods but capable of fellowship with deity. Humans are superior to the other animals, though made from the same earthly substance. The basic attitude of the Creator toward the human creatures is favorable, even when they abuse the gift of freedom to defy the Creator. So long as they acknowledge their dependence on the Creator, they prosper, but they suffer when they greedily grasp for more than is their due. The first human beings were a pair of ordinary peasant type; certainly not any particularly exalted or favored race or class destined to dominate over fellow humans or other lands and cultures. Both P and J, these two originally separate accounts, each exhibiting its distinctive name for Deity, style, vocabulary, and theological teachings, supplement each other admirably.

SUMMARY AND REFLECTION

My long experience of teaching the Bible to Japanese students, beginning with Genesis and creation, became a powerful foundation for my deep conviction that God revealed in Scripture and through Jesus Christ has an eternal plan of reconciliation that is at least as comprehensive as the divine plan of creation. My understanding of Genesis has been liberated from the view expressed by Warfield that God's basic role is righteous lawgiver and judge. The Presbyterian Westminster Larger Catechism (part of Warfield's doctrinal standards) describes the divine-human relationship as a *covenant of works* whereby the human could gain life "upon condition of personal, perfect, and perpetual obedience."[8] This point is unjustifiably read into the text. In a later chapter I deal more fully with covenant, a word that first appears in the Bible in relation to God's unilateral promise of mercy to Noah both before and after the flood (Gen 6:18; 9:8–17).

A traditional interpretation depicts the first human pair created perfect but because of sin fallen into a state of moral corruption called original sin that passes to the whole human race descended from them. Originally immortal, they became subject to biological death, and their sin brought death and corruption to all creation, which was also originally perfect. Augustine, a Roman father in the Latin, or Western Church, is credited with developing this interpretation. Luther, Calvin, Warfield and others, were heirs of Augustine's interpretation, including "double predestination."

Earlier a Greek Father of the church, Irenaeus, understood that the first humans were created in a state of immaturity, not perfection. Endowed with the *image* of God, they were intelligent social animals, with the potential for growth and development through a long period of time toward attaining the *likeness* of God as revealed in Jesus Christ.[9] Irenaeus accepted that since God is the sole Creator and Ruler of the universe, there is no one else to share the responsibility for the origin of evil. Still, he added, we must trust wholly in God, who is not an irresponsible Creator but the loving Father, in whose presence we know that all shall be well.[10] Compared with Augustine's interpretation, that of Irenaeus is more compatible with evolution and with my belief in God for All.

8. *The Book of Confessions*, p 197, "The Larger Catechism" Q. 20.
9. See Hick, *The Second Christianity*, 97–98.
10. Ibid., 102.

5

Biblical Creation, Evolution, and Brain Science

THE DESCRIPTION OF CREATION in Genesis 1:1—2:4a is compatible with modern evolutionary thought. Beginning with a dark, formless chaos, Genesis describes the division of seas and land and an orderly progression from less to more complex forms of life, vegetable and animal, climaxing in the creation of humanity. Of course the biblical authors knew nothing of evolution. They shared the general view of cosmology with their contemporaries, including the belief that the sky was a solid dome. And according to them, each successive stage of creation was a separate divine act imposed from without by the Creator God. Some scholars today question that the authors of Genesis meant the days of creation as literally of twenty-four hours each They certainly were not debating cosmology with pagan contemporaries. The biblical authors were expressing their faith that creation was all the work of one God, Elohim, who they believed was the same as their national god YHWH. They signified their rejection of the mythology of *Enuma elish*, by which Marduk, the chief god of Babylon and his pantheon guaranteed the imperial power that oppressed the Israelites and other peoples.

1. THE AGE OF THE EARTH

Some present day fundamentalists, claiming the literal authority of the Bible in all matters, insist on what is known as a "young earth," which is only six thousand years old. The Irish Archbishop James Ussher (b. 1581, d. 1656) calculated the date of the origin of the world as October 4004 BC.[1] Some versions of the King James Bible add Ussher's dates as marginal notes, but nowadays few people seriously follow Ussher's chronology. Before Darwin published *On the Origin of Species* in 1859, geologists had already presented evidence of a much older earth. Evolution has confirmed the gradual internal development from less to more complex life forms over billions of years of time. Modern astronomy continues to add more knowledge concerning the vastness of the cosmos and its changes during the billions of years since it began with

---

1. Wikipedia, "James Ussher, Reputation."

the big bang. Nobody had such information when Darwin proposed his hypothesis, but he was fully cognizant of the great age of the Earth.

2. CONSERVATIVE CHRISTIANS REJECT EVOLUTION

Thomas Henry Huxley promoted Darwin's hypothesis by aggressively expositing ideas that Darwin only hinted at. Huxley was called "Darwin's Bulldog."[2] He posed the question as *either evolution or God* (a specious stratagem), and some theologians of the time took up the debate on those terms. Even today in the U.S., unfortunately, some still speak of "believing in evolution" as though it were similar to "believing in God." Some claim evolution is only an "unproven theory" and want public school science courses to include Genesis. Others try to smuggle God into science education by proposing that evolution occurred as a result of "Intelligent Design" and that God is the Designer. I think the fundamentalists' denying evolution is not a defense of God so much as an attempt to defend literal biblical authority. In effect, they treat the Bible as though it were God.

Just as the Israelite priests in Babylon accepted the common view of cosmology of their day while declaring faith in God, I, as a Christian, accept the facts of evolution and cosmology and believe in God revealed in Scripture and through Jesus Christ. In my view, there can be no question of the fact of evolution, though specialists continue research on myriad details of the implications of it. In this endeavor there is room for trial and error and for debate. The deciphering of the human genome together with the genomes of other animals has clarified our relations as animals, while affirming human superiority.[3]

3. THE HUMAN BRAIN

Thirty years ago I became aware of the importance of understanding the structure of the human brain in connection with my Bible teaching. Carl Sagan, popularizer of science, summarized the work of Paul MacLean, Chief of the Laboratory of Brain Evolution and Behavior.[4] The most primitive part of our brain, the reptilian complex, contains the basic neural capacities for reproduction and self-preservation, emotions of fear or anger, territoriality and hierarchy, and enabled creatures' survival in a harsh, competitive environment.[5] Recent works by Andrew Newberg and his associates give more detailed information. The reptilian brain, also called the limbic system, centers on the amygdala and thalamus, which after 450 million years of running the show still respond emotionally and with chemicals in the blood to situations of danger, threat, or

---

2. Wikipedia, "Thomas Henry Huxley."
3. Clark and Grunstein, *Are We Hardwired?*
4. Sagan, *The Dragons of Eden.*
5. Sagan, *Dragons of Eden,* 55.

anger—the fight or flight impulse. Our cerebral cortex comprising eighty-five percent of brain mass enables functions more typical of humans, including speech, reason, and abstract thought. The newest feature of our brain is the anterior cingulate between the reptilian brain and the frontal lobe of the cortex to provide balance between feelings and thoughts. Newberg says the anterior cingulate appears to be crucial for empathy and compassion.[6] All this bears directly on the theme of this book, God for All.

4. NEAR-DEATH EXPERIENCE

In recent decades researchers and authors have documented and published authenticated experiences of many people who have had a near-death experience (NDE). One feature common to such experiences is seeing a light. Other details may include an out-of-body experience that permits a surgical patient under anesthesia to observe what doctors and nurses are doing, and hearing their conversation. Some pass through a tunnel into a bright "heavenly" realm where deceased loved ones welcome them. Many have an instantaneous life-review and a sense of total acceptance and well being. Most of those who experience NDE emerge with an abiding sense of confidence, optimism, altruistic concern for others, and interest in spiritual and ethical matters, sometimes accompanied by indifference to organized religion. The details differ from individual to individual, depending on personality and culture, but *the experience of light is a constant*. Researcher Melvin Morse has interviewed persons who, *without* the NDE have had their lives transformed by seeing the light.[7]

Morse interviewed people who experienced "miraculous healings," others had heightened abilities of clairvoyance and precognition—intimations of the death of a loved one, including visual images of the loved one before death.[8] Tom Sawyer, a blue-collar snowplow driver with a high school education, gained insight into nuclear physics, including the mathematical formulas of Max Planck.[9] Olaf Sunden had an NDE as a boy, sensed himself entering into deeper intelligence, and changed from an average student to one almost arrogantly precocious. He wrote that he felt he had total comprehension, which made everything understandable. As an adult he intuited and patented over 100 chemical formulas and had a grasp of nuclear physics including insights into the existence of neutrinos.[10] As one NDEer said, "Just when the door closed on my life and everything was black, another door opened and I walked into a new world. Nothing has been the same since."[11]

---

6. Newberg and Waldman, *How God Changes Your Brain*.
7. Morse, *Transformed by the Light*.
8. Ibid., 3–8.
9. Ibid., 10.
10. Ibid., 11–15.
11. Ibid., 51.

Skeptics have sought for naturalistic, reductionist explanations of all these experiences. Melvin Morse writes:

> The experience of light has no known origin in the brain. Numerous scientific researchers have documented that every element of the NDE—the out-of-body experience, traveling up the tunnel, seeing dead relatives, having a life review, seeing visions of heaven—can be found to reside in the right temporal lobe. The only element that cannot be found in the brain is the experience of light. None of the reductionist researchers have yet been able to find the origin of the light in the brain.[12]

Medical and technical researchers in the field have come to believe that "the right temporal lobe is where the brain, mind, and soul converge in the human body." It is a sort of "receiving system" that allows people to hear voices from outside their bodies. The right temporal lobe contains what Morse calls "the circuit board of mysticism."[13] I take it to be in that sense the physiological locus of mystical experience, for it can be activated by disciplines of meditation of practitioners of different religions. Certain drugs and other stimuli can also produce many of the experiences reported in NDE. Nevertheless, that is not to deny the occurrence of genuine mystical experience. Morse asserts: "The experience of light cannot be activated artificially. It is activated only at the point of death or during some very special spiritual visions. This spiritual vision of the loving light results in the personality transformations that we saw in our study group. The most powerful and lasting transformations were seen in people who saw the light."[14]

Kenneth Ring independently confirms Morse's findings and adds other details.[15] Having interviewed hundreds of NDEers Ring states that the general similarities of their experiences prevail regardless of demographic characteristics such as age, sex, race, social class, educational level, occupation, and the like. Ring calls this "the invariance hypothesis."[16] He writes, "When we come to examine the core of full NDEs we find an absolute and undeniable spiritual radiance. This spiritual core of the NDE is so awesome and overwhelming that the person who experiences it is at once and forever thrust into an entirely new mode of being."[17] In telling their stories, many people refer to this radiance as "a divine being" or a "being of light."[18] One woman reported that she heard reassuring words about an important question, but she was told not to repeat them, and that she would forget them, which indeed she did.[19]

12. Ibid., 67–68.
13. Ibid., 195–96.
14. Ibid., 197.
15. Ring, *Heading Toward Omega*.
16. Ibid., 45.
17. Ibid., 50.
18. Ibid., 57.
19. Ibid., 67.

Practically all the NDEers Ring interviewed reported a sense of total and unconditional acceptance, of forgiveness, and of love. They believed God was calling them to express to others the same love they had experienced. "It is as though the unconditional love many of them felt during their NDE swept away the last vestiges of religious parochialism and opened them up to a vision of humanity united in a faith whose shared foundation is God's limitless love for all."[20]

5. RECENT BRAIN RESEARCH

Other brain experts have produced a vast amount of information concerning how the brain actually works (or fails to work) by reporting how injury or disease disables various areas of the brain. One example is the publication by a long-experienced brain expert writing her account of a serious stroke and eight-year process of recovery. Dr. Jill Bolte Taylor tells how a massive hemorrhage affected the left hemisphere of her brain, disabling her motor abilities, her language centers, and her ability to analyze and order information. She could not think of herself as an individual ego—what she called a "solid"—distinct from other people and the environment. In her unaffected right hemisphere she knew herself as a "fluid" flowing with the life force-energy of the universe. Dr. Taylor rejoiced in the present moment, spontaneous, carefree, and imaginative. She described her state as Nirvana. "I perceived myself as perfect, whole, and beautiful, just the way I was." Freed from left hemisphere dominance, her right hemisphere enabled her to be "completely committed to the expression of peace, love, joy, and compassion in the world."[21]

Dr. Taylor notes that emotions such as anger, anxiety, or fear consist in instantaneous electrical impulses transmitted by nerve cells plus chemicals added to the blood stream by internal glands. The brain receives and processes this electro-chemical input, which persists for about ninety seconds. The most primitive portions of our brains (MacLean's neural chassis and Reptilian Brain that we share with all animals) help process and transmit these impulses. If the left hemisphere with its sense of ego and self-assertion takes over with reactions to defend against perceived threats or opponents, serious negative consequences can result. Since recovery of her left-brain capabilities, Dr. Taylor has learned to let her right brain process such emotions, avoiding the escalation of "fight or flight" instincts and thus enabling compassion, peace, and contentment.[22]

In telling her experience Dr. Taylor referred to another book by brain specialists that bears on my interests.[23] The authors write: "[We] began, as all scientists do, with the fundamental assumption that all that is really real is material. We regarded

20. Ibid., 163.
21. Taylor, *My Stroke of Insight*.
22. Ibid., 131–36.
23. Newberg, d'Aquili, and Rause, *Why God Won't Go Away*.

the brain as a biological machine, composed of matter and created by evolution to perceive and interact with the physical world." Newberg and d'Aquili applied scan technology called SPECT (Single Photon Emission Computed Tomography) to Tibetan Buddhists and Catholic nuns engaged in the practice of meditation. They injected a radioactive substance into the blood, which carried it to the brain. On a computer screen the scan projected the activity of various portions of the brains during meditation, indicating elevated activity in the right hemisphere and passivity in the left, shedding light on the neurological evidence of their spiritual experiences. "It would be possible to believe that we had reduced all spiritual transcendence—from the mildest case of religious uplift, to the profound states of union described by mystics—to a neurochemical commotion in the brain. But our understanding of the brain would not allow us to rest with that conclusion—" They assert that every one of your perceptions, even the most material, such as the floor under your feet, your chair, the book in your hand, is the result of

> secondhand neurological perceptions, as blips and flashes racing along the neural pathways inside your skull. If you were to dismiss spiritual experience as 'mere' neurological activities, you would also have to distrust all of your own brain's perceptions of the material world. On the other hand, if we do trust our perceptions of the physical world, we have no rational reason to declare that spiritual experience is a fiction that is 'only' in the mind.[24]

The authors consider the charge that mystics suffer a mental derangement, but they present abundant contrary evidence. Experiences of epileptics and other mentally disabled people register differently in the brain from the mystics, and their physical and mental experiences affect their daily living in quite different ways.[25]

The authors quote briefly from the writings of mystics of different times and religious traditions—Hindu, Buddhist, Jewish, Christian, Native American, and Muslim.[26] They all report a total absorption of the self, like being swallowed up by the "all" or the "nothing" depending on their culture. Newberg and d'Aquili call this state "Absolute Unitary Being," and continue,

> The neurological realness of Absolute Unitary Being is by no means proof of an absolute spiritual reality . . . What we do suggest is that scientific research supports the possibility that a mind can exist without ego, that awareness can exist without self. In the neurological substance of Absolute Unitary Being, we find rational support for these inherent spiritual concepts, and a scientific platform from which to explore the deepest implications of mystical spirituality.[27] (. . .) Mystical reality holds, and the neurology does not contradict it, that

---

24. Ibid., 145–47.
25. Ibid., 107–11.
26. Ibid., 102–5.
27. Ibid., 126–27.

beneath the mind's perception of thoughts, memories, emotions, and objects, beneath the subjective awareness we think of as the self, there is a deeper self, a state of pure awareness that sees beyond the limits of subject and object, and rests in a universe where all things are one."[28]

At the very time while I was checking my typescript in preparation for publication, another remarkable personal story was published in *Newsweek* magazine, titled "My Proof of Heaven."[29] Dr. Eben Alexander, an experienced neurosurgeon tells how he lapsed into a coma for seven days when *E. coli* bacteria penetrated his brain in spinal meningitis. During the coma Dr. Alexander was on life support and under close scrutiny by other medical experts who by means of various scans and tests ascertained that his higher brain functions were completely shut down. Like other skeptics he had thought near-death experiences resulted from some malfunction of the cortex, but personal experience provided "evidence that consciousness exists beyond the body."

Dr. Alexander writes, "my brain-free consciousness journeyed to another, larger dimension of the universe: a dimension I'd never dreamed existed." He saw the light; he heard the message: "You have nothing to fear." "There is nothing you can do wrong." He describes that new dimension including details of sight and sound, speech and comprehension of an immediacy and clarity completely transcending earth-bound phenomena. "It was as if I were being born into a larger world, and the universe itself was like a giant cosmic womb." He goes on: "Physics tells us that beneath the surface, every object and event in the universe is completely woven up with every other object and event. There is no separation." He continues, "The universe as I experienced it in my coma is . . . the same one that both Einstein and Jesus were speaking of in their (very) different ways." Dr. Alexander says his life has been completely changed, and in his conclusion he says, "I've caught a glimpse of this emerging picture of reality."

SUMMARY AND REFLECTION

An inclination to reject evolution was part of the cultural baggage of my conservative upbringing, which I eventually dumped. More recent knowledge of how the human brain evolved and how that affects understanding the oneness of God and God's plan for the reconciliation of all humankind has stimulated me to try to coordinate evolution and this new knowledge with the teaching of the Bible and my Christian faith. I can't avoid making the attempt as I continue to work on this book.

The OT is concerned for the most part with inhabitants of what we now call the Mediterranean Basin continuing east to the lands of the Persian Gulf. Humankind had accomplished the Agricultural Revolution known also as the Neolithic Revolution, the prehistoric transition from hunting and gathering to settled agriculture, around

---

28. Ibid., 155.

29. *Newsweek* October 15, 2012. All my quotations are derived from this issue.

10,000 years BP (Before the Present). The full-blown manifestation of the Neolithic complex, which in general set the cultural and political background of the OT, is seen in the Middle Eastern Sumerian cities (c 3,500 BCE).[30] The empires of Assyria and Babylonia succeeded the Sumerian cities and built on their accomplishments.

H. and H. W. Frankfort report that the people of the ancient Near East had not exploited the powers of logical, rational thought, (which modern science locates principally in the left hemisphere of the brain). According to the Frankforts, the ancients expressed their attempts to understand and explain the world by use of imagination, poetry, and myth making (which are more typical of right brain functions). The ancients assigned a degree of personhood to every aspect of nature, and they sought to explain events as the effects of activity by many gods along with humans in a total environment that lacked fixed boundaries. Our modern contrast between reality and appearance was meaningless to them. Whatever was capable of affecting mind, feeling, or will had thereby established its reality. The ancients made no sharp distinction among dreams, hallucinations, and ordinary vision. For them, the survival of the dead and their continued relationship with living humans were assumed as a matter of course, for the dead attained some degree of deity and were involved in the reality of people's own anguish and expectations.[31]

In an essay concluding the work of the other authors of the book, the Frankforts summarize the common worldview as consisting in "the fundamental assumptions that the individual is part of society, that society is embedded in nature, and that nature is but the manifestation of the divine. This doctrine was, in fact, universally accepted by the peoples of the ancient world with the single exception of the Hebrews."[32]

I must emphasize that the exception of the Hebrews was neither immediate nor complete. The clear contrast expressed by Professor Ishida in his scheme of "Two Worldviews" (above chapter 2) became evident only after the end of the kingdom of Judah in 587 to 578 BCE. The early Hebrews or proto-Israelites shared the common culture and worldview of the ancient Near East. The agricultural revolution made possible increase of population, settled communities, and surplus of food and bare necessities. Still, humans to some extent behaved in the manner of lower animals. Aggressive males took charge.[33] Among males the stronger accumulated more wealth and property, and lorded it over the weak, some of whom they enslaved. Females, non-aggressive and biologically designed for reproduction, were considered property. A female's owner changed when her father gave or sold her to be wife or concubine of another man. Kings and rulers and any other men who could afford it owned multiple women and produced many children. As tribal communities organized into nation-

---

30. Wikipedia, Agricultural Revolution, Neolithic Complex.
31. Frankfort and Frankfort, *Before Philosophy*, 14–21.
32. Ibid., 241.
33. The genetic makeup of males comprises genes, chromosomes, and hormones that predispose to aggression different from those in females. See Clark and Grunstein, *Are We Hardwired?* 157–75.

states, they promoted national unity and exclusion of others by elevating a particular deity. Each nation-state had its chief god, its war god, and other deities for various other needs.

Careful reading of the OT reveals that its authors lived in this sort of culture and reflected its social and religious practices. Community life and international relations conformed to the general patterns. Like other nation-states Israel had its own God YHWH, especially for times of war, though many Israelites didn't hesitate to seek aid from other deities they considered more appropriate for particular needs, especially fertility of family, of herd, and of field. Compared to other peoples of the ancient Near East, Israel's uniqueness lay in the work of a small minority of zealots, who insisted (sometimes accompanied by deadly violence) that YHWH, who had liberated their forebears from slavery, was sufficient for all their needs. The struggle to advance the YHWH-only agenda amidst a polytheistic culture was a long, arduous process, which is reflected in the OT.

The creation story of Gen 1:1—2:4a (P) is one product of that long process, and it was written down only after Israel and Judah no longer existed as nation-states and their people were subjects of the empires, i.e., some time after 578 BCE. The editorial joining of the P story Gen 1:1—2:4a with the earlier J story Gen 2.4b—3:24 in producing the Pentateuch was much later still. The task I have undertaken is to follow the process of development of the concept of the oneness of God. During the centuries occupied by this process, humanity in general, including Israel whose experience and witness we find in the Bible, gradually learned to check the dominance of the reptilian complex in their brains to give greater play to the more typically human functions of the neocortex (which itself was undergoing development simultaneously). By means of "the circuit board of mysticism" in the neocortex humans became conscious of the God who transcends all races, cultures, and religions, and who in various ways self-manifests in them all. Within the total biblical material itself, OT and NT, one may trace an evolution from fear toward trust in God, from exclusion toward inclusion, from parochial toward universal, and finally, a re-imagining that seems to blur the absolute distinction between God and humankind, as seen in the life, ministry, death, and resurrection of Jesus of Nazareth.

6

The Spread of Population and Sin

THE HEBREW BIBLE (BASIS of the Christians' Old Testament) tells the Israelites' story of their life with the One God. It opens with Genesis, the "book of beginnings." The first eleven chapters, sometimes referred to as the Primeval Events, constitute an introduction that describes the origin of the world that Israel inhabits and the human race of which Israel is only a small part. Therefore the account deals with God and humanity in universal terms. The priestly P account tells the creation of the world climaxing in humanity, and the older Yahwist J story follows, telling of intimate relations between God and humans. Without explanation, the same J source introduces a mysterious third force, Sin (sometimes personified by various figures) that incites human selfish defiance and alienation from the Creator.

1. THE SPREAD OF SIN

The first crime recorded in the Bible is one man's murder of his brother, and in part the motivation arose from a difference over the worship of God. The first human child Cain was a tiller of the ground like his father, and he offered some of his harvest to the deity. The younger son Abel kept sheep, hitherto unmentioned as an occupation, and his offering involved the death of an animal. Cain became angry because YHWH accepted Abel's offering but not his. Without specifying any particular deed or thought, the divine word to Cain implies that he has not done well, but, YHWH says, sin personified as some threatening beast simply lurks outside, waiting for Cain to give it an opportunity to leap in. Cain is not, as some interpreters might have us believe, the victim of a totally depraved nature transmitted from parents by sinful sexual intercourse. We note a striking similarity here to YHWH's pronouncement to the woman: To the woman he said, "Your *desire* shall be for your husband, and he shall *rule over* you" (3:16). To Cain he said, "Sin is lurking at the door, and its *desire* is for you, but you must *master* it" (4:7). The Hebrew vocabulary is the same in both cases. One who *desires* something from another becomes vulnerable to *being ruled* or *mastered* by that other. The woman *desires* her husband to help produce and care for children, and he *rules over* her. Sin *desires* Cain's permission to come to expression; yet Cain can *master* or *rule over* sin by resisting or withholding cooperation.

Cain flings open the door to sin and takes out his resentment upon the brother whose acceptance by YHWH has made him look bad by comparison. Cain strikes Abel dead, alleges ignorance as to his brother's whereabouts, and implies that he has no responsibility as his brother's keeper.[1] This attitude is typical of those who emphasize "individual freedom," which often translates into denial of people's responsibility for the common good. YHWH pronounces upon Cain a punishment similar to that on Adam: YHWH curses the ground and drives him out. Cain complains that now he has become fair game for anyone to kill him, so YHWH places a protective mark upon Cain to spare him. Divine mercy triumphs over strict justice! (4:8–16). "Cain went away from the presence of YHWH" (4:16), to which von Rad comments: "That he still is not abandoned by God but lives expressly in a protective relationship is the most enigmatic part of the narrative, for here God's ordering and protecting will is revealed."[2]

The genealogy of Cain credits him and his descendants with such aspects of human culture as city building, animal husbandry, music, and metal work (Gen 4:17–22). We usually consider them positive accomplishments of civilization, but J hints at their ambiguity (in modern terms read "technology"). Lamech, seventh generation after Cain and father of the metal smiths and musicians, kills a man who struck him and celebrates the deed in song. According to a literal reading of the Bible, the flood wiped out the line of Cain, but their contributions to human culture persist in all their ambiguity. Herman Brichto stresses the universal character of the biblical text. In remarking on God sparing Cain, he states with emphasis: "*And Cain had to live, in this allegory, to father the human race. So that the moral be not lost—Cain, ancestor of all mankind, is your father and mine.*"[3]

Textual ambiguity is even more complicated. Biblical scholars note a connection between Cain (*qayin*) and the Kenites (*qeyni*), itinerant metal workers descended from Tubal Cain, the first smith. The Kenites frequently met and interacted with the Israelites, including their kinship with the family of Moses's in-laws and their possible connection with the introduction of the Name YHWH (see chapter 9.2 "The origin of the Name").

---

1. The Hebrew root of the noun in Cain's question, "Am I my brother's *keeper*?" is the same as that describing the earthling's duty to *keep* God's garden. The basic meaning is to guard, to keep safe.
2. Von Rad, *Genesis*, 105.
3. Brichto, *The Names of God*, 304.

2. THE FLOOD

When J undertook to put the acts of YHWH in the context of world history, he not only began with creation, he also had to take account of a great flood, an event of the ancient Near East that left a lasting residue in every attempt to tell the story.

In the legends and traditions of events occurring in the lower Mesopotamian valley, a flood marks a significant break to which people can point as dividing "before" and "after" in human history as they knew it. The Sumerian King List begins: "When the kingship came down from heaven, the kingship was in Eridu—" The account names cities and rulers: "These are five cities; eight rulers reigned for 241,000 years. (Then) the flood streamed over (the earth)." After the flood, rulers reigned for shorter periods, but still for superhuman lengths of time.[4] Archaeologists Leonard Woolley at Ur and Stephen Langdon at Kish, found thick layers of alluvial deposit separating more recent from much earlier human occupation.[5] At each site, though at different times, a flood had obliterated the earlier civilization. After a break in time humans reoccupied the site and started anew. These traumatic events left their mark on cultural memory.

Translations of fragments of flood myths from different locations and in different languages display a common theme: the gods, for no apparent reason, determine to destroy humanity by means of a flood, but one god reveals the plan to a human, instructing him to save himself and his family by building a vessel. The survivor becomes a legendary hero. Outside the Bible, the best-known and most nearly complete account of a flood is found on Tablet XI of the *Gilgamesh Epic*. Without doubt both J and P were familiar with the ancient myth and used it brilliantly to express their deeply held faith. The flood story now in our Bibles seems to be based on the J source skillfully supplemented by P.

3. THE FLOOD STORY IN GENESIS

The biblical authors take a radically different approach to the flood than any of the pagan myths. Both P and J find the cause of the flood in human depravity and corruption, contrary to the common practice of pagan myths to attribute its cause to the deities and their capricious enmity against humanity. P's explanation is universal—"Now the earth was corrupt in God's sight, and the earth was filled with violence. And God saw that the earth was corrupt; for all flesh [not just humans] had corrupted its ways upon the earth" (Gen 6:11–12 P).

The Yahwist version states that the sons of the gods took wives for themselves from among human women and produced giants (*nephilim*) and warrior heroes

---

4. Beyerlin, *Near Eastern Religious Texts*, 87–89.

5. The destruction of these two cities resulted from separate inundations at different times. See *IDB* II 278–84.

(*gibborim*) (Gen 6:1–4 J). These remind us of Greek and Roman myths of gods and goddesses in sexual union with women and men. The similarity of the Bible verses to such mythology has posed problems for readers and expositors of the Bible. The apocryphal First Book of Enoch, based on the Genesis text and apparently known to both Jews and Christians in the first century CE, contains much fanciful material describing what happened when "the angels, children of heaven," took women as wives. They produced offspring of gigantic size who corrupted and terrorized the earth. This brought on divine judgment through the Deluge (1 Enoch 6–10).[6]

This brief, enigmatic reference in Genesis may be a remnant of primitive belief, which later was contradicted by Israel's experience of YHWH's compassion and justice, and which disappeared elsewhere in Scripture. There was a common belief that the Most High El (or Elohim) had appointed a heavenly deity (one of the "sons of the gods" or one of the "holy ones" for each earthly nation, e.g., "the holy one of Israel" or "YHWH the god of Israel," Chemosh of Moabites, Molech of Ammonites, etc. (see 1 Kgs 11:5–7). The human king of each nation would be the earthly image of the national god and consequently might exercise divine authority over his human subjects. The "heroes that were of old, warriors of renown" of Gen 6:4 could well refer to human potentates who were acclaimed sons of god or who claimed that title by force. Sensitive adherents of YHWH-alone conviction noted that kings and national gods of other nations connived at injustice and favoritism in behalf of the rich and powerful. Even in Israel itself, kings who were considered "son of God"[7] did the same, but injustice and exploitation were not compatible with mature YWHW-alone faith. Earthly potentates and their heavenly sponsors who failed to do justice exposed the falseness of their claim to be gods.

We find in Ps 82 a succinct expression of the conclusion of this way of thinking. The Psalm opens with Elohim, the supreme God, calling the lesser gods to account. They judge unjustly and show partiality. Elohim demands that they rescue the weak and poor from their wicked oppressors (Ps 82:1–4). The psalmist continues his meditation as he reflects on these so-called gods: "They have neither knowledge nor understanding / they walk around in darkness; / all the foundations of the earth are shaken" (82:5). By failing to maintain justice, the gods in heaven and their surrogates in the kingdoms of earth have put world order in danger of collapse. The psalmist now realizes his original error in considering them gods at all. Not only the corrupt earthly surrogates but also the putative gods in the heavenly assembly must die! "I *thought*, 'You are gods, / children of the Most High, all of you; / nevertheless, you shall die like mortals, / and fall like any prince" (Ps 82:6–7 altered).[8] In conclusion, then, the psalm-

---

6. Isaac, trans., "1 (Ethiopic Apocalypse of) Enoch" 6–10, pp 15–19.

7. See 2 Sam 7:17; Ps 2:7; 45:6; 89:26–27; 1 Chr 29:23 for hints that kings of Israel could be called son of God.

8. Ps 82:6–7 NRSV. In translating "I *thought*" instead of "I say" I have followed Dahood, *Psalms II*, 270: In Hebrew, the verb ʾ*amar* = "to say," may mean, "to think" depending on context and construction.

ist utters his fervent petition to the supreme God, Elohim: "Rise up, O God, judge the earth; for all the nations belong to you!" (Ps 82:8).

If Gen 6:1–4 is truly a fragment of ancient mythology overlooked by the postexilic priests who edited Genesis as we now have it, Ps 82 is evidence that elsewhere in Scripture other Israelites of mature understanding proclaimed YHWH-alone faith on the way to the universal faith in God who transcends all gods and embraces all people.

The Yahwist goes on to explain the cause of the flood: "YHWH saw that the wickedness of humankind was great in the earth, and that every inclination of the thoughts of their hearts was only evil continually. And YHWH was sorry that he had made humankind on the earth, and it grieved him to his heart" (Gen 6:5–6 J). The creatures' defiance of the Creator has struck deep into the heart of God, leading to an inclination to destroy them. Yet within YHWH the instinct to preserve outweighs the impulse to destroy: "God is not angered but grieved. He is not enraged but saddened," Brueggemann comments. He notes that the root of the word for "grieved" here is the same as the "pain" of the woman in bearing children (Gen 3:16, twice) and the "toil" by which the man could eat the produce of the ground (Gen 3:17).[9] The concept of YHWH expressing emotion and pain in sympathy with humankind stated here by the author is the fruit of long faith experience, and it should shame any believers who are quick to depict God as ready and eager to punish sin.

Using an expression that describes a free, undeserved gift from God, J adds, "But Noah found favor in the sight of YHWH" (Gen 6:8).[10] The supplemental material from the Priestly version adds, "Noah was a righteous man, blameless in his generation; Noah walked with God" (6:9).[11] Further, God informed Noah of the coming destruction by flood and added, "But I will establish my covenant with you" (6:18 P). Here is the first mention of *covenant*, a concept of paramount importance in the entire Bible. In my view, the author considered the covenant concept so familiar that he felt no necessity to explain it at this point.

4. GOD'S POST-FLOOD PURPOSES OF GRACE

For those interested in comparing the two biblical narratives, J and P, with each other and with the *Gilgamesh Epic* flood story in detail, I provide a chart at chapter's end. Here I wish only to note the conclusions of J and P accounts to emphasize what they say about God. The Yahwist notes that the punishment of the flood effected *no reformation* of the human heart. After the flood, just as before, YHWH observes that "the inclination of the human heart is evil from youth." Precisely *because* this punishment

---

9. Brueggemann, *Genesis*, 77.

10. See Exod 33:12, 13, 16, 17; 34:9. Moses found favor in YHWH's sight after the Israelites worshiped the golden calf.

11. At Gen 7:1 (J) YHWH tells Noah: "I have seen that you alone are righteous before me in this generation."

has been ineffective, YHWH promises never again to destroy every living creature as he has just done, and guarantees regular seasonal change and normal human life on earth (8:21–22 J).

In P, God blesses Noah and his sons and repeats the command of Gen 1:28, "Be fruitful and multiply and fill the earth. The fear and dread of you shall rest on every animal of the earth . . . into your hand they are delivered" (9:1–2). Humans may now eat any animal flesh, though "not with its life, that is, its blood" (9:2–4). All blood, even of animals, is precious to God. Keeping animals under cruel conditions and butchering them for food, plus human encroachment on wild animal habitat may be serious offenses against the divine command to keep/protect the rest of creation. Even more precious is human blood. God says, "—at the hand of every man's brother will I require the life of man" (Gen 9:5b KJV).[12] The text continues, with a poetic fragment: "Whoever sheds the blood of a human / by a human shall that person's blood be shed; / for in his own image God made humankind" (9:6 NRSV). Some people claim this saying to advocate capital punishment. But if we read Gen 9:6 literally, we must see that it is an absolute impossibility. Since *all* humans are brothers and sisters, and *every* human is made in God's image, which human is qualified to shed the blood of another human, even if that other is a murderer? To follow this mandate *literally* would obliterate the entire human race! The controlling concept here is the assertion that all humanity is created in God's image. This text, instead of supporting the death penalty is a powerful argument to abolish it. All too often, U.S. courts administer capital punishment with gross *racial, social, and economic discrimination*. Further, many proponents of capital punishment raise no question of the state's right to wage war, even when a result is mass civilian deaths, euphemistically called "collateral damage."

Next God fulfills the earlier promise of the covenant to Noah. That first mention of covenant in the Bible (Gen 6:18) was made in an almost offhand manner, as though it were something completely familiar. As I explain below, God first established a covenant with one man, Abram and his family, linking deity to humanity in a fictive family relationship (Gen 15:18–21). Thereafter, over many centuries and under many changing circumstances, the concept of covenant persisted and functioned like a lifeline revealing God's unchanging faithfulness despite the people's perennial breaching of obligation. The priestly author in Babylon, having experienced defeat and exile, yet resting confident in what covenant has taught him about the nature of God, is inspired to declare that his God embraces the whole of creation, all the living creatures, the ongoing generations of humanity, and the earth itself in an eternal covenant never again to send a flood to destroy everything. The sign of this covenant will be the rainbow, symbolizing that God has unstrung the war bow and hung it upside down in the heaven as a sign of peace for all, including God, to see. Read for yourself, not

---

12. I cite the KJV for this text as being true to the Hebrew, which indicates total human kinship by reading "every man's *brother.*" NRSV obscures this detail by reading "the blood of *another* "instead of "*brother.*" Here, as often in Scripture "to shed blood" means to kill.

once but at least twice, Genesis 9:9–17 and feel the solemn ponderousness with which God states the divine purpose toward the whole creation, affirming the pledge: "When the bow is in the clouds, I will see it and remember the everlasting covenant between God and every living creature of all flesh that is on the earth." Here is one of the most powerful universal texts in all Scripture!

Immediately after this affirmation of God's universal good will toward every member of the whole creation, Scripture gives an example of the persistence of the evil inclination of the human heart: Noah gets drunk and passes out naked. One of his sons takes advantage of his helplessness to commit some heinous misbehavior that is only hinted at, leaving it to the inclination of our own hearts to imagine the details (9:20–27).[13]

Noah's three sons and their wives proceed to obey the command to "be fruitful and multiply and fill the earth" (Gen 9:1). In what is familiarly known as the Table of Nations, we read a detailed list of their descendants (Gen 10:1–32). Many readers of the Bible tend to skip over the strange-sounding names in this and other biblical genealogies, but to scholars who study them with care they often reveal important information. For societies not organized under a state system, such as the minority of Israelites who returned to Judea under Persian sponsorship, genealogies described the whole social order—rank, status, claims, and expectations of all kinds.[14] Frank Crüsemann dates the Table of Nations to the Persian period and writes:

> We can discern an increasing concentration on Israel as the main line of descent . . . But who this Israel is, can only be grasped within the framework of the whole; this ethnic group is part of the entire coherence of humanity. (. . .) Thus, humanity is represented as *family*. Nothing less is at stake than *the essential unity of all human beings*. Everyone is related to each other; human being as such presents no fundamental differences.[15]

After describing the repopulation of the world through Noah's descendants (10:1–32), the tale of human sinfulness reaches another climax in the story of the Tower of Babel. Perhaps Babel is a parody on the great city of Babylon,[16] which in both the OT and the NT has become the symbol of human arrogance that defiantly pits earthly imperial ambition against God. Humanity (represented by Babylon?) resists the divine command to "fill the earth" and tries to concentrate all people and all power in one human organization that can challenge God. The tower (temple of Marduk?) is so puny that YHWH has to come down to earth even to see what people are doing! YHWH frustrates their plans by confusing their language. "Therefore it was

---

13. Several suggestions of ancient rabbis are noted in *The Torah*, Revised Edition, 74–75.
14. Crüsemann, "Human Solidarity and Ethnic Identity." Note the prominence of genealogies in Chronicles, Ezra, and Nehemiah, all recorded during the postexilic Persian period.
15. Crüsemann, op. cit. 66, emphasis added.
16. *Babel* is the Hebrew word that is always rendered "Babylon" in NRSV except for this one place.

called Babel (=*babel*) because there YHWH confused (=*balal* Hebrew word play) the language of all the earth; and from there YHWH scattered them abroad over the face of all the earth" (11:1–9).

5. THE ANCESTORS OF ISRAEL

At this point the postexilic priestly author(s) insert a continuation of the genealogy of Noah's son Shem (beginning at 10:21–31, resumed at 11:10–26), which forms a bridge linking the Primeval History to the story of Israel. The author(s) are about to make a great leap backward; they will present something like a movie flashback. Drawing on a variety of traditions rising from the mists of prehistory, they will bring on stage a human couple with their share of human weaknesses, the aged Abram and his barren wife Sarai (Gen 11:27–30). These are the unlikely progenitors of the people through whom God will begin his plan to mend the world torn by sin. Ogden Nash spoke for many when he exclaimed, "How odd of God to choose the Jews!" In what follows in the rest of the Hebrew Bible we may sometimes feel as though the means is about to overwhelm the end. Yet for all the special treatment Israel subsequently receives, it is humanity as such that is the object of the One God's reconciliation. With due appreciation for Israel, let us never lose sight of the universal purpose of God for All.

COMPARISON OF THREE VERSIONS OF THE FLOOD STORY[17]

	Gilgamesh Epic Tablet XI	Early Bible Story, Yahwist author (J)	Late Bible Story, Priestly author (P)
Deities	Many in council: hostile Enlil, friendly Enki/Ea; Anu, Ishtar, Adad, Erragal	YHWH (LORD = special Name for Israel's Deity), acts alone	Elohim (generic term for God) the One and Only
Cause	Not stated; decision of gods	Sons of gods marry women; human heart inclined only to evil from youth	All flesh (animals too) had corrupted its way; the earth was filled with violence
Survivor	Utnapishtim, secretly informed by the god Ea	Righteous Noah informed by YHWH, and his family	Righteous Noah informed by Elohim, and his family

17. The *Gilgamesh Epic* version of the flood may be found in English translation in Pritchard, ed., *The Ancient Near East* .I, 65–71. An abbreviated translation may be found in Beyerlin, ed., *Near Eastern Religious Texts*, 93–97. Westermann, *Genesis* 1–11, 395–96, divides the biblical text as follows: (J): 6:5–8; 7:1–5, 10, 12, 16b, 17b, 22, 23a, 23c; 8:2b, 3a, 6–12, 13b, 20–22. (P): 6:9–12; 7:6, 11, 13–16a, 17a, 18–21, 24, 8:1–2a, 3b–5, 14–19, 9:1–17.

Means of survival	Wooden box, 120x120x120 cubits.		Wooden box (ark) 300x50x30 cubits
Taken aboard	Family, kin, silver, gold, craftsmen, domestic & wild animals	Noah's immediate family, 1 pair of unclean, 7 pairs of clean animals and birds	Noah's immediate family, 1 pair of all animals and birds
Source of flood	Storm god Adad sends rain 7 days and 7 nights; Erragal frees water of the deep; gods cower like dogs	Rain falls 40 days and 40 nights	Windows of heaven and fountains of the great deep open, 150 days, water covers all mountains
Waters recede	7 days and 7 nights	40 days; Noah waits 14 days more	150 days. Flood lasts 1 year 10 days before the earth is completely dry
Testing dryness	Utnapishtim sends out a dove, a swallow (both return) then a raven which does not return	Noah sends out a raven (which subsists on carrion?); dove which returns; dove next brings sprig of olive; then dove does not return	Elohim commands Noah and all with him to go out from the ark.
Sacrifice	Utnapishtim offers sacrifice, hungry gods smell it, swarm around like flies.	Noah offers sacrifice, YHWH smells it, and is pleased	
Aftermath	Enlil is angry that humans survived. Gods persuade him to let humans die by natural causes. Ishtar swears by her lapis lazuli necklace to remember.	YHWH promises never again to curse ground, destroy life, for imagination of human hearts is evil from youth. YWHW guarantees orderly progression of seasons for normal life.	Elohim establishes covenant with Noah, all living things, and earth; places the bow (abandoned war weapon) in heaven as sign, swears to remember the covenant never to destroy earth again.

7

The Covenant with Abram

JEWS, CHRISTIANS, AND MUSLIMS all venerate Abram/Abraham as our "father" in one sense or another, and that has left a deep impression on all three monotheistic religions. But Abram, the person, lived long before Israel or the Jews emerged as a self-conscious people among the peoples of the ancient Near East to claim him as their progenitor and his God as their God. The author(s) of the J tradition that we are following just now pre-emptively named Abram's God YHWH,[1] the Name revealed only much later to Moses (Exod 3:13–15; 6:2–3). By the time J was recorded, YHWH was already exclusively the name of "the God of Israel." By contrast, the author(s) of P or the priestly tradition recognized this anachronism; they used Shaddai as the name when God communicated with Abram and the other patriarchs (Gen 17:1; 28:3; 35:11; 43:14; 48:3; 49:25). At Exod 6:2–3 God [Elohim] addressed Moses: "I am YHWH. I appeared to Abraham, Isaac, and Jacob as God Almighty [*El Shaddai*], but by my name YHWH I did not make myself known to them."[2]

Shaddai, or similar names based on the *sh-d* root whose meaning is uncertain, may refer to a class of minor deities that were popular as personal or family guardians throughout the region where Israel's early ancestors lived and moved, according to the research of several scholars.[3] Originally Shaddai was a benevolent spirit who through attachment to Israel's ancestors came to play a role in the concept of the oneness of God. The great Jewish scholar Martin Buber describes it as, "a guardian deity, not a family fetish, but a great guardian deity, hidden and yet manifest." Perhaps this guardian deity at times mediated on behalf of Abram with the higher power, Elohim.

---

1. The J source states that people called on YHWH as early as the third generation after Adam (Gen 4:26).

2. The KJV translation of 1611 CE has fixed "God Almighty" as the translation of El Shaddai, but recent scholars question its accuracy. NJPS transliterates "El Shaddai" with a marginal note "*Traditionally rendered 'God Almighty.'*" NRSV keeps the old translation but adds a marginal note "Traditional rendering of Heb *El Shaddai*."

3. In Akkadian, the language of Babylon, the name is *Shedu*. Bernhard Lang, *Monotheism and the Prophetic Minority*, p 50. In *The Hebrew God*, 105–8 Lang notes a connection with an Egyptian god *Shed*, Lord of the Animals. See also Smith, *Early History of God*, 31 n 42, and Burnett, *A Reassessment of Biblical Elohim*, 38, 47. Cross translates "the mountain one" *Canaanite Myth and Hebrew Epic*, 55.

Buber continues, "The God, Who at the beginning was a guardian deity of a man, will become deity of a community of men, afterwards deity of a people, and finally deity of the peoples; this God, Who at the beginning was the deity of a personal biography, will become the deity of history—"[4] Thus, when the Bible reads YHWH as Abram's God, we should make a mental note "Shaddai." God calls Abram to be mediator of a universal purpose: blessing for all the families of the earth.

> Now YHWH said to Abram, "Go from your country and your kindred and your father's house to the land that I will show you. I will make of you a great nation, and I will bless you, and make your name great, so that you will be a blessing. I will bless those who bless you, and the one who curses you I will curse; and in you all the families of the earth shall be blessed." So Abram went as YHWH had told him. (Gen 12:1–4a)

1. ABRAM THE STATELESS ALIEN

Abram deserves the high praise all three religions give him for his prompt obedience to the divine call. Abram's separation from family, home, and land made him seriously vulnerable. Then, far more than in our society today, the extended family was a person's most important relationship and hope for survival. Each family member was obligated to contribute to the best of his or her ability to the welfare of all the others, and in return each could expect to receive whatever he or she needed for well being. According to A. R. Hulst, at the most primitive level of cognate Semitic languages, the word that came to mean "people" in Hebrew (*ʿam*) originally designated the uncle, the most important paternal relative in the constellation of family kinship.[5] With regard to those outside their family, nobody had either obligations or rights. Indigenous people might consider aliens as threats and attack or victimize them, much as some U.S. citizens today may exploit undocumented aliens.

Typical of disadvantaged minorities who believe their lives to be in serious danger, Abram twice and later his son Isaac once lied to save themselves while being willing to sacrifice their wives. In Egypt (Gen 12:10–20) and again in Gerar (20:1–18), Abram feared the inhabitants might kill him to get possession of his wife who was very beautiful. He introduced her as his sister, and a local ruler gave him rich gifts and took her into his harem. YHWH (Abram's Shaddai) protected Sarai and inflicted illness on the ruler's household till he returned her to Abram. Both times the deceived party sent Abram and Sarai safely away in full possession of the gifts they had given him. Abram, thus enriched, had a considerable household with slaves and flocks and herds. As an alien, he had to enter into formal negotiations with local landowners for

---

4. Buber, *The Prophetic Faith*, 35–36.
5. Hulst, *TLOT* II, 896.

the right to pitch his tents and pasture and water his animals. A formal agreement of this kind was called a covenant (Heb *berit*).

2. COVENANT IN THE ANCIENT NEAR EAST

As noted above, in relatively primitive times a person's extended family was the most important relationship for life and security. In regard to all outsiders, a person had neither obligations nor expectations. From time to time a person might find it necessary or desirable to enter a covenant relationship (*berit*) with an outsider, which would place the parties on the same basis *as if* they were family, not naturally but in a fictive sense. Johannes Pedersen describes *berit* in connection with the Near East family structure. The parties bound themselves to obligations and rights similar to those of members of a natural family.[6] In a society lacking developed legal systems and courts of law, the parties called on their respective deities to witness and enforce the agreement. Perhaps routinely in such ceremonies the parties shared a meal in the presence of the gods. Sharing food with another indicated a relation of mutual trust (see the example at Gen 31:43–54). In some extrabiblical cases, and in one other example in the OT (Jer 34:18–20), the covenant ceremony included cutting animal(s) in two. The parties passed between the pieces, invoking the gods to punish whichever one broke the agreement by cutting him in two.[7]

Pederson shows covenant's effectiveness in enabling peaceful co-existence between people at every level of social and political life. From the personal level of unrelated individuals treating each other as family, covenants grew in complexity to the highest international level, regulating relations between kings, who addressed each other as "brother" (see 1 Kgs 20:30–34, Ahab of Israel and Ben Hadad of Aram; 1 Kgs 9:13, Hiram of Tyre and Solomon.). Both Abraham (Gen 21:22–33), and Isaac (26:26–33), made covenants with Abimelech and Phicol in Gerar to resolve quarrels and guarantee space to settle and obtain pasture and water. Already earlier, Abram had had a covenant relationship with some local Amorites.

3. ABRAM'S COVENANT WITH THE AMORITE BROTHERS

The relationship between Abram the resident alien and three Amorite brothers, Mamre, Aner, and Eshcol, provides some instructive details. "Abram moved his tent,

---

6. See Pedersen, *Israel* Vol. 1–2, 264–310 for a helpful discussion of the broad theme "Peace and Covenant" that includes the matter briefly dealt with here.

7. Harrill offers abundant evidence that similar protocols prevailed throughout the Mediterranean region and were in effect during the time of the emerging Christian church, including such transactions as sale of property. The parties swore truthfulness in all details, and invoked a curse upon themselves in case of perjury. At times a small animal was slain, not in sacrifice but as symbolic of the fate the parties invoked. Such a background would be understood as basis for the story of the deaths of Ananias and Sapphira."Divine Judgment against Ananias and Sapphira (Acts 5:1–11)."

and came and settled by the oaks of Mamre, which are at Hebron, and there he built an altar to YHWH" (his Shaddai, Gen 13:18). Mamre the Amorite owned the local shrine where Abram offered sacrifice to his guardian deity. That would have been impossible without permission from the owner. Indeed we learn that a formal agreement of that nature had taken place, for in what follows, Abram is identified as "Abram the Hebrew" and the aforementioned Amorite brothers are called "allies of Abram" (Gen 14:13). The Hebrew text states, literally, that they were "masters/owners (Heb *baʿalim*) of Abram's covenant." In other words, the alien Abram, in the inferior position of petitioner, had formally requested and received permission to settle on the property of the owners, and this agreement had been sealed by a covenant in the presence of their respective deities at the shrine of Mamre.

A war raiding party captured Abram's nephew Lot and fellow citizens of Sodom. Lot's paternal uncle Abram (his *ʿam*=uncle in primitive terms) fulfilled his family obligation by taking a band of his men and rescuing his nephew and the other captives (Gen 14:14–16). The Amorite brothers, bound to Abram in a fictive family relationship by covenant, went to help him to rescue his kinfolk, and he insisted that they receive some of the spoils of battle, though he himself refused to accept a reward (14:21–24).

4. GOD'S COVENANT WITH ABRAM

According to the biblical account, YHWH (the God of Abram, his personal Shaddai) had promised to give Abram the land and multiply his descendants, though he was both landless and childless (Gen 11:30; 12:2, 7; 13:14–15). Up till now Abram depended on security as an alien on covenant agreements with indigenous landholders. Following the rescue of Lot, when he refused to accept a reward, Abram had a vision in which YHWH (his Shaddai) assured him that he would have a great reward. Abram complained that he was childless, and that one of his servants would inherit his property. God promised him a son of his own, saying that he would have descendants as numerous as the stars of heaven (Gen 15:1–5). Abram believed God, and he reckoned it to him as righteousness (15:6). This attitude of humble trust in the word of promise from God has become for Jews and Christians one of the most important of all religious principles, and we venerate Abram as the prime example of such a personal relation of trust in God (in the NT Rom 4:1–5; Heb 11:8–12).

God said that the reason for bringing Abram to this land was to give it to him as a possession (15:7). The patriarch's trust was not proof against doubt on this point, so in response God proceeded to make a promise to him by means of a covenant. Without question, the final text reflects concerns of God's people over a long period of time, but I offer a plausible explanation of how it all developed out of Abram's encounter with Shaddai understood in terms of *berit* =covenant in the immediate context of his covenant relation with the Amorite brothers. The keepers of Israel's traditions described a covenant making practice with which they were familiar: the participants walked between the parts of a divided animal. It may be that this ceremonial act gave rise to the term J used for the practice: "to cut a covenant." We have no means of recovering the experience of Abram himself, but I suggest a possible process of development of the tradition.

It all started near Hebron at the oaks of Mamre, the local sacred place. Abram had already built an altar to his God and sealed covenant with the Amorite brothers. Here, according to Gen 15:9–21 God cut a covenant with Abram. For Abram it was a visionary experience—"a deep sleep fell upon him" (15:12; cf also 15:1). Couldn't this have been a visionary recollection of his own treaty with Mamre, Aner, and Eshcol? Abram saw himself following Shaddai's instruction, dividing animals in half and laying the parts opposite each other. Then in his vision Abram saw both the deity and himself as parties to the covenant—"a smoking fire pot and a flaming torch"—passing between those pieces. God made the covenant and announced the promise to give that land to Abram's descendants. The ambiguity of the fire pot and smoking torch indicates to me the reluctance of Abram originally and the final author of the account to come right out and say that this actually involved *God*. The God of Abram—Shaddai, YHWH, the Living God of Israel—took a solemn oath guaranteeing to maintain this relationship *on pain of death*. Nothing could be more serious! In my view, though the account underwent revisions reflecting later and more sophisticated situations, covenant rests upon ancient oral tradition that Israel's earliest forebears described the relationship between themselves and their Shaddai in terms that made them fictive family members.

As Frank M. Cross expressed it: "In the religious sphere, the intimate relationship with their family god, the 'God of the Fathers,' was expressed in the only language available to members of a tribal society. Their god was the Divine Kinsman."[8] The Bible preserves this primitive idea in a personal name, Ammishaddai="my kinsman or uncle ('*ammi*) is Shaddai" (Num 1:12). Two other similar names also imply the relationship with the deity: Zurishaddai="my rock is Shaddai" (Num 1:6) and Shedeur="Shaddai is light" (possible meaning, Num 1:5). As the name of the Deity became clearer and more fixed over time, the Israelites naturally came to apply the name YWHW to their Divine Kinsman ('*am*), and to think of Israel as the kin or the people of YHWH ('*am YHWH*).[9] This figure of speech preserves the sense of depth and intimacy of the divine-human relationship without obliterating the distinction between Creator and creature that some pagan myths encouraged by depicting gods as sexually begetting human individuals or a particular ethnic group.

In the final version of the story of the covenant between Shaddai and Abram, the scribe who put the traditions into writing using the name YHWH included details

---

8. Cross, *From Epic to Canon*, 6.

9. The Bible mentions the Moabites, descended from Abram's nephew Lot, as related to their national God in the same way, referring to them as "Moab, people of Chemosh" (Num 21:29; Jer 48:13).

describing the realm claimed for David and Solomon, from the border of Egypt to the Euphrates (Gen 15:18b). It included Kenites and Kenizzites, non-Israelite peoples who affiliated with the tribe of Judah (15:19). The Rephaim inhabited an area southwest of Jerusalem that David captured from the Philistines (2 Sam 5:18, 22; 23:13). Finally, there is the group of six: the Hittites, Perizzites, Amorites, Canaanites, Girgashites, and Jebusites (Gen 15:20-21). These make up a more or less stereotyped list that we find (with slight variations) seventeen times in the OT describing the original inhabitants displaced or absorbed by Israel.[10] All these details guided the hand of the scribe who later recorded this text.

God's self-binding by covenant also resulted in a special characterization of God based on the Hebrew word *chesed*. *Chesed* is so rich in meanings that English translations may use a variety of words to express it: kindness, favor, goodness, love, loving kindness, and mercy. H. J. Stoebe devotes fifteen pages to bring out all its potential richness. He states: "When *chesed* is attributed to God, it concerns the realization of the promises inherent in the covenant."[11] Several modern English versions agree on the phrase "steadfast love" to translate *chesed* for God's unwavering adherence to the covenant.[12] Throughout the story of Israel in the OT, covenant underlies the divine-human relationship, and even when the term covenant does not occur, the more than one hundred references to the "steadfast love" of God presupposes the divine commitment to the human partners. In the OT the most frequent ascription of praise to Israel's God is "His steadfast love endures forever." God's *chesed* remains constant when other metaphors are used to describe covenant, such as the husband-wife marriage contract, the parent-child relationship, or conditions governing relations between a great king and lesser subject kings.

5. ABRAM'S SON ISHMAEL

YHWH (Shaddai) had assured childless Abram that he would have a son of his own as heir but had said nothing about who the mother would be (Gen 15:4). Barren Sarai gave Abram her Egyptian maid Hagar to be a surrogate mother. When Hagar got pregnant and acted haughtily, Sarai treated her so harshly that she fled into the wilderness. The angel of YHWH ordered her to return and submit to her mistress, adding that she would

---

10. This list of six occurs in the late text Neh 9:8 in connection with the reference to YHWH's covenant with Abraham. A similar list of six nations substituting Hivites instead of Girgashites occurs in Exod 3:8; 3:17 (in connection with the revelation of the Name YHWH); Exod 3:8, 17; 23:28; 33.2; 34:11; Deut 20:17; Josh 9:1; 11:3; 12:8; Judges 3:5. Two lists include both Girgashites and Hivites for a total of seven nations, Deut 7:1, Josh 24:11. Ezra 9:1 refers to the nations from which the Israelites failed to separate themselves after their return from exile, namely the stereotypical list minus Hivites and Girgashites, with the addition of Ammonites, Moabites, and Egyptians. In the table of nations, Gen 10:15-18, Hittites, Jebusites, Amorites, Girgashites, and Hivites are listed as descendants of Canaan.

11. *TLOT* II, 451.

12. "Steadfast love" RSV, NRSV, NJPS; "faithful love" in New Jerusalem Bible; "love" New International Version.

have such a multitude of descendants that they could not be numbered (Gen 16:1–10). The angel told her to name her son Ishma-el ["God (El) hears"], "for YHWH has given heed to your affliction" (16:11). Hagar "named YHWH who spoke to her, 'You are El-roi' " (=God who sees me, 16:13).[13] In reporting Ishmael's birth, the Hebrew Bible four distinct times states Abram's paternity (Gen 16:15–16). The descendants of Abram and Hagar make up a numerous Arabian people in the Middle East.

In Genesis 17 (part of the late, postexilic P tradition) YHWH, self-introducing as El Shaddai, commands Abram:"walk before me and be blameless." God promises Abram that he will be progenitor of a multitude of nations; and changes his name to Abraham to symbolize the number (17:1–6). God establishes an everlasting covenant to be the God of Abraham and his descendants, to whom God gives the whole land of Canaan as a perpetual holding. As sign of the covenant God requires the circumcision of all males in Abraham's household, including Ishmael and the slaves (17:7–14). God changes Sarai's name to Sarah and promises Abraham a son by her. He laughs incredulously and begs God's favor on behalf of Ishmael. God repeats that Sarah will bear Abraham a son, whom they must name Isaac (=he laughs), and asserts that it is through Isaac and his offspring that God will maintain the covenant. God will bless Ishmael as Abraham asks and make him exceedingly numerous and a great nation, but God, bypassing Ishmael, repeats that the covenant will be maintained through Isaac and his descendants forever (17:15–22).

The fact that the story of the birth of Ishmael by Hagar to Abram (Gen 16) separates the J account of the covenant with Abram (Gen 15) and the later P account that narrows the human covenant partner to Abraham's descendants through Sarah's son Isaac (Gen 17) is worthy of attention. Ishmael was born to Abram *after* God established the covenant, and he was progenitor of some of the multitude of descendants God promised Abram *before* the covenant (15.1–6). God gave both Hagar and Abram assurances of God's care for Ishmael.[14] Sarah's son Isaac had twin sons Esau and Jacob. Jacob tricked Esau to get the privilege of firstborn, and he deceived Isaac to receive the special blessing Isaac had intended for Esau (Gen 25:29–34; 27:1–40). Henceforth Esau too is omitted from the line of the covenant, and there is much anti-Edomite biblical and extrabiblical material. Still Deut 2:1–6 and 23:7–8 show a positive attitude toward Edomites, "for they are your kin."[15] So we must never think of God abandoning Ishmael and Esau and their descendants. In addition, in a brief account easy to overlook, Abraham married another wife, Keturah, through whom he became ancestor of six other nations (Gen 25:1–4), one of which was the Midianites, who had both friendly and inimical relations with Israel (Exod 2:15–22; 18:1–27; Num 25:1–18). All these are today Abraham's children, and included in God's benevolence.

13. Note the inexact terminology for Deity: YWHW, angel of YHWH, and El, posing difficulty of translation.

14. The list of Ishmael's twelve sons and their territory is at Gen 25:12–18.

15. Esau's descendants as the people of Edom are listed in Gen 36.

SUMMARY AND REFLECTION

The earliest ancestors of Israel were a vulnerable minority in an alien land. It was to their advantage to relate peaceably to their neighbors. Abram had a helpful covenant with the Amorite brothers, and a cordial and respectful meeting with the Jebusite priest-king of Salem (Gen 14:7–20). To bury Sarah, Abraham purchased a cave from Ephron the Hittite (Gen 23:1–20). Both Abraham and his son Isaac settled quarrels with Abimelech of Gerar and made peace by covenants (Gen 21:22–34; 26:12–33). These covenants were possible only because Abraham and Isaac invoked their God Shaddai while the other parties invoked their gods. Shaddai was a dependable Presence as Divine Kinsman, giving Abram the gift of peace and security in a potentially hostile environment.

Eventually Israel became like other nations with king and army, and YHWH superseded Shaddai to become Israel's national God. Israel competed among the nations as YHWH competed among the gods. Under those circumstances YHWH forbade Israel to make covenants with other nations precisely because YHWH would not tolerate the Name being set alongside the names of other gods. YHWH commanded Israel to destroy the images, the shrines, and the sacred places of the other people (Exod 23:23–33; Deut 7:1–6), specifically naming also the Amorites, the Hittites, the Canaanites and the Jebusites with whom Abram had co-existed peacefully.

The events of Abram's life including the birth of Ishmael overlap with the Primeval Events, and all this material constitutes what I call The Universal Matrix. This Universal Matrix establishes the fundamental relationship between Creator and all humanity before the emergence of Israel. God commissions Abram at his call to be a source of blessing for all the families of the earth. An integral part of God's relation to humanity is covenant=*berit*. The first example of covenant in the Bible is universal: God freely and unconditionally committed to preserve the earth, all living animals, and humanity from another total destruction by flood (Gen 9:8–17). In the second example of covenant, God related freely and unconditionally as the Divine Kinsman with Abram and his family (Gen 15). This covenant embraces humanity as such. God had not yet laid the condition of circumcision, which later became a distinction between God's people (ʿ*am*) and the nations (*goyim*). Abram stands as the paradigm of the human who trusted fully in the unseen Deity. God covenanted with Abram, still uncircumcised, in a fictive family relationship that the Divine Kinsman has never betrayed. That is one of the most important aspects of my thesis, God for All. Adding the requirement of circumcision and the Mosaic Covenant at Sinai make possible an apparent conflict with the early covenant with Abram, but that is only apparent, not ultimately definitive.

Psalm 33 reflects post-monarchic times by affirming the futility of a king's trusting for salvation by armed force. YHWH is the Creator, who has fashioned the hearts of all humankind. The whole earth is full of the steadfast love (*chesed*=covenant loyalty) of YHWH (Ps 33:5). The psalmist asks that all earth's inhabitants may come to stand in awe of YHWH. In conclusion the psalmist prays: "Let your steadfast love, YHWH, be upon us, even as we hope in you" (Ps 33:22). Today we can confirm: "We have our hope set on the living God, who is the savior of all people, especially of those who believe" (1 Tim 4:10).

PART TWO

Abraham to the Settlement of Canaan

8

Children of Abraham—Exclusion and Assimilation

THE GENESIS ACCOUNT ABRUPTLY abandons the universal theme of the Primeval Events supplemented by the covenant with Abram and the birth of his son Ishmael to the Egyptian slave girl Hagar (Gen 1–16.). Now God orders Abram to walk blamelessly before him, changes Abram's name to Abraham and Sarai's to Sarah. God requires circumcision of all household males as the sign of the covenant and chooses Abraham's second son Isaac, yet to be born to Sarah, as the "elect" line of descent through which the covenant with Abraham is to be reckoned. Thus begins a new phase (Gen 17). The story narrows further when God rejects Esau, the elder of Isaac's twin sons (ancestor of later Edomites), in preference for Jacob the younger son (Gen 25:19–34; 27:1—28:5).

We will observe other examples of narrowing, within the Israelite community and notably separation of Israelites/Jews from Gentiles. The New Testament contains examples of narrowing—Christians from non-Christians, including Jews, and certain groups of Christians from others. These tendencies toward exclusion persist down to the present time, but the thesis of this book is that the One God, who transcends all lesser gods, who is the Creator of the world and all that is in it, created one humanity and embraces humanity totally in an eternal, universal purpose. But the Bible presents God's universal purpose not in abstract terms but by means of God's particular dealing with one or another people, group, or individual. This may appear to be, and sometimes is erroneously interpreted as, God's *partiality* toward one group or another. Actually, these are concrete examples of what God intends for the whole of creation.

The Bible, basically, is the story of the Sovereign God. God deals with humanity in a special way, compared with the rest of creation (Gen 1:26–27) without contradicting the divine concern for *all* creation. When humans interpret God's choice selfishly, it results in exploitation of creation rather than respectfully keeping it. Within humanity God dealt with Abraham and his descendants according to an elect line of descent differentiated from Abraham's other offspring and from non-Abrahamic peoples, without implying God's indifference to the rest of humanity. In The Universal

Matrix, the earliest chapters of the Bible summarize a long experience of Israelites with God. Besides a deep sense of their own chosenness, the author(s)/editor(s) of Gen 1–16 disclose their conviction that God's purpose embraces all humanity. By means of examples of apparently *special* relations in *particular* cases, I discern God's *universal* purpose for *all* creation. At the end of this book I have appended a diagram to illustrate this concept, Appendix A.

Besides these examples of separation and apparent exclusivism, we also see in the Bible examples of the way in which God begins the relation with those who become the chosen people by bringing together groups that already comprise previously disparate elements. In this total process we may also observe how people's understanding of God changes and develops. Perhaps one might dare to suggest that God also changes and develops in response to human development.

1. A THEME OF UNITY

The biblical narrative focuses on Abraham's grandson Jacob, following the exclusion of Ishmael and Esau. We observe how the unnamed guardian Shaddai, the God of the Fathers who related by covenant as Divine Kinsman first to Abram, gradually revealed the divine character to Jacob.[1] God accompanied Jacob on his wanderings, which he began first as a result of having to leave home for fear of his brother Esau, whom he had cheated out of the privileges and blessings due to the elder son (Gen 25:19–34; 27:1–46). On his way to his mother's family in Haran, part of Aram (later Syria), Jacob bedded down at "a certain place" (*maqom* a local shrine). The Deity introduced himself: "I am YHWH, the God of Abraham your father and the God of Isaac," and gave to Jacob the promises earlier given to them: 1) possession of the land, 2) innumerable descendants, and 3) that through him and his offspring all the families of the earth would be blessed (28:1–15). Jacob now knows that the family guardian (Shaddai) is not limited by space, and in wonder he exclaims, "Surely YHWH [Deity] is in this place!" He sets up a pillar and names the place *Beth-el*, i.e., House of God, and states that YHWH will henceforth be his God (28:16–22).

Jacob arrived at his mother's home in Haran, where he acquired two wives, Leah and Rachel, daughters of his uncle Laban, and two concubines, Zilpah and Bilhah, slave girls of his wives. These four were the mothers of his considerable family that ultimately consisted of twelve sons and one daughter. The account reflects the jealousies and other problems characteristic of polygamous households (Gen 29:1—30:43). The Bible offers this human story of a large family with its inner tensions and all-too-human foibles as the origin of "The twelve tribes of Israel," sons of Jacob, which has become a set phrase to designate the people of God in the OT.

---

1. See Walters, "Jacob Narrative" for an exposition of Jacob as representative of the people Israel.

As this "family story" proceeds, Jacob and his twelve sons and their families go to Egypt to escape famine. They settle there, multiply in number, and prosper. After an Egyptian regime change, the authorities look with disfavor on these Hebrews, as they are called, try to kill off the boy babies, and subject the adults to state slavery (Exod 2:1–10). God raises up Moses, reveals to him the name YHWH, and commissions him to lead the Hebrews from Egypt (Exod 2:1—3:22). Moses leads the fleeing Hebrews from Egypt into the wilderness to Mount Sinai to worship YHWH. YHWH speaks the Ten Commandments directly to the people, plus additional instructions through Moses, which are referred to as "the Book of the Covenant" (20:24—23:19). Moses reads these words to the people, who respond, "All the words that YHWH has spoken, we will do and will be obedient" (24:3). In order to seal the covenant by sacrifice, Moses erects an altar to represent YHWH, and twelve pillars around it to represent the twelve tribes (Exod 24:1–8). Elsewhere in Scripture, as I show later, we see evidence that in fact the twelve-tribe organization did not emerge until long after the settlement in Canaan.

The twelve tribes stay in the wilderness for forty years, during which Moses continues to transmit to them further instructions (*torah*) from YHWH. After Moses's death, Joshua leads the twelve tribes into the land of promise, conquers the seven Canaanite nations, distributes the land to the tribes, and renews the covenant with them (Josh 8:30–35; 24:1–28). As long as Joshua lives, the Israelites faithfully keep the covenant, but after the death of Joshua and the next generation, the Israelites abandon YHWH and worship Baal and the Astartes (Josh 24:31; Judg 2:6–15). YHWH punishes the people by letting them fall into the hands of their enemies, until YHWH's pity is aroused and he sends judges and deliverers to save them (Judg 2:18). So it goes until YHWH allows the Israelites to become "like other nations" and have their own king to lead them out and fight their battles (1 Sam 8:19–21).

2. EVIDENCE OF DIVERSITY

This narrative of "the Twelve Tribes of Israel" told in the form of a family story is very skillfully done, and along the way it is filled with many anecdotes and incidents of inspiring and instructive character. It seems to be, and in some respects certainly is, a real story of real people. Readers of the Bible of all times, Jews and Christians alike, have this twelve-tribe pattern almost indelibly impressed upon our minds. Nevertheless, this is not the whole of the story of Israel contained in the OT. In the Scriptures themselves one finds many genealogical lists devoted to the tribes; and lists of towns and territories assigned to the tribes at different times. These lists all together consist of hundreds, if not thousands, of personal and place names difficult for ordinary folk to pronounce, boring to read, and therefore easy to ignore. Narratives of persons and tribes in action often include small details that, if noticed at all, may raise a slight doubt or question, but they are easily overborne by the weight of the familiar story.

All this additional material, too, is part of the Bible, which for conscientious believers has paramount authority.

In major Bible dictionaries such as *The Interpreter's Dictionary of the Bible* and *The Anchor Bible Dictionary* one may read articles in which scholars have examined in detail the total biblical references to each tribe—all those names too, and details that may be internally contradictory. Scholars have conscientiously tried to come to a reasonable understanding of the total picture. The bibliography of each article in the dictionaries indicates the effort that many people have expended to learn and interpret the mass of biblical material concerning each tribe individually and all the tribes together, that is scattered throughout the OT. One thing becomes clear: Initially the tribes were not united at all, but each had its own prehistory and its own needs and concerns, which often worked against the occasional impulses to join forces with a neighboring group. Examination of the tribal divisions of the land (Josh 13–19 supplemented by notes scattered in Judges) shows that division of land was by no means exact but included some overlapping, which undoubtedly reflects a degree of intertribal competition for territory.[2] The Bible includes stories of bloody battles between and among tribes both before the establishment of the monarchy, and especially after the Israel/Judah split. It was the minority of YHWH-only enthusiasts that maintained the continuity and that made possible the later construction of the family story of unity.

The following account appears reasonable, which I will begin to develop more fully in the next section. A small group of clans in the central highlands of Canaan achieved a degree of cooperation on the basis of kinship and economic and cultic interests. As they grew by assimilating other groups, they sought greater unity by devotion to the god El, whose name appears as a part of their own name Isra-el, bestowed on them by their leader of the same name. El the God of Israel was their unifying force. Some, but not all, of Israel spent time in Egypt, where they learned the name YHWH, the God who delivered them from Egypt and made the covenant at Sinai. They returned eventually to Canaan, bringing the enthusiasm and unity provided by YWHW faith. Some members of the old El confederation that had remained in Canaan joined the exodus group, and it is from this beginning, according to ancient traditions, that eventually the monarchy emerged.

It is worth remembering that within this "family story" we read that the two most powerful of the twelve tribes, referred to as "the house of Judah" (thirty-nine times) and "the house of Joseph" (ten times), each was descended from the foreign spouse of their progenitor. The mother of Judah's sons was a Canaanite woman (Gen 38). "The House of Judah" provided the Dynasty of David that ruled for 500 years (see below chapter 14.3 "David and his tribe of Judah"). "The House of Joseph" was sprung from

---

2. Jerusalem is a notable example: it is assigned to Judah at Josh 15:8, 63 and Judg 1:7–8, but to Benjamin at Josh 18:28 and Judg 1:21. However it is recognized as a city of Jebusites, foreigners, at Judg 19:10–12, and David finally conquered Jerusalem and made it his own city, at 2 Sam 5:6–9.

Joseph's Egyptian wife, a daughter of the Egyptian religious elite. She is mentioned three times with her full identification: "Asenath daughter of Potiphera, priest of On" (Gen 41:45, 50; 46:20).

In Gen 48:1–22 Jacob (here referred to ten times as "Israel") was near death, so Joseph brought Manasseh and Ephraim, his two sons by Asenath his Egyptian wife, for his father to bless them. In blessing them, Israel gave precedence to Ephraim over Manasseh, and asked that they perpetuate his name, i.e. Israel (Gen 48:8–16). Joseph objected that his father demoted the elder, but Israel said, "I know, my son, I know; he also shall become a people, and he also shall be great. Nevertheless his younger brother shall be greater than he, and his offspring shall become a multitude of nations" (48:19). In Canaan, Ephraim occupied the strategic central hill country, and Manasseh, as two half-tribes, occupied land next to Ephraim and east of the Jordan. Siegfried Herrmann suggests that the name "Israel" was first applied to Ephraim and the adjoining tribes that Ephraim was able to gather into an alliance of sorts.[3] The "house of Joseph" became the core of the northern Kingdom of Israel, and a basic rivalry with the "house of Judah" constantly disturbed the people of YHWH. Modern scholars suggest that scribes in the court of King David made the first attempt to describe as "one family" the hitherto diverse peoples struggling for unity as a nation.

David rescued the people from attacks by neighboring warring states and exalted YHWH as their all-powerful victorious national deity. David needed all the help he could get to unify the people under his rule. Royal scribes produced this "family genealogy" by skillfully combining the traditions of these separate clans, linking them all with each other as descendants of the ancestor Jacob. Genealogy became the means of expressing historical relationships. This twelve-tribe pattern survived despite its failure to prevent the split into northern Israel and southern Judah after Solomon c. 922 BCE. In the subsequent centuries the pattern underwent revision according to need. After Judah went down before Babylon as Israel had earlier gone down before Assyria, the leaders used this twelve-tribe pattern to rally the Israelites who were no longer a nation-state but a religious community under the rule of the Persian Empire. See the extensive genealogies in Ezra and Nehemiah and the first nine chapters of 1 Chronicles.

3. A NEW NAME FOR JACOB AND FOR HIS GOD

It is necessary now to return to the "family story" of Jacob and his two wives, two concubines, and numerous children. Genesis tells the story as though it were a single family, but the next events reflect important developments in the affairs of a body of people much larger than just a family.

---

3. Herrmann, *A History of Israel*, 147.

Jacob had parted from his father-in-law Laban and was on his way home to his father Isaac, accompanied by his wives, children, slaves, and numerous livestock. He heard that his brother Esau accompanied by four hundred men was coming to meet him. Fearing Esau's revenge, Jacob sent ahead several herds of livestock as a present to Esau. Jacob then deployed his family and possessions in such a way that perhaps at least half might escape if Esau attacked (Gen 32:3–21). As Jacob waited alone by the Jabbok River, a mysterious "man" wrestled with him all night but could not throw him. As the "man" sought to escape before daybreak, Jacob demanded a blessing, so he changed his name from Jacob ("heel grabber" or "supplanter") to Isra*el*, "for you have striven with god(s) and men and have prevailed." The new name includes the theophoric, or god-bearing element—ʾ*el*. Jacob recognized the divinity of his assailant and named the place Peni*el* (=face of God), "For I have seen God face to face and yet my life is preserved" (Gen 32:22–32). When the brothers met, Jacob humbly prostrated himself, Esau showed no resentment, and the brothers embraced warmly. Jacob said: "Truly to see your face is like seeing the face of God" (33:1–11).

Jacob and "family" went on to Shechem, an important city in the central hill country.[4] He bought a plot of ground where he set up camp and built an altar to El-Elohe-Israel (33:18–20 NRSV).[5] Unfortunately the NRSV obscures the importance of the name by simply transliterating the Hebrew. *Ēl-Elohē-Yisraʾel* means "El the God of Israel." Not only has Jacob received a new name, but so has Jacob's God. Shaddai was not really a name but only a class of family guardian deities. Jacob and the people that follow him are too big for a family guardian; they need a more appropriate name for their God. El is the name of the High God of the Canaanite pantheon, who was capable of moving about freely from place to place, and who was known as "maker of gods and humans." El is also a generic word for god. We have no way of knowing how long this tribal association functioned under El the God of Israel before Moses later introduced the change that led to YHWH the God of Israel. It is worth noting that even when Israel is called "the people of YHWH" their own name includes the name of the God El. We may detect effects of the influence of El in several divine names in the early traditions: El Elyon (Gen 14:17–24), El Roi (16:7–14), and El Olam (21:22–34).

---

4. Shechem played a major role in biblical history. It was site of Abram's first stop and act of worship in Canaan (Gen 12:6–7); the site of covenant renewal by Joshua (Josh 24); at Shechem "all Israel" rejected the house of David and Judah and established their independent monarchy (1 Kgs 11:1–25).

5. The marginal note at this verse is *God, the God of Israel*, but that is of no help without further explanation. Gottwald (*Tribes of Yahweh*, 494–95) suggests that "Israel" designated a coalition of anti-feudal clans in the central mountain area of Canaan before the later adoption of YHWH as the name of a larger, more powerful coalition.

4. JACOB-ISRAEL ASSIMILATES OTHERS

At Shechem, the Jacob-Israel "family" group acts like a coalition of clans. Each of the "brothers" possesses size and strength that permit them to act in semi-independence from Jacob. They come into conflict with the Hivite inhabitants of the region. In an act of treachery, the "brothers" deceive and slaughter all the males and take as booty the women, children, and wealth of Shechem. They have to flee (Gen 34:1–31). The narrative now inserts details from the P tradition, according to which Jacob orders his household (i.e., his "sons") and all who were with him (i.e., the kidnapped Hivite women and children) to give him their foreign gods, evidently including images and fetishes, which Jacob buries under the oak tree at Shechem. With divine protection from retaliation for the crime at Shechem, Jacob leads them to Bethel, where he had encountered God previously (Gen 28:10–22). There Elohim, self-introduced as El Shaddai, changes Jacob's name to Israel and affirms to him the promises to Abraham (35:1–15 P). Jacob's growing company has exceeded mere familial dimensions and requires a more comprehensive religious expression to produce unity out of diversity by loyalty to a single deity, El.

Nothing more is said of the assimilated Hivite women and children. Did some of them accompany Jacob's family when they went to Egypt? When the Israelites left Egypt under Moses's leadership, "a mixed crowd" went up with them (Exod 12:38). Later Moses led the Israelites in war against Midian, in which they killed all the men and took as booty the women, the little ones, and the material wealth (Num 31:1–12). This time Moses in anger ordered the warriors to kill all the male children and the women who had had sexual intercourse, and to save only the females who had not been sexually active (31:13–20). A later law in the *Torah* prescribes the ritual procedure a man must follow in order to render a woman captured in war suitable to be his wife (Deut 21:10–14). In ancient Israel, there was no such practice as conversion from one religion to another. Wives taken from another nation abandoned that god for the god of their husbands. The beautiful speech of Ruth the Moabite to Naomi may reflect a ritual used in such cases (Ruth 1:16–17).

Another non-Israelite group that Israel assimilated was the population of Gibeon, Hivites occupying several cities northwest of Jerusalem. According to tradition, by trickery they evaded Joshua's ethnic cleansing, and as punishment he assigned them to menial labor in the local YHWH shrine (Josh 9:1–27). Gibeonites suffered social discrimination, and later King Saul unsuccessfully tried to wipe them out. Their survivors, by appeal to King David exacted vengeance on seven of Saul's descendants (2 Sam 21:1–10). Before Solomon built the temple in Jerusalem, he worshiped at Gibeon, which was the principal "high place" (1 Kgs 3:4).

God prescribed circumcision as the sign of the covenant with Abraham, but it applied to all the males in the household, "including the slave born in your house and the one bought with your money from any foreigner—" (Gen 17:12). Such circumcised slaves were qualified to partake of the Passover (Exod 12:43–44). Alien residents, provided they were circumcised, could also offer Passover (Exod 12:48). Rolf Rendtorff has made a thorough study of the different terms Israelites used to designate strangers, aliens, sojourners, etc., and whether and to what extent they were integrated into society as citizens.[6] One need not take up all these details; it is sufficient to note that scattered here and there in Scripture is sufficient information to inform us of the wide diversity of folk who came to be known as Israel, the people of YHWH.

Meanwhile, let us not forget that Ishmael was Abraham's first-born son, for whom he asked and received God's favor (Gen 17:18, 20). Ishmael too was circumcised (17:23) and later had twelve sons, "princes according to their tribes" (25:12–18). Isaac's elder son Esau, rejected in favor of Jacob, was ancestor of the Edomite people, who were descended from his three wives, one a Hittite, one a Hivite, and one a daughter of Ishmael (Gen 26:34; 28:9). The Edomites succeeded in forming an organized state before the Israelites (Gen 36:1–42). Despite bloody wars between Israelites and Edomites, it was possible for Edomites to become members of the assembly of Israel (Deut 23:6–7). Keturah, another wife of Abraham, had six sons (including Midian, ancestor of Moses's wife's family), also progenitors of a considerable population (Gen 25:1–4). These "non-elect" lines also must be reckoned among the children of Abraham according to God's promises (Gen 12:2; 13:16; 14:5; 17:5; 22:17).[7]

Leaders of the return of the Israelites after the exile tried to keep a "pure" Israelite character by excluding foreigners, forcing the divorce of foreign wives and sending them and their children away (Ezra 9–10; Neh 13:23–31). This policy highlights the exclusiveness that some people thought to be necessary to maintain the identity of the people of YHWH at that particular time and place. Yet a prophetic message considered to be roughly contemporaneous with Ezra-Nehemiah offers a warm welcome to foreigners and to sexually disabled eunuchs whom Mosaic law specifically excludes from the assembly.[8] In fact the prophetic note states that YHWH will bring near and accept on his altar the burnt offerings of the foreigners who join themselves to YHWH, to minister to him, to love the name of YHWH and be his servants, who keep the sabbath and hold fast the covenant (Isa 56.3–8).[9]

---

6. Rendtorff, "The Gēr in the Priestly Laws of the Pentateuch," 77–87.

7. In the NT Paul interprets God's promise to Abraham as the promise to bless the nations (Gentiles) *not* the promise to give the land: (Rom 4:13, 16; Gal 3:14, 18).

8. See Deut 23:1–6 for the exclusions; vv 7–8 permit inclusion of Edomites and Egyptians after three generations.

9. "To minister" (*sharath*) is a term concerning the cultic duties of the priests and Levites, and "servant" in this context indicates a prestigious honor in the service of YHWH. Jesus cites Isa 56:8 in Mark 11:17.

SUMMARY

A superficial reading of the Bible gives the impression that Israel, descended from *one* ancestor, is *one* people, whom God commanded to keep themselves separate from all others. As I have shown in this chapter, and as will become clearer as I develop the theme of God for All, Scripture tells of One God who is concerned for *all* the members of the *one* humanity. The original Israel of YHWH was a gathering of many different elements, an ancient example of the motto of the United States of America, e pluribus unum—out of many one—the forecast of God's purpose "to reconcile to himself all things, whether on earth or in heaven" (Col 1:20).

9

Moses, the Name, and the Exodus

THE STORY OF JACOB and his family narrates how severe famine compelled Jacob and his household to seek relief in Egypt. As Jacob departed, he received this instruction: "I am God (El), the God of your father; do not be afraid to go down to Egypt, for I will make of you a great nation there. I myself will go down with you—" (Gen 46:2–3). Eventually the descendants of Jacob came under bondage as state slaves to the king of Egypt. "The Israelites groaned under their slavery, and cried out. Out of the slavery their cry for help rose up to God. God heard their groaning, and God remembered his covenant with Abraham, Isaac, and Jacob. God looked upon the Israelites, and God took notice of them" (Exod 2:23–24; see also 6:2–8). In this way, the text presents the Divine Kinsman responding compassionately to the family's need. The text stresses the family aspect of the covenant relation in preparation for the appearance of Moses, who is to lead the Israelites to freedom after receiving the revelation of the special Name YHWH. God instructs Moses to inform Pharaoh: "Israel is my firstborn son. I said to you, 'Let my son go that he may worship me.' (4:22). In the contest between YHWH and Pharaoh, YHWH refers to Israel as "my people"(=my family) seventeen times.

1. MOSES AND THE MIDIANITES

Moses was born in a devout Hebrew family and brought up in the royal Egyptian household. He impulsively killed an Egyptian overseer harassing a Hebrew slave and had to flee. He was welcomed as an alien refugee into the family of a Midianite priest who had seven daughters and who gave one of them to Moses in marriage (Exod 2:1–22). It is reasonable to assume that Moses became an apprentice priest under his father-in-law; at the very least he observed a good deal of religious lore and practice.[1]

---

1. In modern Japan, a family with only daughters may adopt a husband for one of them to be the successor of the family name and affairs. Moses's father-in-law is identified by several names: Reuel at Exod 2:18; Jethro at Exod 3:1 and eight other times in Exodus (once Jether); and Hobab in Num 10:29 and Judg 4:11. Hays suggests the possibility that the Hebrew word translated "father-in-law" may actually apply "to the relationship between a woman's husband and every male member of her family" ("Moses: The Private Man Behind the Public Leader" 21).

The Midianites were related to Israel through Midian, a son of Abraham by Keturah (Gen 25:1–2). They were a nomadic group moving about between the Dead Sea and the Gulf of Aqaba.² Later Midianites and Israelites warred bitterly as enemies (see Num 25, 31; Judg 6–8). In view of that hostility, we can have some confidence that the depiction of early friendly relationships between Israelites and Midianites has a high degree of credibility. Kenites also inhabited this area. Descendants of Moses' father-in-law are called Kenites (Judg 1:16; 4:11).

The Edomites, descended from Esau, Jacob's twin brother, inhabited Seir, comprising Paran and Teman, south of the Dead Sea. We saw in chapter 7 "The Covenant with Abram" that Kenites and a clan of Edomites called Kenizzites were among the groups later forming the tribe of Judah in and around Hebron, site of the Divine Kinsman's covenant with Abram. Several texts state that YHWH came to help his people from the region of Sinai, Seir, and Paran (Deut 33:2), or from Seir, Edom, and Sinai (Judg 5:4–5). Other texts state that it was Elohim who came up from Sinai (Ps 68:7–8), and from Teman and Mount Paran (Hab 3:3). Thus the Bible firmly locates the origin of the name of the God of Israel in the southern wilderness between the Dead Sea and Egypt.

2. THE ORIGIN OF THE NAME

Anson Rainey offers considerable documentation concerning a people called *shasu* as pastoral nomads outside settled political control, who ranged widely from the region inhabited by Moabites and Edomites southeast of the Dead Sea all the way up through Ammonite territory as far as Aram (Syria) in the northeast. Rainey cites an Egyptian papyrus inscription of the late thirteenth century BCE in which an official reports having permitted *shasu* tribes to enter the land, "in order to keep them alive and in order to keep their cattle alive" in a time of drought. Based on this information, Rainey strongly argues that *shasu* type people most likely were among the proto-Israelites. Both Abram and Jacob were pastoralists who ranged from Aram in the northeast to Egypt in the southwest and had ethnic and linguistic affinities with Edomites and Moabites.³

It seems reasonable to think that semi-nomadic peoples such as Midianites and Kenites, and outcast classes such as *shasu* moving about between Egypt and southern Canaan, might well have known of a deity named *YHW*. The Bible places the man Moses precisely in this geographical region in marriage relationship and possible apprenticeship to a Midianite priest. This evidence has given rise to what is known as the Midianite or Kenite hypothesis, that Moses learned the Name from his wife's family.⁴

---

2. So described by Allen Kerkeslager, "Mt. Sinai—in Arabia?" 37.
3. Rainey, "Where Did the Early Israelites Come From" 45-50, and "Who Were the Early Israelites?" 51-55.
4. Rowley, *The Faith of Israel*, 54-55.

There is no evidence that *YHW* belonged to any pantheon or had a consort. *YHW* was solitary, a suitable candidate for the eventual role of the One God of Israel.

In written Semitic languages, consisting only of consonants, the reader must supply the appropriate vowel sounds, and sometimes a particular combination of consonants may produce a different pronunciation and a different meaning depending on which vowels one may supply. The name *YHW* in the extrabiblical text consists of consonants only,[5] so we cannot know exactly how it might have been pronounced, perhaps Yahu or Yau or Yaw. Long after the beginning of the Common Era Jewish scholars called Masoretes devised the vowel points that are now commonly used in written Hebrew. These three consonants *–yhw* occur in hundreds of Hebrew personal names, which by means of short sentences express some aspect of the nature, the activity, or the relation of the Deity. The vowels supplied in the Masoretic Hebrew text for these names give the pronunciation *yahu*. For example, ʾ*eliyahu* means, "My God (is) Yahu," i.e., Elijah, and *yeshaʿ yahu* means, "Yahu (is) salvation" i.e., Isaiah. The English translations obscure the significance of the theophoric or god-bearing elements of these names by omitting the final *u*. Patrick Miller cites evidence that in the sixth century BCE a colony of Jewish mercenary soldiers lived at Elephantine in Egypt (near modern Aswan), and that they had a temple dedicated to YHW. Many of their personal names included *–yhw* as a god-bearing element.[6] This evidence indicates the persistence of the divine name YHW among Jews outside the land of Israel and after the destruction of the Jerusalem temple. A politician named Netanyahu has been a prominent figure in modern Israel in the early twenty-first century.

3. MOSES AND THE NAME

"Moses was keeping the flock of his father-in-law Jethro, the priest of Midian; he led his flock beyond the wilderness, and came to Horeb, the mountain of God [Elohim]. There the angel of YHWH appeared to him in a flame of fire out of a bush; he looked, and the bush was blazing, yet it was not consumed." (Exod 3:1–2). Thus begins the story of Moses at the burning bush. In its final form, the text mingles various names for deity: God (Elohim with and without the definite article), YHWH, and angel of YHWH (*malʾakh yhwh*). We often assume that these names refer to the One God introduced at Gen 1.1 "In the beginning God—" Recent scholars, Jewish and Christian, confirm that even in the time of Jesus Jews thought of at least two deities: Elohim=the Most High God was primary, and the Lord=YWHW was the agent of Elohim.[7] Mo-

---

5. In Hebrew these three *y h w* from early times were among a few consonants that could function also as vowels.

6. Miller, *The Religion of Ancient Israel*, 61–62. See also *ABD* "Elephantine Papyri."

7. Haymon, "Monotheism—A Misused Word in Jewish Studies?" 1–15; and Barker, *The Great Angel,* 126. See my references to these and other works in chapter 34.1 "First century Judaism not strictly monotheistic."

ses's experience took place at "Horeb, the mountain of Elohim," where local people may have venerated a deity known as *YHW*. Meanwhile Moses himself had become the father of two sons. "The name of the one was Gershom (for he said, 'I have been an alien in a foreign land'), and the name of the other Eliezer (for he said, 'The God [El] of my father was my help, and delivered me from the sword of Pharaoh')" (Exod 18:3–4).[8]

The tradition told how Moses encountered here a deity with the self-introduction: "I am the God of your father, the God of Abraham, the God of Isaac, and the God of Jacob"—covering the time from Moses's day all the way back to the unnamed "God of the Fathers" (Gen 46:3; Exod 3:6; also 4:5). Initially, Moses might have assumed this was a revelation from El, the God of Isra*el*. The deity goes on to speak in terms appropriate to the Divine Kinsman's covenant, acknowledging kinship and declaring intention to rescue: "I have observed the misery of my people . . . I have heard their cry . . . I know their sufferings . . . I have come down to deliver them from the Egyptians" (Exod 3:7–8).[9] All well and good, Moses must be thinking. But when God next says, "So come, I will send you to Pharaoh to bring my people, the Israelites out of Egypt," that's a different matter! Moses had already failed miserably in his impulsive act of violence and murder. He immediately demurs. "Who am I?" he objects, to undertake such a project. To this God responds: "I will be with you; and this shall be the sign for you that it is I who sent you: when you have brought the people out of Egypt, you shall worship God on this mountain" (3:11–12).

In view of the lack of clarity concerning the name of the ancestors' God and the multiplicity of gods in the polytheistic culture, Moses naturally asks for a specific identification: "What is his name?" (3:13). This is precisely what the deity will *not* tell. If there is a real distinction between God and not-god, between creator and creature, then to name a name runs the risk of breaching that distinction and making it appear as though the creature might somehow exploit the creator.

4. THE MEANING OF THE NAME

The final story of the revelation to Moses shows evidence that at a much later time when *–yhw* (=yahu) had been incorporated into the personal names of so many Israelites, devout people attempted to explain the significance of the Name for them. But, if Midianites, Kenites, Edomites, and *shasu* peoples in the southern region had venerated *YHW* for a long time, they must have spoken the name without reflecting upon its etymology, even assuming it had one. Buber speculates that "Ya! Hu!" was simply a cry expressing the surprised sense of awe people felt when they encountered

---

8. Hebrew of the sons' names: *Ger*=alien, *shom*=there, and ʾ*Eli*=my God, ʿ*ezer*=help.

9. Twice in this context, 3:8 and 3:17, we encounter the late insertion of the stereotyped list of nations YHWH will displace to give their land to the Israelites. See above chapter 7.4 "God's covenant with Abram" for the first occurrence of the list.

God For All

this mysterious being: "Oh, He!" "This One!"[10] But, it was Moses who had connected *YHW* with both the God of the Ancestors and the liberation of the Hebrews from Egypt. The miracle of the exodus had placed the seal of truth upon that connection. Naturally the story of the deliverance and Moses's part in the entire affair assumed foundational importance for the people who experienced that liberation and for their children after them.

When Moses asked about this God: "What is his name?" God [Elohim] said only, "I Am Who I Am."(*'ehyeh 'asher 'ehyeh*) Say to the Israelites, "I Am (*'Ehyeh*) has sent me to you" (3:14). In itself, this left something to be desired—*'ehyeh* is hardly a name, is it?[11] But prior to that Moses had had God's assurance, "I-will-be (*'ehyeh*) with-you" (*'immakh* 3:12). This assurance of divine "*withness*" was something Moses could understand and cling to, for tradition and experience had taught him that the Divine Kinsman, the God of the ancestors, was a dependable *presence with* undocumented aliens or stateless wanderers, at times assuring both Isaac (Gen 26:3, 24) and Jacob (Gen 26:24; 31:3) "I am with you" or "I will be with you."[12] Therefore the promise Moses heard, "I-will-be with- you," was fully consistent with the character of the God of Moses's family.

However, the attempt to convert all this into a Name for the Deity defies the Hebrew language and the capacity of English to do it justice in translation. English grammatical usage ordinarily requires that a sentence consist of a subject and a predicate that includes a verb, e.g., "I am with you." Hebrew usage requires no verb in such a case, e.g., "I with-you."[13] Hebrew applies the verb "to be" to matters of being or doing, rather than as a mere connective as so often in English: At Exodus 3:12, God said to Moses, *'ehye 'immakh* literally, "I-am with-you" using the verb form of the first personal singular "*'ehyeh*=I-am" plus the preposition with a pronoun suffix "*'immakh*=with-you." The importance of the Hebrew use of the verb "to be" at this point becomes clear when we read the following verses, where *'ehyeh* (I-AM) functions not like an English connective verb form but is turned into a noun that serves as a name for God.

> But Moses said to God, "If I come to the Israelites and say to them, 'The God of your ancestors has sent me to you,' and they ask me, 'What is his name?' what shall I say to them?" God [*'elohim*] said to Moses, "I AM WHO I AM"

---

10. Buber, *The Prophetic Faith*, 37.

11. *'Ehyeh* is the equivalent of English "Am"—the verb form even without a pronoun specifies first person singular of the verb to be.

12. In Hebrew the same grammatical form may be rendered "I am" or "I will be." "Only in wandering does the group become decisively aware of the divinity which belongs to it and which therefore does not stay behind." Buber, *Kingship of God*, 274 n 7.

13. Some editions of the KJV use italics, not for emphasis but to indicate where the translators supplied words not needed in the Hebrew text. In the immediate context we may note the following examples: "Here *am* I" (3:4); "I *am* the God of thy father" (3:6); "Who *am* I that I should go unto Pharaoh—" (3:11); "What *is* his name?" (3:13).

['ehyeh 'asher 'ehyeh]. He said further, "Thus you shall say to the Israelites, 'I AM ['ehyeh] has sent me to you.'" God [Elohim] also said to Moses, "Thus you shall say to the Israelites, 'YHWH the God of your ancestors, the God of Abraham, the God of Isaac, and the God of Jacob, has sent me to you': This is my name forever, and this my title for all generations." (Exod 3:13–15)

In this text we see that the author took note of a possible connection between the three letters of the name *yhw* and the three letters of the root of the verb "to be" *hyh* (or as Cross and others have suggested, a more ancient form of the root *hwy* [14]). "I AM" translates the Hebrew *'ehyeh*, and "I Am Who I Am" translates the Hebrew sentence *'ehyeh 'asher 'ehyeh*. The verb in this case is not a mere connector but conveys special meaning. Hebrew modes of thought focus on the dynamic aspects of what God *does*.[15] As Buber writes, "It means: happening, coming into being, being there, being present, being thus and thus; but not being in an abstract sense."[16] Jack Miles translates simply, "I am what I do."[17] In a fuller manner, Christopher Seitz writes:

> God's name is in fact 'ehyeh 'asher 'ehyeh. That is, God's name is the most personal revelation of God's own character, and as such is not a proper name in the strict sense (like Jim or Sally), but a name appropriate to God's character as God. In this case God's "name" consists of a disclosure of purpose; it "means" something approaching "In the manner that I am, or will be, I am who I am."[18]

In this densely packed text, then, we see a reverent attempt to explain or share or communicate the reality of what the Deity YHWH had meant and could mean: the personal presence of a living, mysterious, powerful "Other" who wills redemption for a people in distress.

Herbert Brichto points out that since *-yhw* in Hebrew personal names is pronounced *–yahu*, that must have been the pronunciation of the divine name YHW. The editors of Exodus made a play on the similarity of YHW and the verb "to be," producing YHWH. When the text was written, there were not as yet any vowel points, so there was no indication how to pronounce YHWH, and so *it never was pronounced*. "A play on the verb 'to be' [gave] new meaning to an old name (which may have had

---

14. Cross, *Canaanite Myth and Hebrew Epic*, 65

15. Cross, op cit, 60–65 presents detailed linguistic arguments supporting the view that "the name *Yahweh* is a causative imperfect of the Canaanite-Proto-Hebrew verb *hwy*" which he would translate "He causes to be." Similarly, Freedman, *Divine Commitment and Human Obligation*, 85 renders it "I create what I create," or more simply, "I am the Creator." I can't help feeling that these scholars have not really discovered the actual linguistic meaning immediate to the mind of the first author. Instead, they have succeeded in expressing their understanding of what YHWH "means" on the basis of their own personal faith, experience, and reverent scholarship.

16. Buber, *Moses: The Revelation and the Covenant*, 52.

17. Miles, *God: A Biography*, 99.

18. Seitz, *Word without End*, 238.

no meaning at all), a name (the new one) unpronounceable and unpronounced."[19] Buber avers that God does not reveal a name to Moses, but gives only an assurance of divine presence when, as, and however the deity wills to be present.[20] Gottwald agrees with Brichto and Buber: "If the name already had a prehistory it cannot be taken for granted that Moses or the first Israelites would have attached any special significance to the name per se. The etymology of Exod. 3:14 is not only a rationalization of the name but also a circumlocution, since it is deliberately vague and cryptic, perhaps thereby insisting on the reticence and mystery of Israel's God."[21]

5. YHWH, GOD OF THE HEBREWS

I should like to call attention to what I see as another attempt to express what YHWH "means." Thirteen times the account in Exodus refers to the Israelite aliens in Egypt as Hebrews, an allusion to their disadvantaged status.[22] The first of these occurs in YHWH's commission to Moses: "You and the elders of Israel shall go to the king of Egypt and say to him, 'YHWH, the God of the Hebrews, has met with us; let us now go a three days' journey into the wilderness so that we may sacrifice to YHWH our God' " (Exod 3:18). Every one of the last five texts specifically identifying YHWH as the God of the Hebrews occurs precisely in the context of confrontation of Moses and Aaron against the Pharaoh, when they convey to him YHWH's demand: "let my people go."[23] In this setting the divine name YHWH "means" the God who champions the Hebrews, this despised, outcast class of nobodies who suffer under the oppression of the Egyptians and their gods, including their king whom they worship as a god.

After YHWH delivered the Hebrews at the Reed Sea,[24] he guided them into the strange geography of desert and the unfamiliar psychology of freedom, satisfying hunger and thirst, and driving off armed raiders (Exod 15:22—17:16).

6. THE MEETING AT THE MOUNTAIN

When Moses first encountered YHWH, the Deity had said, "I will be with you; and this shall be the sign for you that it is I who sent you: when you have brought the people out of Egypt, you shall worship God on this mountain" (Exod 3:12). This act of worship of YHWH in the wilderness was the precise purpose for which Moses had

19. Brichto, *The Names of God*, 30–31.
20. Buber, *Moses*, 53–54.
21. Gottwald, *The Hebrew Bible*, 113.
22. See also Gen 14:13; 39:14, 17; 40:15; 41:12; 43:32.
23. Exod 5:3; 7:16; 9:1, 13; 10:3.
24. Reed Sea is accurate translation of Heb *yam suph*. Red Sea is derived from a mistranslation by the Septuagint.

repeatedly demanded that Pharaoh let them go.[25] The sign is fulfilled in a surprising manner. "Jethro, the priest of Midian, Moses's father-in-law, heard of all that God [Elohim] had done for Moses and for his people Israel, how YHWH had brought Israel out of Egypt" (Exod 18:1). Jethro meets Moses at the camp at the mountain of God [Elohim], bringing Moses's wife and sons with him. When he heard Moses's account of the divine deliverance, "Jethro said: 'Blessed be YHWH . . . Now I know that YHWH is greater than all gods, because he delivered the people from the Egyptians, when they dealt arrogantly with them.' And Jethro, Moses's father-in-law, brought a burnt offering and sacrifices to God [Elohim]; and Aaron came with all the elders of Israel to eat bread with Moses's father-in-law in the presence of God [*ha 'elohim*=the god]." (Exod 18:11–12).

A formal act of communal worship and thanksgiving to their redeemer God is most appropriate and fulfills the sign given Moses. Jethro, the only person at this point who holds recognized priestly office, now takes the initiative in officiating at a sacrifice to God [Elohim] at which Aaron (who only later became "high priest") and the Israelite elders participate. This non-Israelite presides at the Israelites' first worship of their newly recognized Deliverer/Deity at the mountain of God. I note ambiguities in this text. Did YHWH mediate an encounter of the people with himself, or was it not rather with Elohim? Did Jethro now become for the first time a convert to Israel's God, or did he not now see clearly that the deity he already knew as YHW had demonstrated superiority over other gods by this act of deliverance?

Jethro conducts sacrifice and a sacred meal according to laws only later formalized for Israelites, and he advises Moses about establishing a judicial system for the people, delegating some of his authority to respected elders of the people (18:13–27). From early times, Jewish and later Christian students of Scripture puzzled about the prominence of Jethro, a foreigner, a Midianite, as instructor concerning sacrificial cult and judicial procedures.[26] This atmosphere of tolerance and accommodation contrasts strikingly with the fully developed YHWH-alone practice of a later age and the bitter enmity between Israel and Midian. Therefore it is worth noting Propp's comment on the role of Jethro depicted in Exodus 18: "It is astonishing that, at God's very mountain, the priest of a nation later hostile to Israel . . . should invent Israel's legal apparatus and lead the people in worship. The 'Midianite Hypothesis' imputes to Jethro and his people a crucial influence upon formative Israel. How else could tradition have ascribed so great a role to Jethro, were it not historical fact? The force of this argument cannot be gainsaid, but neither can the dearth of evidence."[27]

---

25. Exod 3:18; 4:23; 5:1; 6:11; 7:2; 8:1, 8, 20; 9:1, 13; 10:3; 12:31–32.
26. See Childs, *The Book of Exodus*, 328–34 for a discussion of these questions.
27. Propp, *Exodus 1–18*, 635.

SUMMARY AND REFLECTION

YHWH is fully vindicated. Moses no longer doubts or questions the identity of the deity who called him at the Mountain of God. The people who complained when he led them into the desert, where they were terrified by Egyptian troops in pursuit, have now experienced the deliverance they can only describe as miraculous. The Divine Kinsman has fulfilled the role of Redeemer, delivering from bondage family members incapable of saving themselves, showing *chesed*—steadfast love, complete loyalty—in fulfilling covenant obligations. For my purpose in tracing evidence of God's universal benevolence toward all humanity, it is important to mark the way in which YHWH faith achieved its dominant place in Israelite life by a saving act by the Deity that justified their having accepted the hitherto unfamiliar name YHWH. Of course, YHWH was not a real name like people's names, but the One God is gradually advancing the process of self-disclosure by means of a chosen people, not in words but in deeds. That process involves at the same time appropriation of characteristics of other deities and features of their cults, plus self-adaptation to the people's human limitations. In reflecting on the early stages of this process, the guardians of Israel's traditions couldn't avoid acknowledging that their ancestors had learned sacrificial and judicial processes—that they later accepted as divinely ordained and hence as obligatory—from a foreign people they later came to think of as deadly enemies. God, in turn, allowed such sacrificial and legal practices until real-life circumstances made them either impracticable or impossible.

Although the narrative as told in the OT now focuses narrowly on Israel, one must not forget that much earlier the Jacob coalition had forcibly incorporated the Hivite women and children (Gen 34:28). Moreover, when the Israelites went up out of Egypt, "a mixed crowd went with them" (Exod 12:38).[28] Regardless of terminology to the contrary, "Israel" always included outsiders, and their law accorded them specific recognition. As I trace the growing recognition of the universal divine embrace, we shall see that what so often shows up as special privilege for Israel is, in final terms, particular expression of God's universal intention for all. In the revelation of the Name and the exodus deliverance, we see the growing understanding of the person and work of the One God who transcends all faiths, but who reveals the divine nature most effectively in helping the helpless.

---

28. The meaning of the Hebrew word implies a mixture of uncertain composition at Jer 25:24; 50:27. At Neh 13:3 it refers to those married to foreigners. There was at least one mixed marriage among the Exodus group (see Lev 24:10–12).

10

Moses and the Sinai Covenant

THE GOD WHOM ABRAM had known as Shaddai, whom grandson Jacob/Israel and his tribal coalition had known as El, the God who revealed to Moses the special Name YHWH, showed steadfast love or covenant loyalty (*chesed*) by redeeming his people from bondage in Egypt. The direct descendents of Abraham and Sarah had greatly increased. They had incorporated others into their coalition, including Hittite women and children, the descendants of Joseph and his Egyptian wife, and the mixed multitude that accompanied them out of Egypt. The time had come to expand the covenant to embrace this larger and more diverse body.

For most readers of the Bible, Exodus 19:1–24:18 tells the story of making this covenant. Here the name of the place abruptly changes from Horeb to Sinai, which is maintained through the rest of Exodus and in Leviticus and Numbers.[1] Thus "Sinai" has become fixed in our minds as the symbol for the momentous event and its subsequent interpretation. It is well to keep in mind that Deuteronomy clings to Horeb as the location,[2] and its narrative of covenant making is very brief (Deut 5:1–33). These different traditions present the Ten Commandments, or Decalogue, as the basis of the covenant, yet their respective versions differ in two significant points[3] plus several minor ones. In addition to the Decalogue, many more codes and collections of laws and regulations were subsequently added to the core, and the final version reached its present form only after the exile.

In historical terms, the emergence of the Hebrews/Israelites was comparatively late. Other peoples and nations had long since organized civil and religious systems to establish order in their respective communities, including the Canaanite inhabitants of the land that the Israelites were taking over by a process that included both violent conflict and relatively peaceful infiltration (see chapter 13 "The Conquest and Settlement of Canaan"). Legal systems should probably be seen as originating in primitive

---

1. Sinai is the location in Exodus (13x), Leviticus (5x), and Numbers (12x).

2. Horeb: Deuteronomy and the traditions influenced by it, 1 Kings 8:7; 19:8. Also Ps 106:19, Mal 4:4.

3. 1) The explanation for the Sabbath commandment: Exod 20:11 creation, and Deut 5:15 redemption from Egypt; 2) Exod 20:17 forbids coveting the neighbor's "house" and then lists its contents beginning with wife; Deut 5:21 mentions the wife first and separates her from the neighbor's other possessions.

efforts by Homo sapiens to exploit the capabilities of the neocortex that distinguished them from other animals. From ancient documents it appears that some early people believed the laws governing society were given by the gods, which may explain the priests' role in legal affairs to interpret the divine will in many societies, including Israelite. Scripture has already stated that Moses's father-in-law, the Midianite priest, had conducted cultic worship of God and had advised Moses to delegate authority to respected elders to assist in settling quarrels according to Moses's having made known to them "the statutes and instructions of God" (Exod 18:12–27).

The best-known copy of the famous Code of Hammurabi (also spelled Hammurapi), ruler of Babylon 1728–1686 BCE, is incised on a diorite stela now in the Louvre Museum in Paris. At the top a bas-relief shows the king respectfully standing to receive from the seated sun god Shamash, god of justice, the commission to write the laws.[4] The symbolism implies that the king derived his supreme authority on earth from the heavenly gods. In this way the dominant class of wealth and power in other states emulated Hammurabi's claim to divine authorization. There are many details in biblical law codes that have near parallels in Hammurabi's and other ancient codes of law concerned with proper human relations.[5] The Sinai Covenant is distinguished from other codes by placing first the Ten Commandments, where primary emphasis rests upon the sovereignty of YHWH and the individual's relation to the Deity, before it lays down the fundamental principles of human relationships.

1. THE DIVINE APPEARANCE

YHWH gives Moses instructions to prepare the people for the divine appearance in fire and thunder on Mount Sinai. We need not take literally all details of the awesome depiction of the event; it is an example of a literary/liturgical convention to convey to the worshipers a sense of the power and awesomeness of deity, typical of prescientific cultures. Mythological terminology easily enters into everyday speech without people taking it literally.[6] Since the publication of the Ras Shamra texts Bible students know the extent to which biblical imagery used to describe YHWH appears to have been borrowed almost verbatim from earlier Canaanite poems and myths. Ps 97:2–5 describes the coming of YHWH: "Clouds and thick darkness are all around him . . . Fire goes before him . . . His lightnings light up the world; the earth sees and trembles. The mountains melt like wax before YHWH—." Ps 29 speaks of YHWH in terms that can be paralleled almost word for word in Ras Shamra hymns sung to Hadad the storm god, familiarly called Baal.[7]

---

4. Pritchard, ed., *The Ancient Near East* I, 136 and fig. 59.

5. See Greengus, "Biblical and Ancient Near Eastern Law."

6. Japanese call thunder *kami-nari*, "divine resounding." (Cf "the voice of YHWH" Ps 29.) In Japanese, a dragon causes a solar eclipse *nisshoku* = "sun eating," and a lunar eclipse *gesshoku* = "moon eating."

7. See Gray, *The Legacy of Canaan*, 208.

Mythological language became a convention with biblical authors in anticipating the "Day of YHWH," God's coming for judgment or for rescue. The prophet Joel, stimulated in part by a plague of locusts, brought a message of hope. He prophesied that YHWH would pour out his Spirit on all people, old and young, male and female including slaves, and he continued: "I will show portents in the heavens and on the earth, blood and fire and columns of smoke. The sun shall be turned to darkness, and the moon to blood, before the great and terrible day of YHWH comes. Then everyone who calls on the name of YHWH shall be saved" (Joel 2:30–32a). Peter quoted this text from Joel in full to explain the ecstatic tongue speaking of Jesus's men and women disciples when they were filled with the Holy Spirit on the day of Pentecost. Peter invited his hearers to believe on the Lord and be saved, *and three thousand responded.* Such was the real point of the quotation from Joel, not the presence or absence of darkened sun and bloody moon (Acts 2:14–21, 41. Note: Peter ascribed to the Lord Jesus the same saving function that Joel had ascribed to YHWH.)

I do not suggest that there were no observable natural phenomena associated with the Sinai theophany, the manifestation of YHWH—quite the contrary. But natural phenomena alone have no revelatory significance. Martin Luther believed that a thunderstorm was God's way of calling him to abandon the secular world and become a monk, but the lightning struck at a moment when Luther's own spirit was filled with painful conflict. See also the experience of the prophet Elijah at Horeb the mountain of God (1 Kgs 19:1–12).

As to the Sinai theophany in Exodus, the most plausible suggestion would be that an awesome thunderstorm or earthquake occurred at an impressive moment during Moses's instructions to the assembled people. They were already inclined toward a reverent and receptive attitude by their deliverance at the Reed Sea and being led thus far through the wilderness. A sudden storm could leave an indelible impression on them, which they kept fresh for subsequent generations by means of cultic re-enactment, including beating of drums and sounding of ram's horns in a deafening accompaniment. The final editing of the biblical text came only after many years repeating cultic ceremonies re-enacting the event and reverent reflection upon the significance of the covenant for the people of YHWH.[8]

Despite the prominence that "the Sinai Covenant" has assumed in the Bible itself and in Jewish and Christian tradition, never forget the priority and spiritual significance of the covenant that the Divine Kinsman cut with Abram (Gen 15; see chapter 7 "The Covenant with Abram").

---

8. In my view, the mention of the sound of the trumpet (ram's horn) along with thunder and lightning at Exod 19:16 and 20:18 probably reflects centuries-long practice of the use of the ram's horn to simulate the voice of God in the cultic reenactment of the theophany. It became such a conventional part of religious terminology that it entered naturally into the Exodus narrative based on the cult. See also 1 Thess 4:16 for persistence of the symbolical language of the trumpet as used by Paul in writing of Christian expectation of events at the end of the age.

2. THE DECALOGUE

There is no certain text of the wording of the Ten Commandments. The critical view holds that the Decalogue in its present form with explanatory clauses came long after Moses, expanding the basic principles to reflect conditions typical of a long-settled agricultural people with a social hierarchy including well-to-do families, slaves, and alien residents. The present form attributes the Decalogue to dictation from YHWH and enforces the socio-religious status of the community of YHWH worshippers that came out of Egypt.[9] Some say that a brief form of the ten words could go back to Moses.[10] Moses emphasized the Israelites' exclusive relation to YHWH, commonly called the "First Table" that presents the oneness of God in its more fully developed aspects. The "Second Table," guiding relations among Israelites, contains some general principles common to other religions and societies, but the biblical view is that relations among members of the covenant people depend not on what is common to all humanity but on God, who is not only Creator but also Covenant Lord. Moses had already given "statutes and instructions of God" to guide the people's daily life while they camped at the mountain of God (Exod 18:16). Adam Welch argues that in every stage of its development biblical faith always closely connected the community's ethical behavior to each other with its relationship to the Deity in a manner not typical of the religions of Israel's neighbors.[11]

YHWH's self introduction opens the Decalogue: "I am YHWH your God, who brought you out of the land of Egypt, out of the house of slavery." (20:2).[12] The present form of the self-introduction may reflect a later formulation used in liturgical commemoration for a generation far removed from the personal experience of exodus, e.g., Hos 12:9, Ps 81:10. The self-introduction at this point establishes for all time the principle of divine grace. The words that follow rest upon the fact that YHWH has *already* redeemed this people. Their response is one of gratitude and certainly *not* a

---

9. See Clines, "The Ten Commandments," 26–45.

10. We owe to Deut 5:22 and Exod 32:16 the common view that God wrote precisely these "ten words" on the two stone tablets, the basis of the covenant. By contrast, Exod 24:12 could mean that the covenant comprised the material in Exod 20:22—23:19 that Moses had just written in the book ("The Book of the Covenant"). Exod 31:18 could also refer to all this material; Exod 32:15–16 strengthens this impression by describing the tablets as "written on both sides, written on the front and on the back." Moses broke these tablets because of the idolatry of the golden calf (32:19). He prepared two more tablets, took them up the mountain, where God renewed the covenant with Exod 34:17–26, words significantly different from both the Ten Commandments and the Book of the Covenant. Then "YHWH said to Moses: Write these words; in accordance with these words I have made a covenant with you and with Israel." He was there with YHWH forty days and forty nights; he neither ate bread nor drank water. And he wrote on the tablets the words of the covenant, the ten commandments" (=ten words 34:27–28). This account asserts that at God's command Moses wrote the words of Exod 34:10–26, or at least 34:17–26. The phrase "the ten commandments" (=ten words, 34:28) appears to be an editorial addition harmonizing this account with that of Deuteronomy, which always limits the covenant to the Ten Words.

11. Welch, *Prophet and Priest*, 11–36.

12. According to Jewish reckoning, Exod 20:2–3 together make up the First Commandment, whereas Christians separate the two verses into Self-introduction and First Commandment.

sense of obligation to fulfill conditions in order to merit God's blessing.[13] The verbs of the commandments are in second person singular, stressing the personal involvement of each one. They are expressed in simple future tense, describing community life when each person responds thankfully to God's great blessing.

2a. The first word

You shall have no other gods. (20:3)[14]

For the people with Moses, this first word from the mountain is the most important. It does not deny the existence of other deities or numinous spirits. Paula Fredriksen describes the socio-religious climate of the times: "Gods and humans were the two key populations of ancient society, which could thrive only if gods were happy. Cult was the index of human loyalty, affection and respect. Cult made gods happy, and happy gods made for happy humans. The converse was also true: deprived of cult, gods grew angry. When gods were angry, people paid."[15]

For Israel covenant makes an exclusive demand: For *you, Israel,* Deity must be *YHWH* alone, for to *YHWH* and no other you owe your liberation and life. Exclusive loyalty to YHWH that Moses demands here is the same that father Jacob (newly called Isra*el*) made of his tribal coalition (also named Isra*el*) enlarged by the captured Hittite women and children. Before going to worship only El at Bethel Jacob commanded: "Put away the foreign gods that are among you" (Gen 35:2). It is the same demand that Joshua made of any hitherto unaffiliated tribes that wished to join Israel: "put away the foreign gods that are among you and incline your hearts to YHWH, the God of Israel" (Josh 24:23). The Mosaic covenant is quite in the line of development based on exclusive worship of One God, already begun and still to be continued.

At the mountain of God YHWH brought Israel into an expanded version of the fictive kinship covenant in which the Deity took the initiative to assume the obligation of Divine Kinsman toward this human family, whom he as *go'el,* next of kin, had redeemed from bondage. In one sense, it is correct to say that the Bible's story of Israel is a narrative of the extent to which Israel maintained or violated covenant loyalty. Indeed, violation was more characteristic of Israel than loyalty, and yet YHWH's *chesed*=steadfast love prevailed.

---

13. The unmistakable note of conditionality in Exod 19:5 may reflect a later tendency in that direction, to which I will refer in the next chapter, "Covenant as Gift and Obligation."

14. See Durham, *Exodus,* 276, 277, 285 for the possibility that the words "before me" [Hebrew ʿ*al panay*=*against my face*] are a later addition. Childs, *The Book of Exodus,* 402–3 discusses the difficulties of interpreting these words.

15. Paula Fredriksen, "Judaizing the Nations" 235.

2b. The second word

You shall not make for yourself an idol. (20:4a)

The second word in this short form could well go back to Moses. The word translated "idol" in NRSV is *pesel* ("graven image" KJV; "sculptured image" NJPS). The noun is cognate with *pasal*, to cut, carve, or shape some material to depict the deity (cf. Hab 2:18–20; Ps 115:4–8//135:15–18). Moses prohibits human art and craft from making an image of God. Exactly *that* was the sin of Aaron and the people in making and worshipping the golden calf (Exod 32). Worship without using images is called "aniconic."

People can *symbolize* deity by natural objects. Jacob set up a stone (*'eben*) as a pillar (*matstsebah*) at Bethel (Gen 28:18; 35:14). Moses set up twelve pillars in establishing the covenant at Sinai (Exod 24:4). Joshua set up a stone (*'eben*) at the Shechem covenant (Josh 24:26). Samuel celebrated victory over the Philistines with a stone called "Ebenezer" (NRSV margin, *Stone of Help*), saying, "Thus far YHWH has helped us" (1 Sam 7:12). The psalm in Deut 32 refers to YHWH as the Rock (*tsur*) who gave Israel birth (32:18) and boasts that the enemies' rock is not like Israel's Rock (32:31). The people who inhabited the region where Moses lived among the Midianites and Kenites used standing stones to symbolize deities. Archaeologist Uri Avner has identified nearly 1500 sites dating from the eleventh millennium BCE to the seventh century CE.[16] Early Mosaic religion forbade making images but accepted the practice of the ancestors to *symbolize* God by stones.

The Bible rejects any attempt to *represent* God by means of an artifact to set in a place, to see and to touch to use, or to abuse.[17] An inanimate statue or painting fixes a particular image upon the viewer's mind, which automatically places a limit upon the imagination. Deut 4.6 forbids making any idol in the form of male or female, to protect the concept that Deity transcends gender. Yet linguistic conventions referring to the deity most often in masculine terms has led to fixation upon God as only male, which leads to citicizing those who would re-imagine God by following out biblical symbolism of female aspects of Deity. Fixating on masculine language for God has become idolatrous.

People know YHWH in the events that take place in the course of their following on the way, by means of the sound of words that communicate the divine will, and in the flow of time in which people have their existence. *Hearing* of the word and *movement through space and time* characterize the faith of One God, whereas polytheists tend to emphasize the *sight* of an image or shrine of human construction, *timeless and fixed in place*.[18]

---

16. See Hurowitz, "Picturing Imageless Deities."

17. In the ancient Near East, in time of war the victors would take the images of their enemies' gods as spoils of war. As a boy, I remember reading in the *National Geographic Magazine* about festivals to local saints or patron gods in Latin America. If crops had been poor, or if a major misfortune occurred, the people might take whips to punish the images.

18. See description of differences between Israel and the nations in light of these categories in

2c. The third word

You shall not make wrongful use of the name of YHWH your God. (20:7a)

For centuries students have struggled with translating and interpreting this command. Jewish tradition renders it, "You shall not swear falsely by the name of the LORD your God" (NJPS). Making an oath by the Name invokes divine power for one's personal advantage, to make Deity line up with one's personal agenda.

A related concept is to use a divine name for magic or to invoke a curse, another example of the creature's attempt to manipulate the Creator. Buber notes that the ambiguity of ʾ*ehyeh* ʾ*asher* ʾ*ehyeh* means that Israel cannot be certain that this is a name in the sense that one could use it for magic. While making the divine commitment to be present, God protects the divine freedom. "I do not need to be conjured for I am always with you . . . but it is impossible to conjure me."[19]

2d. The fourth word

Remember the Sabbath day, and keep it holy. (20:8)

"Remember" implies something already known, not mentioned for the first time. Sabbath is named first in the Hebrew Bible at Exod 16:23–29 at the giving of manna in the wilderness. For ex-slaves, one day's rest per week was a munificent gift. Jesus said the sabbath was made for humans, not vice versa (Mark 2:27). Moses spoke authoritatively about the sabbath as if it were something familiar. Nielsen attributes Moses's familiarity with sabbath to the Kenites. Kenite metal smiths could more easily adapt their work to a cycle with one day of rest than could farmers or herdsmen.[20] Nobody knows the origin of the sabbath; the Bible assumes that time belongs to God, not to humans. We should return a set portion of time to God by not using it for our own purposes. In American society Sunday, long set aside for rest from work and for Christian worship, is consumed by sports or labor like any other day, ratcheting up competitiveness, dishonoring God, and ravaging individual health and communal well being.

Aboriginal peoples reckoned time and fixed religious observances according to the phases of the moon.[21] There seems no natural explanation for the seven-day week, which fixed itself upon Israel from earliest times and coexisted with a lunar calendar.[22]

Terrien, *The Elusive Presence*, 133–154. The difference is not absolute, for God's people often succumb to attractions of manageable aspects of polytheism. I object to movies and videos that purport to tell Bible stories. They make a visual presentation of a religious experience or an event that the text relates in terms subject to several interpretations. One specific visualization may preclude other possible interpretations.

19. Buber, *Moses*, 52–53.
20. Nielsen, *The Ten Commandments*, 120.
21. 1 Sam 20:5ff, 2 Kings 4:23, Amos 8:5, Isa 66:23. Except the first reference, new moon and sabbath are mentioned together, like a well-known, familiar expression.
22. "Seven days" and "seven years" occur in the Ras Shamra literature in connection with religious

Jewish high holy days, Christian Easter, and Muslim Ramadan still follow a modified lunar reckoning. Yet from the Jewish Diaspora through globalized Christianity and Islam, the seven-day week has now become practically universal on planet Earth.

The second table of the Decalogue

The Second Table follows upon the First, because the proper understanding and response to God required in the First Table includes the proper relationships among the community of God's people. The Second Table lays down fundamental principles guiding each one's relations to one's "neighbor" (re'a="fellow citizen" in this context), without which one cannot relate properly to God (see Jesus' admonition at Matt 5:23–24). These rules also share some of the most basic principles that all human societies value.

5. Honor your father and your mother. (20:12a)
6. You shall not kill. (20:13)[23]
7. You shall not steal. (20:14)
8. You shall not commit adultery. (20:15)
9. You shall not bear false witness against your neighbor. (20:16)

I see no need to note similarities and differences between biblical law and other ancient codes, or to comment on possible influence from other codes on those in the Bible. In borrowing widely accepted customary teachings and joining them to the unique teachings concerning Israel's peculiar relation to YHWH, the Bible has fixed them in a new dimension.

The tenth word

You shall not covet. (20.17a)

The Hebrew word *hamad,* meaning "desire, yearn for, covet, lust after," has a broad application and points to subjective emotions, a person's interior thought processes, which are difficult to assess in a criminal case.[24]. The Second Table is not a code of

---

observances or events of particular importance; see Gray, *The Legacy of Canaan,* 63, 66, 68. However, I am not aware of any evidence of a seven-day week outside of Israel.

23. NRSV and NJPS among others translate "You shall not murder." The Hebrew verb *ratsah* concerns killing with evil intent, and biblical law permits the death penalty carried out in judicial process and killing enemies in a war of self defense. However, Childs points out that in the OT *ratsah* may also be used of killing in general (*The Book of Exodus,* 419–20). Durham's perceptive comment is worth noting: "[I]ts basic prohibition was against killing, for whatever cause, under whatever circumstances, and by whatever method, a fellow-member of the covenant community" (*Exodus,* 293).

24. I cannot agree with the attempt to heighten the degree of punishment meted out to those who are convicted of "hate crimes," though I sympathize with the general purpose.

criminal law; it prescribes no punishments for violations. Therefore, it appropriately ends with this word, which touches upon selfish desire, a powerful aspect of human nature. Durham comments: "The tenth commandment thus functions as a kind of summary commandment, the violation of which is a first step that can lead to the violation of any one or all the rest of the commandments. As such, it is necessarily all embracing and descriptive of an attitude rather than a deed. It was perhaps set in the Decalogue precisely because of this uniquely comprehensive application."[25]

SOLEMNIZING THE COVENANT

The Exodus 24 account of the covenant making advances the family story (constructed much later) to emphasize the unity of greater Israel as a religious community that emerged out of an originally smaller gathering of diverse elements.[26] Moses reported all the words he had received from YHWH (i.e., Exod 20:23—23:19), and he wrote them in a book. Moses built an altar (symbolizing YHWH) and erected twelve pillars (symbolizing the [later] twelve tribes). He then sent young men of the people (not priests) who offered sacrifices, and Moses poured sacrificial blood at the base of the altar, to symbolize YHWH's partnering. He read the words of the book of the covenant to the people, who said, "All that YHWH has spoken to us we will do, and we will be obedient" (Exod 24.7). Moses completed the transaction by sprinkling blood on the people, to symbolize their partnering in the covenant (Exod 24:3–8).[27] In conclusion, "Moses and Aaron, Nadab, and Abihu, and seventy of the elders of Israel went up, and they saw the God of Israel. Under his feet there was something like a pavement of sapphire stone, like the very heaven for clearness. God did not lay his hand on the chief men of the people of Israel, also they beheld God, and they ate and drank" (Exod 24:9–11), a rare privilege.

SUMMARY

Moses and his work take their place in the canon of Scripture as a focal point upon which a tremendous theological and literary structure has been built, much like an inverted pyramid. Eventually the entire corpus of the Pentateuch was ascribed to Moses. The pilgrimage through life and history of the people of YHWH brought them into new and unfamiliar situations for which they needed new guidance and new interpretations of old traditions and principles. At each crucial stage in this history, those

---

25. Durham, *Exodus*, 299. See Jesus's word in Matt 5:28: "Everyone who looks at a woman with lust has already committed adultery with her in his heart." At Rom 7:7–24 Paul specifics "covet" to describe how Sin has the power to turn God's commandment, meant for humanity's good, into incentive for a human to do evil.

26. See chapter 8 "Children of Abraham—Exclusion and Assimilation."

27. Cf the different wording of the Decalogue at Deut 5.1–22, which alone in that text is the basis of the covenant.

responsible for making and applying new codes added them to what they already had in hand and ascribed Moses's authority to their new understanding, even though in some details they might seem at odds with what had gone before. Concerning this mass of later material Jon D. Levenson expresses an opinion with which more and more serious Bible students, both Jewish and Christian, would agree: "The experience of Sinai, whatever its historical basis, was perceived as so overwhelming, so charged with meaning, that Israel could not imagine that any truth or commandment from God could have been absent from Sinai."[28]

According to tradition in the Scriptures of both the Jews and the Christians, Moses placed the two tablets of the covenant in a sacred box, referred to as the Ark of the Covenant.[29] The box accompanied the people on their trek through the desert, symbolizing YHWH's presence among them, not in the form of an image made by human hands and admired with the eye, but by means of words to be read aloud, to be heard by the ear, and to be obeyed from the heart.

---

28. Jon D Levenson, *Sinai and Zion*, 18–19.
29. Deut 10:1–5; 2 Kings 8:9; Hebrews 9:4; Revelation 11:19.

11

Covenant as Gift and Obligation

YHWH's SELF-INTRODUCTION OF THE covenant that Moses mediated between YHWH and Israel at Sinai clearly links the ineffable Name with the gift that is the foundation on which henceforth the divine-human relationship between YHWH and Israel is built: "I am YHWH your God, who brought you out of Egypt, out of the house of slavery" (Exod 20:2//Deut 5:6). This declaration establishes the gift for all time—Divine initiative in acts of mercy and lovingkindness toward a helpless people. The First and Second Words that follow make human obligation immediately clear: "You shall have no other gods . . . You shall not make for yourself an idol" (Exod 20:3-4//Deut 5:7-8). Unfortunately, there is that in Scripture itself that makes it possible to view gift and obligation as somehow in conflict, and even to imply that obligation is of greater importance than gift (see below). I wish to emphasize the opposite as strongly as possible: Gift sets the terms and far outweighs obligation. The very first covenant in the biblical text, the covenant that Elohim established with Noah, with all living, and with the earth itself, is unconditional and universal: it is a pure gift (Gen 9:8-17). The covenant of the Divine Kinsman with Abram in its original donation (which I view as historically the *earliest* covenant) was also unconditional gift (15:17-18); obligations were added only later (17:1-14).

It was in remembrance of the covenant with the ancestors that the Divine Kinsman redeemed his people from Egypt (Exod 2:24-25; 6:5-7). Between their redemption and their safe arrival at Mount Sinai the people murmured, complained, and even put YHWH to the test (Exod 15:24; 16:2-3; 17:1-7), yet YHWH patiently and mercifully bore with them and supplied their needs (gift). But once they signed on to the covenant at Sinai (obligation), divine wrath was quick to fall on every transgression. The climax came when the people refused to go up and take the land of promise. YHWH declared, "None of the people who have seen my glory and the signs that I did in Egypt and in the wilderness, and yet have tested me these ten times and have not obeyed my voice, shall see the land that I swore to give to their ancestors; none of those who despised me shall see it" (Num 14:22-23). We must consider the evidence that conflict between gift and obligation may touch even the heart of God.

The people promised, "All that YHWH has spoken we will do, and we will be obedient" (Exod 19:8; 24:7), but the narrative reports that at Sinai the people lost little time in violating the obligation.

1. THE GOLDEN CALF

Moses went up the mountain to receive the tablets of the covenant ("written on both sides . . . front and back" Exod 32:15). He was gone forty days for instructions about building the tabernacle (Exod 24:15—31:18). This absence left the people in a state of insecurity. Their natural desire for a material representation of the deity—something that they could see, handle, and set in a sacred place (a *maqom*)—overcame YHWH's desire for a human heart inclined to trust even in the absence of sight, to hear a word, and to obey in real time. Aaron gave in to their request and made the cast image of a bull, the familiar symbol of both El the Most High god of the Canaanite pantheon and of Hadad the storm god, popularly called Baal.

YHWH conformed to the typical behavior of an offended deity, namely, "When gods were angry, people paid."[1] In hot wrath YHWH threatened to consume the people and make of Moses a great nation (Exod 32:10). Moses declined the proffered honor and interceded for the people, reminding YHWH of the promise to the ancestors and appealing to divine self-respect, "And YHWH changed his mind about the disaster that he planned to bring on his people" (32:14). Nevertheless, the general rule still applied—the incident ended with the terse statement, "Then YHWH sent a plague on the people, because they made the calf—the one that Aaron had made" (32:35). Over and over the Israelites paid dearly for their offenses because of the wrath of YHWH.

It was Moses, the human mediator, who by direct appeal challenged YHWH's jealousy and brought about a certain cooling of divine wrath. And yet Moses's anger also burned, and he smashed the two tablets of the covenant (32:19). Moses mobilized the Levites, his fellow tribesmen, to draw sword and go through the camp killing brother, friend, and neighbor. The Levites received a blessing for that act of violence and assured for themselves ordination to the service of YHWH (32:25–29). In like manner, Eleazar, the son of Aaron, won for himself a "covenant of perpetual priesthood" by impaling an Israelite man and the Midianite woman he had brought into the camp during the Israelites' worship of Baal at Peor (Num 25:1–13). One cannot ignore this very deadly, violent element that inheres in the conservative YHWH-alone faith and practice (see also 2 Kgs 10:1–31, especially vv 30–31).

---

1. Fredricksen, "Judaizing the Nations" 235.

2. COVENANT AS GIFT

On the other hand, the sequel of the calf worship at Sinai became the setting for the revelation of another side of YHWH's nature that relates to the gift aspect of covenant. The human mediator, Moses, would not leave YHWH alone but kept after him not to give up on the Israelites (Exod 32:31–32; 33:12–16). Finally Moses begged YHWH: "Show me your glory, I pray." And he said, "I will make all my goodness pass before you, and will proclaim before you the name, YHWH; and I will be gracious to whom I will be gracious, and will show mercy on whom I will show mercy. But," he said, "you cannot see my face; for no one shall see me and live" (Exod 33:18–20).

God will accede only partially to Moses's request. God will not compromise the divine mystery and freedom. YHWH will be present when, as, and however he will, and reserves the right to choose those on whom he bestows grace and mercy. But YHWH commands Moses to prepare two more stone tablets similar to those he broke, in preparation for a renewal of the covenant. When Moses gets to the top of the mountain, YHWH comes down and hides Moses in a cleft of the rock. Moses sees YHWH's "back" (33:22), while he hears the declaration of the Name: "YHWH, YHWH, a God merciful and gracious, / slow to anger, and abounding in steadfast love and faithfulness, / keeping steadfast love for the thousandth generation, / forgiving iniquity and transgression and sin, / yet by no means clearing the guilty, / but visiting the iniquity of the parents upon the children / and the children's children, to the third and the fourth generation" (Exod 34:6–7).[2]

Benno Jacob comments: "Here mercy was emphasized in the richest possible manner, while the justified punishment was only casually mentioned at the conclusion. This comforting presentation was nothing other than the unfolding, natural consequence of the name *y-h-w-h*."[3] Gift is primary, obligation secondary.

We plumb more depths of meaning when we consider the two verbs that God used as self-description in 33:19: "to be gracious" (*nacham*) and "to have mercy" (*racham*). Throughout the Hebrew Bible they occur overwhelmingly with God as subject. This is especially true of "to have mercy," which here first appears in the Bible. To have mercy=*racham* is related to womb=*rechem*, the origin of all human life. H. J. Stoebe writes: "Most statements with *rechem* assume that Yahweh is the Lord of birth and life." Stoebe also notes that *racham* "stands in exclusive opposition to God's wrath or replaces it because wrath suspends the proper relationship to the people of God."[4] The cognate verb and several adjectives all rest upon the attitude of a mother to the child of her womb, an emotion that also can be visceral, gut wrenching.[5] Of the forty-

---

2. I dare not do more than merely observe that, in this context, YHWH's *face* is deadly, but YHWH's *back* is safe.

3. Jacob, *The Second Book of the Bible: Exodus*, 982.

4. *TLOT* Vol 3, 1226, 1229.

5. See Trible, *God and the Rhetoric of Sexuality*, 31–59 for a full treatment of the maternal aspects of Deity.

six occurrences of this verb, subjects other than God appear in only five or possibly six texts. The superlative degree of divine mercy is expressed in a speech of YHWH in answer to a complaint of exiled Israelites that YHWH has forsaken, has forgotten them: "Can a woman forget her nursing child, or show no compassion for the child of her womb? Even these may forget, yet I will not forget you" (Isa 49:15).

In the full description of YHWH in Exod 34:6 we read the two adjectives related to the two verbs mentioned earlier in 33:19: merciful (*nachum*) and gracious (*rachum*). Combining these two adjectives—merciful and gracious—multiplies their force. In the Bible they apply only to God.[6]

The little book of Jonah draws on the golden calf incident to teach YHWH's covenant *chesed* for Gentiles, personified by the hated Assyrians. Jonah the nationalistic Israelite prophet, didn't want to preach in Nineveh, "for I knew that you are a gracious God and merciful, slow to anger, and abounding in steadfast love and ready to relent from punishing" (Jonah 4:2, citing Exod 34:6–7). In response to Jonah's preaching the Ninevites repented, fasting in sackcloth, and "God changed his mind about the calamity he had said he would do, and he did not do it (Jonah 3:10). At Sinai the Israelites did not repent and fast, but Moses offered himself instead of them (Exod 32:31–32) and fasted forty days and forty nights before YHWH (34:28). More fully, Joel Edmund Adamson explicates the detailed similarities between the Jonah story and its related OT texts to emphasize the understanding that YHWH kept covenant loyalty/steadfast love not only with Israel but also with Gentiles[7] (see also Ps 33:5b).

Following Moses's worshipful request once more on behalf of the people, YHWH declares: "I hereby make [cut] a covenant. Before all your people I will perform marvels, such as have not been performed in all the earth or in any nation; and all the people among whom you live shall see the work of YHWH; for it is an awesome thing that I will do with you" (Exod 34:10). Again we see an affirmation of the Divine initiative, the priority of gift in the relationship. (Oddly enough, this renewed covenant, Exod 34:11–26, differs substantially from the Decalogue of Exodus and Deuteronomy, and also from the Book of the Covenant of Exod 20:22—23:19.) The incident closes thus: "He was there with YHWH forty days and forty nights; he neither ate bread nor drank water. And he wrote on the tablets the words of the covenant, the ten commandments [=ten words]" (34:28).[8]

---

6. A possible exception: Ps 112:4 "gracious and merciful" describes the righteous person, in parallel to YHWH in Ps 111:4, although Stoebe, *TLOT* Vol 3, 1229 and Dahood, *Psalms III*, 127–28 apply the adjectives to YHWH in both psalms.

7. Adamson, "YHWH's Surprising Covenant Hesed in Jonah," 3–11.

8. Obviously Moses wrote the words of this covenant on the tablets. The addition of the phrase, "the ten words" seems to be an editorial addition to harmonize with Deuteronomy, which always refers to the ten words, and limits the contents of the covenant only to them, and written by YHWH. See above note 10, note 10.

3. COVENANT AS OBLIGATION

As long as the people of Israel remained a relatively small population, the personal-familial character of covenant relation prevailed. After Israelites became like other nations and established a monarchy (which split into two, Israel and Judah) they came into contact with other monarchies, and their understanding of covenant changed accordingly.[9] Kings of Judah and Israel entered covenants, i.e., treaty relations, with kings of other nations. In such cases they called YHWH as witness and enforcer of the treaty on their side, while the other kings did the same with their gods. In some, but not all, of these treaties, the two parties might act as equals, or the Israelites as superior, but that was not true with regard to Israelites' treaties with the powerful kingdoms of Assyria and Babylonia. Treaties with these latter, sometimes referred to as suzerainty treaties, routinely enforced the sovereignty of the great king of the empire and the subordinate status of the vassal kings. The great king recounted the benefits he had bestowed on the vassals and laid down the duties the vassals owed to him. Those duties involved their absolute loyalty to the king and prescribed terrible curses on disloyal vassals. The treaties also demanded peaceful relations among the vassal kings, with punishments for any who might try to dominate or infringe a neighbor king's rights. The treaties invoked the nations' gods, sometimes in great numbers, as witnesses and enforcers, and the vassals were required to store the documents in the temples of their gods and to bring them out for regular review.

In the twentieth century biblical scholars noted similarities between those treaties and the Sinai covenant. Thus, a suggested interpretation saw YHWH in the role of the Great King, and the deliverance from Egypt as the description of the Great King's beneficence. All the people of YHWH played the part of the vassal kings. Israelites owed absolute loyalty to YHWH, but they also had obligations to each other, all described in detail in the body of the covenant. The covenant was stored in the ark/box and placed in the tent, and it was regularly read and renewed. It became popular for some Bible students to propose that Israel's familiarity with covenant originated from international relations only late in the monarchy and that the concept had been retrojected back to the time of the ancestors. Such interpretations always encountered skepticism, and now consensus is shifting away from seeing exact parallels between the Sinai covenant and extrabiblical suzerainty treaties. Without question there was some influence from outside on the final composition of the biblical accounts of covenant.[10] Nevertheless, picturing YHWH as a Great King and the covenant as his way of imposing his law upon his people inevitably drew attention away from Shaddai as Divine Kinsman in the earliest period.

---

9. I shall take up the matter of Israel "like other nations" in a later chapter.

10. One may see this development by comparing the articles on "Covenant" first in the *IDB* and then the *ABD*.

The book of Deuteronomy, the early version of which modern scholars date from the time of King Josiah of Judah, contains details traceable to treaties of Assyria, which had destroyed northern Israel in 722-1 BCE. Josiah was quite familiar with such treaties, for Judah was also subject to Assyria over more than a century after Israel's fall, even though Assyria declined and eventually gave way to Babylonia. The deuteronomic version of the covenant places the utmost importance on Israel's fulfilling the obligations. "If you will only obey YHWH your God—" a short list of blessings will result (Deut 28:1–14). "But if you will not obey YHWH your God—" a very long list of curses will fall, some of them apparently copied verbatim from Assyrian treaties, including some of the most terrible and frightening calamities imaginable (Deut 28:15–46). The people's failure to fulfill their obligations under the covenant and the law of Moses became a familiar explanation for the fall of the two kingdoms and the people's exile from the land.

Deuteronomy and the historical books influenced by its theology stressed over and over that the sin of Israel was forsaking YHWH and going after other gods. In other words, they laid utmost emphasis on violation of the First Table of the Decalogue, the obligation of loyalty to YHWH alone. In the books of the prophets, Amos and Hosea in northern Israel and Micah, Isaiah, Jeremiah, and Ezekiel in southern Judah, which I will take up later, we note another emphasis. The elite power minority, supported by venal priests, flaunted loyalty to YHWH by lavish expenditures on the sacrifices and offerings required by the cult, while routinely exploiting the ordinary citizens in violation of the Second Table of the Decalogue. The prophets condemned these injustices so strongly as to lead some interpreters to imply their outright condemnation of cult sacrifice. If not that, for them certainly cultic observance was secondary. In any case, the cumulative effect is to make such a show of the human failure to fulfill the obligations of the covenant that the gift—YHWH's unfailing loyalty, compassion, mercy, and grace—grow dim. Finally mercy is seen to take effect only *after* human violation has roused the divine wrath and brought judgment.

4. THE SPECIOUS COVENANT WITH ADAM

The error of placing primary emphasis on human obligation to the effective eclipse of divine gift led to serious misunderstanding of the character of God not only by some within Israel but also by early Christians. First of all, despite the fact that the word covenant=*berit* occurs nowhere in the creation accounts of Gen 1–3, early Christian theologians imposed the concept of covenant, understood as a contract between God and the first human Adam. The Westminster Confession of Faith clearly states the centuries-old belief that has been a common presupposition of Christians whether they express it so clearly or not: "The first covenant made with man was a covenant of works, wherein life was promised to Adam, and in him to his posterity, upon condition of perfect and personal obedience."[11]

I will mention only a few of the objections that can be leveled against this covenant of works: (1) God appears first of all as a strict lawgiver and judge, ignoring and in effect obscuring the divine attitude of good will toward the human creature introduced in Gen 1:26–28 and re-enforced in so many other biblical texts, many of which I referenced above. (2) Traditional Christianity, which insists that human salvation is based on grace and not on works, presupposes that God first required the human to act perfectly, precisely the antithesis of grace. (3) The grace that now makes human salvation possible appeared only afterward and is made available because Jesus, the one sinless human who was the incarnate Son of God, fulfilled perfectly the obligation of the covenant of works, suffered the death penalty all sinners deserve, and thereafter was raised from the dead by God. This scheme of things presupposes *the complete triumph of works over grace, of obligation over gift!*

A second unfortunate result of placing primary emphasis on human obligation is the Christian doctrine of supersession: God rejected Israel after the flesh, the earthly people of God, who consistently violated the covenant and then rejected and put to death Jesus the Messiah. Those of every time and place (including individual Jews) who believe in Jesus Christ as Savior now make up the Church, which has superseded or replaced earthly Israel as the true or spiritual Israel. Christian history is replete with acts of terrible discrimination, cruelty, and genocidal assaults against Jews resulting from this error, which still persists among many Christians even today. Happily, a more enlightened understanding of Scripture is leading some of us to acknowledge Jews and all other humans as sisters and brothers, all of us created in the image of the One God whose eternal plan of reconciliation embraces all of us.

SUMMARY AND REFLECTION

Giving primacy to human obligation presupposes God who is a sort of cosmic Proctor keeping a sharp eye on everybody while we take his exam. Like the Santa Claus of a children's song, "He's making a list and checking it twice, / gonna find out who's naughty or nice." It seems almost to be inherent in human nature to think of God this way. Job calls God "watcher of humanity" and wonders what harm his sin really does to God (Job 7:20). Again Job challenges God: "Your hands fashioned and made me; and now you turn and destroy me" (10:8). This view underlies the anxiety expressed in Ps 139:1–12: "—you hem me in, behind and before . . . where can I flee from your presence?" Still the psalmist derives a degree of personal comfort at the thought of God's creative work in his having been born (139:13–18). Yet even so the psalmist still

---

11. WCF VII.2, *The Book of Confessions*, ¶6.038, p 128.

presupposes the final destruction of the wicked and assures God that he wants to be counted on God's side on the day of judgment (139:19-24).

The theme of separation of "saved" and "lost" runs like a strong thread through Scripture; but there is another thread one must not overlook and other voices one must hear. Psalm 65, a song of joyful praise to God for the bounties of the created earth, opens on the theme of grace: "Praise is due to you, O God, in Zion; / and to you shall vows be performed, / O you who answer prayer! / To you all flesh shall come. / When deeds of iniquity overwhelm us, / You forgive our transgressions" (65:1-3). Psalm 130 gives voice to another who sings the same theme: "If you, O YHWH, should mark iniquities, / Lord, who could stand? / But there is forgiveness with you, / so that you may be revered" (130:3-4).

Having said that, however, it is necessary to recognize that conflicting views of covenant as gift and obligation, and competing conceptions of God as wrathful or merciful, persist through all of Scripture, NT as well as OT. Prophetic books that offer comforting portraits of God as merciful and gracious also highlight divine wrath not only against the enemies of God's special people, but also divine enmity against Israel as well. It is possible to detect a certain degree of inconsistency in the Gospel portrayals of Jesus. My reading of the Bible in its entirety leads me to the conclusion that grace triumphs over wrath.

At the climax of a centuries-long process of development, the Apostle Paul declares: "In Christ, God was reconciling the world to himself, not counting their trespasses against them and entrusting the message of reconciliation to us" (2 Cor 5:19). God is *not* in the business of keeping count of human wrongdoing. God acts to reconcile humans who for one reason or another are alienated from God, and God recruits human partners in the work of reconciliation that embraces the world.

12

From Sinai to Canaan

IN CHAPTER 8 ABOVE, "Children of Abraham—Exclusion and Assimilation," I showed how the most obvious "family story" that runs through the OT was the product of postexilic editors building on efforts originating in the court of David and Solomon to promote a sense of continuous oneness and homogeneity of Israel the people of YHWH. Yet there was other biblical material that gave evidence of a greater diversity and inner tensions among those who became known as Israel. In this chapter I extend that process by briefly summarizing the Israelites' experiences in the wilderness before actually setting out to return to Canaan, followed by other more realistic material.

1. ISRAEL IN THE WILDERNESS

The children of Israel, pictured as the twelve tribes descended from Abraham and Sarah's grandson Jacob/Israel, all heard YHWH speak the Ten Words from heaven. They were all joined to YHWH by the blood of the covenant; they all violated the covenant by worshiping the golden calf; and the survivors all received YHWH's merciful and gracious acceptance when Moses interceded and mediated a renewed covenant (Exod 19–24; 32–34; see above, chapters 10 and 11).

Next the Israelites supplied materials for the tabernacle (often called tent of meeting, NRSV), an elaborate portable shrine administered by priests and Levites, where YHWH dwelt among them (Exod 35:4—40:38). Moses also had a tent outside the camp where he received YHWH's guidance for the people, and where his assistant Joshua stayed (Exod 33:7–11). The details of the tabernacle are thought to describe a structure David prepared later, but this composite text affirms the existence of a portable tent/shrine, the center of the continuous cultic observances that enriched the life of the people in the wilderness. The book of Leviticus, the manual to guide the priests' rituals and to preserve the tabernacle and the people from defilement, interrupts the "family story". Leviticus and the tabernacle are products of more complex and systematized practices of settled life of a later date, but both are based on primitive traditions.[1]

---

1. See *ABD* articles: Friedman, "Tabernacle" and Levine, "Leviticus."

God For All

YHWH commanded Moses to take a census of "every male individually, from twenty years old and upward, everyone in Israel able to go to war," totaling 603,550 men, who were supposed to conquer the land (Num 1:1–46). When they lost heart because of the negative report of the scouts who spied out the land, YHWH declared that all that generation must die in the wilderness (Num 13–14). Forty years later Moses took a second census, 601,730 warriors (Num 26). The Israelites conquered all the land east of the Jordan, including Midianites and Amorites, inflicting almost total annihilation on the inhabitants. Moses allotted this territory to the tribes of Reuben, Gad, and half of Manasseh (Num 31–32). Next Moses gave an idealized description of the land of promise, comprising all of Canaan between the Jordan and the Mediterranean (Num 34:1–15). He next named twelve men, one from each tribe, to help Joshua and the priest Eleazar to apportion the land after the conquest (Num 34:16–29; see Josh 19:51).

Moses then delivered three speeches to the Israelites, which make up the present book of Deuteronomy.[2] He warned them: "If you act corruptly by making an idol in the form of anything, thus doing what is evil in the sight of YHWH your God, and provoking him to anger, I call heaven and earth to witness against you today that you will soon utterly perish from the land that you are crossing the Jordan to occupy; you will not live long on it, but will be utterly destroyed" (4:25–26). Moses's renewal of the covenant (Deut 26:16—28:68) placed great emphasis on obligation, reflecting Israel's experience of subjection to Assyria, as I noted in chapter 11. Besides the book of Joshua, the books of Judges, 1–2 Samuel, and 1–2 Kings show such influence from the doctrine and vocabulary of Deuteronomy that collectively they may be referred to as the Deuteronomistic History. Joshua and Judges should be read consecutively in order to note the contrast: Joshua continues the "family story" and ideally describes the conquest as quick, total, and accomplished by twelve tribes faithfully following Moses's prior orders.[3] Judges tells a realistic story of a painful process involving victories and defeats ending in corruption and degradation before establishing the monarchy (see next chapter). It is well to have a brief description of Canaan before Joshua's "conquest" and an overview of the laws and customs of the early tribes in Israel.

2. CANAAN IN THE LATE BRONZE AGE

Before 1500 BCE towns with outlying farm villages grew up along the eastern Mediterranean coastal plain and in the fertile inland river valleys. Well-armed Hittite invaders gained control of them and organized small city-states. In each, a king and a centralized power bloc exploited the subject people, especially the peasant majority

---

2. The title Deuteronomy is based on a Greek word meaning "second law" or "repeated law." Deuteronomy revises and expands the laws in the Book of the Covenant (Exod 20:24—23:19 see below) to apply to changed conditions.

3. Moses's name appears fifty-eight times in the book of Joshua (NRSV).

from whom they exacted much of their agricultural produce. The rulers supported a non-productive army for defense but also to control the local people. Priests were another non-productive caste, providing divine legitimacy for the power structure, officiating in temples with idols of gold and silver. Peasants were forced into labor gangs to build fortifications, palaces, and temples. Pharaoh Thutmose III (1504–1450 BCE) extended Egyptian control over the area with a feudal system making each local vassal-king pay tribute to Egypt. Egyptians repulsed an invasion by Philistines coming by land and sea from the Aegean, but incorporated them as managers of the feudal system of Canaan. Hittite inhabitants of the land interacted with the ancestors (Gen 23:1–20; 26:34), and they appear in the list of peoples the Israelites were supposed to annihilate, but whom they left and with whom they intermarried (Judg 3:5–6).[4]

Information concerning conditions in Canaan came to light with the discovery in 1887 CE of Egyptian diplomatic correspondence written in cuneiform on clay tablets. They were unearthed at the Egyptian town of El Amarna, which had been the site of the short-lived capital of Pharaoh Ikhnaton and Queen Nefertiti, best known for the attempt to promote monotheism c. 1376 BCE. These Amarna Letters comprise correspondence sent to the Egyptian court when some feudal kings of Canaan felt neglected by the Pharaoh.[5] The Amarna Letters enable students to reconstruct conditions of Canaan in the Late Bronze Age (LBA) when the proto-Israelites were emerging.

Violent competition among Canaanite city-states erupted as Egypt's control waned. Local kings reported that armed bands exacerbated the violence. The Amarna Letters call these bands *hapiru* or *habiru* (possibly ʿ*apiru*), which some scholars would connect with Hebrews (=ʿ*ibri*), a name applied to some proto-Israelites. We read of "Abram the Hebrew" in Gen 14:13, and Joseph and his family in Egypt are called Hebrews.[6] In the Amarna Letters *habiru/hapiru* were outside of and resistant to normal governmental control. They were foreigners or refugees without settled homes. Some were robbers or brigands, some were mercenaries, and others were little more than slaves. Some *habiru/hapiru* may have become Israelites, but not all Israelites were *habiru/hapiru*.[7]

Some of the exploited underclass in the Canaanite city-states may have revolted or simply escaped from their stifling environment to join the Israelites in the hills. The Gibeonites who tricked Joshua into an alliance that preserved them (Josh 9) may have been motivated in part by the weight of servitude to Egyptian feudal overlords. Even though the highlands were more difficult to cultivate than the lowlands, Israelites could keep their produce from being confiscated as tribute. They didn't have to

---

4. See above chapter 7 note 10, also *ABD* "Hittites In The Old Testament."

5. See *ABD* Nadav Na'aman, "Amarna Letters."

6. See *ABD* articles on "Hebrew and Habiru," "Hapiru" and above chapter 9.5 "YHWH the God of the Hebrews."

7. Gottwald, *The Tribes of Yahweh*, 401–9.

perform forced labor or support parasitic armies and priests. Some of those whom the Israelites liberated and others who willingly attached themselves to Israelites could experience liberation from Egyptian power without having participated in the exodus, but they joined forces with those who had actually come out of Egypt. As the Israelites developed an identity, it contrasted strikingly with city-state feudalism dominated by Egypt and their Philistine surrogates.

Norman K. Gottwald describes the emerging Israelite community and adds that the most powerful unifying force was their mono-Yahweh religious cult:

> Among those who entered Israel in the thirteenth–twelfth centuries, indeed those who formed its ideological and organizational spearhead, were congeries of ʿapiru and mixed agriculturalists and pastoralists, some of whom had fled from Egypt. *Consequently, Israel is most appropriately conceived as an eclectic composite in which various underclass and outlaw elements of society joined their diffused antifeudal experiences, sentiments, and interests, thereby forming a single movement that, through trial and error, became an effective autonomous social system.*"[8]

Baruch Halpern criticizes Gottwald for overemphasizing revolution and the egalitarianism of the society that Israel created, but he agrees that the common religious belief in YHWH and shared festival observances strengthened their self-conscious resistance against the exploitative threats of city-state kings.[9]

Many Bible students think that "the Book of the Covenant" that Moses read to the people and which they promised to obey (Exod 24:7) refers to the body of laws following the Decalogue (Exod 20:24—23:19). Though there is no sure way of proving it, the material in the Book of the Covenant seems suitable for early Israelite tribes in Canaan such as Gottwald described, before the establishment of the monarchy.

3. THE BOOK OF THE COVENANT AS GUIDE FOR THE TRIBES

The social organization reflected in the Book of the Covenant lacks any indication of a firmly united people under a single authority. It hints at a growing belief that YHWH was the supreme authority. The Book of the Covenant shows evidence of gradual compilation before it was later incorporated into the narrative of covenant making in Exodus. It is divisible into Part One (20:24—22:16) that names YHWH once, and Part Two (22:17—23:19) that names YHWH three times.

The opening sentences reflect primitive Israelite conditions in contrast to the feudal Canaanite city-states: "You shall not make gods of silver alongside me, nor shall you make for yourselves gods of gold. You need make for me only an altar of earth

---

8. Gottwald, *The Tribes of Yahweh*, 491, emphasis original. See also "Egyptian Imperialism and Canaanite Feudalism" 391–400 and "The ʿApiru Adaptation in Amarna Canaan" 401–9 in *The Tribes of Yahweh.*

9. Halpern, *The Emergence of Israel*, 100–3.

and sacrifice on it your burnt offerings and your offerings of well-being, your sheep and your oxen; in every place where I cause my name to be remembered I will come to you and bless you." Altars of natural undressed stone were also permitted (Exod 20:23–26). There is no mention of priests or temples. At the earliest period these local shrines had powerful influence in exalting YHWH and unifying the people. The local option, however, could lead to a variety of practices, competing priestly families, and possible corruption. Later the royal and priestly establishment of King Hezekiah tried to eliminate these local sanctuaries (2 Kgs 18:29//Isa 36:22). Deuteronomy 12:2-28 limits sacrifice to only one place. King Josiah was the first to centralize the cult completely, and that only shortly before his death and the end of the kingdom (2 Kgs 22–23). The Deuteronomistic History criticizes altars outside Jerusalem, especially those of the northern kingdom of Israel, but the History itself mentions many altars that were unquestioned in their time (e.g., Judg 11:11; 20:26–28; 1 Sam 1:3; 7:15–16; 1 Kgs 18:30–31; 19:10, 14).

Jay W. Marshall provides a detailed analysis of the Book of the Covenant that demonstrates how local Israelite society functioned in the time of the settlement of Canaan.[10] [Page numbers in brackets refer to Marshall's work.] The Book of the Covenant reflects a sedentary population in hill country like that of central Canaan in the pre-monarchical period of the Late Bronze and Early Iron Ages (thirteenth to twelfth centuries BCE). Marshall summarized scholarly studies of other societies living under comparable social and economic conditions to clarify those of Israel.

This decentralized society lacked an organized judicial system, but it had means to settle disputes on three levels: (1) family law, ruled by the senior male or patriarch; (2) an intermediate court system made up of village elders to settle disputes between families; and (3) a third level to settle disputes between larger groups, which may have been headed by a recognized chief [p 138]. The two upper levels of judgment took place at a shrine, for people depended on religious sanctions to enforce judgments. Family law included the death penalty for striking or cursing father or mother (21:15, 17) and for premeditated murder (21:12) [p 135]. Primitive hunter-gatherer bands did not wage war, but they permitted individuals or families to exercise self-redress.[11] Israel limited personal vengeance by relying on legal procedures. In case of accidental death a killer could seek refuge at a shrine (22:13). If investigation proved that the refugee had killed with intent, the law demands, "you shall take the killer from my altar for execution" (21:14). The *lex talionis*, "eye for eye and tooth for tooth" (21:21–23) attempted to assure equivalence of injury and punishment, to prevent the injured party from inflicting excessive injury as revenge. If men in a scuffle caused a pregnant woman to have a miscarriage, an appropriate monetary fine was paid according to the

---

10. Marshall, *Israel and the Book of the Covenant*. In my comments the page numbers in brackets refer to Marshall's work.

11. Fry, *Beyond War*, 214.

fetus's stage of development (21:22). If the woman herself was injured, the *lex talionis* applied.¹²

The Bible has laws to ameliorate but not abolish slavery. Hebrew male bondservants were to be set free at the end of six years. At the second level the Book of the Covenant dealt with a bondservant who chose to remain in servitude even though he qualified for freedom. "His master shall bring him before God (Heb ʾel-ha ʾelohim; sing or plu). At the doorpost his master shall pierce his ear with an awl; and he shall serve him for life" (21:5-6).

Interpretation of the Hebrew ʾel-ha ʾelohim is difficult. NJPS and some Christian translations (NRSV, RSV, NJB) render it literally "before God" with a marginal note that it might be "to the judges." KJV and NIV render it "to the judges" but with marginal note "before God." Marshall says that ʾel-ha ʾelohim / "to the judges" refers to a divinely legitimated human authority that mediates between families [p 138]. Childs says some have suggested the practice may have taken place before "the private house gods," but he says, "before God" is "a stereotyped term signifying the nearest sanctuary."¹³ Bondwomen were not included in release, yet they had certain rights, for they were assumed to have become wives or concubines in the master's household, (Exod 21:7–11). A later revision included release of female slaves (Deut 15:12–17). Another later law permitted Israelites to own non-Israelite slaves as permanent property (Lev 25:44–46). In the Book of the Covenant, an owner was not held equally accountable for injury or death of his slave as for a free person (Exod 21:20–21).

The phrase ʾel-ha ʾelohim / "to the judges" occurs twice in Exod 22:7–9 (H 22:6–8) concerning cases of two parties making opposite claims. They come before the gods/judges, and the one whom the gods/judges condemn shall pay double (22:9 H 22:8). According to Martin Noth, the occurrence of plural gods with plural verbs here indicates that Israel borrowed these rules from Canaanites and left the forms unedited.¹⁴ In the only specific naming of YHWH in Part One of the Book of the Covenant, a similar dispute is settled by an oath before YHWH (22:10–11 H 22:9-10). Without a state mechanism to enforce the decision, the system depended upon all parties accepting the supreme authority of YHWH the God of Israel. The one denying wrongdoing took an oath subject to divine retribution should he be lying. The code does not specify the authoritative human functionary in these cases.

Part Two of the Book of the Covenant states: "You shall not revile God (Elohim), or curse a leader (*nasiʿ*) of your people" (22:28 H 27). In late material *nasiʿ* (="one lifted up") refers to a high official of undefined authority. According to the structure of the text, the authority of this "leader" was similar to that of God. Except for this

---

12. Some people speciously claim that an ovum fertilized by a sperm immediately constitutes a human person, and therefore an induced miscarriage or abortion constitutes murder, for which they would apply the *lex talionis*. This argument has been extensively used to try to curtail women's reproductive rights.

13. Childs, *Exodus*, 448; 469.

14. Noth, *The Laws in the Pentateuch*, 20–21.

single example, Part Two places unambiguous emphasis upon the supreme authority of YHWH, who occasionally speaks directly.

"Whoever sacrifices to any god, other than YHWH alone, shall be devoted to destruction" (22:20). "Do not invoke the names of other gods; do not let them be heard on your lips" (23:13). "Three times in the year all your males shall appear before the Lord YHWH" (23:17). "The choicest of the first fruits of your ground you shall bring into the house of YHWH your God" (23:19). "The firstborn of your sons you shall give to me. You shall do the same with your oxen and with your sheep: seven days it shall remain with its mother; on the eighth day you shall give it to me" (22:29b–30 H 2:28b–29).

The Book of the Covenant makes no exception for human firstborn. Jon Levenson examines all relevant texts and concludes that Exod 22.29b (H 22:28b) contains an authentic demand by YHWH for the firstborn sons. Levenson says YHWH's ordering Abraham to offer Isaac, but then stopping him and allowing substitution of a goat, would be an example of special exemption (Gen 22:1–19). Ezekiel acknowledged that YHWH gave the command, which he said was "not good" (Ezek 20:25–26), but Jeremiah vigorously denied it (Jer 7:31; 19:4–6; 32:35).[15] Marshall theorizes that economic survival was so uncertain that Israelites limited population and consumption to maintain balance with the environment [p 166].

A similar sense of necessity may lie behind the command to let the land lie fallow for one year out of seven in order to preserve fertility [Marshall, 157–8]. A humanitarian aspect also was included in that the poor and the animals could freely consume what grew of itself (23:10–11). The requirement to rest one day in seven was also initially practical and humanitarian: it protected the strength and energy of free citizens, bond servants, resident aliens, and work animals (23:12) [p 158–9]. In the Book of the Covenant itself, there is no cultic or religious reason given for the sabbath commandment; such connections have to be imported from later biblical texts.

Besides the growing prominence of YHWH in Part Two, we find mention of the exodus from Egypt as background for a particular command: "You shall not wrong or oppress a resident alien (*ger*); you know the heart of an alien, for you were aliens in the land of Egypt (23:9; also 22:21). Marshall says that besides a foreigner a *ger* may be a fellow Israelite from a different tribe [pp 148–9]. The *ger* lacks the security of a family and is thus vulnerable to exploitation. Widows and orphans had lost the protection of the male household head. They should have been cared for on the family level, but apparently neglect was common enough to call forth this admonition handed down from a higher level, which threatened religious sanction. "You shall not abuse any widow or orphan. If you do abuse them, when they cry out to me, I will surely heed their cry; my wrath will burn, and I will kill you with the sword, and your wives shall become widows and your children orphans" (22:22–24). Without mechanisms for

---

15. Levenson, "Child Sacrifice in the Hebrew Bible: Deviation or Norm?" *The Death and Resurrection of the Beloved Son*, 3–16.

enforcement, the Book of the Covenant depends upon communally accepted religious practice to persuade people's willingness to do justice.

Not only does YHWH speak in first person in Part Two of the Book of the Covenant. In the command to lend to the poor without charging interest, YHWH speaks as the Divine Kinsman referring to them as "my people" (22:25), and promising to heed their cry of distress, "for I am compassionate" (22:27). The Book of the Covenant calls for evenhanded justice, not showing special partiality to the poor (23:3), yet demanding that they actually receive justice instead of the wealthy paying bribes or joining with other citizens to pervert justice due them (23:6–8).

The Book of the Covenant requires that all males must appear before YHWH (i.e., at a sanctuary) three times in a year (23:17), and it presupposes that the shrine would be fairly near the men's homes. At these festivals officials could give instruction on social and religious issues, tell the story of YHWH's mighty acts, and celebrate the covenant with YHWH. Each sanctuary would tend to develop its own liturgical forms and practices.

SUMMARY

The Book of the Covenant begins the process that gradually developed into the complex of laws and rituals of a later time. The various materials included in the total Sinai complex are so diverse that it is impossible to state exactly what was in the Mosaic Covenant after all. Sinai comprises many diverse traditions that developed over time at some of the more prominent local sanctuaries dating back to premonarchical times.

Together with information from the Amarna Letters and other extrabiblical documents, we get a realistic view of Israelite life in the hill country of central Canaan, where life was by no means easy, but at least it was an improvement on that of populations subject to Egyptian domination of the small city-states on the coastal plains and river valleys. People gained a deepening sense that YHWH was a God of compassion and liberation. Principles of justice developed during this earliest stage powerfully influenced the prophets of eighth and seventh centuries in Israel and Judah, when the two kingdoms had become so much like other nations that the prophets dared confront not only the political but also the religious power structure (see below chapter 18 "The Prophets and the End of the State").

13

The Conquest and Settlement of Canaan

FOLLOWING THE PLAN OF the previous chapter, I begin with the "family story" in Joshua, the idealistic account of total conquest of Canaan in a few short years and its distribution to the twelve tribes. Following that Judges gives a more realistic account of Israelite life before the monarchy.

1. THE CONQUEST BY JOSHUA

The biblical account of Joshua's conquest begins with extermination of every living human and animal in Jericho. Joshua "devotes" them as burnt offerings to YHWH (Josh 6). Such a practice was not unknown in the ancient Near East where each nation had its war god, to whom it might sacrifice enemies to celebrate victory. During the ninth century BCE King Mesha of Moab celebrated conquest of several Israelite towns by devoting their inhabitants to his god Chemosh. In 1868 CE archaeologists discovered a stone recording Mesha's victory.[1] Some Israelites thought that YHWH among the gods also desired similar human sacrifices. The Joshua account tells us more about a conception of deity that Israel held in common with other ancient Near Eastern peoples than it does about the God whom we see revealed in the whole of Scripture, especially in Jesus of Nazareth.[2]

Interrupting his military campaign, Joshua renewed the covenant between YHWH and the whole congregation in the valley between two mountains, Ebal and Gerizim. Joshua wrote the law of Moses on stones, which he read to the people, including blessings and curses (Josh 8:30–35). The city of Shechem lay in this valley. Both Abram (Gen 12:6) and Jacob (33:18–20) had worshiped at Shechem. Perhaps some of Jacob's people, adherents of El the God of Israel who had not gone to Egypt,

---

1. See "Moabite Stone" *IDB*. The article contains an English translation of the inscription and explains the connection with contemporary events in Israel about 850 BCE.

2. The contrast of Jesus and Joshua is clouded by the fact that the Greek translation of the OT (Septuagint, LXX) spells Joshua exactly the same as the NT Greek spells Jesus. At Acts 7:45 and Heb 4:8 KJV renders Joshua as "Jesus."

participated in the ceremony. That would account for Joshua's being able to conduct the covenant renewal in peace (see more on covenant renewal below, Josh 24).

Following this covenant renewal, Joshua completed conquering the whole land and its peoples: "For it was YHWH's doing to harden their hearts so that they would come against Israel in battle, in order that they might be utterly destroyed, and might receive no mercy, but be exterminated, just as YHWH had commanded Moses... So Joshua took the whole land according to all that YHWH had spoken to Moses; and Joshua gave it for an inheritance to Israel according to their tribal allotments. And the land had rest from war." (Josh 11:16-23).

In all fairness one must acknowledge that Scripture itself, both in Joshua and elsewhere, supplies ample evidence to contradict this description. The community for which the book of Joshua was written had experienced defeat and exile from the land their people had long inhabited. Their leaders (who produced the deuteronomistic writings) reflected on Israel's centuries-long experience in the land. They reminded their people that possession of the land had been YHWH's gift and that defeat and exile resulted from their failure to keep covenant. Still, YHWH had not abandoned them, for they had another opportunity to return and reoccupy the land.

Many Christians tend to limit reading Joshua to the "family story" in the first eleven chapters and to skip the lists of names of persons and places. It is just here that we find some of the data to support a more realistic account of what the main narrative has presented in idealistic terms. I offer only a few of many examples.

Joshua 12:7-24 lists thirty-one kings (actually thirty) on the west side of Jordan whom Joshua overthrew, implying that Israel took over those cities then, but Scripture supplies other data. (1) There are conflicting notes about which tribe got *Jerusalem* (Judg 1:5-8, 21); but the city remained independent till David captured it (2 Sam 5:6-12). (2) Pharaoh gave *Gezer* to Solomon when Solomon married Pharaoh's daughter (1 Kgs 9:16). (3) Deborah and Barak defeated the king of *Hazor* (Judg 4:1-2), and in Deborah's time the Canaanites still possessed *Dor, Taanach,* and *Megiddo* (Judg 1:27). Immediately after the list of those kings, YHWH told Joshua, "You are old and advanced in years, and very much of the land still remains to be possessed" (Josh 13:1). Several indigenous peoples remained and lived among the Israelites, who failed to dislodge them (Josh 13:13; 15:63; 16:10). Joshua sent scouts to survey the territory and to mark off seven portions so he could cast lots to distribute it. The whole congregation set up the tent of meeting at Shiloh, where Joshua, Eleazar the priest, and heads of the families of the twelve tribes supervised the division by lot (Josh 19:59; see Num 34:16-39). Some boundaries were vague and overlapping, and some cities were assigned to more than one tribe (Josh 18:1—19:51).

The Book of Joshua closes with an impressive covenant ceremony. "Joshua gathered all the tribes of Israel to Shechem" (Josh 24:1). He reminded them that Terah and Abraham served other gods, as did the Israelites in Egypt (24:2, 14). Joshua recounted YHWH's blessing of Abraham, the redemption from Egypt, and the gift of the bountiful land (24:2–13). Joshua urged the people to put away other gods and serve only YHWH. He asked them to choose among YHWH, or the ancestors' former gods, or the gods of the indigenous Amorites. Joshua concluded, "but as for me and my household, we will serve YHWH" (24:14–15). The people protested that they would indeed serve only YHWH, and after once more demanding that they put away the foreign gods, "Joshua made a covenant with the people that day and made statutes and ordinances for them at Shechem" (24:25).

The covenant making described here shortly before Joshua died involved *all* the tribes (24:29), who supposedly had experienced the total conquest. In view of the equivocal nature of this text, some biblical students have proposed a different setting: Joshua and his household are the group bound to YHWH through exodus and Sinai covenant. Others in the assembly include tribes of the Jacob/Israel confederation united by faith in "El the God of Israel" near Shechem (Gen 33:18–20) who had not gone to Egypt. Still others may have been Canaanites who now had the option of joining the confederation by pledging loyalty to YHWH.[3] Here also is evidence of the constant efforts of the leaders in every generation to strengthen unity by promoting YHWH-alone faith. Such a quest for unity became especially important after the exile.

2. IN THE DAYS OF THE JUDGES

The book of Judges provides detail about real conditions in tribal Israel. In its present canonical order and editing in the Deuteronomistic History, Judges describes Israel's cyclical decline into apostasy and corruption following the idealized account of Joshua's success in winning and distributing the land to the twelve tribes.

Judges repeats almost verbatim the conclusion of Joshua: "The people worshipped YHWH all the days of Joshua, and all the days of the elders who outlived Joshua, who had seen all the great work that YHWH had done for Israel" (Judg 2:7// Josh 24:31). The account continues, "Another generation grew up after them, who did not know YHWH or the work that he had done for Israel" (Judg 2:10b). It tells how the people committed idolatry, suffered defeat and subjection to enemies, cried out to YHWH, who sent a judge to save them, but after the death of the judge they repeated the same cycle and ended up worse (Judg 2:11–19).

Judges states that YHWH grew tired of the recurring cycle of apostasy, repentance, rescue, and relapse. YHWH decided on purpose to leave the nations Joshua left so as to give the Israelites experience of war and to test whether they would obey YHWH, concluding: "So the Israelites lived among the Canaanites, the Hittites, the Amorites, the Perizzites, the Hivites, and the Jebusites; and they took their daughters as wives for themselves, and their own daughters they gave to their sons; and they

---

3. Gottwald, *The Tribes of Yahweh*, 566–67.

God For All

worshipped their gods" (Judg 2:20—3.6). This is a very believable description of the actual conditions of Israel's settlement of the land of Canaan.

There was a blurring of distinction between YHWH and the storm god Hadad, who was popularly called Baal, (a title, depending on context, meaning "owner" or "lord" or "husband"). While most Israelites called YHWH *Adonai*=Lord, it was easy to adopt the title *Baal* instead. In early days it was acceptable to address YHWH as Baal, i.e., "master" or even "husband" of Israel, and include *baal* as a god-bearing element in personal names.[4] Later this practice was condemned and the record was edited to reflect a more acceptable practice.

2a. Gideon, Judges 6–9

The story of Gideon (composed by joining several traditional sources) reveals syncretism of the cult of Baal and worship of YHWH. Gideon's father Joash, a wealthy landowner of Manasseh, owned a shrine "under the oak at Ophrah" (Judg 6:11), which included an altar to Baal and a wooden pole symbolic of Asherah, who could be considered the consort of Baal or YHWH. People could worship either YHWH or Baal or both at the shrine owned and managed by Joash. There the angel of YHWH[5] appeared to Gideon, who complained that YHWH had cast off his people and sold them to the Midianites. YHWH commanded Gideon to destroy his father's Baal altar, and chop down the pole. This act caused uproar among the people, who demanded death for Gideon. His father defended him saying, "If Baal is a god, let him contend for himself." This was said to be the origin of the name Jerubbaal, resulting from a typical Hebrew play on words, applied to Gideon at this point (Judg 6:30–32).

The present account implies that Gideon was the son's name but was changed to Jerubbaal because of this incident. Originally the opposite was probably the case. Gideon means "hacker" or "chopper" a nickname based on his chopping down the Asherah pole. The son's original name was probably Jerubbaal, which means something like "Baal multiplies." As Joash was known as the owner or master (*baʿal*) of the local sanctuary where both YHWH and Baal were worshiped, Jerubbaal would be a perfectly acceptable name for his son, to be edited only at a later date.[6]

Gideon balked at YHWH's call to fight the Midianites, but YHWH assured him, "I will be with you" *ʾehyeh ʿimmakh* (Judg 6:16), the same promise to Moses at Exod 3:13). After Gideon defeated the Midianites the Israelites wanted him to establish a royal dynasty, but he refused, "I will not rule over you, and my son will not rule over you. YHWH will rule over you" (8:22–23). Gideon's behavior belied his

---

4. Saul named a son Ishbaal, and Saul's son Jonathan had a son Meribbaal. David named a son Beeliada (1 Chron 14:7). In a later negative reaction, editors changed some of the names substituting "bosheth" or "besheth"="shame" for baal, e.g., Ishbosheth and Mephibosheth.

5. In this account the Deity's name varies among YHWH, angel of YHWH, and angel of Elohim.

6. The name is rendered Jerubbaal 2x in Judg 8, 9x in Judg 9, and once in 1 Sam 12:11.

pious-sounding protestation. He requested the gold booty the militia took in battle. "Gideon made an ephod of it and put it in his town, in Ophrah; and all Israel prostituted themselves to it there, and it became a snare to Gideon and to his family" (8:27). The meaning of "ephod" in this context is not clear.[7] Gideon used it as a cultic object at his family shrine, for he perceived that a priestly function gave him the power to announce the will of YHWH, the true but invisible King.[8] "As soon as Gideon died, the Israelites relapsed and prostituted themselves with the Baals, making Baal-berith their god" (Judg 8:33).

One of Gideon's sons, Abimelech (his name means "my father is king"), went to Shechem and appealed to people there, who supported him with silver from the temple of Baal-berith. He killed all but one of his thirty brothers and declared himself king in Shechem. He died in a bloody civil war during which he burnt the temple of El-berith, the refuge of some of his opponents (9:1–46). So much for human attempts to usurp YHWH's kingship!

2b. Deborah, Judges 4–5

The king of Hazor oppressed two tribes, Zebulun and Naphtali, which had failed to dislodge the Canaanite inhabitants (Judg 1:27–35). A prose account introduces Deborah in terms highlighting her female gender: *Deborah, woman, prophetess, wife of Lappidoth, she, she-judged Israel at that time* (Judg 4:4 literal translation of Hebrew). Deborah called Barak to rally Naphtali and Zebulun, promising YHWH's help, but he insisted she accompany him. She agreed, but warned him that a woman would accomplish the victory (4:6–9). The battle took place in the Kishon River valley, location of Taanach and Megiddo, cities that Manasseh had failed to occupy (Josh 17:11–12). Elite Canaanite warriors had chariots, but YHWH caused them to be ineffective (4:15). The commander Sisera escaped on foot and took refuge in the tent of Jael a Kenite woman, with whose clan he had a peace treaty (4:11, 17). Jael welcomed him, but while he slept she killed him (4:18–20).

An ancient poetic account, called the song of Deborah (Judg 5), supplements the story. YHWH, called the "one of Sinai," came in power from his original location south in Edom and Sinai (5:4–5). The song presupposes the covenant of the Divine Kinsman. Twice YHWH is called "the God of Israel" (5:3, 5) and Israel "the people of YHWH" (5:11, 13). The peasant militia was lightly armed (5:8b) but they won victory because YHWH sent rain that flooded the Kishon valley, rendering the chariots inoperable (5:20–21).

This episode makes clear that the idealized twelve-tribe union did not yet exist. Zebulun and Naphtali, most deeply involved in the Deborah-Barak campaign, had

---

7. See *IDB* article "Ephod."

8. See Buber, *Kingship of God*, 73 and 168 n 31. On Gideon and the power of the sacral cult, see Halpern, "The Uneasy Compromise" 76-7; also Halpern, *The Emergence of Israel*, 217-18.

help from Ephraim, Benjamin, and a portion of Manasseh called Machir (5:14). Another portion of Manasseh called Gilead refused to participate, as did Dan and Asher (5:17). Reuben in the far southeast did not participate (5:15b–16), and Judah and Simeon farther south go unmentioned. At this early time, Judah was isolated and in process of assimilating Simeon and other clans before David solidified Judah's identity when he succeeded Saul as ruler of the gradually emerging kingdom (see the following chapters).

2c. Jephthah, Judges 11

Jephthah had been expelled from his family as a prostitute's son and became chief of a band of brigands. The king of the Ammonites accused the Gileadites (part of Manasseh east of the Jordan) of occupying Ammonite territory. The Gileadites appealed for help to Jephthah, who made them promise before YHWH at the shrine of Mizpah that they would accept him as chief if he succeeded (11:1–11). Jephthah then sent a message to the Ammonite king arguing that his claim to the land was not correct, for YHWH had defeated the Amorites and given the land to Israel. "Should you not possess what your god Chemosh gives you to possess? And should we not be the ones to possess everything that YHWH our God has conquered for our benefit?" (11:12–28). Before the battle Jephthah vowed to YHWH that if he won, he would sacrifice to YHWH whoever came out of his house to welcome him. In the event, it was his only child, a daughter, who came out. Despite his genuine distress, Jephthah felt obligated to fulfill his vow, which he did, probably at the YHWH shrine at Mizpah. His daughter submitted obediently, and her sacrifice became the origin of an annual commemoration by other young women of the area (11:34–40).

3. DECLINE AND DEGRADATION OF TRIBAL ISRAEL, JUDGES 17–21

Judges concludes with two stories to illustrate general conditions: "In those days there was no king in Israel" (18:1; 19:1). An Ephraimite named Micah stole silver from his mother, and when she pronounced a curse on the thief he returned it to her. She blessed him in the name of YHWH and used some of the silver to make an idol, which Micah placed in a household shrine. He made his son a priest until a Levite from Bethlehem in Judah, Jonathan a descendant of Moses, happened by in his search of employment. Micah installed him as priest and declared, "Now I know that YHWH will prosper me, because the Levite has become my priest" (17:1–13). Some of the tribe of Dan, expelled from their own territory by Philistines in the south and looking for a safe place to settle, stole the idol and kidnapped the priest to establish a tribal cult in their new location at Laish, a peaceful people whom they massacred and dispossessed. They renamed the place Dan, which became the northern extremity of the traditional land of Israel, "from Dan to Beersheba." Descendants of Jonathan officiated at the shrine till the destruction of the kingdom in 722-21 BCE (Judg 18:1-31).

Another Levite from Ephraim took a concubine from Bethlehem. On their way home, in the town of Gibeah of Benjamin an old man of Ephraim who lived there as an alien welcomed them into his home. To escape homosexual rape by local ruffians, the Levite pushed his concubine outside, where they abused her all night. In the morning he found her collapsed outside the door, cut her body in twelve pieces, and sent them through the land as a call to war (19:1–30). The tribe of Benjamin was nearly annihilated, but not before it had inflicted grievous losses on the rest of Israel (Judg 20–21). Alice A. Keefe has called attention to the biblical interpretation of the symbolic importance of woman's body as source of fertility and life in relation to family, land, and the entire social structure. The Benjaminites committed a "vile outrage" (19:23; 20:6) causing the fission of Israelite society symbolized by dismemberment of the woman's body.[9]

Some of the few hundred survivors of Benjamin were provided wives from Jabesh-Gilead, from which Israelites captured virgins for them (21:1–14). The rest were allowed to abduct girls participating in a grape harvest festival at Shiloh (21:15–24). The incident and the book as a whole conclude: "In those days there was no king in Israel; all the people did what was right in their own eyes" (21:25).

SUMMARY AND REFLECTION

Joshua presupposes that YHWH is the true king-leader of his people who gives them total success. Judges begins with YHWH as king who provides human leaders when necessary, although those leaders were not exactly the type of person one would ordinarily expect. Ehud (3:2–39) was a lefthander, though all cultures consider something is basically wrong with lefthanders—they are thought to be awkward, unlucky, backwards. Deborah and Jael were women. Gideon was a coward and an idolater whose son proved the folly of human kingly ambitions. Jephthah was chief of a robber gang who made a human sacrifice of his daughter. Samson was a popular folk hero, a muscular jokester with more brawn than brain. He was a womanizer who preferred Philistine women who betrayed him and caused his downfall (Judg 13–16). By the end of the book of Judges, exercise of individual freedom had resulted in such spiritual, social, and political chaos that one couldn't help thinking that, after all, what Israel really needed was a king like other nations.

---

9. Keefe, *Woman's Body and the Social Body*, 169–70. This interpretive principle comes into play again in the story of Amnon's rape of Tamar (2 Sam 13) and the message of the prophet Hosea, below.

PART THREE

The Monarchy from Beginning to End

14

Like Other Nations: David's Monarchy

BY THE END OF the book of Judges, Israel the people of YHWH is in a very degraded state, politically, economically, and religiously. Apparently one cause was its form of government: "In those days there was no king in Israel; all the people did what was right in their own eyes" (Judges 21:25; see also 17:6; 18:1; 19:1). In the Hebrew Bible the books of Samuel and Kings follow immediately and tell the story of how the people of YHWH became "like other nations" by establishing a kingdom, around 1050 BCE, and follow the story of Israel among the nations and YHWH among the gods for over half a millennium.

1. THE TRANSITION TO MONARCHY

The effective center of authority for the tribal coalition was at Shiloh, where earlier Joshua and Eleazar the priest had set up the tent of meeting before YHWH and completed the distribution of the land (Josh 18:1—19:51). Now, besides the tent and the ark, the text mentions the house of YHWH (1 Sam 1:7, 24; 3:15), which is also called the temple of YHWH (1:9; 3:3). Perhaps the Israelites had taken over a Canaanite temple and continued some fertility rites from its previous users. When men of Benjamin needed wives, they kidnapped young virgins participating in a festival of the grape harvest at Shiloh (Judg 21:19-23). Hannah, a wife in a polygamous family, despondent because she was barren, prayed for a son at Shiloh, and the priest Eli reported God's favorable approval (1 Sam 1:17-20). Sons of Eli "lay with the women who served at the entrance to the tent of meeting" (2:22). Such practices persisted for centuries in southern Judah.[1] The Israelites venerated the ark as a representation of YHWH's presence; to violate the ark could bring instant death. The ark was Israel's equivalent of the idol images of other nations' gods.

---

1. The practice is mentioned in the time of Rehoboam, Solomon's son (1 Kgs 14:23); Asa, third generation after Solomon, (1 Kgs 15:12), Jehoshaphat, Asa's son (1 Kgs 22:46), and Josiah's major reformation (2 Kgs 23:7).

Hannah dedicated her son Samuel to YHWH at Shiloh, and he was apprenticed to Eli, though he was not of priestly lineage.[2] When the Israelites resisted an attack by the Philistines, they brought the ark to the battlefield, attended by Eli's sons, thinking to guarantee the presence and help of YHWH. YHWH, unwilling to be manipulated, allowed the Philistines to win the battle, kill Eli's sons, and place the ark as spoil of war in the temple of their god Dagon, whom they believed had defeated and captured Israel's God. YHWH's presence caused the fall and breakage of Dagon's idol and brought pestilence and death to the Philistines, so they sent the ark back, but not to Shiloh (1 Sam 4:1—7:2). It may be that the Philistines had destroyed the Shiloh temple (see Jer 7:12; Ps 78:60).

Israel's defeat and the loss of the ark and his two sons shocked Eli to death. Samuel succeeded him, but he ignored the ark, built an altar to YHWH at his home in Ramah, and made Mizpah his base (1 Sam 7:15-18). In Buber's view, Samuel inaugurated a new phase in the life of Israel under the leadership of YHWH. Samuel is best known as a prophet (*nabi'*), who announced God's word *apart from* the ark and *apart from* the shrine that housed it. Samuel played a key role in establishing the kingship, which eventually tried to displace divine leadership with human political power. Samuel was the first of the line of prophets through whom YHWH continued to impose critical and judgmental checks on monarchy.[3]

2. THE KINGDOM ESTABLISHED

The final editing of the Deuteronomistic History took place after the monarchy had come crashing down, when hindsight might lead to a negative view of the entire enterprise. In the present biblical account, the story begins with a speech of Samuel in typical deuteronomic style. He demands that the Israelites get rid of the Baals and Astartes and serve YHWH only. They do this, and YHWH gives them immediate miraculous victory over the Philistines and "all the days of Samuel" (1 Sam 7:3-13). Samuel also regained towns taken by the Philistines and kept peace with the Amorites (7:14-17). Against this background of divine protection, when Samuel has grown old and his sons prove corrupt, the elders of Israel ask for a king "like other nations." Samuel resents this as a rejection of himself, but YHWH replies that ever since he saved them from Egypt they've rejected *him* as king but says to listen to them anyhow (8:1-9).

At YHWH's order Samuel informs the elders of the "ways of the king." Six times Samuel says, "he will take" and describes how the king will build a military dictatorship that will end up making them slaves, but then their cry to God will be in vain

---

2. 1 Sam 1:1 lists the genealogy of Samuel's father, Elkanah, going back four generations in the tribe of Ephraim. In the late book of 1 Chron 6:33-38, Samuel is given a genealogy of twenty generations all the way back to Levi, son of Jacob/Israel. Thus through his important role in cultic and national affairs, Samuel achieved recognition as a Levite, and the record keepers produced a genealogy for him.

3. Buber, *The Prophetic Faith*, 60-70.

(8:11–18). The people insist: "No! but we are determined to have a king over us, so that we also may be like other nations, and that our king may govern us and go out before us and fight our battles" (8:20). The Israelites were no longer willing to wait for YHWH to respond to a crisis before raising up a military commander to lead the peasant militia. They wanted an ever-ready king prepared to go to war every spring if necessary (see 2 Sam 11:1). The Hebrew Bible makes a distinction between the people (ʿam) of YHWH and the nations (goyim pl., goy sing.). For Israel to be like other *nations* is to question their special status as YHWH's *people*. Having got their wish for a king to fight their battles, they found themselves almost constantly at war. In the end the empires destroyed Israel, and they lost their status as a *nation*. Whether spoken with foresight or written from hindsight, 1 Sam 8:11–18 accurately describes the militarized state of the *people* of YHWH once they became like other *nations*.

First Samuel 9–11 preserves another tradition that describes YHWH's positive response to Israel's present danger and urgent need. In words reminiscent of the call of Moses, YHWH speaks as the Divine Kinsman and informs Samuel that he will send him a man from the tribe of Benjamin. "You shall anoint him to be the ruler over my people Israel. He shall save my people from the hand of the Philistines; for I have seen the suffering of my people, because their outcry has come to me" (9:16). The Spirit of God (Elohim) fills Saul and he has great early success (1 Sam 10–11). A brief summary concludes that Saul "rescued Israel out of the hands of those who plundered them" (14:47–48). Yet at the end of a career marked by ups and downs, during which he incurred rejection by YHWH and Samuel, Saul and three of his sons fell as the Philistines administered a massive defeat on "the army of YHWH and the house of Israel" (2 Sam 1:12).

Saul was hardly more than a military leader like those in Judges. He took the first tentative steps to transform Israel the people of YHWH from a loose confederation of tribes into a nation-state, but he could not break free of the old order, and he lacked the personal qualities to do more. YHWH raised up Saul in a time of crisis, empowered him by an inrush of ecstatic energy to win early military victory, and confirmed him as king. (1 Sam 11:1–15). Immediately after that joyous occasion, Samuel called "all Israel" together and delivered a farewell address in typical deuteronomic style. Samuel recounted his own virtuous leadership, YHWH's mighty acts of deliverance, and Israel's incessant faithlessness, including their latest sin in demanding a king. Samuel warned the people, in the presence of the king, that unless they faithfully served YHWH, both they and their king would be swept away (12:1–25). In the end, by a combination of Saul's own weaknesses and frustrations beyond his control, he could not complete the process of establishing a kingdom worthy the name. In his personal religious character and behavior Saul failed to fulfill Samuel's expectations. YHWH too "was sorry that he had made Saul king over Israel" (15:35). In reading the whole story of Saul it is possible to interpret it in some sense as YHWH's deliberate purpose to punish the Israelites for demanding a king by sending them a loser. God's word spoken by Hosea for a later time seems applicable: "I gave you a king in my anger, and I took him away in my wrath" (Hos 13:11). While Saul still reigned, YHWH sent Samuel to choose David to replace him. "The spirit of YHWH came mightily upon David from that day forward . . . Now the spirit of YHWH departed from Saul and an evil spirit from YHWH tormented him" (1 Sam 16:13–14). It was YHWH, who by means of inscrutable election and uncritical support of David, finally raised up Israel as a nation among the nations, which in turn facilitated the ascendancy of YHWH among the gods. David, YHWH's chosen one, presents us with one of the most complex characters in the entire Hebrew Bible.

3. DAVID AND HIS TRIBE OF JUDAH

David sprang from the tribe of Judah, which, according to the more realistic stories in the book of Judges and elsewhere, was not affiliated with other tribes in the time of Deborah and Gideon. Comparison of all sources within the Bible leads to the conclusion that originally peoples of ethnic diversity, occupying mountain and desert regions in the south of Canaan, isolated from "all Israel" in the central highlands, eventually became "Judah."[4] Legends about the ancestor Judah told how he separated from his brothers, married a Canaanite woman, and later had twin sons by his daughter-in-law Tamar (Gen 37). One of those twins, Perez, was an ancestor of David. A genealogical note in the book of Ruth 4:13–22, supplemented by notes in Matthew 1:3–6, lists among David's forebears besides Perez, one Salmon, husband of the Canaanite prostitute Rahab, and the Bethlehemite Boaz, who married Ruth a Moabite woman. If David's personal family history was typical, the whole tribe of Judah must have been a rather diverse mixture.[5]

Only in David's time did Judah begin to interact seriously with all Israel. I would like to suggest that one factor encouraging cooperation between these two entities was a common familiarity with the divine Name YHWH. Among the groups that made up the Israelite tribal confederation the most energetic were descendants of the

---

4. See entries for Judah in *IDB* and *ABD*. Knoppers affirms the complex makeup of "Judah" in ancient Israel, "Intermarriage, Social Complexity, and Ethnic Diversity in the Genealogy of Judah" 15-30. By a close examination of the genealogies preserved in Chronicles, Knoppers demonstrates that the clan relations, the family background, and the actual practice of the great hero David were the very opposite of the ethnic exclusiveness promoted by the authors of Ezra and Nehemiah in the postexilic restoration.

5. Noth, *The Laws in the Pentateuch*, 32–33; Herrmann, *A History of Israel*, 148–49. Flanagan, "Judah in All Israel," 101–16, took up all the occurrences of the phrase "all Israel" in the Hebrew Bible. His analysis indicates that until David achieved a personal coalition of his own tribe of Judah with "all Israel" (2 Sam 5:1–5) the two entities were quite distinct. The Davidic rule over "all Israel" with Judah continued through Solomon's reign, but on the breakup following Solomon's death, the original tribes comprising "all Israel" resumed their previous status separate from Judah. Flanagan also cites texts to support the conjecture that even Benjamin may not have been a part of "all Israel" before Saul and David achieved greater inclusiveness. It is worth noting that despite the conflict between David's men (Judah) and the remnants of Saul's regime (Benjamin), when the federated kingdom split, Benjamin remained with Judah, separate from "all Israel."

YHWH-alone exodus group. Others who had been part of the original Jacob/Israel coalition that worshiped El the God of Israel at Shechem (Gen 33:18–20) but had not gone to Egypt had reunited with the exodus Israelites (Josh 24:1–28). Traditions concerning Jacob and these El-worshiping Israelites are preserved in a biblical source designated E (for El, Elohim, and Ephraim). The Judah of David had not been part of that early history, but being from the south and including southerners such as Kenites and Kenizzites, they could also have known of a southern deity originally called YHW. As we have seen earlier, the J or Yahwist material contained southern traditions concerning Father Abram and named YHWH as his God, even though that special Name was not revealed until the time of Moses in Egypt. Our present Hebrew Bible contains a literary composition combining J and E (JE), which was not completed until long after David, but he is the key to understanding the process. A person of undoubted genius,[6] David combined his personal abilities with genuine (even though at times exploitative) devotion to YHWH.[7] He forged a fragile coalition of disparate Israelite and Judahite interests and forces. With them David established a small empire dominating the minor states lying between the power centers of Egypt and Mesopotamia when the empires were in coincident decline. Though the Bible does not specify it, we must understand that whenever David forced a conquered nation to pay tribute, or when he made a peace alliance with another state (cf 2 Sam 8:2, 6, 14; 10:19) it was a covenant (*berit*) that appealed to YHWH and the deities of the other partners for enforcement. As David and Israel's power and authority grew among the nations, so also YHWH's power and authority grew among the gods. Under Solomon David's empire began to fall away, but YHWH's authority over the nations formerly allied to David persisted. The messages of Amos 1:1—2:6; 9:1–12 reflect that conviction (see below in chapter 18.1 "Amos and the extension of YHWH's sovereignty.").

4. DAVID SOLIDIFIES THE YHWH CULT

David became leader of a band of malcontents while he was a fugitive from Saul, (1 Sam 22:2), and during his stay with the Philistines some fighters from there had also joined him, forming a formidable private fighting force. After the death of Saul, David led his army to Hebron, where "the people of Judah" anointed him king (2 Sam 2:1–4). No doubt King David appropriated the traditions about father Abram, the oaks of Mamre where the Divine Kinsman established the covenant, and the cave of Machpelah where the ancestors were buried.

Saul's successors failed to act effectively to maintain rule over Israel after his death, "So all the elders of Israel came to the king at Hebron; and King David made

---

6. Brueggemann, *Power, Providence, and Personality* describes David in the chapter "Sport of Nature."

7. According to de Moor's statistical count, *The Rise of Yahwism*, 32–33, personal names including the god-bearing element *yeho-* or *-yahu* increased noticeably after the time of David, in contrast to the preponderance of names with *el* prior to David).

a covenant with them at Hebron before YHWH, and they anointed David king over Israel" (2 Sam 5:3). This covenant, ratified "before YHWH" as witness, united King David of Judah and the elders of Israel. After they anointed him the king of Israel, David reigned over a dual kingdom consisting of "all Israel and Judah" (5:5; see also 3:10), and he ruled each directly. David then set about to consolidate his realm. (The events listed in 2 Sam 5:6—6:19 do not follow chronological order.)

David's personal army captured Jerusalem, a hitherto independent Jebusite enclave that lay between Judah to the south and all Israel in the central hills (5:6-10). "David took the stronghold of Zion, which is now the city of David" (5:7). As David's personal possession, Jerusalem became his third kingdom.[8] He made it the administrative capital of his total realm, accomplishing geographical unification among its parts. Later David established Zion the dwelling place for YHWH. Picking up verses and hints in Scripture it appears that David adopted some of the religious and political policies of the Jebusite city. Some scholars incline to the view that David simply assumed much of the political and religious establishment of Jerusalem, incorporating and adapting it to his own purposes. The scribes retrojected this new situation into the tradition of Abram's encounter with Melchizedek, priest-king of Salem, who blessed Abram "by God Most High, maker of heaven and earth." Abram recognized Melchizedek's God as his God YHWH (Gen 14:17-24). From David's time, YHWH becomes identified with the Most High and gains recognition as "maker of heaven and earth" (Ps 134:3). "Most High" as a title of YHWH occurs in psalms originating in the Jerusalem cult.[9] The religious authorities allied with David gave divine approval for the king who reigned in Zion, to function as "priest after the order of Melchizedek" (Ps 110). David himself acted as priest when he brought the ark to Jerusalem (2 Sam 6:17-19), as did Solomon when he dedicated the Temple he built for YHWH (1 Kgs 8:54-55).

King Hiram of Tyre sent materials and workers to build David a royal palace, the start of a long relationship between the houses of David and Hiram (5:11-12). According to protocol, such a relationship would have necessitated a covenant or treaty that involved pledging mutual obligations witnessed by YHWH and the gods of Tyre.

David took many wives and concubines and had numerous sons to broaden his alliances and increase his reputation (2 Sam 3:2-5; 5:13-14). One wife was the daughter of the king of Geshur, northeast across the Jordan near Damascus (3:3). Multiple wives and sons in a royal dynasty almost inevitably led to conflict and bloodshed in the struggle for succession. Three of David's first four sons died prematurely, two violently, and Solomon, although only tenth in order of birth, achieved the throne through a palace coup in which David was complicit (1 Kgs 1:1—2:35).

David drove the Philistines out of the regions closest to Jerusalem (2 Sam 5:17-25). He could now recover the ark that had remained in Kiriath-jearim (or Baale-Judah), which may have been under Philistine control until then (cf 1 Sam 6:1-16).

8. Myers, "David" 6. King at Jerusalem, *IDB* 1:776a.
9. Ps 7, 9, 18, 21, 46, 47, 50, 56, 57, 73, 77, 78, 82, 83, 87, 91, 92, 97, 106, 107.

David set out to bring up the ark, mobilizing "all Israel" (2 Sam 6:1, 5, 15, 19; no mention of Judah). With some difficulty and delay, because one person was struck dead when he inadvertently touched the ark, David finally succeeded in retrieving it and installing it in a tent he had provided for it (6:1–15). David himself officiated as priest. The account still includes phrases indicating alternation between YHWH and Elohim as names for the Deity, and this event functioned powerfully toward solidifying the YHWH-alone trend. In bringing the ark to this former Canaanite city that was now his personal possession, David gave Jerusalem powerful symbolic value as YHWH's dwelling place. Shamai Gelander comments: "Bringing the Ark up to Jerusalem, David's desire to build a permanent domicile for the Lord, and the acquisition of the Araunah threshing floor (2 Sam 24:18–25) are all part of an effort to change the nature of the deity from an 'itinerant' God to a 'permanently settled' one . . . After the Ark is brought up to Jerusalem, there is no more evidence of David's asking the Lord for guidance—."[10]

Among his highest cabinet officers David appointed two priests (2 Sam 8:17; 15:24). One, Abiathar/Ahimelech, was descended from Eli and the Shiloh priesthood, and he had accompanied David in his flight from Saul (1 Sam 23:6). Concerning the other priest, Zadok, biblical texts are ambivalent.[11] Some scholars conjecture he may have been priest of El Elyon in Jerusalem. More plausibly Zadok had been priest at Gibeon, a venerable southern high place. David's brilliant move united two ancient traditions concerning "YHWH the God of Israel." Psalm 132, which was composed to commemorate the event, elevates the drama and the effort David expended to recover the ark and states YHWH's response: "This is my resting place for ever; here I will dwell, for I have desired it" (Ps 132:14). The psalm concludes with a blessing upon David's dynasty. The author(s) of the psalm belonged to the priestly establishment that mediated the will of the Deity. Naturally, it was to their advantage to promote the national shrine where they ministered and to support the king who supported both them and the shrine.

5. DAVID, TEMPLE, AND DYNASTY

Like any victorious founder of a successful empire, David wished to build a temple for the god who had been his divine guide and ally. He mentions his desire to Nathan the prophet, stating that the ark (as if it were YHWH) "stays in a tent" (2 Sam 7:2). After initially approving the proposal, Nathan brings word that YHWH has always

---

10. Gelander, *David and His God,* 137. See below, 14.5 "David, temple, and dynasty."

11. Articles in *IDB* and *ABD* on Zadok and Abiathar (sometimes confused with Ahimelech) deal with all references to these individuals and try to arrive at an understanding of their origins and functions under David. 1 Chron 16:1–49 states that David placed the ark in the tent he prepared (at Jerusalem), and that Zadok served the altar at the high place of Gibeon, where the tabernacle of Moses was. Zadok anointed Solomon as king on David's order (1 Kgs 2:39). Before he built the Temple, Solomon used to sacrifice regularly at Gibeon, which was "the principal high place" (1 Kgs 3:4).

moved about in a tent wherever his people have wandered and has never commanded any of them to build him a house (7:5–7). God seems to refuse a permanent house. In historical fact Solomon *did* build the temple, and people came to think of it as essential to the being and the worship of YHWH. It *must* have had divine approval. So, concerning David's son, the text states, "he shall build a house for my name" (7:13). Only after the temple was destroyed, people understood that it was not an absolute necessity. A. A. Anderson takes the view that the original oracle approved the temple building concept but gives weight to the negative implications of vv. 5–7 and attributes them to an editor after the destruction of the temple.[12] Brueggemann comments: "Maybe all the kings build temples, and all the gods like temples, but not this God and therefore not this king."[13] One should recall the early insight into the character and nature of YHWH, who took the initiative to call a people and accompanied them as he promised Moses, "surely I-Am (is) with you" (Exod 3:12).[14]

YHWH announces, in return, that he will build David a house, i.e., a dynasty, continuing in his descendants. The clause, "I will be a father to him, and he shall be a son to me" (7:14a) indicated not only Solomon but also all davidic kings: The same title is implied for David in Ps 89:26–27. Psalm 45:6, addressed to the king, may be read, "Your throne, O God, endures for ever."[15] Like rulers of other nations, the king of Israel was called God's son. A new dimension of social exaltation is introduced as Israel becomes like other nations.

6. THE MYSTIQUE OF DAVID

David the outsider ruled diverse elements that kept El, Elohim, and YHWH traditions, and he used those traditions to hold together a fragile state of which he made YHWH the national God.[16] This effort had such vitality that after the nation split and eventually fell, YHWH faith survived. David exploited raw power, violence, and religious sentiment, but his accomplishments underlie the Bible's positive portrait of him while exposing his human fallibility. Nothing succeeds like success!

Psalm 78 encapsulates the David story in a liturgical poem. The introduction calls on parents to teach children lessons of history so as not to repeat the sins of the

---

12. Anderson, *2 Samuel*, comment on 2 Sam 7:5–7.
13. Brueggemann, *David's Truth*, 73.
14. See Gelander's comment above, note 10.
15. In the NT Hebrews 1:8 quotes this rendering of the verse and applies it to Christ the Son.
16. The Hebrew of Ps 50 begins: "*El, Elohim, YHWH* speaks and summons the earth . . . out of Zion" (i.e., the dwelling that David and Solomon provided for YHWH. Yet it is only Elohim who speaks, calling Israel "my people" saying "I am Elohim, your Elohim (v 7). I take this as an example of the effort to unify traditions using different names for God. See also Josh 22:1–34 for a quarrel when the West Jordan tribes accuse the East Jordan tribes of unfaithfulness. Defending themselves the East Jordan tribes shout: "*El, Elohim, YHWH; El, Elohim, YHWH!* He knows!" (v 22) and they go on to satisfy their accusers. English translations usually amalgamate the Hebrew *El Elohim YHWH*, which, of course, was the ultimate objective of the original authors of these texts.

Like Other Nations: David's Monarchy

ancestors (78:1–8). The poem uses the name *Ephraim* to bracket the entire recital of the ancestors' ingratitude and God's grace (78:9–66). The tribe of Ephraim, to which Joshua and Samuel belonged, and which for centuries had been the leader of "all Israel" is singled out for blame. "The Ephraimites, armed with the bow / turned back on the day of battle. / They did not keep God's covenant / but refused to walk according to his law" (78:9–10). The recital lists many examples of forgetfulness, ingratitude, and rebellion in the desert and in the land of promise (78:11–64). God punished their idolatry severely: "He utterly rejected Israel. He abandoned his dwelling at Shiloh, the tent where he dwelt among mortals . . . He gave his people to the sword . . . young men, girls . . . priests . . . widows." *But all was not lost!* The psalm concludes:

> 65 Then the Lord awoke as from sleep,
> like a warrior shouting because of wine.
> 66 He put his adversaries to rout;
> he put them to everlasting disgrace.
> 67 He rejected the tent of Joseph,
> he did not choose the tribe of Ephraim;
> 68 but he chose the tribe of Judah,
> Mount Zion, which he loves.
> 69 He built his sanctuary like the high heavens,
> like the earth, which he has founded forever.
> 70 He chose his servant David,
> and took him from the sheepfolds;
> 71 from tending the nursing ewes he brought him
> to be the shepherd of his people Jacob,
> of Israel, his inheritance.
> 72 With upright heart he tended them,
> and guided them with skillful hand.

Psalm 78 uses eight names for Deity, though English obscures their distinctiveness:

1. *yhwh* (YHWH) vv 4, 21
2. *ʾelohim* (God, plural used as singular) vv 7, 10, 19, 22, 31, 35, 59
3. *ʾel* (God, singular, name of chief Canaanite god) vv 7, 8, 18, 19, 34, 41
4. *ʿelyon* (Most High, first applied to Canaanite El) v 17
5. *ʾel ʾelyon* (God, singular, Most High) v 35
6. *ʾelohim ʾelyon* (God, plural form, Most High) v 56
7. *qadosh yisraʾel* (Holy One of Israel) v 41
8. *ʾadonai* (Lord) v 65

Each name pertained to some divine being before Israel adopted it, including two that may seem exceptions. (#1) YHWH originated from *yaw* or *yhw*, known to semi-nomadic people such as Kenites and Midianites. (#7) Holy Ones were subordinate members of the heavenly council whom El assigned to various nations, so that "Holy One of Israel" was originally only one among many. As the concept of the oneness of God and the people of God grew in the faith and life of Israel, they appropriated and adapted the characteristics and powers of other gods one by one into their national God YHWH. Great David played a key role in this process.

In his person and in his tribe David epitomized the great diversity of the peoples whom YHWH welcomed and who were assimilated into Israel, the *people* of YHWH. David knew that diversity could destroy the unity he sought. David's scribes used the traditions of the more prominent tribes and devised the twelve-tribe scheme to describe Israel, linked by genealogies of the early ancestors.[17] David did as much or more than any individual to solidify YHWH alone as Israel's national God.[18] Within the kingdoms of Israel, Judah, and Jerusalem, David absorbed Canaanite cities and people, some of whom assimilated, while others remained resistant.

On the other hand, David did more than anyone to conform Israel to the Canaanite pattern of *nation*. David ordered his war commander Joab to take a census of all males of fighting age in Israel and Judah, and also included the Hittites, Hivites and Canaanites (2 Sam 24:1–9). The census was the basis for taxation, military conscription, and forced labor, sometimes called corvée (a non-monetary tax on people). In David's cabinet, Adoram administered the corvée (2 Sam 20:24). Solomon exploited this census, using forced labor from "all Israel" to build the temple for YHWH (1 Kgs 5:13–18). He made state slaves, a permanent status, of the remaining Canaanites (9:15–22). Solomon completed what David had begun, to make Israel like the nations.

---

17. Gottwald credits David for having devised the twelve-tribe organizational model, citing the great wealth of material that indicates early traditions of several of the tribes with which David had to reckon: *Tribes of Yahweh*, 155–75.

18. David did not eliminate the influence of lesser deities on the family and local level. He and his wife Michal had a household idol (Heb *teraphim*) in their private home (1 Sam 19:12–13).

15

Like Other Nations: Solomon's Shadows

SOLOMON COMPLETED WHAT DAVID had begun, to make Israel like other nations. He had a long, relatively peaceful reign: "Judah and Israel were as numerous as the sand by the sea; they ate and drank and were happy" (1 Kgs 4:20). "During Solomon's lifetime Judah and Israel lived in safety, from Dan even to Beer-sheba, all of them under their vines and fig trees" (4:25). "Solomon conscripted for slave labor" the survivors of the indigenous Canaanites (9:21). Solomon waged no major wars but spent great sums on public works, including fortifications and advanced weapons including chariots, which per unit were the most costly weapon both for procurement and for maintenance. Solomon went so far into debt to Hiram King of Tyre that he ceded to him part of the land of promise, twenty towns in the land of Galilee (9:10–13). The temple he built for YHWH helped define Israelite faith and practice for centuries. Solomon prayed for wisdom to be "able to discern between good and evil" (3:9). So wise was he that long after his time scribes attributed various wisdom works to Solomon's authorship. No doubt Solomon deserved some praise, but we must read between the lines and note the shadows cast by the brilliance of his portrait.

1. SOLOMON'S WIVES

The coup that put Solomon on the throne and the violent cleanup afterward finally ended (1 Kgs 1:1—2:46a). "So the kingdom was established in the hand of Solomon. Solomon made a marriage alliance with Pharaoh king of Egypt; he took Pharaoh's daughter and brought her into the city of David, until he had finished building his own house and the house of YHWH and the wall around Jerusalem" (1 Kgs 2:46b—3.1). Mentioning the Egyptian princess first hints at her special prominence, though she mysteriously disappears from the record. "King Solomon loved many foreign women along with the daughter of Pharaoh: Moabite, Ammonite, Edomite, Sidonian, and Hittite women" (1 Kgs 11:1). They were hostages to guarantee their countries' peaceful relations in David's empire, yet Solomon had to treat them courteously and respect their religions. Solomon built and maintained high places where they observed their

God For All

native cults (11:7–8), and he participated in their worship (11:5, 33). The Deuteronomistic History blames these wives for tempting Solomon in his old age and names his apostasy as cause of the kingdom's rupture (11:11). Nevertheless, from earliest days, Solomon's entire royal governance violated the standards of justice and equity set by the YHWH-alone covenant. Was Psalm 72 written to guide Solomon as its introduction suggests? "Of (or for) Solomon / Give the king your justice, O God, / and your righteousness to a king's son. / May he judge your people with righteousness / and your poor with justice" (Ps 72:1–2). Solomon's royal policies contrasted starkly with this divine standard.

2. SOLOMON'S TEMPLES

Solomon built high places "for all his foreign wives" (2 Kgs 11:8), which survived three hundred years until King Josiah defiled them in his reform movement (2 Kgs 22:13).

Although the Bible does not record her name, the daughter of Pharaoh was evidently Solomon's chief wife, yet he did not build a high place for her as he did for the others. The Jerusalem temple for YHWH faced east, so that at spring and fall equinox the sun shone directly in, just as in Egyptian temples. Thus, the Egyptian princess might worship her sun god there, while the Israelites worshipped YHWH, merely *symbolized* by the sun.[1] The record falls silent about the fate of Pharaoh's daughter; she was not the mother of the crown prince. The Deuteronomistic History doesn't name Rehoboam's mother when it reports his succession to the throne (1 Kgs 11:43) Instead it tells of Jeroboam's reign in Israel (1 Kgs 12:20—14.20). Only after that the text identifies Rehoboam's mother, Naamah the Ammonite (1 Kgs 14:21). Undoubtedly the archives contained much more about the Egyptian princess than the final editors of the text wished to transmit.[2]

The chief emphasis of the story of Solomon is his construction and dedication of the temple for YHWH (1 Kgs 5:1—9:9). David's success at empire building and dynasty founding, the adoption of mythological elements of the Jebusite cultural traditions of Jerusalem, and influences from Egypt and Tyre came to a focus in this house for David's patron Deity YHWH. The people at large viewed Solomon as God's Son, the human manifestation of the God who actually lived in the temple on Mount Zion, next door to the king. The king provided the building, the upkeep, the daily and special sacrifices, and compensation for the priests. They in turn supported the king's regime by constant petitions for divine aid on his behalf. Herrmann calls the temple,

---

1. Voegelin, *Israel and Revelation*, 318–19.

2. Hadad prince of Edom escaped to Egypt when Joab massacred Edomite males. Pharaoh welcomed him and gave him a royal princess as wife. She bore him a son named Genubath (1 Kgs 11:14–22). He later ended Edom's subjection to Solomon. Jeroboam of Ephraim fled to Egypt after rebelling against Solomon and remained there till Solomon died. The Septuagint tells more of Jeroboam's stay in Egypt than does the Masoretic text of the Hebrew Bible.

like Jerusalem as a whole, "an alien body in the state, in contrast with accepted cultic practice during tribal times."[3]

Solomon depended on Tyre for the design and building of his temple as well as for the cedar and other valuable timber. The plan closely followed a pattern for temples in Phoenicia, full of mythological symbolism. The two large gold-covered cherubim[4] whose wings overshadowed the ark were the most exotic. More cherubim were carved on the inside walls and doors of the temple together with open flowers and palm trees, all overlaid with gold. A palm tree often represented the mythological tree of life, which figured so prominently in all ancient Near East religions.[5]

Even though the hill of Zion is overshadowed by higher hills on either side, in mythological terms Zion now becomes the highest mountain, the center of the cosmos, because it is the dwelling place of YHWH. A liturgical psalm used in the Jerusalem worship reflects this theme: "Like the utmost heights of Zaphon is Mount Zion, the city of the Great King" (Ps 48:2b NIV; cf NJPS). In this psalm, "the utmost heights of Zaphon" refers to a high mountain in the far north, which in Ugaritic mythology was the abode of the gods like Olympus in Greek myths (cf Is 14:13). The psalmist calls Mount Zion "Zaphon" to declare, "*Zion* is the *real* Mount Zaphon where the *true* supreme God dwells."[6]

The most distinctive feature of Solomon's temple was the total absence of an image of the deity. Solomon brought in the ark, the chest containing the stone tablets on which were inscribed the words of the covenant. Solomon seems not to have paid serious attention to the covenant; in his day its ethical standards suffered a serious eclipse. In the eyes of many, the ark itself must have served almost the same function as an idol. Now it was shut away in the innermost room of a house of stone and cedar, just where an idol would stand in any pagan shrine. Solomon fulfilled David's desire to change YHWH from an itinerant God to a settled one. Solomon declared: "YHWH said that he would dwell in thick darkness. I have built you an exalted house, a place for you to dwell in forever" (1 Kgs 8:13). Here, writes Buber, "we meet the unreserved expression of the aim of the early kingdom to confine YHWH's sovereignty within the cultic sphere alone."[7] YHWH, who had always moved about with his people and who neither needed nor wanted a house of cedar, was now shut away in such a house. Ironically, to build this house, Solomon had drafted forced labor from all Israel, YHWH's own people (1 Kgs 5:13–18).

---

3. *A History of Israel*, 179.
4. *Cherubim* (plu) *cherub* (sing), mythological figure with human head, bull body, and eagle wings.
5. *IDB* III 646 "Tree of Life."
6. Clifford, *The Cosmic Mountain*, says that most of the epithets applied to Zion in Psalm 48 originally referred to Zaphon in Ugaritic literature. In ordinary Hebrew, *tsaphon* means simply "north" (Pss 89:12; 107:3).
7. *The Prophetic Faith*, 82.

David, incited by YHWH, had commanded Joab (over the latter's objection) to take a census that included not only Israel and Judah but also the remnants of the Canaanites and Hivites. Joab had implied that this was wrong, but David overruled him (2 Sam 24:1–17). Even though YHWH sent a plague upon the people as punishment, the practical results remained, for the census facilitated taxation, military conscription, and forced labor. David's overseer of forced labor was named Adoram/Adoniram (2 Sam 20:24). A son or grandson with a similar name filled the same post under Solomon (1 Kgs 4:6; 5:14; 12:19).

3. THE KINGDOM RESISTED, DIVIDED, AND PLUNDERED

Hadad of Edom and Rezon of Damascus successfully broke away from Solomon. Hadad and a few companions escaped when David's commander Joab tried to kill all the males in Edom, and Rezon similarly survived a slaughter by David (1 Kgs 11:14–25). David's terrorist foreign policy led to violent retaliation that ultimately brought negative results, for Edom attacked from the south, and Damascus from the north.

At home, two men from Ephraim joined forces against Solomon (11:26–40). First, Jeroboam the son of Nebat was overseer of the forced labor of "the house of Joseph," i.e., Ephraim and Manasseh, the power base of all Israel. Draft labor always fell on the poor and disadvantaged, while the rich and well connected evaded it.[8] Perhaps Jeroboam was among the disadvantaged. The fact that his mother was a widow, and perhaps also a leper as her name Zeruah might indicate, would be an economic handicap. Jeroboam won promotion by his ability, but he used his position to oppose Solomon. The second, Ahijah, a prophet from the old cultic center of Eli and Samuel at Shiloh, justifiably resented the radical changes in the "old time religion" and charged Solomon with apostasy and worshipping foreign gods. Ahijah told Jeroboam that YHWH would make him king over the ten tribes, but would leave the house of David to rule over Judah and "Jerusalem, the city that I have chosen out of all the tribes of Israel" (11:32). Solomon tried to arrest Jeroboam, but he escaped to Shishak in Egypt where Hadad of Edom had already received hospitable treatment.

Rehoboam, Solomon's heir, went to Shechem to gain approval from the Israelites in order to assume the throne. When he rejected their request for lighter burdens and arrogantly threatened to increase them, they declared independence from the house of David. Rehoboam sent Adoram the supervisor of forced labor, whom they lynched on the spot (12:1–19). Jeroboam became king of all Israel with divine approval expressed by the prophets Ahijah and Shemaiah (12:15, 21–24). Though this averted

---

8. That was certainly the case in the U.S. during the Vietnam War. See, for example, MacPherson, *Long Time Passing*, which draws the contrast between the large numbers of African-Americans and poor whites who were drafted and the extreme paucity of sons of Congresspersons. The cases of presidents Clinton and Bush and Vice President Cheney to avoid the draft later attracted publicity and criticism.

war at that point, the people of YHWH, now having become two nations, maintained a deadly rivalry with almost continual warfare until Assyria destroyed northern Israel.

Pharaoh Shishak, perhaps already angry about Solomon's neglect of his Egyptian wife, gave refuge and aid to Hadad and Jeroboam in their successful struggles for independence from Solomon, which left Judah very feeble. Five years after Rehoboam came to the throne, Shishak led an attack on Judah and Jerusalem: "He took away the treasures of the house of YHWH and the treasures of the king's house; he took everything. He also took away all the shields of gold that Solomon had made" (1 Kgs 14:26). A great deal of that gold ended up as donations to temples of gods and goddesses in Egypt.[9] A later biblical text says Shishak took the fortified cities of the south, and that Judah had "to be his servants" (2 Chron 12:2–8). Becoming "like other nations" made Solomon's realm vulnerable to the vicissitudes of fickle international power politics.

4. THE ORIGIN OF THE J MATERIAL

These harsh blows against what had so recently been an apparently prosperous and powerful society became the motivation for thoughtful temple scribes to write the document that modern scholars have designated the Yahwist or J material. Beginning with what is now Gen 2.4b, J tells the story of humankind from creation through Israel's history under the lordship of YHWH. A major motive was to justify divine providence that prepared the way for David. The author wanted to reassure the people of Judah that since YHWH now dwelt in Zion, the City of David, they could be sure YHWH had not abandoned them. Postexilic editors, who opened their final work with the P creation story of Gen 1:1—2:4a, added to that the overture of the older J document (now Gen 2:4b—3:24) as introduction to the entire Pentateuch. The J description of the first humans in Eden is based on Tyrian mythology. One can discern a remarkable overlap of linguistic and mythological detail in three extended biblical texts: Genesis 2.4b—3:24, Ezek 28:1–19, and 1 Kgs 3–10. I see an implied rebuke of Solomon's sycophants (or perhaps of Solomon himself) who thought of him as divine—the first humans were not royal, but mere peasants. Not the king alone but every human person, in dependence on the Creator, can name animals and plants and can discern between good and evil, though that is most important for kings. The account critiques polygamy and excessive wealth (see the chart at the end of this chapter).

---

9. See Kitchen, "Where Did Solomon's Gold Go?" 30 and "Shishak's Military Campaign in Israel" 32–33 *BAR*. Apparently Shishak plundered a number of cities, both south and north, on this same expedition, according to Egyptian records. See also Levin, "Did Pharaoh Sheshonq attack Jerusalem?" (42–52) *BAR*.

SUMMARY

The story of Israel "like other nations" confirms my earlier contention that pre-monarchical tribal Israel was already a diverse mix, and the policies of David and Solomon encouraged a great degree of assimilation of foreign peoples and cultures. David had solidified the YHWH-alone faith so firmly that it was able to withstand threats from the many pagan elements Solomon introduced. Not even the split into separate nations could destroy YHWH faith. The Deuteronomistic History repeatedly states that despite all the weaknesses and failings of Judah during the following three hundred years, YHWH spared the kingdom for the sake of David and of Jerusalem, where YHWH had chosen to place his Name (1 Kgs 11:12–13, 32, 34, 36; 2 Kgs 8:19; 19:34).

First, however, I think it important to consider the consequences that ensued from the fact that David and Solomon had effectively transformed the people of YHWH so that they became like other nations. They split into two nations, each claiming YHWH as their national deity. How did YHWH respond to that new situation? How does it affect the biblical message of God for All?

CONTACT POINTS AMONG GENESIS 2.4b—3:24, EZEKIEL 28.1-19; 1 KGS 3-11

Item	Genesis	Ezekiel	1 Kings
1. A garden in Eden, in the east	2:8		
2. The garden of Eden	2:15; 23-4		
3. In Eden, the garden of God		28:13	
4. Tree of life	2:9; 3:22		
5. Palm trees (=Tree of Life? cf. *IDB* III 646)			6:29, 32, 35
6. The knowledge of good and evil	2:9,17; 3:22		
7. To discern between good and evil, a quality desirable for kings			3:9; (2 Sam 14:17, 20)
8. Human names *cattle* (= *animals* in #9), *birds*, field animals	2:20		
9. Solomon speaks of *animals, birds*, reptiles, and fish			4:33 (Heb 5:13)
10. Man leaves parents, *clings* to wife	2:24		
11. Solomon *clung* to foreign wives			11.2:
12. Man and woman not ashamed	2:25		
13. Blameless when you were created		28:15	
14. Solomon loved YHWH, as did David			3:3
15. Like God, knowing good and evil	3:22		
16. You said, "I am a god"		28:2	
17. You consider yourself wise as a god		28:2	
18. The tree desirable to make one wise	3:6		
19. You were wiser than Daniel		28:3	
20. Solomon was wiser than anyone else			4:31
21. By wisdom you increased your wealth		28:5	
22. Solomon's wealth through commerce with Hiram of Tyre and arms trade.			9:26-28; 10:22; 10:26-29
23. Solomon richest and wisest king			10:23
24. Gold	2:11-12	28:4,13	34 times
25. Precious stones		28:13	10:2,10,11
26. Blame laid on the woman	3:12, 17		11:3-4
27. YHWH God expelled him from Eden	3:23		

28. The guardian cherub drove you out		28:16	
29. Guardian cherub in the mountain of God		28:14, 16	
30. Cherubim guarded way to tree of life	3:24		
31. Cherubim in Solomon's temple			6:23–29, 32, 35
32. Everyone is astonished at the downfall		28:19	9:7–9

16

The People of YHWH Like Other Nations

THE RUPTURE OF THE monarchy poses a problem in tracing Scripture's teaching of the Oneness of God and God's concern for all people. After Solomon the *people* of YHWH became *two nations*. The Deuteronomistic History is the main narrative source of our knowledge of the relations between the two nations, but the document reached its present form only many centuries later after the end of both kingdoms. One concern of the author(s) was to judge the basic religious and political policies of each king and the impact on relations between the two sister nations and with other nations.

"All Israel" ruled by Jeroboam occupied the central region of Canaan northward into Galilee bordering Tyre and Sidon, plus the territory of Gilead east of the Jordan River. YHWH continued to refer to them as "my people Israel" (1 Kgs 14:7; 16:2).[1] Judah ruled by Solomon's son Rehoboam occupied Jerusalem and the southern region hemmed in by the Philistines on the west, Edom on the south, and the Jordan River and the Dead Sea on the east. YHWH never called them "my people Judah." Now two nations invoked YHWH/Elohim as war god, thus invoking the deity to complicity in their war crimes and atrocities. As the history of the divided kingdom unfolds, it is obvious that YHWH is not bound to either one of these two nations. Sometimes Judah prevailed over Israel (1 Kgs 15:16–24), but other times it was Israel over Judah (2 Kgs 14:8–14). As Abraham Lincoln said of the North and the South in the American Civil War, both sides prayed to the same God, but God couldn't grant the petitions of both. Among the many Psalms that ask for help against enemies some appeal to YHWH and some appeal to Elohim/El. Were they fighting each other and begging Divine help against the sister nation, who were also people of YHWH? In the end, YHWH allowed both nations to go down before the great empires.

---

1. See also "YHWH the God of Israel" referring to the northern kingdom: 1 Kings 14:13; 15:30; 16:26,13; 17:1,14; 22.53; 2 Kings 9:6; 10:31; 14:25.

1. NATIONS MADE FOR WAR

From the very beginning, being like other nations required that kings mobilize the people on a constant war-making basis. (Review 1 Sam 8:10–18 and chapter 12.2 "Canaan in the Late Bronze Age" above for a quick overview of what characterized "other nations.") Saul, the first king, was at war constantly, always on the hunt for men to induct into his army (1 Sam 14:52), and seeking ways to reward his partisans (22:6–8). Saul and three sons fell in the final massive defeat delivered by the Philistines. David and Judah struggled for several years against Saul's remnant before he secured the crown. Thereafter David had to fend off attacks from Philistines and Edomites among others, before he could gradually move on to wars of aggression by which he carved out his small empire. In later years David fought two civil wars, one in defense against third son Absalom. David failed to plan for his successor; he ended up a bedfast old man entangled in a questionable plot that put number ten son Solomon on the throne.

Solomon fought no wars, but his realm began to disintegrate during his lifetime, and after his death it split in two between Rehoboam in Judah and Jeroboam in Israel/Ephraim. Of the nineteen kings of northern Israel, nine took the throne by violence. In Judah the davidic dynasty continued more or less stable, but still, of its twenty rulers, five were assassinated, and one queen, Athaliah daughter of a northern Israelite king, usurped the throne of David for several years.

The Deuteronomistic History takes no realistic account of the fact that from the time of David and Solomon the population of both Israel and Judah included large minorities of Canaanites who had not fully assimilated to the YHWH-only faith. Solomon had exploited them as state slaves, and it is highly likely that a number of them were active military officers or soldiers. On a small scale Saul had utilized chariots, but under David and especially Solomon a cadre of elite, highly privileged military officers monopolized this extremely expensive armament. David had used many foreign mercenaries in his private army, and it is likely that foreign mercenaries played prominent roles in the armed forces of all the kings. They restricted expenditures that would benefit the ordinary people in order to pay high military expenses. Royal security undercut national well being.

Through prophetic messengers, YHWH violently changed the ruling house in northern Israel several times. First, the prophet Ahijah encouraged Jeroboam to break away from Solomon and Rehoboam, but later rejected him. Next, the prophet Jehu roused Baasha to massacre Jeroboam's family, but later rejected him (16:1–7). The commander of half of Israel's chariots slaughtered Baasha's royal house and seized the throne, but there was no prophet agent to give YHWH's approval. This set off a bloody conflict within the officers' ranks that finally resulted in the army commander Omri taking the throne of a severely weakened Israel (1Kgs 16:1–23).

Omri's name is not typically Israelite, and some expositors theorize he may have been a Canaanite professional soldier.[2] The Deuteronomistic History dismisses Omri briefly and negatively, but he ended the war with Judah. He was a very able administrator and restored Israel to domestic stability and strong international relations. Assyria's foreign annals referred to Israel as "the House of Omri" for many years after his own dynasty had been eradicated.[3] Omri bought the hill of Samaria on which he built a completely new national capital (1 Kgs 16:24). This land must have belonged originally to an indigenous Canaanite property owner, which Herrmann takes as a positive sign that Omri improved domestic relations among Israelite citizens and remnants of the Canaanites. He may have included in his policy greater tolerance of Baal, which his son Ahab continued.[4] Omri engaged in friendly relations with Tyre and Sidon, taking Jezebel, daughter of King Itobaal of Tyre, as wife of his son Ahab. With Phoenicia at his back, Ahab was able to take the field against the Arameans/Syrians on the North. The company of the prophets gave aid to Ahab in this war, and they condemned him severely because he did not defeat the enemy as thoroughly as they wished (1 Kgs 20:1–43).

Ahab figures prominently in the Deuteronomistic History as the object of the prophet Elijah's bitter opposition. Ahab and Jezebel gave their children names with the god-bearing element *-yahu*, but Jezebel persecuted YHWH prophets and Ahab helped her actively promote the cult of Baal and Asherah. This may have been a concession to the mixture of Israelites and Canaanites among his people. The regimes of Omri and Ahab put in sharp focus the incompatibility between YHWH-only cultic practice and domestic tranquility for a religiously diverse population and for secure international relations.

2. THE QUESTION: WHERE IS YHWH?

The Deuteronomistic History that narrates the story of the divided kingdom imposes upon that history a much later point of view, which in many details was different from the life experienced by the two nations. The deuteronomists presupposed that only YHWH's *Name* dwelt in the temple, and that the temple in Jerusalem had the only altar for sacrifice to YHWH. Starting in tribal times and continuing until near the end of southern Judah, however, people had sacrificed to YHWH/Ēl at *many* local shrines (Exod 20:24–26), and the organization of cultic personnel became a strict hierarchy only slowly over time.[5] When David brought the ark to Jerusalem and Solomon installed it in the temple he had built, they encouraged the belief that the Deity in person was actually there, enthroned on the cherubim (Pss 80:1; 99:1). Therefore, when

---

2. Gray, *I & II King*, 330.
3. Bright, *A History of Israel*, 222.
4. Herrmann, *A History of Israel*, 206–7.
5. See chapter 12.3 "The Book of the Covenant as guide for the tribes."

the kingdom split, the literal belief about YHWH's presence persisted. The people of YHWH who lived in the northern kingdom still had to go to Jerusalem "to seek the face" of YHWH. Jeroboam feared that pilgrimages to Jerusalem could have the political side effect of drawing away his people to the ruler of the house of David who, as the son of God, reigned in Zion, where the God actually dwelt.

Jeroboam devised a festival calendar later than that in the south, one perhaps more appropriate to the northern climate pattern and agricultural seasons, and he broke the monopoly of the Levites on cultic service. Jeroboam placed bull images for YHWH's throne in national shrines at Bethel and Dan as a theological bulwark against pilgrimages to Jerusalem. He declared, "You have gone up to Jerusalem long enough. Here are your gods, O Israel, who brought you up out of the land of Egypt" (1 Kgs 12:26–33). Bethel was far older than Jerusalem as a shrine for Israel's God. Jacob (with the new name Israel) had led his people to worship El the God of Israel at Bethel (Gen 35:1–7). Ancient traditions referred to Jacob's Deity as "the Mighty One of Jacob" (*'abir ya'akob*), but with a slight change of pointing it could be read *'abbir*="The Bull" of Jacob.[6] The bull was a more appropriate symbol (because indigenous) than the alien cherubim in Solomon's temple. Both symbols were meant to represent a pedestal or throne for the invisible Deity. The deuteronomists denounced the bulls as "other gods" (1 Kgs 14:9) and "idols" (16:13), and fixed Jeroboam's identity as "Jeroboam the son of Nebat who made Israel to sin." All the kings of the northern kingdom were tarred with the same brush.

Of all the Israelite kings, Ahab gets the severest criticism from the deuteronomists, because of his official tolerance of Tyrian Baal in addition to his own YHWH faith. Ahab, in effect, promoted two Gods for Israel: YHWH the god of exodus and desert, and Baal the god of agricultural prosperity. In Canaanite mythology, Baal died in the hot, dry summer, but rose again when the winter rains resumed. I assume Baal priests enacted an annual ritual to facilitate their deity's resurrection.[7] Abruptly, without any introduction, the prophet Elijah confronted Ahab and challenged the Baal mythology with the declaration: "As YHWH the God of Israel lives, before whom I stand, there shall be neither dew nor rain these years, except by my word" (1 Kgs 17:1). With YHWH there is no dying and rising. YHWH lives and rules both fertility and sterility; and YHWH sends the drought as punishment for worshipping Baal and Asherah. In flight for his life, Elijah fled to Sidon, territory supposedly cared for by Baal. YHWH's drought extended even there and impacted a widow of Zarephath. Elijah rewarded the widow's hospitality by keeping her family alive during the drought and restoring her son to life when he died (1 Kgs 17:8–24).[8]

---

6. Gen 49:24; Ps 132:2, 5; Isa 49:26; 60:16. Bulls symbolized Canaanite gods El and Baal. It's possible "bull" may be original, and "mighty one" a later adaptation to avoid a perceived impropriety.

7. Kagawa Prefecture, Japan, where I lived many years, has less than average rainfall. The ancient ritual prayer for rain, dramatized by the battle of good and bad dragons, accompanied by booming drums and clanging cymbals, has been revived as a modern tourist attraction.

8. The care of the widow is an example of God's concern for Gentiles cited by Jesus in Luke 4:25–27.

Elijah returned in time to interrupt the ritual of Baal's prophets on Mount Carmel invoking their god to end the prolonged drought. He challenged the people: "How long will you go limping with two different opinions? If YHWH is God, follow him; but if Baal, then follow him" (18:21). It was a stark either/or choice: YHWH or Baal, whichever could send rain. The Baal prophets danced, limped, self-mutilated, and cried in vain. To Elijah's prayer, YHWH answered with lightning and abundant rain. The people confessed, "YHWH indeed is God!" and carried out Elijah's command to slaughter the prophets of Baal (18:30–40).

Elijah's dramatic victory was short-lived and incomplete at best. The worship of Baal was not so easily extirpated, and even some YHWH worshippers did not accept YHWH's sovereignty over agriculture. One was Jehonadab the son of Rechab (see more below). In his first appearance the text tells us only his name, but in later texts we learn details about him and the descendants who faithfully adhered to the traditions he established (see Jer 35; according to 1 Chron 2:55, the Rechabites were descendants of Kenites). Jehonadab single-mindedly chose YHWH only, deity of exodus and wilderness, and left to Baal the care of settlement and agriculture. Jehonadab's people would live only in tents and pursue nomadic herding, leaving the planting of fields and vineyards (and the drinking of wine) to those who chose Baal. One may compare these ancient fundamentalists to some present-day believers who hold so strictly to the literal interpretation of the Bible's creation stories that they reject the scientific evidence for evolution. Radical monotheism ascribes to the One God sovereignty over every aspect of reality, whether in connection with redemption, with agricultural practice, or with evidence concerning the origins and development of life in nature.

King Ahab lost his life fighting the Arameans, and some years later his son Joram had to retire from the war to recover from a serious wound. The prophet Elisha sent a young member of the prophetic guild to anoint as king Jehu, the commander of Israel's army that was still engaged in the campaign, with the command to extirpate the house of Ahab (2 Kgs 9:1–13). As Jehu drew near the royal residence, Joram went out to meet him, accompanied by King Amazaiah of Judah, who had come to visit him. Jehu killed them both forthwith and proceeded immediately into town where he overran Jezebel under his chariot when some of her own attendants threw her out of a window as he approached the palace. With a thoroughness that modern day terrorists would appreciate, Jehu annihilated all the family and close partisans of Ahab plus some fifty Judean connections of King Ahaziah who showed up in all innocence during the bloodletting. Next Jehu, pretending to honor Baal, assembled his worshippers into the temple of Baal at Samaria, shut them in, and let loose his guards to massacre them all. He then destroyed the temple of Baal and turned it into a public latrine (2 Kgs 9:1—10:27). Jehu found an enthusiastic partner for these atrocities in the person of Jehonadab ben Rechab, the YHWH-only fundamentalist (2 Kgs 10:15–17). YHWH rewarded Jehu for all this: "Because you have done well in carrying out what I consider right, and in accordance with all that was in my heart have dealt with the house of

Ahab, your sons of the fourth generation shall sit on the throne of Israel" (10:30). Jehu's was the longest dynasty in the northern kingdom.

The mother of Ahaziah, the Judean king whom Jehu had killed, was Athaliah, a daughter or granddaughter of Ahab. When she heard that her son had died she killed the other seed royal and usurped the throne in Jerusalem for seven years. The priestly family had secretly rescued Joash, an infant prince, and secretly nurtured him until age eight. In a carefully executed plot the YHWH party crowned Joash and executed Athaliah, thus restoring the davidic dynasty (2 Kgs 11:1–20).

3. DAVID SETS THE STANDARD

Throughout the Deuteronomistic History the editors uphold David as the supreme standard by which to judge all the following kings. Before Solomon actually began building the temple, YHWH addressed him, "if you follow my decrees, carry out my regulations and keep all my commands and obey them, I will fulfill through you the promise I gave to David your father. And I will live among the Israelites and will not abandon my people Israel" (1 Kgs 6:12–13). When Solomon finished the building, YHWH spoke again, repeating the conditions of David and forecasting the consequences of failure: "I will cut Israel off from the land that I have given them; and the house that I have consecrated for my name I will cast out of my sight; and Israel will become a proverb and a taunt among all peoples" (1 Kgs 9:4–9). Solomon worshiped the gods of his foreign wives (1 Kgs 11:1–8), so YHWH took the kingdom out of Solomon's hand in the days of his son, but not entirely—YHWH left him a reduced state for the sake of David and Jerusalem (11:12–13).

The prophet Ahijah of Shiloh urged Jeroboam to rebel against Solomon, making the same promise of kingship on condition that he follow the example of David (11:32, 34, 36, 38), but Jeroboam also failed. In Judah eight kings received approval for doing "right in the sight of YHWH:"[9] I will take note of four of them. As I consider what the text reports of their rule, it leaves me with serious questions why their policies so pleased YHWH and the deuteronomists.

(1) Asa (913-873 BCE), grandson of Rehoboam, "put away the male prostitutes out of the land, and removed all the idols that his ancestors had made. He also removed his mother Maacah from being queen mother, because she had made an abominable image for Asherah" (1 Kgs 15:9–13). Asa continued the war with Israel that had gone on since the split (14:30), but he raised it to a more destructive level. Baasha of Israel was fortifying the town of Ramah to impede communications with Jerusalem. Asa took the treasures in both temple and palace and bribed Ben Hadad of Damascus to break his treaty with Israel and go on the attack. Ben Hadad responded by taking the major towns in the region of Naphtali and Dan (15:6–20), the first in

---

9. Asa (1 Kgs 15:11), Jehoshaphat (22:43), Jehoash (2 Kgs 12:2), Amaziah (14:3), Azariah (also called Uzziah, 15:2), and Jotham (15:34), plus Hezekiah and Josiah at great length.

a series of debilitating wars that eventually ate up Israelite territory in the north and east. Meanwhile Asa mobilized his entire people (forced labor?) to collect the building materials and apply them to his own purposes of defense elsewhere (15:22).

(2) Amaziah (800-783 BCE). Although the Deuteronomistic History does not credit Israelite kings with making peace with Judah, apparently Omri ended the mutually destructive wars. Under Ahab Israel seems to have been in a superior position, with friendly relations including marriages of Israelite princesses to Judean kings. The text reports that Jehoshaphat of Judah had cooperated as an ally with Israelite kings in military campaigns (1 Kgs 22:1–4; 2 Kgs 3:4–7). Amaziah reversed this policy of cooperative co-existence. Emboldened by victory over Edom, Amaziah challenged Jehoash of Israel. Jehoash defeated and captured Amaziah, broke down the northern section of the Jerusalem wall, plundered the treasures of the royal palace and YHWH's temple, and took hostages to Samaria (2 Kgs 14:1–14). Amaziah was one of the five Judean kings who were assassinated (14:17–21).

(3) Hezekiah (715-687/6 BCE). During the reign of Hezekiah's father Ahaz, Assyria began overrunning all the minor states in the west on the way to Egypt, and Israel and Damascus attacked Judah to force them to join in resisting Assyria. Ahaz had fought back desperately and appealed to Assyria for help (2 Kgs 16:5–9). Assyria destroyed Damascus and was attacking Israel when Hezekiah succeeded Ahaz as king. The text states that Hezekiah "did what was right in the sight of YHWH just as his ancestor David had done. (. . .) He trusted in YHWH the God of Israel; so that there was no one like him among all the kings of Judah after him, or among those who were before him. (. . .) YHWH was with him; wherever he went, he prospered. He rebelled against the king of Assyria and would not serve him" (2 Kgs 18:3–7). Even after Assyria destroyed Israel (according to the Deuteronomistic History, 18:9–12, this was the well-deserved punishment of YHWH),[10] Hezekiah continued his resistance. King Sennacherib occupied and plundered all the fortified cities of Judah and gave them to the Philistines, besieged Jerusalem, and demanded a great amount of silver and gold, which Hezekiah paid by stripping the temple and royal treasury. Despite this payment, the Assyrian army officers sent a letter demanding complete surrender. Hezekiah spread the letter before YHWH in the temple, and the prophet Isaiah sent a message of assurance that YHWH would save Jerusalem for the sake of David. In what Hezekiah considered a divine miracle, the Assyrians withdrew without actually taking the city (2 Kgs 19:1–37).[11] Hezekiah kept his throne, but he remained a vassal of Assyria, and his realm consisted only of Jerusalem and slight outlying areas. Meanwhile the exiles of Israel and the remnant of the people of YHWH in Judah suffered great deprivation and misery. Hezekiah never ceased machinations against Assyria, which the prophet Isaiah told him would eventuate in the fall of his dynasty (2 Kgs 20:12–19).

---

10. For more detailed account see 2 Kgs 17:1–23.
11. The total biblical text is not clear, and scholars still wonder whether Assyria besieged Jerusalem once or twice.

(4) Josiah (640-609). Assyria continued to dominate Judah, and Hezekiah's son, Manasseh, remained submissive during his reign of forty-five years. The Deuteronomistic History calls Manasseh the worst of all Judah's kings. He was so bad that even the good things his grandson Josiah did could not please YHWH enough to prevent the kingdom's fall and exile (2 Kgs 23:26–27). Assyrian power began to fade as the New Babylonian Empire budded, and Josiah started to clean out all remnants of Assyrian effects on the YHWH cult. Josiah's priests, while cleaning up the temple, found a book of the law, which turned out to be an early version of what is now the Book of Deuteronomy. Following instructions in the book, Josiah led all the people in a covenant renewal service and then carried out a radical religious and cultic reorganization, which included destroying the YHWH shrines outside Jerusalem, including those at Bethel and Samaria that Jeroboam had established at the beginning of the split (2 Kgs 23:1–24a). "[H]e established all the words of the law that were written in the book that the priest Hilkiah had found in the house of YHWH. Before him there was no king like him, who turned to YHWH with all his heart, with all his soul, and with all his might, according to all the law of Moses; nor did any like him arise after him" (23:24b–25).

At that very time, Assyria and Babylon met in a final showdown, and Pharaoh Neco with his Egyptian army passed through Judah to join the fray. Josiah tried to intercept Neco, but he killed Josiah, and for a brief time Egypt ruled over Judah (2 Kgs 23:28–35). Babylonia beat Assyria in the big war and took Judah away from Egypt (24:7). For a decade a faction of pro-Egypt diehards struggled on, but in 597 BCE Babylon imposed the first exile followed by final destruction of Jerusalem and the temple and further phases of exile in 587-6 BCE and beyond (24:18—25:21).

It's ironic that Hezekiah and Josiah, the two Judean kings who get the highest praise from the deuteronomist authors, combined YHWH-only cultic zeal with power politics and international war that caused the greatest degree of defeat and economic hardship for the people of YHWH. David's personal genius at exalting YHWH-only faith and cult, reinforced by his success as a warrior in subduing the surrounding small states, had made possible his consolidation of the Federated Kingdom, but David had to contend only with other minor states while all three of the major empires happened to be simultaneously in decline. Conditions were significantly more difficult for those who followed David, yet the deuteronomists still held David up as the supreme example.

4. YHWH'S CONCERN FOR NON-ISRAELITES

The Deuteronomistic History includes several incidents that demonstrate YHWH's concern for non-Israelites, which find an echo in the teaching of Jesus. (1) Elijah worked together with the widow of Zarephath in Sidon to survive the famine and raised her son from a fatal illness (1 Kgs 17:8–24). (2) Naaman, the army commander of the enemy king of Aram, frequently defeated Israel and made slaves of Israelite captives, yet Elisha healed him of a serious disease. Naaman vowed to sacrifice only to YHWH, but Elisha gave him permission to bow to Rimmon whenever he had to accompany his king to that god's temple (2 Kgs 5:1–19).[12] (3) Elisha employed divine clairvoyance to notify the king of Israel of the plans of the king of Aram to mount raids against Israel, enabling Israel to avoid these deadly conflicts. When the king of Aram learned of Elisha's activity he sent an armed troop to capture him. Elisha invoked divine aid to confuse the troop and led them inside the walls of Samaria. When the king of Israel saw them he said to Elisha, "Father, shall I kill them? Shall I kill them?" The prophet strictly forbade such an act and insisted, "Set food and water before them so that they may eat and drink; and let them go to their master." The king prepared a feast for them and let them go, and for a while the Arameans stopped their raids (2 Kgs 6:8–23).[13]

SUMMARY AND REFLECTION

It should be clear that in the two centuries during which the people of YHWH co-existed and often fought each other like other nations, and the following century when Judah alone survived as a nation, the concept of the oneness of God and the divine plan for the reconciliation of all humanity made but small progress, at least as reported in the Deuteronomistic History. Examples of YHWH's concern for non-Israelites contrast with the central message of the Deuteronomistic History that the people of the two kingdoms fell before the power of the empires and lost possession of the land because they had failed to keep YHWH's covenant.

We are fortunate to have the messages of prophets who had more concern for the older aspects of covenant—that YHWH, the Divine Kinsman related to the people ('am=family) more in terms of the personal relation as husband-wife and parent-child than as a stern Sovereign Master imposing exclusive conditions. One has to search the prophets' messages to discover their words of comfort and encouragement, for they lack the consistency of the Deuteronomistic History's narrative. As powerfully impressive as we may find the narrative, Scripture speaks other words from the prophets to enable us to say, "But on the other hand—"

---

12. In his hometown synagogue at Nazareth Jesus mentions the widow and Naaman as examples of God's concern for non-Israelites. That made the people so angry they wanted to lynch him (Luke 4:16–30).

13. See Jesus' teaching, "Love your enemies...so that you may be children of your Father in heaven..." (Matt 5:44–45), and Paul's citation of Prov 25:21 "If your enemies are hungry, give them bread to eat; and if they are thirsty, give them water to drink" (Rom 12:20).

17

The Covenant as Family Relation

A GREAT DEAL OF attention to the biblical concept of covenant has focused on that which Moses mediated at Sinai (Exod 19–24). The Divine Kinsman, with the newly revealed Name YHWH, redeemed his people out of slavery and brought them to the Mountain of God. In gratitude the people pledged to have YHWH only as their God and Sovereign, and to obey his laws as his people. Over time such a vast body of tradition collected around this aspect of covenant—including portions of Exodus and Numbers, all of Leviticus and Deuteronomy—that it is impossible to isolate just what was the content of that first Sinai covenant. The Jewish scholar Jon D. Levenson expresses an opinion with which more and more serious Bible students would agree:

> Modern scholars date these various codes to different periods of Israel's history, all of them post-Mosaic. What their common ascription to Moses on Sinai suggests is that the Sinaitic "event" functioned as the prime pattern through which Israel could re-establish in every generation who she was, who she was meant to be. The experience of Sinai, whatever its historical basis, was perceived as so overwhelming, so charged with meaning, that Israel could not imagine that any truth or commandment from God could have been absent from Sinai.[1]

A less formal but no less important aspect of covenant relates to the near-at-hand relationship between the Divine Kinsman and human partner as family, husband-wife, and parent-child. In the ancient Near East, covenant relations on the personal level regulated many aspects of social life, especially marriage, which was not a romantic attachment between a man and a woman as a couple but a socio-economic relationship between families. The family of the husband accepted the woman from the outside into its most intimate sphere. Once the concept of covenant between deity and humankind became familiar, it was only natural that some people would think of it in terms of marriage. The Divine Kinsman played the role of husband, and Israel that of wife, the outsider brought into the most intimate relation by covenant=*berit*. The prophetic

---

1. Levenson, *Sinai and Zion*, 18–19.

literature includes texts that show how marriage as metaphor developed over time. Prophets depicted Israel in the role of wife as betraying YHWH by worshipping other gods, particularly the fertility god Baal, and by making covenants=treaties with foreign powers that necessitated at least the acknowledgement if not subservience to the gods of the other nations. YHWH as husband temporarily divorced unfaithful Israel, but to the end kept faith, ultimately receiving back and restoring the errant spouse.

A second aspect of family relationships is that of parent and child, which the prophets depict as playing out in the same way—YHWH as father/mother expressing deep sorrow and even anguish over the delinquency of first-bon son Israel, yet ultimately unable to give him up. In the ministry of the prophets Hosea, Jeremiah, Ezekiel, and Second Isaiah we trace the development of that process.

1. HOSEA LIVES THE COVENANT

The prophet Hosea was a native of northern Israel in the eighth century BCE, who probably lived to see Israel's end in 721. He often referred to his country as Ephraim, the name of the most prominent of the ten tribes. Hosea knew the daily life and religious practices of rural villagers inside and up close, where farm festivals celebrating fertility encouraged excessive drunkenness and sexual licentiousness of both men and women. Free sex undermined marriage relations and family life and degraded public morality (Hos 4:1–19). The Israelites who prospered from burgeoning material prosperity of that time attributed their good fortune to Hadad, the Canaanite god of fertility, popularly called Baal, a title that means "owner" or "master" or "husband" depending on context. Israelites might also use the title Baal to refer to YHWH. They pretty much forgot the traditions of YHWH's saving their ancestors out of Egypt and caring for them in the desert (Hos 13:4–6). In Hosea's view those acts of redemption were YHWH's wooing of Israel (or perhaps even paying a bride price). YHWH's relation with Israel was a marriage contract. The Divine Kinsman thus was the husband, but the people Israel, the wife, had betrayed the husband with lovers. Hosea refers to the fertility Baals as plural (2:17), perhaps suggesting that the farmers attributed ownership of each field or farm to a different local manifestation of Baal, the Canaanite power of fertility, just as Japanese farmers acknowledge the god=*kami* of each field by placing an upright rock or a small pile of stones in a corner. In Hosea's words, to worship Baal was to commit adultery against YHWH.[2]

Chapters 1 and 3 of Hosea contain fragmentary references to Hosea's personal life, but my understanding is as follows: Hosea felt called by YHWH to live out in his own marriage YHWH's experience of being betrayed by unfaithful Israel (Hos 1:2;

---

2. Women scholars have noted the misogyny implied in likening Israel to an adulterous wife. Space here does not permit adequate consideration of the question, but for a helpful discussion of the issue in a broader context I recommend Keefe, *Woman's Body and the Social Body in Hosea*. See above chapter 13.3 "Decline and degradation."

3:1). Hosea married Gomer, and "she bore him a son" (1:3) named Jezreel, presumably his own child. The second, a daughter, was apparently illegitimate, whom he named Lo-ruhamah="Not-pitied," and likewise a second son named Lo-ammi="Not-my-people" (1:6, 8–9). These two names symbolize YHWH's rejection of Israel. Hosea 2:2-15 (Heb 2:4-17) is a poetic narrative of the betrayed husband's appeals to the unfaithful wife. YHWH [Hosea?] declares: "She is not my wife, and I am not her husband" (2:2 H 2:4). YHWH threatens Israel, for she has gone after lovers=Baals, who, she thought, gave her plentiful crops. YHWH will cause crop failures, for which Israel will blame Baal and say, "I will go back to my first husband, for it was better with me then than now" (2:7 H 2:9). In spite of all the poor harvests that she experienced, however, she kept going after her lovers (2:8-13 H 2:10-15). Therefore—therefore what? Even more severe punishment? No! YHWH will start the courtship all over again! YHWH will woo her, as in the early wilderness days after bringing Israel out of Egypt (2:14-15 H 2:16-17).

In the restoration, Israel no longer will call YHWH "My Baal" (an honorific title for "husband/master"), but will call him "my man" (which in Hebrew context means *husband*).[3] YHWH promises Israel a restoration of fruitful earth and abolition of war. "I will take you for my wife in righteousness and in justice, in steadfast love, and in mercy. I will take you for my wife in faithfulness; and you shall know YHWH" (2:16-20 H 2:18-22). Though temporarily divorced ("I will drive them out of my house. I will love them no more" 9:15), YHWH will renew the marriage and accept the illegitimate children. "I will have pity on Lo-ruhamah, and I will say to Lo-ammi, 'You are my people'; and he shall say, 'You are my God'" (2:21-23 H 2:23-25).

So YHWH said to Hosea, "Go, love a woman who has a lover and is an adulteress, just as YHWH loves the people of Israel, though they turn to other gods ..." (3:1). Hosea responded by mending his marriage—broken by her abandonment and by his divorce. Hosea took the initiative and spent his meager resources to buy her back from whatever kind of bondage she had fallen into (3:23). Now the brother is called Ammi=My people, and the sister Ruhamah=Pitied (2:1). Here is a significant example of healing the ineffectiveness of mere punishment, which has no reforming effect on human character. YHWH's *chesed*—faithful, gentle, loving kindness, and Hosea following the divine example, accomplish the desired reconciliation.

During Hosea's lifetime Israel fell into chaos: Between the death of Jeroboam II in 746 and the end of Israel in 722/1 BCE, six kings ruled, and four of them were assassinated. YHWH charges, "They made kings, but not through me; they set up princes, but without my knowledge" (8:4a). Accumulating weapons and military forces proved counterproductive: "Because you have trusted in your power and in the multitude of your warriors, therefore the tumult of war shall rise against your people ..." (10:18-19).

---

3. In Japan "husband" is *otto*, but the honorific word for husband is *shu-jin*=lord-person. The Japanese Bible uses the Chinese character for *shu* =lord to translate both YHWH and *Adonai*.

Hosea uses the adultery metaphor to criticize Israel's international relations. Making treaties and alliances with the great powers for security and commerce involved assuming a subordinate role and acknowledging the deities of dominant nations, but it also meant the economic exploitation of the masses of the people, whose produce the king confiscated in order to pay tribute (2 Kgs 15:19–20; 17:1–4). "Ephraim has become like a dove, silly and without sense; they call upon Egypt, they go to Assyria" (7:11). The frequent regime changes reflected the conflict between the pro-Egypt and the pro-Assyria parties. Thus to Hosea, Israel's illicit lovers are not only the local Baals, but also the gods of the great powers. "Israel is swallowed up; now they are among the nations as a useless vessel . . . Ephraim has bargained for lovers . . . " (Hos 8:8, 9b). Accusations such as these underlie the theme that YHWH has divorced Ephraim/Israel. The end of the northern kingdom came after Assyria's brutal three-year siege of Samaria (2 Kgs 17:5–6).

Besides the metaphor of the betrayed spouse to describe the YHWH-Israel relationship, Hosea uses that of the parent betrayed by an ungrateful, delinquent child. "When Israel was a child, I loved him, and out of Egypt I called my son. The more I called them, the more they went from me; they kept sacrificing to the Baals and offering incense to idols" (Hos 11:1–2). Exile to Egypt and Assyria and the ravages of war followed (11:5–7). But YHWH cannot leave it at that. "How can I give you up, Ephraim? How can I hand you over, O Israel? . . . My heart recoils within me [lit, my bowels are turned upside down]; my compassion grows warm and tender . . . for I am God and no mortal, the Holy One in your midst" (11:8–9). God, who is gradually being revealed in the story of YHWH and Israel, sets the example for us human children to follow: no one is too far-gone simply to be rejected. The One who told Hosea, "Go, love a woman who has a lover and is an adulteress, just as YHWH loves the people of Israel, though they turn to other gods . . . " now at the end declares: "I will heal their disloyalty; I will love them freely, for my anger has turned from them" (14:4).

In my personal spiritual pilgrimage, Hosea's declaration of God's unconditional love for sinful Israel struck me forcefully in contrast with the prophet Amos's message of God who judges surrounding sinful nations impartially (Amos 1:3—2:3) and then turns on the chosen people: "You only have I known of all the families of the earth; therefore I will punish you for all your iniquities" (Amos 3:3). Surely the One impartial God who judges all sinful nations including Israel, will in the end impartially show to all the nations the special love lavished on sinful Israel!? Just when I was meditating on Amos and Hosea, one of those terrible typhoons struck Bangladesh. Powerful winds drove tidal waves over outlying islands and far inland over the river delta to drown countless thousands of victims. I wondered, could the God revealed in Scripture condemn these masses of poverty-stricken Muslims to eternal damnation simply because they had never confessed faith in Jesus Christ as Savior? No! One God must be God for all. To strengthen this conviction of mine, I note that Amos's message concludes that eventually God *will* restore David's fallen booth, repair its breaches and ruins, to restore dominion over the nations formerly ruled by David and called by YHWH's name (9:11–12). At Acts 15:16–17 the earliest Jesus people cited this text from Amos to give Scriptural approval for receiving Gentile believers directly without making them first convert as Jews.[4]

2. JEREMIAH CONFIRMS HOSEA'S MESSAGE

Northern Israel and Southern Judah had co-existed for a long time, both claiming YHWH/Elohim as national god but often locked in bitter and mutually destructive warfare. When Assyria destroyed Israel and deported many of its citizens in 721 BCE, some people in Judah felt smug satisfaction, and in line with the metaphor of marriage, they concluded that YHWH must have divorced wife Israel and sent her away. Inevitably people made comparisons between lost Israel and surviving Judah. Still, in Jeremiah's day, though calling itself an independent nation, Judah found itself in the same crisis, dominated by Egypt and Assyria at first, only soon to face a resurgent Babylon.

Building on Hosea's basic metaphor that the covenant is a marriage, Jeremiah appeals to Israel: Thus says YHWH: "I remember the devotion of your youth, your love as a bride, how you followed me in the wilderness, in a land not sown. Israel was holy to YHWH . . . " (Jer 2:2–3). The message goes on to state how the people, once settled in the land, stopped inquiring after YHWH and went after Baal (2:4–8). The prophet passes over the intervening centuries and states that that early unfaithfulness underlies their present crisis. They have forsaken YHWH, the fountain of living water, to drink from the waters of the Nile and the Euphrates (2:9–19). Long ago they gave themselves up completely to involvement in the fertility cults, from which they now cannot break free (2:20–25). Moral, social, and political corruption is rampant, and dependency on foreign powers will bring no help (2:26–37).

A new poetic section introduces an important issue. In the Mosaic law a rule strictly forbids a man from taking back a wife whom he divorced if she had married another man in the meantime; such an act would be "abhorrent to YHWH" and "bring guilt on the land" (Deut 24:1–4). In view of this, could Israel return to YHWH even if she wanted to? Could YHWH go against his own law and receive Israel back? YHWH seems to answer negatively. "You have played the whore with many lovers; and would you return to me? Look up to the bare heights and see where have you not been lain with? " Israel refuses to be ashamed but shifts the metaphor by appealing, "My Father, you are the friend of my youth—will he be angry forever?" (Jer 3:1–5).

In the next paragraph Jeremiah reports that YHWH ordered him to compare Israel and Judah. Judah had seen that Israel as an unfaithful wife had betrayed YHWH,

---

4. There is great variation of Amos 9:11–12 in Hebrew, the Septuagint, and the citation in Acts 15:16–17. See Beale and Carson, eds., *Commentary on the New Testament Use of the Old Testament* 589b–593a.

and that YHWH "had sent her away with a decree of divorce (viz., defeat by Assyria), yet her false sister Judah did not fear, but she too went and played the whore." Yet, in the end, Israel proved less guilty than Judah (3:6–11). Therefore YHWH ordered Jeremiah to go proclaim these words "to the north" and say:

> Return, faithless Israel, says YHWH. I will not look on you in anger, for I am merciful, says YHWH; I will not be angry forever. Only acknowledge your guilt, that you have rebelled against YHWH your God, and scattered your favors among strangers under every green tree, and have not obeyed my voice, says YHWH. Return, O faithless children, says YHWH, for I am your [husband];[5] I will take you, one from a city and two from a family, and I will bring you to Zion (Jer 3:12–14).

With divine freedom, YHWH ignores the Mosaic law and offers to receive back as "wife" the survivors of the former northern kingdom, however few they may be, even though people thought YHWH's "divorce" was irremediable. The passage goes on to anticipate eventual reunion of the separated kingdoms (3:15–18). As I show below, the prophet Ezekiel declares YHWH's restitution of the "adulterous" wife even more graphically and strenuously, but for the moment I will note another example of Jeremiah's speaking of YHWH and Israel as bound in an unbreakable family relationship.

Jeremiah witnessed the deterioration and demise of his beloved homeland and the tragedy that overtook its people, events that caused him intense pain and sorrow. In Jeremiah's speeches, we observe a sort of melding of his personal emotions and those attributed to YHWH, as Hosea's relationship and emotional involvement with Gomer at times mirrored YHWH's with Israel. YHWH forbade Jeremiah to marry (16:2), but in a sense he was wedded to the people. Stern when confronting their wrongdoing, he was privately devastated by their tragic fate:

> My anguish, my anguish! I writhe in pain. Oh, the walls of my heart! My heart is beating wildly; I cannot keep silent; for I hear the sound of the trumpet, the alarm of war. Disaster overtakes disaster, the whole land is laid waste, suddenly my tents are destroyed, my curtains in a moment. How long must I see the standard, and hear the sound of the trumpet? "For my people are foolish, they do not know me; they are stupid children, they have no understanding. They are skilled in doing evil, but do not know how to do good." (Jer 4:19–22 NRSV)

The Heb text graphically describes the wrenching of the guts, the palpitations of the heart—the very real physical effects of emotional distress. Who is speaking here? NRSV suggests it is Jeremiah at first, but by placing quotation marks around 4:22 implies that YHWH speaks now. The Hebrew is equivocal. Does this not express YHWH's

---

5. NRSV reads "maker." I read "husband" to agree with the KJV, NIV, and NJPS. The Hebrew word is based on the root *baʿal*, and here, as in many contexts, *baʿal* presupposes the concept of marriage and implies husband.

emotional involvement that Jeremiah personally shares? For depth of sorrow over the fate of his people Jeremiah has been called the weeping prophet, and tradition (incorrectly) named him author of the book of Lamentations. *Here, YHWH weeps!*

Elsewhere, YHWH expresses a similarly impassioned attachment to the people: "I have loved you with an everlasting love; therefore I have continued my faithfulness to you" (31:3) "I have become a father to Israel, and Ephraim is my firstborn" (31:9b). Later YHWH speaks in maternal terms: "Is Ephraim my dear son? Is he the child I delight in [or dandle]? As often as I speak against him, I still remember him [emphatic form]. Therefore I am deeply moved [my bowels are in an uproar] for him; I will surely have mercy on him," says YHWH (Jer 31:20). In Jeremiah YHWH speaks of Israel as "my people" (*'ammi*—my kin, my family) a total of thirty-eight times, displaying divine pathos over a broad range of emotions expressing the Divine Kinsman's commitment to the covenant, at the same time as venting anger over the Israelites' betrayal. Unfortunately, space here does not permit the detailed treatment that all these texts deserve, but the conclusion of Jeremiah is inescapable: *YHWH will not give up his people.*

3. EZEKIEL AFFIRMS GOD'S TOTAL COMMITMENT

Ezekiel was among the captives taken to Babylon several years before the final fall of Jerusalem in 586 BCE. Jeremiah was a contemporary of his who remained behind. They were both priests, though Ezekiel was apparently of the elite Jerusalem family of Zadok in contrast to Jeremiah's upbringing in rural Anathoth. We have no evidence that they met each other personally, but they have many themes in common. Ezekiel was a very strange person whose role as YHWH's messenger immersed him totally. Of the many aspects of this difficult but fascinating prophet, I am interested in his contribution to our understanding of how the One God embraces all.

Ezekiel uses metaphorical and allegorical parables to describe the relationship between YHWH and his people in terms of marriage, but each separate example has its unique details and application, which it is impossible to combine into one unified, harmonious whole or to interpret literally. Nevertheless the basic message is clear: Israel has repeatedly broken the marriage covenant and betrayed YHWH, but after severe and deserved punishment of the betrayers, YHWH will restore them by means of a renewed covenant.

(1) Ezekiel reports a first-person autobiographical story as told by YHWH (Ezek 23). There were two sisters, Samaria—capital of northern Israel—and the younger Jerusalem—capital of southern Judah, who became YHWH's wives[6] (Ezek 23:1–4). Thus YHWH appears as a polygamist who ignores the legal prohibition of marrying

---

6. HCSB note: The strange names assigned to the two cities apparently allude to the royal shrines dedicated to God at the national capitals: Samaria=Oholah (her tent) and Jerusalem=Oholibamah (my tent is in her).

sisters (Lev 18:18). The narrative accuses them both of whoredom by equating their treaties with foreign nations as adultery. YHWH called Assyria to destroy Samaria, and although Jerusalem saw it, she committed adultery in the same way only worse. Therefore Jerusalem must suffer the same fate (23:5–49).

(2) A second parable is a sort of historical sketch of the city of Jerusalem. David conquered the city, absorbed its people, and made it his capital (2 Sam 5:6–10). Ezekiel says it was a Canaanite enclave of Amorites and Hittites (16:1–3). Ezekiel describes original Jerusalem as an unwanted girl child whose parents abandoned her, but YHWH rescued her and made a marriage covenant with her when she grew up (16:4–8). Despite all the gifts YHWH lavished on her, she betrayed him repeatedly with foreign lovers, which Ezekiel describes in almost pornographic terms (16:9–34). Therefore YHWH will vent his fury and bring her lovers to destroy her (16:35–43a). In an odd turn, YHWH continues to address Jerusalem as one of three sisters, the others being Samaria in the north and Sodom in the south. The other two committed the same kinds of sins, but Jerusalem was so much worse that she made them look good by comparison (16:43b–52). Nevertheless YHWH declares that he will "restore the fortunes" of all three, Sodom, Samaria, and Jerusalem in order to make them ashamed of all that they have done. YHWH will return them all to their former state, though they will have to bear the penalty of their lewdness (16:53–58). In conclusion YHWH declares he will remember his covenant and will make it an eternal covenant with Jerusalem (addressed as second person feminine singular). YHWH will give Samaria and Sodom to Jerusalem as daughters, but will not include them in her covenant. Then shall Jerusalem remember and feel shame, after YHWH has forgiven her (16:59–63).

(3) When elders of the exiles came to inquire of YHWH from the prophet, Ezekiel speaking for YHWH gives a brief summary of Israel's history from the days of oppression in Egypt. YHWH announced he would deliver them and urged them to abandon their idols in Egypt, but they refused. YHWH was ready to destroy them, but he relented for the sake of his name, that it should not be profaned in the sight of the nations (20:1–9). So YHWH led them out of Egypt into the wilderness, gave them laws and statutes, but they refused to follow them. Again he relented for the sake of his name (20:10–17). The same process was repeated over and over. Each time YHWH spared them and gave them another chance, for the sake of his name (20:18–26). Therefore, YHWH informs these elders in exile, he will not be consulted by them (20:19–32). Yet, once again in an unexpected turn, YHWH announces the divine intention to gather his people now scattered in exile throughout the nations and bring them back to their land, purge and purify them, and manifest his holiness among them before the nations (16:33–42). They shall remember their evil deeds and repent. "And you shall know that I am YHWH, when I deal with you for my name's sake, not according to your evil ways or corrupt deeds, O house of Israel, says the Lord YHWH" (20:43–44).

4. ISAIAH CONFIRMS THE RESTORATION

The prophet of the exile called Second Isaiah adds his voice to answer the complaint that YHWH must have divorced his wife and sold his children: Thus says YHWH: "Where is your mother's bill of divorce with which I put her away? Or which of my creditors is it to whom I have sold you? No, because of your sins you were sold, and for your transgressions your mother was put away" (Isa 50:1). The prophet appeals to the original covenant: "Look to Abraham your father and to Sarah who bore you, for he was but one when I called him, but I blessed him and made him many" (Isa 51:2). In a great hymn of rejoicing YHWH, the Divine Kinsman, assures the abandoned wife that she will have many children and recalls the covenants with Abraham and Noah (in the time that I refer to as The Universal Matrix):

> Your Maker is your husband, YHWH of Hosts is his name; the Holy One of Israel is your Redeemer, the God of the whole earth he is called ... For a brief moment I abandoned you, but with great compassion I will gather you. In overflowing wrath for a moment I hid my face from you, but with everlasting love I will have compassion on you, says YHWH, your Redeemer. Just as I swore that the waters of Noah would never again go over the earth, so I have sworn that I will not be angry with you and will not rebuke you. For the mountains may depart and the hills be removed, but my steadfast love shall not depart from you, and my covenant of peace shall not be removed, says YHWH, who has compassion on you. (Isa 54:1–10)

SUMMARY AND REFLECTION

I wish to stress the supreme importance of family relationship as the key to interpreting the concept of covenant to describe the divine-human relationship. Divine gift prevails, and we best understand God and respond to him as devoted spouse or loving parent. In chapter 11.3–4 I noted the tendency to place unjustified emphasis upon legal aspects and the necessity of human obedience to the covenant in western Christianity. When the prophets take up the question, they put the emphasis where it belongs: on the *personal* relation. God is the dependable Divine Kinsman and humankind is God's family. The Divine Kinsman, whether spouse or parent, maintains steadfast love, is utterly and ultimately faithful. Though resentful at repeated betrayal and disobedience, and though allowing the disobedient partners to suffer the consequences of their wrongdoing, with parental compassion God bestows restoration to the guilty ones, through no virtue of theirs, but solely by the gracious parental will. As we shall see, Jesus of Nazareth seldom mentioned covenant, and even then not in any legalistic sense. Jesus most often called God Father.

In their writings the prophets still think of Israel as the one people of YHWH though separated north and south and dispersed among the nations. This people is the human partner in the covenant between Deity and humanity, and a strong sense of Israel's specialness and exceptionalism pervades. Yet the God whom Israelites increasingly acknowledge as the One and Only Creator cannot limit divine favor to Israel alone. Ezekiel says that even though YHWH would not include Sodom and Samaria in the special covenant with Jerusalem, he would restore their fortunes and return them to their former state. Isaiah brings us back full circle to the days of Noah. YHWH assures doubtful Israel that he will never remove his covenant of peace from her, and for proof cites the universal everlasting covenant with all flesh never to destroy the earth again by waters.

Taking full account of what I have written above, I must note that in Scripture, alongside the theme of divine compassion and grace, we find a theme of wrath, vengeance, enmity, judgment, and the terrorism of barbaric war commanded by YHWH. Hosea depicts God as a bear robbed of her cubs, ready to rip the hearts out of those who rouse her anger, or as a lion ready to maul and devour its prey (Hos 13:9). To what extent was Hosea projecting his own anger toward Gomer on to YHWH, before YHWH's compassion led him to restore Gomer?

Jer 10:23—12:17 is a collection of prose and poetry, some perhaps from Jeremiah himself, others from later editors. In deep love for his people Jeremiah appealed to YHWH to pour out wrath on the nations that did not know him, who were devouring and wasting Jacob (Jer 10:23-5). Then in deuteronomistic style, YHWH condemns Israel for breaking the covenant and worshiping other gods. YHWH will bring disaster on the people and challenges them: see what those no-gods can do for you then! (Jer11:1-13). Thrice God forbids Jeremiah to pray for the people (11:14; 7:16; 14:11), yet the prophet continues to do so. But despite his intercessions for them, some people seek his death, so he asks YHWH to obliterate them and their innocent children (11:18-23; 18:18-23). Twice YHWH calls his people "my beloved" (11:14), "the beloved of my soul=*nephesh*" (12:7). You can't get more intimate than that! Yet YHWH abandons them to their enemies for near complete destruction (11:9-17). Jeremiah's desire for personal revenge and his desire for annihilation of Israel's enemies spill over into his portrait of God.

The section ends offering the possibility that the nations that caused Israel to sin with Baal may one day swear by Israel's God, "As YHWH lives," and thus "be built up in the midst of my people" (12:14-17). One must reckon with the inner biblical conflict as one searches the Scriptures to trace the growing understanding of God through many generations. Only thus can we come to see that the special love for Israel that the prophets proclaim is, in truth, God's love for all humanity, embraced in God's eternal plan for total reconciliation of all (Ephesians 1:9-10; Colossians 1:19-20).

18

The Prophets and the End of the State

THE PROPHETS PUT PROPER emphasis upon the nature and character of God as compassionate and faithful partner in the covenant relationship with Israel, but they by no means overlooked the aspect of human obligation. The prophets did not, however, express that obligation in legalistic terms of subject to overlord, but rather of children of the same family relating to each other under the compassionate oversight of the parent. The prophetic emphasis on the obligation of mutual peaceful co-existence applied not only to Israelites as ethnically and religiously related, but also to nation states under supreme divine sovereignty.

1. AMOS AND THE EXTENSION OF YHWH'S SOVEREIGNTY

Amos was originally among the shepherds of Tekoa, a few miles south of Bethlehem, i.e., an area steeped in the davidic and Judahite traditions. He states his point of view with the first blast of his message: "YHWH roars from Zion and utters his voice from Jerusalem—" (Amos 1:2a). YHWH's true dwelling place is in Zion, and from there the divine word goes forth. In Amos's mouth, YHWH's word goes out in the form of judgment against all the lands once ruled by David or bound to him by treaty: Damascus, the Philistines, Tyre, Edom, Ammon, and Moab (Amos 1:3—2:3). Even though davidic authority no longer reaches these peoples, YHWH's word still prevails, and YHWH holds them and their rulers responsible for crimes against common standards of humanity. Max Polley says the scene recalls a great king's treaty laid on client kings—not only do they owe loyalty to their overlord, but they must also relate to each other as brothers. The little kingdoms in Palestine have committed heinous crimes against each other and deserve the judgment of their Divine Sovereign.[1] Amos includes Judah and Israel in YHWH's condemnation (2:4–8). Amos further displays his inclination toward universalism by asserting that Israel's God looks upon Israel no differently than upon the exotic black Ethiopians; and just as YHWH had led Israel

---

1. Polley, "Amos' Oracles against Foreign Nations," *Amos and the Davidic Empire*.

from Egypt, so had he led the Philistines from Caphtor and the Arameans from Kir (9:7–8).

Amos goes beyond the prophets recorded in the Deuteronomistic History, Elijah, Elisha, and the prophetic guilds.[2] Amos transcends their national chauvinism to declare YHWH's impartial judgment of *all* the nations, making no exception. "Hear this word that YHWH has spoken against you, O people of Israel, against the whole family that I brought up out of the land of Egypt: You only have I known of all the families of the earth; therefore I will punish you for all your iniquities" (3:1–2). The divine "I" speaks as subject of verbs a total of ten times describing a series of disasters, sent as judgment: famine, drought, blight, locusts, pestilence, war, and earthquake. "I sent" all these, yet in every case, "you did not return to me, says YHWH. Therefore thus I will do to you, O Israel; because I will do this to you, prepare to meet your God, O Israel!" (4:6–12). Meet God *how*? Will God now bring the *last* and most fearful judgment? But no! "For lo, he who forms the mountains, and creates the wind, and declares to man what is his thought . . . YHWH, the God of hosts, is his name" (4:12–13). People may now meet the Creator not only in the works of creation and natural disasters but especially as incarnated in a fellow human being through whom the Divine Kinsman shares his *thought*—musing, meditation, complaint[3]—with the family he has chosen. This message is designed to appeal to the human heart and conscience, not to stir instinctive fear, for punishment has no power to bring reformation and reconciliation.

2. THE GAP BETWEEN RICH AND POOR

As Israel's development like other nations progressed since David's policy of assimilating indigenous people, the gap between rich and poor widened with the adoption of customs of land ownership and exploitation common to the Canaanites. The prophets addressed the problem posed by the growing inequality between the few and the many, a contradiction of the more egalitarian conditions that ideally should prevail where one God is acknowledged and followed by all.

Amos condemns those who for mere trivial debts seize the property or even the persons of the debtors (Amos 2:6–7a). The Book of the Covenant mandates a release of male debt slaves after seven years (Exod 21:2), but Amos gives no hint of any release. As for a female slave, ordinarily the master or one of his sons would take her as wife or concubine (Exod 21:7–10), but Amos charges that both father and son simply used such girls for sex (Amos 2:7b). If a creditor took a poor person's garment in pledge for a debt, he should return it by nightfall (Exod 22:25–27). The rich used such garments as ground cover to loll about at feasts "in the house of their god," drinking

---

2. Elijah, Elisha, and the prophetic guilds opposed rulers judged to be idolatrous, but they fervently supported the state and even abetted idolatrous rulers whenever they fought enemy states, but not so Amos.

3. The Hebrew is unclear—see BDB and commentaries.

wine bought with money that they had taken by means of fines imposed on the poor (Amos 2:8).

Andrew Dearman describes how both the wealthy class and the royal court used their power to demand from the smaller farmers money and various kinds of agricultural produce in the form of levies or taxes for their own enrichment. In many cases, such payments forced the farmers into debt slavery, resulting in loss of property and citizenship rights. Few if any sales of land were made voluntarily. The powerful could give a plausible legality to these transactions by means of an administrative judicial system imposed from above. It made use of military officers stationed throughout the land. In the absence of detail in the various laws of the Book of the Covenant, these royal officials could draw up documents with a stamp of approval and appearance of legality.[4] Accumulation of lands and building of larger and more luxurious houses comes in for condemnation by prophets in both nations (Isa 5:8; Amos 3:15; 5:11; Mic 2:2; 6:9–16). Amos is especially incensed at the conspicuous luxury and total indifference of the wealthy to the sufferings of the poor (Amos 4:1). He predicts that the pampered wives of the rich will be marched away to "Harmon"—perhaps hinting at the "harem" of their captors (6:4–6). Isaiah says the dowagers who love to flaunt their finery will lose all their costumes and jewelry and end up stinking, baldheaded, and draped in sackcloth with a rope for a sash (Isa 3:16–24). When the state is defeated, universal poverty will level all classes, conspicuous difference between "high" and "low" will disappear, "and YHWH alone will be exalted in that day" (Isa 2:11, 17; 5:15).

3. YHWH REJECTS THEIR CULTIC SACRIFICES

The power elite lavished their surplus wealth on ostentatious religious observances, but these prophets saw through this attempt to buy God's indulgence of a life style that weighed so cruelly on the masses of people. In his opening message to Jerusalem Isaiah reports YHWH's totally negative response: "I have had enough of burnt offerings . . . I cannot endure solemn assemblies with iniquity . . . your new moons and appointed festivals my soul hates . . . I will not listen," and he concludes with this demand: "Seek justice, rescue the oppressed, defend the orphan, plead for the widow" (Isa 1:10–17). In northern Israel Amos strikes a similar note: "I hate, I despise your festivals . . . But let justice roll down like waters, and righteousness like an ever-flowing stream" (Amos 5:21–24). Hosea calls the bull images mere human handiwork; they are not God and will become spoils of war (Hos 8:4–6; 10:5–6; 13:2). Twice Jesus referred to

---

4. Dearman, *Property Rights in the Eighth-Century Prophets*. "More was at stake than simple ownership of property. Participation in the cultic life . . . required the presentation of tithes and offerings so that the loss of house and field would be humiliating to a former owner who could no longer meet his previous sacral obligations" 40–41. See 19–25 for detailed treatment of Amos's accusations, 78–82 for the corrupt centralized judicial system, and 85–90 for the involvement of the military in the judicial system. Dearman bases his study on Hosea, Isaiah, and Micah in addition to Amos. Guatemalans of Spanish ancestry use the same fabrication of legal papers to deprive indigenous Mayan peasants of ancestral lands farmed communally.

Hosea's famous words: "For I desire steadfast love and not sacrifice" (Hos 6:6a; Matt 9:13; 12:7). Micah predicted the destruction of holy Mount Zion and its temple, that most sacred place, which, in the Deuteronomistic History, was the only place where YHWH could be sought and for the sake of which YHWH would keep covenant with David unconditionally. Micah chanted a litany of economic violence, corruption, and exploitation, committed by the rich and powerful, while the religious establishment assured them, "Surely YHWH is with us! No harm shall come upon us!" (Mic 3:9–11). To that Micah responded: " Therefore because of you / Zion shall be plowed as a field; / Jerusalem shall become a heap of ruins, / and the mountain of the house a wooded height"(Mic 3:12).

This prediction was not fulfilled at once, however, for apparently the power structure in the person of King Hezekiah took the message seriously, as we learn in the book of Jeremiah. About a century later Jeremiah faced a capital charge from priests and prophets, i.e., the religious authorities, because he too foretold the end of the temple. Jeremiah escaped death then, only because people remembered Micah's words and quoted them in his defense (Jer 26:17–19).

4. PROPHETS AND THE REJECTION OF WAR

YHWH gave the firmest possible sign of opposition to the state as such by condemning the use of military power. Nations have proven time and again that when they possess military forces and supplies, they sooner or later put them to use: "Because you have trusted in your power and in the multitude of your warriors, therefore the tumult of war shall rise against your people—" (Hos 10:13b–14a). The prophets all foresaw war as the inevitable end of unjust states. Isaiah calls on the people of YHWH to abandon quest for security by trusting in arms. The man Isaiah was active in Jerusalem in the period of Assyria's assault on Aram and Palestine, the destruction of Israel in 721-20, and the attack on Judah and Jerusalem in 701 BCE. The book of Isaiah contains material relevant to the people of YHWH through three centuries: the events of Isaiah's time, the destruction of Jerusalem in 587-6 BCE, the Babylonian exile, and the restoration of Jerusalem and its temple under the Persian Empire, down to the 400s BCE.

John D. W. Watts treats the entire book of Isaiah as a religious drama produced around 430 BCE in Jerusalem. He identifies speakers and audiences throughout. Watts supplies historical background to support his interpretations. Watts's thesis is this: Beginning with the victorious advance of the Assyrians in the reign of Ahaz in Jerusalem about 734 BCE, the people of YHWH faced a new set of circumstances that called for radically different response. "The former things" to which people were so much attached were the "glory days" under David, the highest point of national prestige. Henceforth the people of YHWH must abandon ambition for independence like other nations; they must take the role of servant people within the larger international

God For All

world, which by YHWH's permission was subject to Assyria, Babylonia, and Persia. Isaiah of Jerusalem was the first to understand the divine will for this new age, and the entire book in its final form appealed to Judahites under Persian rule to take a vital lesson from the past and adapt to it in their own time. "Yahweh's strategy assigns to the world empires the task of managing and policing the world and invites his elect, saved, and called people to be his servants in worship, witness, and mission."[5]

When Israel and Aram/Syria felt the force of Assyria's campaign toward the west, they tried by armed attack to compel Judah to join their alliance to resist. Isaiah advised King Ahaz: "Take heed, be quiet, do not fear, and do not let your heart be faint because of these two smoldering stumps of firebrands . . . Thus says the Lord YHWH: It shall not stand, and it shall not come to pass" (Isa 7:4, 7). Ahaz exceeded the prophet's counsel of non-resistance and appealed to Tiglath-pileser of Assyria for help: "I am your servant and your son," typical language of a treaty of submission (2 Kgs 16:7) The Deuteronomistic History considers Ahaz one of the worst davidic kings. It reports that he even made his son pass through fire, which would have been a desperate expedient at this time of crisis (cf. the case of Edom's king, 2 Kgs 3:26–7). In any case, Judah and the davidic dynasty survived for a century and a half, while Assyria destroyed Damascus in 733 and Israel in 721-20.[6]

As Watts says, Isaiah was the first to grasp and try to convince others of this insight into the being and power of YHWH God of Israel. Their Deity, without abandoning his own people, controlled the affairs of the nations of the world. YHWH used Assyria—"the rod of my anger"—to discipline Israel and Judah for their arrogance, ambition, and failure to execute justice (Isa 10:5–6). Isaiah 9:1–7 presupposes that northern Israel has fallen to Assyria, but it quotes the expectations of the royal party that through the zeal of YHWH of hosts (the ancient warrior God) Israel will participate in a bright new day, encouraged by a new king in the line of David (probably Hezekiah). The throne-names indicate the extent to which Jerusalem and Judah elevated their human king to near-divine status: "Wonderful Counselor, Mighty God, Everlasting Father, Prince of Peace" (9:6).[7] These hopes are consistent with 2 Sam 7:12–14 and royal psalms such as 2, 45, and 72, but they are not to be fulfilled. YHWH will deal with Assyria when its usefulness for chastisement has ended (Isa 10:12). Meanwhile, only a remnant will escape from Israel to the mighty God, i.e., the refugees who flee to Jerusalem when Samaria falls (10:20–23). YHWH assures those who dwell in Zion, "Do not be afraid of the Assyrians when they beat you with a rod," for YHWH will remove the yoke of Assyria (10:24–27). As Watts comments, "With God being the activist, Jerusalem's (and Israel's) role was a passive one. This Ahaz accepted and was

---

5. Watts, *Isaiah 1–33*, p lvi. For fuller explanation see "This Commentary's Approach to Isaiah" pp xli–lvii.

6. This summary of events is based on 2 Kgs 16:1–9, Isa 7:1–9, and extrabiblical material cited by commentators.

7. See Watts *Isaiah 1-33*, 135–6 for his interpretation of these words in their original historical context.

rewarded."[8] This evaluation of Ahaz contrasts with the negative view of 2 Kgs 16:1–20, greatly heightened and exaggerated in 2 Chron 28.

After Ahaz, Hezekiah ascended the throne in Jerusalem, and the Deuteronomistic History lauds him with high praise: "He did what was right in the sight of YHWH just as his ancestor David had done . . . He trusted in YHWH the God of Israel, so that there was no one like him among all the kings of Judah after him, or among those who were before him . . . YHWH was with him; wherever he went, he prospered. He rebelled against the king of Assyria and would not serve him" (2 Kgs 18:3, 5, 8). Isaiah had a less flattering opinion of Hezekiah. First, Isaiah condemned socioeconomic injustice by the power elite in Jerusalem, a point generally ignored by the Deuteronomistic History. Second, Hezekiah's religious zeal for YHWH was wedded to intense nationalism backed by a buildup of arms. He violated the treaty of submission to Assyria signed by Ahaz. Typically Judah, along with other small states, would turn to Egypt when plotting resistance to Assyria. A prominent theme in Isaiah is blaming the "rebellious children" who allied with Egypt without consulting YHWH (30:1–17; 31:1–3). To ally with Egypt was to make "a covenant with death" (Isa 28:15, 18), because the treaty invoked Osiris, the Egyptian god of the underworld, a stark contrast with YHWH the living God. The prophet's advice to Hezekiah was the same as to Ahaz: "In returning and rest you shall be saved; in quietness and in trust shall be your strength. But you refused and said 'No! We will flee upon horses' " (30:15–16). "The Egyptians are human, and not God; their horses are flesh, and not spirit" (31:3). In the end, the Egyptians provided no help at all.

"In the fourteenth year of King Hezekiah, King Sennacherib of Assyria came up against all the fortified cities of Judah and captured them" (2 Kgs 18:13). The Deuteronomistic History (but not Isaiah) reports that Hezekiah stripped all the treasures of the palace and temple to buy off Sennacherib, but his army laid siege to Jerusalem anyhow. The Assyrian annals state that Sennacherib captured forty-six outlying cities and their villages, plundered them, and turned them over to Philistines. He claims to have carried away 200,150 captives and to have shut up King Hezekiah in Jerusalem "like a bird in a cage."[9] Humanly speaking it was a hopeless situation. Yet Isaiah told the king "Do not be afraid" and gave him YHWH's assurance that Sennacherib would lift the siege and return home without any action by Hezekiah (Isa 37:5–7). "The angel of YHWH set out and struck down one hundred eighty-five thousand in the camp of the Assyrians," Sennacherib withdrew, returned home, and eventually his own sons assassinated him (Isa 37:36–38//2 Kgs 19:35–37). The Deuteronomistic History considers this a great victory, and the Assyrian annals affirm the escape of Jerusalem, but still Hezekiah remained a vassal of Assyria and his realm comprised only Jerusalem and a few suburbs.

---

8. Watts, *Isaiah 1-33*, 156.
9. Pritchard, *The Ancient Near East* I, 200.

God For All

The saving of Jerusalem has made an indelible impression, especially upon people already influenced by the deuteronomists' high evaluation of Hezekiah.[10] Christopher Seitz has labored to absolve Hezekiah of all blame, emphasizing his positive character in contrast to that of Ahaz, and crediting his prayers for the salvation of Jerusalem.[11] Today, Bible readers in comfort and security may rejoice in Jerusalem's providential escape and the death by pestilence of the Assyrian army, while overlooking the tragedy suffered by most of the people of Israel and Judah. I suggest a different judgment. Sennacherib had nothing more to gain by occupying Jerusalem, for he had already collected the treasures of Jerusalem and captured all the other cities of Judah and given them to the Philistines. But consider the fate of the vast majority of the Judeans who suffered the consequences of Hezekiah's stubborn resistance to Assyria. Were not these victims also people of YHWH? Hezekiah showed no concern for them. I am reminded of information coming to light several decades after the end of World War Two indicating that the general population of Tokyo was approaching a state of rebellion because Emperor Hirohito prolonged their suffering by refusing to surrender, allowing the massive fire bombing of Tokyo.[12]

This deliverance of Zion and the closing account of Hezekiah's reign, hinting at eventual defeat and exile in Babylon (told in slightly different parallel versions in Isa 36–39 and 2 Kings 18.13—20:19), became the nucleus from which the great scroll of Isaiah grew.[13] Despite Zion's destruction in 587 (which the audience of the completed Isaiah scroll well knew without being reminded), Zion's later restoration symbolized the continuing divine presence. To Jerusalem people of all nations will come on pilgrimage and from Zion YHWH will send forth his teaching (*torah*) to arbitrate among the nations and preside over a world without war (Isa 2:2–4). In Isaiah, this becomes the universal vision that motivates everything else that follows in the scroll.

A century after the fall of Israel and Samaria to Assyria, Judah and Jerusalem came under the heavy yoke of Babylon. I will confine myself to a brief account of efforts of the prophet Jeremiah, the most authentic spokesman of God during that final crisis. Jeremiah acted in the spirit of Isaiah to urge the royal house and the religious establishment to recognize the futility of trying to behave like other nations in international power politics and to concentrate on social justice rather than mere dependence on cultic sacrifice. He charged the elite with trusting in a sort of magical chant: "This is the temple of YHWH, the temple of YHWH, the temple of YHWH." They thought their sacrifices bought impunity from the just punishment they deserved for their depraved and cruel criminal acts. Speaking for YHWH Jeremiah reported, "You are turning my

---

10. E.g., Lord Byron's thrilling poem, "The Destruction of Sennacherib."
11. Seitz, *Isaiah 1–39*, 242–260.
12. Bix, "Japan's Delayed Surrender."
13. Seitz agrees: *Zion's Final Destiny*. See especially his Conclusion, "The Hezekiah-Isaiah Narratives and the Growth of the Book of Isaiah," 193–208.

The Prophets and the End of the State

house into a robber's hideout, so I'm going to destroy it as I destroyed the shrine at Shiloh" (Jer 7:1–15). The prophet barely escaped with his life at that time (Jer 26:16–19).

The Judean court was constantly plotting rebellion, but that resulted only in Babylon deposing King Jeconiah and taking him, the royal family, and most of the power elite into exile. It was a popular opinion that those taken away to Babylon were cursed, and they could no longer worship YHWH, but those left behind were blessed, for they could worship in Zion, where YHWH properly dwelt. Jeremiah saw the true situation as exactly the opposite (Jer 24).

Nebuchadnezzar of Babylon had set up hapless young Zedekiah as a puppet king, but he couldn't withstand the party of hard-core resistance. Representatives of neighboring kings came to plot against Babylon, but Jeremiah, wearing an ox-yoke, confronted them all and announced:

> Thus says YHWH of hosts, the God of Israel: This is what you shall say to your masters: It is I who by my great power and my outstretched arm have made the earth, with the people and animals that are on the earth, and I give it to whomsoever I please. Now I have given all these lands into the hand of King Nebuchadnezzar, my servant, and I have given him even the wild animals of the field to serve him . . . Any nation that will bring its neck under the yoke of the king of Babylon and serve him, I will leave on its own land" (Jer 27:1–6, 11).

Jeremiah went on to urge not only these foreign delegates but also his own king Zedekiah, and the priests and all the people to wear the yoke of Babylon and abandon all thoughts of armed resistance. Jeremiah was almost alone in rejecting the superstition going back to the "miraculous" deliverance in Hezekiah's day that YHWH would never allow Jerusalem to fall.

Another prophet, Hananiah by name, took Jeremiah's yoke and broke it, prophesying ("Thus says YHWH") that God would break the yoke of Babylon, the captives would return, and authentic cult would be resumed in the temple, but Jeremiah branded him a liar (Jer 28:1–17). Other prophets in Babylon kept the captives constantly stirred up with dissatisfaction at their lot and with hopes for a quick return home. To them Jeremiah sent a letter urging them not to listen to those prophets. The real word of YHWH was that they should expect to be there for a long time. Settle down, build homes, plant gardens, have families and multiply. "Seek the welfare [*shalom*] of the city where I have sent you into exile, and pray to YHWH on its behalf, for in its welfare you will find your welfare" (29:1–14). Peaceful co-existence is preferable to constant agitating and opposition.

Jeremiah expressed a concept of God that far surpassed that of the intensely nationalistic, parochial people of Judah, their rulers, and religious spokespersons such as the prophet Hananiah. Most of the exiles who had already been carried away to Babylon had the same opinions, but a small number of those exiles who shared Jeremiah's understanding of God were the authors of the creation story we now read in Genesis 1:1—2:4a (see above chapter 2 "The Beginnings of Monotheism."

More than once Jeremiah was accused as a traitor because he consistently opposed armed resistance. In the Hebrew and English versions of the book, chapters 46–51 contain a series of messages concerning other nations. Here Jeremiah's theme is the tragic destructiveness of war. There is nothing good about war. Nations that do not practice justice but engage in self-aggrandizing policies inevitably bring judgment upon themselves in the form of war. (For other pacifistic prophetic texts see Micah 5:1–5a, early, and Zech 9:9–10, late.)

5. THE NEW COVENANT

One of the most significant passages in the entire OT is Jeremiah's prophecy that in days to come YHWH will cut a new covenant with the house of Israel and the house of Judah (Jer 31:31–34). This brief notice is part of a collection of poetic and prose texts that have become popularly known as the "Book of Consolations" (Jer 30–33). Scholarly analysis concludes that this "book" comprises material originally addressed to northern Israel/Ephraim as well as later words addressed to Judah also. It was assembled and placed here after the destruction of 586 to bring consolation and hope. Some scholars say Jeremiah proclaimed only the poetic passages, but the deuteronomists edited or even composed the prose material.[14] Without entering this debate I point out that throughout this brief "book" the relation between YHWH and Israel does not emphasize human obligation typical of the deuteronomists but the prophetic emphasis on YHWH's initiative toward faithless people, (see chapter 17 "The Covenant as Family Relationship" above). Jeremiah uses terminology that reflects the Divine Kinsman's role of *go'el*=(next of kin, redeemer), YHWH as parent, and YHWH as spouse.

YHWH will rescue Jacob from the yoke of slavery, indeed has ransomed and redeemed him (Jer 30:7b–8; 31:11). YHWH speaks as "father" and acclaims Ephraim as "my firstborn" and "my dear son" (31:9b, 20). YHWH addresses "virgin Israel" and reminds her of the everlasting love experienced by those who escaped into the desert (31:2–3; cf. also 2:2–3). It is in this total context we consider the "new covenant": "It will not be like the covenant that I made with their ancestors when I took them by the hand to bring them out of the land of Egypt—a covenant that they broke, though I was their husband," says YHWH (31:32). The exodus was not a military victory but the groom lovingly taking the bride's hand and leading her out.

As for the new covenant, "I will put my law [=*torah* teaching] within them, and I will write it on their hearts; and I will be their God, and they shall be my people. No longer shall they teach one another, or say to each other, 'Know YHWH,' for they

---

14. Notably Nicholson, *Preaching to the Exiles*.

shall all know me, from the least of them to the greatest, says YHWH; for I will forgive their iniquity, and remember their sin no more" (31:33–34). It remains for the people of the New Covenant to interpret the significance of this promise (1 Cor 11:25; 2 Cor 3:6; Heb 8:1–13).

SUMMARY AND REFLECTION

The Deuteronomistic History offers a lengthy explanation why YHWH punished Israel by allowing them to be defeated and taken into exile by Assyria and Babylonia, but the emphasis is almost totally focused on their abandonment of YHWH to follow other gods and worship idols (2 Kgs 17:7–20). Only by reading the prophets do we get a better-balanced description of the real situation. People in both kingdoms worshipped gods other than YHWH, especially Baal and the queen of heaven, but the YHWH cult was practiced with great lavishness by the wealthy and powerful. They thought YHWH their war God would reward them for this, while they exploited the weak and poor. The prophets condemned such practices. Micah was the first to say that the temple of YHWH itself would be destroyed. Jeremiah affirmed that prophecy and witnessed its fulfillment.

By becoming like other nations, Israel lost its distinctiveness as the people of YHWH. Therefore Israel began to feel the heavy hand that YHWH had previously laid on other nations for the benefit of his people Israel. At the same time, YHWH was showing to some among other nations a compassion similar to that which hitherto had been considered to belong exclusively to Israel. In other words, as Israel blurred the distinction between people and nations, ʿam and *goyim*, from YHWH's side the distinction between *goyim* and ʿam likewise began to fade. The process of movement of the concept that God is One and that One God is for all seems to be glacially slow, but it moves—it moves!

PART FOUR

From Exile to the Time of Jesus

19

Exile: Re-imagining God and Humanity

THE BABYLONIAN CAMPAIGN AGAINST Judah dragged on excruciatingly for over a decade, bringing famine, disease, and death to uncounted thousands.[1] Babylon destroyed Jerusalem, its walls, and the temple of YHWH and major buildings and took captive the royal house and most members of the elite power structure and artisan class. Left behind were the poor and the powerless. Jeremiah chose to remain with them. They were ready to give up on YHWH, who they thought had not been able to save his people from defeat. When Jeremiah condemned their idolatry they retorted that so long as they had followed the age-old and universal practice of worshipping the Queen of Heaven, everything had been all right. Defeat came only when they stopped (in conformity with Josiah's reform movement), so they were determined to resume the old cult (Jer 44:15–19). Away in Babylon, exiles wondered how they could any longer sing the songs of Zion (Ps 137). Facing constant reminders that Marduk had conquered YHWH, other exiles were tempted to transfer allegiance to the more powerful deity. Defeat challenged the foundation of the national self-image, Israel the people of YHWH, YHWH the God of Israel. A small minority stepped into the breach to offer new ways to understand deity and deity's relations to Israel and to the other nations. (See the P creation story, Gen 1:1—2:4a)

1. EZEKIEL: YHWH'S GLORY AND JUDGMENT

Ezekiel was among the captives taken away to Babylon about 597 BCE along with King Jehoiachin (Jechoniah) several years before the final fall of Jerusalem. I have already presented Ezekiel's contribution to the concept of YHWH's covenant with Israel as marriage, divorce, and remarriage, in chapter 17.

Ezekiel's prophecy opens with a straightforward statement: "In the thirtieth year, in the fourth month, on the fifth day of the month, as I was among the exiles by the river Chebar, the heavens were opened and I saw visions of God [Elohim]" (Ezek 1:1).

---

1. The Deuteronomistic History, 2 Kings 15–22, covers the destruction of northern Israel by Assyria and southern Judah by Babylon. The book of Jeremiah contains additional information on the fall of Jerusalem and Judah, Jer 19–29, 34–44.

God For All

If Ezekiel had had any doubts whether his God was present in Babylon, this inaugural experience overwhelmed him with the reality. What he saw combined features of God seated on the cherubim and riding on the storm cloud. He was so overcome with awe that he could not adequately describe it. In the midst of a great bright cloud with continually flashing fire he saw a chariot throne. It was supported by "something like four living creatures . . . they were of human form (Heb *demuth 'adam*)." Each had four wings for freedom of movement and four faces: human, lion, ox, and eagle (four categories of living beings: humans, wild animals, domestic animals, and birds). Ezekiel's vision of the cherubim throne contains details not susceptible of exact translation. The Hebrew words for "living creature" and for "likeness" are both feminine, but in about a third of the examples where they are subjects of verbs, the verb forms are masculine. Such details have puzzled commentators. Walter Wink notes that since Ezekiel is reporting his vision of God, the mixing of masculine and feminine forms points to the understanding that the One God transcends and embraces both genders.[2] Ezekiel identifies these creatures as cherubim (10:15, 20). "Over the heads of the living creatures there was something like a dome [Heb *raqiʿa*, cf Gen 1:6–7) shining like crystal, spread out above their heads . . . and above the dome over their heads there was something like a throne . . . and seated above the likeness of a throne was something that seemed like a human form . . . Like the bow in a cloud on a rainy day, such was the appearance of the splendor all around. This was the appearance of the likeness of the glory of YHWH" (Ezek 1:22, 26, 28). The detail of the bow borrows a feature of the ubiquitous illustrations of the Assyrian god Assur in a flowing robe seated in the midst of the winged sun, holding a drawn bow in his hands, flying above the Assyrian king in his chariot to lead the way in battle against their common enemy.[3] In Ezekiel's vision the deity is YHWH, coming with drawn bow, but here the deity's earthly partner is not a heavily armed royal figure but Ezekiel, whose weapon is the word of his God, spoken in judgment against a rebellious people (2:3–7).

Ezekiel's hesitancy in telling his vision, using equivocal words and phrases—appearance like, something like, looked like, something that seemed like—shows that he felt himself incapable of doing full justice to what he saw; or perhaps it may also suggest that Ezekiel could not bring himself to come right out and say, "I saw God, who looked like a human." For Ezekiel this was an intensely personal experience, not like legends about Father Abraham whom YHWH visited as a human (Gen 18:12). The narrative continues: "When I saw it I fell on my face, and I heard the voice of someone speaking. He said to me: O mortal [Heb *ben 'adam*=son of man], stand up on your feet, and I will speak with you" (1:28b—2:1).

The Hebrew of YHWH's address to Ezekiel, *ben 'adam*, is rendered "mortal" in NRSV and NJPS, but in the familiar KJV, NIV, and most other English translations it

---

2. Wink, *The Human Being*, 29.

3. Mendenhall, *The Tenth Generation*, 32–56 has a full explication of the mythology and many illustrations.

is literally "son of man." The Hebrew expression "son of X" or "child of X" indicates a member of a class. An arrow is a son of the quiver (Job 41:28) or a child of the bow (Lam 3:13). In Ezek 3:11 YHWH commands Ezekiel to go and speak "to your people," literally "the children of your people." In the KJV we read hundreds of examples of "the children of Israel," which in modern translations is "Israelites." Thus "son of man" means simply "human" or "human one." In Ezekiel's vision "human form" applies both to the living creatures representing sentient life and to the divine Presence on the throne. Now for the first of ninety-three times in the whole book, God addresses the prophet as "son of man" or "human," and never in any other way. It does not go beyond the linguistic limits of the text to understand that God addresses Ezekiel as the son of that One in human form who encountered him in the vision. Leslie Allen says calling Ezekiel *ben ʾadam* "relates him to the supernatural beings, Master and servants, whose forms were humanlike (1:5, 26) but who by their very likeness were distinct from humanity. A chasm of essence separates Ezekiel from them and especially from the God whom the spoken words eventually reveal the speaker to be (see 2:4)."[4]

What Allen here calls "a chasm of essence" that separates humans and nature from God is a fundamental difference between monotheism and polytheism as Professor Ishida distinguished them.[5] But as I probe more deeply into the biblical text itself, and as I anticipate the Christian understanding of God's incarnation in the human Jesus, I have to adopt a more nuanced understanding of this "chasm." On the one hand we have certainly become deeply, even painfully, aware that humankind is indissolubly bound up in the bundle of life that embraces all creation—all that I referred to as "not-god." But the vision that Ezekiel saw (when considered in the total biblical context) begins to blur the lines of distinction between deity and humanity. In my view, the Christian encounter with pantheism may have provoked in us too much of a negative reaction. We should seriously try to learn what reality lies behind the pantheist's experience. At least Ezekiel suggests we might begin to think in reverse: not that *everything is God*, but that in some very real sense we dare not deny that God is in all of life, and that *God is at least human*, although obviously much more than human. Gerd Theissen says we should stop looking for "the 'missing link' between primates and human beings; . . . we ourselves could be the 'missing link' between the animal world and true humanity."[6] It is God who must show us who and what true humanity is. Wink agrees with Theissen and remarks that serious word play is involved. The One who appears in human form addresses Ezekiel as "child of the human One" (or, alternatively, "son of Adam"); "the human child is also the child of the Divine Human. 'Child of' thus stresses the intimacy of their relationship."[7] We see, as the biblical

---

4. Allen, *Ezekiel 1-19*.

5. See above chapter 2.1 "Two worldviews."

6. Theissen, *Biblical Faith*, 47.

7. Wink, *The Human Being*, 32. See his whole treatment of Ezekiel's vision, pp 25–34. Wink brings out various possibilities that become clear only as we take up other OT texts and the NT story of Jesus.

story unfolds, that gradually God withdraws from the scene and turns more and more responsibility over to humankind, God's image, God's co-regent to rule the world.[8]

The God whom Ezekiel introduces as having appeared as "something that seemed like a human form" and who addressed him as "child" certainly displayed some less than pleasant human-like characteristics. Twenty-eight times Ezekiel mentions YHWH's wrath, but mercy only once: "Now I will restore the fortunes of Jacob, and have mercy on the whole house of Israel; and I will be jealous for my holy name" (39:25). God's concern for "my holy name" occurs nine times, and it is that more than anything else that motivates YHWH to refrain from annihilating his people and risking a bad reputation among the nations. A similar spirit inhabits Ezekiel's statement of YHWH's declaration that he will remember the covenant, even though Israel repeatedly broke it. (The special covenant term *chesed*=steadfast love does not appear in Ezekiel.) "I will establish my covenant with you, and you shall know that I am YHWH, in order that you may remember and be confounded, and never open your mouth again because of your shame, when I forgive you all that you have done, says the Lord YHWH" (16:59–63). This final conclusion implicitly acknowledges that all the punishment YHWH in wrath inflicted upon Israel had no reformative effect. Only the final, gratuitous restoration of the apostate nation would make them conscious of their failures and grateful for divine mercy.

2. THE PROPHET OF THE EXILE: RE-IMAGINING SERVANTHOOD

Scholars and commentators unanimously agree that beginning with Isaiah 40 the scroll suddenly leaps from the time of King Hezekiah in Jerusalem about 685 BCE to well over a century later, concerning conditions during and after the exile. Isaiah 39 ends with Hezekiah's foolhardy reception of envoys from Babylon's King Merodachbaladan and Isaiah's rebuke and forecast that the royal house, persons, and property will eventually become booty for Babylon. Immediately Isaiah introduces a strangely new, heart-lifting message (in the beloved text used in Handel's *Messiah*): "Comfort ye, comfort ye my people, saith your God. Speak ye comfortably to Jerusalem, and cry unto her, that her warfare is accomplished, that her iniquity is pardoned" (Isa 40:1–2).

John D. W. Watts imagines this word issuing from the heavenly court addressed to someone(s) among the Babylonian exiles, instructions to preach good news to the miserable survivors in the old homeland. Watts identifies this abrupt change of tone as introducing a new era in the relationship among YHWH, Israel, and the nations. (1) YHWH's role as Creator and Sovereign of all is the principal theme; (2) but Israel's part is to witness to YHWH's power and grace among the nations; (3) while the rulers of empires become YHWH's agents to carry forward the divine purpose on the political level.[9]

---

8. See below chapter 19.3a "Humankind, the image of Elohim" and chapter 35 "Humanity in God's Plan—1."

9. Watts, *Isaiah 1-33*, "Yahweh's Strategy," lv–lvi.

2a. Israel, servant people

No longer a kingdom like other nations constantly entangled in warfare and international intrigue, Israel in dispersion is still "my servant" (Isa 41:8–9) to witness to the One living God. But first YHWH must rouse a downcast people that feel forsaken by the God they thought could not protect them from the armies and the gods of Babylonia. They think God abandoned them: "My way is hidden from YHWH, and my right is disregarded by my God," they complain (Isa 40:27), but YHWH claims total responsibility for all creation and for all the nations. YHWH is leading the way back to Jerusalem, and he will give strength even to the faint and powerless (40:28–31).

Babylon is tottering on the brink of collapse from internal weakness and dissatisfaction with King Nabonidus.[10] Cyrus the Mede has emerged from his eastern base and, bypassing Babylon, has won easy victories in the west. Everybody wonders when Cyrus may turn on Babylon. This uncertainty plays into the hands of religious hucksters, prompting people to seek out soothsayers and diviners, and those who can afford it to make new and better idols. Some of YHWH's own people were not immune from idolatry. Such is the background of the speeches against idols in Isa 40:19–20; 41:6–7, 21–24; 42:17; 44:9–20.

Israel as such has few if any qualifications as witness. They are still deaf and blind, so YHWH had given them over to the spoiler and poured out wrath on them in war, but they did not understand (42:18–25). "But now thus says YHWH, he who created you, O Jacob, he who formed you, O Israel: Do not fear, for I have redeemed you; I have called you by name, you are mine" (43:1). As always, punishment failed to reform, so YHWH changed tactic to mercy and grace, promising deliverance even when they pass through fire and water. "Do not fear, for I am with you" (43:2–7). YHWH calls these blind and deaf people to witness that he is God, the One who alone foretells events before they occur, the only Savior. He will send to Babylon, break down the gates and walls, and lead his people through the desert (43:8–21). Again, after further encouragement YHWH insists: "Remember these things, O Jacob, and Israel, for you are my servant; I formed you, you are my servant; O Israel, you will not be forgotten by me. I have swept away your transgressions like a cloud, and your sins like mist; return to me, for I have redeemed you" (44:21–22). Redemption and forgiveness from YHWH come first; grateful response from Israel follows, and all nature, from heaven to depths of earth, mountains and forests, rejoices together (44:23).

Continuing this theme of reassurance YHWH proceeds to name Cyrus, "He is my shepherd, and he shall carry out all my purpose" to rebuild Jerusalem and the temple. YHWH calls Cyrus "my anointed" and promises him success "for the sake of my servant Jacob and Israel my chosen" (44:28—45:7, see below). However, Israel is stuck in the past, clinging to "the former things." Israel cannot imagine that this foreigner will restore what David had once accomplished. Thus in 45:9–19 YHWH

---

10. For this information see Watts, *Isaiah 34–66* "Historical Background" 73–75.

upbraids those who would question him about his plans and his agents. Stubborn adherence to what is past and refusal to accept YHWH's new thing are forms of idolatry.

2b. Cyrus, servant emperor

YHWH now exercises sovereignty over the affairs of nations by means of empire. Before the fall of Jerusalem YHWH had already assigned full authority to "King Nebuchadnezzar of Babylon, *my servant*" (Jer 27:5–7). Now YHWH has chosen *another servant*, Cyrus, the rising star who gained control over Media, then Persia, and was on the way toward overpowering Babylon. YHWH first introduces Cyrus *without naming him*: "Who has roused a victor from the east, summoned him to his service? He delivers up nations to him—" (Isa 41:2). This introduces a polemic against idols and an appeal to Israel not to fall into fear like others but to trust YHWH. "You are my servant, I have chosen you . . . do not fear" (41:9–10). YHWH again refers to Cyrus, still unnamed: "I stirred up one from the north, and he has come—" (41:25). These events threw people everywhere into a dither and drove them to seek guidance from their idol gods and even to bring their images for safety within Babylon. YHWH declares that it is he alone who announces the decree (41:26–29). The divine speech describes more specifically this one from the north: "Here is my servant, whom I uphold, my chosen, in whom my soul delights."[11] He will not make a display of arrogant power but will accomplish his purposes by patient endurance. He will establish treaties in justice, bring enlightenment, and set prisoners free (42:1–7). YHWH calls Cyrus by name and identifies him as "my shepherd" and "my anointed" both eminent titles traditionally applied to Israel's rulers (44:28—45.1). By means of Cyrus YHWH will accomplish his purposes "He shall build my city and set my exiles free" (45:13).

In actual fact, Babylon fell to Cyrus practically without resistance, and he symbolically took the hand of Marduk, to demonstrate that he was the new protector of the chief god of Babylon and that he had now received sovereignty over the realm. In the Isaiah drama YHWH asserts that it was he who had made possible Cyrus's easy victory, and promises him also Egypt, Ethiopia, and the Sabeans, who will acknowledge that YHWH truly is with Cyrus alone (45:14). YHWH, creator and regulator of heaven and earth, invites all those shamed by their idols to accept the new order he will bring through Cyrus: "Turn to me and be saved, all the ends of the earth! For I am God, and there is no other. By myself I have sworn, from my mouth has gone forth in righteousness a word that shall not return: To me every knee shall bow, every tongue shall swear" (45:22–23). In the Isaiah drama, YHWH announces this universal purpose to be accomplished through his servant/agent Cyrus. At this point, Cyrus will

---

11. Centuries of time difference and of Jewish and Christian interpretation have obscured the meaning of "servant" in this original context. Even more than Nebuchadnezzar (Jer 27:5–7), rulers of Persia are YHWH's servants, first Cyrus, who also is called "my shepherd" and YHWH's "anointed", but also Darius and Artaxerxes are true servants to fulfill YHWH's purpose. See Watts, *Isaiah 34-60*, 117.

wield political and economic authority from which all who submit to him will benefit. The spiritual blessings YHWH will offer through servant Israel are to be explained later in Isaiah 55 and 66.[12]

Kings of Assyria and Babylonia demoted gods of conquered nations to minor deities in their national pantheons. By contrast, Cyrus recognized all local deities as manifestations of his god Ahura Mazda, God of Heaven. Cyrus subsidized other gods' cults, demanding only that people pray for him and his imperial house. Cyrus was, in fact, one of the most enlightened leaders of ancient times. He reversed the cruel, divisive, and oppressive policies of Assyria and Babylonia, permitted deportees to return home, and allowed subject nations a high degree of local autonomy.[13] Ezra 1:1–4 records a version of Cyrus' decree that encouraged any of YHWH's people who desired to do so to go back to Jerusalem "and rebuild the house of YHWH, the God of Israel—he is the God who is in Jerusalem" (Ezra 1:1–4; cf 2 Chron 36:22–23). The community of returned exiles lived in relative tranquility and security under Persian rule. The royal court heavily subsidized both the construction of the Second Temple and its daily upkeep, exempting the priests and other temple staff from taxation (Ezra 6.3–6; 7:11–26). Cyrus merited the title of servant of YHWH and of YHWH's people.

2c. YHWH, servant Deity

Since Israel has ceased to be like other nations she now reverts to the premonarchic condition in which YHWH was her *melekh*=king. Without mentioning "king" the herald gives orders to "prepare the way of YHWH" as people prepare for any king's visit—smoothing the road, shaving off the bumps, and filling in the potholes (40:3–4).[14] In Isaiah 40–66 "king" occurs only three times, all referring to YHWH, emphasizing supernatural characteristics.[15] YHWH King of Jacob challenges the so-called gods of the nations to prove themselves, concluding, "you are nothing!" (41:21–24). YHWH promises deliverance from Babylon, with the self-identity, "I am YHWH, your Holy One, the Creator of Israel, your King" (43:15). This deliverance will surpass "the things of old" i.e. the exodus (43:16–20). Finally, a self-identification: "Thus says YHWH, the King of Israel, and his Redeemer, YHWH of hosts: I am the first and I am the last, besides me there is no god" (44:6–8).

---

12. See Watts, *Isaiah 34-66*, 158–163, for translation and explanation of Isa 45:14–25.

13. See Young, "Cyrus (Person)," *ABD*, "Such a policy of remarkable tolerance based on a respect for individual people, ethnic groups, other religions, and ancient kingdoms must have seemed amazing to people who had grown accustomed to the governing techniques of the Neo-Assyrian and Neo-Babylonian empires, in which ruthless destruction, the deportation of people, and the forced integration of the conquered into the conqueror's political system had been common practice."

14. When I lived in the provincial town of Marugame, Japan, in 1951 I saw work gangs (including many women) out repairing the streets and prettifying the place in preparation for a visit from Emperor Hirohito.

15. The meaning of the Heb for king in 57:9 is disputed. It is not YHWH.

God For All

All but one of these descriptions of King emphasize some transcendent quality—judge of deities, Holy One, Creator, YHWH of hosts, first and last, Only—ringing the changes on themes of power and sovereignty. But with Redeemer we return to the earthy level, that of Deity's self-abasement to enter as Divine Kinsman into covenant with humans. In that role YHWH fulfills the obligation of *goʾel*, the next of kin, to rescue family members from captivity, debt, or servitude.[16] To ransom his people and to pay for Israel's being freed from captivity, YHWH their Redeemer will give Egypt, Ethiopia, and Seba to Cyrus. "Because you are precious in my sight, and honored, and I love you, I give people in return for you, nations in exchange for your life" (43:3–4). In a similar vein, but with a deep touch of tenderness, the herald who first speaks says, "He will feed his flock like a shepherd; he will gather the lambs in his arms, and carry (Heb *nasaʾ*) them in his bosom, and gently lead the mother sheep" (40:11).

The word "he will *carry*" in this text leads to a complex of terms that Isaiah uses to contrast Israel's God with the two chief gods of Babylon, Marduk (called Bel=Baal) and Nebo his son. The prophet scoffs: "Bel bows down, Nebo stoops, their idols are on beasts and cattle; these things you *carry* are loaded as *burdens* on weary animals. They stoop, they bow down together; they cannot save the *burden*, but themselves go into captivity" (46:1–2). On festival days, beasts of burden or even human laborers have to *carry* these idol-gods, so carefully *made* and richly bejeweled. The porters have to *carry* them to safety in war, for the idols can't *save* themselves. Contrast the description of YHWH: "Listen to me, O house of Jacob, all the remnant of the house of Israel who have been *borne* by me from your birth, *carried* from the womb; even to your old age I am he, even when you turn gray I will *carry* you. I have *made*, and I will *bear*; I will *carry* and will *save*" (Isa 46:3–4) Israel's God does for his people exactly what Babylon's people have to do for their gods! The true Sovereign of the universe, the creator of all things, the King of Israel, condescends to fill to perfection this role of servant, "for the sake of my servant Jacob, and Israel my chosen" (45:4) to bear, to carry, and to save.

In this portion of Isaiah we find a very high concept of the uniqueness of Israel's God—"Besides me there is no other"—repeatedly argued by the Deity in person, as though protesting against doubt or denial. At 40:18 someone asks: "To whom then will you liken (*damah*) God, or what likeness (*demuth*) compare with him?" YHWH himself asks a similar question at 40:25 and 46:5, all three in the context of demonstrating the futility of idols. Seeing an idol, nobody would instinctively think of YHWH. Many credit the author of Isaiah with true monotheism, but I question that. In Isaiah YHWH is still the particular God of Israel, even though also the Creator of the ends of the earth and the Lord of all nations. From the very beginning Israel has been blind and deaf, a traitor and a rebel (48:8), but YHWH has protected, led, saved, carried, and will preserve Israel, but only for YHWH's own sake, that his Name not be

---

16. In Is 40–55 forms of the root *gʾl*=redeem occur twenty-four times, all referring to YHWH.

profaned (Isa 48:9–11; see Ezek 20.44). When all is said and done, the final editor of the Isaiah vision makes YHWH, in effect, the servant of Israel, favoring Israel above all others. YHWH God of Israel and Israel people of YHWH still implies exclusiveness and discrimination among humankind that are not compatible with universalism.

3. THE UNIVERSAL ELOHIM

At this point it is appropriate to revert to the creation story in Genesis 1:1—2:4a, the sublime account of the creative work of the universal God.[17] Judean priests in exile in Babylon composed that creation story. They must have been daily provoked by the sight of numerous idols of gods and goddesses and disgusted by acts of superstition and ignorance. Further, they would have experienced the contempt of those who exalted Marduk, the chief god of Babylon, the conqueror of the gods of all the minor states, including YHWH of Israel. Provocation, disgust, and anger may have driven them to more fervent devotion to their God and inspired the writing that modern scholars have designated the P material. I am convinced that the author(s) of P were zealous partisans of YHWH-only faith. They were self-confident in the sense of chosenness that ran through the story of their people from Abraham and Sarah down to their own time and place in captivity. They reflected that mature faith in what they wrote. But when they began their story they introduced the Creator not as Israel's God YHWH but simply as Elohim=God, that is God in the generic or universal sense of the term.[18] It is in that sense that I interpreted God earlier in this work, and how I want to emphasize it in what follows.

3a. Humankind, the image of Elohim[19]

Next to the concept of the universal God in the creation account, the concept of humankind is most important. "Then God said, Let us make humankind in our image (*tselem*), according to our likeness (*demuth*)—" (Gen 1:26). These two words describe humans' similarity to Elohim. About the first man Adam we read "he became the father of a son in his likeness (*demuth*), according to his image (*tselem*) and named him Seth" (Gen 5:3 P).[20] There could be no doubt that the son was of the same human nature as the father. While it would be a mistake to say that the similarity between Deity and humanity is the same as that between Adam and Seth, on biblical evidence

---

17. See above chapter 2 "The Beginnings of Monotheism."

18. Some modern scholars explain this by noting that in the total scheme of the Priestly history, they did not know the special name YHWH before the revelation to Moses in Egypt (Exod 6:2–3).

19. See below chapter 35.1 "Humanity, the image of God."

20. Both *tselem* and *demuth* of God appear in 1:26 and apply equally to humanity, although only *tselem* = image appears in 1:27 and only *demuth* = likeness in 5:1. Seth's similarity to his father Adam is expressed by both likeness and image in 5:3.

God For All

we must acknowledge that there is a similarity between God and humans that distinguishes humans from other creatures. Humankind belongs to the created order, yet in some way partakes of the divine.

Tselem basically means a carved figure to represent something or someone. The Philistines suffered plagues of boils and mice, which they attributed to the power of YHWH, whose ark they had captured. They made images of gold, presumably full-scale models of boils and mice, and sent them back to Israel as an offering with the ark (1 Sam 6:5, 11). During a religious reformation, Israelites broke in pieces the images of Baal (2 Kgs 11:18). Depending on the skill of the artisans who made the images of mice and of Baal, people seeing them would have no doubt what they represented. The king of an empire could not be physically present everywhere in his realm, so he would set up images of himself at strategic places to represent his authority. The image of the king stamped on coins indicated the royal authority over the monetary system. Similarly a god's image represented the god. Wildberger writes: "One may determine, then, that the origins of the concept of humanity's divine image [*tselem*] are associated with ancient Near Eastern concepts of the king as the son, the representative, viceroy, proxy of God on earth."[21]

Genesis P negates elitist concepts and applies the divine image and likeness to male-and-female humankind to serve as God's representative to rule over the other living beings. Joel Green writes: "[T]he creation account imbues humanity with royal identity and task, but this is a nobility granted without conquest; its essence is realized in coexistence with all of life in the land, and in the cultivation of life."[22] In the final editing of the Pentateuch, this P description of humankind is placed before J, the older Yahwist account. The Yahwist also had negated royalty's claims to superiority in the order of creation and assigned it instead simply to a peasant-like man and his woman, to the earth creature, male and female, flesh of the same flesh and bone of the same bone (Gen 2:15–24).[23] Members of a tiny minority of Judean exiles, victims of empire and almost overwhelmed by imperial claims to divinity and divine authority, dared confess their faith in the one supreme Elohim who transcended all such authorities and in whose sight all humankind stood on the same level.

Ancient people made idols that were helplessly immobile and therefore were the likeness(=*demuth*) of no-gods, but no human can *liken* YHWH to the *likeness* of an idol (Isa 40:18). People do not see YHWH when they see an idol. In Genesis the P author states that Elohim by creation made humankind, male and female, the authentic representative *image* and *likeness* of God. Therefore when we see a human, any human—man, woman, or child—we ought to think of God. When Ezekiel saw in a vision something that looked like the appearance of a human *form* [Heb *demuth*] he thought he saw God. Or perhaps it was the opposite: when Ezekiel had a vision of

21. *TLOT* Vol 3, 1083.
22. Green, *Body, Soul, and Human Life*, 62.
23. See above chapter 4.3 "Out of the garden into the real world."

God, he thought he saw a human. There is something mysteriously human-like about God, and something mysteriously god-like about a human. In the Genesis context human god-likeness consists more in function than in essence. As Brueggemann writes: "The image images the creative use of power which invites, evokes, and permits. There is nothing here of coercive or tyrannical power, either for God or for humankind."[24]

Gen 9:5–6 points to another aspect of humans' God-likeness: the high value of human life. The P account asserts the supreme sacredness of human life precisely because it is made in the image of God. Murder is the greatest of all crimes; it is fratricide, killing a brother or sister. Elohim declares: "At the hand of every man's brother will I require the life of man . . . for in the image of God made he man" (Gen 9:5b, 6b KJV).[25] The post-exilic priestly author, speaking for Elohim and describing pre-abrahamic conditions, declares the universal family relationship of all people as bearers of the divine image, and thus all human life is sacrosanct. In my view this is the governing principle for us today. A brief balanced couplet has been inserted at 9:6a, which interrupts and appears to weaken this principle: "Whoso sheds the blood of man, by man shall his blood be shed" (9:6a KJV). Advocates of the death penalty glibly quote this verse to claim biblical authority to oppose abolition of the death penalty. If we take Scripture seriously, we have to ask ourselves: What human being, finally, has the authority to shed the blood of another human being, even the blood of a murderer, since the murderer too is created in God's image? Further, we have to make the concept of the image of God the greater context in which we relate to fellow human beings who don't fit our generally accepted norms such as ethnicity or skin color, or who show evidence of perceived abnormalities, such as Down syndrome, cerebral palsy, different sexual orientations, etc.

3b. Elohim's universal covenant

In the course of this study I have traced the concept of covenant (Heb *berit*) between God and humankind. It began at the simplest personal level when the Deity condescended to relate to Israel's ancestor Abram as the Divine Kinsman. Deity pledged loyalty, or steadfast love (Heb *chesed*) to fulfill the obligation to contribute everything possible for the well being of the other members of the family. This basic concept persisted, no matter how population growth and socio-political circumstances changed over the centuries, or how different interpreters might understand the symbolism of covenant. After revelation of the special Name YHWH, covenant might consist of a set of rules governing worship of YHWH and communal life of a tribal population (the Decalogue and the Book of the Covenant); or later it might signify a much more

---

24. Brueggemann, *Genesis*, 32. See also von Rad, *Genesis*, 56.
25. The Heb text includes the word "brother" which is obscured by NRSV translation, "each one for the blood of another. NIV also obscures "brother" by translating: "I will demand an accounting for the life of his fellow man."

comprehensive set of laws (e.g., in Deuteronomy) similar to the treaty between an emperor (e.g., of Assyria) and subordinate client kings. Covenant might suggest the relationship of husband and wife, involving courtship, marriage, divorce, and reconciliation. In all of this, two points remain constant: the human partner persistently violates the covenant obligations, but the Divine Kinsman always maintains steadfast love. Even when the human partner's infidelity leads to the tragedy of defeat and captivity, the Divine Kinsman takes the role of *go'el*, the next of kin making any necessary sacrifice to redeem the lost family member.

In my view, all of the above is reflected in the priestly account of the Flood. Elohim announces to Noah a flood of universal proportions: "Everything that is on the earth shall die. But I will establish my covenant with you" (Gen 6:17b–18a). Although this is the very first mention of covenant=*berit* in the entire Bible, the writer tosses in the term as though it were the most familiar thing possible (which, of course, it was to him!). When the flood was dried up, Elohim established "my covenant" (foretold at 6:18) never again to destroy the earth with a flood. Elohim made the covenant not only with Noah and his descendants but also with every living creature and with the earth itself (9:8–13). In contrast to the bow drawn for war by Assur, and by YHWH in Ezekiel's vision, Elohim has now unstrung the bow and hangs it upside down in the heaven as a sign of peace (9:12–17). In P's account the sovereign Elohim acts altogether unilaterally to establish this rainbow covenant unconditionally with all flesh and with the earth. Elohim sees the bow; Elohim remembers.

As other material intrudes into the story it may obscure this universal theme, which, temporally speaking, is the climax of a previous history. In the biblical documents what appears to contradict the universal partakes of the earlier preparatory events leading toward the universal. Even P itself falls into ethnocentric discrimination in describing the covenant sign of circumcision that Elohim establishes with Abraham at Gen 17, narrowing the covenant concept of Gen 15. Although Abraham and Sarah's calling will result in blessings for many nations and peoples, their lineal descendants will still be superior. Genesis 1 and Second Isaiah lift the concept of the oneness of God to a level not previously attained; yet they never achieve universal monotheism.

SUMMARY

In my view, the development of the concept of the oneness of God in the OT has reached a practical zenith at this time. In the life of the people of YHWH after the exile, the construction of the Second Temple, and solidifying of priestly authority under the patronage of the Persian Empire, the concept of the divine purpose of reconciliation for all suffered a period of stagnation and even decline, to which I shall turn next.

20

Return, Rebuild, Retrench

A QUICK REVIEW OF post-exilic biblical history makes it clear that without a sovereign political state, the people of God had a comparatively peaceful existence for several centuries. Under the patronage of Persian King Cyrus and his successors, a minority of Jews returned to the Province of Judea (Heb *Yehud*) in 539-8 BCE. The Persian court kept authority to appoint the High Priest and the governor, but granted the Jews a degree of self-governance and religious freedom. Without going into great detail, my concern here is to consider such aspects as relate to the question of growth of the concept of the oneness of God and of God's concern for all humanity. In the postexilic period one may note certain circumstances that advance this thesis, yet in my view there were notable steps backward.

1. TEMPLE AND PRIESTHOOD RESTORED UNDER PERSIAN RULE

King Cyrus of Persia introduced a new and enlightened religious policy. Rather than degrading the gods of conquered peoples to minor rank in the empire's pantheon, Cyrus recognized them all as local manifestations of his one supreme God of Heaven, Ahura Mazda. Cyrus made support of major temples everywhere in his realm a key policy to win the loyalty of adherents of the respective cults. Cyrus believed that loyalty of the peoples based on their contentment concerning his religious tolerance was more dependable than that of the local political leaders. In 538 BCE, the first year of his reign in Babylon, Cyrus gave permission for all those who wished to do so to return to Jerusalem and rebuild the temple (2 Chron 36:22-23; Ezra 1:2-4). We get the impression that a group gathered at once and went to Jerusalem (Ezra 1:5-11). Trusting in Cyrus's decree they set up an altar and resumed sacrifice according to Mosaic law at the ruins of the First Temple, collected an offering, and began to assemble building materials (Ezra 3:1-13).

The Bible gives little detail, but the reconstruction was delayed for a while. Some Jews seemed content without a temple. Other residents, including some who had lived in and around Samaria continuously, offered to help but were rebuffed, and reacted by

God For All

opposing the project.[1] When Cyrus died his successor Cambyses reigned only eight years, principally occupied with pacifying Egypt. Cambyses's death set off a violent contest for the succession, and Darius had to fight a bitter war to consolidate his claim to the throne. This interlude of uncertainty seems to have encouraged some Jews to hope the time had come to re-establish the kingdom of David.[2]

In the second year of Darius (520 BCE), the prophet Haggai mobilized enough returnees, the governor Zerubbabel (a grandson of King Jehoiachin), and the priest Joshua (also called Jeshua, a descendant of Zadok), to start the work again (Hag 1:1–15). The result appeared rather paltry compared to the first temple, but Haggai proclaimed YHWH's promise: "In a little while . . . I will shake all nations, so that the treasure of all nations shall come, and I will fill this house with splendor" (Hag 2:1–9). In conclusion, the prophet gave the governor a message from YHWH predicting Zerubbabel's personal role in the new era: "I am about to shake the heavens and the earth, and to overthrow the throne of kingdoms . . . On that day I will take you, O Zerubbabel my servant, son of Shealtiel, says YHWH, and make you like a signet ring; for I have chosen you, says YHWH of hosts" (Hag 2:21–23; see Jer 22:24 referring to the king as YHWH's signet).

This promise *implies* a royal establishment with Zerubbabel, a descendant of David, destined for a kingly role. The contemporary prophet Zechariah urged Jews still in Babylon to hurry back to participate in the coming prosperity (Zech 2:6–13). He gave YHWH's word that Zerubbabel would finish building the temple and overcome all obstacles, "not by might nor by power, but by my spirit, says YHWH of hosts" (Zech 4:6–10). The prophet also *hints* at a messianic role for Zerubbabel in the near future, as "my servant the Branch" (3:8; 6:12).[3] He proposes to prepare crowns of gold for both Zerubbabel and Joshua the priest (Zech 6:9–13). The present text of Zechariah is tantalizingly ambiguous, suggesting that originally Zerubbabel had been designated specifically for royal office, but that since no such result occurred and Zerubbabel disappears completely from the biblical record, a later editor must have removed Zerubbabel's name from some of the texts. Darius eventually put down all his opponents, solidified his control of power, and had a lengthy and successful reign. The Jews' hopes for a rebirth came to nothing like those of other nations. Darius ordered complete subsidy to rebuild the temple (Ezra 6:1–22), and the Jews remained a religious community centered on the Second Temple in Jerusalem, but dependent upon the Persians.

Watts, in his commentary on Isaiah, introduces extrabiblical information concerning international affairs at the time of the accession of Darius and the difficulties the Jews faced in restoring the temple. Watts suggests that local opponents of the Jews

---

1. They claimed to have been "sacrificing to him" ever since the king of Assyria brought them there (Ezra 4:2). Biblical sources take a negative attitude toward Samaritans (see 2 Kings 17:24–41).
2. Bright, *A History of Israel*, 351–55.
3. "Branch" is a messianic title from earlier prophecies of restoration (Jer 23:5; 33:15).

may have brought about Zerubbabel's death during the controversies hinted at in Ezra 4:2-4 and 5:1-17. But Darius later acknowledged that killing Zerubbabel was an act of injustice, and in the end it worked out to the advantage of the Jews. In such a case, Zerubbabel may be the real-life person behind the portrait of the Martyred Servant of Isa 53, whose sacrificial death brought about benefits for his people.[4] Whatever the circumstances of the fate of Zerubbabel, in reality for the people of YHWH, Israel never again existed like other nations with a throne occupied by a descendant of David.

Darius appointed Ezra, a Jewish priest with Aaronite genealogy and scholarly reputation, to be teacher and enforcer of "the law of your God" among those who lived in Judah and Jerusalem (Ezra 7:14, 26). The result of this imperial policy was a "democratization" of the Torah, which had hitherto been the special possession of the priests.[5] Artaxerxes I (465-424), following the policy set by Cyrus and Darius, decreed almost unlimited subsidy not only for the temple and its staff but also for Jerusalem (Ezra 7:11-26). During Artaxerxes's lengthy reign, Jerusalem enjoyed greater peace and prosperity than anyone could remember. All this forms the background of Isaiah 60, which (with a strong tinge of idealism) describes the extent to which Jerusalem prospered from extensive commercial trade encouraged and protected by the empire.[6] Jerusalem was not the only city whose temple enjoyed such royal support and special privilege, but Scripture speaks only of YHWH's favor to the Jews begun by Cyrus and abundantly fulfilled by Darius and Artaxerxes. Please note that the Jewish community, no longer a nation state, was spared the overwhelming burden of supporting a royal military establishment and suffering almost endless warfare.

The Second Temple, after its dedication in 515 BCE, continued to be the most authoritative center for Judaism in the postexilic period. Richard Nelson writes: "The ... restoration of the temple and ritual system demanded a sweeping redesign of the shattered priesthood" that "entailed a good deal of jockeying for power by competing priestly groups," the final settlement of which was a compromise.[7] The compromise was a hierarchical structure in which different parties occupied their places in the cultic service of YHWH. The word for this service is based on the Hebrew root *sh-r-t*, which "indicates an inferior's attendance upon a superior."[8] It may be translated by "to serve" or "to minister to" the superior. It was YHWH to whom the priests ministered and rendered service, but they occupied distinct ranks. The High Priest (descended from Aaron through Zadok) occupied the top rank,

---

4. Watts, *Isaiah 34-66*, "Zerubbabel" 201-203; "The Sufferer/Martyr of 50:4-9 and Chapter 53" 227-29.

5. Bickerman, *From Ezra to the Last of the Maccabees*, 18. He says the law of their God was imposed "by the decree of their pagan sovereign."

6. Watts, *Isaiah 34-66*, 288-98.

7. Nelson, *Raising Up a Faithful Priest*, 7. For a brief account of the complexities of priesthood see Nelson 1-15, and for a more detailed treatment see Rehm, "Levites and Priests" in *ABD*

8. *TLOT* III 1406.

and in postexilic times he was anointed, as had been the kings during the monarchy. The other priests ministered to the High Priest, and the Levites (who during the monarchy had been priests at some of the rural temples, or high places) ministered to the priests. Lesser ministers were singers, gatekeepers, and other minor functionaries. The Septuagint (LXX) translates *sh-r-t* using the Greek word *leitourgein*, which originally described public works rendered to the state by wealthy citizens at their own expense. There is no exact equivalent in either the OT or the NT, in both of which *leitourgein* is applied exclusively to service to God.

In the absence of a royal davidic restoration, the High Priest became the most authoritative person representing the Jews before the Persian power. The priesthood became a tool of the Persian and later Greek rulers to maintain imperial status quo, since the emperor controlled the right to appoint the high priest as well as the governor. Eventually candidates for high priest paid big bribes to gain the privilege, and the common people, who had to bear the weight of tax and tribute, began to view the priestly power structure as well as the imperial rulers as enemies and oppressors.

In the sixth and fifth centuries BCE during the Persian period, a contingent of Jewish mercenary soldiers and their families had a fairly stable settlement at Elephantine in Egypt (near the first Nile cataract at Aswan), including a temple dedicated to YHW, also called God of Heaven, to whom they offered sacrifices. Textual evidence includes a number of personal names with the god-bearing element –*yahu*. There were also names of other deities originally connected with Palestine, such as Anath, Anath-bethel, and even Anath-yahu.[9] That temple was destroyed, apparently due to spite or plots of Egyptian priests, and local Jews petitioned for permission to rebuild it, to both the Persian and Jerusalem authorities. After considerable correspondence, Jerusalem permitted the rebuilding, but forbade any blood sacrifices.[10] Despite our ignorance of all the details, it's obvious that these Jews, far distant from their homeland and challenged by alien cultures and religions, sought a sense of identity and security in their own religious traditions.

During the Second Temple era, the ethnocentric exclusivism of the Jews began to intensify. Zerubbabel and heads of families returning from Babylon had repulsed locals who wanted to help build the temple (Ezra 4:1–3), and when the priest/scribe Ezra came later he more stringently enforced a policy of exclusion. As an expert in the law of Moses, Ezra may have based his policy on Deut 23:1–6 that excludes a man whose genitals are injured or missing, illegitimate children, and foreigners such as Moabites and Ammonites. Ezra found that many of the leaders, including even priests and Levites, had married foreign women. He persuaded all such persons to divorce their foreign wives and send them and their children away (Ezra 9–10). One has to assume that they were willing to do that only because they already had Jewish wives and children.

9. Miller, *The Religion of Ancient Israel*, 61–62.
10. Bickerman, op. cit., 39–40.

Within the whole community of the returned, there were some who had a more open and generous attitude. In the scroll of Isaiah YHWH positively welcomes persons who might otherwise be excluded, specifically naming eunuchs (who may represent all physically handicapped persons) and foreigners. Such persons who "maintain justice and do what is right . . . who keep the sabbath . . . and refrain from doing any evil . . . and hold fast my covenant" can come in and be ministers and servants of YHWH. "For my house shall be called a house of prayer for all peoples.[11] Thus says the Lord YHWH, who gathers the outcasts of Israel, I will gather others to them besides those already gathered" (Isa 56:1–8). Zechariah also envisioned "many nations" joining themselves to YHWH and becoming his people (Zech 2:11).

2. YHWH'S PARTIALITY TOWARD ISRAEL

In my rationalistic description of monotheism I have emphasized the basic equality of all that is "not-God" in the presence of the One and only God. Yet in the course of tracing the growth of the conception of the divine oneness, one can't escape the prominence of the scriptural emphasis that the line of the Hebrews/Israelites/Jews enjoys a special status of divine favor.

In the messages of the prophet of the exile, "Second Isaiah," we note texts that more specifically than any others seem to assert monotheism: "I, YHWH, am first, and will be with the last" (41:4b). YHWH totally dismisses all other so-called gods: "You, indeed, are nothing and your work is nothing at all; whoever chooses you is an abomination" (41:24). "I am YHWH, who made all things, who alone stretched out the heavens, who by myself spread out the earth" (44:24b). "For thus says YHWH, who created the heavens (he is God!), who formed the earth and made it (he established it; he did not create it a chaos, he formed it to be inhabited!): I am YHWH, and there is no other" (45:18). "There is no other god besides me, a righteous God and a Savior; there is no one besides me" (45:21b; see also 43:10–11; 44:6; 45:6–7, 12; 46:9).

When we array these verses beside the priestly creation story in Gen 1:1—2:4a we have an impressive argument for the monotheistic worldview. However, if we examine each of Isaiah's texts in their proper context we see that YHWH addresses a skeptical people Israel and bends every effort to persuade them that YHWH, the national God they thought had let them down, was really the Lord of Creation who was managing world affairs *for their sake*. Gerald O'Collins says this is not *true* universalism (which he calls "decentralized universalism") but only *apparent* universalism centered on Israel, (which O'Collins calls "centralized universalism").[12] I believe the same was true in the mind of the editor of Genesis: What P says about Elohim at 1:1—2:4a *appears* to be expressed in universal terms, but it is immediately contradicted by the addition of the Yahwistic creation account in 2:4b—3:24. The divine subject here is YHWH

---

11. Jesus cited this verse when he hinted at the destruction of the temple, Mark 11:17.
12. O'Collins, *Salvation for All*, 12.

Elohim, none other than the YHWH who was Israel's national/war God, who spoke through Isaiah and other Israelites to declare that YHWH makes Israel Number One (see also, e.g., Joel 3:1–17 H 4:1–17; Zeph 3:20; Zech 14:16–19).

In Second Isaiah we read other promises of YHWH that show special favoritism to Israel: "Kings shall be your foster fathers, and their queens your nursing mothers. With their faces to the ground they shall bow down to you, and lick the dust of your feet. . . I will make your oppressors eat their own flesh, and they shall be drunk with their own blood as with wine" (Isa 49:23, 26). The whole of Isaiah 60 speaks in especially extravagant terms of the glory of Jerusalem: "Arise, shine, for your light has come, and the glory of YHWH has risen upon you. . . Nations shall come to your light, and kings to the brightness of your dawn" (60:1, 3). "For the nation and kingdom that will not serve you shall perish; those nations shall be utterly laid waste" (60:12). "Your sun shall no more go down, or your moon withdraw itself; for YHWH will be your everlasting light, and your days of mourning shall be ended. Your people shall all be righteous; they shall possess the land forever. They are the shoot that I planted, the work of my hands, so that I might be glorified" (60:20–21). I have already cited Watt's extensive background information describing Artaxerxes's contributions to the great prosperity of Jerusalem, which Scripture here interprets ethnocentrically (see above n. 6).

3. JEWS UNDER GREEK AND ROMAN RULE

Jews enjoyed a fair degree of self-governance and religious freedom until the fall of the Persian Empire to Alexander the Great of Macedonia in 333–332 BCE. History and legend report that Alexander treated the Jews with favor on his way south to subdue Egypt and afterward on his return north. After Alexander died in 323 BCE his four generals divided up his realm. Of concern to the Jews, Ptolemy took Egypt and Seleucus took Syria, which included the former Assyria and Babylonia. Large communities of Jews lived in Babylonia and in Egypt, and for a while Jerusalem and Judea were under the relatively benign rule of the Ptolemies of Egypt. The favored status of the temple gave the High Priest authority recognized by all Jews. In what Elias Bickerman calls "the paradoxical combination of universal monotheism and particularism," the Jews believed that the sole Lord of the Universe dwelt on Mount Zion in Jerusalem.[13] With their hearts set on Jerusalem even though they lived far away, Jews could still worship YHWH without assimilating to the cults of the lands where they lived. They gathered in meeting places to pray and study Torah. Thus they became accustomed to worship YHWH without the central sanctuary and without sacrifice. YHWH became known everywhere as the God of Heaven, and YHWH was not represented by any idol. These facts attracted to Jewish meeting places many serious-minded Gentiles who were dissatisfied with polytheism.[14] Some Gentiles became converts (proselytes),

---

13. Bickerman, op. cit., 8.

14. Such meeting places are now popularly called synagogues (a term of Gk derivation), though

but others stopped short of undergoing circumcision and were known as "God fearers." Many of the latter responded to the appeal of the later Jewish cult of the Nazarene, or the Way of Jesus.

Ptolemy II (282 to 246 BCE) encouraged translation of the Torah (Pentateuch) from Hebrew into Greek, while other cults kept secret their most important teachings.[15] Other Scriptures were translated for the Greek Bible, now known as the Septuagint (symbol LXX), but additional Jewish writings as well became available to the wider public that, since Alexander's efforts, now benefited from Greek culture, or Hellenism.[16] What may be more important for our present purposes, the Greek Bible transliterated the ineffable Name but pronounced it *kyrios*=Lord, the same Greek word used in the NT to address Jesus. Septuagint eliminated many distinct names for God, substituting "the God" or "the Almighty." "In this way the particular God of Abraham, Isaac and Jacob becomes in Greek the Supreme Being of mankind."[17]

In 200 BCE the Seleucids of Syria gained control of Judea, and in 176 after severe civil war, Antiochus IV secured the throne. He called himself Epiphanes, personification of the Olympian god Zeus, and he began a campaign to promote Greek language and culture, including religious customs. Intra-Jewish struggles intensified, with competing candidates for the office of High Priest offering big bribes to win the appointment. Antiochus appointed first Jason and then Menelaus, candidates that cooperated with hellenization. Other Jewish elites also cooperated, but great popular resistance and even violent conflict erupted among Jewish parties. Antiochus massacred Jews, burned scrolls, and forbade study of Torah, Sabbath observance, and circumcision. He stopped the daily sacrifices and desecrated the temple by offering swine's flesh on the altar (the "abomination of desolation" Dan 9:27, referred to in Mark 13:14). Imperial agents went about to enforce royal orders. In the village of Modein a minor priest named Mattathias killed a Jew offering pagan sacrifice and then struck down the officiating officer. Mattathias and his five sons escaped to the hills and began a violent guerrilla campaign targeting the "renegades"—those Jews who compromised. Many "pious ones" (Heb *chasidim*) joined Mattathias in his resistance; they are thought to be the forerunners of the Pharisees.

When Mattathias died, his second son Judas, nicknamed the Maccabee (the Hammerer, after whom his family became known) achieved such popular success that government troops tried unsuccessfully to suppress him. In 164 Judas and his forces recaptured, purified, and rededicated the temple, which became the origin of the Jewish Hanukkah festival. Antiochus acknowledged the failure of his persecution policy and

---

their origin has never been definitively determined.

15. Rabbis from Jerusalem east to Babylon refused to record their oral interpretations of Torah lest Gentiles take them over and claim to be Israel. This practice led to Paul's itinerating among Gentiles in the west, rather than the east. Mendels, "Why Paul Went West" 49–54.

16. Bickerman, op. cit., 74–75.

17. Ibid., 77.

God For All

called it off. Other problems in the empire beckoned, and he died during a distant campaign in 163. With freedom of worship restored, most of the pious ones abandoned the fight, but the Maccabees and their partisans fought on. Later, as the Maccabees became more violent and corrupt, many pious ones turned to active opposition.

The heroic story of Mattathias and his sons is told in the Septuagint books of 1 & 2 Maccabees and included in the deutero-canonical books that Roman Catholics accept as authoritative to some extent, but that Protestants generally reject and include only for information in some printed editions of their Bibles. The Hebrew Bible omits Maccabees and other Greek documents, but it includes the book of Daniel (written partially in Hebrew and in Aramaic), chief example of a new literary genre called apocalypse, which arose from the circle of the pious ones as a response to the extreme conditions of the time. Paul D. Hanson defines apocalypse as a literary genre in which "a *revelation* is given by God through an otherworldly *mediator* to a *human seer* disclosing *future events*" (emphasis original).[18] In many cases, the future events include final victory and vindication for the people of God. The futuristic aspect of apocalypse is referred to as *eschatology*, a word of Greek derivation that means teaching about the end.

The book of Daniel is a pseudonymous composition of around 163 BCE, the time when Antiochus was fighting the Maccabean resistance. The human seer Daniel is depicted as a Jewish wise man in the court of Nebuchadnezzar of Babylon (d. 562).[19] The book includes dreams and visions concerning the future, which actually describe the course of events leading up to the time of the author. Nebuchadnezzar's dream of a great statue represents four empires, Babylonian, Median, Persian, and Greek (the latter divided into Egyptian and Syrian). A stone cut out "without hands" strikes the statue's feet, totally destroys it, and fills the whole earth. Daniel tells the king: "In the days of those kings the God of Heaven will set up a kingdom that shall never be destroyed. . . It shall crush all these kingdoms and bring them to an end, and it shall stand forever" (Dan 2:31–45). In a vision Daniel sees four beasts rising out of the sea (ancient symbol of chaos) each representing one of the same four empires as those of the great statue. A small horn representing Antiochus IV violently emerges from the fourth beast and speaks arrogantly (7:2–8). An "Ancient One"(God) passes judgment and destroys the beast. Then one like "a human being" (lit. "a son of man") comes to the Ancient One and receives "an everlasting dominion that shall not pass away, and his kingship is one that shall never be destroyed" (7:9–14). The rest of Daniel 7 describes the acts of Antiochus to persecute the Jews and change their laws but states that God will act soon to replace the beastly empires with a more human-like kingdom, given "to the people of the holy ones of the Most High; their kingdom shall be

---

18. Hanson, "Apocalypses and Apocalypticism," *ABD*.

19. If one interprets Daniel literally as historical fact, the Jewish Daniel was chief wise man in the court of Nebuchadnezzar, who destroyed Judah and Jerusalem in 587–6.

an everlasting kingdom, and all dominions shall serve and obey them" (see especially Dan 7:23-27). Led by the one like a son of man, the Jews enjoy world dominion.[20]

The book of Daniel gives no hint of approval of the Maccabees' violent armed resistance and prefers to leave matters up to God, who will establish divine sovereignty "without hands" in the near future. Other "visions of the future" appear in Dan 8-12, which generally summarize the historical events culminating in the persecution by Antiochus, ending in his overthrow and the triumph of God's people. In these visions there is frequent mention of the impending "time of the end" (Dan 8:17, 19; 11:35; 12:4, 9) and "end of days" (10:14; 12:13). Clearly the author expected some spectacular fulfillment of the hopes of the Jews who remained steadfast during the torture and death they underwent at the hands of Antiochus.

Meanwhile, the Maccabees continued the struggle, taking advantage of uprisings in various places and intra-dynastic struggles that weakened the Seleucid rulers of Syria. In 161 BCE, Judas Maccabeus sent envoys to Rome, which gave "the nation of the Jews" a grant of freedom. "For the first time since the Exile the Jews were recognized as an independent power, and by the very people that ruled the world." Of course, such recognition was really not yet Rome's to grant, but the Maccabees had "accommodated devout Judaism to the ways of the world."[21] The people of YHWH had once more become like other nations. As clients of Rome they continued to resist the Seleucids.

Judas's youngest brother Jonathan succeeded him as military commander and later had himself recognized by the Jews as High Priest, even though he was not of Zadokite lineage. The Seleucid king Demetrius II recognized Jonathan's de facto authority as the effective governor of the Jewish minority centered on Jerusalem and affirmed him as High Priest. Modern scholars refer to the family now as the Hasmonean Dynasty. Jonathan's usurpation of the High Priest's office aroused opposition from Zadokites and their sympathizers. When suppressed, they retreated to the desert and formed the Qumran community that came to be known as Essenes. These strict separatists intensely emphasized priestly purity, liturgical practices, and biblical interpretation to support their position. They anticipated divine action to overthrow the "wicked priests" and restore themselves to their rightful place.[22]

After Jonathan died in 142 BCE, his brother Simon, last of Mattathias's five sons, became king, military commander, and High Priest. Simon convened a great assembly of priests, elders, and heads of the nation. They passed a decree, inscribed on a bronze tablet on Mount Zion, proclaiming that the high priesthood was given to Simon's

---

20. In Dan 8:1-25 Daniel sees a similar vision and its interpretation that tells the same story in different terms. A goat with one horn (Alexander) destroys a ram with two horns (the kingdom of the Medes and Persians). The goat's horn is broken (Alexander's death) and replaced by four lesser horns. From one of those a king shall arise (Antiochus) who will persecute the holy ones, but "he shall be broken, and not by human hands" (8:25).

21. Bickerman, op. cit., 133.

22. Cross, *Canaanite Myth and Hebrew Epic*, "The Early History of the Apocalyptic Community at Qumran" 326-42.

house forever. For three generations in succession (143–76), Simon Maccabeus, John Hyrcanus, and Alexander Jannaeus monopolized power in their own hands, proclaiming the Kingdom of Judea and issuing coins. They conquered all Palestine, a realm approximately equaling the kingdom of David. They forced Edomites (Idumeans) and Galileans to convert to Judaism. As fruits of these conquests, an Idumean, Herod, and a Galilean, Jesus of Nazareth, entered history as Jews.[23]

Alexander Jannaeus (103–76 BCE) became increasingly despotic and faced growing Jewish opposition. The Pharisees withdrew their support and many of the common people opposed him. Jews asked Demetrius III to put down Jannaeus,[24] but he retained power. Jannaeus wreaked terrible revenge on his enemies. He crucified eight hundred fellow Jews and massacred their families before their eyes while he and his concubines feasted sumptuously. When Jannaeus died he bequeathed his rule to his wife Salome Alexandra, who reigned for nine years. On her death, her two sons contended for power in a bloody stalemate. In 63 BCE the Roman general Pompey conquered Syria and occupied Jerusalem with a great slaughter. Rome now seized authority to appoint the High Priest. In 40 BCE Rome appointed the Idumean Herod (later called the Great) King of the Jews.

Herod had to confirm his title by force against remnants of the Hasmoneans, which resulted in death and slavery for thousands of Jews. Fenn notes that Herod was a Hellenized Edomite by ethnicity but a Jew by religion, owing his position of authority to Rome. Trying to improve his legitimacy in the eyes of the Jews, Herod married Mariamme, a prominent daughter of the Hasmonean line, but she proved "a fifth column within his regime," fomenting conflicts between Herod's Idumean kin and the Hasmoneans, and finally joined a plot against him.[25] Herod became more ruthless as he grew older, killing any who opposed him or whom he merely suspected, including Mariamme and their two sons. Matthew 2:16–18 charges Herod with responsibility for massacring the baby boys in Bethlehem in the attempt to dispose of Jesus, whom he considered a possible challenger. Herod's death, followed by an interim before Rome approved Archelaus as his successor, stirred a Jewish attempt at independence, resulting in a massacre of at least 3000 Jews by Archelaus assisted by Rome. Fenn's general thesis is that Herod's reign was so plagued by intermixtures of religious, ethnic, and psychological conflict that his death inaugurated a period of general dysfunction, which brought about the Jewish rebellion of 63 CE that resulted in the destruction of the temple in 70 and ultimate dispersion of the Jews.

For about a century, the Hasmoneans flaunted the trappings and characteristics of nations, involved in constant warfare, both external and internal, steeped in intrigue, corruption, and cruelty, with great negative consequences for the ordinary people. Though they were of priestly lineage they were not Zadokites. Simon's Assembly

---

23. Fenn, *The Death of Herod*, 6.
24. Cross, *Canaanite Myth and Hebrew Epic*, 336.
25. Fenn, *The Death of Herod*, 9.

had abrogated biblical law to legitimize high priesthood for the Hasmoneans, but they of course made no pretense of davidic descent for their royal claims. Their entire dynasty rested on a blatant application of the principle that "might makes right." This was the last example of the Jews becoming like other nations, until the declaration of the state of Israel in 1947 CE as client of the United States. Chaim Weizmann, who became the first president, had written, "our relations to the other races and nations would become more *normal*"; "We shall revert to *normal*... 'like unto all the nations.'"[26]

SUMMARY

Haggai and Zechariah, who inspired the Jews to build the Second Temple, expressed the expectation that YHWH would soon act to establish a messianic kingdom under Zerubbabel, the scion of David's line, and Joshua, the Zadokite High Priest. It didn't happen. About three hundred fifty years later, the Maccabees rescued the Temple from desecration and Jews from persecution by Antiochus IV of Syria. The author of Daniel proclaimed the hope that God would act, without human hands, to establish at last the kingdom of the holy ones of the Most High, who would possess "an everlasting kingdom, and all dominions shall serve and obey them" (Dan 7:27). It didn't happen.

What did happen was that the Maccabees went on from triumph to triumph by force of arms and skillful diplomacy, aided by the authority of the high priesthood, until they gained Rome's recognition as the Kingdom of Judea. The Hasmoneans' skill at the ways of pagan empires brought collapse of their state in a welter of suicidal corruption. Rome became their imperial master, and for another hundred years the Temple system survived, but it never escaped the taint of being the tool of exploitation. The militarized priestly theocracy of the Hasmoneans was a serious setback to the development of the biblical concept of the oneness of God and God's concern for all humanity. Still, the expectation of the imminent establishment of the Kingdom of God persisted and grew among the people of God. The stage was set for their response to the next cataclysmic blow. Once more deprived of a state, what could the Jews do after the Romans destroyed the Temple, their most powerful religious symbol?

---

26. Citations of Weismann's words, with emphasis, in Rose, *The Question of Zion*, 76.

21

Roman Palestine in the Time of Jesus

HEROD THE GREAT SOUGHT to win the Jews' approval by lavishly refurbishing the Second Temple building in Jerusalem, but most Jews questioned his authentic Jewishness and his legitimacy as their ruler. Herod felt himself so insecure that "surveillance as well as secrecy were twins" of his regime and "made that society a virtual prison for many, perhaps most, of its citizens."[1]

1. SOCIAL AND POLITICAL CONDITIONS

Gaalya Cornfeld succinctly sets the stage for the life and ministry of Jesus in his summary statement: "The end of Herod's reign marked a turning point in the social and political development of the Jewish community. In addition to the ascendancy of the new aristocratic and landed gentry who owed allegiance to Herod's successors and to Rome, with whom they wished to coexist without disturbance, the basis was also laid for an anti-Herodian opposition—"[2]

1a. The successors of Herod

Herod's death did not end the climate of fear, but it added a crisis of succession. Herod had already executed his two sons by Mariamme amid highly questionable proceedings, and shortly before his death he executed his eldest son, whom he had led to believe would be his successor. The surviving sons had such serious quarrels among themselves that instead of appointing one to succeed Herod, Caesar Augustus divided his realm among three of them. Augustus gave Archelaus approximately half of Herod's realm—Judea, Samaria, and Idumea (Edom), with the title ethnarch (=ruler of a people) rather than King. He made Antipas tetrarch (=ruler of a fourth)

---

1. Fenn, *The Death of Herod*, 7, 2.
2. Cornfeld, *Josephus, The Jewish War*, 135B. For events leading to making Judea a Roman province, see Josephus's text and Cornfeld's comments, 132–142.

over Galilee and Perea (part of East Jordan). Antipas had tried unsuccessfully to get Rome to declare him King of the Jews like his father.[3] Philip, another son of Herod, was tetrarch of Iturea, a region including former Aram/Damascus. Jesus's ministry took him to all of these regions.

Archelaus had started to act like a king as soon as Herod died. The funeral coincided with Passover (celebration of liberation from Egypt), when many pilgrims gathered in Jerusalem. A delegation begged Archelaus to lighten the tax burdens of his father, to which he gave a positive response. This emboldened them to demand reparations for Herod's having burned to death the Jews who had destroyed the golden eagle Herod had placed over the main temple gate, and to remove a High Priest they considered illegitimate. They refused to negotiate with representatives from Archelaus, so he sent troops that massacred some three thousand and scattered masses of pilgrims camped outside the city.[4] When Archelaus went to Rome to seek Augustus's approval of his rule, opposition began to stir everywhere. The Roman general Varus anticipated trouble and brought a Roman legion to Jerusalem, where a riot broke out in the temple area among pilgrims who had come for Pentecost (celebrating Moses's giving of the Law and the covenant at Sinai). Jews vastly outnumbered the Romans, but the soldiers cut down many. Varus brought more legions through Galilee, killing and plundering as they came, and relieved the Romans in Jerusalem with even greater slaughter of Jews. Varus crucified as many of the perceived leaders as he could capture.[5] One must not overlook the religious/cultic aura suffusing these popular uprisings.

Other uprisings among the lower social strata outside Jerusalem during the interregnum of Archelaus' absence in Rome had a noticeable "messianic" aspect, although that term was not used. Cornfeld writes of "the old eschatological roots of their aspirations for the restoration of the ideal Jewish ruler descended from the house of David." More than that, "their strongest yearnings were for the reinstatement of the ancient theocracy ruled by a high priest."[6] Josephus mentions Judas son of an earlier leader of resistance, Hezekiah in Galilee; a former slave Simon in Perea, who burned the Herodian palace in Jericho; and the shepherd Anthrongaeus who crowned himself and with his four brothers survived for several years before Archelaus destroyed them after his return from Rome.[7]

Delegations of both Jews and Samaritans traveled to Rome to ask Caesar to remove Archelaus and to make them a self-governing territory attached to Syria. Because of the Jews' peculiar religious and cultural characteristics, Augustus made Archelaus's realm a Roman province under a Roman governor in 6 CE. This new

3. HCSB Luke 3:1 note.
4. Cornfeld, *Josephus, The Jewish War*, 128–29.
5. Ibid., 133–34.
6. Cornfeld, *Josephus, The Jewish War*, 135B.
7. Ibid., 135–36.

form of rule called for a census to update the tax system, which in turn spurred new resistance. One Judas in Galilee aided by Zaddok a Pharisee, stirred the resistance of the people by insisting that Jews should not be subject to rule by a foreign power. The current high priest succeeded in calming the people.[8] Most governors served short three-year terms. The fifth, Pontius Pilate (26-36 CE), was notably arrogant and cruel, contemptuous of the Jews, indifferent to their special sensibilities, and swift to respond to the least sign of trouble.

As subjects of Rome the Jews of Palestine experienced the same consequences of political and economic subjugation to empire that others all over the Mediterranean world endured. The Roman Empire was in an almost chronic state of war and had to contend with a multitude of internal struggles. Endemic poverty of the most severe kind was the principal cause of unrest everywhere. The Jewish historian Josephus makes clear that the basic distinction in Jewish society was that between the royal house and priests on the one hand, and the people as a whole on the other. The very small minority of social elite was powerful and rich, directly served by a small, educated social stratum called retainers. The mass of the population was weak and poor, uneducated and voiceless.[9] The steady accumulation of land by the wealthy minority meant that more and more people had to get a living from less and less land. Rome took approximately 40 percent of the peasant tenant farmers' crops in addition to what they paid the owners, and the tithes and the temple tax they owed as Jews. The relatively poor "suffered no need but had nothing left over," which made them vulnerable to drought or illness that could drive them into debt. This swelled the number of those who were absolutely poor or destitute (Gr *ptōchoi*), lacking assurance of adequate food, clothing, and shelter, the barest necessities of life.[10]

1b. Jewish opposition movements

The poverty of the masses and the indifference of the elite meant that from Herod's rise to power in the last decade BCE until the rebellion that broke out in 66 CE, social banditry was likely to be carried on sporadically throughout Jewish Palestine. Some desperate people took to stealing out of sheer necessity, but here and there organized bands carried on more systematic operations, targeting wealthy Jews and robbing royal stores where possible. The masses of peasants who themselves did not participate in banditry provided cover and gave aid to the activists, who often responded with gifts to the poor like ancient Robin Hoods.[11]

---

8. Ibid., 143.

9. The summary of Josephus's general portrayal of these conditions is found in. Stegemann and Stegemann, *The Jesus Movement*, 53–54 and elsewhere throughout.

10. Stegemann and Stegemann, *The Jesus Movement*, 89.

11. Horsley and Hanson, *Bandits, Prophets, and Messiahs*, 63–85.

Some of the larger and longer-lasting bandit enterprises took on a quasi-royal caste. The Hasmonean dynasty had flouted the genealogical standards for both priestly and royal office, and Herod had only complicated the issue. There is no documented popular "messianic expectation," but even illiterate peasant Jews could not have been unaware of the tradition that David the shepherd had been leader of a group of malcontent fugitives from royal rule that became his private army before he was recognized as king by popular acclaim. The term "son of David" could mean not necessarily a lineal descendent but any individual with talents and exploits like David. The Jesus movement had no direct connection with such movements, characterized as they were by militant violence, but Jesus's appeal to the poor people of the lower strata was an important factor in his popularity.

John the Baptist led a movement primarily against the corrupt Jewish religious establishment, but it also had strong overtones of opposition to the Herodian political establishment. I will describe John's ministry in more detail below in chapter 23.1 "The call of Jesus."

2. COSMOLOGY AND ANTHROPOLOGY OF THE MEDITERRANEAN PEOPLES

Before we take up Jesus in the socio-economic and political setting of his time, we must consider the reigning anthropological and cosmological worldview of the peoples of the Mediterranean basin, including the Jews with their particular differences. Theirs was what is called the "pre-scientific age"—they all lived many centuries before the European Enlightenment, before Galileo, Descartes, Kepler, Newton, Darwin, Marx, Freud, Einstein, Hubble, and many others. Their cosmos was three-storied: heaven, earth (separated by the solid dome), and the underworld (cf Exod 20:4//Deut 5:8). We cannot put ourselves completely in the thought environment of Jesus and his contemporaries, but it helps to have a general idea of their worldview, lest we misunderstand or misinterpret Jesus owing to our scientific ways of thinking.

2a. The great chain of being

The view of reality (even for Jews) was close to the polytheistic worldview described by Professor Ishida (above chapter 2.1 "Two worldviews"). They did not posit an absolute distinction between God and not-God. The multitude of inhabitants of heaven and earth was connected in a hierarchy that scholars call the "great chain of being," though the exact distinctions are fuzzy. At the top were the gods, the *Eternals*. Below them were the *Immortals*, lesser divine/spiritual beings who served the gods, but also some human heroes of outstanding accomplishment (some of whom were thought to be offspring of sexual relations between gods and humans), and in the lowest rank were the *Mortals*, ordinary human beings.

God For All

For Jews the only *Eternal* was the Most High God. Among the *Immortals* was the Most High's vizier or chief agent YHWH, and other angels or heavenly beings, who were lesser ministers of the *Eternal* Gods. Among the *Immortals* other famous characters of the OT were counted: "Enoch walked with God; then he was no more, because God took him" (Gen 5:24). A whirlwind took Elijah up to heaven (2 Kgs 2:11). Moses died, literally, "by/at the mouth of God" (Deut 34:5) and thus was considered immortal. From Maccabean times the faithful dead were believed to be immortal "sons of God." Satan was YHWH's constant and powerful adversary, who could infect creation and tempt and destroy humans whom he tried to prevent from trusting YHWH and may or may not have been considered *Immortal*. Numerous demons were Satan's assistants.

The Great Chain of Being[12]

	Mediterranean Chain of Being	Israelite Chain of Being
Eternals	Multitudes of Gods	The Most High God
Immortals	Diamones: many spiritual beings Offspring of gods and humans Heroes, famous kings, etc.	God's Vizier=YHWH | Satan Angels | Demons Moses, Enoch, Elijah, et. al. "sons of God"=faithful dead Ancestors, Heroes
Mortals	Humans	Humans

2b. Human beings

In ancient conception, everything in all creation, including humans, consisted of differing combinations of the four elements, all of which were substances, or some sort of "stuff": air, earth, water, and fire. As Pieter Craffert writes,

> The human being was a "commingling of substances," and the primary substances were body-stuff and soul-stuff . . . materiality was a spectrum of more or less (or different configurations) of these elements and not in a dichotomy with nonmatter . . . Therefore to say that something was incorporeal (like a soul or spirit) did not translate to being immaterial. The human being was an "animated body," but there was no consensus on the exact distribution of the elements in the human. Ancient literature, including that of the Bible, can speak of different body/soul/spirit configurations.[13]

---

12. Based on description and chart in Craffert, *The Life of a Galilean Shaman*, 169–87, supplemented by Haymon, "Monotheism—A Misused Word in Jewish Studies?"

13. Craffert, *The Life of a Galilean Shaman*, 188, summarizing a number of expert references.

People considered dreams to be real experiences, and the human soul/spirit could depart the body and travel to the locus of the dream. Visions could reveal reality, and one could have a vision in a state of ecstasy or trance, without going to sleep. Modern scholars refer to such experiences as "altered states of consciousness" (ASC), which still can be observed in some cultures in the world of today. An ASC may come upon a subject involuntarily, or it may be induced in a number of ways—solitary meditation, breath control, fasting, monotonous chanting or drumming, mountain climbing, or by ingesting hallucinogens such as natural substances (e.g., peyote or certain mushrooms) or various artificial or chemical concoctions sought out by thrill seekers. An ASC ("trip"?) may be good or bad depending on sources and circumstances, and judged by its results.

3. THE RELIGIOUS PATTERN BASED ON ALTERED STATES OF CONSCIOUSNESS (ASC)

Some societies have provided the cultural environment in which certain individuals have been known for their extraordinary accomplishments while undergoing ASCs, including healing diseases or exorcizing evil spirits, in clairvoyance, in controlling weather, and in imparting special information and wisdom. The earliest examples of such persons to be seriously reported by scholarly observers were the shamans in hunter/gatherer societies of Siberia. But subsequent researchers have identified individuals with similar talents living and working in different particular cultures and called by different titles, but reporters have generally settled on "shaman" as the generic title. Craffert writes, "The *shamanic complex* is the shorthand phrase for the features and practices associated with an ASC-based religious pattern."[14] Authentic shaman-type practitioners do not seek the office but believe themselves called or possessed by a spirit or force from outside themselves, often as the result of a serious illness or some other traumatic life-threatening experience. They do not work for their own advancement but for the benefit of their people. A shaman works effectively because the people are steeped in the tradition and continual observation of the results, and therefore they trust him or her.

Craffert is not the first to apply the title shaman to Jesus,[15] but he has done extensive research of shamanism and ASCs, and he makes the results readily available. In my view Craffert does a believable job of demonstrating how we can understand many of the features of the Gospel stories of Jesus by seeing them in the light of the

---

14. Craffert, *The Life of a Galilean Shaman*, 135 emphasis original, with fuller explication extending through p 153.

15. See note on shaman at the end of this chapter. I first encountered Jesus called shaman in Ashton, "The Religious Experience of Jesus." Ashton suggests Jesus thought of himself as what people today call a shaman. Ashton cites *Possession* by Erika Bourguignon, who observed spirit-possession in all but 90 of the 488 societies she surveyed. Craffert also cites several works by Bourguignon, p 428.

God For All

shamanic complex in the spirit world that Jesus inhabited. I will apply this information as I take up certain of the texts concerning Jesus later in this book.

4. NOTE ON SHAMAN

Some people may think it inappropriate to call Jesus a shaman, (or a magician, as does Morton Smith, *Jesus the Magician*.) Those who do so do not seek to diminish Jesus in the least, but noting his work and comparing it to known activities of other human figures, they use the only English vocabulary available. A Peruvian-born American, Carlos Castaneda wrote about a Mexican shaman-like-figure in his 1968 book *The Teachings of Don Juan*, with many similarities to shamanic complex cultures described by scholars such as Craffert. Castaneda made no mention of Jesus and apparently was driven by personal ambition. See Wikipedia, the Free Encyclopedia.

PART FIVE

Jesus of Nazareth

22

Introduction to Jesus and the Gospels

ONE OF THE JEWISH sects that came into being during the dysfunctional period between the death of Herod and the Romans' destruction of the temple in 70 BCE was that which early on called itself the Way, that is, the way of life laid out by word and deed of Jesus of Nazareth.

Jesus and his immediate followers were all Jews, originating in Galilee ruled by Herod Antipas, but they couldn't avoid comings and goings to the territory ruled by Herod Philip, as well as to Jerusalem under the Roman governor Pilate. Jesus and his followers were influenced by the Hebrew writings and practices that tended toward the exclusive attitude of Ezra and Nehemiah. They were also influenced by the apocalyptic expectations of direct divine intervention to establish the Kingdom of God on earth and affirm the priority of Israel as the people of God, which the book of Daniel and other late documents had stirred up during the preceding century and a half of rapid and drastic changes. The current political and economic dysfunction was steadily pushing the Jewish people toward the revolution that finally burst out in 63 CE, thirty-some years after Jesus.

The earliest Jesus movement grew out of the common people's experiencing Jesus's works of healing and exorcism, hearing his teaching, and resonating to his criticism of the religious and political power structure. As his following grew in numbers, some began to hope he might be the long-expected one to renew the Kingdom of David. The Jewish religious establishment centering on the Temple and responsible to Rome for keeping order among the Jews arrested Jesus and accused him as a royal pretender before Pilate, who crucified him as a rebel about 30 CE. Jesus's disciples claimed that Jesus was raised from the dead and really was the Messiah, or Anointed One, but they cited texts from the Greek translation of the Hebrew Bible to argue against nationalistic expectations and portrayed a Messiah who was to die for his people. They enthusiastically spread the word about Jesus, which they called the gospel, or the good news, which attracted popular response from the people and opposition from the powers. The Jesus movement was one of several Jewish sects in Palestine in mid-first century CE. It spread rapidly after Rome destroyed the Second Temple in 70 CE during the Jewish revolts of 63 to 135 that ended in Rome's driving most Jews out of Palestine.

1. THE STORIES OF JESUS

Jesus never wrote anything, and traditions about what he did and said circulated in oral form for several decades before people began to make selections from available material and organize them into written versions of the story, each intended to meet the needs and conditions of a particular body of believers. These documents came to be known as Gospels. Jesus himself spoke Aramaic, the language of the common Jewish people in Palestine, but the Gospels were all written in Greek. That fact indicates the rapidity with which the Jesus movement had broken free of Jewish limitations, but it warns us that except for a very few words and phrases, we have no record of Jesus's exact words. By the mid-second century CE a number of Gospels circulated fairly widely. People noted discrepancies among them and began to make discriminations about comparative value. By the end of the second century the four that now comprise the first section of the NT had received general acceptance: Matthew (Matt), Mark, Luke, and John. The authors' names depend upon traditions for which we have no certain proofs. Scholars have discovered all or parts of other documents that did not gain acceptance, but some of them may supplement what we have in the Four Gospels. Some NT scholars place high value on the Gospel of Thomas, which contains principally sayings of Jesus.

Analyzing the origins, composition, and relationships among the Gospels has exercised scholars for centuries. I offer only a brief summary of the generally agreed view. Mark is considered earliest, completed at the height of the Jewish rebellion about 70 CE for a community of believers in Syria (perhaps), whether just before or just after the fall of Jerusalem and the Temple.[16] Matthew was written for Jewish and Luke for Gentile believers after the end of the Temple. They were later than Mark by at least a decade and had Mark as a source. Generally speaking Matthew and Luke follow Mark's chronological order, but they may alter that and also edit Mark's material to suit the needs of their communities. Matthew and Luke have in common many teachings of Jesus not found in Mark; derived from a supposed "sayings source" (Q), and some of this material may have been earlier than Mark. Matthew and Luke also have special material of their own, (M) and (L). Because of their many similarities, Matthew, Mark, and Luke are called Synoptics, because they can be viewed side-by-side ("syn-optically") and compared very easily by means of a synopsis.[17] The Gospel of John was completed about 90 CE and differs markedly from the Synoptics in so many ways that it is generally treated separately. In my view, the author of John depended on sources other than the Synoptics, which he appears not to have known in their present form.[18]

16. Boring allows for either alternative in his work, *Mark: A Commentary*.
17. Throckmorton, ed. *Gospel Parallels*.
18. On the Synoptic Problem and on individual Gospels see articles in *ABD* or *IDB*, or in the

A second response to the multiplicity of gospels was to compile a unitary account of the story of Jesus, the best known of which is that by Tatian, around 170 CE. His work has been called *Diatessaron*, from the Greek word that means "through four," i.e., the Four Gospels. Tatian summarized multiple accounts of the same incident, harmonized contradictions, and "corrected" omissions detected in his sources. In a time when copying documents by hand was laborious and expensive, Tatian's *Diatessaron* provided a convenient and relatively cheap book for evangelists to use in their travels. People used this popular document for several hundred years, but by mid-fifth century CE it was finally suppressed in favor of the canonical four.[19] Without denying the limited usefulness of the *Diatessaron* and of modern attempts at harmonizing the gospels, we can all be glad that the four survived, so that we can study and compare all of them rather than just the results of one man's selection and amalgamation of material, leaving only a limited scope for interpretation.

Modern study of the Gospels includes minute attention to the differences of wording, emphasis, chronological order, and other details that lead scholars to speculate on the social type of community for which each gospel was prepared and what its special needs and problems might have been. A slightly different portrait of Jesus appears in each Gospel. This troubles people who prefer uniformity and final certainty. Church councils in the fourth century CE produced statements of faith declaring the full deity of Jesus and the trinitarian theology of God. For centuries people brought those theological perspectives to their study of the Gospels and read them back into the text, which they read in a harmonizing manner. The view adopted here attempts to deal with the text as it is and leaves room for differences, trusting in the assistance of the Holy Spirit as earnest believers and inquirers work alone and together to discover Jesus's significance for faith and life today. I hope that examining the role of Jesus in the process of the growth of the oneness of God and God's concern for all humanity may bring new insight to the total understanding of .the Bible.

2. JESUS THE JEW

In recent years the Jewishness of Jesus has drawn a good deal of attention.[20] Animosity between Christians and Jews had erupted before the Gospels were accepted as authoritative, and they may have downplayed that aspect of Jesus's person. Still, it is worthwhile considering a few examples.

Harper Collins Study Bible or the New Oxford Annotated Bible.

19. For more detail on these points see *ABD* articles on "Canon" and "Diatessaron."

20. An important book dealing at length with this subject came to my attention only after I had finished my work, but I wish to acknowledge its great value: Daniel Boyarin, *The Jewish Gospels: the story of the Jewish Christ*. New York: The New Press, 2011. See especially his chapter 3, "Jesus Kept Kosher" for one important point.

God For All

The very first words of the NT hit the reader with a list of over seventy names, mostly unfamiliar and difficult to pronounce. These make up Jesus's genealogy. It goes from Abraham to King David to the end of the kingdom. After that the names keep going to the time of Jesus the Messiah (Matt 1:2–17). Many readers ignore this genealogy and go directly to Matt 1:18–25, a story of the birth of Jesus. Thus they may fail to appreciate the Jewishness inherent in this Gospel.

Jesus showed his Jewish ethnicity and sense of superiority. On one occasion Jesus sought privacy while on a trip near Tyre, but a foreign woman found him and humbly begged Jesus to heal her demon-possessed daughter. In an insulting manner Jesus said, "Let the children be fed first, for it is not fair to take the children's food and throw it to the dogs." She said, "Sir, even the dogs under the table eat the children's crumbs." Impressed by this sharp reply, Jesus praised the woman and healed her daughter (Mark 7:24–30). Jesus clearly stated Jewish superiority—"children first"—and actually used insulting language toward her. However, unlike many Jews, Jesus did not exclude Gentiles, but he allowed for their participation in the divine benefits mediated by Jesus.[21] One may see this as a learning experience for Jesus, for he changed his attitude after conversing personally with this anxious mother.

In Matthew's version of this encounter (Matt 18:15–28), the author heightens the difference between Jew and Gentile. Matthew calls the woman a Canaanite, a term of opprobrium from OT times.[22] He describes her as vociferously and repeatedly beseeching Jesus, and the disciples urging him to drive her off. Jesus flatly states: "I was sent only to the lost sheep of the house of Israel."[23] Matthew's version, written for a Jewish Christian community, heightens Jewish superiority, yet also makes clear that Gentiles may receive blessings through Jesus.[24] There is no hard evidence of Jesus's having made a purposeful attempt to minister to Gentiles; the fact that the post-resurrection community had serious disputes over the status of Gentiles tells against it. Still, Jesus did respond positively to non-Jews when he met them (see, e.g., Matt 8:5–12; Mark 5:1–20; Lk 17:11–19).

A scribe, i.e. an expert in details of Mosaic law, asked Jesus's opinion on a question under perennial debate, namely, which of all the commandments of the Torah (six hundred thirteen by scholarly count) was the first, that is, which was so important as to override all others. Jesus answered, "The first is, 'Hear, O Israel: the Lord our

---

21. In Jewish society dogs were unclean outside scavengers, not pets. That this woman could speak of dogs as inside pets under the family dining table indicated her relative affluence. See Boring, *Mark*, 213–14.

22. In Israel today, some Israelis contemptuously refer to Palestinians as Canaanites.

23. In Matt's account of Jesus's sending out the disciples to preach, he tells them: "Go nowhere among the Gentiles, and enter no town of the Samaritans, but go rather to the lost sheep of the house of Israel" (10:5–6).

24. The visit of the Magi to find the baby Jesus (Matt 2:1–12) and Jesus's final commission to the disciples (Matt 28:16–20) put the entire Gospel in a mode that emphasizes Matthew's importance for non-Jews.

God, the Lord is one; you shall love the Lord your God with all your heart, and with all your soul, and with all your mind, and with all your strength.' The second is this, 'You shall love your neighbor as yourself.' There is no other commandment greater than these" (Mark 12:29–31).[25]

Jesus cites the *Shema*—Deut 6:4–5, the daily confession of faith of pious Jews affirming the oneness of God and the total sovereignty of God over all aspects of a person's life. He then adds the obligation to love one's neighbor as oneself, quoting Lev 19:18. Commentators have noted that this combination of texts is not original with Jesus. Nevertheless it attests to Jesus's conviction concerning the oneness of God and the authority of the Scriptures, and it shows his own view that love rules over all the laws. In the parable of the Good Samaritan, Jesus signaled that his interpretation of the term "neighbor" transcended distinctions of ethnic identity, religion, and social class (Luke 10:25–37).

In the previous chapter I provided general information on the political and economic conditions of Jews under Roman rule, and the cosmological and anthropological features of the worldview of the peoples of the lands of the Mediterranean basin. Within that general context I wish to present examples of Jesus's conflict with certain Jewish practices of his time. It is here that we see more clearly what is special and unique about Jesus and, I believe, advances our understanding of the oneness of God and God's concern for all. In subsequent chapters I shall call attention to such points.

---

25. Matt 5:23–28 and Luke 10:25–28 have versions of the question of the great commandment, but only Mark includes Jesus's confession of the oneness of God.

23

The Call of Jesus

THE FOUR GOSPELS THAT open the New Testament and offer their several portraits of Jesus begin their accounts of Jesus's public appearance by introducing the ministry of John the "Baptizer" (Mark 1:2–6; "Baptist" Matt 3:1–6; Luke 3:1–6, John 1:19–23). Christian tradition adapted John's ministry to that of Jesus, but here I depend on more comprehensive works on John that develop his portrait by means of references to him in the NT documents supplemented by extrabiblical sources to round out his particular historical and cultural context.[1] In this way we see that John is an indispensable link between the general Jewish stance of opposition to Roman rule abetted by the corrupt Jewish religious establishment on the one hand, and the ministry of Jesus, who began as a disciple of John and absorbed much of John's political and religious thought. Jesus began his public ministry only after the death of John, and during that ministry he departed significantly from his early mentor, but it is important for us to understand John as an important element in the religious context in which Jesus lived and worked.

1. JOHN THE BAPTIST

John was son of Zechariah, a member of the lower order of priests who lived outside Jerusalem but served occasionally (by lot) at the temple (Luke 1:8–9). They suffered discrimination and economic hardship at the hands of the elite priests in Jerusalem. The Hasmoneans had accumulated great power and wealth. They increased the head tax each Jew paid for temple support from one-third shekel (Neh 10:32) to one-half shekel. Under the Ptolemies and Seleucids, in addition to being rivals bidding for the high priest's office, they also competed for the right to lease the collection of taxes.[2] John did not follow the priestly calling of his father but withdrew to the wilderness for a time (Luke 2:80). He may have imbibed teachings of the separatist Essenes, who were severely opposed to the status quo of the Temple priesthood.

---

1. Hollenbach, "John the Baptist" *ABD*; Kraeling, *John the Baptist*.
2. Stegemann and Stegemann, *The Jesus Movement*, 115, 114. They sub-let tax collection to others on regional and local levels.

The Call of Jesus

According to one Christian tradition, the theme of John's message was, "Repent, for the kingdom of heaven has come near" (Matt 3:2).[3] John's vision of the coming rule of God stressed God's imminent imposition of wrath on unrepentant apostate sinners. Like Amos of old, John announced God's judgment even upon the chosen people; Jews' claim of descent from Abraham meant nothing (Matt 3:9//Luke 3:8). John appeared in public dressed as an ascetic, alienated figure, reminiscent of Elijah (Mark 1:6). Malachi is the last book in the OT according to the Septuagint and Christian order. Malachi condemns a corrupt priesthood (Mal 1:6—2:9) and threatens YHWH's imminent coming as a purifying fire (4:1–3 H 3:19–21). Malachi ends with the promise: "Lo, I will send you the prophet Elijah before the great and terrible day of YHWH comes" (4:5 H 3:23). A target of John's criticism was Scribes and Pharisees, religious elite, whom he called a "brood of vipers" (Matt 3:7).[4] John offered a way of escape by means of repentance and baptism,[5] followed by a life demonstrating a complete change of attitude and behavior.

John commanded citizens who had more than their absolute needs (poor, but with two tunics and with food on hand) to share with the *ptōchoi*, the destitute, who had nothing. Tax collectors and soldiers asked what he required of them. To the former he said not to take more than the legally required tax, and to the latter he forbade using their superior force to exploit the unarmed masses and to cease agitating for greater pay (Luke 3:10–13). Paul W. Hollenbach notes the significance of these two groups, for "the two main functions of ancient aristocratic governments were taxation and warfare." Tax collectors were Jews who pre-paid a lump sum to the top bidders and kept as much as they were able to extort from their own people. Soldiers often assisted in collecting the tax, in addition to fighting the wars of the rulers and suppressing popular risings. If tax collectors and solders took seriously John's advice, both empire and temple would be seriously affected.[6] John's attack on the politico-religious power structure appealed to the poor masses who hailed him as a prophet. They admired John so fervently that religious authorities were afraid to contradict their views openly (Mark 11:32//Matt 21:26//Luke 20:6). John's broad popularity, together with his charge that Herod Antipas had violated Mosaic law by marrying the divorced wife of his brother, led to Antipas imprisoning and executing John (Mark 6:17–29//Matt 14:3–12).

Although the Gospels all tend to diminish John's ministry in comparison to Jesus's, it is beyond question that Jesus accepted baptism at John's hand and was for a while among John's followers. Jesus himself showed nothing but admiration for John and never criticized him. Like John, Jesus expected the imminent inbreaking of the

---

3. In Matt, Kingdom of Heaven=Kingdom of God.

4. Luke 3:7 broadens this accusation by applying it to "the multitudes."

5. I know of no definitive explanation why John advocated baptism. Jewish cultic customs required ceremonial baptisms in some cases, and Gentiles who wished to convert fully as Jews underwent baptism.

6. Hollenbach, op.cit., "Ethical Criticism and Obligation"

rule of God. Nevertheless, whereas John preached imminent judgment and destruction, Jesus preached healing and acceptance now. "Jesus did not see the judgment of God as already realized, but saw instead the kingdom of God as having come and, not coincidentally, to people who were in need."[7] Jesus experienced his divine call at the moment of his baptism by John.

John the Baptist's sphere of activity was apparently on the eastern shore of the Jordan River at the edge of the desert near where it entered the Dead Sea. According to the oldest Gospel report, the crowds who came out to John were all from Judea and Jerusalem (Mark 1:5). Rumors of the ministry of this prophet-like person reached north, all the way to Galilee, home of Jesus of Nazareth, who evidently heard something that resonated with him. If John really should be a prophet, a spokesman for God, this pious young Jew would have to respond.

2. THE BAPTISM OF JESUS

Jesus made his way to where he could hear John in person. He heard John's call to undergo baptism for the forgiveness of sins (Mark 1:4//Luke 3:3). He heard John's denunciation of sinners; he heard John's prediction that one stronger than he would come, who would baptize with fire, whereas John used only water; one who was ready to chop down and burn up all unfruitful trees (Matt 3:7–10//Luke 3:7–9). Jesus did not take his stand shoulder-to-shoulder with John to condemn the crowds, but in solidarity with the crowds Jesus submitted to total immersion by John *into* the Jordan (Mark 1:9 literal Gk). Besides the thunderings of John, the Gk text of Mark is replete with the vocabulary of violence. As Jesus came up out of the water, the heavens were torn open for him, the Spirit went down like a dove *into* him, and a voice came from heaven, "You are my Son, the Beloved; with you I am well pleased" (Mark 1:9–11).

We moderns with our concordances can identify OT texts that convey these ideas, but Jesus had no immediate leisure to reflect on such details. He was a "Spirit possessed" person,[8] and the Spirit drove him into the wilderness, the home of dangerous wild animals, where disembodied spirits find no hospitable refuge (see Matt 12:43–45; Luke 8:29–31). There in solitude Jesus spent a long period of fasting, and he underwent a severe ordeal. Given Jesus's religious culture, that ordeal had its special character: if Jesus were truly YHWH's Son, he would have to contend with YHWH's chief adversary, Satan, who constantly opposed God and the people of God. John Ashton says Jesus was called as a prophet with an apocalyptic vision similar to that described in the first chapter of Ezekiel.[9] Craffert, in keeping with his voluminous

---

7. Stegemann & Stegemann, *The Jesus Movement*, 204.

8. Boring, *Mark*, 45. Later Jesus' own family thought he was out of his mind and tried to restrain him, while the legal experts (scribes) accused him of being possessed by Beelzebub and under control of the ruler of the demons, i.e., Satan (Mark. 3:20–22).

9. Ashton, "The Religious Experience of Jesus," 17d–18a. See above chapter 19.1 "Ezekiel: "YHWH's

research on the subject, suggests that Jesus experienced an altered state of consciousness (ASC) and that the baptism was Jesus's initiation as a shamanic figure.[10] Mark's brief account indicates that while in the desert Jesus successfully passed the ordeal, the wild beasts did him no harm, and angels (YHWH's ministers among the Immortals) rendered him service (Mark 1:12–13).

As the Synoptic Gospels show, Jesus credited John with being the one through whom he had had a life-changing experience that bestowed on him authority to challenge "the authorities" (Mark 11:27–33//Matt 21:23–37//Luke 20:1–8). I accept the term ASC (altered state of consciousness) as an appropriate way of describing this experience through which Jesus was given an unshakable conviction of a relationship to God so intimate that he could address God familiarly as ʾ*abba* (=father in Aramaic, Mark 14:36).[11] The prophet Hosea had taken the lead in understanding the covenant with the Divine Kinsman in the most intimate of personal terms—as husband and wife, but also as father and son (Hos 2:16–20; 11:1).[12] On other occasions YHWH referred to the Israelites as "my son," as when he sent Moses to confront Pharaoh, declaring, "Israel is my firstborn (Heb *bechor*) son" (Exod 4:22); and when Jeremiah announced YHWH's affirmation of the defeated northern tribes, "I have become a father to Israel, and Ephraim is my firstborn (*bechor*)" (Jer 31:9). Vincent Taylor points out the general semantic equivalence of Heb "firstborn"=*bechor* and Gk "beloved"=*agapētos*.[13] When Jesus accepted John's baptism, he took his place as one among the others of the people of YHWH to whom the term "my son" applied, but his private experience led him farther—Jesus completely internalized his relation to the Divine Kinsman as his Father God.

These words from heaven that were mediated to Jesus through ancient traditions preserved in Scripture plunged him into a dilemma. Jesus knew that to be Son—Beloved/Firstborn—implied a privileged status (Matt 17:24–27). Yet what did it mean for Jesus to be "son of God" in terms of the hand-to-mouth daily existence among the poverty-stricken Israelite people of Roman Palestine? In my view, the temptation of Jesus consisted precisely in the contradiction between Jesus's personal experiences at his baptism. Was his call to *majesty* or to *meekness*?

---

glory and judgment."

10. Craffert, *The Life of a Galilean Shaman*, 214–15

11. Jeremias, *The Prayers of Jesus*, "Abba," 11–65. Jeremias has much more detailed critical examination of the terms, "my Father" and "your Father" plus the significant absolute usage by Jesus of "the Father."

12. See above, chapter 16 "The Covenant as Family Relationship" section 1 "Hosea lives the covenant."

13. Taylor, *The Gospel According to Mark*, 161.

3. THE TEMPTATION OF JESUS

Matthew and Luke share lengthier accounts of the temptation, which scholars attribute to the Sayings Source Q (Matt 4:1–11//Luke 4:1–13). The Q account also shows similarities to shamanic culture, since it describes Jesus engaged in spirit travel, accompanied or driven by his adversary. During his solitary stay in the wilderness, engaged in struggle with Satan, Jesus had to choose between biblical themes that could support either uniqueness and privilege in relation to God (majesty) or the poverty and uncertainty implied by solidarity with the people (meekness). Matthew and Luke each adapted the Q material to his own needs, including different order of the three episodes, plus differences in detail. This would seem to indicate the passage of time and more leisurely reflection on the scriptural basis and its meaning for Jesus and his disciples.

Without attempting to determine which version is original, I will follow Luke, and I call attention to a special feature in Luke's Gospel, which scholars agree was meant for a non-Jewish community of believers. Luke interrupts the logical connection between baptism and temptation by inserting his genealogy of Jesus just here. In the Gk text Luke's genealogy reads thus: "Jesus was the son of Joseph, of Heli, of Matthat . . . [on and on] . . . of Seth, of Adam, of God" (Luke 3:23–38). In writing this, Luke universalizes the scope of Jesus's self-identity with people. What Luke's genealogy says of Jesus is no different from what could be said of any human being. Every one goes back to Adam and hence to God. By common humanity all people are God's children.

One OT text underlying the original declaration was addressed to a davidic king on the occasion of his coronation, "You are my son; today I have begotten you," followed by a promise: "Ask of me, and I will make the nations your heritage, and the ends of the earth your possession. You shall break them with a rod of iron, and dash them in pieces like a potter's vessel" (Ps 2:7–9). Another OT reference only complicates the matter: "With you I am well pleased" occurs in the introduction of the Servant of YHWH, who is filled with the Spirit and commissioned to bring justice to the Gentiles (Isa 42:1). The further development of the Servant figure leads to his innocent death on behalf of others (Isa 52:13—53:12). The fuller account of Q includes three temptations, dealing with separate issues, but all related to the question, "If (or since) you are the Son of God—."

3a. The first temptation

The devil said to Jesus: "If you are the Son of God, command this stone to become a loaf of bread" (Luke 4:3). In other words, you have a direct supply line from heaven, and you don't have to live hand-to-mouth.[14] But how could Jesus identify with the

---

14. Missionaries from affluent Western nations face a similar temptation when they go to developing countries.

people if he got special treatment while so many lived on the edge of starvation? Jesus would not allow privilege to come between him and the rest of humanity. He would live as a beggar, dependent on others' generosity. Jesus answered, "It is written, 'One does not live by bread alone' " (4:4), a reference to Deut 8:3. In OT context, Moses is making his farewell address to the Israelites before they enter the land of promise, speaking to each individual (Heb 2 pers. sing.). He reminds them of the bitter experiences in the desert—the hardship, the pain, the humility of realizing they were at the end of their rope and couldn't do a thing to help themselves. Moses says God treated you that way on purpose, so that you would learn to trust and obey God. God let you hunger and fed you with manna "in order to make you understand that one does not live by bread alone, but by every word that comes from the mouth of YHWH . . . Know then in your heart that as a parent [Heb father] disciplines a child [Heb son] so YHWH your God disciplines you" (Deut 8:3, 5).

God never said bread was unimportant. God provided the miracle of manna. But more important is one's trusting in God alone. Jesus would not ask a miracle on his personal behalf, when the masses were starving. Later on, Jesus opened his table fellowship to all comers without distinction. He fed the masses and told his disciples to do so too. Sonship to God means to be in solidarity with the other children of Adam, who are also children of God.

3b. The second temptation

The devil showed him all the kingdoms of the world and said, "To you I will give their glory and all this authority; for it has been given over to me, and I give it to anyone I please. If you, then, will worship me, it will all be yours" (Luke 3:5–7). One of the privileges of sonship according to Ps 2 is world dominion by a son of David. This promise and this hope were on the minds of many Jewish people, including Jesus's intimate disciples. Near the end, the Zealot party believed they could force God's hand by starting a large-scale uprising. Jesus had demonstrated his solidarity with the people, who longed so desperately for freedom. How far was he willing to go in that solidarity—as far as marching at their head as they rose against their oppressors? This must have been an especially strong temptation to Jesus.

But throughout world history, and especially throughout Israel's history, the imperial use of armed force had always ended in tragedy. Isaiah and Jeremiah, especially among the prophets, had urged their kings not to resort to arms and to trust in God, but all to no avail.[15] The author of Daniel had not supported the Maccabees' war of resistance. Yet the Jews could still cry out, "O that you would tear open the heavens and come down, so that the mountains would quake at your presence . . . so that the

---

15. See above chapter 17.4 "Prophets and the rejection of war."

nations might tremble at your presence" (Isa 64:1–2; also Ps 144:5–8). It didn't happen; there was no divine act of redemptive violence

Jesus answered, "It is written, 'Worship the Lord your God, serve only him' " (Luke 4:8), a second allusion to Moses's speech. Moses warns the people that when they enter Canaan they will find more prosperity than they have known, and they may think the local deities had made such affluence possible. They must not worship those gods. "YHWH your God you shall fear; him you shall serve, and by his name alone you shall swear" (Deut 6:10–14). That's to say, YHWH is giving you the land, but on YHWH's terms and not those of the local deities.

If after all, in some manner, God's promise to the Son includes world dominion, the Son must trust God to grant that dominion in God's own time and by God's own means. To try to impose dominion by military aggression is to worship the devil, the god of violence, instead of the God whom Jesus knew as ’*abba*. Sonship does not permit one to assert one's rights and grab for the promise. One must act patiently, giving worship, loyalty, and obedience to God alone. At his baptism, Jesus saw the heavens torn apart, but what came down was the Spirit like a dove, a creature with no weapons of attack or of self-defense, the sign of God's mercy after the flood, a universal symbol of peace. At his first public appearance, Jesus Son of God was possessed by the spirit of nonviolence. In this respect Jesus's ministry differed significantly from John's expectation of divine violent action.

3c. The third temptation

If sonship requires denial or surrender of special privilege, how can one be certain of sonship? Like the other temptations, the devil lifts this one right out of the Bible. Whoever fully trusts God will be kept safe in every danger. While pestilence and warfare mow down the multitudes all around, the one who really trusts God will be unscathed. "He will give his angels charge of you, to guard you, and on their hands they will bear you up, lest you strike your foot against a stone" (Ps 91:11–12). Here's the promise; check it out! Since you are the Son of God, put yourself in a position of danger, and see if God won't make good on the promise.

Jesus answered, "It is said, do not put the Lord your God to the test" (Luke 4:12). The citation is from Deut 6:16, where Moses warns the people: "Do not put YHWH your God to the test, as you tested him at Massah." The Massah incident is found in Exod 17:1–7. After being delivered from Egypt, the people arrived at Rephidim but found no water to drink. They complained to Moses and demanded water. They asked: "Is YHWH among us or not?" After deliverance at the Reed Sea, after the gift of the manna, the people could still demand more proof. That time Moses struck the rock and brought forth water, but in his farewell speech he warned them never again to put YHWH to the test, doubting the divine presence or good will.

SUMMARY

When John baptized Jesus, Jesus was given a special awareness of sonship to God, of intimacy with God as ʾ*abba*. But he had taken a stand, not with John in judgment over against the people, but by baptism in solidarity with them. In the temptation Jesus understood that sonship meant no special privileges for him, but only reinforced his sense of trust in ʾ*abba* and his oneness with the people. On this principle we must read the Gospel accounts of Jesus. I believe that whatever is consistent with this attitude of total surrender to God and nonviolent service to humanity shows us the authentic Jesus. Any hints of violence or sense of superiority reflects a later attitude of disciples incapable of accepting Jesus in his full humanity.

24

Jesus's Ministry as Healer and Exorcist

WHEN WE READ THE Gospel accounts of Jesus's baptism and temptation in the light of abundant evidence from research describing shamanic figures functioning in the types of culture that support such a personage, we must concede that Jesus must have undergone what modern researchers call altered states of consciousness (ASC; see above chapter 23). The cosmic view common to the peoples of the Mediterranean basin, called "The Great Chain of Being" as described above in chapter 21, saw nothing unbelievable about spirits of prominent ancestors of old from the realm of the Immortals, or other spirits whether good or bad entering into human individuals and taking over or empowering them, or of such persons in dream or vision traveling temporarily to a superior realm.[1]

Jesus's experience brought about changes in his behavior such that people could wonder what had happened to him. Among the people in general, some thought Jesus was indwelt by the martyred John the Baptist, or Elijah, or Jeremiah, or one of the other prophets (Matt 16:13–14//Mark 8:27–28//Luke 9:18–19; 9:7–9). His immediate family thought Jesus was out of his mind and tried to restrain him (Mark 3:21); he also thought of himself as a prophet who was rejected by his own people (Mark 6:4; John 4:43; 7:3–5). Partisans such as the Gospel writers called his empowering spirit Holy, i.e., from the God of Israel (Mark 1:12–13//Matt 4:1//Luke 4:1). Jesus's opponents said that Beelzebul, the evil prince of demons possessed him (Mark 3:22//Matt 12:24//Luke 11:15). As for Jesus, hearing God call him "My Son, the beloved," he felt himself endowed with such power and confidence that he immediately began to use that power for the benefit of the poor masses of people of Galilee by healing their diseases and liberating them from the evil spirits that could make them sick or drive them to violent, anti-social behavior.

---

1. Note the broken line separating Eternals and Immortals, and that separating Immortals and Humans in the Great Chain of Being chart. Lines of separation were not absolute and impassible. The whole system was porous to a degree.

1. EVALUATING JESUS'S ACTS OF HEALING AND EXORCISM

Traditional orthodox or conservative readers of the Gospels believe that "Jesus is God" and so they entertain no questions about his ability to heal any and all diseases and to overpower evil spirits. On the other hand, deep skepticism arises among critical scholars trained in the scientific approach based on the Enlightenment, "that revolutionary movement which held that there are 'eternal, timeless truths, identical in all the spheres of human activity—moral and political, social and economic, scientific and artistic; and there is only one way of recognizing them: by means of reason.'"[2] A chief motive of Craffert in interpreting Jesus as a Galilean shaman was precisely to offer a corrective to the tendency of those who from the rationalistic enlightenment point of view discount the factuality of the healings by Jesus of Nazareth. By his cross-cultural comparative study and research, Craffert offers a much more credible approach to understanding the biblical texts.[3]

Jesus's first healing act according to the earliest Gospel occurred in the synagogue of Capernaum, where Jesus went with his first disciples. "Just then there was in their synagogue a man with an unclean spirit, and he cried out, 'What have you to do with us, Jesus of Nazareth? Have you come to destroy us? I know who you are, the Holy One of God.' But Jesus rebuked [it] saying, 'Be silent, and come out of him!' And the unclean spirit, convulsing him and crying with a loud voice, came out of him" (Mark 1:23–26).[4] Both Jesus and the afflicted man were indwelt by spiritual powers, which were capable of recognizing each other as of mutually hostile character. Jesus's success in restoring the man to health was proof not only of his superior power, but that that power was good.

After leaving the synagogue, Jesus and his disciples went to the home of Simon and found his mother-in-law sick abed with a fever. "He came and took her by the hand, and the fever left her" (Mark 1:30–31). In Luke's parallel account, Jesus rebuked the fever, as though it had some quasi-personal quality, and it left her (Luke 4:38–39). A similar cultural context is assumed in the healing of a deaf man with a speech impediment. "He took him aside in private, away from the crowd, and put his fingers into his ears, and he spat and touched his tongue. Then looking up to heaven, he sighed and said to [it][5] 'Ephphatha,' that is, 'Be opened.' And immediately his ears were opened, his tongue was released,[6] and he spoke plainly" (Mark 7:33–35). Jesus

---

2. Davies, "The Rationalization of Suffering," quoting Isaiah Berlin, *The Proper Study of Mankind*, 334. See below for more on Davies.

3. Craffert, *The Life of a Galilean Shaman*, Part 1: A Paradigm Shift in Historical Jesus Historiography, 3–135.

4. Most likely, Jesus rebuked the unclean spirit, *it*, rather than the man, *him*, as in NRSV.

5. Jesus commanded the infecting spirit, *it*, rather than the sufferer, *him*. See above on the unclean spirit, Mark 1:23–26.

6. Literally, "freed from its bond"—the hostile power that prevented the patient from proper use of his faculties. Cf Luke 13:16; Jesus sets free a woman whom Satan had bound for eighteen years so that she could not stand up straight.

is in the region of Decapolis ("Ten Towns") with Greek-speaking Gentile population. Jesus's Aramaic command "Ephphatha" may have sounded like a magic word to the patient. Jesus's looking toward heaven and his sighing (praying?) reflect his dependence upon the divine power of his ʾ*abba* Father. He also performed acts and gestures of other shamanic-type persons. The Gk text states that the man's tongue was set free from its bondage. This is "the language of exorcism," reflecting "not only the general connection between sickness and demons in ancient understanding (see Luke 13:16), but also Mark's conception of Jesus's ministry as a whole as a divine liberating onslaught against the demonic powers that bind human life, the victory of God over demonic power in the Christ-event as a whole."[7]

Note that in Mark's Gospel this healing in the Decapolis occurs next after Jesus had healed the possessed daughter of the Syro-Phoenecian woman (Mark 7:24–30 and //; see above chapter 22.2 "Jesus the Jew"). As I noted at that point, Jesus made no specific campaign of ministry to the Gentiles, but whenever Jesus traveled among Gentiles, he shared with them also the divine gift of redemption from disabling illnesses and binding satanic powers. In Mark the very first Gentile healing was that of the Gerasene demoniac after Jesus and his disciples had crossed the sea of Galilee to the eastern shore that was inhabited by Gentiles (Mark 5:1–20). Boring emphasizes that just as Jesus's first exorcism among Jews took place in the religious setting of the synagogue, so the first exorcism among Gentiles took place near the tombs, a familiar location for some pagan religious rituals in addition to being the abode of the dead.[8] The Gentile demoniac who lived in the tombs, like the Jewish one in the synagogue, correctly identified Jesus and recognized him as a threat. This time the demons begged to be allowed to enter a herd of pigs feeding nearby, and when so allowed the whole herd rushed into the sea and was drowned. The pigs highlight the non-Jewish setting and thereby reinforce the Gospel's message that the liberating ministry of Jesus has universal implications.

Moderns in North America and Western Europe who discount these healing stories as mythological constructions are accustomed to consider diseases according to the *biophysical paradigm* based on Enlightenment rationalism that sees "disease as physical, the solution as technical, and the spectrum of human illnesses as universal."[9] This general approach owes a great deal to the influence of René Descartes, the seventeenth century French philosopher and author of the well-known aphorism, "I think, therefore I am." Descartes was a thoroughgoing rationalist, insisting that reason is the only reliable method of attaining knowledge. Applying this principle consistently led him to posit a distinct dualism between the body, which he likened to a machine

---

7. Boring, *Mark*, 217.
8. Boring, *Mark*, 149.
9. Craffert, *The Life of a Galilean Shaman*, 251.

following laws of nature, and the mind, or soul, which was nonmaterial and did not follow the laws of nature.[10]

Antonio Damasio has undertaken to demonstrate Descartes' error by means of his extensive research and experimentation on the actual structure and function of the human brain.[11] Descartes' error lies precisely in his proposal that thinking and feeling can be separated. Damasio points out that in evolutionary development, we were feeling beings long before we became thinkers, as brain structure seems to demonstrate. After presenting his evidence, Damasio summarizes his hypothesis: "I suggested that feelings are a powerful influence on reason, that the brain systems required by the former are enmeshed in those needed by the latter, and that such specific systems are interwoven with those which regulate the body . . . Feelings do seem to depend on a dedicated multi-component system that is indissociable from biological regulation. Reason does seem to depend on specific brain systems, some of which happen to process feelings."[12]

In Damasio's argument, the human mind is a unity of the body and the brain; I understand him to call "mind" what Descartes and many others were accustomed to calling "soul," with religious overtones that have become taboo in secular scientific circles. In a Postscriptum Damasio comments on the extent to which Western medical practice, especially that in the U.S., has maintained the dichotomy of Descartes and ignored the human mind. "The result of all this has been an amputation of the concept of humanity with which medicine does its job."[13] Damasio highlights a serious problem, which is gradually attracting attention in proper circles of authority, but which as yet shows few positive results.

James Davies is a practitioner and teacher of psychotherapy in the United Kingdom. He writes of his early acquaintance with two women who suffered debilitating depression. A psychologist had diagnosed the first as manic-depressive and prescribed medication. On her first visit with Davies she declared that her God had abandoned her. "As I hate the idea of a cruel god, I have decided there is no God. There is just me, my pain, these pills, and now you." After eight sessions, the woman departed, a confirmed atheist. Another woman suffered such grief at the death of her husband that a psychiatrist overcame her objections and persuaded her to take antidepressant pills. Medication improved her general condition, but she never recovered her joy and vivacity, though she still attended church as a formality. She was bound to the doctor and she sought pharmacological rather than religious relief. At the time, Davies

---

10. See also Wikipedia on René Descartes, Dualism.

11. Damasio, *Descartes' Error*. In his chapter 11 "A Passion for Reasoning" 244–252 Damasio applies to Descartes the considerable data related to brain structure and activity that he had presented in the previous chapters.

12. Damasio, *Descartes' Error* 245.

13. Ibid., 255.

approved the outcomes for the two women: "as the psychiatric vision increasingly colonized their outlook, their dependence upon the Christian vision decreased."[14]

After considerable further study, research, and observation, Davies has come to appreciate the aspect of Christian faith that helps people recognize suffering and pain as means of grace whereby they grow in spiritual depth and understanding and become better persons.[15] Many modern Western people seem to be abandoning that view and consider suffering as a negative affliction that can be alleviated medically. This has given rise to a multi-billion dollar pharmaceutical industry that profits from identifying various kinds of discontent, mental or spiritual, as medical conditions for which they can provide chemical cures. As a result, antidepressants are "the most prescribed medication in the United States today (and the most prescribed medication in U.S. medical history)."[16] Indeed, great numbers of Christians, including members of conservative, evangelical denominations, take such medications, which may be seen by some as a denial of basic Christian faith in God, but by others as a new gift ultimately from God, which believers are fully justified in accepting thankfully.[17] Davies himself takes a broad view that recognizes values in both aspects of suffering and its relief, and discourages a stark either/or secularist or religious approach to the question. On this point, the ministry of Jesus is helpful.

In actual fact, the vast majority of today's world population lives in cultures to which the biomedical paradigm is foreign, and to which healings, spirit possession, and exorcisms are commonplace. This is especially true in Africa. In the early decades of the twentieth century when the King of the Belgians considered the Congo his personal possession, an African named Kimbangu achieved fame as an exorcist. He had been educated as a boy and given the name Simon by missionaries from Europe, who trained him as an evangelist. Simon felt that they failed to respect him as an African and tried to control him, so he deserted them to act independently. One day a woman who was obviously "possessed" confronted him and demanded that he exorcise the demon. Simon said he was not an exorcist, but she insisted, so he pronounced words appropriate to exorcism and the demon departed. The woman then charged: "If you could exorcise a demon, you could also impose one." Despite this inauspicious beginning, Simon gained a wide reputation as a healer and exorcist and was believed to have raised the dead. He always claimed that he was acting in the Spirit of Jesus and for the benefit of the people. His popularity drew the attention of the Belgian authorities, who discounted his Christian ministry and accused him of plotting a popular uprising. They arrested him in 1921 and took him in chains nearly a thousand miles from his home, where they kept him imprisoned till he died in 1951. To the end Simon

---

14. Davies, "The Rationalization of Suffering" 49–50. See above note 2.

15. See, e.g., Rom 5:3–4: "We also boast in our sufferings, knowing that suffering produces endurance, and endurance produces character, and character produces hope."

16. Davies, "The Rationalization of Suffering" 53.

17. "The Rationalization of Suffering" 54–55.

denied political ambitions and persisted in his Christian witness. His sons continued his ministry, and today the Kimbanguist Church in Congo numbers approximately three million members.

A college friend of mine, Henry Crane, who grew up in Congo, son of Presbyterian missionaries, returned as a missionary to Congo and became acquainted with the Kimbanguists. Unlike some other indigenous African self-promoted Christian sects, the Kimbanguist maintained its faithful exaltation of Christ and avoided deifying its founder. Simon always insisted that he was another Simon who helped bear the cross of Jesus. His successors applied for membership in the World Council of Churches, and my friend Henry Crane assisted the investigation that verified the authenticity of the Kimbanguists and enabled their reception into membership of the World Council in 1969.[18] Still today, many years later, the Kimbanguist Church remains a partner of the Presbyterian Church (USA). The Anglican and the Roman Catholic dioceses in Africa are among Christian denominations there that have flourishing charismatic wings. Some Westerners view them as threats, while others wish to remain open to the possibilities of ministries that are compatible to the indigenous culture as well as to the faith of Christ.

Skeptics have also dismissed the Gospel reports of Jesus raising the dead (Matt 9:23–25//Mark 5:35–43//Luke 8:49–56; 7:11–17). It should be noted, however, that even today with technological aids available to medical experts, it is sometimes difficult to determine whether or not a person is biologically or legally dead. In non-scientific cultures, it is eminently possible for a sick person to present every indication of having expired, but for some of them to have been restored to life and activity in response to ministrations of prophets such as Elijah (1 Kgs 17:17–24) and Elisha (2 Kgs 4:18–37), as well as by Jesus, Peter (Acts 9:37–41), and Paul (Acts 20:7–10). Jesus considered himself a prophet, and others acclaimed him such. One cannot summarily dismiss accounts of Jesus raising the dead.

Other notable healings of Jesus include cleansing so-called lepers[19] (Mark 1:40–45//Matt 8:1–4; Luke 5:12–16; 17:11–19), and healing a woman with a twelve-year flow of blood (Mark 5:25–34//Matt 9:20–23//Luke 6:43–48). Jewish law complicated these particular conditions by declaring the persons ritually unclean and necessitated their isolation from religious worship and normal social contact.[20] Add the possibility of popular belief that the victims were suffering punishment for sin, and the cases

---

18. Unfortunately, Henry Crane had been seriously wounded in World War Two and died at a fairly young age. His elder brother Sidney, also my personal friend, shared with me this information about Henry and the Kimbanguists. See also Wikipedia entry on Simon Kimbangu for more information.

19. The terms leper and leprosy in the Bible result from an error in translating the OT Lev 13–14 and related texts into Gk. The OT deals with a variety of skin conditions in people including fungus, some of which could also be detected in linen, wool, or leather goods. *Lepra* for the disease and *lepros* for the person affected refer to a specific disease now scientifically identified as Hansen's disease, not specifically that dealt with in the OT. See *ABD* "Leprosy."

20. In pre-modern Japan, some rural villages had special places where menstruating women were segregated during their "period."

become even more complicated. The causes and cures of this kind of disease are not amenable to explanations on the basis of the modern biomedical paradigm. Craffert assembles documentation indicating that some recent expert opinion raises serious questions about the inadequacy of the biomedical paradigm and that employs a biopsychosocial paradigm that "offers an alternative framework for dealing with illness and healing in Western as well as in cross-cultural situations."[21]

2. JESUS RESPONDS TO CRITICISM AND QUESTIONS

Pharisees and experts in the Law charged that Jesus could expel demons only because the ruler of the demons enabled him to do it. Jesus promptly retorted that if such were the case, it was a sign that the realm of Satan was involved in a self-defeating civil war. Besides, he asked, how is it that some of *your* people cast out demons? The fact of the matter, Jesus insisted, was that somebody stronger than Satan had come to bind Satan as a captive and was in process of plundering Satan's house. "But if it is by the finger of God [Luke//Matt "Spirit of God"] that I cast out demons, then the kingdom of God has come to you" (Matt 12:24–29//Mark 3:22–27//Luke 11:15–22).

It is necessary to read together all the Gospel accounts listed here, each in its broader context. The numerous differences in detail, which I have conflated in the summary, indicate that oral traditions circulated of multiple occasions of this charge against Jesus, and that many different followers remembered and communicated their witness before the Gospels were written. One should also note that Jesus makes subtle references to several OT texts in his response to his critics. The reference to the "finger of God" points to the remark of Pharaoh's magicians when they had to admit that the power given to Moses and Aaron was greater than theirs—it was the finger of God (Exod 8:16–19). Jesus's claim that he has bound Satan and robbed him of his human prey recalls YHWH's declaration to Israel in exile that he will free them from the mighty tyrants who hold them captive (Isa 49:24–25).

A passage in Q (Matt 11:2–6//Luke 7:18–23) centers on a saying of Jesus that references several OT texts: While John the Baptist still languished in prison, he heard about Jesus's activities and sent some of his disciples to ask, "Are you the one who is to come, or are we to wait for another?" The text does not specify John's motive, but evidently the reports about Jesus did not suit his own sense of calling and mission, which had emphasized threats of imminent divine punishment. In reply to the questioners, Jesus offered a brief resumé of his work: "the blind receive their sight, the lame walk, the lepers are cleansed, the deaf hear, the dead are raised, and the poor have good news brought to them" (Matt 11:5). This list reflects the main features of many texts in Isaiah that speak of YHWH's restoration of exiled and discouraged Israel, especially Isa 35:5–6, but also 26:19; 29:18; 42:7, 18).

---

21. Craffert, *The Life of a Galilean Shaman*, 260.

Another restoration text from Isaiah featured Jesus' discourse in his home synagogue at Nazareth; "The Spirit of the Lord is upon me, because he has anointed me to bring good news to the poor. He has sent me to proclaim release to the captives and recovery of sight to the blind, to let the oppressed go free, to proclaim the year of the Lord's favor" (Luke 4:18–19; Isa 61:1–2). In his subsequent remarks Jesus referred to the OT examples of Elijah preserving the life of a Sidonian widow during famine (1 Kgs 17:1–16), and Elisha healing the leprosy of Naaman, the military commander of Aram, the chief enemy of Israel (2 Kgs 5:1–14). These references to YHWH's concern for Gentiles, when many Israelite sufferers were bypassed, so enraged the congregation that they were prepared to lynch Jesus (Luke 4:16–30).

In answer to another question, Jesus again specifically linked himself with the entire concept of the kingdom of God and its actual presence in his own person "Once Jesus was asked by the Pharisees when the kingdom of God was coming, and he answered, 'The kingdom of God is not coming with things that can be observed; nor will they say, "Look, here it is!" or "There it is!" For, in fact, the kingdom of God is among you' " (Luke 17:20–21). In the Gospel records, Jesus's teaching about the kingdom of God, especially in his use of parables, lacks any sense of organization or system, but that may be precisely because in the consciousness of Jesus he himself personified, localized, and manifested the kingdom, and his teachings concerning the kingdom were often offered only in connection with his acts of healing and exorcism.

As Craffert writes with emphasis, "in most instances the term *kingdom of God* (or derivatives) can be seen as the *experience of the powerful presence of God in and through the life and activities of Jesus as a shamanic figure*. 'Kingdom of God' is a code word, if you like, for the state or condition of God's powerful presence mediated by Jesus's (shamanic) activities."[22]

SUMMARY

A careful study of the life and teaching of Jesus as preserved in the Gospels reveals the great extent to which Jesus cited the OT in support of what he was doing and saying. Sometimes it was by means of specific quotations (as in the case of his references to Deuteronomy in his temptation by Satan), but often simply by general allusion as in the case of his response to the question from John the Baptist. As Ben F. Meyer writes, "Jesus is seen as intent on listening to the Scriptures for the orientation of his life and mission . . . with an economy of revelation that withheld the secret of his person and destiny out of realism and wisdom respecting his listeners."[23]

---

22. Craffert, *The Life of a Galilean Shaman*, 349.
23. Meyer, "Jesus and the Scriptures," 174. Meyer employs a full range of critical techniques in reaching this conclusion. My MTh thesis of 1954, *Christ and the Scriptures* was uncritical and somewhat unsophisticated, but I feel that Meyer and I are "on the same page" as the saying goes.

God For All

The conclusion of Meyer's statement refers to the fact that not only the general population but also his own disciples had fixated ideas based on nationalistic hopes that Jesus refrained from exciting by openly identifying himself by means of words and titles, especially that of Messiah/Christ that they would misinterpret tragically. I shall deal with this question more specifically below in chapter 27; meanwhile I shall call attention to the influence of the concept of the oneness of God upon the ministry of Jesus.

25

Jesus and the Oneness of God

JESUS AFFIRMED THE ONENESS of God in quoting the Shema and declaring that love of God was the greatest of all the laws. By adding the command to love one's neighbor as one's self, Jesus affirmed the basic equality of all humanity before the One God. I have insisted that radical monotheism implies the basic equality of all contingent existence in the presence of the One Creator God, but as seen above, chapter 21.2 "Cosmology and anthropology of the Mediterranean peoples," Jesus's contemporaries were still far from that radical conclusion. Yet Jesus himself demonstrated that he was making progress toward that point as we see when we examine his words and deeds. Jesus affirmed the essential value and sacredness of everything God created.

1. AFFIRMING THE GOODNESS OF THE MATERIAL WORLD

After the construction of the Second Temple and the policies of the Hasmoneans, the elite cadre of priests concentrated power in their hands and mobilized the people of YHWH as a separated community bound by complex rules and regulations of pure/impure and clean/unclean. We note Jesus in conflict on this issue all through the gospel accounts. Jesus boldly laid hands on a leper to cleanse him (Mark 1:40–45//Matt 8:1–4; cf Luke 5:12–16), and he praised a hemorrhaging woman who surreptitiously touched him for healing (Mark 5:25–34//Matt 9:20–22//Luke 8:43–48), even though mosaic law and legalistic interpretation would judge him to have become unclean by these contacts.

The priests, approaching most closely to the presence of God, had to keep purity laws scrupulously, but it was difficult for people whose work put them in "unclean" environments and whose poverty limited their choice and preparation of foods. Some Pharisees would like to apply priestly standards to themselves, and in their own gatherings for meals they might limit their fellowship to others who kept the same standards of personal cleanliness, food purity, and payment of tithes. According to the OT, the land belonged to YHWH, and the Israelites were only "aliens and tenants" (Lev 25:23). In order that all might enjoy the fruitfulness of the land, payment

God For All

of tithes helped share the wealth with those in need (Deut 26:12). The Jewish temple elites, profiting from the extractive system of imperial Rome, enriched themselves from tithes collected from peasants. Peasants, who were unable to resist Roman tribute because of military enforcement, became either unable or unwilling to pay tithes, which rendered them impure according to the Pharisees.[1]

Jesus adopted the common-sense view of food that it goes into the stomach and thence into the sewer, without causing any ritual defilement. Instead, what issues from heart and mind in the form of evil thoughts, words, and acts causes real defilement (Mark 7:1–23//Matt 15:1–20). Jesus made no distinctions on the basis of clean/unclean in welcoming all comers to share meals with him, and he got a bad reputation for eating with "tax collectors and sinners," two classes that epitomized all the undesirables (Mark 2:13–17//Matt 9:9–13//Luke 5:27–32; 15:1–2). By personal example Jesus took the lead in acknowledging and appreciating the essential goodness of all that God created (Gen 1:31).

2. AFFIRMING HUMAN EQUALITY

Jesus's practice of open table fellowship was a challenge to the hierarchy of persons. For people in Western societies that respect democracy and equal rights, it is difficult to imagine the extent and the complexity of structural hierarchy and discrimination in the society of first century Palestine as Jeremias describes it.[2] Distinctions were rigid, and there was practically no opportunity for upward social mobility. That makes Jesus's egalitarian behavior all the more remarkable.

Within his most intimate group of disciples Jesus included at least two who might be considered sworn enemies (Mark 3:13–19; Matt 10:1–4; Luke 6:12–16). One was a tax collector (Gk *telōnēs*). Herzog defines a *telōnēs* as a toll collector, a very minor functionary, probably a Jew who was so destitute that he hired out to a wealthy retainer who had contracted to collect some of the many tolls and tariffs the power structure had imposed on every sort of enterprise. He had to gouge the payers and was thus the immediate object of their hatred and social rejection.[3] Through this disciple, Jesus became accessible to many other toll collectors and people branded as "sinners" because of their inability to conform to the higher standards of purity (Mark 2:15). Another of Jesus's disciples was a Cananaean,[4] later called Zealot, a member of a group pledged to resist to the death not only Roman domination but especially Jews whom they considered collaborators (see below on the destruction of the temple).

---

1. Herzog, *Parables as Subversive Speech*, 183–84.
2. Jeremias, *Jerusalem in the Time of Jesus*, Part Three "Social Status" and Part Four "The Maintenance of Racial Purity."
3. Herzog, op.cit., 187.
4. Taylor, *Mark*, 234, "an adherent of the party later known as 'the Zealots', and is correctly rendered by Luke *zēlōtēs* (Luke 6:15)."

The rest of the disciples were ordinary folk, and both Jesus and his followers were considered uneducated according to current intellectual standards (Jesus: John 7:15; disciples: Acts 4:13). Quarrels marred the personal relations among the disciples, and more than once Jesus upbraided them for arguing about rank. He ordered them not to adopt the model of political hierarchy typical of royal courts (Mark 10:35–45//Matt 20:20–28; cf Luke 22:24–27).

In the NT itself we detect hints that early on a sort of hierarchy began to take form among the disciples. Matt 23:1–36 comprises a stringent criticism by Jesus against the Pharisees, beginning with their love of ostentation and rank, including warnings to the disciples not to fall into the same pattern. "Call no one your father on earth, for you have one Father—the one in heaven. Nor are you to be called instructors, for you have one instructor, the Messiah. The greatest among you will be your servant. All who exalt themselves will be humbled, and all who humble themselves will be exalted" (Matt 23:9–12). This saying reached its present form post-resurrection, as indicated by placing in the mouth of Jesus the term Messiah applied to himself (see below chapter 27). But it is an authentic reminder that Jesus had characterized his followers as a family of equals under one father/teacher, that is God. The saying on being humbled or exalted recalls the words of some of the OT warnings on the downfall of the proud (e.g. "Pride goes before destruction, and a haughty spirit before a fall. It is better to be of a lowly spirit among the poor than to divide the spoil with the proud" (Prov 16:18–19), and it is fully appropriate as a warning of Jesus to his followers.

The very first of Jesus's parables, that of the sower (Matt 13:1–9//Mark 4:1–9//Luke 8:4–9), aptly illustrates Jesus's non-discriminatory attitude toward people. The farmer in this parable appears utterly stupid from the point of view of practical farming. He throws the precious seed not only in the well-prepared soil but everywhere else, including the hard-trodden pathway, rocky ground, and patches of weeds. Like that farmer, Jesus spreads his message everywhere without attempting to judge whether a particular individual or class of persons will or will not respond—"Let anyone with ears listen!" (Mark 4:1–9//Matt 13:1–9//Luke 8:4–8).

2a. Women disciples

People who refuse women ordained office in the church today point out that nowhere does Jesus specifically appoint women disciples. They consider this crucial, for "disciple" was a technical term denoting a special relation between a teacher and a learner. We have no evidence or reason to believe that Jesus followed a formal protocol in accepting a person as disciple in the same way as the rabbis. The Gospels mention a number of women in Jesus's company, some of whom traveled with them "through cities and villages" (Luke 8:1–3; cf Mark 15:40–41), something scandalous in that society. In Acts "disciple" refers to any and all followers of the resurrected Jesus both men and women, no doubt reflecting Jesus's own practice.

The story of Jesus with Martha and Mary (Luke 10:38–42) implies that Jesus recognized Mary as a disciple. Martha (this may be a nickname, Aramaic for "Mistress"), who had welcomed Jesus into *her* house, busied herself with proper hospitality for a respected male guest, as society demanded. By contrast, Mary *also*, or *even* Mary (Gk *kai*) sat *at Jesus's feet*, in the posture proper to male disciples who may have been present as well. Usual translations of the text ignore *kai*, but *kai* calls specific attention to Mary. She deserves this attention, since the rabbis were very insistent *not* to take women disciples.

In the writings of Luke/Acts the author stressed this posture of disciples *at the feet of* a teacher. Paul identifies himself as having been educated *at the feet of Gamaliel*, an illustrious rabbi (Acts 21:3). In Luke's version of the healing of the Gerasene demoniac (8:26–39), the author adds a detail not in his source (Mark 5:1–20). Luke says people found the healed man *sitting at the feet of Jesus* like a disciple. Jesus does not allow him to join his immediate band, but instead sends him back home with a commission to bear witness to what God has done for him (in strict construction, being sent by Jesus on a mission made him an apostle, in the NT a special calling beyond that of disciple).

Martha busies herself with many *tasks* (Gk *diakonia*=service) and complains that Mary has left her to *do* all the *work* (Gk *diakonein*=to serve). Jesus responds kindly to Martha, because of her worry and anxiety over *many things*. As the large number of variations in the Gk text indicates, copyists found it difficult to grasp the implications of what Jesus said next. The best attested is, "Few things are needed, or one" referring to food. In other words, "A simple meal is quite sufficient." Jesus suggests that Martha need not spend so much time, energy, anxiety, and expense on an elaborate banquet when simple fare, even only one dish, would be enough. As for Mary (same name as Moses and Aaron's sister Miriam the prophet, Exod 15:29), Jesus approves her choice to be a disciple and insists that it not be denied her. Mary is free to cross the customary limits for women, while Jesus appreciates the indispensable work that homemakers like Martha do.

In Mark 10:43–45//Matt 20:26–28 Jesus describes his own work and that to which his disciples should devote themselves using the very word that appears in the Martha/Mary story, the word rendered in Greek *diakonein* and translated in English as "to serve." This verb and its cognate nouns, *diakonos*=servant and *diakonia*=service, had no religious connotations until Jesus introduced it. Serve, servant, service all related to the most menial of work, ordinarily done by slaves or women or by the youngest in an all-male group. The culture demanded that one avoid labor of any kind and see to it that only an inferior would be saddled with such chores. In effect Jesus turns the hierarchy of service upside down:

"You know that among the Gentiles those whom they recognize as their rulers lord it over them, and their great ones are tyrants over them. But it is not so among you; but whoever wishes to become great among you must be your servant (*diakonos*), and whoever wishes to be first among you must be slave (*doulos*) of all. For the Son of Man came not to be served but to serve, and to give his life a ransom for many." (Mark 10:42b–45). Even if, as some contend, the wording of this text shows evidence of post-resurrection editing, unquestionably Jesus was the originator of the fundamental point about service. For my central aim in this study, it is important to note that Jesus's teaching and example stand in stark contrast to the concept of service/ministry in the postexilic priestly hierarchy based on the Hebrew word *sh-r-t* and employed by the Hasmoneans.[5]

2b. Women and divorce

Among Jews adultery consisted in a man having sexual intercourse with the wife of another man, for he had damaged the man's property. It was not an offense against the offender's own wife. The aggrieved man could divorce his wife, but she had no such right, even in cases of his infidelity or abuse. Jewish rabbis differed concerning proper grounds for divorce, Hillel placing practically no conditions on the husband, and Shammai restricting divorce to cases of the wife's infidelity.

According to Mark 10:2–9 Pharisees asked Jesus's opinion on the basic question: "Is it lawful for a man to divorce his wife?" Jesus responded with a question, "What did Moses command you?" They replied that Moses said a man should write her a certificate of dismissal and to divorce her (a reference to Deut 24:1–4). Consider Jesus's reply in detail: "Because of your hardness of heart he wrote this commandment for you. But from the beginning of creation, 'God made them male and female.' For this reason a man shall leave his father and mother and be joined to his wife, and the two shall become one flesh. So they are no longer two, but one flesh. Therefore what God has joined together, let no one separate" (Mark 10:5–9).[6]

Jesus states that husbands' obtuse sinfulness led to Moses's requirement. Men had always divorced wives, but Moses gave some relief to a divorced woman. A certificate of divorce proved that she had been married and was not a common unattached female. But, said Jesus, divorce was contrary to God's original purpose. He cited Gen 1:27 where God created male and female together simultaneously in the image of God (followed by giving them joint dominion over the rest of creation). Jesus then cited Gen 2:24, which requires the man to give greater loyalty to his wife than to his own birth family. Sexual union between husband and wife thus becomes, in God's original purpose, indissoluble by divorce. In one fell swoop, citing the creative purpose of God, Jesus acknowledges for women the original divine intention of equality with men and strips from men the exclusive privilege they had grasped to own, dominate, abuse, and dismiss their women.

Through the centuries Christians interpreted Jesus's words legalistically, turning Jesus into a stricter lawgiver than Moses, and many states enforced laws forbidding

---

5. See above chapter 20.1 "Temple and priesthood restored under Persian Rule" notes 7 and 8.
6. See chapter 4.1 "YHWH God, the garden, and the first humans."

divorce. (In Matthew's version, 19:10, the disciples, making the absolute interpretation of Jesus's words, opined that it would be better for a man not to marry at all!).[7] What follows in Mark takes the form of private teaching to the disciples: "Whoever divorces his wife and marries another commits adultery against her; and if she divorces her husband and marries another, she commits adultery" (Mark 10:11–12). These verses probably express the interpretation of the Markan community that preserved and valued them. They certainly acknowledge the implications of Jesus's teaching on the equality of women and men. Hardness of heart in both genders persists, and divorce happens. But the saying affirms women's full equality with men, for good or for ill. Conditions change over time, and mercy must triumph over judgment. Even YHWH did not abide by the law! After divorcing Israel for unfaithfulness, YHWH took her back again (Hos 2:2–20; Jer 3:1–14; chapter 17 "Covenant as Family Relation").

Through his non-discriminating treatment of people, Jesus undermined the hierarchical structures of superordinate and subordinate in human society under God. Jesus bestows on all people the dignity implied in the Genesis account of creation: Men have no right to dominate women, and even the dominion originally intended for male and female alike is rather to be voluntarily surrendered for the role of mutually serving one another.

3. THE TRUE VALUE OF TIME: THE SABBATH CONTROVERSIES

A particularly sharp difference of opinion between Jesus and religious authorities concerned how to honor the sabbath day. Strict constructionists of Mosaic Law—do no work—fenced the sabbath about with prohibitions of all sorts of activities, with the result that in practical terms one might be prevented from performing an act of kindness or humanitarian benefit for fear of violating some restriction on "work." Jesus's way was to perform acts of healing and mercy on this very day despite risking criticism for a presumed offense. The Gospels describe Jesus defending his disciples' plucking handsful of grain to eat (Mark 2:23–27//Matt 12:1–8//Luke 6:1–5); healing a man with a withered arm (Mark3:1–6//Matt 12:9–14//Luke 6:6–11); a bent over woman (Luke 13:10–17); and a man with dropsy (Luke 14:1–6).

Christians today might interpret the controversy in an anti-Jewish manner, contrasting Jesus's championing of freedom against Jewish legalism. But the real issue was not *whether* to keep sabbath but *how best* to keep it. Thus, Jesus challenged his critics: "Is it lawful to do good or to do harm on the sabbath, to save life or to kill?" (Mark 3:4). For Jesus, keeping sabbath could be subsumed under the two great commandments, to love God and to love one's neighbor as oneself. Doing good by taking initiative on behalf of hungry or sick or disabled people—saving life—was the fulfillment of

---

7. Matt 19:1–9 reflects the use Jewish Christians made of this story, viz, Shammai's conservative *grounds* of divorce, only in case of the wife's infidelity.

the sabbath law. Failing to show mercy, or prohibiting it when given the opportunity, was, in effect, to do evil, to kill.

All three synoptic versions of the grain-plucking incident end with the declaration, "The Son of Man is lord of the sabbath." Taking the title Son of Man exclusively to refer to Jesus, Christians may tend to think that faith in Jesus relieves Christians of responsibility for keeping the sabbath holy. However, "Son of Man" is susceptible to interpretation as a representative figure including humans in general, thus placing responsibility on each one to decide in his or her own situation.[8] This understanding becomes more compelling if we note Mark 2:27, which Matthew and Luke omitted: Then he said to them, "The sabbath was made for humankind, not humankind for the sabbath." As Wink observes, "Law structures freedom. If we are serving that which the law serves, then we have freedom of choice, even if it means breaking the law (or, as here, interpreting for oneself what constitutes violation of the law)."[9]

Schottroff and Stegemann cite the economic condition of first century Palestine. Under double exploitation by Roman overlords and the Judean power structure that acted as Rome's surrogates in exploiting the people, a sizeable proportion of the population lived on the edge of starvation. Matthew makes clear what is presumed, that the disciples were *hungry*. "In God's eyes the hunger of the poor is more important than the Sabbath and imposes a more important religious duty than does even the Sabbath . . . The intention is not to attack or relativize the importance of the Sabbath, but rather to use the Sabbath to bring out the importance of alleviating hunger."[10]

We read that at the end of the incident of healing the man with the withered hand, the authorities went out and tried to find a way to destroy Jesus (Mark 3:6). In terms of real time, it may have been too early in Jesus's ministry for his opponents to reach such an extreme decision, but theologically it is altogether understandable. The hardness of their hearts (3:5) was such that not only would they deny healing to a disabled brother or sister; but they would eventually seek the death of the one who seriously challenged their authority.

4. THE ASSAULT ON THE TEMPLE, THE HIERARCHY OF SPACE

According to Mark 11:15–19, the basis of the synoptic account, Jesus's assault on the temple marked the point of no return, for from that moment the religious authorities sought how to destroy him. At his trial, the first accusation was his threat to the temple (Mark 14:57).

The minority who returned to Judea from Babylon tried to separate themselves spatially by borders and walls and by driving out all those thought to be ethnically

---

8. Crossan, *The Historical Jesus*, 257. "Son of man" carried the ordinary generic meaning that every human being is lord of the sabbath.

9. Wink, *The Human Being*, 71.

10. Schottroff and Stegemann, "The Sabbath Was Made for Man," 125.

mixed (Ezra 10, Neh 13). As a people holy to YHWH they occupied a holy land. Space outside and Gentiles who inhabited it were unclean. In Jesus's time, priestly authorities divided space into fourteen areas of decreasing holiness from the temple in the center. God's glory dwelt in the Holy of Holies, "a mythologically conceived space where heaven, earth, and underworld were believed to come together." Only the high priest could enter this space, and he only on the annual Day of Atonement. Lesser priests could enter the adjacent Holy Place daily to offer incense. Outside, Levites ministered to priests doing their sacrificial duties. Farther out were courts where Jewish men could come, then Jewish women, and finally Gentiles, who were forbidden on pain of death to cross over into more holy space.[11]

The Temple, center of this hierarchy of holy space, was also the economic and political nerve center for Jews both in Judea and in the diaspora. Every Jew regardless of status or residence had to pay an annual temple tax. The poor widow who put her very last bits of cash—"everything she had, all she had to live on"—was not exempt (Mark 12:41–44//Luke 21:1–4). Wealthy people, who may have made their fortunes precisely by preying on helpless people like her (Mark 12:40//Luke 20:47), could easily afford to put in much more. Great landowners and moneylenders used the temple as a bank to safeguard their wealth. The temple kept records of loans made at usurious rates to peasants and small landholders. The elite priestly class was fully complicit in this exploitation of fellow Jews.

With that background we can better understand what was at stake when Jesus entered the temple, overthrew the tables of the moneychangers, and drove out the animals available for sacrifice. "He was teaching and saying, 'Is it not written, My house shall be called a house of prayer for all the nations (=Gentiles)? But you have made it a den of robbers.' And when the chief priests and the scribes heard it, they kept looking for a way to kill him; for they were afraid of him, because the whole crowd was spellbound by his teaching" (Mark 11:17–18).

Jesus cites two prophetic texts: First, "My house shall be called a house of prayer for all the nations (=Gentiles)" cites Isaiah 56:7, which I considered in noting opposition to the exclusivist policies of the postexilic Judean priestly power elite (see above, chapter 20.1 "Temple and priesthood restored under Persian rule"). Jesus affirms his approval of that earlier (apparently unsuccessful) attempt to establish a more inclusive policy. In Jesus's appreciation of the implications of the oneness of God, the holiness of this place should not serve to exclude anyone, but should offer a place where people of any human condition could meet God. Second, "You have made it a den of robbers" paraphrases Jer 7:11, spoken in the context of Jeremiah's sermon against the temple in the waning days of the kingdom of Judah. The authorities got the point that Jesus was implying that the temple of his day would be destroyed as was the temple of Jeremiah's time, and for the same reason. Instead of furthering the cause of justice in the true

---

11. Maier, "Self-Definition, Prestige, and Status of Priests," 146. See the diagram on p 143 showing 14 concentric degrees of holy space.

service of God and neighbor, people had degraded the holiness of the temple into a robbers' hideout, where they could stash their swag and escape just punishment for their crimes.

Jesus himself was deeply sensitive to the widespread poverty of the people and the systemic evils that drove them into poverty and kept them there. He had special sympathy and assistance for the poor, especially the paupers (*ptōchoi*) who literally had nothing. Jesus also had nothing good to say for rich people—"How hard it will be for those who have wealth to enter the kingdom of God" (Mark 10:23//Matt 19:23//Luke 18:24). Jesus might have believed as some people do today that wherever there is great wealth, there has been a great crime. Conditions got worse after the death of Jesus, and general dissatisfaction and unrest developed into a situation calling for Roman military intervention. Meanwhile, peasant rebellion and brigandage grew to such a height that under the leadership of the Zealots they invaded the temple, destroyed the debt records, and looted the wealth. The Zealots chose their own high priest by casting lots among candidates from the old Zadokite genealogy rather than the Hasmonean usurpers. They killed off so many of the Jewish religious and political power structure that the Romans had no one with whom to negotiate for a surrender and settlement, so they destroyed Jerusalem and its temple altogether.[12]

The power structure rightly saw that the end of the temple would not only overthrow the religious system that had nourished them and their people for centuries, but also it would destroy their base of political and economic power. Therefore in self-defense they had to get rid of Jesus. In Jesus's view, the end of the temple would mean the end not only of people's debasement of religious cult to cover their criminal acts, but it would also break down barriers of exclusion and open up the possibility of universalizing the worship of the One God.

5. JESUS'S ONE GOD: THE FATHER

Jesus's preferred name for God was Father, a term he used over 170 times.[13] His understanding of the divine-human relationship was not based on the Sinai covenant modeled on the Assyrian suzerainty treaties, picturing God as a despot threatening terrifying punishment for disobedience (Deut 28:47–68).

People whose human fathers have abused or neglected them may balk at calling God Father. A colleague told me that a popular Japanese saying linked earthquake, volcano, and father—all could be unpredictably capricious and violent, but none was of permanent significance! It is truly sad that some people have negative experiences of father; but for Jesus experiencing God as Father and encouraging the rest of us to do the same is a wonderful contribution to the betterment of the human condition.

---

12. Crossan, *The Historical Jesus*, 210–218 "A Revolution Within a Revolution."

13. See Gulley and Mullholland, *If Grace is True*, 55–61 for touching examples of deep love of human fathers for their children.

God For All

For Jesus, God as the Divine Kinsman, specifically the parent who loved unconditionally and who freely restored the wayward child (Hos 11:1–10) was the most compatible concept of God. Based on God's call at his baptism and his triumph over temptation by complete trust in God, Jesus lived and died and rose again in the divine embrace. The Father of Jesus is Lord of heaven and earth (Matt 11:26//Luke 10:21), who sends sun and rain on good and evil, just and unjust alike (Matt 5:45), who is kind to the ungrateful and selfish (Luke 6:35). The Father knows the needs of his children before we ask (Matt 6:8), and will outdo even the most generous of imperfect human fathers (Luke 11:11–13). Since the Father is merciful and undiscriminating in his dealing with people, Jesus told us to love our enemies and pray for those who abuse us (Matt 5:44//Luke 6:27), and he set us a personal example. Thus, Jesus's concept of God as Father, and the life of Jesus completed in that relationship, provide a fitting example for all of us as we accept our relationship to the God and Father of our lord Jesus Christ and let ourselves be guided by our trust in God for all.

26

Jesus Challenges the Domination System

As a result of recent scholarly research and publishing, it is ever more clear that Jesus posed a fundamental challenge to the accepted order of his day. Keep in mind that the Gospels were written post-resurrection and after the destruction of the Temple in 70 CE. By then the Jesus people may have to some extent escaped the utter and desperate poverty of the masses of people among whom Jesus walked and talked. The Q material includes many sayings of Jesus that Matthew and Luke have utilized in their Gospels, but each in its own distinct manner. Each opens with a series familiarly called The Beatitudes, which turn accepted wisdom upside down.

1. THE BEATITUDES

Blessed are the poor in spirit, for theirs is the kingdom of heaven.	Blessed are you who are poor, for yours is the kingdom of God.
Blessed are those who mourn, for they will be comforted.	Blessed are you who are hungry now, for you will be filled.
Blessed are the meek, for they will inherit the earth.	Blessed are you who weep now, for you will laugh.
Blessed are those who hunger and thirst for righteousness, for they will be filled.	Blessed are you when people hate you, and when they exclude you, revile you, and defame you on account of the Son of Man.
Blessed are the merciful, for they will receive mercy.	
Blessed are the pure in heart, for they will see God.	Rejoice in that day and leap for joy, for surely your reward is great in heaven; for that is what their ancestors did to the prophets.
Blessed are the peacemakers, for they will be called children of God.	
Blessed are those who are persecuted for righteousness' sake, for theirs is the kingdom of heaven.	But woe to you who are rich, for you have received your consolation.
	Woe to you who are full now, for you will be hungry.
Blessed are you when people revile you and persecute you and utter all kinds of evil against you falsely on my account.	Woe to you who are laughing now, for you will mourn and weep.
Rejoice and be glad, for your reward is great in heaven, for in the same way they persecuted the prophets who were before you. (Matt 5:3–12)	Woe to you when all speak well of you, for that is what their ancestors did to the false prophets. (Luke 6:20–26)

Luke's version is particularly relevant to the poor and destitute (*ptōchoi*), and it adds the woes against the rich and powerful. Luke's version continues at this point with a saying that adds a cautionary note to what has just been said: "But I say to you that listen, Love your enemies, do good to those who hate you, bless those who curse you, pray for those who abuse you" (Luke 6:27–8). The oppressed are warned not to gloat over the downfall of their oppressors but rather to pray for them.

2. OTHER SAYINGS FROM Q

The reversal of accepted wisdom reaches its climax in what follows: "But love your enemies, do good, and lend, expecting nothing in return. Your reward will be great, and you will be children of the Most High, for he is kind to the ungrateful and the wicked. Be merciful, just as your Father is merciful" (Luke 6:35–36). Jesus addresses fellow Jews who know God as Father just as he does. Yet Father God is also the Most High, the One Creator God, who is kind to the ungrateful and the wicked—without specifying ethnicity or class and making no moral requirements.

Matthew has, "But I say to you, Love your enemies and pray for those who persecute you, so that you may be children of your Father in heaven; for he makes his sun to rise on the evil and on the good, and sends rain on the righteous and on the unrighteous . . . Be perfect, therefore, as your heavenly Father is perfect" (Matt 5:44–45, 48). Like the majority of English translations, NRSV here uses "perfect" to render the Gk word *teleios*. This is misleading, for perfection is impossible even for the best of us. The LXX uses *teleios* to translate Heb *tamim*, which at Deut 18:13 NRSV translates, "You must remain completely loyal to YHWH your God." In Matt 5:45 the Revised English Bible rendering is, "There must be no limit to your goodness, as your heavenly Father's goodness knows no bounds."[1] The One whom the Jews called Father in Heaven is the Creator of All, who embraces all in divine goodness and mercy, and whom Jesus makes our example. Walter Wink comments: "We are not to be perfect, but, like God, all-encompassing, loving even those who have least claim or right to our love. . . We are to regard the enemy as beloved of God every bit as much as we."[2]

Wink comments on another text in Matthew that is subject to misunderstanding: "But I say to you, 'Do not resist an evildoer. But if anyone strikes you on the right cheek, turn the other also; and if anyone wants to sue you and take your coat, give your cloak as well; and if anyone forces you to go one mile, go also the second mile" (Matt 5:39–41). Wink points out that "do not resist" is a mistranslation of Gk *antistēnai*, which more appropriately might be rendered "retaliate." One should not respond *in kind* or *in like manner* when one has been insulted or wronged in these ways. Wink

---

1. REB Matt 5:45.
2. Wink, *Engaging the Powers*, 269.

suggests, "Do not mirror evil." (The Apostle Paul expressed the same concept more specifically, "Do not be overcome by evil, but overcome evil with good" Rom 12:21).

Jesus speaks of experiences common to people on the bottom of the social pyramid. A superior might give a backhand slap to one's right cheek, a gesture of pure contempt. The peasant has been socially conditioned simply to cower silently and take it. Jesus advises that by standing up straight and offering the other cheek to be struck, he is affirming his human dignity and thereby confusing his attacker and putting him on the defensive. In the same way, a superior might use a compliant court system to make a fraudulently legal claim to take one's outer garment. The written Torah required that a peasant's cloak could not be taken in pawn permanently, but must be returned at sundown (Exod 22:26–27). The oppressed peasant, therefore, should strip off the undergarment also and hand it over, shaming the offender by standing naked in public. A Roman soldier could force a Jew to carry his pack one mile, but if the Jew refused to surrender it and insisted on going a second mile, the soldier would be thrown into confusion, for even he was subject to discipline if he exceeded stated limits of exploitation.[3] Jesus encouraged the lowest of the low to assert their worth in the eyes of God, the giver of the law, whose divine will the legal experts had subverted by specious reinterpretations of written Torah by so-called oral tradition, which they claimed had also been entrusted to Moses at Sinai.

3. RECOVERING THE SOCIAL CONTEXT OF JESUS'S PARABLES

By the time the Gospels were written down, the members of the Jesus movement had already emerged to some extent from the utter poverty of the masses of people. One might imagine that the authors of the Gospels were sufficiently removed from the real-life situation of the *ptōchoi*, the indigent disposables of the society, that they could not grasp the sharp bite of the parables, which the truly poor recognized. The parables would stimulate them to discuss, question, and begin to think in new ways. The earliest Gospel, Mark, says that Jesus spoke in parables precisely to confuse people outside, while to his inner circle Jesus explained everything (Mark 4:10–12//Matt 13:10–15// Luke 8:9–10). This seems hardly in character for the Jesus whom his enemies accused of being a friend of tax collectors and sinners (Luke 15:1–2). Surely Jesus spoke so that they understood!

William R. Herzog II has assembled a great amount of information concerning the actual social and economic conditions of agrarian empires of the first century CE that shine light on the probable situations depicted in many of Jesus's parables. Herzog studied interpretations of the parables by dozens of commentators, ancient and modern, to profit from their historical, literary, redaction, and other critical techniques to cast reasonable doubt upon the authenticity of the actual setting of particular parables

---

3. Wink, *Engaging the Powers*, 175–85

in the Gospels. By elucidating the real-life situation of the peasants under increasing pressure from the exploitative power elite, Herzog has made a convincing argument for the title of his book, *Parables as Subversive Speech: Jesus as Pedagogue of the Oppressed*.[4]

3a. The Pharisee and the tax collector, Luke 18:9–14[5]

Luke's context, separated from its original social setting, makes a universal theological point of a person's humility and willingness to acknowledge one's sin in the presence of God. Important as that may be, Jesus's story had a different point. Herzog titles this "The Parable of the Pharisee and the Toll Collector" because the Gk word *telōnēs* refers to a very minor operative who did the dirty work of collecting the many tolls, imposts, and duties that Rome imposed on every kind of enterprise. A toll collector might well be a Jew who was so destitute that his only hope for subsistence was to hire out to a wealthy person who had bought the contract for collection. To keep this meager job the Jew had to play the game and gouge the public. Socially a Jewish toll collector was hated, shunned, denied some judicial rights, and religiously he was declared unclean, alien from the redemptive media of the temple. Jesus had at least one toll collector in his intimate disciple band, through whom he attracted others (Matt 9:9–13; Luke 15:1).[6]

Herzog characterizes the Pharisee also as a type of toll collector, because he participated in interpreting the Torah so as to render unclean the poor peasants who defaulted on paying tithes, which instead of assisting the poor enriched the temple elite—"he and the toll collector belong to parallel systems of tributary exaction."[7] The Pharisee and the toll collector go up to the temple at the afternoon sacrifice, while priests are burning the incense symbolic of the people's prayers. The Pharisee has seen the toll collector standing apart, and he prays aloud, comparing himself favorably to others, who are thieves, rogues, and adulterers (i.e., who, in OT terms have broken covenant with YHWH), such as this toll collector. He brags that he exceeds the Torah requirements for fasting and tithing. The toll collector acknowledges the portrait of himself, but instead of sneaking away in shame he cries out, "God, be merciful to me, the sinner!" Jesus declares: "I tell you, this man went down to his home justified rather than the other" (Luke 18:14a).

Herzog emphasizes the brazen incongruity of Jesus's verdict. How could the toll collector be justified without making reparation? How could he be acquitted? He has not rebutted the Pharisee's charge but has conceded it and thrown himself on God's mercy. "By his bold and audacious prayer, the toll collector challenges the claim of the

---

4. Herzog, *Parables as Subversive Speech*.
5. Herzog, ibid., 173–93.
6. See chapter 25.2 "Affirming human equality"
7. Herzog, op. cit., 191.

Pharisee, the Temple, and the redemptive media, and claims God's ear for himself . . . If the toll collector is justified by a mercy as unpredictable and outrageous as this, then who could not be included? And if toll collectors and sinners are justified in the very precincts of the Temple itself, then how is one to evaluate a Temple priesthood and its scribes who declare that nothing of that kind is possible?"[8]

3b. The widow and the unjust judge, Luke 18:1–8[9]

By his setting and conclusion Luke encourages people to unceasing prayer, even in times when it appears as though God may have forgotten us, for despite all appearances, God will eventually do right for us (18:1, 6–8). By contrast, Herzog, drawing on the socioeconomic conditions of agrarian empires and building on extensive research of other scholars, suggests a more realistic setting in Jesus's own time.

The widow is involved in a legal controversy involving property of her late husband, perhaps including the dowry her father had paid when she married, which was supposed to be her safety net. A party or parties are trying to cheat her. She comes alone before the judge because she has no male kinsperson to represent her, and she certainly has no wherewithal to offer a bribe. Contrary to Torah and Mishnah requirements, there is only one judge, and by his own admission he "neither feared God nor had respect for people." In other words, he was thoroughly corrupt, and the fact that he was acting alone is because the other parties were using a possibly extralegal means to defraud the widow. Yet the judge has delayed decision, and the widow keeps after him. Perhaps he has been holding out, hoping to get a bigger bribe from her adversaries. The persistence of the widow has put him in such a shameful public position that he considers it more profitable in the long run to grant her rights and be done with her. Jesus encourages widows to stand up for their rights when defrauded, a practice that the legal experts (scribes) engaged in so blatantly as to attract Jesus's condemnation (Mark 12:38–40; Luke 20:46–47). As usual, Jesus recognizes the basic equality of persons before the One God, and he encourages even the least valued members of society to claim their rights and dignity.

Luke's setting encourages the reader to think of the unjust judge as somehow a God figure, a problem that many expositors acknowledge. The usual solution is that God may seem to delay, but if even such a self-described scoundrel as that judge will eventually end up doing right, how much more will God do right. This suggested solution cannot completely erase the inappropriateness of any comparison between the ʾabba Father of Jesus and a judge who does not fear God or have respect for people.

---

8. Herzog, *Parables as Subversive Speech*, 192-93.
9. Herzog, ibid, 215–32.

3c. The Parable of the talents, (Matt 25:14–30; Luke 19:11–27)[10]

Both Matthew and Luke have placed this parable in an eschatological context, encouraging believers to faithful service and expectation, even though the kingdom consummation and the return of the Son of Man may be delayed. Herzog offers a different reading. In contemporary socio-economic context, everybody from highest to lowest assumed a system of scarcity or limited supply—for one to gain meant that another lost. The master in Matthew is an absentee landlord, and in Luke a nobleman who is going away to receive authority as a king, some of whose subjects objected. These characters are prominent in the exploitative system that increases the riches of those with enough resources and smarts to beat down the less able, and most particularly the vast majority of people who had next to nothing and from whom the powerful could take even what they thought they had (Matt 25:29//Luke 18:26). The amounts of money the wealthy entrusted to their household bureaucrats (talent in Matthew, pound=*mna* in Luke) are beyond the imagination of the poorest in society, but in comparison with the rich man's total assets, they are "little." The master commends the first two stewards in each case, who had gained anywhere from 100 percent (Matthew) to 1,000 percent (Luke). Given the reality of the system, the only way to make such high profits was by exploiting and bankrupting others, chiefly small landholders. The parable assumes that Jesus's hearers would know that the stewards had also raked off for themselves enough to increase their own wealth without rousing suspicion of their masters, who well knew what they would be doing anyhow.

In Jesus's parable, the third servant in each case is the main focus. Herzog calls him the whistle blower. When he renders account, he says to his master: "I knew that you were a harsh man, reaping where you did not sow, and gathering where you did not scatter seed; so I was afraid, and I went and hid your talent in the ground. Here you have what is yours" (Matt 25:24–25). The master repeats the charges without denying them. The polite and congratulatory exchanges between the master and the "faithful servants" have masked the sordid reality that underlay their success. The master says that at least this servant should have invested the money with the bankers and have produced interest. But that, too, would be possible only because the legal experts had devised methods of getting profit from loans to people in need without calling it interest, which was forbidden by Torah (Exod 22:25; Lev 25:36–7; Deut 23:19–20).

The whistleblower, as so often happens, was summarily dismissed, which in this case was a virtual sentence of death—he was reduced to the level of a dispensable day laborer. The weeping and gnashing of teeth, says Herzog, was the condition of the poor, who wept when they had to send their surplus children away, or when their property was foreclosed, and their teeth chattered when they lacked warm clothing in winter and gnashed when malnutrition led to painful illnesses. Jesus's parable must have posed many unanswerable questions to its original hearers, says Herzog,

---

10. Herzog, ibid., 150–68.

questions that I think people today need to consider seriously. But at least one thing should be clear: It is altogether inappropriate to see these wealthy persons as God figures, especially the king in Luke's parable, who commands that those who opposed him should be slaughtered in his presence (Luke 19:27).

3d. The laborers in the vineyard, Matt 20:1–16

In Matthew's setting, the parable follows the incident of the rich man who refused to give up his riches and follow Jesus, and Jesus's reassurance to Peter and the other disciples who have left everything to follow him (Matt 19:16–30). The parable stresses that God receives all believers equally, whether early or late. It may address a question in the Jewish congregation of Matthew, concerning late-coming Gentiles—"many who are first will be last, and the last will be first" (19:30); "so the last will be first, and the first will be last" (20:16).

Jesus's story presupposes a big operation—large-scale wine production for local or export sale. Harvest requires more laborers than daily upkeep, and the owner takes care to hire only enough to meet the harvest need. In the first instance, the owner offers the "usual daily wage." Later in the market place, he finds people standing around whom he calls "idlers," but they say, "no one has hired us"—no employment, no income. To these he promises only "whatever is right," and they are in no position to bargain.

At sundown the owner tells his steward to pay the workers, beginning with those hired only an hour previously, and so on to the first, paying them each a denarius. The first hired complain about being discriminated against, since they worked all day in the heat. The owner addresses one of them, speaking with mock politeness, "Friend (*hetairos*=pal or buddy), I am doing you no wrong; did you not agree with me for the usual daily wage? Take what belongs to you and go; I choose to give to this last the same as I give to you. Am I not allowed to do what I choose with what belongs to me?" (20:13–15). The master thus sets the exploited workers against each other, a common practice among modern colonial powers and capitalist bosses as well as ancient agrarian empires. He dismisses the one called "friend" with the implication that he won't be hired again for day labor. I have actually heard libertarians cite the master's claim to free use of his wealth to support laissez-faire capitalism! However, in the true-to-life situation of Jesus's day, the master has violated the Torah and claims ownership of what Torah says actually belongs to YHWH (Lev 25:23).

Herzog says that having the master go out to hire the laborers, ordinarily a job for the steward, was an unusual detail in Jesus's story; it makes clear the master's responsibility for the injustice, which the laborers usually blamed on stewards. The owner was the real source of exploitative malice, and he may have developed this vineyard by combining smaller plots foreclosed from some of the very men who were forced to hire out by the day.

3e. Other parables briefly

A similar background underlies the parable of the wicked tenants (Matt 21:33-46//Mark 12:1-12//Luke 20:9-19). The landowner who develops a new vineyard in the manner described is commercializing a large tract of land he has accumulated by foreclosing many peasants, with the same goal of commercialization as that of the vineyard owner who exploited the day laborers (Matt 20:1-16). Some of these tenants may have originally owned parts of that land, and Herzog cites expositors who researched various possibilities the tenants thought might enable them to regain title. It was all in vain, however, for the rich man was so powerful that he could muster enough force to quell any overt move they might attempt and still find other tenants desperate enough to work for him.

The Gospel writers allegorized Jesus's parable: Israel is God's vineyard (cf Isa 5:1-7), and the tenants are the Jewish rulers. They killed the prophets and God's son, and therefore God took the authority from them and gave it to the Jesus movement, now showing signs of strength and growth. Christians have used this parable to justify replacement doctrine, that the church has replaced Israel as the true people of God. A similar allegorization is seen in the parable of the wedding banquet for the king's son at Matt 22:1-14, immediately following the wicked tenants (21:33-46).[11] The king is a God figure, and his son is presumably Christ. But the king's behavior toward his opponents—destroying them and burning their city, and throwing out a guest who lacks a proper wedding garment—is not consistent with Jesus's other teachings about God. Following Herzog's lead, one must question the suitability of some of the Gospel settings of Jesus's parables that present a rich landowner or a king as a metaphor for God.

4. JESUS AND NICODEMUS, JOHN 2:23—3:12

In my view Nicodemus is another figure in the elite Jewish power structure who really is a negative character, despite the common practice of commending him for coming to learn from Jesus. The break between John 2:23-25 and 3:1-12 obscures the fact that Jesus knew what was in every person, and that he would not commit himself to any, so Jesus was forearmed. Whether Nicodemus is a historical person or a figure of the author's creation; he represents the elite power structure that did away with Jesus. He is a Pharisee, a leader (Gk *archōn*=ruler) of the Jews, and Jesus calls him *the* teacher of Israel (Gk text of 2:10). Immediately we note two points in Nicodemus's disfavor. First, he comes at *night*, which in John has negative, even ominous significance (see 9:4; 11:10; 13:30; 21:3). Second, he says of himself and his associates: "*We know* that you are a teacher come from God." But in John, every time Jesus's opponents claim *we know* something about him, they are mistaken (6:42; 7:27; 8:52; 9:24). Nicodemus is John's counterpart to the Synoptics' hypocritical Pharisees and Herodians who came

---

11. See notes on both parables in HCSB that assume the allegorical nature of the present text.

to trap Jesus with the trick question about paying taxes to Caesar, beginning with the flattering address: "Teacher, *we know* that you are sincere, and teach the way of God in accordance with truth—" (Matt 22:16).

We have to imagine that Nicodemus was sure he was one of God's chosen people. Jesus doesn't let him pose whatever provocative question he may have had in mind—Jesus "knew what was in everyone" (2:25). Jesus takes the initiative: "No one can see the kingdom of God without being born from above." Jesus does not say that instead of trying to fulfill the Law of Moses a person must get saved by a once-for-all confession of faith in Jesus and being "born again." Jesus demands a complete change in Nicodemus's worldview and Jewish maintenance of power based on drawing lines of exclusion and contempt for ordinary folk.

Nicodemus appears again in 7:45–52, when the Council flat out rejects Jesus and says the crowd who follow him is accursed. Nicodemus asks: "Our law does not judge people without first giving them a hearing to find out what they are doing, does it?" Some people interpret this in Nicodemus' favor. I think it is possible to see a negative motive. As a boy growing up in white supremacist North Carolina, I heard stories of lynching. On one occasion the crowd had caught their prey and were about to kill him on the spot. One prominent man objected: "Naw, don't lynch that N---. Let's take him to town, give him a fair trial, and then string him up." Isn't that what Jesus got? Hearing that Jesus was dead, Nicodemus brought a hundred pounds of spices to embalm the body (John 19:39). Was such a large amount an act of generosity? Maybe it was; but maybe Nicodemus wanted to make dead sure this troublemaker stayed good and dead.

The Gospel is ambiguous; it does not specify Nicodemus's final state one way or another. Since I believe One God embraces all, then God's embrace includes Nicodemus. Jesus's encounter with the Samaritan woman supports my view (John 4:1–42). As a Samaritan the woman had no nationalistic hopes concerning Messiah, so Jesus did not hesitate to take that identification for himself. The disciples were astonished by his behavior, which challenged the system—he should not speak to a lone, strange woman in a public place, and he shouldn't drink from her jar. After she bore witness to her fellow Samaritans, and when they met Jesus in person, they declared, "*We know* that this is truly the Savior of the world" (4:42).

SUMMARY AND REFLECTION

"The domination system" is Walter Wink's name for socio-economic policies that enrich the elite and impoverish the masses, his definition of "the world" in John's Gospel. Wink, Herzog, and others help us to see more clearly the extremes that characterized the domination system during Jesus's earthly ministry, how Jesus opposed and challenged it, and how he stood in solidarity with those who suffered most from its exploitation. Jesus unmasked the greed of the religious elite and their subversion of

Torah and the prophets' calls for justice. In increasing numbers the people responded positively to Jesus, and the power structure grew progressively fearful of the looming threat. If they lost control of the people, the Romans could oust them and take direct control. As the Council, i.e., the Sanhedrin or highest court, was dithering about what to do, the high priest is reported to have told them, "You do not understand that it is better for you to have one man die for the people than to have the whole nation destroyed," whereupon "from that day on they planned to put him to death" (John 11:47–53). Rome could not allow the crowds to get out of hand either, and Pilate readily did his part to stop Jesus. This two-headed monster was quick to destroy Jesus as an example of a threat to the supremacy of imperial Rome abetted by the complacent Jewish religious elites.

In light of all this, we must take care to avoid the lingering tendency we find even in Scripture, to depict God as an authority figure similar to the kings and wealthy magnates who oppressed the poor and were responsible for the death of Jesus.

27

Who Did Jesus Say that He Was?

IT SEEMS CLEAR THAT Jesus thought of himself as son to God as Father—as a member of the Israelite people of God, but also in a unique sense of sonship revealed to him at his baptism and strengthened through testing. Jesus did not go about announcing such a claim, and he spoke and acted as though other human beings also were children of that same Father. He healed the sick and cast out demons as a result of his empowerment by God's Spirit, but he commissioned his disciples and they did the same (Mark 3:14–15// Matt 10:1; Mark 6:7//Luke 9:1–2; Luke 10:17). Not only so, he assumed the effectiveness of exorcists other than those of his own followers (Mark 9:38–39//Luke 9:49–50; Matt 12:27//Luke 11:19 [Q]). But who did Jesus say that he was? When questioned by others, he implied that the kingdom of God was present in his ministry to the poorest (*ptōchoi*) by healing and exorcism. But who did Jesus say that he was?

1. THE MESSIAH?

According to Mark's chronology, perhaps halfway through a public ministry in which his teaching and activity in line with his relationship with the One God had attracted the multitudes but brought him into conflict with the authorities, Jesus asked his disciples: "Who do you say that I am?" Peter answered him, "You are the Messiah." And Jesus sternly ordered them not to tell anyone about him (Mark 8:27–30). As Herman C. Waetjen points out, the Gk text of 8:30 literally reads: "And he rebuked them that they speak to no one about him." It is not that Jesus rejected the title of Messiah, but that the title was susceptible to misinterpretation.

> The Messiah or Christ title, as its history indicates, is essentially elitist. . . . It denotes a king who is seated at the pinnacle of the socioeconomic pyramid over which he rules. To perpetuate his reign he maintains an army, collects taxes, and supports a temple that is serviced by a priesthood committed to the preservation of the divine order of his rule. (. . .) The structures of the society

that he governs are vertical and therefore, because they foster oppression and dispossession, are dehumanizing.¹

In Peter's mind, that is what Messiah means, and Jesus brusquely rebukes him and orders them not to tell anyone. To accept Peter's understanding of Messiah would be to solidify with putative divine approval a mere rearrangement of rankings within the same dehumanizing structure. Jesus's own sense of call was to precisely the opposite, to express his oneness with the people. And what Jesus said next to Peter and the others expressed the completeness of that oneness: "Then he began to teach them that the Son of Man must undergo great suffering . . . and be killed" (Mark 8:31).² Such a fate was inconceivable for the Messiah of Peter's expectation, and he rebuked Jesus. Jesus now rebuked Peter, calling him Satan—the devil, that accuser, that deceiver, that tempter with which Jesus had had to struggle in the wilderness (Matt 4:10). Jesus *could not* publicly claim to be Messiah.

Near the end, as Jesus stood alone and bound in the presence of the Jewish court, the High priest asked, "Are you the Messiah?" Only then did Jesus publicly acknowledge it, yet again he changed the terminology, "I am, and you will see the Son of Man seated at the right hand of the Power, and coming with the clouds of heaven" (Mark 14:61–2. Matt 26:64 and Luke 22:67–69 leave it ambiguous, for Jesus does not make the unequivocal answer, "I am.").

2. THE SON OF MAN?

When Jesus rebuked Peter's confession of him as Messiah, he immediately changed the terminology, saying, "The Son of Man must suffer" (Mark 8:31). According to the familiar English translations of the NT, Son of Man is the self-identification Jesus used most frequently, but he never clearly explained what he meant by it. In both the OT and the NT, someone may use "son of man" as a modest personal reference, "I" or "me," and some have suggested that that was Jesus's practice, but the issue is much more complex. In the OT "son of man" may refer to humankind in general, fourteen times in poetic parallelism with man, e.g., "what is man that you are mindful of him, the son of man that you care for him?" (Ps 8:4 NIV). "Son of man" may refer to an individual person, such as the prophet Ezekiel, whom God addressed exclusively as "Son of man" (Ezek 2:1 and throughout (KJV and NIV), and Jesus certainly thought of himself as a prophet.

---

1. Waetjen, *A Reordering of Power*, 144-5. In Gk, "rebuke" in Mark 8:30, 32, 33 is the same word Jesus used when confronting the unclean spirit at Mark 1:25 and when stilling the wind at 4:39.

2. Boyarin *The Jewish Gospels*, chapter 4 "The Suffering Christ as a Midrash on Daniel" asserts that Jesus self-consciously thought of himself as Son of Man depicted in Daniel 7, a human with divine qualities subordinate to the Ancient One (=the Most High) but with authority to rule a universal, everlasting kingdom Dan 7:13-14. Boyarin says there was at least a minority of Jews who thought of a coming savior who would suffer and die for people. Jewish Christians accepted Jesus in that role, while others objected.

The NRSV often renders "son of man" as "mortal," or "human being" in the OT. In Daniel, "one like a son of man" (NRSV "like a human being") received from God everlasting "dominion and glory and kingship, that all peoples, nations, and languages should serve him" (Dan 7:13–14). In further interpretation, this one like a son of man represents (or *is*?) "the holy ones of the Most High" (Dan 7:14, 18, 22, 25, 27), apparently meaning the faithful Jews. Jesus's reference to himself as the son of man indicates at least the sense of solidarity with his fellow Jews that he demonstrated by accepting baptism from John.

The narrator of the visions in the book of Daniel, the work of an Israelite who was undergoing visionary experiences that a modern scholar like Craffert would call an altered state of consciousness (ASC), identifies himself as "I, Daniel" (8:15, 27; 9:2; 10:2, 7; 12:5). At one point he says he is unable to understand one of the visions, but. the heavenly guide, Gabriel, was sent to him. "As he came near the place where I was standing, I was terrified and fell prostrate. 'Son of man,' he said to me, 'understand that the vision concerns the time of the end'" (Dan 8:17 NIV). It is notable that in the text of Daniel, the one who *saw* the vision that featured "one like a son of man" *was himself addressed* as "son of man."

A similar case is that of the author of "The Book of Similitudes,"[3] part of a collection of writings composed in the late centuries BCE. "Enoch" who is purported to have had these visions was the seventh generation from Adam. "Enoch walked with God; then he was no more, because God took him" (Gen 5:24). In his visions Enoch saw a transcendent heavenly figure designated as the eschatological judge and the vindicator of the righteous and elect people of God. The text refers to that person variously as "the Chosen One" (his primary title), "the Righteous One," "that son of man," and God's "Anointed One." As these designations indicate, the descriptions of this figure are the fruit of speculations on the biblical texts about "one like a son of man" (Daniel 7), the "servant of YHWH" (Isa 42, 49, 52–53), and the davidic king (Ps 2 and Isa 11).[4]

First Enoch 48 states that "that Son of Man" existed before the creation of the heavenly bodies, and that the Lord of Spirits has made him the chosen, righteous one, to save his people and punish kings of the earth and the mighty landowners who have oppressed them.[5] At the climax of these visions, an angel from among the host accompanying the Lord of Spirits addressed "Enoch" himself as "son of man" and assured him that "that Son of Man" shall bring peace to the righteous ones in the name of the Lord of Spirits forever and ever.[6]

In both Daniel and 1 Enoch, the visionary who sees or who learns about the/ that Son of Man reports that one of the heavenly beings addressed him also as "son of

---

3. Isaac, trans. 1 Enoch, "Similitudes" 29–50.
4. Nickelsberg, "Enoch, First Book of," The Book of Parables (or Similitudes 37–71). In *ABD*.
5. 1 Enoch 48, "Similitudes" 35–36.
6. 1 Enoch 71 ibid, pp 49–50.

man." Jesus may not have known 1 Enoch, but he knew Daniel, and he was familiar with the various OT concepts of Messiah, Servant of the Lord, davidic king, and Son of Man that 1 Enoch combined into an appointed figure who saved the people of God and judged their oppressors. Accepting Craffert's employment of shamanic culture and contemporary Mediterranean cosmology as the context in which to understand Jesus of Nazareth, one may imagine that in an ASC Jesus had been transported into the heavenly realm where he received insight and understanding that affected his self-image and his actions. We have already seen that Jesus saw a direct relationship between his ministry of healing and exorcism with the presence of the Kingdom of God. The same may be said concerning his self-identification as Son of Man.[7] On the one hand, the title implied a multifaceted calling as an agent of God, yet it was also a way to refer to himself modestly because of his consciousness of his subordination to and complete dependence upon God—Father, 'abba.

The words of Jesus as recorded in the Gospels present judgment as one of the functions of the Son of Man, who will come in glory with the angels, sit on his throne, and judge the nations (=Gentiles). The standard of approval or disapproval is whether or not they have given aid to the hungry, thirsty, strangers, naked, and prisoners, *with whom Jesus personally identifies*: "just as you did it to one of the least of these who are members of my family [brothers], you did it to me." (Matt 25:31–46). Perhaps it is precisely because of Jesus's sense of solidarity with neglected and needy people that the Father "has given him authority to execute judgment, because he is the Son of Man" (John 5:27). Compared to the ethnocentric character of the dominion that shall be given to the Danielic one like a son of man—the kingdom of the holy ones of the Most High (Dan 7:14, 27)—Jesus's depiction of judgment has a universal aspect, and Gentiles who have acted compassionately are greeted as "blessed by my Father" even though they may have acted without any direct knowledge of Jesus. Moreover, totally absent from Jesus's judgment is the verbose, oft-repeated vengeful attitude toward those who are not members of God's elect, which is characteristic of 1 Enoch.

Therefore I question whether Jesus himself spoke of the Son of Man consigning those at his left hand to "the eternal fire prepared for the devil and his angels" (Matt 25:41, 46). This text inspired the painting of the judgment in the Vatican's Sistine Chapel: Jesus sits on the throne and with the right hand directs the blessed up to heaven, while with his left he consigns to hell—depicted in frightening detail—those who are cursed. Such a future role for the Son of Man is totally out of character with Jesus of Nazareth. It seems much more typical of the author of Matthew, who makes the exploitative master in the parable of the talents into a god figure (Matt 25:14–30, followed immediately by the judgment of the Son of Man, 25:1–46).[8]

---

7. See above n 2, Boyarin's affirmation that Jesus thought of himself as Son of Man as in Dan 7.
8. See chapter 26.3 "Recovering the social context of Jesus' parables" and Matt 20:1–10, 21:33–46, 22:1–14.

Jesus's call was to express his own humanity to the fullest extent in reliance upon God and to enable his disciples, and through them to enable others as well to realize and express their own humanity to the fullest potential. For Jesus, that was the true meaning of the reign of God, the challenge and the overthrow of the dehumanizing domination system. Therefore Waetjen calls Jesus the New Human Being to express more clearly the significance of his self-identification as the son of man. "As the New Human Being, he is the ultimate human being, the one who is so completely and perfectly human that the image of God will become transparent in his life and activity."[9]

I have already noted the importance Wink gives to Ezekiel's inaugural vision of God appearing as what seemed to be a human.[10] When God addressed Ezekiel as "son of man" it must be in some sense as son of that One who appeared to him in the likeness as it were of a human (Ezek 1:26). The insight prompted by Ezekiel's ancient vision is reflected in what one may hear now and again today, when people refer to God as "the Man upstairs," or simply as "the Man." Between Ezekiel and twenty-first century folk, Jesus referred to himself as "the son of the man." Wink describes the process thus: "If the 'son of the man' has God as his Father, then Jesus is, by inference, the Son of God. This line of christological development might have gone like this: God as the Human One / Ezekiel as the son of that Human One / Jesus as the son of that Human One / Hence Jesus as the Son of God, the Human One."[11]

As I showed by my interpretation of Jesus's baptism and temptation, Jesus *was* convinced that he was son of God in a relational sense, but not as implying his deity, for he knew his fellow Jews, the people of YHWH, were also children of God in that relational sense, although to a lesser conscious degree than Jesus himself experienced. Thus, the self-designation "the son of man" *followed later and built upon his son-of-God conviction* originating at his baptism, but he expressed it in ambiguous terms.

3. WHY ALL THIS AMBIGUITY?

In this study I have taken the position that Jesus did, in some sense, think of himself as Messiah, one anointed by God's Spirit, but he would not use the term or allow his disciples to do so because so many people held erroneous, nationalistic views of Messiah. Jesus knew himself as Son of God because of his conviction that God was his ʾ*abba*, and because he cast out demons "by the finger of God" (Luke 11:20). But he refrained from going about publicly making the claim, since others also were children of ʾ*abba*. Jesus cloaked his claim in the enigmatic self-designation "the son of man."

In my view, this obvious diffidence on the part of one who otherwise spoke and acted with such power and authority represents an advance in the biblical transformation

---

9. *A Reordering of Power,* 72. Myers, *Binding the Strong Man,* 37 adopts "Human One" as substitute for son of man. See also Wink's *The Human Being.*

10. See above chapter 19.1 "Ezekiel: YHWH's glory and judgment."

11. Wink, *The Human Being* p 256.

of the conception of God described primarily in terms of coercive power. Others are children of "the Man" too, but they need to recognize this for themselves and then live accordingly. God is ready to pour out the Spirit on *all* flesh, making them anointed or messianic figures in the company of Jesus. But Jesus could not, would not compel or impose that self-realization on others. As Wink says: "Jesus *could not* tell others he was the Messiah. For if he told them, they would not have to discover the Messiah within themselves. And if they did not discover the Messiah within themselves, they would not learn that they had such powers of discovery within themselves. And if Jesus did not enable them to discover such powers within themselves, he was not the Messiah."[12]

Jesus will not do anything to hinder his followers from making their own decisions, even though they decide wrongly. Creative Deity itself is human enough to respect the humanity of the creature. As is well known, from time to time the OT depicts God in human terms. God will listen and respond to Abraham pleading for a few innocent people in a crowd of the guilty (Gen 18:22–33). God will change his mind about destroying a people in response to the pleading of Moses (Exod 32:11–14), or in spite of the anger of Jonah (Jonah 3:10). Jacob saw the face of God in the man that had wrestled with him and had named him Israel (Gen 32:24–30). Immediately afterward, seeing Esau, the brother whom he had wronged but who now was reconciled to him, Jacob saw the face of God (Gen 33:10). God is like a spouse betrayed by the marriage partner, yet cannot finally let the betrayer go but starts the courtship all over again (Hos 2:14–20). God is like the parent of a persistently rebellious child, but God's inner being is turned upside down, so that God cannot abandon the rebel (Hos 11:1, 8–9). God is like the brother who was maliciously deprived of elder son's rights, yet who embraced the wrongdoer without seeking revenge. By gifts of grace beyond deserving, by working warmly within to cajole and persuade, and if need be by exhilarating infusions of divine Spirit—ASCs—and even by adapting to the creatures' weakness, God, the Truly Human One, seeks to enable the human creatures willingly to work the Creator's will.

4. TO ERR IS HUMAN, TO FORGIVE DIVINE

One way that Jesus, the New Human Being, drew fellow human beings into the sphere of action of God, the Truly Human One, was to bestow on them forgiveness of sins and the authority to forgive sins. In Mark 2:1–12 a group of four brought to Jesus a paralyzed friend lying on a pallet. Such a crowd filled the house where Jesus was that they had to go up on the flat roof, dig through the mud and wattle plaster, and lower the man through the hole down into the presence of Jesus. Jesus was so impressed by this display of bold confidence that he declared: "Son, your sins are forgiven." Myers writes, "The man's lack of bodily wholeness would have been attributed to either his own sin, or, if a birth defect,

---

12. Wink, *The Human Being*, 127, emphasis original.

inherited sin; he was thus denied full status in the body politic of Israel"[13] (see also John 9:2). The man made no confession of faith or word of repentance, yet Jesus unconditionally declared all his sins forgiven—"a total cancellation of the past that will remove the destructive effects of the action and reaction cycle of sin."[14]

Jesus's amazing statement brought immediate negative reaction from the legal experts: "Why does this fellow speak in this way? It is blasphemy! Who can forgive sins but God alone?" (Mark 2:8). According to their piety, the only sins Jesus could forgive were offenses against him personally, but this blanket remission of plural sins was the prerogative of God alone. Besides, it infringed on their authority as interpreters of Torah to determine type or degree of sinfulness, and it bypassed the temple and the priesthood who controlled the sacrificial system. One can't help recalling Hosea's charge against the religious establishment of his day: "They feed on the sin of my people; they are greedy for their iniquity" (Hos 4:8). Throughout history, the arbiters of the forgiveness of sin can wield almost unassailable power over the credulous, while profiting handsomely from it.[15]

To assert his authority to forgive, Jesus (according to Mark) for the first time uses his preferred self-identification: "So that you may know that the Son of Man has authority on earth to forgive sins"—he said to the paralytic—I say to you, stand up, take your mat and go to your home." The crowd is amazed when the man does so: "We have never seen anything like this!" (Mark 2:11–12). Of course, the natural reaction is the full acknowledgement by Christians of Jesus's authority to forgive sins, and if we had only Mark's account our tendency to limit the power to Jesus might be excusable. However, Matthew's account of this incident ends on a different note with tremendous potential that we sadly neglect: Matthew's Gospel was written for a Jewish community whose own language was much closer to that of Jesus. They got the point: "They glorified God, who had given such authority to human beings" (9:8). The author of Matthew and his community understood Jesus's self-designation "the son of man" or "Human Being" in a collective sense. Wink comments, "The early Christians understood that the authority to forgive sins is not restricted to Jesus as son of man, but that it is an authority given to all human beings, the authority to heal and to forgive sins."[16]

From a different source and angle, we get confirmation of this point from John's account of the first appearance of the risen Jesus. Jesus appears unexpectedly in the presence of the cowardly disciples who had abandoned him, and one of whom, Peter, had thrice denied him with a curse. Jesus says simply, "Peace be with you." This is the gift of forgiveness. It is unconditional; they have not confessed their guilt nor offered

---

13. Myers, *Binding the Strong Man*, 155.

14. Waetjen, *Reordering of Power*, 87.

15. King Henry IV standing for three days outside the castle at Canossa, doing penance to seek cancellation of an edict of excommunication by Pope Gregory VII, Wikipedia, Henry IV Holy Roman Emperor.

16. Wink, *The Human Being*, 78.

repentance, yet a second time Jesus confirms it: "Peace be with you." He then commissions them as his messengers, empowers them with Holy Spirit, and states: "If you forgive the sins of any, they are forgiven them; if you retain the sins of any, they are retained" (John 20:19–23). The Risen Lord Jesus gave this charge to his people there present, unnamed and of unspecified number. In due time, church authority sought to limit the recipients of such power to an elite few and to define the conditions and effects of forgiveness. In my view, it should be left vague and general, interpreted in conjunction with Matthew 9:8. God gives authority to forgive sins to all God's human children. In the exercise of this authority, we participate in the divine nature that Jesus reveals and imparts. My friend Grayson Tucker explained the text this way: "If we forgive others' sins, those sins go away and the relationship is healed. If we refuse to forgive, the sins remain and continue to poison the relationship."

SUMMARY AND REFLECTION

On the basis of Scripture I cannot affirm that Jesus thought of himself in the way that church doctrine later described him as "very God of very God." In my view Scripture does not support the confession of those who insist, "Jesus *is* God." For some who insist on such a confession, they then define Jesus's deity by giving him the same powers as those of YHWH the God of Israel, the war god who led armies and commanded genocide. The deity of Jesus means that post-resurrection we must rethink our conception of God and understand deity in keeping with Jesus's modesty, Jesus's solidarity with humanity, and Jesus's total obedience to the Father. Certainly Jesus reveals God to a degree hitherto unknown, but God is more than even Jesus reveals. Through the testimony of Jesus, the author of John has clearly experienced the reality that lay concealed behind the ambiguous terms Messiah, Son of God, and Son of Man. In the Gospel of John, Jesus makes all the "I am" statements and says, "The Father and I are one" (John 10:30). If this seems to blur the distinction between Jesus and God we must remember that Jesus prays for the disciples and all who will believe through them, "that they may all be one. As you, Father, are in me and I am in you, may they also be in us, so that the world may believe that you have sent me. The glory that you have given me I have given them, so that they may be one, as we are one, I in them and you in me, that they may become completely one" (John 17:20–23).

Thus, the oneness with God that Jesus asserts for himself embraces the oneness of all believers with him and with God. So oneness with the Father as Jesus experiences and expresses it cannot mean deity for Jesus in the classical doctrinal sense any more than it would mean deity for all believers. As a Jew of the first century CE who was bound by the conviction that God is One, Jesus democratized the special relation he had with God so that all participated in a non-hierarchical way. The distinction between God and not-God remains, even for Jesus, who says, "The Father is greater than I" (John 14:28).

To the disciples the risen Jesus sends word through Mary Magdalene: "I am ascending to my Father and your Father, to my God and your God" (20:17).

In the Calvinistic tradition that nourished me, the Westminster Shorter Catechism asks: "Who is the Redeemer of God's elect?" The answer: "The only Redeemer of God's elect is the Lord Jesus Christ, who, being the eternal Son of God, became man, and so was, and continueth to be, God and man, in two distinct natures, and one Person forever."[17] The Westminster divines were struggling to express classical Nicene Christology, but if we deconstruct their answer we discover something different. If the Lord Jesus Christ is "very God" from eternity, then in becoming man God underwent change, which contradicts Westminster's basic tenet that God is unchangeable.[18] If God became human, there must be that in the divine nature that is capable of humanity. Likewise, there must be that in human nature that is capable of deity. In Jesus of Nazareth people saw a man who realized the human capacity for deity to the fullest extent. Through Jesus, mediated to us by the witness of his disciples and the indwelling of his Spirit, we too may realize our capacity for deity. Generic god does not become generic human, nor does generic human become generic god. But because of Jesus we understand what human is meant to be and that the chasm separating god and human is not so deep as monotheists like me have traditionally assumed. Because of Jesus you and I gain empowerment for our own possibilities. As we approach more nearly our potential as human beings, we come that much nearer to the likeness of God, best revealed in Jesus.

---

17. *The Book of Confessions* Shorter Catechism Q. 21: 7.021, p 177.
18. *The Book of Confessions* Shorter Catechism Q. 4, 7.004, p 175.

PART SIX

Paul, Apostle to the Gentiles

28

In Quest of Saul/Paul

A DECADE OR TWO before any of the Four Gospels was written down, the Apostle Paul had traveled widely in the lands of the Mediterranean basin proclaiming the message of Jesus as Messiah and Savior. He had written letters to the believers' groups resulting from his ministry that are included in the New Testament and which, in point of time, pre-dated any of the Gospels.[1] While the early followers of the Jesus Way were debating what to do about Gentiles who responded to the message about Jesus—shouldn't they be required to become Jews first?—Paul was preaching that the One God, the God of Israel, included the Gentiles in the divine plan of reconciling humankind, and that the plan of redemption of people from the powers of sin and the Devil included Gentiles as well as the people of Israel.

Paul never personally knew Jesus while he lived and walked in Galilee and Judea, nor had Paul any contact with the members of the original disciple band until some time after the death and resurrection of Jesus. A careful reading of the letters of Paul and the Book of the Acts of the Apostles detects serious differences between Paul and the original disciples who were now elevated to the status of Apostles (ones whom Jesus himself had appointed to specific missions). Paul considered himself an Apostle, but it seems almost beyond doubt that the original Apostles never fully accepted him as their equal.

Paul by his own testimony was once a strict Jewish Pharisee who persecuted the church that emerged from the post-resurrection witness to Jesus (Gal 1:13–14; Phil 3:5–6). And yet Paul was more responsible than any other human being for making way for the primitive Jewish sect centering on Jesus to become a universal monotheistic world religion. Without question, Paul's self-declared encounter with the resurrected Jesus transformed him from persecutor of the church to propagator of the message about Jesus. But before Paul became an apostle of Christ, he already held a strong conviction of the oneness of God, based on his thorough knowledge of

---

1. I consider Romans, 1 and 2 Corinthians, Galatians, Philippians, 1 Thessalonians, and Philemon as authentic Pauline letters. He exercised powerful influence on the writers of Ephesians, Colossians and 2 Thessalonians.

the Jews' Bible. This, I believe, was a major factor in preparation for his special call. As a Pharisee, (first introduced as Saul, Acts 7:58, a native of Tarsus in Asia Minor, Acts 9:11; 22:3),[2] Paul derived his worldview from the same Scriptures as did those other Pharisees who brought to birth the religion now known as Judaism, after the destruction of the Jerusalem temple in 70 CE. The rabbis preserved the Jewish people by pressing the theme of divine election of Israel by the God YHWH revealed in the emerging monotheistic worldview of the Hebrew Bible. Paul, however, underwent a painful trauma that wrenched him out of the familiar matrix he shared with them into a new locus that enabled him, while reading the same Scriptures, to see that this God included the other nations—Gentiles—in the ultimate divine redemptive purpose.

1. PRE-CHRISTIAN SAUL OF TARSUS

Before his conversion Saul encountered several enigmatic questions raised by claims of the followers of Jesus of Nazareth: (1) that Jesus was the Messiah of Israel who had to suffer and die, (2) that Jesus had been raised from the dead, and (3) that they addressed Jesus as Lord in prayer and devotion. Saul shared the belief that God was capable of raising the dead, and that resurrection would be a reward for saints who died for the faith, but the other two points he must reject. Except for the Jesus people, no Jews of that time expected a suffering Messiah, and as for the title Lord, that was the way Jews referred to YHWH the God of Israel. Such claims provoked zealous opposition from Saul.

In his post-conversion personal confession in Phil 3:6 Paul says that his religious *zeal* impelled him to persecute the Christians. He uses a word that appears in the LXX account of the jealous/zealous wrath of YHWH toward the Israelites who joined the idolatrous worship at Baal-peor (Num 25:1–13). Many other texts in the OT use words of this root to describe God's zeal/jealousy as vengeful, burning, or destructive, against those who betray God.[3] In Gal 1:13 Paul writes, "I was violently persecuting the Church of God and was trying to destroy it."[4] In view of these words of Paul himself, I dare make some conjectures as to his actions toward the followers of the Jesus movement, all of whom were originally Jews.

Paul almost certainly told stories of his pre-Christian life to people among whom he ministered. The Christians' earliest confession of faith "Jesus is Lord" recognized Jesus for them as the equal of YHWH=LORD for the people of Israel. As an adept Pharisee combating the idea of a crucified Messiah, Paul could cite a text from Torah: "Cursed is every one who hangs on a tree" (Deut 21:22–23). Therefore one cruel

---

2. Acts was written several decades after Paul's letters, in which he never refers to himself as Saul.

3. In the Decalogue Exod 20:5 // Deut 5:9; also Exod 34:14; Num 25:11; Deut 4:24; 6:15; 29:20; Josh 24:9.

4. For citation of various OT texts commending lethal action against apostate Israelites that might have inspired Paul, see Longenecker's comments on this verse in his commentary on *Galatians*.

means of persecuting Christians would be to try to force them to declare, "Let Jesus be cursed!" Saul himself, in his role as zealous, violent persecutor, could easily have cried, "Let Jesus be cursed!" After meeting the risen Christ and becoming his apostle, Paul can now cite this same text from Torah with a *Christian interpretation*: It is true that the crucified Christ *was* cursed, but only in the sense that he bore the curse that rested upon the Israelites who failed to fulfill the Torah, with the added result that the blessings of Abraham might *also* come to the Gentiles (Gal 3:10–14).

We see a hint of some such pre-Christian incident when Paul writes: "You know that when you were pagans [lit. Gentiles], you were enticed and led astray to idols that could not speak. Therefore I want you to understand that no one speaking by the Spirit of God ever says, 'Let Jesus be cursed!' and no one can say 'Jesus is Lord' except by the Holy Spirit" (1 Cor 12:2–3). C. K. Barrett and other expositors wonder how Paul could possibly suppose anybody in the Corinthian congregation, even under ecstatic excitement, could ever call for a curse on Jesus.[5] I don't think Paul considered that possibility. He has just reminded them that in their own pre-Christian life ecstatic demonic spirits could carry them away during worship of idols, without specifying what sorts of utterances they might make. Out of *his own* background, with which they are now familiar, he alludes to his experience of having been led to curse Jesus, or to try to force believers to curse Jesus, making use of this text from the Torah. But now that the risen Christ has possessed him, everything has changed.

After the vision of the resurrected Jesus effected the change from Saul the persecutor to Paul the propagator, Paul must have recited his pre-Christian ideas and actions to demonstrate the greatness of divine grace: "I am the least of the apostles, unfit to be called an apostle, because I persecuted the church of God. But by the grace of God I am what I am, and his grace toward me has not been in vain" (1 Cor 15:9–10a). If God did it for Paul, God can do it for anybody! In the next generation, a writer representing Paul expanded this theme as a means for encouraging Gentiles to accept the grace of Christ Jesus, who came into the world to save sinners "of whom I am the foremost" (1 Tim 1:12–17).

2. THE RELIGIOUS ENVIRONMENT OF SAUL/PAUL

For centuries, especially after the Reformation, Christians presupposed the direct inspiration of Paul "from above" without having knowledge of or access to extrabiblical materials to shed light on the cultural milieu and personal experiences that might influence Paul's writings. Also, many people searched Paul's letters for teaching concerning the deity of Christ and the question of the conflict between faith and works as the grounds of salvation. Today many resources can fill in the broader background and explain details in the writings that may have seemed obscure or less important.

---

5. Barrett, *First Epistle to the Corinthians*, 279–81.

God For All

Gentiles would probably have paid little attention to Paul's teachings based solely on the Jewish Scriptures, and they would have had little reason to save his letters, if he had not been a very powerful and successful wonderworker, one who might be called spirit-possessed in a positive sense. I owe to John Ashton appreciation of this point. Acts tells stories of works that can only be called miracles performed by Paul: healing (Acts 14:8–10), exorcism (16:16–18), and resuscitation of one apparently dead (20:8–10). In Ephesus "God did extraordinary miracles through Paul, so that when the handkerchiefs or aprons that had touched his skin were brought to the sick, their diseases left them, and the evil spirits came out of them" (Acts 19:12). The account describes Paul's besting seven other exorcists and stating that practitioners of magic, overwhelmed by Paul's superior powers, became believers and burned their books (Acts 19:14–20). Ashton writes with thinly veiled contempt for modern expositors who dismiss these stories as exaggerated legends.[6] Ashton cites extrabiblical sources that confirm the accuracy of the description of the kinds of things that were going on constantly in the contemporary society. Even in modern times, such phenomena are common in many African and East Asian societies.[7]

Paul modestly says very little about his wonderworking but enough to show that miraculous deeds were integral to his ministry. In 1 Thess 1:5 he writes, "Our message of the gospel came to you not in word only but also in power and in the Holy Spirit and with full conviction." He asked the Galatians: "Having started with the Spirit, are you now ending with the flesh? . . . Does he who supplies the Spirit to you and works miracles among you do so by works of the law, or by hearing with faith?" (Gal 3:3, 5 RSV). Ashton inclines toward seeing this as a reference of Paul to himself.[8] We would never know that Paul spoke in tongues except for a brief notice where he urges voluntary limitations on excessive use of this gift: "I thank God that I speak in tongues more than all of you" (1 Cor 14:18). Paul asks: "Are all prophets? Are all teachers? Do all work miracles? Do all possess gifts of healing? Do all speak in tongues? Do all interpret?" (1 Cor 12:29). The question assumes that *all* these types of activity were familiar features of their gatherings; no doubt Paul set the example.

Paul writes of "a person in Christ" of his acquaintance who experienced being caught up to the third heaven, whether in the body or not, he didn't know; he was caught up to Paradise, in or out of the body, and "heard things that are not to be

---

6. Ashton, *The Religion of Paul the Apostle*, 174–77. Crossan and Reed insist that Paul's ministry targeted "God-fearers," pious Gentiles already familiar with Judaism through synagogue fellowship, who could understand his scriptural arguments, *In Search of Paul*, 38–41 and frequently throughout. That might seem to question Paul's ministry among Gentiles unfamiliar with Judaism, but Ashton makes that altogether credible.

7. See above chapter 24.1 "Evaluating Jesus's acts of healing and exorcism" for one example, that of the Congolese church of Simon Kimbangu.

8. *The Religion of Paul the Apostle*, 201–2. NRSV supplies "God" as the subject, with a marginal note that the subject is really *he*. A similar possibility occurs in 1:6 where Paul says, "I am astonished that you are so quickly deserting *the one* who called you in the grace of Christ—." This could be Paul's reference to himself.

told, that no mortal is permitted to repeat" (2 Cor 12:2-4). Paul speaks as though of a third party, but most commentators agree that he really recounts his personal experience. This is an example of what Craffert and others refer to as "altered states of consciousness" (ASC). Jewish apocryphal literature of the first century CE is full of stories of "celestial travel" by famous characters of the Bible, such as Enoch, or Moses, or Melchizedek. They are caught up to heaven where they receive special messages of assurance of God's control despite appearances to the contrary. Some of these characters, especially Enoch and Moses, receive power to assist God as partners, but not quite co-equal with God. Philo can even call Moses "a second God." This kind of material circulated broadly at the time, and Paul gives evidence of acquaintance with at least some of it.

Recently published Qumran documents offer instruction on techniques to induce visions. Paul's personal testimony of his own experience is only one testimony of Jews' belief in the possibility of such experiences. Some rabbis prohibited speaking about "partners" for God and tried to suppress mysticism (perhaps owing to rapid growth of the Jesus movement), but by the third century CE some Jews were circulating secret documents teaching techniques of inducing visions and heavenly ascent similar to those found at Qumran.[9] Alan F. Segal describes Paul as "a Jewish apocalyptic-mystagogue of the first century."[10] Ashton calls Paul "a mystic, an apostle, a prophet, a charismatic," and states that the most appropriate modern term to describe Paul is "shaman."[11] Of special importance is the influence on Paul of Jewish merkabah mysticism to which I have already referred in commenting on Ezekiel and on Jesus as "the son of man."[12] It is particularly pertinent in understanding and interpreting the conversion experience of Saul/Paul.

As I read Paul's testimony in his letters. I am struck by the similarities of his experience compared with those of a number of people whom scientific experts have interviewed and who have had what is known as "near-death experience" (NDE). In the next chapter I will present a plausible case for thinking that at the time of his call, Paul underwent a near death experience that determined his sense of call to be "the Apostle to the Gentiles."

---

9. Alan F. Segal, *Paul the Convert,*" 36.

10. Idem, 35.

11. *The Religion of Paul,* 74. For extensive demonstration of the striking similarities between Paul and shamans of many different cultures see chapter 8 "Paul the Possessed," 214–37 in the same work.

12. See above chapter 19.1 "Ezekiel: YHWH's glory and judgment" and chapter 27.2 "The Son of Man?"

29

The Death of Saul and Birth of Paul

PAUL USES AN EXPRESSION that most expositors relate to his conversion experience, but that they tend to interpret symbolically or metaphorically: "For through the law I died to the law, so that I might live to God. I have been crucified with Christ; and it is no longer I who live, but it is Christ who lives in me. And the life I now live in the flesh I live by faith in the Son of God, who loved me and gave himself for me" (Gal 2:19–20 NRSV).[1] Ashton emphasizes Paul's use of the term *crucified*, "the sheer horror of this barbarous form of execution," which to us moderns is so remote. Surely for Paul it must have had some immediate and intimate meaning. Ashton suggests that Paul may refer to "his actual experience of an agonizing death that preceded a new kind of life. This is in fact what Paul says (!)"[2] Comparing Paul with shamans, Ashton cites examples of the initiatory ceremonies some shamans undergo, which may be considered symbolic "suffering, death, and resurrection." In my view Ashton presses shaman experience too far to explain Paul. A more appropriate comparison would be that of a near-death experience, NDE (see below and above chapter 4.4 "Near death experience"); but first we must consider the crisis undergone by Saul, the pre-Christian Paul.

1. THE DEATHLY CRISIS OF SAUL

In Rom 6–7 Paul takes up in detail, illustrated by his own experience, the power of Sin, what Ashton describes "as a kind of cosmic force doing battle with grace on a global scale, and possessing the frightening capacity of taking up residence in the human soul."[3] In Rom 6:12–14 Paul can range Sin versus God as one of two possible masters that rule people. Sin has power to distort and abuse even the divinely given law.[4] In

---

1. NRSV margin suggests what I consider a better rendering *by the faith of the Son of God* here and *by the faith of Christ* at 1:16.
2. *The Religion of Paul the Apostle*, 232.
3. Ibid., 213.
4. Paul uses the Gk word *nomos*=law in several ways, not always clear. Law may comprise the whole Pentateuch, the Law of Moses. At other times "works of law" seems to designate the rules of Jewish identity rather than the moral law. Sometimes law is more like a "general principle" as in Rom 7:21; 8:2, etc.

Walter Wink's study of "the powers" he specifically deals with the way in which the purity regulations and other marks of ritual practice embedded in Jewish law could serve as means of separation, exclusion, discrimination, and oppression.[5] I believe that we can think of the entire Mosaic Law as though it too is one of those many "powers" that Wink described, created by God originally for human order and well being, but corrupted by Sin.

In Rom 7:7–25 Paul speaks of *law* not just as Jewish identity markers but as perhaps the deepest and most subtle aspect of the moral law: "You shall not covet." Twice Paul says "Sin, seizing an opportunity in this commandment" bred covetousness in him (Rom 7:8), deceived him, and through it killed him. "The very commandment that promised life proved to be death to me" (7:10). Despite all this, Paul can still insist, "The law is holy, and the commandment is holy and just and good" (7:12), and "the law is spiritual" (7:14). Just as Sin can corrupt God-ordained governing agencies to oppress a whole people, so also apparently Sin can abuse the Torah in such a way as to force Paul (and therefore also anybody else) to do sinful deeds against his own will and to be unable to do good deeds he earnestly desires to do (7:15–20a).[6] Acknowledging this malign bondage Paul can only cry, "It is no longer I that do it, but Sin that dwells within me" (7:20b). This is not a flippant, self-justifying excuse, "The Devil made me do it." For Paul, it was literally a life-and-death matter: "Wretched man that I am! Who will rescue me from this body of death?" (7:24–25).

At the height of the spiritual and psychological struggle of his divided self the onset of an additional physical trauma of injury or disease[7] might conceivably have resulted in clinical, not merely metaphorical death. I am willing to believe that Paul had a near-death experience (see below). In any case, when Paul was in the very depths of despair he was transformed utterly.

As Paul continued his narrative to the Romans, he exulted, "Thanks be to God through Jesus Christ our Lord! So then, with my mind I am a slave to the law of God, but with my flesh I am a slave to the law of sin. There is therefore now no condemnation for those who are in Christ Jesus. For the law of the Spirit of life in Christ Jesus has set [me] free from the law of sin and of death" (Rom 7:25—8.2).[8]

---

5. Wink, *Engaging the Powers*, 115–117. See next chapter, n. 10.

6. Satan tempted Jesus in the wilderness by citing Scripture (see above Chap 22.3 "The temptation of Jesus").

7. See various commentaries on the question of Paul's physical infirmities (cf. Gal 4:13; 2 Cor 12:7).

8. NRSV reads "has set you free" with marginal note indicating the pronoun is singular, and that other ancient mss read "me" and some read "us." I take the view of those who think Rom 7 describes Paul's personal experience, and the continuation into what is now separated into Rom 8 was unbroken in his thought and dictation, so that at this point he is still expressing his personal sense of relief at having been set free.

2. THE APPEARANCE OF JESUS TO SAUL

In my view Paul underwent what is now known as a near-death experience (NDE). In chapter 5.4 "Near-death experiences" I gave a fuller treatment of this phenomenon, so here I will mention those features that seem most applicable to Saul/Paul.

In the documented NDEs *the experience of light is a constant*.[9] Without doubt the light overwhelmed Paul, and he believed that God revealed the resurrected Jesus in (or *as*) the light. Using a more generalized style of expression, I believe Paul reflects his own experience: "The God who said 'Let light shine out of darkness,' has shone in our hearts to give the light of the knowledge of the glory of God in the face of Jesus Christ" (2 Cor 4:6). Paul links his transformation by the light to God's first act of creation; "let there be light" (Gen 1:3)! In asserting to the Corinthians his apostolic authority he asks, "Am I not an apostle? Have I not seen Jesus our Lord?" He assumes an affirmative answer. Paul saw Jesus. He says the risen Christ "appeared to [or was seen by] me" (1 Cor 15:8). Kenneth Ring says concerning those he interviewed who had seen the light, "we find an absolute and undeniable spiritual radiance. This spiritual core of the NDE is so awesome and so overwhelming that the person who experiences it is at once and forever thrust into an entirely new mode of being."[10] Ring comments further: "It is as though the unconditional love many of them felt during their NDE swept away the last vestiges of religious parochialism and opened them up to a vision of humanity united in a faith whose shared foundation is God's limitless love for all."[11] In my view that is an accurate description of Saul/Paul.

For Saul, therefore, the vision of the resurrected Jesus convinced him that Jesus truly lived, though in a changed state. The resurrection body is no longer physical but has been transformed into a spiritual body (see his later statement on this point, though without offering any specifics, 1 Cor 15:44). Through personal experience Saul now had confirmation of his faith in resurrection in general and proof of the specific case of Jesus's resurrection. Now he could accept the truth of the Christians' claims that he had resisted so violently: the *crucified* Jesus was *the Messiah*, and Saul could now confess, *Jesus is Lord*. As Lord (equivalent to YHWH=LORD of the OT) Jesus in human form reveals the Most High God whom no one has ever seen. Ashton and others whom he cites interpret Paul's experience in terms of the *merkabah* mysticism, that is, the vision of the chariot throne. "It is reasonable to infer that his vision was basically of the same order as those of Ezekiel and others whose experiences followed a similar pattern."[12]

Seeing the resurrected man Jesus of Nazareth in that great light, Paul shared Ezekiel's vision of "the appearance of the likeness of the glory of YHWH" (Ezek 1:28b).

---

9. Morse, *Transformed by the Light*, 67–68.
10. Ring, *Heading toward Omega*, 50.
11. Ibid., 160.
12. Ashton, *The Religion of Paul the Apostle*, 85.

From the Christian community that Paul joined, he learned of Jesus's self-designation as "the son of man." Since that title would mean nothing to Gentiles, among them Paul called Jesus the Son of God, having made the deduction that Jesus had enigmatically expressed, i.e., his self-consciousness as the son of *that man* represented on the throne, namely *God*. The risen Jesus, Son of God, becomes the latest and most effective revealer of God. For Paul, Jesus is the glory of God; Jesus presents the authentic image of God. According to some current thought of that time, the first human Adam had lost the divine image because of the "fall." Paul shows familiarity with that thought by contrasting Adam as having a physical body, but Christ (resurrected) having a spiritual body. "Thus it is written, 'The first man, Adam, became a living being' [Gen 2:7], but the last Adam [Christ] became a life-giving spirit. But it is not the spiritual that is first, but the physical, and then the spiritual. The first man was from the earth, a man of dust; the second man is from heaven. As was the man of dust, so are those who are of the dust; and as is the man of heaven, so are those who are of heaven. Just as we have borne the image of the man of dust, we will also bear the image of the man of heaven" (1 Cor 15:45–49). In all this, Paul describes his own experience and his interpretation of it, generalizing for all believers, whether or not they had the same experience he did: "For as in Adam all die, so all will be made alive in Christ" (15:22; see Rom 5:14, 18).

Paul is the only NT writer to give personal testimony to having seen the risen Jesus. All the gospels were written considerably after Paul, and none presents an eyewitness account. Just as we may observe a progressive heightening of the concept of Jesus as Son of God in the Gospels, so we see a heightening of the material aspects of the resurrection. In Mark, the earliest, nobody saw the risen Jesus. In Matthew, Jesus met several women who had gone to the tomb, and they "took hold of his feet and worshipped him" (Matt 28:9). Later the "eleven disciples" met him on a mountain in Galilee; "when they saw him, they worshipped him, but some doubted" (28:17). In Luke Jesus, unrecognized, walked the Emmaus road with two disciples, sat at table with them, and broke bread before suddenly disappearing (Luke 24:13–31). Jesus later appeared to assembled disciples, denied he was a specter, invited them to touch him and see that he had flesh and bones, and ate a piece of broiled fish in their presence (24:39–43). Jesus invited doubting Thomas to put his finger in the nail holes and his hand in his side (John 20:27). According to Segal, "The motif of realistic appearances in Luke is similar to a Graeco-Roman apologetic designed to impress critics and friends with the power of Jesus's resurrection, whereas the ecstatic visions of Paul are more in line with the original Jewish apocalypticism out of which Christianity arose."[13]

Writing to the Galatians Paul states that it pleased God "to reveal his Son *en emoi*," a Gk phrase that can be rendered either *to me* as in NRSV, or *in me* (Gal 1:16). Grammatically either English preposition is possible. (The Revised English Bible renders *in and through me*.) Following Longenecker I prefer *in me* as more suitable in

---

13. Segal, *Paul the Convert*, 35.

the Galatians context.[14] Paul was convinced that through God's revelation, the resurrected Jesus now "*lives in me*," (Gal 2:20). This spiritual reality makes possible here and now a transformed human existence, which Jesus with a flesh-and-bone body that consumed fish could never provide. Therefore Paul can confidently declare: "If the Spirit of him who raised Jesus from the dead dwells in you, he who raised Christ from the dead will give life to your mortal bodies through his Spirit that dwells in you" (Rom 8:11). Whether or not the author of John knew the work of Paul, it seems to me he comes close to Paul's meaning when he writes the words of Jesus's prayer to God on behalf of those who will come to believe in him, "that they may all be one. As you, Father, are in me and I am in you, may they also be in us, so that the world may believe that you have sent me. The glory that you have given me I have given them, so that they may be one, as we are one, I in them and you in me, that they may become completely one" (John 17:20–23).

3. THE BIRTH OF PAUL

There can be no doubt that Paul had a life-changing encounter with light. Whether the light shone on him during a crisis of illness (and scholars generally agree that Paul had some sort of physical disability), or whether it occurred during a spiritual/psychological crisis, we cannot say. Like an NDE it was apparently instantaneous in one sense, but the actual outworking of its results came about over time as Paul reflected on it and as his personal experiences triggered or elicited memories of it. From Paul's own testimony it must have seemed a real death experience. It worked in him a transformation distinguished from those of twentieth century NDEers only in degree of intensity modified by culture and personal circumstances, and in leading to the emergence of Christianity as a world-wide faith tradition.

In Paul's self-understanding, he saw the resurrected Jesus either *in* that light or *as* that light, and he became somehow amalgamated with Jesus. One might say that in his relation to Christ, the Spirit of Christ *possessed* Paul. This possession enabled him to perform miraculous works, including overcoming and driving out other, evil spirits. In non-rational and non-scientific cultures where shamans operate effectively even today, a spirit possesses each shaman and enables him or her to promote their own interests but especially to help others.[15] Though showing similarities to shamanism, in Paul's case the Spirit of Christ mastered him and he became the slave of others in order to build them up and not to advance his own interests (see 2 Cor 4:5; 10:8; 12:19; 13:10).

Here we see a particularly important example of the effect on Paul of having been transformed by the light. *Saul, the persecutor*, acting violently as a destroyer (Gal 1:13)

---

14. See Longenecker, *Galatians*, comment on 1:16. He notes the distinction between "reveal in" here as internal and "see" in 1 Cor 9:1 and "appear to" 1 Cor 15:8 as more objective.

15. Ashton, *The Religion of Paul*, 213.

sought energetically to assert his authority and either force his religious convictions on dissenters or destroy them altogether. *Paul, the propagator*, having been accepted by God, was now motivated by love, *agapē*, prepared to make personal sacrifices on behalf of those to whom he ministered. Freed from narrow religious parochialism, he became a citizen of the world. Other parallels between Paul and NDEers include heightened prophetic insights, healing powers, and undaunted courage and endurance in the midst of hardship and danger, with liberation from the power of destructive fleshly appetites and from fear and anxiety.

In light of what we now know of brain science, it seems beyond question that Paul's experience involved neurobiological changes that resulted in significant transformation of behavior, what Paul considered a work of God through Christ that he described as living by the Spirit and not according to the flesh. I incline toward the view that Paul's initial NDE involved instantaneous and nearly total reorientation, so total that Paul described it as death. I agree with Colleen Shantz that it was not a once-for-all event, but that Paul had frequent subsequent mystical ecstatic experiences that reinforced and perpetuated his encounter with the light.[16] Brain science uses twenty-first century terminology, but Paul used first century Jewish and cultural terms to describe it:

> Live by the Spirit, I say, and do not gratify the desires of the flesh. For what the flesh desires is opposed to the Spirit, and what the Spirit desires is opposed to the flesh; for these are opposed to each other, to prevent you from doing what you want. . . Now the works of the flesh are obvious: fornication, impurity, licentiousness, idolatry, sorcery, enmities, strife, jealousy, anger, quarrels, dissensions, factions, envy, drunkenness, carousing, and things like these. I am warning you, as I warned you before: those who do such things will not inherit the kingdom of God. By contrast, the fruit of the Spirit is love, joy, peace, patience, kindness, generosity, faithfulness, gentleness, and self-control. There is no law against such things. And those who belong to Christ Jesus have crucified the flesh with its passions and desires. If we live by the Spirit, let us also be guided by the Spirit. Let us not become conceited, competing against one another, envying one another. (Gal 5:16–26)

In all his letters, either briefly or at length, Paul urges his audience to live by the Spirit according to the pattern described above. The entire chapter of Rom 12:1–21 is an extended essay on the subject. Basic to all that Paul writes is his conviction that Jesus Christ is the model, and that his own personal experience included a physical element he equated with Christ's crucifixion (Gal 2:19). Paul uses the same language at least metaphorically to apply to believers (Rom 6:16; Gal 5:24).

---

16. Shantz, *Paul in Ecstasy*, "Paul's Brain: The Cognitive Neurology of Ecstasy" 67–110. Shantz researched brain science in great depth in her preparation to apply it specifically to the study of Paul, detecting evidence of his ecstasy and altered states of consciousness (ASC).

Both Paul's personal testimony and the later accounts in Acts make it clear that he did not seek his transforming experience; God initiated it. Other ecstatic states may also have come unbidden, yet it is possible that Paul engaged in devotional disciplines that could induce them. Certainly today, in both Christian and other religious traditions, people experience ecstatic states unbidden, while spiritual disciplines have been developed to induce them.

In my reading of Paul, I see no evidence that he expected everybody else to have the same sort of traumatic experience that transformed him, but he considered others capable of imitating him (1 Cor 4:16; Phil 3:17) as he imitated Christ (1 Cor 11:1). That meant, at least, willingness to surrender one's personal advantages for the benefit of others. Paul listed a number of privileges he might rightly claim as an apostle, but he declined them all (1 Cor 9:4–12). In Corinth there was evidence of popular ecstatic experiences in a competitive atmosphere, and people seemed to think that speaking in tongues was the best. Paul insisted that the better gifts were those that benefited the community, not just the private person. In this context Paul inserted the hymn extolling the supremacy of love (=*agapē*, 1 Cor 13:1–13), which he said was the best gift of all, and he urged everybody to follow the way of love (14:1). Without discouraging any spiritual gift, Paul insisted that each person should exercise self-control to avoid sheer chaos in public worship that would result if everybody let emotion get the best of them. Humans are not hardwired to follow mere animal instincts!

In my view, the most important transformation in Paul was the basic change in his understanding of the essential nature of God. In the next chapter, "Paul's New Understanding of God" I take up this point extensively and connect it with the emerging biblical concept of the oneness of God.

30

Paul's New Understanding of God

As noted in the previous chapter, in his own way Paul had an experience similar to those of people who have reported near-death experiences (NDEs), as summarized by Ring: "It is as though the unconditional love many of them felt during their NDE swept away the last vestiges of religious parochialism and opened them up to a vision of humanity united in a faith whose shared foundation is God's limitless love for all."[1] As young Olaf Sunden believed that his NDE gave him a sort of "total comprehension,"[2] so Paul may have gained a grasp of the divine plan, as he knew it from his immersion in the study of the Bible as a Pharisee. Immediately Paul sensed that divine love embraced him, the former persecutor of God's church. He sensed also that this love was for all people. He felt an irresistible force driving him to share his experience of God's love with the Gentiles, whom Jews generally despised, and whose paganism had kept them in bondage.

Paul clearly refers to his call to mission when he wrote, "—God who had set me apart before I was born and called me through his grace was pleased to reveal his Son [to/in] me, so that I might proclaim him among the Gentiles—" (Gal 1:15–16). God put Paul in the company of the prophets Jeremiah and Isaiah. Paul's ancestral tribe was Benjamin, the land of Jeremiah, who heard God's call: "Before I formed you in the womb I knew you, and before you were born I consecrated you; I appointed you a prophet to the nations" (i.e., Gentiles; Jer 1:5). Details of Isa 49:1–6 appealed especially to Paul: "YHWH called me before I was born, while I was in my mother's womb he named me . . . And now YHWH says, who formed me in the womb to be his servant, . . . 'It is too light a thing that you should be my servant to raise up the tribes of Jacob and to restore the survivors of Israel; I will give you as a light to the nations [Gentiles] that my salvation may reach to the end of the earth.'"

Saul had shared Peter's concept of an all-conquering Messiah,[3] but Paul, having met the crucified and risen Christ, understood how wrong he had been. His entire concept of deity based on overwhelming and irresistible power had been wrong! In

1. Ring, *Heading Towards Omega*, 163.
2. Morse, *Transformed by the Light*, 12.
3. See chapter 27.1 "The Messiah?"

God For All

writing to the Corinthians, Paul now actually speaks of the *foolishness* and *weakness* of God! For at Corinth, the Roman capital of the Greek province of Achaia, Paul confronted a personal and ministerial crisis that forced him to articulate his new understanding of who God is and how God works.

1. PAUL'S MINISTRY AT CORINTH

After what seemed an ambiguous result of Paul's brief visit to Athens, he went on to Corinth, where he met a Jewish couple Aquila and Priscilla, who were tentmakers like him. They welcomed him to work in their shop (Acts 18:1–3), and he argued with Jews and Greeks in the local synagogue. Silas and Timothy joined Paul, bringing financial support from the believers in Philippi (Macedonia), and when Jewish opposition intensified, Paul was able to move his ministry next door to the house of a God-fearing Gentile named Titius Justus, where he was joined by two synagogue leaders, Crispus and Sosthenes. Thus Paul came in contact with prominent local people, both Jews and Gentiles, but during his eighteen months' ministry, most of those who became believers were ordinary folk, including a number of slaves and freed persons, renters, shopkeepers, and others who depended in some way on the better-off believers. In later references, Paul acknowledges several other people, who in all likelihood hosted gatherings of believers in their homes (Acts 18:5–11).[4] Paul refrained from becoming dependent on any of these people, although later that proved to be a cause of criticism against him. The Jews' opposition intensified to such an extent that they brought charges against Paul before the Roman proconsul Gallio, but he, noting that this was a Jewish religious debate with no relation to Roman law, dismissed the charges and idly observed the crowd's abuse of some of the Jews (18:12–17). Gallio's tenure in Corinth is known to have been between 51 and 53 CE.

Paul, with Priscilla and Aquila, moved on to Ephesus, where they met an Alexandrian Jew named Apollos. The couple (led by the wife Priscilla) instructed Apollos more exactly concerning Jesus, and they recommended him to the church at Corinth, where Apollos had a fruitful ministry for a while during Paul's further journeys and ministry in Ephesus (Acts 18:24—19:1). Meanwhile various problems arose in Corinth. Paul wrote a letter that is now lost, in which he criticized Corinthians severely for tolerating various kinds of immorality, especially sexual (see 1 Cor 5:9–13 for a reference to that letter). From Ephesus Paul made a quick trip in person, but he was rebuffed, and then wrote a severe letter of criticism and advice, which brought about good results as reported by Paul's messenger Titus (2 Cor 2:1–17).[5] In any case, what

---

4. See Crossan and. Reed, *In Search of Paul*, 316–37, for archaeological and sociological background of the typical kind of house church and patron/client relation typical of Greco-Roman society of Paul's day.

5. It is impossible to achieve consensus on the exact number of Paul's letters and visits to Corinth. See articles in *IDB* and *ABD*, and introductions to 1 & 2 Corinthians in HCSB.

appears in our Bibles as 1 Corinthians contains Paul's response to reports concerning the situation there and to specific questions sent from the church.

The first problem Paul addresses deals with the appearance of factions among the believers, based on their admiration of various leaders. One group followed Paul, the founder, a second group liked Apollos, who had come later and apparently seemed a very gifted speaker, and still another group claimed to follow Cephas, that is Peter (1 Cor 1:10-12). Scholars debate whether Peter had come in person to Corinth, or whether some representatives had vigorously promoted what they claimed for Peter against Paul. A basis for such divisions was the typical Greco-Roman patron-client social hierarchical system, ruled at the top by the Emperor, most powerful and considered divine in his own person. By attachment to a particularly powerful patron, lesser folk could get access to more personal prestige and advantage. In Paul's new worldview, this power structure was based on each person's selfish ambition for more money and power. Thus, to correct it Paul spoke of the weakness and foolishness of God (1 Cor 1:18-25).

2. CHRIST CRUCIFIED TURNS THE WORLD'S POWER SYSTEM UPSIDE DOWN

In both the Nicene and Apostles' Creeds, Christians affirm: "I believe in God the Father Almighty." The Westminster Confession of Faith, to whose system of doctrine I gave general consent at my ordination, speaks of God as "almighty and most wise." I believe Paul would respond, as he sometimes did in his letters, "Yes, but—." To the Corinthians he actually wrote, "God's foolishness is wiser than human wisdom, and God's weakness is stronger than human strength" (1 Cor 1:25). Someone may think that if we grade strength and wisdom on a scale of a hundred, say, and if we could imagine God as having any weakness or any foolishness at all, they would still be above the highest achievement of humans. That, however, would be to misunderstand Paul, for he does not apply the same scale to *God* and *not-god*.

In the polytheistic Mediterranean culture, deities and humans shared the same environment.[6] Deities took their place in hierarchies of most powerful down to little household guardians, and people had similar rankings from high to low. The most powerful people were like the greater gods (some, such as the emperor, might even be called gods, or immortals). Ordinary folk might "catch a ride" with a particularly powerful person, a hero, a king, a priest, a wonder-worker, or a skillful scribe or debater (like a clever lawyer), who could help them get special advantages. Apparently in Corinth some members appeared ready to split into factions, each elevating a leader in competition with others: Paul, Apollos, and Cephas [i.e., Peter] along with Christ (1 Cor 1:12). Paul was shocked at this tendency that might lead to ranking him among the lesser gods. He objects: "Was Paul crucified for you? Or were you baptized in the

---

6. See chapter 21.2a "The great chain of being."

name of Paul?" (1:13). For Paul, Jesus, the crucified Messiah, has turned upside down the conception of God as using sheer power to impose the divine will, and to enable people to get what they want by cleverly working the religious system. Paul avers:

> Has not God made foolish the wisdom of the world? For since, in the wisdom of God, the world did not know God through wisdom, God decided, through the foolishness of our proclamation, to save those who believe. For Jews demand signs and Greeks desire wisdom, but we proclaim Christ crucified, a stumbling block to Jews and foolishness to Gentiles, but to those who are the called, both Jews and Greeks, Christ the power of God and the wisdom of God. For God's foolishness is wiser than human wisdom, and God's weakness is stronger than human strength. (1 Cor 1:17–25)

When Paul mentions the Jews' demand for signs, he undoubtedly alludes to the nationalistic aspect of belief in "YHWH the God of Israel"—YHWH who split the sea for the Israelites and drowned the Egyptians; YHWH who drove out seven nations and gave their land to Israel; YHWH who won the primeval battle over the chaos monsters and guaranteed success in war to the davidic king.[7] When YHWH seemed to have forgotten his people, they could cry out: "O that you would tear open the heavens and come down . . . so that the nations might tremble at your presence" (Isa 64:1a, 2b). The cross was a stumbling block to Jews, for in popular thought one who could not save himself was certainly *not* the Messiah (Mark 15:31b–32).

The Greeks, Paul observes, desire wisdom—that is, in popular terms, the sophists' teachings of the sort of wisdom that enabled the practitioner, "the debater of this age," to win every argument and get the best of any opponent. The best-known sophist, Protagoras, claimed that there were two contradictory arguments about everything, and that he could make the weaker cause the stronger.[8] To Greeks, therefore, the cross was foolishness. Though depending on different techniques, both Jews and Greeks sought their own advantages by means of imposition of dominating wisdom and power, or through affiliation to a wiser and more powerful patron. This worldly concept of power is precisely that which God, through Christ, overturns by the very opposite, the weakness and foolishness of nonviolent self-sacrificing love of Jesus on the cross.

Paul cites the OT in support: "I will destroy the wisdom of the wise, and the discernment of the discerning I will thwart," an approximation of Isa 29:14b. King Hezekiah had sent messengers to Egypt to secure armaments and joined a coalition against Assyria with full backing of the religious establishment, but Isaiah strongly opposed this war policy. Isaiah argued: The prophets and seers go into their trances, but it's only drunkenness or sleepy stupor, for they can't discern the signs of the times (Isa 29:9–10). The priests fervently draw near with lip service and rote ceremony, but their hearts are far from God (29:13). "The wisdom of their wise shall perish, and the

---

7. 2 Sam 22 and Ps 18, near-identical poems, describe YHWH's cosmological power now manifested in King David.

8. Voegelin, *The World of the Polis*, 296; see also Wikipedia, Protagoras, Philosophy.

discernment of the discerning shall be hidden" (29:14). Prophets and wise men think they can manipulate YHWH; they turn things upside down like the pot questioning the potter (29:15–16). But YHWH will bring about a reversal by which the deaf, the blind, the meek, and the neediest of the people shall be blessed, for "the tyrant shall be no more," and those "who cause a person to lose a lawsuit and without grounds deny justice to the one in the right" shall be cut off (Isa 29:17–21).

Paul reminds the Corinthians that they themselves are living proof of God's policy of reversal. Not many were wise, not many were powerful, not many were of noble birth. "But God chose what is foolish in the world to shame the wise; God chose what is weak in the world to shame the strong; God chose what is low and despised in the world, things that are not, to reduce to nothing things that are, so that no one might boast in the presence of God. He is the source of your life in Christ Jesus, who became for us wisdom from God, and righteousness and sanctification and redemption, in order that, as it is written, 'Let the one who boasts, boast in the Lord' " (1 Cor 1:26b–31).

Paul's second citation is from Jer 9:24, when King Zedekiah was plotting rebellion against Babylon. Like Isaiah before him, Jeremiah opposed war and proposed surrender, but the king gave in to the religious and court power elite who counseled resistance, till the whole nation fell. In that situation, Jeremiah put his finger precisely on the authors of that fatal policy: "Thus says YHWH: Do not let the wise boast in their wisdom, do not let the mighty boast in their might, do not let the wealthy boast in their wealth; but let those who boast boast in this, that they understand and know me, that I am YHWH; I act with steadfast love, justice, and righteousness in the earth, for in these things I delight, says YHWH" (Jer 9:23–24). The value system of the world—that which is not-god—brings only ignominious failure.

The way of the world and the way of God, 1 Cor 1:18—3.4

The way of the World	The way of God
The wisdom of the world, the wise, the scribe, the debater, (1:20–21)	The foolishness and weakness of God (1:18–24)
By human or fleshly standards: the powerful, the wise, those of noble birth (1:26)	God chooses the foolish, the weak, the low and despised, the "nothings" (1:27–28)
The wisdom of the rulers of this age, who are doomed to perish, led to crucifying the Lord of glory (2:6, 8)	The hidden wisdom of God, has now been revealed by the Spirit (2:7)
The spirit of this world (2:12)	The Spirit of God (2:10, 12)
Natural persons (2:14)	Persons who are spiritual (2:15)
People of the flesh (=sarx 3:1, 3) merely human (3:4)	Those who have the mind of Christ (2:16)

It may seem exaggerated for Paul to refer to matters of international politics in ancient Israel when addressing a quarrel in a private association of near nobodies in Corinth. But as he continues his argument, Paul himself puts the issue precisely in the political realm. "We speak God's wisdom, secret and hidden, which God decreed before the ages for our glory. None of the rulers of this age understood this; for if they had, they would not have crucified the Lord of glory" (2:7-8). Worldly wisdom prompted the high priest to advise, "It is better to have one man die for the people than to have the whole nation destroyed" (John 11:50). Worldly wisdom dictated Pilate's decision to crucify Jesus. Worldly wisdom was what Jesus rejected when he said, "My kingship is not from this world" (John 18:36), and why he would not appeal to the Father for legions of angels (Matt 26:53).

3. THE REIGN OF CHRIST (PHIL 2:5-11)

Paul more clearly teaches the essence of godhead revealed by the lordship of Christ by his use of what many scholars believe is an early hymn sung by believers even before Paul joined the Way. While encouraging the members of the Philippian community to avoid selfish ambition but to love and serve others rather than self, Paul offered Christ as an example:

> Let the same mind be in you that was in Christ Jesus, who, though he was in the form of God, did not regard equality with God as something to be exploited, but emptied himself, taking the form of a slave, being born in human likeness. And being found in human form, he humbled himself and became obedient to the point of death—even death on a cross. Therefore God also highly exalted him and gave him the name that is above every name, so that at the name of Jesus every knee should bend, in heaven and on earth and under the earth, and every tongue should confess that Jesus Christ is Lord, to the glory of God the Father. (Philippians 2:5-11)

Unlike the first ancestors of the human race, who grasped at the possibility of becoming "like God," the human Jesus neither sought such equality nor tried to exploit his privileged position as Son for his own advantage.[9] Jesus's voluntary humiliation on behalf of the many resulted in God's exalting him above all others and giving him "the name that is above every name," so that "at the name of Jesus every knee should bend, in heaven and on earth and under the earth, and every tongue should confess that Jesus Christ is Lord [=YHWH] to the glory of God the Father."[10]

---

9. See chapter 23.2 "The temptation of Jesus."

10. "Indeed, the adoption/adaptation of the Old Testament cultic expression to connote devotion to Jesus is probably to be seen as indicating that these early Christians intended a direct association and analogy between their devotion to Jesus and the Old Testament cultic devotion to *Yahweh*." Hurtado, *At the Origins of Christian Worship*, 79. "For a Jew this phrase can only mean that Jesus received the divine name Yahweh, the tetragrammaton YHWH, translated as the Greek name *kyrios*, or Lord. We have seen

Paul's New Understanding of God

For Paul, the Jewish Pharisee now become apostle to the Gentiles, the resurrected Christ is the LORD=YHWH, and for believers in Christ among the subjects of Rome, Jesus Christ is Lord *even over Caesar*. Christ is now Lord not only of the individual and the church but also of the world, and at the end he will "hand over the kingdom to God the Father, after he has destroyed[11] every ruler and every authority and power. For he must reign until he has put all his enemies under his feet. The last enemy to be destroyed is death" (1 Cor 15:24–26). Paul's inclusion of death as an enemy to be deprived of power makes it clear that he has not lapsed back into the mode of worldly wisdom and the literal imposition of violent force to achieve Christ's final victory. Only life can defeat death, and through Christ, God effects not the destruction of opposition but the life-giving reconciliation of all things, even enemies, including death! To the Philippians Paul wrote, "Our citizenship is in heaven, and it is from there that we are expecting a Savior, the Lord Jesus Christ. He will transform the body of our humiliation that it may be conformed to the body of his glory, by the power that also enables him to make all things subject to himself" (Phil 3:20–21). "When all things are subjected to him, then the Son himself will also be subjected to the one who put all things in subjection under him, so that God may be all in all" (1 Cor 15:28). "All in all" implies, indeed necessitates, abandoning the popular concept of imposition of divine power from above or from without and destroying all opposition. Now we understand that through the immanent Spirit God works in human spirits and in all created nature to persuade and enable the creatures willingly to work the Creator's will.

---

that sharing in the divine name is a recurring motif of early Jewish apocalypticism, where the principal angelic mediator of god is or carries the name Yahweh, as Exodus 23:20 describes the angel of God." Segal, *Paul the Convert*, 62.

11. In my view the word "destroy" (15:24, 26) inappropriately implies violence, whereas the Gk word *katargein* in its more than twenty occurrences means to render powerless or ineffective. Powers and authorities are part of creation and hence are not to be destroyed, but to be reconciled. See chapter 31 "Universal Grace in Romans."

31

Universal Grace in Romans[1]

WE MUST TAKE SERIOUSLY the universal reconciliation that Paul introduces in Corinthians and Philippians as I explained in chapter 30 above, "Paul's New Understanding of God," which later Paulinists such as the authors of Ephesians 1:9–10 and Colossians 1:15–20 express more succinctly. We must rethink the concept of salvation by faith and the idea that every individual human must either be saved or lost depending on whether or not one has believed in Christ as Savior. In popular Christian belief and practice, the act of faith itself has become the necessary condition of salvation and hence the determiner of eternal destiny. Benjamin B. Warfield bluntly called it "autosoterism," a scholarly word meaning saving oneself.[2] Such does not represent Paul's gospel. Is faith meaningless, then? By no means! By faith we open ourselves to the grace, mercy, and peace that God gives us, and of which we may be deprived by lack of trust or by indifference, rebellion, or ignorance. We must understand "save" and "salvation" primarily in terms of sharing in the resurrection life of Christ and enjoying here and now the blessings of healing, restoration, liberation, and preservation. Without attempting further elucidation, or addressing the questions of freedom of will and "second chance" after death, I simply offer these words of G. H. W. Lampe: "What we mean by salvation from sin is . . . nothing less than the conversion of hostility to God, with its accompanying lovelessness towards the rest of his creation, into a new spirit of freely willed trust in God and love towards his creatures—the victory of God's Spirit within man over the sin which is the misuse of his freedom."[3] We shall, indeed, enjoy these blessings in fullest measure in God's eternity, but those who do not now believe are not thereby cut off from God forever, because as part of the one world created by the one God, they are embraced in the one plan of reconciliation. We can confidently leave the details of that to the God revealed through Jesus Christ and interpreted by the Apostle Paul.

---

1. My understanding of universal grace in Romans has been sharpened by reading Staples, "What Do the Gentiles Have to Do with 'All Israel'?"

2. See chapter 1.1 "Benjamin B. Warfield." See also Westminster Larger Catechism Q 32 ". . . requiring faith as the condition—."

3. Lampe, *God as Spirit*, 21.

I have shown enough of Paul's thought to support a theology of universal reconciliation. It remains now to note how Paul threads this theme through his letter to the Romans. Paul's sense of eschatological urgency, his expectation of the Lord's early return, never allowed him the leisure to write down his message all in order. Paul was continually applying his understanding of God to new situations, and he couldn't know the exact detail until he faced each real-life problem. Romans is the closest Paul came to an ordered statement, but we still detect evidence of polemics on a number of issues. I will not take up these issues, but if we better understand his grasp of the one God and the divine plan for all humanity, one can work out some of the details on lesser issues. In tracing Paul's theme, keep in mind the universal reconciliation I have just posited as I focus on Paul's use of the word *all* at significant points in his letter to the Romans.

1. ALL ARE UNDER THE POWER OF SIN

As Paul's argument develops, we see that he views Sin as what Ashton describes "as a kind of cosmic force doing battle with grace on a global scale, and possessing the frightening capacity of taking up residence in the human soul."[4] From Rom 1:18—3:20 Paul states his well-known and much-studied description of human sinfulness. Following my seminary Greek teacher (and some printed editions of the NT) I used to read Rom 1:18–32 as describing specifically the failure of the Gentiles, but this introduces a distinction that Paul does not make. From the first, Paul speaks of Jews *and* Gentiles (Rom 1:16; 2:9–10); he insists that God is God of both Jews and Gentiles (3:29) and that God shows no partiality (2:11). Paul speaks of "all ungodliness and wickedness of those who by their wickedness suppress the truth" (Rom 2:18). The Greek underlying NRSV "those who" is the generic word for human=*anthrōpos*. The list of sins is often considered typical of Gentiles whom some Jews simply dismissed as "Gentile sinners" (see Paul's own unabashed use of the expression, Gal 2:15). But in this context the general term, *anthrōpos* means anybody, and the OT gives ample evidence that the special people of YHWH could be as guilty as anybody else of everything in Paul's catalogue. All sins flow from the basic sin: "They exchanged the truth about God for a lie and worshiped and served the creature rather than the Creator" (1:25).

Among humans, Jews have the advantages of God's gifts of the law and the divine oracles, and some Jews boasted, comparing themselves to Gentiles. Still, any perceived superiority was God's gift, not personal accomplishments by Jews as individuals or as a people. There are Gentiles who naturally keep the (moral) teachings of the law. "They show that what the law requires is written on their hearts" (2:15) Here Paul includes Gentiles as beneficiaries of the new covenant that YHWH promised for the house of Israel and the house of Judah, according to which God would put the law

---

4. *The Religion of Paul*, 213. See chapter 29 "The Death of Saul and the Birth of Paul" notes 2 and 3.

within them and remember their sins no more (Jer 31:33). There are indeed Jews who break the law, but God deals the same with all: "to those who by patiently doing good seek for glory and honor and immortality, he will give eternal life; while for those who are self-seeking and who obey not the truth but wickedness, there will be wrath and fury. There will be anguish and distress for everyone who does evil, the Jew first and also the Greek, but glory and honor and peace for everyone who does good, the Jew first and also the Greek. For God shows no partiality" (Rom 2:7–11).

Paul knew that there were Gentiles in synagogues throughout the Diaspora who had not converted but who had abandoned idolatry and lived moral lives. Paul's believers in Thessalonica had "turned to God from idols, to serve a living and true God, and to wait for his Son from heaven—" (1 Thess 1:9–10). Paul advanced a Jewish view that Paula Fredriksen describes: "When God establishes his Kingdom, then, these two groups will together constitute 'his people': Israel redeemed from exile, and the Gentiles redeemed from idolatry. Gentiles are saved as Gentiles; they do not, eschatalogically, become Jews."[5] For the time being, though, Paul writes, "we have charged that all, both Jews and Greeks, are under the power of sin—" (3:9). Then what is God's answer to this universal sinfulness, the captivity of all God's human children to sin?

2. JUSTIFICATION FOR ALL WHO BELIEVE

In 3:21—5.11 Paul begins to answer the question of God's response to human need, "the righteousness of God through the faith [of] Jesus Christ for all who believe. For there is no distinction, since all have sinned and fall short of the glory of God, they are now justified by his grace as a gift, through the redemption that is in Christ Jesus, whom God put forward as a sacrifice of atonement by his blood, effective through faith" (3:22–25a). The Gk of these verses is susceptible of many interpretations. In the immediate context, *all* appears to be limited only to those who believe (but see §3 below). "Through faith in Jesus Christ" is a genitive construction that may be rendered *through the faith of Jesus Christ* (3:22 NRSV margin). The marginal reading is to be preferred, for the other reading traditionally places emphasis on each individual's act of faith, whereas it is God who takes the initiative and guarantees its effect through Christ. Redemption is deeply related to the covenant concept in the OT as we have seen, especially YHWH's fictive kinship with Israel. The Divine Kinsman took responsibility as *go'el*, next of kin, to redeem family members in economic or physical bondage *from which they could not save themselves*.[6] Making salvation depend on the sinful individual's faith in Christ turns the whole biblical concept of redemption upside down.

Paul experienced enslavement to Sin and divine liberation in his own life (Rom 7:9—8:2). Still, God is not indifferent to individual sins and transgressions, and in the OT the high priestly sacrifice on the Day of Atonement took away the people's sins.

5. Fredriksen, "Judaism, the Circumcision of Gentiles, and Apocalyptic Hope," 547.
6. See chapter 7.4 "God's Covenant with Abram" and chapter 9 "Moses, the Name, and the Exodus."

Now the death of Jesus is interpreted also in terms of atonement (3:25). This is the single example of Paul's use of the technical term *hilastērion* translated "atoning death" in NRSV. It was probably already in use among believers before Paul's conversion; he makes more effective use of the concepts of redemption and reconciliation. As Paul says, God in his divine forbearance had passed over the sins previously committed, that is, before Christ (Rom 3:25). In 2 Cor 5:19 Paul said that in Christ God was reconciling the world, "not counting their trespasses against them." Although the wording is different, I see no distinction between "not counting their trespasses" in Corinthians and "passed over the sins previously committed" in Romans. Both are evidence of divine grace, and they highlight Paul's new understanding of God.

Paul offers Abraham as the prime example of justification by faith. Abraham believed God, and God counted his trust as righteousness (Rom 4:3). This happened before God commanded circumcision as seal of the covenant, the identifying mark of the Jew. God promised Abram his descendants would be as numerous as the stars of heaven (Gen 15:5, see 22:18) but Paul universalizes it: "the promise that he would inherit *the world*[7] (Gk *kosmos*)" was not according to law (4:13). God promises that Abraham and his descendants shall produce many *nations* (Gen 17:5–7; 35:11; 48:19). Paul understands it in the sense of *Gentiles*. In both his Gentile and his Jewish existence, Abraham lived by trusting in the God "who gives life to the dead and calls into existence the things that do not exist" (Rom 4:17b). This is the God who guarantees his promise to Abraham by grace (Rom 4:16–18). All who believe in the God who raised Jesus from the dead will also be reckoned as justified (4:24–5). Near the end of Romans Paul affirms the effectiveness of Christ in God's plan for the Gentiles: "Christ has become a servant of the circumcised on behalf of the truth of God in order that he might confirm the promises given to the patriarchs, and in order that the Gentiles might glorify God for his mercy," adding citations of OT texts devoted to the Gentiles (Rom 15:7–12: Ps 18:50; Deut 32:43 LXX; Ps 117:1; Isa 11:1, 10).

By faith we have peace with God, which enables us to surmount any earthly tribulation and to grow in the process. Once we were enemies, but God has reconciled us through the death of his son, so that we are saved by his life (5:1–11). Here I must note another misinterpretation of Paul, namely, that enmity between God and sinners is mutual, and that both God and humans need to be reconciled, specifically that Christ had to die to satisfy divine justice.[8] Not so! *We* are God's enemies, but God takes the initiative to show grace and mercy to *us*, to overcome *our* enmity or fear of God—"Do you not realize that God's kindness is meant to lead you to repentance?" (Rom 2:4; see also 2 Cor 5:11–20; Ezek 20:43–44).

---

7. Paul's use of *kosmos* apparently follows late Jewish interpretations of the promise as "all the earth" in Sirach 44:21, Jubilees 22:14 and 32:19. Paul never mentions the promise of the *land*=Canaan, which is so prominent in the OT and among those who today support the Israelis in occupying the territories of the Palestinians.

8. Westminster Larger Catechism Q 38: "to satisfy God's justice, procure his favor"; Q 40: "to reconcile God."

3. CHRIST RESTORES WHAT ADAM LOST

Romans 5:12–21 is the key passage containing the *all* that transcends the apparent limit of the *all who believe* in 3:22 and 4:24. In contrast to our modern obsession with rights and responsibilities of individuals, Paul considers all humanity as one solidary, interrelated entity. Paul adds detail concerning the way Sin dominates humankind. Adam (Heb ʾ*adam* also means humanity), representing the whole race, committed the sin of disobeying God, which allowed Death to gain dominion over all, for all likewise sinned. But in response to the reign of Sin and Death, God had a more effective response: Grace and Life bestowed as free gifts. Jesus Christ, representative head of renewed humanity, by his act of obedience brought about the total reversal of the consequences of Adam's disobedience: "But the free gift is not like the trespass. For if the many died through the one man's trespass, much more surely have the grace of God and the free gift in the grace of the one man, Jesus Christ, abounded for the many" (5:15). The use of the definite article in the phrases "the one" and "the many" has the effect of equaling *all*. For example, a classroom teacher (the one) and her pupils (the many) equals all.[9] Rom 5:18 makes this clear: "Therefore just as one man's trespass led to condemnation for all, so one man's act of righteousness leads to justification and life for all." In 1 Cor 15 Paul gives more detail on the Adam figure that reinforces the universal scope. "For as in Adam all die, so all will be made alive in Christ" (1 Cor 15:22). "Thus it is written, 'The first man, Adam became a living being' [citing Gen 2:7]; the last Adam [Christ] became a life-giving spirit" (1 Cor 15:45)

in Adam	in Christ
Sin	Grace
Death	Life
trespass	act of righteousness
condemnation	justification
disobedience	obedience
sinners	righteous
living being	life-giving spirit
all die	all will be made alive

Romans 5:12–21 deals entirely with Christ's accomplishment in reversing for *all* humanity the deadly effects of what Adam had done for *all*. Let Paul's statements stand: "where sin increased, grace abounded all the more" (5:20). Only thus can Christ's superiority to Adam be assured, for if Adam's act affected *all*, but Christ's act affected only a limited number of believers, then Christ is less effective than Adam. No sincere person could ever accept Adam's superiority to Christ.

---

9. The same principle applies in vv 16 and 19 also where *the one* and *the many* = *all*.

4. GOD'S MERCY ON ALL

The goal of universal grace in Romans is that God will grant mercy to *the entire* human race, without exception. Between Christ repairing Adam's disobedience for *all* (5:18), and the statement that "God has imprisoned *all* in disobedience so that he may be merciful to *all*" (Rom 11:32), Paul's argument in Rom 9–11 gets complicated. I shall try to keep to the main theme.

Paul opens this much-debated section of his letter with a heartfelt cry of distress because many of his fellow Jews have not accepted Christ. Even so, he lists the great blessings that are theirs: "They are Israelites, and to them belong the adoption,[10] the glory, the covenants, the giving of the law, the worship, and the promises; to them belong the patriarchs, and from them, according to the flesh, comes the Messiah" (9:1–4). Yet in spite of these obvious privileges, not all of Abraham's descendants participate in them. Indeed, from among Abraham and Isaac's children, God chose Jacob and rejected Esau on purely arbitrary grounds (9:6–13). God hardened Pharaoh's heart in order to demonstrate divine power in saving Israel from Egypt (9:16–18).[11] One might question why God finds fault with wrongdoers, since the divine decree is irresistible, but Paul will not permit anyone to question God's sovereignty. Paul's vehemence in this matter hides, I think, an unexpressed doubt about God's vaunted impartiality. "What if" the divine Potter makes of the same clay vessels for destruction and vessels for honor? (9:19–23). Indeed, vessels for honor, says Paul, include "us whom he has called, not from the Jews only, but also from the Gentiles" (9:24). To support this last statement Paul gives a paraphrase of several texts from Hosea: "Those who were not my people I will call 'my people,' and her who was not beloved I will call 'beloved.' And in the very place where it was said to them, 'You are not my people,' there they shall be called children of the living God." (Rom 9:25–6; Hos 1:6, 9; 2:23b. See chapter 16.1 "Hosea lives the covenant"). In Hosea, these words apply *precisely* to Israel, whom God had cast off because they were inextricably mixed with Gentiles: "Israel is swallowed up; now they are among the nations [Gentiles] as a useless vessel" (Hos 8:8). Yet Hosea concludes with YHWH freely forgiving Israel and restoring them again. According to Jason Staples, Paul argues that in order to restore Israel, God has to include the Gentiles who have swallowed them up and among whom they are intermingled.[12] The texts that called Israel "my people" *after* YHWH had once called them "not my people" now apply also to the Gentiles, who previously never had been called God's people. Gentiles who have been justified by the faithfulness of Christ belong to God's people—without becoming Jews by circumcision—but most of Israel seems to have stumbled (9:30–33).

---

10. That is, the status as "my son" (Exod 4:22–23; Hos 11:1).
11. Think what the effect on the biblical story might be if Pharaoh had said, "All right! Go!"
12. Staples, "What do the Gentiles Have to Do with 'All Israel'?" 380–83 (see note 1 above).

Again, Paul expresses heartfelt hope that his fellow Jews might be saved (10:1), but by the time he reaches the end of his argument, it has become clear that he is not thinking of saved/lost in absolute categories of eternal separation. In line with his starting point "*all* are under the power of sin," Paul writes: "For there is no distinction between Jew and Greek; the same Lord is Lord of *all* and is generous to *all* who call on him. For, 'Everyone who calls on the name of the Lord shall be saved' " (10:12–13, citing Joel 2:32). Here "Lord" has a double meaning. Of old those who called on the name of YHWH were saved, and now those who call on the name of the Lord Jesus are saved. But of old as now, not all who heard believed the message. Citing several OT texts, Paul says God has been found by Gentiles, while vainly stretching out hands toward indifferent Israel (10:19–21).

This poses the question: "I ask, then, has God rejected his people? By no means! . . . God has not rejected his people whom he foreknew" (11.1a, 2a). Paul's declaration did not deter those Christians who claim that God *has* rejected the Jews for their failure to keep the law and to accept Jesus, and that Christians now comprise the true people of God. Augustine provided the argument that dominated the Western Catholic view for centuries, and Luther and Calvin, both originally Augustinians, saddled the Reformation with the same error. The term "foreknew" plays a significant part in "double predestination" according to which God knew beforehand those who would believe in Christ, *precisely because* God had chosen them and ordained their salvation. Romans 8:29–30 develops the thought: "For those whom he foreknew he also predestined to be conformed to the image of his Son, in order that he might be the firstborn within a large family. And those whom he predestined he also called; and those whom he called he also justified, and those whom he justified he also glorified." These words came to be limited to the elect, and later *only* to those who by believing fulfilled the condition to complete their salvation. But this turns Paul's argument upside down!

It turns out, says Paul, that God always maintained by grace a faithful remnant in Israel, while the rest were hardened. In fact, "God gave them a sluggish spirit, eyes that would not see and ears that would not hear, down to this very day" (11:8, a rough approximation of Deut 29:4 H 29:3; see also Isa 6:9–10). The purpose, however, is that Israel's stumbling will make possible the salvation of the Gentiles, which will, in turn, excite Israel's jealousy. "Now if their stumbling means riches for the world, and if their defeat means riches for the Gentiles, how much more will their full inclusion mean!" (11:12).

Here Paul picks up on either an actual or a potential situation in which Gentile believers may be congratulating themselves and feeling a bit condescending toward Jews. Don't forget, he says, that Israel is the root and trunk of the olive tree, and you Gentiles are only wild branches grafted in contrary to nature. If God removed some of the natural branches, "how much more will these natural branches be grafted back into their own olive tree." (11:25). Staples says the natural branches that were cut off were the Israelites, mixed in with the Gentiles, who will be restored. And even though the Gentiles are wild, they are still olive branches.[13] Paul continues: "I want you to understand this mystery: a hardening has come upon part of Israel, until the full number of the Gentiles has come in. and so all Israel will be saved' (11:25b-26a). Staples connects the phrase "the full number of the Gentiles" to Gen 48:19, where patriarch Israel foretells of Ephraim that his offspring shall become a multitude of nations [Gentiles], and with Hosea 8:8 where Israel is swallowed up among the Gentiles as a useless vessel. By saving the Gentiles, God will save Israel that is among them.[14] It is on this basis that Paul continues with his conclusion: "For God has imprisoned *all* in disobedience so that he may be merciful to *all*" (11:32).

In Romans 9–11 Paul has struggled with the complications brought about when previously segregated Jews and Gentiles unite in one religious community united by faith in Jesus Christ. He has attained the summit of conviction that the one God's mercy embraces all humanity entire. Paul now bursts forth in praise to the Sovereign God: "O the depth of the riches and wisdom and knowledge of God! How unsearchable are his judgments and how inscrutable his ways! 'For who has known the mind of the Lord? Or who has been his counselor?' 'Or who has given a gift to him, to receive a gift in return?' For from him and through him and to him are all things. To him be the glory forever. Amen" (11:33–36).

SUMMARY AND REFLECTION

Admittedly it is difficult to follow the universal thread through Romans, particularly if one is obsessed with individual salvation by faith and Christianity's replacement of Judaism. Paul insists on God's complete freedom and sovereignty. God has revealed wrath on *all* ungodliness. There is *no* distinction, for *all* have sinned and fall short of the glory of God. God has imprisoned *all* in disobedience. God can have mercy on whom he will and harden whom he will. Some expositors such as Warfield conclude that the Sovereign God determined from all eternity that some would be saved and the rest lost. But Paul insists that with God there is *no* partiality (2:11; see also Gal 2:6). Paul backs up that claim by arguing that God enfolds several examples of *apparent* partiality in a total plan to show mercy to *all*. It is a plan for the redemption of the whole creation (Rom 8:20–21; 2 Cor 15:24–28). God's sovereignty is a sovereignty of grace!

The question of salvation by faith or by obedience to law must be addressed in light of Paul's universal presupposition. Christian interpreters set Christianity as the religion of grace based on faith in Christ against Judaism as the religion based on obedience to law. E. P. Sanders convinced me and many others that this was a false dichotomy. Jews knew themselves saved by divine grace and took on the obligation

---

13. Staples, op. cit., 383–85.
14. Ibid., 385–90.

to keep the law as their grateful response. Sanders called this "covenantal nomism."[15] When Paul condemns Gentiles who insist on "works of the law" he means the particular laws that set Jews apart, e.g., circumcision, kosher, and sabbath observance. That made the former Gentile a Jew and therefore obligated him to observe all the law, both ritual and moral. Seyoon Kim has contributed much to the exposition of key texts in Paul's letters by persuasively showing how they relate to his Damascus road encounter with the risen Christ. But Kim seems fixated on defending not only the contrast of faith vs law but also the view that Christ's death was the necessary atoning sacrifice that made it possible for God to reconcile sinners. Kim writes, "At this 'conversion' experience, Paul himself appropriated Christ's atonement by faith in him so that he came to be 'in Christ' and received God's forgiveness of his sins."[16] Kim presents Paul's conversion almost as an act of autosoterism, and it certainly contrasts negatively with Jesus's healing and forgiving the paralytic (Mark 2:1–12) and the experience of Jesus' disciples as summarized in John 20:19–22 (see above chapter 27.4 "To err is human, to forgive divine").

Paul and the early Christians exalted Jesus Christ, Son of God, suffering Messiah, and Savior as the supreme agent for God at work in the world. The Christians viewed Jesus much the same way as some contemporary Jews saw Enoch, Moses, and other ancient heroes as exalted agents of God, but Christians venerated Jesus by honors not accorded those others. They included Jesus the Son along with God the Father in their worship, they prayed to him, sang hymns to him, and called on his name as Lord=YHWH.[17] For Paul Jesus Christ is the best and truest revealer of the God whose judgments are unsearchable and whose ways are inscrutable. Yet Jesus is not the God whom he reveals. For Paul, God is still God the Father and Jesus Christ is the Son. Christ is the viceroy ruling over *all* until God will have put all things in subjection under his feet, at which time the Son will be subjected to God, who then will be *all* in *all* (1 Cor 15:27–28).

---

15. Sanders, *Paul and Palestinian Judaism*.

16. Seyoon Kim, *Paul and the New Perspective*, 234. Kim occupies much of his book debating J. D. G. Dunn, who coined the term "new perspective" to characterize Sanders's insights. In footnotes on page 1 Kim lists Dunn's books and articles that he will try to refute.

17. Hurtado, *One God One Lord*, 17.

32

Paul and the Oneness of God

IN CHAPTERS 28 THROUGH 31 I described how Paul's understanding of God changed because of his meeting with the risen Jesus, and how his conviction of being appointed Apostle to the Gentiles led him to conclude that God's final plan includes all, both Jews and Gentiles. In this chapter I will explore further the agreement I see between Jesus and Paul, who in his own way responded to his call from God and his conviction that God is one.

1. FORGIVENESS OF SIN

I have already described how Jesus, both in his ministry and in his resurrection state, forgave sins and encouraged or commissioned people to forgive the sins of others (see chapter 27.4 "To err is human, to forgive divine"). The example and gift of Jesus went against common Jewish belief and practice. Sanders collected examples of rabbinical teachings that repentance is always necessary for God's forgiveness[1] and notes that a criticism of Paul is the almost total lack of mention of repentance in his writings.[2] I believe Paul's view is practically the same as Jesus's, and it rested upon his personal experience of having been unconditionally accepted when he encountered the light of Christ. In his doctrine of reconciliation, Paul asserts that God does not count our transgressions against us (2 Cor 5:19). The crucified Christ proves that the sin question has been settled once for all—we are forgiven; therefore we can and should forgive. One may become flippant regarding such a serious matter, but that is always a danger when we talk about God's unconditional grace.

We need the discipline of private and corporate reflection upon the extent to which we do those things we ought not to do and leave undone those things we ought to have done. But neither Jesus nor Paul threatens people with God's wrath if they don't repent properly. It is unfortunate to find the following statement in a popular

---

1. Sanders, *Paul and Palestinian Judaism*, 174. See other citations on 158, 161, 165.
2. Ibid., 5.

and generally dependable source: "Divine forgiveness is dependent on the loving nature of God. But while offered to all, pardon is not given to all. . . . Rather, forgiveness is the exception to God's wrath which will fall upon all but the pardoned."[3] For both Jesus and Paul, God's acceptance of all is unconditional.

2. DESACRALIZING MATTER, TIME, AND SPACE

Paul calls attention to his imitation of Jesus and asks others to imitate him (1 Cor 11:1; Phil 3:17). Paul appreciated that the one God is Creator and Sovereign over all, and all else stands on the same level before God. Like Jesus, Paul resisted the tendency to set up a hierarchy of values among matter, time, and space. Paul's task was complicated by the geographical spread of his field of labor, the ethnic, national, and economic diversity of his Gentile followers and the difficulty of trying to bridge the gulf between Jews and Gentiles.

2a. Meat offered to idols

Most people of the Mediterranean world of the first century CE ate meat only at special times, usually in a religious context. When they brought an animal for sacrifice, part was burnt on the altar and sent up in smoke to the deity, the person who brought the sacrifice ate part of it (with family and fellow worshippers), and the officiating priests received part as their commission. The priests couldn't eat all they received, so they sold the surplus. Selling meat was big business for pagan temples, allowing some people to buy meat at a reduced price and eat it in a non-religious setting.

Observant Jews scrupulously avoided eating such meat. Paul's Gentiles participated in the covenants of God without becoming Jews, so they were exempt in this matter. A problem surfaced when Gentile and Jewish believers participated in the common life of a single congregation. Jewish believers maintained their scruples, and Gentiles might offend them by ignoring regulations about clean and unclean, particularly eating meat from the temple markets. Some Gentiles had not fully grasped the significance of their freedom, and old emotions embedded in idolatrous practices made them sensitive about eating food offered to idols.

Either by word of mouth or by letter, some people in Corinth had asked for guidance. In reply Paul gave his opinion (or summarized their views):[4] We all have knowledge (1 Cor 8:1); there is no idol in the world, there is only one God (8:4). Therefore eating meat offered to idols is left to individual judgment (8:8), according to the principle "all things are lawful for me" (6:12; 10:23). Paul had broken down the distinction between sacred and secular in view of the oneness of God, shown by his paraphrase of Ps 24:1, "The earth and its fullness are the Lord's" (1 Cor 10:26).

---

3. Shogren, "Repentance in the New Testament" *ABD* CD.
4. Without punctuation, the Gk text may represent Corinthians quoting Paul's previous teaching.

While stressing the sovereignty and oneness of God, Paul did not deny other spiritual powers, which pagans called gods. Paul quoted the Corinthians (who quoted Paul?) that "there is no God but one" (1 Cor 8:4). Paul responds, Yes, but—: "Indeed, even though there may be so-called gods in heaven or on earth—as in fact there are many gods and many lords—yet for us there is one God, the Father, from whom are all things and for whom we exist, and one Lord, Jesus Christ, through whom are all things and through whom we exist" (8:5–6). Paul's view is similar to that found in the Hebrew Bible, namely, that while other nations have their gods, for Israel YHWH alone is God.

In connection with meat offered to idols, Paul adduces the practice of the Lord's Supper (1 Cor 10:14–22). Here, believers partake of the body and blood of Christ in analogy to the Israelites' sharing in the altar sacrifices. Paul agrees that idols are nothing, yet he says, "I imply that what pagans sacrifice, they sacrifice to demons and not to God. I do not want you to be partners with demons" (10:20). In Gk culture a *daimon* was a spirit that might be benevolent or not. Socrates spoke appreciatively of the *daimon* (=demon NT) that accompanied and guided him. But in the NT the word always implies an inimical spiritual being. Paul recognizes the existence of demons, but since they belong to the created world they are "not God", and Christians must not worship them.

Without taking back his principle of freedom, however ("Yes, but—"), Paul appeals to his readers to be guided by love. Not all sisters and brothers have such knowledge, and they may be offended or even have their faith undermined if they are urged to act against conscience. He urges people to act freely by voluntarily surrendering their individual rights to eat such meat in order to build up the whole community of believers. In 1 Cor 9:1–12 Paul offers his personal example as one who will not claim his right as an apostle to be supported at the expense of the members, but instead offers the gospel free of charge by working for his living. In conclusion he writes: "So, whether you eat or drink, or whatever you do, do everything for the glory of God. Give no offense to Jews or to Greeks or to the church of God, just as I try to please everyone in everything I do, not seeking my own advantage, but that of [the] many, so that they may be saved. Be imitators of me, as I am of Christ" (1 Cor 10:31—1:1). Addressing a similar question in Rome, Paul wrote: "I know and am persuaded in the Lord Jesus that nothing is unclean in itself; but it is unclean for anyone who thinks it unclean. If your brother or sister is being injured by what you eat, you are no longer walking in love" (Rom 14:14–15).

2b. Observing special days

Apparently the Jewish believers in Rome wished to keep up their observance of sabbath and Jewish holy days. "Some judge one day to be better than another, while others judge all days to be alike" (Rom 14:5a). In reality, the hierarchy of time typical of

Jewish practice has been abolished. Yet once again the principles of mutual respect and acting in love prevail: "Let all be fully convinced in their own minds. Those who observe the day, observe it in honor of the Lord. Also those who eat, eat in honor of the Lord, since they give thanks to God; while those who abstain, abstain in honor of the Lord and give thanks to God" (14:5b–6). None has the right to pass judgment on the other, but all stand on the same level before the one God. "For it is written, 'As I live, says the Lord, every knee shall bow to me, and every tongue shall give praise to God.' So then, each of us will be accountable to God" (14:11–12, paraphrasing Isa 45:23).

In Galatia, Paul addressed a superficially similar problem that called for a different answer. Here some Gentile believers, having been persuaded to accept circumcision and keep the law, had begun to observe "special days, and months, and seasons, and years" (Gal 4:10). Paul disapproved this as evidence of their having fallen from grace by faith in which they had begun their life in Christ. They were now striving for a supposed advanced level of religious accomplishment through works of law. To Paul, this was tantamount to returning to their pre-Christian status of enslavement "to beings that by nature are no gods" and "to the weak and beggarly elemental spirits" (4:8–9) according to which humans must placate the deities. On this issue he could not grant Gentiles the same tolerance as he did for Jewish Christians. Not only have they erected a hierarchy of time; they have restored the hierarchy of deities typical of polytheism.

Regarding the expression "works of the law" in such contexts, Markus Barth agrees with Sanders, showing that it refers not to the totality of Mosaic law but only to the special commandments laid on Jews to mark their status as the covenant people: circumcision, dietary rules, and sabbath observance. Jews participate in the covenant through divine grace, and they respond by keeping these rules as marks of identity. Gentiles likewise are saved by grace, and they respond by faithful trust in Christ and following the moral precepts. Gentiles should not take on the marks of identity as Jews but should cherish the principle of freedom bestowed on them by God's grace.[5]

2c. Holy space, God's true dwelling

As a diaspora Jew Paul had few opportunities to participate in the temple observances, but he knew that it was possible to be an observant Jew totally apart from Temple worship. Nevertheless, according to Acts 21:17–36, when in Jerusalem, Paul fully participated in Temple practices and respected the boundaries separating Jews and Gentiles in the Temple precincts.[6] Even before his conversion Paul must have known that the

---

5. Barth, *Ephesians 1–3*, 246–47. See also Segal, *Paul the Convert*, 124–25 for fuller explanation of the importance of identifying marks for Jews and Christians.

6. In Paul's day the Temple still stood and exercised a powerful influence on Paul's theology and his teaching of the Gentiles. See the argument of Fredriksen, "Judaizing the Nations," 232–252. Stressing

Paul and the Oneness of God

Temple was not an absolute necessity to the faith of his forebears. The first Temple had had both a beginning and an end, and Jewish worship had continued with or without the rebuilt structure. After encountering Jesus a new understanding on this matter could grow upon the foundation of Paul's earlier experience and observation. One of Paul's great contributions to the Jesus movement was to locate the true Temple, that is, the locus of the divine presence, not in a building but in the people.

Responding to the threat of divisions in Corinth, Paul tried to prevent splitting into factions by encouraging members to appreciate the gifts and contributions of all those who had ministered to them instead of valuing one above another (see chapter 30.2 "The crucified Christ turns the world's power system upside down"). Their ministers were all servants, working with God as farmers or as construction workers. "You-all are God's building," Paul says (1 Cor 3:9). Going further he says, "Do you not know that you-all are God's temple and that God's Spirit dwells in you-all? If anyone destroys God's temple, God will destroy that person. For God's temple is holy, and you-all are that temple" (3:16–17; I think the translation "destroy" implies too final a state to be appropriate here; "render ineffective" would be better).

Besides factionalism, the Corinthians tolerated at least one case of gross immorality, a man's incest with his stepmother. Paul cautioned that like yeast working in dough, this unchecked misbehavior could corrupt the whole congregation (1 Cor 5:1–8). Besides that, if not already in evidence, it was possible that some might take advantage of their new-found freedom to engage in sexual libertinism—"All things are lawful for me," they were saying. (6:12). Paul's answer to this claim was to insist that union with Christ sanctified every individual member of the congregation, and each person's body was a member of Christ. They should therefore not devote their bodies to immoral sexual relations. "Or do you not know that your body is a temple of the Holy Spirit within you, which you have from God, and that you are not your own? For you were bought with a price; therefore glorify God in your body" (6:19–20).

Yet a third time in his Corinthian correspondence, Paul identified the body of believers as God's temple. Paul mentions briefly a number of issues, all related to the importance of shunning any sort of "partnership" with unbelievers that could corrupt the believers' moral and ethical behavior or entice them into idolatry. "What agreement has the temple of God with idols? For we are the temple of the living God; as God said, 'I will live in them and walk among them, and I will be their God, and they shall be my people'" (1 Cor 6:16). Paul cites part of Lev 26:11 LXX, but he omits mention of anything that could imply a material structure, placing greatest emphasis on God's living in them and walking with them. Here we see the recovery of the primitive feature of Israel's faith in a God who needs no permanent structure of cedar and stone, who is not rooted to one location, but who is free to move about with and within people. Paul's conception of God's presence in all believers, together and individually,

---

Paul's emphasis on God's oneness Fredriksen writes: "Precisely in and through its ineradicable Jewishness, Paul's gospel brings the good news of universal redemption," 250 note 52.

thus prepared hearts and minds of believers to withstand the shock of the fall of Jerusalem and the destruction of the Temple, which occurred a few years later.

3. PAUL'S EGALITARIANISM

In Paul's writings we can see residual evidence of hierarchialism, but in my view his conviction of the oneness of God enlightened by Christ led him more in the direction of egalitarianism than any of his contemporaries, and certainly more than later generations, from NT times until the present.

3a. Equality within the fellowship of believers

Since believers each and all comprise God's holy temple, Paul referred to all believers as saints (Gk *hagioi*=holy ones). Paul democratized a term used in the Hebrew Bible and the Septuagint for members of the divine council, of whom YHWH was one, and later for the Jews who remained faithful under persecution. For Paul, *all* of God's people are saints. Through the centuries many Christians have allowed a return of elitism. They call saints people who have shown a degree of holiness or virtue above the ordinary, offering them special respect or veneration as members of a special class. It is not wrong to respect and emulate such people, but one must not overdo it. Christian tradition and legend became so densely populated by saints that following the Second Vatican Council the Roman Catholic authorities purged many dubious ones, but the late Pope John Paul II "created" hundreds of new saints. The translators of the New Jerusalem Bible (NJB) under Catholic influence avoided the term saint(s) and rendered *hagioi* (=saints) by some variation of "God's holy people" (see, e.g., Rom 1:7; 1 Cor 1:2; 2 Cor 1:1). In a polytheistic culture people thought they could more closely approach a deity by becoming attached to individuals of superior spiritual power, people who themselves might even be considered in some sense divine (see above chapter 30 "Paul's New Understanding of God").

From early times Christians began to refer to the apostle as "Saint Paul," but in his own day he would have none of it. Later in 1 Corinthians Paul reverts to the supposed rivalry between him and Apollos. "What then is Apollos? What is Paul? Servants (*diakonoi*) through whom you came to believe" (1 Cor 3:5). Although each has a particular function assigned by the same Lord, they are *one* (Gk *henos* 3:8). Paul continues: "For we are God's *co-workers*" (3:9). According to the literal translation of Paul's words, there is a basic unity and equality of Paul and Apollos. They might even be called co-workers of God as well as of each other.[7]

Paul concludes his discussion of factionalism in Corinth with a warning, "So let no one boast about human leaders [lit, about people=*anthrōpoi*)]," and a sweeping

---

7. *Are one* is the literal translation of the Gk *hen eisin* (3:8). NRSV interprets the phrase as "have a common purpose," which while not incorrect obscures the equality and unity that Paul emphasizes.

declaration: "For all things are yours, whether Paul or Apollos or Cephas or the world or life or death or the present or the future—all belong to you, and you belong to Christ, and Christ belongs to God" (3:21–23). For myself, I take Paul's statement to encompass every field of human endeavor or knowledge. The One God is the source and guarantor of all that is, and in keeping with monotheism's principle of human equality and the essential goodness of creation, each believer—each saint—has the freedom to draw from any and all of these rich springs—Copernicus, Galileo, Hubbell, Darwin, Marx, Freud, Einstein, whoever, whatever—"all belong to you." The fact that we belong to Christ (have "the mind of Christ" 2:16) and Christ belongs to God, means that our appropriation of such universal knowledge is for the glory of God and the common good, not for our selfish exploitation.

3b. Paul's co-workers

The presumed competition among leaders in Corinth suggests a logical entry into Paul's basic attitude of equality toward all his partners in mission. Despite the obvious differences among them and evidence of Paul's greater accomplishments, he always spoke of them in the most respectful terms. As we saw above, Paul said he and Apollos were one (Gk *hen*), and that they were co-workers (*synergoi*) both with each other and with God. *Synergoi* is a combination of the preposition "with" and the noun "workers." In referring to his associates, Paul used a great many nouns and verbs compounded with *syn* (=with), which the NRSV represents by "co-" or "fellow" or some other indication of equal partnership.

Reference	Name	Description
Rom 16:1–2	Phoebe (f)	Deacon
Rom 16:3	Prisca (f) and Aquila	who work with me [my fellow workers]
Rom 16:7	Andronicus and Junia (f)	in prison with me [fellow-prisoners] among the apostles
Rom 16:9	Urbanus	our co-worker
Rom 16:21	Timothy	my co-worker
1 Cor 1:1	Sosthenes	our brother
1 Cor 16:10	Timothy	doing the work of the Lord, just as I am
1 Cor 16:12	Apollos	our brother
2 Cor 1:1	Timothy	our brother
2 Cor 8:23	Titus	my partner and co-worker in your service
Eph 6:21	Tychicus	a dear brother and faithful minister
Phil 1:1	(Paul &) Timothy	servants [slaves] of Christ Jesus
Phil 2:22	Timothy	like a son with a father he has served [slaved] with me

Phil 2:25	Epaphroditus	my brother and co-worker and fellow soldier
Phil 4:2-3	Euodia (f), Syntyche (f)	struggled with me in the work of the gospel
Phil 4:3	Clement (and others)	the rest of my co-workers
Col 1:1	Timothy	our brother
Col 4:7	Tychicus	a beloved brother, a faithful minister, and a fellow servant [slave]
Col 4:9	Onesimus	the faithful and beloved brother
Col 4:10	Aristarchus	My fellow prisoner
Col 4:10-11	Mark and Jesus called Justus	My co-workers
Col 4:12	Epaphras	a servant [slave] of Christ Jesus
Phm 1	Timothy	our brother
Phm 1	Philemon	our dear friend and co-worker
Phm 2	Archippus	our fellow soldier
Phm 23	Epaphras	my fellow prisoner in Christ Jesus
Phm 24	Mark, Aristarchus, Demas, Luke	My fellow workers

Paul never referred to himself as teacher nor to any of his converts as disciples, a formal term used in contemporary society. In the entire NT with only one doubtful exception, disciple refers only to followers of Jesus. Acts 9:19b–25 tells of a threat to Paul's life while he stayed in Damascus after his conversion, concluding by saying (literally), "but his disciples took by night and let him down through an opening in the wall—." This account was written *about* Paul many years after the fact. A later Gk manuscript changes *his* to *him* and so smoothes the wording and corrects the impression that Paul had disciples of his own, as shown by the New Jerusalem Bible: "But the disciples took him by night and let him down from the wall—."

3c. Paul and women

In his letters Paul specifically named fourteen individual women, including six among those he recognized as co-workers (see chart above). Paul appreciated the importance of women in the culture and life of the Christian fellowship. Perhaps best loved of all Paul's sayings on the subject is Gal 3:26–28: "—for in Christ Jesus you are all children of God through faith. As many of you as were baptized into Christ have clothed yourselves with Christ. There is no longer Jew or Greek, there is no longer slave or free, there is no longer male and female; for all of you are one in Christ Jesus." Paul is arguing against those who advocated observing Jewish laws including circumcision. Circumcision applied only to Jewish males, but Christian baptism is for all, both female and male.

We observe Paul struggling against some older hard-line traditions in the question of women's equality in the Christian fellowship. We can imagine that some men might object to women's display of freedom at Corinth. In Jewish synagogue custom, women were not only segregated and silenced but might even be kept out of sight. Paul takes up this question following his command: "Be imitators of me as I am of Christ" (1 Cor 11:1). Paul begins by describing a hierarchy of "heads" (presumably "authorities"): "Christ is the head of every man, and the husband is the head of his wife, and God is the head of Christ" (11:3)—in effect, God, Christ, man, wife. Further, a man "is the image and reflection [lit. *glory*] of God; but the woman is the reflection [*glory*] of man" (11:7). Paul does not deny that woman also bears the image of God, though he does not specifically state it here. This male/female hierarchy rests on the story of God's making the woman from the man's rib—"man was not made from woman, but woman from man. Neither was man created for the sake of woman, but woman for the sake of man" (1 Cor 11:8–9; Gen 2:18, 21; woman was the help needed to do what man could not do for himself, namely produce babies). Many people stop at this point and use Paul to assert men's supremacy over women, but Paul must go on, "yes, but—." Paul's honesty and his belief about the God revealed by Christ leads to an amelioration of stark male supremacy by pointing to essential equality based on the new relationship "in the Lord" and the absolute necessity of mutual assistance: "Nevertheless, in the Lord woman is not independent of man or man independent of woman. For just as woman came from man, so man comes through woman; but all things come from God" (11:11–12). In this way, Paul affirms women's freedom and equality on the basis of original creation, the principle of the oneness of God, enlightened by the Lord Jesus Christ.

Next, Paul takes up the question of women praying and prophesying in the Church, and despite cultural details difficult for us to understand today, there is no question: Paul *presumes women's right to pray and prophesy in public*; he requires *only* that they veil their heads. In this text, hair occupies a prominent place, and Paul obviously follows popular understanding of what is "natural" (though today we would not necessarily agree). "Does not nature itself teach you that if a man wears long hair, it is degrading to him, but if a woman has long hair, it is her glory? For her hair is given to her for a covering" (1 Cor 11:14–15). The word translated "covering" is Gk *peribolaion*. Troy Martin, in his thorough research of *peribolaion* in Paul's cultural milieu, found the word not only in medical literature but also in popular stories, plays, and in both serious and ribald satirical usages. In the plural, *peribolaia* meant male testicles. In the singular *peribolaion* applied to a woman's hair, which was thought to be a gland with power of suction to draw in male semen during intercourse. Belief that women's hair was part of their genital endowments would *naturally* require that they veil their hair in public.[8] Perhaps some women in Corinth took Christian liberty so far as to remove the veil in the family atmosphere of the Christian fellowship, leading Paul to

---

8. Martin, "Paul's Argument from Nature for the Veil," 75–84.

insist on their remaining veiled. This was the *only* condition placed upon women's liberty in Christ to pray and prophesy in church.

When Paul describes worship in Corinth (12:1—14:33) we get the impression of great variety and great energy with no distinction between men and women. Paul writes, "When you come together, each one has a hymn, a lesson, a revelation, a tongue, or an interpretation" (14:26). But apparently the winds of the Spirit swept through the gathering so vigorously that all were doing their thing at the same time without consideration for others and risking ridicule from outsiders. Paul does not forbid anybody, man or woman, from exercising whatever spiritual gift they have received. As he had previously instructed women to keep their heads covered when praying and prophesying, now he asks that everybody exercise order and restraint. "You can all prophesy one by one, so that all may learn and all be encouraged. And the spirits of prophets are subject to the prophets, for God is a God not of disorder but of peace, as in all the churches of the saints" (14:31-33). I read 14:33b not as belonging to what follows, but together with 33a as concluding Paul's call for order in worship as common to all churches.

The following verses present a problem if taken as Paul's personal opinion: "Women should be silent in the churches. For they are not permitted to speak, but should be subordinate, as the law also says. If there is anything they desire to know, let them ask their husbands at home. For it is shameful for a woman to speak in church" (14:34-35). These words directly contradict what Paul has just been saying about public worship in Corinth, where he says that *all* may prophesy, and the fact that earlier he had affirmed the right of women to pray and prophesy. I cannot accept that these words express Paul's own view. Recall that ancient Gk manuscripts had no punctuation marks and the words ran together without spaces. It is reasonable to think that here Paul quotes directly the opinion of some of the Corinthian men, which they themselves would immediately recognize when they heard it.[9] Far from handing the men this sort of stick to beat women, Paul affirms what he has just said by bluntly refuting their view. The sentence that follows (14:36), introduced by the Gk particle translated "or" but possibly also "what?" sounds much more like Paul's response to men's pretentious opinion: "Or? What? Did the word of God originate with you? Or are you the only ones it has reached?"[10] As 14:37-40 indicates, Paul continues by claiming his authority to give them commands from the Lord, still encouraging *all* of them to exercise spiritual gifts, but insisting that "all things should be done decently and in order" (14:40).

---

9. See 1 Cor 6:12-13 and 7:1 in NRSV, where words originally thought to be Paul's are now set in quotation marks and considered to be opinions expressed by people in Corinth.

10. See 1Cor 6:16 and 6:19, where Paul responds to a suggestion from Corinth that he had to refute very strongly, introduced by the same Gk particle: "Or?" "What?"

SUMMARY AND REFLECTION

The appearance of the crucified and resurrected Christ to Saul gave the transformed Paul a new understanding of the implications of his Jewish conviction concerning the oneness of God, for the One God is the Creator of all. God did not exhaust his creative power "in the beginning" but works creatively still. Exhilarating newness occurs when one is incorporated into Christ: "If anyone is in Christ, there is a new creation: everything old has passed away; see, everything has become new! All this is from God, who reconciled us to himself through Christ" (2 Cor 5:17–18). Despite the intervention of Sin and human alienation from God, in a basic sense all created things are good (Gen 1:31; Ps 24:1). This goodness is realized in Christ. (1) There is a basic equality between male and female. (2) The Church, comprising the assembly of the disciples of Jesus, each and all of whom Paul called saints, is the new family in which all can exercise their newfound freedom. (3) In Christ each believer is free to enjoy the fruits of wisdom and knowledge (including latter day science and technology) wherever they may be found and no matter who discovered and propagated them.

We should not impose on subsequent creative acts the concept of "creation out of nothing," for despite the sense of sudden transformation as in some individuals' experience of conversion, there is much more a process of renewal propelled by the divine Spirit. What is true for the believers is the eventual destiny of all creation.

> For the creation waits with eager longing for the revealing of the children of God; for the creation was subjected to futility, not of its own will but by the will of the one who subjected it, in hope that the creation itself will be set free from its bondage to decay and will obtain the freedom of the glory of the children of God. We know that the whole creation has been groaning in labor pains until now; and not only the creation, but we ourselves, who have the first fruits of the Spirit, groan inwardly while we wait for adoption, the redemption of our bodies. (Rom 8:19-23)

Paul knew about entropy, how things deteriorate if left on their own, a state that he called "futility" (the same Gk word translated "vanity" in Ecclesiastes 1:2 and throughout). But Paul believed further that both humankind and the total environment in which we live had fallen captive to inimical powers from which we need to be redeemed. Paul makes no attempt to explain the source of evil or why Sin exerts such power in opposition to God, but he insists that the Creator has established a countervailing power of redemption and renewal, which in the end will embrace the whole creation. Paul was mistaken in thinking this final consummation would occur during his own lifetime (see 1 Cor 15:50–57; 1 Thess 4:13–17). Nearly two thousand years have passed, and the end is not yet. But I take my stand with Paul that the One God is Sovereign over all and embraces all in divine love.

PART SEVEN

After Jesus and Paul

33

The Jesus Movement's Breakout

THE AUTHORITATIVE SCRIPTURE OF Christianity, the New Testament, begins with four canonical Gospels called by the names assigned them by ancient tradition as Matthew, Mark, Luke, and John. Together they bear witness to Jesus of Nazareth, whom they present as Son of God, Messiah of the Jews, and Savior of the world. Luke originally addressed his work to Theophilus, otherwise unidentified, who may have been a Roman, a patron of the author (Luke 1:1–3, HCSB note). Luke also sent Theophilus the sequel, now known as the Acts of the Apostles, to describe how the post-resurrection Jesus Movement spread from Jerusalem to Rome. There is no evidence that the two-volume work (Luke-Acts) circulated together. By the time other gospel-type writings had been winnowed out leaving only the Four, Acts was already placed between the Four Gospels and the letters ascribed to Paul.

Acts is the most familiar source of knowledge of the growth of the primitive Church and the break with Judaism. Acts first focuses on the largely Galilean group of Jesus believers now settled in Jerusalem and led by Peter and later by James, brother of Jesus. Later chapters focus on Paul's turning to Gentiles when rejected by Jews, his missionary journeys, and eventual arrival at Rome.

Acts shows that Jesus Movement membership had expanded to include some besides the desperately poor or indigents who crowded about Jesus, and in Acts and in the letters of Paul, care for the poor in Judea was a major concern. Activity of the Holy Spirit, resulting in visions, altered states of consciousness, premonitions, etc., continued to influence events.[1]

Until the development of historical-critical approaches to biblical studies, most readers of the NT tried to fit details from Paul's writings into the framework of Acts. Modern scholars give priority to Paul's writings. (1) The letters accepted as genuinely Pauline—Romans, 1–2 Corinthians, Galatians, Philippians, 1 Thessalonians, and Philemon—were all written *before* any of the four Gospels.[2] Acts, the later sequel to the Gospel of Luke, dates well over a generation *after* the events it narrates. (2) In Acts there

---

1. See above chapter 21.3 "The religious pattern based on altered states of consciousness (ASC)."
2. For estimated dating of Paul's letters see HCSB, 2113.

is little indication of tensions among the believers and between the Peter-Jerusalem group and Paul, but a close reading gives hints of both kinds of problems. (3) Before the Apostles and believers in Jerusalem had agreed how to accommodate Gentile believers—shouldn't they be required to become Jews first?—Paul had already established communities comprising both Jewish and Gentile believers in several Greek cities. Paul had also written his most comprehensive letter to the church in Rome, which neither he nor the Jerusalem apostles had established, and which none of them had visited.

1. DIVERSITY AND TENSION IN THE PRIMITIVE JESUS MOVEMENT IN JERUSALEM

According to Acts, the apostle group asked the Lord to choose a successor to Judas, and Matthias was chosen by lot, thus completing "the twelve" (Acts 1:15–26). About 120 believers were together on the day of Pentecost or Feast of Weeks, a major festival seven weeks (fifty days) after Passover. The season was favorable for travel, and multitudes of pilgrims gathered in Jerusalem. The disciple band experienced a sudden onset of Spirit possession, which may be compared to some episodes of ecstatic frenzy typical of bands of YHWH prophets in ancient Israel (Num 11:24–29; 1 Sam 10:1–14; 19:18–24; 2 Kings 3:13–17). The believers streamed out in public, evincing strange physical and psychological symptoms, most noticeable of which was speaking in tongues (Acts 2:1–4). Pilgrims from afar said they heard these Galileans proclaiming the acts of God in their own languages, but scoffers accused them of being drunk (2:5–13).

Peter declared that this was fulfillment of the prophecy of Joel that God would pour out his Spirit on all flesh, even slaves, men and women, old and young, who would prophesy, and all who called on the name of the Lord would be saved (Acts 2:14–21; Joel 2:28–32 in LXX version with slight variations). In response to Peter's sermon some three thousand became believers and underwent baptism in the name of Jesus Christ (2:22–41). Subsequently leaders and members alike experienced inrush of the divine Spirit inducing altered states of consciousness that enabled them to act fearlessly in face of opposition and to give bold witness to Jesus (e.g., 4:23–31).

At first the believers, including better-off persons and property owners, lived a voluntary life of sharing all possessions in common, to the extent of selling property and contributing the assets for the benefit of all (2:42–47; 4:32–37). This communistic life-style did not last long, perhaps because of delay in the expected early return of the Son of Man, but also because of internal problems. One couple professed to have contributed the total sale price of their property while keeping back a part of it (Acts 5:1–11), but they died suddenly when their lying conspiracy became known.[3]

---

3. Harrill puts this incident in broader cultural context, explaining the pervasive custom of oath-taking before gods and invoking curses in case of perjury: "Divine Judgment against Ananias and

Different language and culture also caused problems: "When the disciples were increasing in number, the Hellenists complained against the Hebrews because their widows were being neglected in the daily distribution [Gk *diakonia*=service] of food" (Acts 6:1. See HCSB note: "*Hellenists* probably refers to Jewish Christians from the Diaspora whose native language was Greek and who spoke little or no Aramaic; *Hebrews*, by contrast, would be Christians from among those Jews who spoke only or primarily Aramaic. Conflict could arise from their social and cultural differences—."). Consequently "the twelve" instructed the assembly to choose "seven men of good standing, full of the Spirit and of wisdom, whom we may appoint to this task [Gk *diakonia*=service]." The seven thus chosen and "ordained" by laying on of hands all had Greek names. The last, Nicolaus was "a proselyte of Antioch" (6:2–6). Nicolaus, originally a Gentile, had already made one major change to become a fully observant Jew; he then joined the Jesus Way. His hometown Antioch was later a prominent scene of Paul's ministry (see below). A subtle distinction between "the twelve" and "the seven" originates here, indicated by the use of the Greek words for serve and service.[4] The apostles said it was not suitable for them to serve [*diakonein*] tables, but they should devote themselves to prayer and to service [*diakonia*] of the word, so they delegated serving tables to the seven. Stephen and Philip, two of the seven, were prominent in preaching the word, undergoing opposition, and increasing membership beyond the limits of narrow Jewishness.

2. OPPOSITION, DISPERSION, AND EXPANSION

Stephen, one of "the seven," is honored as the first martyr to have given his life in witness to Jesus. (The Greek word for witness is the origin of martyr in English.) Stephen was first besides the apostles to work signs and wonders (7:8). He argued powerfully with Jews from Northern Africa and Asia Minor (7:9–10). Judging from their charges against Stephen, they evidently concluded that faith in Jesus would ultimately result in a break with the Mosaic Law and the Temple, and they accused Stephen before the council (7:11–14).

In an altered state of consciousness (ASC)—"his face was like the face of an angel" (6:15)—Stephen began by summarizing how God had called Abraham and given him promises (7:2–8). His theme soon focused on how Israelites from patriarchal days had rejected God's chosen ones, Joseph and Moses, and lapsed into rebellion and idolatry, but God continued to deal mercifully with them (7:9–44). Ignoring the Temple and emphasizing the tabernacle in the wilderness, Stephen climaxed his speech accusing the council members of hardheartedness like their ancestors who killed the prophets, for they had betrayed and killed the Righteous One (7:44–53). The council interrupted Stephen, who then said he saw heaven opened and the Son of

---

Sapphira," 351–69.

4. See above Chapter 25.2a "Women disciples."

Man standing at God's right hand. They dragged him out and lynched him by stoning, but as he died he prayed for their forgiveness (7:54–60). Devout men (not necessarily disciples) buried and mourned Stephen (8:2).

In NT canonical order we find the first mention of Saul (later Paul), in connection with the death of Stephen (7:58) and the subsequent persecution, in which Saul was a leader, perhaps primarily targeting the Hellenist believers (8:1, 3). Among those fleeing Jerusalem was Philip, another of "the seven," who had a fruitful ministry of signs, wonders, and preaching among Samaritans (8:4–13). This success was a further step away from Jewish exclusiveness, involving a people ethnically and religiously related to the Jews, but separated by an ingrained mutual hatred. In the Gospels Jesus made several favorable references to Samaritans (Luke 10:33; 17:16; John 4:9, 39, 40), but the Jerusalem apostles thought it necessary to send Peter and John to review conditions following Philip's ministry. When they laid hands on the believers and prayed, Samaritans too were filled with the Spirit, probably made manifest by ecstatic tongue speaking (8:14–18).

Philip next was instrumental in the conversion of an Ethiopian, a high-ranking eunuch in the court of the queen of Meroe in Nubia (Acts 8:27 HCSB note). As a Gentile and a sexually mutilated male he was doubly excluded from Israel (Deut 23:1), yet he was obviously a devout seeker who had made a pilgrimage to Jerusalem and had obtained a copy of the scroll of Isaiah (in Greek). Philip encountered him as he rode in his chariot and read aloud from Isa 53:7-8, a text related to the "suffering servant." Philip began with this text, applied it to Jesus, and the Ethiopian dismounted to receive baptism in a roadside pool (8:34–40). The Ethiopian returned home, where tradition says he became a missionary, and Philip went north through the towns along the coast till he came to Caesarea (8:39–40; see the next mention of Philip, 21:8).

Acts next tells Saul's "Damascus Road" conversion experience (9:1–20). The suddenness of the event, seeing the light, and what Paul writes personally, are consistent with my conjecture that he had something like a near death experience (NDE; see chapter 29 "The Death of Saul and Birth of Paul"). Threats from Jews in Damascus prompted Saul to flee to Jerusalem, where Barnabas vouched for him. Arguing with Hellenistic Jews there roused further opposition, and so the disciples sent Saul to Tarsus. For the author of Acts, Saul's conversion was a momentous event for the primitive church, as indicated by Paul's having told it twice in defending himself against accusations from the Jewish authorities (Acts 22:1–21; 26:1–29). In his own writings Paul never narrates this story.

Peter likewise needed a divine vision plus personal interaction with Gentiles to shake him loose from Jewish prejudice. A devout Roman officer stationed at Caesarea, Cornelius, saw a vision instructing him to send for Peter, who was staying with a tanner named Simon in Joppa (10:1-8). The significance of thrice identifying Simon as a tanner (9:43; 10:6, 32) lies in the fact that his trade rendered him unclean in Jewish eyes, yet Peter stayed in his home. While Cornelius's delegation was approaching,

Peter was praying. In a trance he saw a large sheet descending from heaven filled with four-footed animals, reptiles, and birds. A voice told him to kill and eat. He demurred saying he had never eaten anything unclean, but the voice commanded, "What God has made clean, you must not call profane." This happened thrice, and the voice further instructed him to welcome the visitors.

Despite his traditional and personal reluctance but instructed by the vision, Peter took six other disciples with him and went to Cornelius's house. There he expressed his new understanding: "You yourselves know that it is unlawful for a Jew to associate with or to visit a Gentile, but God has shown me that I should not call anyone profane or unclean . . . I truly understand that God shows no partiality, but in every nation anyone who fears him and does what is right is acceptable to him" (10:28, 34–35). While Peter was still making his witness to Jesus Christ—Lord of all, his death and resurrection and forgiveness through him—the Holy Spirit fell on the whole company that Cornelius had gathered for the occasion, and they spoke in tongues. Peter and his companions recognized this as the same gift they themselves had received, so Peter ordered the Gentiles to be baptized in the name of Jesus Christ (10:34–48). Among the disciples in Jerusalem some (described simply as "of the circumcision") criticized Peter for staying and eating with uncircumcised men (11:1–3). Peter recounted his vision and how the Gentiles had been baptized with the Holy Spirit. "Who was I that I could hinder God?" he asked. So the assembly praised God, saying: "God has given even to the Gentiles the repentance that leads to life"'(11:4–18).

Taking up the activity of the believers scattered following the death of Stephen, Acts reports that some of them moved north through Phoenicia and Cyprus, settling in Antioch in north Syria, where they had notable success among Gentiles. Jerusalem sent Barnabas to check it out, and he sought out Saul to come and help in the ministry. Antioch was a cosmopolitan center with residents from many locales, where people of similar nationality, language, or craft might form associations of common interest. At Antioch believers were first called Christians, a name probably given them by outsiders, who took note that they proclaimed Christ, transcended ethnic groups, and included Jews, generally noted for exclusive tendencies. Lucius of Cyrene (North Africa), Menaen of the court of Herod Antipas, and Simeon nicknamed Niger (=Black) were also members. Here is evidence of the growing diversity of the Jesus movement in Antioch (11:19–26; 13:1).

From this point Acts takes up Saul/Paul's ministry, but it is impossible to harmonize the events in Acts with Paul's biographical notes in his letters, especially in Galatians (see below). A famine prompted a gift of aid for Jerusalem's poor, sent from Antioch by Barnabas and Saul (11:27–29). King Herod Agrippa, grandson of Herod the Great, killed James son of Zebedee and planned to kill Peter also, who had a miraculous escape, followed later by the death of Herod. One should resist the impression that Barnabas and Saul were in Jerusalem all this time (Acts 12:1–25). Back in Antioch the believers commissioned Barnabas and Saul as itinerant missionaries. Community

God For All

fasting and prayer, probably contributing to an altered state of consciousness, led to this decision (13:1–4).

3. QUESTIONS OF POLICY TOWARD GENTILES

From Antioch in Syria via Cyprus, where Saul's name change to Paul is noted, they went on to Antioch in Pisidia and Iconium (Konya in modern Turkey) and other inland towns, where the two had a fruitful ministry on what has come to be known as Paul's First Missionary Journey. Besides positive response from many Gentiles they met Jewish opposition and even violent persecution of Paul, who gradually took over leadership from Barnabas. According to Acts, negative reaction from Jews prompted Paul's turn to the Gentiles (13:46–7). Back in Syrian Antioch Paul and Barnabas reported how God "had opened a door of faith for the Gentiles" (13:4—14:28).

Disciples of Pharisee background came to Antioch from Judea and insisted that Gentiles must be circumcised in order to be saved (15:1). This led to the "Jerusalem Council" to debate the issue. Paul and Barnabas reported on the numerical success of the Gentile mission, and Peter again told his experience with Cornelius, which settled the question of salvation. There is no distinction. "We believe that we will be saved through the grace of the Lord Jesus, just as they will" (15:2–11).

James (brother of Jesus, who seems now to have assumed the role of leader) quoted Amos 9:11–12, prophecy of the restoration of David's dwelling to include the nations that once were under David and YHWH's authority.[5] The NT citation follows the LXX more closely than the Heb and makes it universal: "so that all other peoples may seek the Lord, even all the Gentiles over whom my name has been called." Howard Marshall has dealt in great detail with the many questions related to this citation and the differences among Heb, LXX, and NT wording, and concludes: "The use of the citation establishes that 'the Gentiles do not have to become Jews in order to join the eschatological people of God and to have access to God in the Temple of the messianic age.'"[6]

The question remained how to manage fellowship among Jewish and Gentile believers in the same community. To facilitate it, James proposed a few restrictions on Gentiles: "we should write to them to abstain only from things polluted by idols and from fornication and from whatever has been strangled and from blood" (15:20). The assembly approved a letter to this effect and sent it by Judas and Silas, who also transmitted the decision orally to the believers in Antioch (15:22–35). Significantly, the several Acts texts of the letter are not the same verbatim and are subject to debate as to the meaning of terms. Paul never mentions the decision of the Jerusalem Council; he

---

5. See above Chapter 18.1 "Amos and the extension of YHWH's sovereignty."

6. See Marshall in Beale and Carson, eds. *Commentary on the New Testament Use of the Old Testament*, 589a–593a. Marshall quotes Baukham, "James and the Gentiles" in Witherington, ed., *History, Literature and Society in the Book of Acts*, 178.

allowed believers to eat meat offered to idols, while cautioning that individuals should act in love and forego that privilege if it might offend other believers.[7]

In his letter to the Galatians Paul took pains to insist that the Gospel he preached was given directly by revelation from Jesus Christ and not from humans, not even from Cephas (Peter) and James (the Lord's brother), whom he met briefly three years after his conversion (Gal 1:11–24). This declaration by Paul is consistent with evidence of near-death experiences, in which subjects have an instantaneous life-review and sudden burst of comprehensive insight.[8] Paul wrote that he again went to Jerusalem fourteen years later,[9] presumably in connection with the Jerusalem Council of Acts 15, but Paul's account differs from Acts. He took with him a Gentile believer named Titus, and he refused a demand from "false brothers" to circumcise Titus "so that the truth of the gospel might always remain with you" (Gal 2:3–5).[10] Paul speaks somewhat slightingly of James, Cephas, and John, who were "supposed to be acknowledged leaders (what they actually were makes no difference to me; God shows no partiality)—those leaders contributed nothing to me" (Gal 2:6). Paul went on to say that Peter and the Jerusalem people agreed to preach the gospel to "the circumcised" and gave Barnabas and Paul "the right hand of fellowship to go to the Gentiles." In addition, Paul agreed to "remember the poor" which he had already been doing (2:7–10).

At some time after the Jerusalem Council Peter (Cephas) came to Antioch and freely ate with Gentiles until "certain people came from James," but then "he drew back, and kept himself separate for fear of the circumcision faction." Other Jews including Barnabas also acted with what Paul calls hypocrisy, "not acting consistently with the truth of the gospel" (Gal 2:11–14). In Paul's words, "the truth of the gospel" has two aspects: (1) salvation by grace is without condition, regardless of race, ethnicity, or previous religious affiliation (Gal 2:3–4); and (2) there must be no barriers separating Jewish and Gentile believers, i.e., of different ethnic or cultural background (Gal 2:13–14).

In his letters Paul never referred to the decision of the Jerusalem Council, but one can't help thinking that Paul actually lost this contest. After Peter's visit, Paul had no further contact with the church at Antioch, and he broke his partnership with Barnabas over an issue which, according to Acts 15:36–41, seems rather inadequate, but which is fully understandable in light of Barnabas's hypocrisy in separating from the Gentile believers. (Gal 2:13).

---

7. See above chapter 32.2a "Meat offered to idols."
8. See detail in chapter 29 "The Death of Saul and Birth of Paul."
9. The time is uncertain: fourteen years after conversion, or after the first visit? In any case, Paul speaks of many years of separation from the Jerusalem leaders.
10. Paul circumcised Timothy, son of a Greek father and Jewish mother, who became one of his co-workers (Acts 16:1–3).

4. PAUL'S ONGOING MINISTRY

There are too many differences of details in Acts and Paul's letters to occupy us here. The familiar Acts account narrates a Second and a Third Missionary Journey of Paul (Acts 15:36—19:41), during which he encountered both success and opposition. Paul personally writes of having gone much farther—to Illyricum in Dalmatia (Rom 15:19)—and to have undergone much more suffering than Acts reported (1 Cor 4:9–13; 2 Cor 11:21b–29). Paul lays greater emphasis on collecting relief funds for the poor in Judea than does Acts (see 1 Cor 16:1–4; 2 Cor 8–9; Rom 15:22–33). He emphasized the offering to promote the oneness of the Gentile and Jewish believers, but he had a constant struggle against divisive influences that dogged his ministry everywhere. Moreover, there was accusation that Paul was not really an apostle of Jesus Christ (he did not fulfill the conditions laid down by Peter to choose the twelfth apostle to replace Judas, Acts 1:21–22). From what Paul says in self-defense we have to deduce what his critics had said.

"I want you to know, brothers and sisters, that the gospel that was proclaimed by me is not of human origin; for I did not receive it from a human source, nor was I taught it, but I received it through a revelation of Jesus Christ. . . But when God, who had set me apart before I was born and called me through his grace, was pleased to reveal his Son to me, so that I might proclaim him among the Gentiles, I did not confer with any human being, nor did I go up to Jerusalem to those who were already apostles before me" (Gal 1:11–12; 15–17). Opponents denied Paul's status because he supported himself instead of demanding support from believers. "Am I not free? Am I not an apostle? Have I not seen Jesus our Lord? Are you not my work in the Lord? If I am not an apostle to others, at least I am to you; for you are the seal of my apostleship in the Lord" (1 Cor 9:1–2). If others doubted his claim, at least believers in Corinth were proof of his apostolic effectiveness.

Evidently people claiming to be apostles, or having letters of recommendation from apostles, had come to Corinth to contradict Paul's message of pure grace and oneness in Christ. "For if someone comes and proclaims another Jesus than the one we proclaimed, or if you receive a different spirit from the one you received, or a different gospel from the one you accepted, you submit to it readily enough. I think that I am not in the least inferior to these super-apostles" (Cor 11:4–5). Paul hinted of an altered state of consciousness experience, being caught up to "the third heaven" and receiving unspeakable revelations (2 Cor 12:1–10). But then he regretted this boasting: "I have been a fool! You forced me to it. Indeed you should have been the ones commending me, for I am not at all inferior to these super-apostles, even though I am nothing" (2 Cor 12:11). Paul does not name these "super-apostles," but there is a strong hint of some connection with Peter, James, and John, or at least with the conservatives in Jerusalem who had contributed to the troubles in Antioch.

Acts reports that as Paul traveled toward Jerusalem delegates from churches among the Gentiles went with him, no doubt as companions to carry the donation to the poor (Acts 20:4; 2 Cor 8:16–24). Along the way Paul had hints of trouble awaiting him in Jerusalem, but he went on (Acts 20:22–25; 21:8–13). In Jerusalem, James told Paul that many Jewish believers still kept Torah, and had heard that Paul forbade Jewish believers to circumcise their children and keep Torah. To prove his own Jewishness Paul agreed to join some brothers in fulfilling a vow in the Temple, but while there he was arrested, being accused of bringing in Gentiles (Acts 21:17–36). The rest of Acts narrates the several trials Paul faced, in which he always insisted that the basic issue related to resurrection, which some Jews believed, but Sadducees and powerful Temple authorities denied. Acts emphasizes Paul's innocence of any capital crime, but that persistent Jewish accusers and venal Roman officers forced him, as a Roman citizen, to appeal his case to the Emperor in Rome (Acts 26:30–32). After a hazardous voyage to Rome, Paul was left as a prisoner under guard in his own lodging, free to meet with all comers (Acts 28:30–31). The author must have known that Paul died in Rome, but he leaves the account open-ended, to emphasize that the gospel spread was ongoing.

SUMMARY AND REFLECTION

Peter's vision, his experience with Cornelius, and his self-defense before critics (Acts 10:1—11:18; 15:7–11) gives a powerful and lasting example to overcome ever-erupting tendencies toward narrowness and separation even down to the present day, just as Peter later erred by trying to segregate Jewish and Gentile believers. Moreover, the Jerusalem Council in Acts 15 appears to wield a central authority impossible at that time. The Gospels had not yet been written; and each of the communities for which a Gospel was later written was separated by distance from the others; believers could be found in synagogues throughout the Diaspora;[11] there was no means to enable a central authority to act for all Christians. Compared to details in Paul's letters, the breakout of the Jesus movement was not nearly so straightforward as Acts describes it. The Palestinian-based churches did not know Paul's letters, nor did Paul and his churches know the fuller traditions of Jesus that later became the Gospels. Paul wrote all of his letters while the Temple still stood, and he expected the return of Christ during his own lifetime (1 Thess 4:15–17; 1 Cor 15:51–52). Paula Fredriksen argues that, in his expectation of the early return of Christ to establish the eschatological kingdom, Paul envisioned *one* people of God embracing both Jews and Gentiles. By his ministry

---

11. Allison takes at face value that the recipients of the Epistle of James 1:1 were synagogues of the Diaspora, where believers in Jesus may have been objects of a growing practice of criticism and cursing that later was formalized in the *Birkat ha-minim*, the twelfth of the eighteen benedictions commonly used against the Christians in the synagogues. See "Blessing God and Cursing People: James 3:9-10," 397–405.

God For All

Paul sought to prepare the Gentiles for that event.[12] It didn't happen. In the chaos that followed the Roman destruction of the Temple and the end of Judaism built on the system of sacrifice to One God alone, plus the concurrence of many factors even now not fully known or understood, the Christian Church and rabbinic Judaism went their separate ways.

---

12. Fredriksen, "Judaizing the Nations," 232–52. See above, chapter 31 "Universal Grace in Romans."

34

Jesus of Nazareth in God's Plan

JESUS OF NAZARETH IS worshipped as Son of God and Savior, the Christ whose title identifies the Christian faith. According to the Nicene Creed, Jesus the Christ is considered to be both human and divine, God the Son, the Second Person of the Trinity, together with God the Father and God the Holy Spirit. Church councils made these declarations of faith in response to theological, cultural, and political requirements of a day and time several centuries after the life, ministry, and death of Jesus and the completion of the documents of the NT. In this chapter I concentrate on the testimony of the NT and evidence from some contemporary extrabiblical documents, ending with some negative and positive results of the Nicene Creed.

1. FIRST CENTURY JUDAISM NOT STRICTLY MONOTHEISTIC

Jews for many centuries have held that attributing deity to Jesus violates fundamental Jewish monotheism. In recent decades both Jewish and Christian scholars have acknowledged evidence that the claim by Jewish rabbis of a violated monotheism was actually based on evidence dated much later, when controversy between Jews and the growing number of Christians was intensifying. It is now recognized that the Judaism of the first century CE was not the pure monotheism that was claimed. Peter Haymon writes that until the Jewish philosophers of the Middle Ages, Judaism presupposed at least two divine entities, "one the supreme creator God, the other his vizier or prime minister, or some other spiritual agency, who really 'runs the show', or at least provides the point of contact between God and humanity."[1] The identity of the vizier was never clearly defined, and there came to be many a "little Yahweh."[2] According to belief in the afterlife following the Maccabees, "the faithful would join the heavenly assembly and become like the 'angels', the 'sons of God', the 'stars,' "—an assembly to which YHWH also belonged. Later Judaism considered YHWH king of this heavenly

---

1. Haymon, "Monotheism—A Misused Word in Jewish Studies?" 2.
2. Ibid., 12.

host, though without being different from them in kind.³ Haymon notes that biblical literature preserves language concerning Lady Wisdom (Heb *hokmah,* Gk *sophia*) that reflects earlier belief that YHWH had his *Asherah,* or female consort. Wisdom was the first of YHWH's creative acts and was present with him in creating everything else (Prov 8:22-31). In the apocryphal book Wisdom of Solomon (Wis 9:4), Wisdom sits by God's throne, i.e., she is God's consort.⁴ According to Philo, the Alexandrian Jewish philosopher roughly contemporary with Paul, Wisdom "is the 'divine mother of all things.' "⁵ Further, Haymon writes, "In Philo this figure becomes the Logos which he can even describe as a 'second god.' " Haymon says, "The fact that functionally Jews believed in the existence of two gods explains the speed with which Christianity developed so fast in the first century towards the divinization of Jesus."⁶

2. EVIDENCE FROM HELLENISTIC JEWISH DOCUMENTS

The Wisdom of Solomon is a Hellenistic Jewish Greek book that expands upon the identity and function of Wisdom as described in Prov 8:22-31. The document originated in Alexandria, Egypt after Rome conquered the city in 30 BCE. This book was written to comfort and encourage the Jews during persecutions that followed.⁷ Not only did Wisdom aid YHWH in creation but she also acted *instead of YHWH* on behalf of humankind from the time of Adam through the election of the patriarchs, the salvation from Egypt, and the leadership by Moses (Wis 10:1—11:14). Philo, the Jewish philosopher in Alexandria whom Haymon cites, wrote many volumes in Greek to introduce Israelite Jewish thought to Gentiles, attempting to demonstrate its superiority to Greek philosophy. Philo used the Greek word *logos* to designate the "second god" who acted as YHWH's agent in relation to humankind. Greek *logos* is usually translated "word," but it has multiple meanings, among them analogy, explanation, rule, or principle. One immediately recognizes Logos as an identification of Jesus Christ in John 1:1-14. Philo wrote at great length on many subjects and is not always consistent in detail, but his general approach is clear.

Margaret Barker devotes an entire chapter of her book to the evidence of Philo, carefully sifting through his many volumes to present pertinent information.⁸ Among

---

3. Ibid., 5.

4. Ibid., 14.

5. Ibid., 14; Haymon cites Philo *Leg. All.,* II.49.

6. The two quotations are found in Haymon, op cit., 14. See also Boyarin, *The Jewish Gospels,* which I encountered too late to utilize fully in this book.

7. See introduction to Wisdom of Solomon HCSB, 1497-8. Together with other documents that today are popularly called the Apocrypha, Wisdom of Solomon plus the Greek translation of the Hebrew Bible, the Septuagint, was the Bible of the earliest Christians, most of whom were Jews.

8. Barker, *The Great Angel,* 114-32. Barker cites Philo's work in the Harvard University Loeb Classical Library multi-volume edition, but in citing Barker, I will not repeat all her specific citations from Philo. Here I indicate Barker's page references in square brackets.

many other details of Philo's writings Barker lists nine characteristics that belong to both Wisdom and Logos [Barker 130–131]. Philo uses many names for the Logos: King, Shepherd, High Priest, Covenant, Rider on the Divine Chariot, Archangel, and Firstborn Son [Barker 118]. Philo recognizes Elohim and YHWH as different aspects of one God [Barker 128], but Elohim is *the* Most High God while YHWH is God only in a subordinate sense. Philo writes, "Nothing mortal can be made in the likeness of the Most High One and Father of the Universe but (only) in that of the second God, who is his Logos" (*Questions on Genesis* II.62) [Barker 116]. In the OT it was YHWH who in human form appeared to (lit. "was seen" by) Abraham (Gen 18:1). YHWH is this second God whom mortals can see while no one can see the Most High God.

Philo comments on Jacob's return to Bethel, where God commands him to build an altar to the God who appeared to him when he fled from Esau (Gen 35:1). Philo takes "Beth-el" to be "place of *a* god" which he distinguishes from *the* God who appeared to Jacob. "Accordingly the holy word in the present instance has indicated Him Who is truly God by means of the articles saying 'I am the God', while it omits the article when mentioning him who is improperly so called.'" [Barker 119].

3. EVIDENCE FROM THE NEW TESTAMENT

Observe the term "the Logos" in a literal translation of the Greek prologue to the Gospel of John (the italicized words represent the Greek definite article that English translations omit): "In the beginning was the Word, and the Word was with *the* God, and the Word was God. He was in the beginning with *the* God" (John 1:1–2). We have no way of knowing whether Philo's distinction between "the God" and "God" was present to the mind of the author of the Prologue, but here the Greek states twice that the Word was *with the* God. The Word and the God are two, not one, and though the Word has a high status, being called God, the Word is not *the* God. Jesus calls the God Father and himself the son, but consistently he stresses the son's subordination to the Father, while still acting as the Father's appointed agent. As late as the third century CE Origen of Alexandria (184 to 253) reflected on this text. Origen taught that the Father was absolutely God (Gk *ho theos*) applying the definite article, but he called the Word a second God and referred to him as *theos*, without the article.[9]

As will become clear, the Johannine Jesus speaks and acts in accordance with a principle based on what is taught in a particular OT text. At Sinai, God said to Moses: "And behold, I send my angel before thy face, that he may keep thee in the way, that he may bring thee into the land which I have prepared for thee. Take heed to thyself and hearken to him, and disobey him not, . . . for my name is on him" (Exod 23:20–21, LXX, Brenton's translation). In John, as in the NT as a whole, Jesus acts like this "angel" or messenger, who bears God's name and who acts for God to lead the people.

---

9. Rusch, *The Trinitarian Controversy*, 14.

"The Father loves the Son and has placed all things in his hands" (John 3:35). "The Son can do nothing on his own, but only what he sees the Father doing; for whatever the Father does, the Son does likewise. The Father loves the Son and shows him all that he himself is doing . . . as the Father raises the dead and gives them life, so also the Son gives life to whomever he wishes. The Father judges no one but has given all judgment to the Son, so that all may honor the Son just as they honor the Father . . . For just as the Father has life in himself, so he has granted the Son also to have life in himself" (5:19–23, 26). In his long prayer to the Father Jesus says, "this is eternal life, that they may know you, *the only true God*, and Jesus Christ whom you have sent" (John 17:3, emphasis added).

Jesus may seem to contradict these sayings that indicate his subordination with the following claim: "The Father and I are one" (John 10:30), but by this Jesus does not claim to be ontologically the equal to the Father nor to possess the same degree of deity as the Father. In chapter 21:2 above I described the cosmology and anthropology that were common to the Jews and other Mediterranean peoples of Jesus's day. They did not make an absolute distinction between God and not-God, and they believed there was frequent traffic between earth and heaven by the multitude of spiritual entities in the great chain of being. Visions, mystical experiences, and altered states of consciousness were frequent for some people, especially for Jesus. Brain science and research by Newberg and d'Aquili confirm experiences among mystics of many religious traditions who testify to having been totally absorbed by, or lost within, the All, or the Nothing. Newberg and d'Aquili call this "Absolute Unitary Being."[10] Among Jewish, Christian, and Muslim mystics, not one has claimed that such an experience *transformed them into* the God of their encounter. Of course we have no record of Jesus's brain function, but as a human being, Jesus's brain must have functioned as do the observed functioning of the brains of mystics. I have every reason to believe that Jesus had mystical experiences of oneness with God.

Jesus prays to the Father on behalf of his disciples ". . . that they may all be one. As you, Father, are in me and I am in you, may they also be in us, so that the world may believe that you have sent me. The glory that you have given me I have given them, so that they may be one, as we are one, I in them and you in me, that they may become completely one" (John 17:21–23). Jesus here makes no claim either for himself or for his disciples that they are ontologically one with God the Father. So far as this Gospel witness is concerned, Jesus could express his conviction of a special relationship as son to God the Father, yet without claiming equality. Indeed, Jesus declared: "The Father is greater than I" (14:28). In John, the relation of Father and Son guarantees that the Son's work will be effective because of the Father's supreme will and because of the Son's humble obedience.

In Paul's letters he frequently refers to Jesus Christ as Lord (=Gk *kyrios*). In the Septuagint Greek translation of the Hebrew Bible familiar to Paul and other Jewish

10. *Why God Won't Go Away*, 126–27.

Christians, *kyrios*=lord is used to represent the Hebrew consonants Y,H,W,H. Thus, in the primitive hymn that Paul cites in Phil 2:5–11, the Jewish Christians already gave Jesus Christ the title Lord, ordinarily used to distinguish YHWH from Elohim, the Most High God. The hymn concludes, "at the name of Jesus every knee should bend, in heaven and on earth and under the earth, and every tongue should confess that Jesus Christ is Lord, to the glory of God the Father" (Phil 2:10–11).[11] While this hymn is rightly treasured for the high praise it offers to Jesus in ascribing to him the Ineffable Name Lord=YHWH, that praise does not stop with Jesus but ascribes glory to God the Father, the supreme Most High God, the Creator (note agreement with the Gospel of John). The usage indicated by Phil 2 confirms that for the primitive Jewish/Christian communities, Jesus fulfilled the function of what Philo called the second God, the agent or vizier of the Most High, commissioned to act in relation to humankind.

In his letters to churches Paul begins by invoking on his audience blessing from God the Father and the Lord Jesus Christ (Rom 1:7; 1 Cor 1:3; 2 Cor 1:2–3; Gal 1:3; Phil 1:2; 1 Thess 1:1, 3; Phm 3). All these instances presuppose the supremacy of God the Father and the secondary status of Jesus Christ as Lord. The matter is beyond doubt when Paul, writing to Corinth, addresses the problem of meat offered to idols, and whether such sacrifices were made to actual gods or not. Paul wrote, "Indeed, even though there may be so-called gods in heaven or on earth—as in fact there are many gods and many lords—yet for us there is one God, the Father, from whom are all things and for whom we exist, and one Lord, Jesus Christ, through whom are all things and through whom we exist" (1 Cor 8:5–6). Without unequivocally denying the existence of "other gods," Paul insists that for Christians there is One God and One Lord. The Father is the one God *from whom* are all things, and Jesus, acting for the Father, is the one Lord *through whom* are all things. Paul writes in conformity to the Jewish belief in the two powers.

The most convincing text affirming the Son's pre-eminent role in human affairs together with his subordination to the Father is found in 1 Cor 15, Paul's chapter on the resurrection. Here Paul speaks of the climax of the work of the risen Christ: "For he must reign until he has put all his enemies under his feet. The last enemy to be destroyed is death[12] . . . When all things are subjected to him, then the Son himself will also be subjected to the one who put all things in subjection under him, so that God may be all in all" (1 Cor 15:25–26, 28).

The little Epistle of Jude may seem strange to us because of its virulent condemnation of false teachers within the Christian community, who apparently taught that Christian freedom removed all moral restrictions, and perhaps because of its citation of texts from the apocryphal documents 1 and 2 Enoch and Jubilees.[13] But the doxol-

---

11. See chapter 30.3 "The reign of Christ."

12. Note: rather than "destroyed" a better translation of *katargeitai* is "rendered ineffective, nullified, cancelled."

13. See Baukham, "Jude, Epistle of" in *ABD*.

ogy and the ascription of praise with which the letter ends admirably demonstrate the current Christian faith based on contemporary Jewish belief: "To the only God our Savior, through Jesus Christ our Lord, be glory, majesty, power, and authority, before all time and now and forever. Amen" (Jude 25).

The distinction between God the Father and Jesus as Lord went back to the early days when Jewish believers in Palestine used Aramaic in worship. They had often heard Jesus address God familiarly just as a child would, saying 'abba (Mark 14:36). Christian evangelists used a few Aramaic terms with Greek-speaking Gentiles, so that in Rome and in Galatia they also knew to address God as 'abba (Rom 8:15; Gal 4:6). By contrast, the primitive Jewish believers acknowledged Jesus as Lord, using the Aramaic word *mar*. In the excitement of their worship they might often cry out in Aramaic, *Our Lord, come!* Paul himself was so accustomed to doing this that as he dictated his letter to the Corinthians he cried out "*maranatha!*" and his secretary simply transliterated the sound in Greek letters, assuming that the Corinthians would understand.[14] The author of the book of Revelation, who predicts the imminent coming of Jesus, uses the same prayer, although he translates the original Aramaic phrase into Greek as he exclaims: "Amen! Come, Lord Jesus" (Rev 22:20). These short prayers seem to have been typical of the worship of the Jewish Palestinian believers, eagerly entreating Jesus the Lord to come and set up the kingdom of God on earth, as they had been led to expect by late apocalyptic writings such as Daniel, and apparently by Jesus himself.[15] Barker cites many OT texts in which people appealed to YHWH for help and expected him to come soon and deliver them, or to establish his kingdom. These early Jewish believers made similar appeals to Jesus as Lord (*mar*), while acknowledging God as Father ('*abba*).[16]

4. JESUS AND THE WORSHIP OF GOD

Into the first century CE the Jews, even as minorities in Diaspora, carefully maintained worship of their God only, even though they acknowledged the existence of other peoples' gods and were known to participate in civic ceremonies in the names of those gods. For such Jews, the operative principle was sacrifice. They refused to sacrifice to any but their own God, and Gentiles throughout the Greco-Roman world recognized this practice as distinctive of Jews.[17] As is well known, many Christians also refused sacrifice to Roman gods even under persecution when refusal meant death.

---

14. KJV has "Maranatha"; NIV has "Marana tha"; NJB has "Maran atha"; NRSV has "Our Lord, come!" with a marginal note: "Gk *Marana tha*. When these Aramaic words are read *Maran atha*, they mean *Our Lord has come*."
15. See above chapter 20.3 "Jews under Greek and Roman Rule."
16. Barker, *The Great Angel*, 215.
17. McGrath, *The Only True God*, 27–35.

McGrath writes: "Within early Judaism and throughout the New Testament, no other figure is simply placed on the same level as God Most High and considered to be his equal. (...) The only form of Jewish monotheism that existed was different from what later generations of Jews and Christians called monotheism."[18] The earliest Jerusalem believers regularly attended worship at the Temple (Acts 2:46; 3:1), and at the Temple Paul participated in a ritual involving sacrifice with several Jewish brothers who had undertaken a vow (Acts 21:23-24, 26). But these believers never proposed that anyone should offer sacrifice to Christ as they did to God. The status of Jesus became a problem only after the destruction of the Jerusalem Temple, when sacrifice no longer served Jewish Christians as the exclusive marker for the Only True God. Among rabbis an authoritative voice gradually emerged to oppose the once acceptable view of "two powers in heaven," as Christians were moving in the direction of divinizing Jesus. McGrath notes, "Belief in a principal divine agent or angelic mediator was probably not condemned until groups with Gnostic tendencies began to distinguish between the supreme God and the creator of the world, and/or until Christians began to regard the 'second power' as coequal with God and equally worthy of worship."[19] McGrath says the Christian response was to draw a dividing line between God and creation, which they had not done previously. The Logos (whom Philo had described as "neither uncreated... nor created") stood between God and creation. By the time of the Council of Nicea, "Arius and other non-Niceans drew the line between God and the Logos, whereas the Niceans drew the line between the Logos and the creation."[20]

5. THE NICENE CREED

The NT does not present a full deity of Jesus, but by the end of the second century CE Christians were sharply divided over defining the Son's relation to the Father. In the war to gain full control of both the Western and Eastern domains of the Roman Empire in 312 CE, Constantine believed he had a heavenly vision of a cross and a command from Jesus to win victory by means of the sign of the cross. He commanded his army to put the cross on their shields and banners and thereafter won a series of what he considered miraculous victories against great odds. As he sought to consolidate his power, Constantine made Christianity the official religion. He believed the disagreement about Christ hindered his purposes, which he expressed as "One God, one Lord, one church, one empire, one emperor." Constantine convened the Council of Nicea in 325 CE, but debate didn't end until the Council of Constantinople in 381 made some revisions and additions that produced what is now known as the Nicene Creed.[21]

18. Ibid., 94, 97.
19. Ibid., 94.
20. Ibid., 92.
21. A brief note on Constantine and his motto is from *The Constitution of the Presbyterian Church (U.S.A.) Part I* "The Nicene Creed," 2.

One can't escape a feeling of revulsion on reading the story of the controversies that plagued both the church and the state for decades.[22] Constantine dominated the first Council, expecting to use a united and compliant church to consolidate his imperial power, but he was badly mistaken. A sticking point was the Greek philosophical term *homo-ousion*, (literally, "the same *being*" or "*essence*"), which Nicenes interpreted to mean that Son and Father were ontologically equal, while the school of Arius rejected it as denying the humanity of Christ. The sides were almost equal in number. Partisans mobilized mobs for violent and sometimes lethal street rioting. Each side convened local councils to condemn and anathematize their opponents as instruments of the devil and antichrists. The emperor intervened to appoint, exile, or restore bishops here and there.

On Constantine's death three sons divided his realm but fought till the survivor, the Arian Constantius II ruled supreme. He chose a nephew Julian as his associate and successor. When Julian became ruler he got fed up with Christian infighting and tried to unite his realm by restoring the cult of the ancient gods, which got him his epithet "the Apostate." That ended when Julian died on a campaign against the Persians. Next, Emperor Valens, an Arian sympathizer, suffered a massive defeat at the hands of the Goths. Apparently many people thought the end of these anti-Nicene rulers was God's sign of disapproval. Theodosius, a non-Christian Spanish military commander who became Emperor of the East, requested Christian instruction from Ambrose of Milan, a Nicene bishop. After baptism Theodosius threw his weight behind what already seemed to be a trend in the Nicene direction. Theodosius sponsored the Council of Constantinople that affirmed the Nicene Creed with *homo-ousion* and additional emphasis on the Holy Spirit in the doctrine of the Trinity. Thedosius ruled all non-Niceans apostates liable to the death penalty.

Well over half of the creed focuses on Jesus, beginning with his ontological oneness with God: "We believe in one Lord, Jesus Christ, the only Son of God, eternally begotten of the Father, God from God, Light from Light, true God from true God, begotten, not made, of one being (*homo-ousion*) with the Father; through him all things were made." As for the humanity of Jesus, the creed takes an anthropocentric approach: "*For us and for our salvation* he came down from heaven . . . and became truly human. *For our sake* he was crucified under Pontius Pilate—."[23] The focus shifts from God to "us" and "our salvation." It encourages people to make Jesus (as God) the means by which Christians "attain" salvation or eternal life, as the Pew Trust reported.[24] The Creed leaps from the resurrection of Jesus to his ascension to the right hand of the Father, and ends by declaring, "He will come again in glory to judge the living and the dead, and his kingdom will have no end." The creed says nothing about Jesus revealing God's compassion for the poor by his teaching and healing. The creed

---

22. The following summary is based on Rubenstein, *When Jesus Became God*.
23. Ibid., 3 (emphasis added).
24. See the Introduction to this book.

totally omits Jesus's challenge to the religious and political ruling powers as a factor in his crucifixion as a state criminal. The shorter Apostles' Creed is subject to the same criticism. The effect that these omissions have had on the history of Christendom prompted Jack Nelson-Pallmeyer to write his bitingly critical book with its provocative title, *Jesus Against Christianity*.[25]

Following Constantine, throughout history armed forces of self-declared Christian nations have made the cross their battle emblem, including the shields of the Crusaders, the Thirty Years' War between Protestants and Catholics (1618 to 1648), the insignia on warplanes of Nazi Germany, and the highest honor awarded to individual warriors for bravery in war, such as the Victoria Cross of Great Britain, the Croix de Guerre of France, and the Russian Cross of St. George. The creed also gave leave for theologians of feudal Europe to interpret Jesus's death as a substitutionary atonement by which God the Father offered his divine and perfect Son to bear the death penalty that all of "fallen" humanity deserved, because human sin was such a terrible insult to God-the-Father's honor that nothing less than a sacrifice of equal value, namely that of God-the-Son, could suffice to satisfy God's justice. Many Christians today cling to this distorted interpretation of the deity of Christ and make their act of acceptance of Christ's sacrifice their mark of distinction from (and implied superiority to) all who refuse it or those who never heard of it. For some believers, the deity of Jesus means that he had perfect knowledge and was without error in any thought, word, or deed. Since Jesus is co-equal with God people may attribute to him all the powers of Elohim/YHWH, including leadership in battle and inerrant inspiration of the Bible. In the Sistine Chapel at the Vatican Jesus is graphically depicted enthroned as final judge; he sends the righteous to heaven with the right hand, while with the left he casts the damned headlong into hell.

Even so, I acknowledge that the Nicene Creed may have had a positive result as a principle of interpretation of the concept of divine love. The statement "God is love" (1 John 4:8, 16) is the climax of a theme that runs through both the OT and the NT and is basic to Christian faith. A monotheism of God's absolute singleness is thought inadequate for this concept, since love requires both a subject and an object in mutual relation. This is one factor leading to the belief that Jesus as Son participates equally with God the Father and the Holy Spirit in Trinity. This comprises the all-sufficient divine community perfectly united by love, into which by grace God also embraces humanity. Here I wish to recognize two Christian authors for whom the deity of Christ in Trinity had great significance to my theme "God for All": German Lutheran Dietrich Bonhoeffer and Scots Presbyterian Thomas F. Torrance.[26]

(1) Dietrich Bonhoeffer joined the theology faculty of the University of Berlin in 1931. After Hitler's rise to power in 1933 Bonhoeffer ardently criticized the

---

25. Jack Nelson-Pallmeyer, *Jesus Against Christianity*.

26. Articles devoted to both these men in Wikipedia, the free encyclopedia, provide easy introduction to them and their work.

nazification of the National Church that acquiesced in de-Judaizing Christianity by rejecting the OT, denying the Jewishness of Jesus, and by persecuting Jews. Bonhoeffer considered this a *status confessionis,* an issue serious enough to distinguish between true and false Christianity. He joined the Confessing Church, which came together to protest these false doctrines and policies and whose Theological Declaration of Barmen (1934) asserted, "Jesus Christ, as he is attested for us in Holy Scripture, is the one Word of God which we have to hear and which we have to trust and obey in life and in death."[27] The Nazis forbade Bonhoeffer to speak publicly or publish, but he taught in an underground seminary as long as he was able. He was appalled and outraged by Nazi atrocities against Jews, the physically disabled, Poles and other Slavic peoples. Bonhoeffer joined the *Abwehr,* a German military intelligence organization that harbored a secret plot to assassinate Hitler, who many high-ranking military figures considered the root of the inhumanity that would ultimately destroy Germany. Bonhoeffer was arrested and imprisoned in 1943 and hanged in April 1945 shortly before Germany's surrender.

Jesus Christ as the perfect revealer of God was central to Bonhoeffer's life and work. Like Luther he taught, "If you want to see God, look at Jesus" (see Jesus's word: "Whoever has seen me has seen the Father" John 14:9). As we see from Bonhoeffer's poem, the crucified God in vs 2 is the source of universal grace in vs 3 that answers universal human need in vs 1.

> 1. All go to God in their distress,
> seek help and pray for bread and happiness,
> deliverance from pain, guilt and death.
> All do, Christians and others.
>
> 2. All go to God in His distress,
> find him poor, reviled, without shelter or bread,
> watch him tormented by sin, weakness and death.
> Christians stand by God in His agony
>
> 3. God goes to all in their distress,
> satisfies body and soul with his bread,
> dies, crucified for all, Christians and others,
> and both alike forgiving.[28]

(2) Thomas F. Torrance, born in China of missionaries, spent most of his career as Professor of Christian Dogmatics at New College, Edinburgh. A Reformed churchman and theologian, Torrance worked for harmony with Anglicans, Lutherans,

---

27. On the Barmen Declaration see Presbyterian Church (USA) *Book of Confessions,* 245–50.

28. From Edwin Robertson, translator and editor, Dietrich Bonhoeffer's Prison Poems. Grand Rapids MI: Zondervan, 1999. Used by permission.

Eastern Orthodox, and Roman Catholics, and established friendly relations with Jewish leaders. Torrance contributed to the dialogue between science and theology and participated in translating Karl Barth's voluminous writings into English.

Torrance saw great significance in the Nicene Creed's statement of *homo-ousion*, "the oneness of being, or sameness in being, between the incarnate Son and God the Father—."[29] As Mediator, Jesus "fulfilled the covenant from both sides: 'I will be your God and you will be my people' " [Torrance 77]. Jesus has a two-fold ministry, God to humanity and humanity to God, but Jesus does not merely represent the two sides; he actually *presents* God to humanity and humanity to God. Jesus can reveal God to us because he is of the same substance as God. In the sacrifice of the Son was the sacrifice of the Father [Torrance 117]. On the other side, Torrance reminds us "the *real text* of New Testament revelation is *the humanity of Jesus*" [Torrance 78 emphasis original]. In offering himself, the man Jesus offers all humanity. Jesus took our full humanity—"he bore not just upon his body but upon his human mind and soul the righteous judgments of God and resurrected our human nature in the integrity of his body, mind and soul from the grave" [Torrance 85].

Torrance comments that the fundamentalists who tell sinners that their salvation depends on their accepting the sacrifice of Christ has "the effect of telling poor sinners that in the last resort the responsibility for their salvation is taken off the shoulders of the Lamb of God and placed upon them" [Torrance 93]. In the introduction to his book Torrance notes: "Some people evidently feel that the stress I have laid upon unconditional grace undermines the integrity of the response we are called to make in repentance for sin and in acceptance of Jesus Christ as our personal Saviour. . . unconditional grace is too costly, for it calls in question all that we are and do, so that even in our repenting and believing we cannot rely upon our own response but only upon the response Christ has offered to the Father in our place and on our behalf" [Torrance *xii*].

SUMMARY AND REFLECTION

In the New Testament, Jesus of Nazareth, a Jewish man of flesh and blood reveals the God whom he familiarly called Father.[30] The authors of the NT writings that witness

---

29. Torrance, *The Mediation of Christ*, 113.

30. I am aware that many women and increasing numbers of men sincerely believe that for us to call God "Father" may perpetuate a patriarchal social order that is demeaning to women and girls. My wife Margaret Hopper assisted me to have an attitude adjustment on this and other questions. Yet as I have tried to show in this book, in the OT understanding of covenant, calling God Father in a family relationship was significantly superior to calling God King who imposed strict legal requirements on human subjects. Given his own cultural context and OT background, Jesus's calling God Father with the familiar Aramaic word ʾ*abba* indicates his choice of family over royal legal relationship to express his belief about the Creator. I sympathize with and enthusiastically support present day attempts to oppose any implied misogynist abuse of masculine terminology for God.

to Jesus believed Jesus the Son was divinely appointed agent to do the works of God the Father to demonstrate the divine good will toward humankind. I firmly believe that Jesus himself was personally convinced of his calling. God confirmed the words and work of Jesus by raising him from the dead after his ignominious death. As Scripture states, the God whom Jesus revealed by his words and work is the One True God who created humans in the divine image, who grants humans a degree of freedom of choice even to defy the Creator, yet whose unconditional benevolence toward human creatures is such that God embraces each and all of us in the plan of reconciliation. Jesus of Nazareth reveals the God who is God for All.

35

Humanity in God's Plan—1

THE STORY OF CREATION that opens the Bible of Jews and Christians (Gen 1:1–31 P) presents God (*elohim*) as Creator, superior to and above creation, and also the Spirit of God (*ruach elohim*) closely present to creation (Gen 1:1–2 P). Scripture as a whole develops a fuller understanding of God as awesomely Other, both creative and judgmental, a power whom humans may fear even with a sense of terror. Yet God is also a mysterious spiritual Presence, working subtly within to effect the divine purposes. We have thus come to speak of human awareness of God as both transcendent and as immanent, and over time humanity grows in trusting that God's transcendent power is tempered by immanent mercy.

1. HUMANITY, THE IMAGE OF GOD

The transcendent/immanent God creates creation in successive stages, climaxing with humanity, male and female together, created in the divine image and given dominion over the rest of creation (Gen 1:26–27 P). Jon D. Levenson writes that God "appoints the entire human race as God's royal stand-in" and speaks of "the co-regency of God and humanity."[1] Gerhard von Rad interprets humanity as "God's sovereign emblem ... God's representative, summoned to maintain and enforce God's claim to dominion over the earth."[2] Joel B. Green writes, "the creation account imbues humanity with royal identity and task, but this is a nobility granted without conquest; its essence is realized in coexistence with all of life in the land, and in the cultivation of life."[3] I concur in the interpretation of the biblical description of humanity created in God's image as expressed by these scholars, one Jewish and two Christian. To me it says that God has given humanity a mediating role between Deity and creation.

The biblical passage introduces what I have called *The Universal Matrix* (Gen 1:1—16:16), the stage setting of God's plan for *all* creation and *all* humanity, before

---

1. Levenson, *Creation and the Persistence of Evil*, 116–17.
2. Von Rad, *Genesis*, 58.
3. Green, *Body, Soul, and Human Life*, 62.

the later distinction between Israel and the nations. Humanity, personified in Adam and Eve, tried to grasp and exploit their high status without acknowledging the responsibility (Gen 2:4b—3:24 J). Israel's ancestor Abram was called and blessed by God so that through him and his descendants the rest of humanity would experience the blessing (Gen 12:1–3) and, I would say, be inspired to fulfill the responsibility. As I have shown in this book, it was late in the history of Israel before people began to have intimations of this universal plan. Beginning at Gen 17:1 the rest of the OT reflects the more ancient struggles of humanity, personified by Israel the people of YHWH. It was only a small minority of priests/scribes who began to express God's aims in universal terms as in Gen 1.

Genesis presents a Triad (or is it a Trio?): God the Creator transcendent, God the Spirit immanent, and God's co-regent Humanity as Partner. This is not trinity. Humanity is creature, formed from the ground out of which YHWH God made all plants to grow, from which YHWH God formed all animals, to which all plants and animals return (Gen 2:7, 9, 19, 21–23; 3:19 J). Evolution reinforces the biblical description of the basic oneness of planet Earth with its marvelous diversity and the uniqueness of humankind, with whom, the Bible teaches, God establishes a *mutual relationship*. Even humans' disobedience did not negate their divine image, and God did not revoke their role as God's royal stand-in with a responsibility toward the rest of creation.[4]

God appears *first* in Scripture, sovereign and most important, but the account soon reports that God endowed humanity with high dignity and responsibility. This is an altogether *positive* evaluation of humanity, but traditional interpretation has almost completely eclipsed it. Many years have passed and still its universal significance has not been fully appreciated.

2. THE HUMAN RESPONSE TO GOD

What does seem to be almost universally assumed is that people must give something to a god or do something for the god in order to merit the god's favor. The ruler of a state wanted divine help, especially for war, and maintained functionaries including magicians, fortune-tellers, diviners, or seers who practiced techniques designed to learn what the gods wanted, and others who presided at altars and conducted the cult accompanying the sacrificial offerings designed to please the gods. As the Babylonian *Enuma elish* poem demonstrates, the gods wanted palaces to live in and food to eat. The power elite, who controlled the means to learn the gods' demands, exploited the masses of people, while enriching themselves in the process. Ordinary folk who could afford it sought the aid of sorcerers, witches, or magicians, and paid fees for their advice. They also offered sacrifices of valuable possessions, sometimes including children.

---

4. See above chapters 3 and 4, and chapter 19.3.a "Humankind, the image of Elohim."

As a latecomer on the world scene, Israel absorbed influence from Canaanite culture and adopted some of its practices and terminology.[5] At the primitive level tribal Israelites were told: "You need make for me only an altar of earth and sacrifice on it your burnt offerings and your offerings of well-being, your sheep and your oxen; in every place where I cause my name to be remembered I will come to you and bless you" (Exod 20:24). This text does not specify who officiated—perhaps at first only a household head, but gradually professionals emerged as the functionaries.[6] People could resort to the shrines to give thanks, to offer sacrifice and worship, to ask the deity's decision on debated questions, and to receive guidance in personal relations, even if only to ask the deity to determine the answer by casting lots.[7] In earliest times some customs and cultic acts were similar to Canaanite practices. But Israel's fundamental religious conviction was quite different. Israel's God YHWH had delivered them from oppression in Egypt and therefore expected them to conduct their cult practices and daily life in the spirit of thanksgiving to YHWH, not primarily out of fear of God or of trying to wheedle some favor from God. So at the shrines two related features were common: presiding at the sacrificial offering, telling the acts of YHWH, and teaching about community life, including mediating quarrels and answering individual inquirers' requests for advice.

In the OT, these two functions are already developed and called priest and prophet.[8] Cult priests usually tend to be conservative. Adam C. Welch describes how more progressive prophets could encourage changes in cultic practices and customary behavior in more appropriate ways.[9] Welch sees Ps 81 as celebrating the festival of Tabernacles, commemorating the giving of the law. Following an opening of praise by vocal and instrumental music, a prophetic voice representing deity reminds the people that YHWH saved them from slavery in Egypt, insists on exclusive loyalty to YHWH, and promises blessings (81:6–13).[10] Psalm 95 begins with praise to YHWH as creator and king, urging people to hear his voice, followed by an appeal and warning expressed by a prophet (95:6–11). Primitive practices such as human sacrifice and cultic prostitution were originally accepted in Israel, but prophetic circles came to see them as inappropriate for YHWH-only faith, and with priestly concurrence they were eliminated.[11]

---

5. Lev 21 calls sacrificial offerings "bread" meaning food. Psalm 50 criticizes the view that God needs food.

6. These professionals may have comprised the group originally called Levites who took up positions wherever they could find employment. See examples in chapter 13.3 "Decline and degradation of tribal Israel, Judges 17–21."

7. See chapter 12.3 "The Book of the Covenant as guide for the tribes."

8. The subject of prophet and prophecy in Israel is extremely complicated and even today not fully understood (see *IDB* and *ABD* articles.)

9. Welch, *Prophet and Priest in Old Israel*.

10. Welch, op. cit. 124–27

11. Ibid., 78–85.

3. PRIESTS AND PROPHETS IN ISRAEL

We see in Scripture these two functions, prophetic and priestly, with considerable overlap. In early times women called prophets played important parts: Miriam the sister of Moses and Aaron helped to preserve the infant Moses and to celebrate the exodus from Egypt (Exod 2:1–10; 15:20–21); Deborah acted as judge in Ephraim and motivated several tribes to throw off Canaanite domination (Judges 4–5); King Josiah sent to consult Hulda concerning a scroll of the Law discovered during repair of the temple (2 Kings 22:10–14). Originally there was no clear distinction between the two roles. When Saul wanted advice about some lost donkeys, he went to ask advice from the "man of God" Samuel, to whom he paid a fee (1 Sam 9:1–9). Samuel was one who, originally called a "seer" gave personal advice, but later was called a "prophet"—Heb *nabi'* a person who engaged in ecstatic speech and behavior. Samuel, an Ephraimite, gave advice, offered sacrifice, acted as judge, and gained the name of prophet speaking for YHWH to establish the kingship and to criticize the king. Prophets were particularly active during the monarchy, emphasizing the vital characteristics of YHWH-only tradition (chapter 17 "Covenant as Family Relationship") and pronouncing judgment against the power structure (chapter 18 "Prophets and the End of the State"). Some of the most notable prophets were of priestly families, such as Jeremiah, Ezekiel, and probably Isaiah, who criticized not only injustice and corruption but also priests and cultic practices.

King David and King Solomon acted as priests, but priesthood became limited to a highly specialized, hereditary, exclusive, and ultimately privileged power class. After the exile without a king and under foreign rule, the high priests assumed the greatest political as well as religious power among the Jews (chapter 20 "Return, Rebuild, Retrench"). They grew increasingly prominent and powerful and liable to arrogance and corruption. Throughout Israel's history, competition for the authority attached to offices of both prophet and priest became intense. Incidents in the book of Numbers usually affirm the power structure, while Scripture includes hints of "democratization." While women act as prophets, we have no evidence if women priests in Israel.

3a. Priests.

YHWH affirmed control by the power structure when Korah and Levites demanded the privilege of priesthood along with descendants of Aaron, and when Reubenites Dathan and Abiram challenged Moses and Aaron's rule. The three charged: "You have gone too far! All the congregation are holy, every one of them, and YHWH is among them. So why then do you exalt yourselves above the assembly of YHWH?" (Num 16:3). Fire from YHWH burned up Korah and 250 Levites who tried to offer incense, and the earth opened and swallowed Dathan, Abiram, their households, and their possessions (Num 16:18–40).

The editors of the Pentateuch reflected on the discrepancy between priests specializing in sacrifice and exploiting power on the one hand and a whole people's life of faithful trust and obedience to God in the service of others. Thus we read in the Sinai narrative that God through Moses chose the Israelite people, saying, "You shall be My treasured possession among all the peoples. Indeed, all the earth is Mine, but you shall be to Me a kingdom of priests and a holy nation" (Exod 19:5–6 NJPS). Young men of the people offered the sacrifice to effect the Sinai covenant (Exod 24:5). Rome's destruction of the Jerusalem Temple in 70 CE made cultic sacrifice impossible and the class of priests superfluous, a particularly traumatic blow to Jews but also to early Christians, whose understanding of the death and resurrection of Christ had been influenced by the sacrificial system. But end of Temple in no way cancelled the priestly role of humanity; it only closed a dead end. Jews and Christians, each in their own way, moved to occupy the resulting vacuum.

3b. Prophets

Against a challenge from Miriam and Aaron, YHWH affirmed Moses's authority is chief spokesperson for YHWH, superior to all prophets (Num 12:1–15). In my view the incident also reflected a growing trend in Israel to deprive women of authority in public affairs. Moses told the Israelites that God would raise up from among them a prophet like him, whom they must hear (Deut 18:16). This brief statement had long-lasting repercussions.

An earlier episode in the wilderness seems to make a point favorable toward sharing prophetic gifts more broadly. YHWH took some of the spirit on Moses and put it on seventy chosen elders who began to prophesy (apparently to speak ecstatically). Two of the chosen were absent when this happened, but they also prophesied where they were. Joshua urged Moses to stop them, but he responded: "Are you jealous for my sake? Would that all YHWH's people were prophets, and that YHWH would put his spirit on them!" (Num 11:26–29). Elsewhere Scripture declares that YHWH will do exactly that, but will make the gift of the Spirit universal. "Then afterward I will pour out my spirit on all flesh / your sons and your daughters shall prophesy, / your old men shall dream dreams, / and your young men shall see visions. / Even on the male and female slaves, / in those days I will pour out my spirit" (Joel 2:28–29 H 3:1–2). Thus the OT records at least the expectation, if not the actualization, of humanity's role as prophet, represented by Israel.

4. PROPHETS AND PRIESTS IN THE NT

4a. Prophets.

Paul thought his call as apostle to the Gentiles was comparable to the call of the prophets Jeremiah and Isaiah (Gal 1:16-17; Jer 1:1, 5; Isa 43:5-6). Paul never called himself a prophet, and for him prophecy was a potential gift for every believer. In his ministry among Gentiles, Paul listed prophecy among spiritual gifts distributed among believers (Rom 12:6-8; 1 Cor 12:8-10). The Corinthians valued ecstatic speech, but Paul emphasized prophecy. He urged all the Corinthians to strive for prophesy, for whereas the tongue-speaker addressed only God in words nobody understood without an interpreter, prophecy brought benefits to the whole congregation by "upbuilding and encouragement and consolation," (1 Cor 14:1-5).[12] Paul strongly affirmed that women could prophesy as well as pray during the service, but required only that they cover their hair to conform to cultural propriety (1 Cor 14:1-12; 11:4-16).[13] Philip, one of the Jerusalem "seven" who later settled in Caesarea had four daughters who were known as prophets (Acts 21:8-9). Agabus foretold the coming of a famine, and he also predicted that Jews in Jerusalem would bind Paul hand and foot when he went there (Acts 11:27-30; 21:10-11).

The events of the Day of Pentecost highlight the coming of the Spirit on the believers and their speaking in tongues (Acts 2:1-4). Evidently this was ecstatic speech, for some bystanders said they were drunk (2:13). But this was not mere tongue speaking, for the crowd declared, "we hear them speaking about God's deeds of power" in our own tongues (Acts 2:11).[14] Peter declared that this was precisely the fulfillment of the OT promise that God would pour out the Spirit on "all flesh" so that they would prophesy (2:15-18; Joel 2:28-29 H 3:1-2). In Acts, tongue speaking was an important sign of the Spirit being poured out not only on Jewish believers but also on Samaritans and on Gentiles (Acts 8:14-17; 10:44-48).

4b. Priests.

Writing to "exiles of the Dispersion" (probably including both Jewish and Gentile Christians), the author of 1 Peter urged them, "Let yourselves be built into a spiritual house, to be a holy priesthood, to offer spiritual sacrifices acceptable to God through Jesus Christ. . . You are a chosen race, a royal priesthood, a holy nation, God's own

---

12. Paul does not further explain these terms, but it is believed that in some sense prophecy in NT worship had some basis in understanding and applying teaching from the OT, especially wisdom. See *IDB* Sup 700.

13. See chapter 32.3c "Paul and women."

14. There seems to be a difference between this Pentecost phenomenon and tongue speaking which is said to be incomprehensible to others in Corinth. I am not aware of a satisfactory explanation of this difference.

people—" (1 Peter 1:1; 2:5, 9; see Exod 19:5-6). The author of the book of Revelation alludes to the same texts in his doxology of praise to Jesus Christ "—who freed us from our sins through his blood, and made us to be a kingdom, priests serving his God and Father—" (Rev 1:5-6). In another hymn the author praises Jesus the Lamb for having ransomed by his blood and made priests to his God from among "every tribe, language, people, and nation—" (5:9-10).[15]

In the Bible, the function of all God's people could be called a priesthood. Unfortunately the Christian Church erred by trying to re-invent the Israelite priesthood and ended with another hierarchy of pope, bishops, and priests elevated as "clergy," possessing authority to admit or exclude the "laity" from divine favor.[16] Scripture still maintains the ideal of the priesthood of all believers. Considering all Scripture, I claim that the Bible gives to all humanity the role of priestly mediators between God and creation. Israelites and Christians are but partial representatives of the whole.

5. JESUS AS PROPHET, PRIEST, AND IMAGE OF GOD

Jesus received his call through the prophet John the Baptist, and he knew himself to be a prophet (Mark 6:4; Matthew 13:57; Luke 4:16-21). The disciples believed that Jesus, human as they knew him, was the anticipated prophet like Moses whom they must hear,[17] for he was the unique revealer of the One True God. The Gospel of John calls Jesus the Word, who in the beginning was with the God and who was God (1:1-14). "Long ago God spoke to our ancestors in many and various ways by the prophets, but in these last days he has spoken to us by a Son—" (Heb 1:1-2). The titles Word and Son function in a special way to emphasize Jesus's prophetic ministry, to speak for and to make God known. As believers contemplate Jesus as the best revealer of God, the greatest of all prophets, we may hesitate to think of ourselves also as prophets, since we compare so feebly with him. But that by no means cancels the role that the Creator God (The father of our Lord Jesus Christ) bestowed upon us as members of the one family of humanity, who bear the divine image (Gen 1:26-27).

The author of Hebrews introduces the Son of God, "the reflection of God's glory and the exact imprint of God's very being," who "made purification for sins" (Heb 1:3). Later the author, drawing on the cultic laws of the Pentateuch that were operative in the Tabernacle/Tent of Meeting in the wilderness,[18] lists similarities between the

---

15. I reject every attempt to use these texts with others to claim Christians replace Jews as God's people.

16. Ironically, "laity" is derived from the inclusive Gk word *laos*=people. "Laity" now separates the people from the "religious"—those with special ordination, including priests. "Priest" is derived from Gk *presbyteros* = "elder."

17. Mt 21:11; Lk 7:16; 13:37; 24:19; 4:19; 6:14; 7:40; 9:17; Acts 3:22-24.

18. Hebrews gives no hint that the Temple has been destroyed, but most expositors assume the book is post 70 CE. The author was perhaps a Hellenistic Jew who had no direct Temple experience. He uses the Pentateuch's description of the Tabernacle and the laws related to its cult. See also Stephen's speech,

Aaronic High Priests and Jesus. God appointed them; they offered sacrifices for the people's sins; and they had to be truly human to sympathize and deal gently with the people (Heb 5:1–6). The author emphasizes that Jesus "had to become like his brothers and sisters in every respect, so that he might be a merciful and faithful high priest" (2:17). Jesus even faced every kind of testing/temptation without sinning (4:15). That is, Jesus, though exceptional, was *truly human*. There were significant differences: Aaronic high priests served generation after generation; they offered animal sacrifices for their own as well as the people's sins; they offered sacrifices repeatedly because animal blood was unable to remove sin; and they served in a tabernacle that was only a copy of the real one in heaven. Jesus belonged to Judah, not the tribe of the Levitical high priests; Jesus had no sins needing sacrifice; he made his own life blood the effective sin offering once for all; and he bore it into the heavenly sanctuary (8:1–7).

In doing all this Jesus became the mediator of the New Covenant foretold in Jeremiah, according to which God promised, "I will write my law on their hearts and I will remember their sins no more" (Hebrews 8:12; Jer 31:34). Through Jesus God replaced the former covenant, not because it was bad, but because it was temporary and only typified the later covenant, which Jesus fulfilled. Again, we may tend to ignore the priesthood of all believers simply because Jesus, the High Priest, is so prominent by comparison.

In the NT Christ is "the image of the invisible God" (Col 1:5; see 2 Cor 4:4). The Son is the image according to which God will conform those whom he chooses and elects (Rom 8:29). One text states that man (Gk *anēr*) is the *image* of God (1 Cor 11:7, without denying the same for woman) and another text states that people are made in the *likeness* of God (James 3:10). Still another text views the image of God in the believer as a *process of renewal* by the Creator (Col 3:10), but it doesn't deny the *status* given by creation. Still, the NT exalts Christ as superior to other humans in general in respect of the image of God. Herman Waetjen, rephrasing the title son of man, writes, "As the New Human Being, he is the ultimate human being, the one who is so completely and perfectly human that the image of God will become transparent in his life and activity."[19]

6. THE CONSTANTINOPLE COUNCIL PROCLAIMS THE DEITY OF JESUS

It is obvious that for believers Jesus is a special human. As time went on after his death and resurrection, and especially after the destruction of the Temple, as believers experienced Jesus's excellence and reflected on it, emulating the Jewish precedent of recognizing a "second God," it was not unexpected that Christians tended to think of Jesus as divine. But what *was* the relationship between Jesus the Son and God the

---

Acts 7:44–50.

19. Waetjen, *A Reordering of Power*, 72.

Humanity in God's Plan—1

Father? As I briefly recounted in the previous chapter, over some decades councils of bishops debated the issue, with the line of division separating the Arians who insisted on the humanity and the implied subordination of the Son, and the Nicenes who insisted that the Son was of the same being and essence as the Father and hence equally God.[20] Constantine's calling the Council of Nicea in 321 CE did not resolve the debate; it continued to fester for decades, often with deadly consequences. In general, Arianism declined somewhat in the meantime but was still a viable option.

In 381 CE the ruling Emperor Theodosius acted soon after he gained control of the Eastern Empire and deposed Arian bishops in several important cities. Theodosius convened a Council at Constantinople to settle the fight that had simmered since Constantine's day. Voting members of the Council were bishops largely from the Greek East, each of whom ruled a diocese centering on a metropolitan area. Bishops had ecclesiastical and political power that was denied to lower orders of priests, elders, and deacons, and to ordinary members (the "laity"). The bishop delegates were under intense pressure from the strongly anti-Arian emperor. It was this politico-religious body of men whose decision determined the Nicene Creed by which they declared the full deity of Jesus the Son, of equal being and substance with the Father and the Holy Spirit in the Trinity. Following final approval of the Creed, Theodosius undertook suppression of all Arians and other Christian minorities who would not accept official Nicene dogma.

7. THE BREAK WITH JUDAISM

The next step was only to be expected. Since the state could punish non-Nicene Christians by death, why not pagans also, and especially the Jews, who were accused of having denied and killed Jesus in the first place? Bishop Ambrose of Milan, who had first instructed Theodosius in the Christian faith, began a fire-breathing campaign to annihilate the Jews. When Theodosius announced that he would rebuild a destroyed Jewish synagogue, Ambrose defiantly told him not to do it. At mass, when the emperor was present, Ambrose interrupted the liturgy and refused to continue unless the emperor relented. Fearing excommunication, the emperor obeyed.[21] This incident is typical of what followed, in James Carroll's account of Christianity's relentless persecution of Jews and Judaism that climaxed in the Nazi Holocaust that tried to annihilate the Jews along with the physically and mentally handicapped, homosexuals, and others considered not to be of proper Aryan stock.

Nicea solidified an impulse that had long grown among Christians, to reject their common origin with the Jews. Paul addressed the tendency in his letter to the Romans, where he reminded Gentile Christians that they were but wild olive shoots grafted onto the trunk and root of God's people Israel (Rom 11:13–24). Paul's lengthy

---

20. See above chapter 34.4 "Jesus and the worship of God" and 34.5."The Nicene Creed."
21. Carroll, *Constantine's Sword.*

argument in Rom 9–11 leads to the conclusion that God's final plan is for Gentiles to partake fully in God's covenants and blessings for Israel without having to become Jews—"so all Israel will be saved" (Rom 11:26).[22] As if this were not sufficient, Paul (or someone deeply influenced by Paul) wrote to remind Gentiles that at one time they were

> without Christ, being aliens from the commonwealth of Israel, and strangers to the covenants of promise, having no hope and without God in the world. But now in Christ Jesus you who once were far off have been brought near by the blood of Christ. For he is our peace; in his flesh he has made both groups into one and has broken down the dividing wall, that is, the hostility between us. He has abolished the law with its commandments and ordinances, that he might create in himself one new humanity in place of the two, thus making peace, and might reconcile both groups to God in one body through the cross, thus putting to death that hostility through it." (Eph 2:12–16).

The death of Christ made it possible for Gentiles to participate fully in "the commonwealth of Israel" without becoming Jews. The two, who had formerly been bitter enemies, have now been made "one new humanity in place of the two." God's plan is to "reconcile both groups to God in one body through the cross." Sad to say, where Christ had broken down the wall of partition between Jews and Gentiles, after Nicea Christians fortified the wall and made Christ a narrow door through which Jews might enter into what they claimed to be the new people of God. The cross, which made reconciliation and peace, Christians turned into a sword of division and death. Even the Jews who entered the door were suspected of dishonesty and treated with suspicion. Small wonder that most Jews have consistently refused to join the Christians, who, in terms of our own Scriptures, should have joined Israel. The details of the break between the Christians and the Jews are not clear. The NT says that Jews persecuted and harassed Christians (who themselves were Jews). The accusations may have been exaggerated though the facts cannot be denied. Neither Judaism nor Christianity has possessed a central leadership sufficient to engage in negotiations. There appear to have been few if any incentives for the two sides to try to work out a way whereby they could become one body, and today it is difficult to imagine what the new "body" would look like. Yet in God's sight, we Christians and Jews are one new humanity. And, I would add, we represent all humanity.

According to Richard Rubenstein, until the Nicene decision declaring the full deity of Jesus, Jews and Christians could still talk to each other, discuss, and debate. "They disagreed strongly about many things, but there was still a closeness between them. They participated in the same moral culture." Rubenstein admits to a personal fascination with Jesus, despite having suffered personally the violent hatred against Jews that centuries of Christian prejudice instigated. Rubenstein thinks that the figure

---

22. See above chapter 31 "Universal Grace in Romans."

of Jesus may play an important part in healing divisions. "I think his life teaches us what it really means to be members of the human family," he writes.[23]

REFLECTION

Humanity as such, God's sovereign emblem and royal stand-in, forms a Triad together with God Transcendent and God Immanent, which in some way may seem to blur the distinction between God and not-God. Though created in the image of God humanity is mortal, and capable of great evil as well as of great good. Should we not thank God for any good the royal stand-in does? Is God somehow accountable for the stand-in's evil? God gives humanity a mediating role toward creation, which I consider both a priestly and a prophetic office. Both Jews and Christians have to some extent fulfilled the calling, but neither with full satisfaction. Both Jews and Christians are people of God, yet like the kingdoms of Israel and Judah of old, we are separate, and we tend to think of each other as rivals if not enemies. Meanwhile, as of old, God shows mercy to both, as well as to people who are neither Jews nor Christians and who may be hostile to us. Thus we see some other members of the human family, who yet accomplish good or at least avoid doing terrible evil, while resisting and trying to repair the evil some other humans do. Shall we not honor them for this?

At the center of this mutuality of God and humanity we find Jesus. In the NT Jesus presents such a high example as a human that later Christians insisted on declaring him God. But promoting the deity of Jesus resulted in a tragic fate for many non-Christians, especially for Jews. Is it not time for us to focus more specifically on the way in which the human Jesus may lift all humanity to a higher level of humanness and to enable us to follow in his Way, assisted by the Spirit within, and welcome all others who, in their way, fulfill the role God assigned to humanity in Genesis 1:26–27?

---

23. *When Jesus Became God* xiv, xv.

36

Humanity in God's Plan—2

There is one God;

there is also one mediator between God and humankind,

Christ Jesus, himself human,

who gave himself a ransom for all ...

(1 Timothy 2:5-6)

Jesus confirms to all who believe the good news of God's love that *all* humankind participates in the Triad with God Transcendent and God Immanent. Every human is involved in this Triad simply by the fact of human existence, and as I have developed at length, everyone is also embraced in God's redeeming love. Obviously not everybody knows this. We believers have received this awesome divine gift and the commission to make known the God revealed by Jesus. "The saying is sure and worthy of full acceptance. For to this end we toil and struggle, because we have our hope set on the living God, who is the Savior of all people, especially of those who believe" (1 Tim 4:9–10).

1. THE COSMIC TIME FRAME

Many Christians have been indoctrinated in the belief that the world is about six thousand years old, that it's getting worse, but that Jesus will return in power at any time to establish a thousand-year reign on earth—a misguided hope for a demonstration of redemptive violence. After two thousand years it hasn't happened. Some people never learn from each disappointed expectation, but they revise their calculations and wait expectantly again. The fact is that brevity characterizes each human's existence in the multi-billion year time frame. The likely prospect is that barring some astral collision or self-annihilation through nuclear bombs or irreversible degradation of global ecology, life on earth will go on for millions of years.

Eastern religions presuppose a much longer existence for the world. Ancient philosophers thought that the world undergoes cycles of creation and destruction. Each cycle lasts a *kalpa*, a Sanskrit term for the Hindu and Buddhist concept of a period of 4,320 million human years. We need not agree to these calculations, yet the concept is compatible with what we are learning about the cosmos since the big bang and evolution. Instead of waiting anxiously for Jesus's return we should devote ourselves to sharing with others the true meaning of the Jesus Way every day.

2. THE GLOBAL SCOPE OF THE JESUS WAY

Christians have spread the good news of Jesus in every land. At times this endeavor has collided with other religions and abetted colonial policies, but it has had a powerful attraction for many people, some who have become Christians, but others who, while declining to join an organized church, have taken Jesus seriously and have followed in his Way. Here I take up what may be the best known of many examples.[1]

Mohandas K. Gandhi, a Hindu by birth, was the champion of nonviolent resistance against British colonial power in India and a leader of the independence movement. As a young lawyer in South Africa, Gandhi learned of Jesus from Quaker and Baptist missionaries. Jesus's Sermon on the Mount was his favorite Scripture. Gandhi almost converted to Christianity, but he was repelled by the exclusive claims of the proselytizers and by the racism of most whites. Gandhi credited the Christians with having stirred his quest for spiritual enlightenment.

Several authors whose faith and life were somewhat to the left of Christian orthodoxy exerted formative influence on Gandhi. John Ruskin's book *Unto this Last* based on Jesus's parable of the laborers in the vineyard (Matt 20:1–15), was an attack against industrial capitalism that dehumanized labor. From Ruskin Gandhi absorbed the principles that the good of the individual was contained in the good of all, and that the life of a craftsman or a plowman was a life worth living. Gandhi founded a communal farm in a rural setting (he called it an *ashram*) where people could live a simple, self-sustaining life [Weber, 36–38]. When he returned to India from South Africa, Gandhi founded *ashrams* where many people had first-hand experience of his life and teaching.

Gandhi reported that Leo Tolstoy overwhelmed him with his book, *The Kingdom of God is Within You: Christianity not as a Mystical Doctrine but as a New Understanding of Life*. Tolstoy portrayed Christ as teacher and example. He emphasized the law of love and advised passive resistance as the best policy for those seeking independence from the British [Weber 38–42]. After Gandhi had begun his nonviolent endeavors

---

1. Here I depend largely on Weber, *Gandhi as Disciple and Mentor*. Without attempting in-depth research, I have drawn on Weber's study of original sources for what follows. Page numbers in square brackets indicate references to Weber's work. Information drawn from other sources will be cited in footnotes. Weber gives many more examples of Gandhi's influence than I have included here.

he read Henry David Thoreau's *Essay on Civil Disobedience*. Gandhi adopted the term "civil disobedience" as more appropriate than "passive resistance" to express his own term *Satyagraha*, Truth Force or Soul Force [Weber 42–45].

Gandhi's vision was of *Ramrajya*, "the Kingdom of God, where even the lowliest person could get swift justice without elaborate and costly procedures, where inequalities that allowed some to roll in riches while the masses did not have enough to eat were abolished, and where sovereignty of the people was based on pure moral authority rather than on coercive power" [Weber 121]. Based on his own understanding and emulation of Jesus, Gandhi exerted powerful influence on many others, including Christians, who adapted Gandhi's way to their own place and time.

1. Martin Luther King, Jr. in the USA [Weber 165–173]. Many people know that Gandhi influenced the martyred leader of the civil rights movement that has had such a positive, though still unfinished, effect in the USA. Human rights activists A. J. Muste and Bayard Rustin introduced Gandhian thought early in the civil rights movement. King stated in *Stride Towards Freedom* that early in life he believed that when Jesus taught, "love your enemies" and "do not resist evil," it applied only at the personal level. On reading Thoreau's *Essay on Civil Disobedience* he began to see a broader application of Jesus's teaching, but Gandhi showed him the true power of love and the practical value of nonviolence in the struggle for civil rights. King's assassination prevented his planned visit to Gandhi

2. Joseph Jean Lanza del Vasto [Weber 173–189] was born of an aristocratic family of Sicily. He converted to Catholicism while studying Thomas Aquinas's work on the Trinity, but he could find no satisfaction in life. Del Vasto abandoned wealth for voluntary poverty, trusting in God. After reading a biography of Gandhi, he spent time at Gandhi's *ashram*, imbibing his teachings, including Gandhi's declaration that peace and nonviolence were central to Christianity. In France del Vasto established an *ashram* called the Community of the Ark. Branches now are found in Italy, Spain, Morocco, Belgium, Argentina, Canada and the USA. Del Vasto formulated Gandhian principles for the Ark communities, and he led movements against nuclear arms and power generators. Weber calls del Vasto "a true Gandhian Christian."

3. Arne Næss and deep ecology [Weber 191–202]. Næss grew up in the mountains of Norway and admired the mountain people. He read Gandhi on the principles of nonviolence and the basic oneness of all life. As professor of philosophy at the University of Oslo Næss taught that humans can achieve Self-realization (with a capital S) only when we understand that our "ecology should not be concerned with man's place in nature but with every part of nature on an equal basis. . . Indeed, humans could only attain 'realisation of the Self' as part of an entire ecosphere."[2] This concept Næss called "deep ecology" contrasted with "shallow ecology" that protects the environment primarily for human benefit. Næss explained that Gandhi "made manifest the

---

2. *Guardian* Newspaper, England, obituary for Næss January 14, 2009.

internal relation between self-realisation, non-violence and what sometimes has been called 'biospherical egalitarianism' " [Weber 196].

4. Johan Galtung and peace research [Weber 203–217]. As Næss's assistant he co-authored with him a book on Gandhi's political ethics, and he cited Gandhi as probably his most important influence. [Weber 209]. Galtung defined peace as more than mere absence of war. Peace is the condition that eliminates mental and spiritual dimensions of violence and promotes human development. Galtung noted that Gandhi was the only author or politician who clearly fought against both direct violence inflicted by perpetrators, and the continuous, not necessarily intended, violence built into social structures such as institutionalized racism and sexism, in which a regime prevents individuals from achieving their full potential. He called this *cultural violence* and its antithesis *cultural peace*, based on Gandhian doctrines of the unity of life and the unity of means and ends [Weber 204–207]. One of Galtung's several negotiations for international peace was that between Ecuador and Peru in 1995. Conflict over an uninhabited and resource-poor border region had simmered off and on for nearly 200 years. Galtung proposed to convert the area to a bi-national park, and both sides, together with neighboring nations, found this an acceptable solution.

5. Gene Sharp and civilian-based defense [Weber 232–246]. Gene Sharp was son of a Protestant minister. As an idealistic student of Gandhi, Sharp wrote his first book in 1953, *Gandhi Wields the Weapon of Moral Power*, for which Albert Einstein wrote an introduction. Sharp explained Gandhi's *Satyagraha* nonviolent action, and apparently he numbered himself among those who believed in changing society by love. During doctoral studies at Oxford University Sharp organized an international Civilian Defense Study Conference. Sharp cited Gandhi's observation that oppressive regimes succeed only by the passive acquiescence of the oppressed people.

Sharp became convinced that the spiritual-religious aspects of Gandhi's thought and his expectation of converting opponents to his views were not only unrealistic but also unsuitable as a nonviolent alternative to war. Sharp said, "I found that people didn't need to *believe* right to engage in nonviolent struggle." He believed that nations as well as individuals could practice nonviolence. In his *The Politics of Nonviolent Action*, Sharp lists 198 "acts of protest and persuasion, noncooperation and nonviolent intervention designed to undermine the sources of power of the opponent in order to bring about change." [Weber 232–39]

The Lithuanian, Latvian, and Estonian governments used Sharp's writings on "Civilian-Based Defense" during their separation from the Soviet Union in 1991. His 1993 handbook *From Dictatorship to Democracy* was first published in Burma, fourth edition in 2010. It has been translated into at least thirty-one other languages and served as a basis for campaigns in Serbia, Georgia, Ukraine, Kyrgyzstan, and Belarus. In local translations posted on the web and also circulated by hand, *From Dictatorship to Democracy* has played a role in the "Arab Spring" in the Middle East and North Africa. It circulates widely in the "Occupy" movement in the USA since 2010.[3]

The authentic Jesus way, taken in and lived out by the Hindu Gandhi reflected back and strengthened the thought and ministry of the Christians, Martin Luther King, Jr., Lanza del Vasto, and Gene Sharp. It's not clear whether Arne Næss and Johan Galtung were formally Christians, but it is clear that their life and work show evidence of the example of Jesus refracted through Gandhi and undoubtedly influenced by Christian aspects of European culture.

3. THE JESUS WAY WITHOUT JESUS

We must now be willing to go a step further and appreciate the life and work of many people who are not Christians and who perhaps know little if anything of Christianity. Peter, enlightened by a vision, told a Gentile audience, "I truly understand that God shows no partiality, but in every nation anyone who fears him and does what is right is acceptable to him (Acts 10:34–5). Paul wrote that some Gentiles had the law of God written on their hearts and did authentic works of the law without even knowing it (Rom 2:14–15). Jesus became so engrossed in his compassionate ministry to the masses of indigents that his family thought him out of his mind and set out to restrain him (Mark 3:20–21). Critics said he could cast out demons only if the Prince of Demons allowed it. Jesus exposed such hypocrisy by referring to the success of some Pharisees at expelling demons, concluding that such acts proved that Satan's rule was being overthrown (Mark 3:22–30). As for his family members outside looking for him, Jesus said: "Who are my mother and my brothers? . . . Whoever does the will of God is my brother and sister and mother" (Mark 3:31–35). Jesus places no limitation on his human family kinship except to do God's will, and we have abundant evidence as to what Jesus himself considered was God's will. John tried to prevent a man from doing exorcisms in Jesus's name because he didn't belong to their group. Jesus disagreed and expressed appreciation for such good works, regardless of who does them, adding, "Whoever is not against us is for us" (Mark 9:38–40).

My seminary professor Dr. Rule taught me the Calvinistic term "common grace" that is set beside "saving grace." The latter is God's grace that saves sinful humans, but common grace is God at work in all that is good in human life, thought, and society. I personally universalize God's grace to embrace both salvation for all people, *and* whatever other good we may see anywhere. Let us continually emphasize the role of humanity as such as it is described in the Universal Matrix of the Jewish and Christian Scriptures: God has made all humanity stand-ins and co-regents in relation

---

3. Gene Sharp, Wikipedia, the free encyclopedia.

to creation, so good deeds done by any human are worthy of praise. A friend of mine shares this example:

> A doctor who teaches in a nearby medical school told me about a man in his country who devoted his entire life to the education of nomadic children whose families follow their herds.
>
> The hero of my friend's story was a man who, even though his noble birth afforded him a formal education in law and fluency in English, German, and French, never forgot that he himself was born in a tent, the son of a tribal chieftain. And so he went and pitched a "white school tent" among a nomadic people. From that simple beginning, as others joined him, there began a movement that grew so rapidly during the 1950s, 60s, and 70s that, by the end of his life, having established 550 nomad schools, a half million nomads could read, with the most promising students going on to a nomad college that graduated 9,000 trained teachers (many of them women), with other graduates moving on to careers as physicians, lawyers, and engineers.
>
> Of course, this man's movement encountered strong opposition, particularly because the education of so many women threatened the status quo of those for whom an uneducated populace, raised by illiterate mothers, was a source of profit and power. So threatening was the success of his work that, finally, his enemies paid him the supreme compliment: they accused him of being a CIA operative! When he died in May of 2010, the gratitude of his graduates was so overflowing that, at his funeral, 24,000 mourners were in attendance.
>
> Such stories somehow don't make our front pages—maybe because all of this took place in Iran, and his name was Mohammad Bahmanbeigi, and he was a Muslim. Rather surprisingly, however, this man devoted his life to something strangely and beautifully Christ-like. Like the Word in John's gospel, who became flesh and "pitched his tent among us," this man stepped down from a higher, nobler place and "pitched his tent" among a people deeply in need of the light of literacy.[4]

4. AN ANSWER TO WAR

While Jesus was a child in Nazareth, Herod's son Archelaus went to Rome to secure his rule over Judea. Jews who opposed him started a revolt.[5] The Roman general Varus, on the way through Galilee to relieve the Roman garrison in Jerusalem, crucified hundreds of Jews, destroyed the city of Sepphoris, and sold its population into slavery. The city of Sepphoris was located a mere four miles from Jesus's hometown Nazareth. Archelaeus's brother Antipas, ethnarch of Galilee, immediately began to rebuild

---

4. F. Morgan Roberts, "Does it matter if Mohammad Bahmanbeigi was not a Christian?"
5. See Chapter 21.1.a. "The successors of Herod."

Sepphoris, mobilizing craftsmen and laborers from all the surrounding towns.[6] This circumstance suggests that Jesus's father Joseph may have been employed in the work at Sepphoris. If so, why not Jesus also? In any case, Jesus had to be aware of those tragic events, and they must have influenced his antiwar and nonviolent views. Jesus resisted the temptation to be a military Messiah. He consistently opposed the Jews who longed to fight Rome, and he accurately predicted what would happen if they tried it (see Luke 12:54—13:5; 13:34; 21:5–6, 20).

Jesus affirmed the summary of Jewish law, to love God with heart, soul, mind, and strength, and to love one's neighbor as oneself, but he included Samaritans as neighbors (Mark 12:29–31//Matt 22:37–40; Luke 10:25–37). Jesus went further to add, "Love your enemies and pray for those who persecute you, so that you may be children of your Father in heaven; for he makes his sun rise on the evil and on the good, and sends rain on the righteous and on the unrighteous" (Matt 5:44–45). God's undiscriminating benevolence toward people, whether good or bad, led Jesus to extend the scope of loving enemies beyond a mere personal level. Jesus cited the example of the prophet Elisha healing the Aramean army general Naaman of leprosy (Luke 4:27; 2 Kgs 5:1–19). Elisha also commanded the king of Israel to feed and then release the Aramean raiders who had been lured into captivity (2 Kgs 6:8–23).

The impulse toward nonviolence and antiwar typically originates among minorities who lack the numbers and resources for warfare, or among people who have personally experienced or observed the terrible consequences of war and who advocate the way of peace as did the prophets Isaiah and Jeremiah.[7] That was the case with Jesus, and we may observe it in other religions and cultures worldwide. Their cumulative wisdom is preserved for us in many variations of what we call "the golden rule."

5. THE UNIVERSAL GOLDEN RULE [8]

1. Everything you should do you will find in this: Do nothing to others that would hurt you if it were done to you. ~ Mahabharata 5:15–17 (Hinduism)
2. Do not offend others, as you would not want to be offended. ~ Udanavarga 5:18 (Buddhism)
3. The successes of your neighbors and their losses will be to you as if they were your own. ~ T'ai-shang Kan-ying P'ien (Taoism)
4. Is there any rule that one should follow all of one's life? Yes! The rule of gentle goodness: That which we do not wish to be done to us, we do not do to others. ~ Analects 15:23 (Confucianism)
5. That which you do not wish for yourself you shall not wish for your neighbor. This is the whole law; the rest is only commentary. ~ Talmud Shabbat 31 (Judaism)

---

6. Strange, "Sepphoris" in *ABD*.
7. See Chapter 18.4 "Prophets and the rejection of war."
8. Entry for February 24, 2011 in *Reflections for Nonviolent Community*.

6. In everything do to others as you would have them do to you; for this is the law and the prophets. ~ Matthew 7:12 (Christianity)
7. None of you shall be true believers unless you wish for your brother the same that you wish for yourself. ~ Sunnati (Islam)
8. Do one of the above, and live in such a way that you will enrich, and not diminish our relatives in the Earth family of animals and plants, soil, air and water. ~ Earth wisdom

The last originates from people who may not affiliate with a particular religion, but who are familiar with the implications of evolution, which enables appreciation for the basic unity of life on earth. Each of the other expressions of the golden rule is the product of an ancient culture, the fruit of practical observation of what really promotes general human well being. The Christian statement of the rule is attributed to Jesus, but he only reflected Jewish precedent. The monotheistic cultures acknowledge God, but the principle is basically humanistic. Simply as a human, each in his or her own way can contribute to general well being by conscientiously following this rule in the context of any religion or non-religion. For Christians in the twenty-first century, we should accept it as our calling, following the example and the command of our Lord and Savior Jesus Christ ("go and do likewise"), to make this rule the guiding principle of our own faith and life.

6. SOME GROUNDS OF HOPE

6a. Reduction of war and violence

Douglas P. Fry, a specialist in anthropological evolution, observes: "Although war and other types of violence may be very noticeable, a close examination of cross-cultural data reveals that people usually deal with conflict without violence. Humans have a solid capacity for getting along with each other peacefully, preventing physical aggression, limiting the scope and spread of violence, and restoring peace following aggression."[9] Fry writes that our hunter-gatherer forebears did not engage in war, though personal violence and self-redress occurred. Evolving over two million years without war, Homo sapiens is not pre-programmed for it. Warfare in the proper sense occurred only 10,000 years BP (before the present) after the change from simple hunter-gatherer societies to sedentary, materially rich and socially stratified communities, that is, after the agricultural revolution.[10]

Steven Pinker, a specialist in psychological evolution notes that news media distort our perceptions by their watchword, "If it bleeds, it leads." Pinker asserts that all sorts of violence have been on the wane for centuries. Pinker uses the data others

---

9. Fry, *Beyond War*, 21.
10. See chapter 5, "Biblical Creation, Evolution, and Brain Science."

helped him compile to argue that the world of the past was much worse than now. Today we may be living in the most peaceable era in the existence of our species. Assisted by over a hundred named individuals, Pinker presents data in dozens of figures and charts to support his thesis. Some examples: Homicide, torture, slavery, and capital punishment, domestic spousal and child abuse have steadily declined, giving way before increasing moral repugnance. The frequency of wars between the great powers, their duration, intensity, and loss of life have declined markedly over the last 500 years. Better conditions of human life such as improved diet and life expectancy, education and literacy, empathy and reason have greatly improved.[11] Like Fry, Pinker credits human evolution with making such progress possible, but he insists there is no guarantee of inevitable improvement.

Fry notes that once humans settled into larger, organized communities they developed legal processes to replace private revenge or self-redress. In general, killing and family feuding gave way to the establishment of law and order and the organization of police and courts to deal with crime. Even now, however, nation states still operate on the principle of self-redress by war in international relations, a situation Fry compares to the old American Wild West before the coming of the sheriff and the judge. Fry celebrates the better way of dealing with private revenge, and he believes the human race may eventually succeed in establishing an international system of judgment with a global scope that can lead us beyond war. The data in Pinker's book demonstrating the decline of violence reinforces Fry's hope, and in fact we have actual evidence of progress in that direction.

6b. The International Criminal Court

On 17 July 1998, the international community reached an historic milestone when 120 states adopted the Rome Statute, the legal basis for establishing the permanent International Criminal Court (ICC). The Rome Statute entered into force on July 1, 2002 after ratification by sixty countries. (The United States signed the Statute but did not ratify it.) A web site gives regular reports on activities of the ICC including the names and profiles of people formally accused of crimes against humanity now under investigation.[12] Not all states cooperate with the ICC, so that it is very difficult to proceed against some of the accused, but the court is committed to following international protocols to respect the human rights of everyone involved. In *Mother Jones* magazine Mac McClelland's article "To Catch A Warlord" gives some

---

11. Pinker, *The Better Angels of our Nature*. Pinker is an articulate non-believer who seems to delight in giving examples of violence in the Jewish and Christian Scriptures. He follows a literal reading typical of fundamentalists. In my book I have acknowledged the violence, especially that ascribed to YHWH the war God of ancient Israel. Unlike Pinker I take a critical approach that reads biblical documents in their cultural setting and traces the progress of improvement for the better over time.

12. International Criminal Court, <http://www.icc-cpi.int/Menus/ICC/About+the+Court/>.

idea of the extreme difficulty of fulfilling the objectives of the Court.[13] Yet there are some successes. In May 2012 the Court convicted Charles Taylor, former president of Liberia, of all eleven counts of war crimes and crimes against humanity for aiding and abetting Sierra Leone's Revolutionary United Front during the country's brutal 1991 to 2001 civil war. One must remember that this is only the beginning of doing what Fry anticipated, to bring the sheriff and the judge into the "wild west" situation of international relations. In the cosmic time frame, we need patience and persistent effort, accompanied by fervent hope, educational effort, and energetic action.

6c. Improvement in the status of women

We are constantly bombarded with news of armed bands that force children to become soldiers and routinely rape and torture women and girls in combat zones in Africa and Asia. But there is no denying that consciousness of the plight of women and efforts to improve their lot are on the increase worldwide. As representative of this improvement I mention only the women recipients of the Nobel Peace Prize. Since 1901 twelve women have been peace laureates. As of this writing, Aung San Suu Kyi of Myanmar (Burma) gets international attention because the repressive government has changed enough to allow her to receive the Nobel Peace Prize she was awarded over twenty years ago.

In the past decade five women have received the Peace Prize: Shirin Ebadi of Iran, a human rights lawyer in 2003; in 2004 Wangari Maathai a peace activist of Kenya who mobilized women to plant millions of trees. In 2011 there were three: Tawakkul Karman, who has led the struggle for women's rights and for democracy and peace in Yemen, and two African women of Liberia, Ellen Johnson Sirleaf, the president and Leymah Gbowee, both of whom worked indefatigably to restore peace in Liberia after the violent regime of aforementioned president Charles Taylor.

Liberian Laureate Leymah Gbowee said, "The world is functioning on one side of its brain" because women's skills and intelligence are "not being used to advance the cause of the world." Throughout world history men monopolizing weapons and over-endowed with testosterone have controlled affairs and relegated women to subordinate status and often to victimhood. Today, even in societies where women seem to have the fewest rights and their abilities are least appreciated, things are changing, and the Nobel awards are bound to provide greater encouragement and opportunity for women everywhere, spurring expectations of a better future for the world.

Leymah Gbowee's remark calls attention to bioneurological differences that make women more nurturing and compassionate than men, and hence able to contribute to better conditions of human life when they can apply their talents on a broader public scale. Reports of recent neurological research indicate that every individual, whether

---

13. McClelland, "To Catch a Warlord" *Mother Jones*.

male or female, whether religious, secular, or atheist, can actually change own brain structure and function to become less self-serving, more compassionate, and better able to contribute to a greater degree of general human well being.

6d. Brain science and mystical experience

In chapter 5 "Biblical Creation, Evolution, and Brain Science" I noted the personal witness of Dr. Jill Bolte Taylor. A severe stroke disabled the left hemisphere of her brain, locus of her sense of self in distinction from others and her environment, but her right brain enabled her to think of herself as a liquid, part of the eternal and universal flow of life, in harmony with herself and all other people, for whom she felt deep sympathy and compassion. I cited testimony of people who have undergone near-death experience (NDE) showing that the human brain can transcend the inherent animal instincts of self-preservation, conflict, and dominance. Many NDEers lost all vestiges of religious parochialism and felt themselves opened to a vision of humanity united by a confidence in God's limitless love for all. In some instances, the same changes occurred in persons who did not have an NDE, but who encountered the light. This was the life style of Jesus, and of the Apostle Paul who called it "living by the Spirit" in contrast to living "according to the flesh" (Gal 5:13–26).

Besides Jesus, Paul, and many believers, individuals of traditions other than the Judeo-Christian have entered mystical states and left reports of their experience to enrich the literature of world religion. Brain research scientists Newberg and d'Aquili monitored both Roman Catholic nuns and Tibetan Buddhist mystics in the practice of meditation that climaxed in their sense if being absorbed in oneness with the mystical presence that indwells all existence. Newberg and d'Aquili call this *Absolute Unitary Being*. To me, it seems a great deal like the state that people enter by a near death experience. Apparently relatively few adepts of all traditions have that absolute degree of mystical union, but it is possible for ordinary people to benefit from meditation.

Meditation practice has proven to be beneficial, not merely for one's personal health and well being, but also for compassion for others and more peaceful personal relations. Soka Gakkai, a lay organization of Japanese Nichiren Buddhism, promotes peace, culture, and education on a worldwide scale since the 1950s. In Boston I attended a public meeting of the local group featuring a sermon by the executive director of Soka Gakkai's USA region that reminded me of a Billy Graham evangelistic service. People from as far away as New York City testified to having been set free from drug and alcohol addiction, from destructive habits, and from hopelessness and depression by being welcomed into the fellowship and meditating.[14]

Calvin Malone, who wrote while an inmate of the prison system of Washington State, described the life-changing effects of Zen Buddhist meditation.[15] Malone,

14. For information on Soka Gakkai go to http://www.sgi.org/.
15. Malone, *Razor-Wire Dharma*.

self-described as a violent, angry man when he began his prison sentence, found in the prison library a book on Buddhism. When he wrote to an address he found there, he received a prompt reply and materials to guide meditation practice. That changed his life completely and enabled him to help many fellow prisoners. Malone calls prison "a setting where hate-mongers sit in wait for a chance to capitalize upon your vulnerability... Since everything is so transitional in the world of the incarcerated, it is rare that prisoners dare to explore the realm of sincere friendship."[16] Malone dared to show kindness to other prisoners, sustained by meditation and encouragement from Buddhists outside. He arranged for welcoming Buddhist groups to help released prisoners readjust to life outside.

Andrew Newberg, M.D., co-author of the book *Why God Won't Go Away*, has written with Mark Waldman another book further describing details of the evolution of the human brain, documenting the physical, mental, and social benefits of meditation, and giving instruction in practices that anyone can follow to bring about measurable improvement in one's life.[17] The neurological key to the advantages of meditation is the anterior cingulate, found only in humans and a few primates, that has existed for only about 15 million years. The authors write that the anterior cingulate is the true "heart" of the neurological soul, enabling one to feel greater tolerance and acceptance toward others. Meditation allows one to experience God as compassionate, and it suppresses reptilian brain emotions of anxiety, guilt, fear, and especially anger, which is the most destructive emotion.[18]

SUMMARY AND REFLECTION

Humanity as such, when studied in the context of the total evolutionary process, has indeed been at least partially fulfilling the priestly role that Genesis 1:26–27 assigns us. If we concentrate on the progress and give thanks for it on a daily basis, it will actually cause a positive change in the neurons of our brains. Following the golden rule, positively and sympathetically responding to others, regarding them, like ourselves, as members of the one humanity that the One God created and embraces, that too will have a self-reinforcing influence on our lives. And that, in turn will have a positive effect on our world.

---

16. Malone, "A Little Closer Home," *Fellowship*, 28–30. The entire *Fellowship* issue is devoted to the theme "Transformation of/in Prisons."

17. Newberg and Waldman, *How God Changes your Brain*, chapter 9 "Finding Serenity, a personalized brain enhancement program."

18. They recommend "Meditations for Christians, "a CD by James Finley. http://www.soundstrue.com/shop.

Afterword

"If God is for us, who is against us?"
(Rom 8:31b)

AT THE END OF this book, I can confidently say that this short, rhetorical question of the Apostle Paul summarizes what I have written at length. Like Paul, I expect the answer, "Nobody can be against us, because God is for us!" Yet it is still a question, for neither Paul nor I can demand unanimous agreement. In other rhetorical questions Paul names circumstances that might prompt disagreement: "Who will separate us from the love of Christ? Will hardship, or distress, or persecution, or famine, or nakedness, or peril, or sword?" (8:35). Paul himself has suffered almost unspeakable harassment and hardship. He recalls the words of a fellow Jew of many centuries past, who found himself and his people overwhelmed by disaster despite their faithful adherence to the covenant. Almost as an accusation the psalmist cries out to God: "For your sake we are being killed all the day long; we are accounted as sheep to be slaughtered" (Rom 8:36=Ps 44:22).

Paul knows that the psalmist didn't abandon hope, though he ends with this desperate plea: "Rise up, come to our help. Redeem us for the sake of your steadfast love" (Ps 44:26).[1] Paul knows that the inclusion of the psalm in the Scriptures of his people means that the Divine Kinsman answered, even though it may not have been exactly as the psalmist wished. So Paul answers his own question: "No, in all these things we are more than conquerors through him who loved us. For I am convinced that neither death, nor life, nor angels, nor rulers, nor things present, nor things to come, nor powers, nor height, nor depth, nor anything else in all creation, will be able to separate us from the love of God in Christ Jesus our Lord" (8:37–39)

Immediately following this enthusiastic declaration Paul set out in Romans 9–11 to demonstrate from Scripture that this love of God is universal, "For God has imprisoned all in disobedience so that he may be merciful to all" (11:32; see above chapter 31 "Universal Grace in Romans"). Christians take great comfort from Paul's words in Romans 8, and we often read them at funerals or memorial services. That was done at the service for my wife Margaret Ruth Hopper, who died of lung cancer at age sixty-three after surviving a mere two years following surgery, chemotherapy, and radiation treatment. She said, "How can I ask 'Why me?' for this? I would have to ask 'Why

---

1. See chapter 17, "The Covenant as Family Relationship."

me?' for all the blessings God has given me." Margaret's witness is typical of many Christians, and it always gives me a warm feeling of gratitude when I remember her.

For many of us Christians, however, we have tended to think that Paul's words, addressed to fellow Christians in Rome, describe the privilege *only* of Christians. Yet to think that is to read an erroneous tradition of exclusion into the text that distorts its meaning. Paul asserts his confident statement of trust in God's total sovereign control over any and all circumstances of life. Paul says there is nothing, *nothing* in all creation—not even *death*—that can separate humanity from God's love in Christ.

Those few paragraphs form a sort of climax, almost a conclusion, of Paul's reflection on Israel's experience of God enlightened by his personal experience of being transformed by the light of the risen Christ. Israel's experience began in the mists of prehistory where primitive humans all began, terrified by mysterious non-human forces that they couldn't understand, but to which they attributed human-like needs, wants, and desires. Battered by storm, flood, fire, disease, and other calamities people assumed ill will or enmity from these mysterious beings.[2] Our fellow humans devised means of trying to learn the will of these powers, to placate them for our protection, and if possible to gain their favor to help us satisfy our needs. An old Latin aphorism succinctly summarizes it: *do ut des*—"I give so that thou mayest give."

Over time some people progressed beyond those primitive concepts, and Paul, aided by his own transformation by the light, knew that that primitive fear of the gods, to whom we must give in order that they give to us, is a great mistake. Paul advanced to his climax by declaring that God the Creator, the God who is *one*, is merciful to *all*. Once more he asks rhetorically: "Who has given a gift to God, to receive a gift in return?" (Rom 11:35). Again Paul assumes the answer "Nobody!" Yet it is still a question, because of the persistence of that ancient idea. Even now, unacknowledged, it infects much popular Christian belief: God's demand is so great that only "Jesus paid it all." We then *give* God our agreement, so that God *can give* us Jesus's completed work. No!

God, from the beginning, created humankind, each and all, in God's own image to be co-regents, partners, mediators, priests, and prophets in relation to everything else that God made. Instead of accepting with thanks this subordinate role and acting to fulfill it, we exploit the privilege and try to be "like God." Thus we make ourselves God's rivals. From our side, rivalry with God becomes fear, enmity, and alienation. We personified these mysterious forces with names and attributes—Satan, the Adversary, the Devil, or a spiritual entity Sin (with a capital S). By reflection on his people's history focused by his own experience, Paul knows that our alienation and fear result from *our* selfishness and ignorance, *not* from God's side. Paul teaches: While we were enemies Christ died for the ungodly. In Christ God was reconciling the world to God-self, not counting our trespasses against us (Rom 5:6, 10; 2 Cor 5:19). God relates to us with steadfast love as Divine Kinsman in a family relationship. Our work is not

---

2. Pagan accounts of the flood attributed its cause to enmity of the gods, see chapter 6.2 "The flood."

something we give to God in order to receive his blessing. It is, rather, our grateful response as family members to do whatever we can for the benefit of the whole family, in gratitude to the Family Head. This is the basic truth of Scripture that we need to rediscover and reaffirm.

Both Jesus and Paul's favorite name for God was Father, a term they took positively describing a parent who had the children's best interests at heart, though in the patriarchal culture that was not always the human experience. Nowadays some people recoil from calling God Father, because it calls to mind the abuses of patriarchy that even now characterize human culture in so much of the world. To some sensitive minds, "Father" seems to preclude "Mother" but even these terms imply gender roles that the only God transcends. Moreover, referring to Jesus as God's "only begotten Son" carries an implication of sexual reproduction, an idea that is repulsive to other monotheists such as Jews and Muslims.

I don't wish to deprive or offend anyone who receives comfort and reassurance by thinking of God as Father/Mother/Parent, but I think there are other ways to think of God that may be acceptable to people who have not been nurtured by faith in the fatherhood of God and who take seriously the implications of science and evolution. Non-religious people may wonder, "Is the universe friendly?" I hope that those who may read this book can be persuaded that the universe may be friendly.

I take my text from the account of Paul's appearance before the Mars Hill council in Athens, as recounted in Acts 17:16–33. I accept the text as a believable example of how Paul, a well-instructed Jew with extensive knowledge and personal experience of Greek language, culture, and thought, might have approached a sophisiticated body of intellectuals that included adherents of both the Epicurean and the Stoic philosophical schools in Athens, the intellectual center of first century Greece. The scene is set by telling how Paul was turned off by seeing idols and altars to so many gods everywhere in the city. He argued with Jews and devout persons in the synagogue, but also in public he spoke about Jesus and resurrection (=Gk *anastasis*; Anastasia is a name for girls even today). Some thought these were "new deities," so they called him to Mars Hill for a more formal presentation. Paul began with his observation of the evidence of the Athenians' *religious sensitivities* (17:22). The word he uses appears only here in the NT, and most English versions render it in a neutral sense such as "very religious," though the KJV interprets it pejoratively, "too superstitious." The extent of Athenians' religious sensitivity is seen in the fact that they didn't want to run the risk of neglecting any of the deities, so they had an altar on which offerings could placate "the unknown god." Paul used this as the springboard to introduce his presentation. His sophisticated hearers would generally agree with Paul's opening remarks, for he states approvingly several of their typical views in contrast to the religion of the masses.[3]

---

3. See the articles on Epicureans and Stoics in *ABD* and *IDB*.

> What therefore you worship as unknown, this I proclaim to you. The God who made the world and everything in it, he who is Lord of heaven and earth, does not live in shrines made by human hands, nor is he served by human hands, as though he needed anything, since he himself gives to all mortals life and breath and all things. From one ancestor he made all nations to inhabit the whole earth, and he allotted the times of their existence and the boundaries of the places where they would live, so that they would search for God and perhaps grope for him and find him—though indeed he is not far from each one of us. For "In him we live and move and have our being"; as even some of your own poets have said, "For we too are his offspring."[4] Since we are God's offspring, we ought not to think that the deity is like gold, or silver, or stone, an image formed by the art and imagination of mortals. (Acts 17:23b–29)

Paul begins from the sovereignty of God, maker and owner of all things (*kosmos,* heaven, and earth). This all-sufficient God does not live in a shrine nor is he *served* by human hands as though he needed anything. Paul uses the word *therapeuetai* only here in the sense of *to be served* ("worshiped" in KJV). In forty-six other places in the NT the verb is translated "to heal" or "to be healed" and refers to acts by Jesus, his disciples, and others. In Greek *therapeuō* is used primarily as "1. *serve a divinity* . . . 2. *care for, wait upon, treat* (medically) . . . "[5] The concept of healing conveyed by this verb and its cognates in Greek was so pervasive that it has come into English in words that relate specifically to restoring health, such as "therapeutic" and "therapy." It is clear, therefore, that Paul's rebuttal of the Athenians' scrupulous religiosity aims at their assumption that humans have to do something for the gods (not even excluding the possibility of thinking that if gods get sick, they need human help to get well!). Paul completely reverses the whole idea. Far from needing anything from humans God gives to *all* mortals life and breath and *all things.* This thought was compatible with some Stoic thought and may be a citation by Paul.

Paul develops this thought by stating God's sovereignty over all people of every race everywhere on the face of the Earth, all derived *from one* (which he leaves otherwise undefined).[6] Paul describes human nature as involving the divinely instilled impulse to seek and grope for God, though God is not far away from anyone. The multiplicity of religions and differing conceptions of deity worldwide even now give support to Paul's statement, and evolutionary data provide moderns with scientific confirmation of the unity of humanity. Both Epicureans and Stoics would probably sympathize with the general view of Deity and humanity that Paul has offered so far. Paul cites an ancient source, perhaps Epimenides, "for we humans live and move and have our being in God" (17:25). As I interpret that idea today in full biblical context,

---

4. See HCSB on Acts 17:28: these citations may be from Greek intellectuals Epimenides and Aratus.
5. Arndt and Gingrich, *Greek-English Lexicon,* 359b.
6. Greek: *ex henos*="from one," Some English translations add as follows: NRSV "ancestor"; KJV "blood"; NIV "man"; NJB "single principle."

our total physical and spiritual environment is God. Every human person lives in that environment. We have a degree of freedom of choice that permits us to go our way in enmity or indifference to God and to suffer the consequences if we do. Yet even the most rebellious is never outside God. Paul shows further agreement with his hearers by affirming some sense of affinity between deity and humanity as he cites the Stoic Aratus, who said, "for we are his offspring." Like the Greek philosopher, Paul uses "offspring" metaphorically, just as did the OT writers who used *berit*=covenant to describe the family relation with the Divine Kinsman.

Practically everything Paul said was in general agreement with the Epicureans and Stoics. They had a low view of popular idolatry; they spoke of god(s) not personally but metaphorically; and they tended to think of some degree of unity of humanity. Paul continues by stating that God has patiently allowed people hitherto to live in ignorance, but now God has set a time of judgment (soon?) when God will call on everyone to repent, i.e., to change their erroneous views and behaviors. God has entrusted this righteous judgment to a man, whom God approved by raising him from the dead (17:32). Here Paul lost his audience. Greeks, in common with most people, assumed some sort of life after death, as has been demonstrated since prehistoric times by human burial practices.[7] Bodily resurrection was not an acceptable idea for Greeks, who assumed a dualism of immortal soul trapped in material body from which it would be liberated at death.

Today we should take care not to impose modern ideas on Paul and his Greek audience. As I reported in chapter 21.2a "The great chain of being" there was no conception of what we think of today as "pure" spirit or soul in contrast to body. Scripture generally supports the view that a human is an "animated body." But as Craffert explained it, everything consisted of "stuff"—different degrees or combinations of the four elements earth, air, fire, and water. The human being was a commingling of "stuff," but ancient literature, including the Bible, shows no unanimity about the configuration of body, soul, and spirit.[8] Today chemistry has identified a multiplicity of elements, and since Einstein, physics tells us that all the substances that to us appear so solidly material are really only different manifestations of energy.

The Christian creeds state belief in "the resurrection of the body," which usually is interpreted materially. Yet the biblical testimony is not clear.[9] Luke's account is grossly physical: Jesus appears to gathered disciples, who fear they see a ghost. Jesus shows them that he has flesh and bones and eats a piece of fish (Luke 24:36–43). Paul's take is different: "The kingdom of God is not food and drink" (Rom 14:17), and "flesh and blood cannot inherit the kingdom of God" (1 Cor 15:50). Paul speaks of a "heavenly" body in contrast to the body made from earth. He says the resurrection

---

7. Hick, *Death and Eternal Life* describes the views and practices of the world's major religions.
8. Craffert, *The Life of a Galilean Shaman*, 188, summarizing a number of expert references.
9. Green, *Body, Soul, and Human Life*, 140–81 and bibliograpy.

body is spiritual and has undergone transformation from corrupt to incorrupt, from perishable to imperishable, from weakness to strength (1 Cor 15:35–49).

Despite differences in detail, Paul, Greeks, and most world religions believe in some sort of life-after-death.[10] Even though our present text barely touches it, they also have some idea of an ultimate judgment of good and evil. Both these ideas bring us into a realm of mystery beyond finite human comprehension and therefore beyond the scope of my work. Christians can derive hope and encouragement from the witness of NDErs and from books in which people have described personal experiences "in heaven" that confirmed for them the reality of life-after-death. Yet all those who have given their personal witness "came back" again to live on earth, and they can only expect that eventually their physical bodies will succumb to death, and their biological existence on earth will end. There is no absolute and compelling "proof" that can convince every person. Rhetorical questions that seem to require particular answers are still questions to which there are no undebatable answers. There is far too much mystery in the infinity that God is for finite humans to comprehend fully.

Since the enlightenment, some people have thought that religion and science are "at war," but some sincere adherents of religious faith and some experts in science find our respective fields of interest meeting and are engaged in dialogue to explore areas of agreement, or at least maintain open and sympathetic minds toward the views of their counterparts. The biblical evidence and my personal study and experience are sufficient to convince me that there is One God who transcends all religions, the One God who created all humans in the divine image, the One God who embraces all humankind in the plan of total reconciliation. The scientific description of evolution convinces me of the oneness of humanity, which is an integral part of total creation. I believe that Dr. Eben Alexander's experience indicates that human consciousness exists and persists even when the human brain no longer functions. Dr. Andrew Newberg convinces me of the Absolute Unitary Being, whom I call God, the One God who is for all.[11] For Christians certainly but for many others throughout the world, Jesus is the man who represents the best of humanity, who reveals God to other humans, and by whose help humans can be enabled to participate in God's plan for reconciliation of humanity living at peace in a sustainable creation toward which God has called us to be God's co-workers.

---

10. Covered at great length by Hick, *Death and Eternal Life*.
11. On Alexander and Newberg see above chapter 5.5 "Recent brain research."

Appendix A

A SCHEMATIC REPRESENTATION OF the one God's plan for the one world as deduced from Scripture

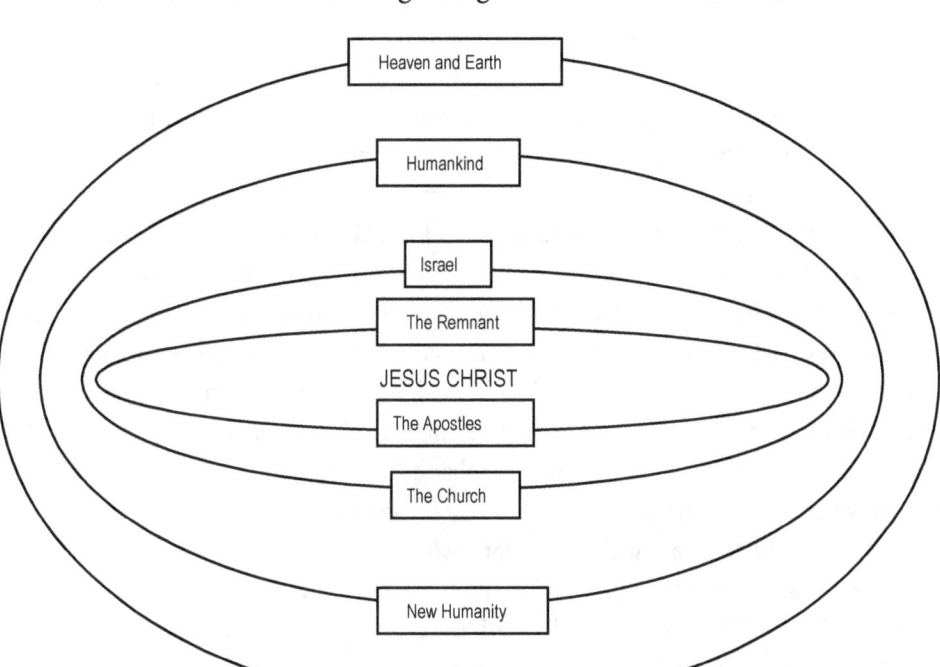

Genesis 1:1
In the beginning God Created

God shall be all in all
(1 Corinthians 15:28)

I have presented the major theme of the Bible that there is only one God, the Creator of All, who shows special favor to humanity, hence the title, *God for All*. The entire Bible is a record of God's self-revelation to certain people and their response. Growing out of polytheistic ideas about deity, the biblical revelation, over time, reaches the point at which it can declare, quite simply, "God is love" (1 John 4:8, 16). According to this way of understanding the comprehensive teaching of the Bible, both Old and

Appendix A

New Testaments, the God who is Love has revealed to humanity the divine purpose of redemption and reconciliation for the creation.

The diagram above represents the divine plan schematically: The God who exists eternally began a work of creation, which includes everything, expressed by the Hebrew "Heaven and Earth," which in the thought of the biblical writers comprised what we call Planet Earth. The totality of created being is therefore the product and the object of divine love.

To show more specifically what divine love involves, the Bible teaches that God entered into a special relationship with Humankind (male and female) different from relationship with the rest of creation, by commissioning humankind to share God's responsibility for creation. As seen in the Bible, reflecting human reality, humankind became alienated from God, having refused to accept dependent status as creature and rejected the loving authority of the Creator.

Confronted with the sin of human creatures, God acted to overcome sin by initiating a process of forgiveness, redemption, and reconciliation. That relation is expressed in the biblical concept of covenant, by which God related unconditionally to humanity in a fictive kinship through Abram as though members of one family.

In order to make more explicit the divine love, God entered a special relationship with one group of people—family, race, nation—Abraham's descendants who came to be known as Israel. God redeemed the Israelites from slavery in Egypt and then established with them another covenant similar to that between a king and his people. God had shown favor to Israel, and they pledged loyalty to him alone as God. To guide their worship and life in covenant relation, God gave them the divine teaching (Torah). Even though Israel habitually violated the covenant and often suffered the consequences, God remained faithful and never abandoned faithless Israel.

God made use of a faithful Remnant within Israel to make even more explicit what relationship with the One God means. Through the Remnant, particularly the prophets, God made known the divine judgment upon sin and God's will for reconciliation. As a result, there arose the expectation that God would bring eventual redemption of Israel through an anointed leader, a Messiah.

One should not misinterpret what might appear like a narrowing of the divine concern, from Heaven and Earth→ to Humankind→ to Israel→ to a Remnant. God did not neglect the rest while showing favoritism toward some, even though there was always a temptation for beneficiaries to see it in that way. God, who is Love, in order to make more and more clear the divine love for all creation, acted in more and more particular ways with and through Humankind, Israel, and the Remnant. They became, in a sense, paradigms of what God intends for Heaven and Earth, for All.

Out of the faithful remnant of Israel there came the man JESUS CHRIST. In him the revelation of the loving purpose of God for all creation finds its central focus, and at the same time Jesus becomes the supreme paradigm for humanity subject to God. Jesus was crucified, the victim of human political and religious authority alienated

Appendix A

from God. But God raised Jesus from the dead. Those who had known him and who experienced him as resurrected and alive acclaimed Jesus the Messiah/Christ of expectation. They saw the death and resurrection of Jesus as the sign that God does not keep records of human sin but purposes human reconciliation to God and to each other.

The close associates of Jesus who witnessed the resurrection were, like him, members of the Remnant of Israel. Jesus appointed them Apostles, ones sent to bear witness to what they had seen and heard. Very soon, not only others of Israel but also many non-Israelites, or Gentiles accepted the message about Jesus and became believers/disciples/followers. From that time to the present, the body of these believers constitutes the church, which has received from the risen Christ the commission to proclaim the good news of God's reconciliation to all people with the goal of a New Humanity.

At present humanity is troubled by conflicts and divisions of many kinds, but a long view of history gives evidence of some improvement over time and hope for more progress. In the Bible Christians have one example of how the one God has been at work in the world. The Bible supplemented by evolution enables Christians to discern signs of peace and reconciliation in other cultures and religious traditions. As the church faithfully carries out its mission empowered by the Spirit of God, Christians can recognize signs of progress toward world peace and human reconciliation manifested in any and all other religious and cultural traditions. God's reconciling purpose as revealed in the Bible is reinforced by our understanding of the basic oneness of all creation as shown by evolution. Christians are a paradigm by which God's purpose of total reconciliation may progress toward culmination in the New Heaven and New Earth. As expressed in 1 Corinthians 15:20–28, the way of the risen Jesus becomes a spiritual impulse and force working within the cultures and religions of humanity toward realization of the one God's reconciliation of all things in what the Bible calls the New Heaven and New Earth in which God will be All in All.

Appendix B

Other Books

OVER THE LAST DECADE or so a number of authors have written books that either suggest or insist that God has a gracious plan for the final redemption of all humanity. Here I offer the main points of several of them, which I find interesting and helpful.

1. WHO ARE THE CHOSEN PEOPLE? THE MEANING OF CHOSENNESS IN JUDAISM, CHRISTIANITY, AND ISLAM.

Rabbi Reuven Firestone describes the historical and cultural conditions that led the adherents of the three major monotheistic religions to declare themselves specially chosen by the one God. Over time the three have engaged in violent conflict, each making an exclusive claim to chosenness. Yet there has always been a minority within each religion that offers a more inclusive interpretation of their sacred scriptures. People everywhere are gradually coming to recognize each individual's right to choose or reject religious faith. Rabbi Firestone concludes his book with this question: "If God created everyone to be absolutely unique, are we not all chosen?"

2. THE GOSPEL OF INCLUSION: REACHING BEYOND RELIGIOUS FUNDAMENTALISM TO THE TRUE LOVE OF GOD AND SELF.

Bishop Carlton Pearson identifies himself as an African-American, fourth-generation traditional Pentecostal holiness preacher raised in the tradition of sin and damnation.

He was a graduate of Oral Roberts University and a member of its Board of Visitors, and also pastor of a megachurch in Tulsa, Oklahoma. One evening while watching TV news of the conflict between Tutsis and Hutus in Africa, Pearson engaged God in conversation, complaining that God didn't send enough missionaries to convert those people. God replied that missionaries never saved anybody. God through Christ is Savior of the world. Those people are already saved; they just don't know it. It's up to believers to get that message spread abroad. Pearson began to read the Bible from that point of view and to proclaim that everybody is saved, but not everybody knows it. As a result he lost the pastorate of his church, Oral Roberts broke off relations with him, and his own denomination revoked his ordination status. Sympathetic members of other churches such as Episcopalian and particularly those of the lesbian, gay, bisexual, and transgender community have given support and encouragement to Pearson in his continuing ministry of writing and speaking on his universal theme.

3. IF GRACE IS TRUE: WHY GOD WILL SAVE EVERY PERSON AND IF GOD IS LOVE: REDISCOVERING GRACE IN AN UNGRACIOUS WORLD.

Co-authors Philip Gulley and James Mulholland are pastors of Quaker churches in Indianapolis. Formerly a Catholic and a Protestant, they became friends in seminary and similar pastoral experiences have drawn them closer together. They describe how, little by little, their eyes were opened to new insights into the Scriptures that led toward universalism. Their books are rich in personal examples that show deep sympathy and understanding for people to whom they've ministered. Many had personal backgrounds or experiences that gave them negative feelings about God and organized religion. Some eventually became Christians; others never "got saved" in the popular sense, but the authors honor them all and are assured that they are fully embraced by God. In many respects they are of superior faith and character than some arrogant and aggressive conservative believers.

These two books supplement each other and clarify the meaning of the terms love and grace. The authors note that many people think God's love is limited and conditional; they think "God's love becomes a reward, not a divine commitment... Grace, in contrast, is not connected to our behavior... Grace is God's commitment to love us regardless." Gulley and Mulholland stress that the realization of God's universal love should change our behavior. One example: If God loves everyone so much, we should do the same. Reflecting on Jesus's command, "Love your enemies," we must realize that God who loves us loves our enemies too.

4. ROB BELL, LOVE WINS: A BOOK ABOUT HEAVEN HELL, AND THE FATE OF EVERY PERSON WHO EVER LIVED.

Bell, founder and pastor of a megachurch in Grand Rapids, Michigan, was motivated to write this book because of some Christian's assertion that Mahatma Gandhi is in hell. Bell opens his book with a slew of questions about people who could make such a judgment, what kind of authority they had, what sort of God they believed in, etc. He has a knack for taking a familiar Bible verse that most Christians think they understand quite well and teasing out a point that we haven't really noticed previously and setting it beside other overlooked points in other texts that appear to call it in question or raise ambivalence. In this way Bell devotes a chapter each to examining in detail what the Old and New Testaments have to say about heaven and hell. He demonstrates the misleading error of assuming they are both places prepared as the final destination of human beings, some of whom end up in one place and the rest in the other.

The fact is that all too many Christians seem quite willing to consign the vast majority of people to hell, while only a minority (including themselves, of course) will end up in heaven. Who makes it into heaven, and how? The popular idea is that each individual must pray the proper prayer or repeat the proper formula or undergo the proper ritual to be able to qualify. Most evangelicals stress that Jesus died for everybody and God wants everybody to be saved, but it all depends on the decision of each individual. That puts God's desire in question. Bell asks, "Does God get what God wants?" Then he marshals evidence from a broad range of biblical sources to demonstrate God's power and concludes: "In the Bible, God is not helpless, God is not powerless, God is not impotent." Bell refers to many biblical texts that speak of God's will, God's plan, God's grace and favor for all. He asks: "Which is stronger and more powerful, the hardness of the human heart or God's unrelenting, infinite, expansive love?"

In the end, Bell concedes that genuine love permits freedom, so the final question is, "Do we get what we want?"—even if we want nothing to do with light, hope, love, grace, and peace. But if we really want those, God bestows them in abundance. "God says yes, we can have what we want, because love wins."

Bell's tone is positive, upbeat, enthusiastic, and inviting. I think that he really believes that the God of the Bible, supremely revealed in Jesus Christ, does ultimately save every person who ever lived. But he never makes that a categorical pronouncement—it's left up to the reader. Bell never uses the word that means God actually does save everybody: universalism. The staff of his church prepared material to help church members respond to critics, noting that the book does not promote universalism, which many Christians consider heretical.

Many evangelicals do consider Bell a heretic. One prominent author tweeted: "Farewell, Rob Bell." Church membership dropped significantly during the ensuing turmoil. According to an article in a recent **New Yorker,** Bell resigned as pastor of the Mars Hill Bible Church and has moved to California. He is seeking other possibilities for ministry while continuing to present his case wherever audiences will give him a hearing.

Bibliography

Adamson, Joel Edmund. "YHWH's Surprising Covenant Hesed in Jonah," *Biblical Theology Bulletin* 42/1, 2012
Alt, Albrecht. *Essays on Old Testament History and Religion*. Sheffield: JSOT Press, 1989
Allen, Leslie C. *Ezekiel* 1–19. Waco: Word, 1986
———. *Psalms* 101–150. Waco: Word, 2002
Allison, Jr. Dale C. "Blessing God and Cursing People: James 3:9–10" *SBL* 130/2, 2011
Anderson, A. A. *2 Samuel*. Dallas: Word, 1989
Arndt, William F. and F. Wilbur Gingrich. *A Greek-English Lexicon of the New Testament and Other Early Christian Literature*. Chicago: University of Chicago, 1957
Ashton, John. *The Religion of Paul the Apostle*. New Haven: Yale University Press, 2000
———. "The Religious Experience of Jesus" The William James Lecture for 2002–03. In *Harvard Divinity Bulletin* 32/1, 2003
Barker, Margaret. *The Great Angel: A Study of Israel's Second God*. Louisville: Westminster/John Knox, 1992
Barth, Markus. *Ephesians* 1–3. Garden City: Doubleday, 1974
Barrett, C. K. *A Commentary on the First Epistle to the Corinthians*. New York: Harper & Row, 1968
Baukham, Richard. "Jude, Epistle of." In *ADB* 3:1098–1103
Beale, G. K. and D. A. Carson, editors. *Commentary on the New Testament Use of the Old Testament*. Grand Rapids: Baker, 2007
Berry, Wendell. *Life is a Miracle: An Essay against Modern Superstition*. Washington DC: Counterpoint, 2000
Beyerlin, Walter. *Near Eastern Religious Texts Relating to the Old Testament*. Philadelphia: Westminster, 1978
Bickerman, Elias. *From Ezra to the Last of the Maccabees: Foundations of Postbiblical Judaism* © 1949. New York: Shocken Paperback, 1962
Bix, Herbert P. "Japan's Delayed Surrender: A Reinterpretation." In *Diplomatic History* 19/2, 1995
Boling, Robert G. *Judges: Introduction, Translation, and Commentary*. Garden City: Doubleday, 1975
Boring, M. Eugene. *Mark: A Commentary*. Louisville: Westminster/John Knox, 2006
Brenton, Launcelot Lee, translator. *The Septuagint Version, Greek and English*. London: Samuel Bagster and Sons, no date
Brichto, Herbert Chanan. *The Names of God: Poetic Readings in Biblical Beginnings*. New York: Oxford, 1998
Bright, John. *A History of Israel*. London: SCM, 1960
Brooks, Melvin. *Transformed by the Light: The Powerful Effects of Near Death Experiences on People's Lives*. New York: Villard, 1982
Brown, Francis, S. R. Driver, and Charles A. Briggs. *A Hebrew and English Lexicon of the Old Testament*. Oxford: Clarendon, 1976
Brueggemann, Walter. *David's Truth in Israel's Imagination & Memory*. Philadelphia: Fortress, 1985
———. *Genesis, A Bible Commentary for Teaching and Preaching*. Atlanta: John Knox, 1982
———. *Power, Providence, and Personality*. Louisville: Westminster/John Knox, 1990
Buber, Martin, *Kingship of God*. 3rd ed., translated by Richard Scheimann. New York: Harper & Row, 1967)
———. *Moses: The Revelation and the Covenant*. Harper Torchbooks #27, 1958
———. *The Prophetic Faith*. Harper Torchbooks #73, 1960

Bibliography

Burnett, Joel S. *A Reassessment of Biblical Elohim.* Atlanta: Society of Biblical Literature, 2001
Butler, Trent C. *Joshua.* Waco: Word, 1983
Buttenwieser, Moses. *The Psalms, Chronologically Treated with a New Translation.* New York: KTAV, 1969 reprint of 1st ed. 1938
Carman, John B. *Majesty & Meekness: A Comparative Study of Contrast and Harmony in the Concept of God.* Grand Rapids: Eerdmans, 1994
Charlesworth, James H, ed. *The Old Testament Pseudepigrapha I, Apocalyptic Literature and Testaments.* Garden City: Doubleday, 1983
Chilton, Bruce D. and Craig A. Evans, eds. *Authenticating the Activities of Jesus.* Leiden, Boston: Brill, 1999
Carroll, James. *Constantine's Sword: The Church and the Jews.* Boston, New York: Houghton Mifflin, 2001
Childs, Brevard S. *The Book of Exodus: a Critical, Theological Commentary.* Philadelphia: Westminster, 1974
Clabeaux, John J. "Marcion." In *ABD* 4:514–516
Clark, William, and Michael Grundstein. *Are We Hardwired? The Role of Genes in Human Behavior.* New York: Oxford, 2000
Clifford, Richard J. *The Cosmic Mountain in Canaan and the Old Testament.* Cambridge: Harvard University Press, 1972
Clines, David J. A. "The Ten Commandments." In *Interested Parties: The Ideology of Writers and Readers of the Hebrew Bible.* Sheffield: Sheffield Academic, 1995
Cornfeld, Gaalya, Gen. Ed. *Josephus, The Jewish War: Newly Translated with Extensive Commentary and Archaeological Background Illustrations.* Grand Rapids: Zondervan, 1982
Craffert, Pieter F. *The Life of a Galilean Shaman: Jesus of Nazareth in Anthropological-Historical Perspective.* Eugene OR: Cascade, 2008
Craigie, Peter C. *Psalms 1-50.* Waco: Word, 1983
Cross, Frank Moore. *Canaanite Myth and Hebrew Epic: Essays in the History of the Religion of Israel.* Cambridge MA: Harvard University Press, 1973
———. *From Epic to Canon: History and Literature in Ancient Israel.* Baltimore: Johns Hopkins University Press, 1998
Crossan, John Dominic, and Jonathan Reed. *In Search of Paul: How Jesus' Apostle Opposed Rome's Empire with God's Kingdom.* HarperSanFrancisco, 2004
———, *The Historical Jesus: The Life of a Mediterranean Jewish Peasant.* HarperSanFrancisco, 1992
Crüsemann, Frank. "Human Solidarity and Ethnic Identity: Israel's Self-Definition in the Genealogical System of Genesis." In Mark G. Brett, ed. *Ethnicity and the Bible.* Leiden, New York: Brill, 1996
Dahood, Mitchell. *Psalms III 101-150: Introduction, Translation, and Notes.* Garden City: Doubleday, 1970
Damasio, Antonio. *Descartes' Error: Emotion, Reason and the Human Brain.* London: Vintage Books, 2006
Davies, James. "The Rationalization of Suffering: Contrary narratives of emotional discontent interplay in complex ways." In *Harvard Divinity Bulletin* 39/1 & 2, 2011
Dearman, John Andrew. *Property Rights in the Eighth-Century Prophets.* Atlanta: Scholars Press, 1988
Dever, William G. *What Did the Biblical Writers Know and When Did They Know It?: What Archaeology Can Tell Us about the Reality of Ancient Israel.* Grand Rapids: Eerdmans, 2001
Dungan, David. *Constantine's Bible: Politics and the Making of the New Testament.* Minneapolis: Fortress, 2007
Durham, John I. *Exodus.* Waco: Word, 1987
Fenn, Richard. *The Death of Herod: An Essay in the Sociology of Religion.* Cambridge UK: Cambridge University Press, 1992
Flanagan, James W. "Judah in All Israel." In Flanagan and Anita Weisbrod Robinson, eds. *No Famine in the Land: Studies in Honor of John L. McKenzie.* Claremont: Scholars Press, 1975
Frankfort, H. and H. A., John A. Wilson, Thorkild Jacobsen. *Before Philosophy: The Intellectual Adventure of Ancient Man.* Baltimore: Penguin, 1963
Freedman, David Noel. *Divine Commitment and Human Obligation.* Grand Rapids: Eerdmans, 1997
———, ed. *The Anchor Bible Dictionary,* New York: Doubleday, 1997, 1992

Fredriksen, Paula. "Judaizing the Nations: The Ritual Demands of Paul's Gospel." *New Testament Studies* 56, 2010

Fry, Douglas P. *Beyond War: The Human Potential for Peace.* New York: Oxford, 2007

Garr, W. Randall. *In His Own Image and Likeness: Humanity, Divinity, and Monotheism.* Leiden: Brill, 2003

Gelander, Shamai. *David and His God: Religious Ideas as Reflected in Biblical Historiography and Literature.* Jerusalem: Simor, 1991

Gottwald, Norman K. "Israel's Emergence in Canaan." *Bible Review* V:6, 1989

———. *The Hebrew Bible—A Socio-Literary Introduction.* Philadelphia: Fortress, 1985

———. *The Tribes of Yahweh: A Sociology of the Religion of Liberated Israel 1250-1050 B.C.E.* Maryknoll NY: Orbis, 1979

Gray, John. *I & II Kings: A Commentary.* Philadelphia: Westminster, 1963

———. *The Legacy of Canaan: The Ras Shamra Texts and Their Relevance to the Old Testament.* Leiden: Brill, 1957

Green, Joel B. *Body, Soul, and Human Life: The Nature of Humanity in the Bible.* Grand Rapids: Baker, 2008

Greengus, Samuel. "Biblical and *ANE* Law" Under "Law." In *ABD* 4:242–52.

Gulley, Philip, and James Mulholland. *If Grace is True: Why God will Save Every Person.* New York: HarperOne, 2004

Halpern, Baruch. *The Emergence of Israel in Canaan.* Chico: Scholars Press, 1983

———, "The Uneasy Compromise: Israel between League and Monarchy." In Baruch Halpern and Jon D. Levenson. *Traditions in Transformation: Turning Points in Biblical Faith.* Winona Lake: Eisenbrauns, 1981

Harrill, J. Albert. "Divine Judgment against Ananias and Sapphira (Acts 5:1–11): A Stock Scene of Perjury and Death." *JBL* 130/2, 2011

Haymon, Peter. "Monotheism—A Misused Word in Jewish Studies?" *Journal of Jewish Studies*, 42/1, 1991

Hays, J. Daniel. "Moses: The Private Man Behind the Public Leader." *Bible Review* XIV:4, 2000

Herrmann, Siegfried, *A History of Israel in Old Testament Times.* London: SCM, 1975

Herzog, William R. *Parables as Subversive Speech: Jesus as Pedagogue of the Oppressed.* Louisville: Westminster/John Knox, 1994

Hick, John H. *An Interpretation of Religion: Human Responses to the Transcendent.* New Haven: Yale University Press, 1989

———. *Death and Eternal Life.* New York: Harper and Rowe, 1976

———. *The Second Christianity.* London: SCM, 1983

Hollenbach, Paul W. "John the Baptist." In *ABD* 3:887–89

Horsley, Richard A., and John S. Hanson. *Bandits, Prophets, and Messiahs: Popular Movements in the Time of Jesus.* Minneapolis: Winston, 1985

Hurowitz, Victor. "Picturing Imageless Deities: Iconography in the Ancient Near East" *BAR* VII/3 1997

Hurtado, Larry W. *One God One Lord: Early Christian Devotion and Ancient Jewish Monotheism.* Philadelphia: Fortress, 1988

Isaac, E. translator. "1 (Ethiopic Apocalypse of) Enoch." In James H. Charlesworth, ed., *The Old Testament Pseudepigrapha I.* Garden City: Doubleday, 1983

Ishida, Ei-ichirō. "Futatsu no Sekaikan" ("Two Worldviews") *Tō-Sai Shō*: In *Nihon, Seiyō, Ningen (East-West Miscellanies: Japan, the West, Humanity).* Tōkyō: Chikuma Shobō, 1967

Jacob, Benno. *The Second Book of the Bible: Exodus.* Hoboken: KTAV, 1992

Jeremias, Joachim. *Jerusalem in the Time of Jesus.* Philadelphia: Fortress, 1969

———. *The Prayers of Jesus.* London: SCM, 1967

Keefe, Alice A. *Woman's Body and the Social Body in Hosea.* Sheffield: Academic, 2001

Kerkeslager, Allen. "Mt. Sinai—in Arabia?" *Bible Review* XVI/2, 2000.

Kim, Seyoon. *Paul and the New Perspective: Second Thoughts on the Origins of Paul's Gospel.* Grand Rapids: Eerdmans, 2002

Kitchen, Kenneth A. "Where Did Solomon's Gold Go?" and "Shishak's Military Campaign in Israel Confirmed." *BAR* XV/3, 1989

Kraelin, Carl H. *John the Baptist.* New York: Charles Scribner's Sons, 1951

Bibliography

Knoppers, Gary. "Intermarriage, Social Complexity, and Ethnic Diversity in the Genealogy of Judah." *JBL* 120/1 2001

Lampe, G. H. W. *God as Spirit.* Oxford: Clarendon, 1977

Lang, Bernhard. *Monotheism and the Prophetic Minority.* Sheffield: Almond, 1983

———."No God but Yahweh! The Origin and Character of Biblical Monotheism." *Concilium* 177/1, 1985

———. *The Hebrew God: Portrait of an Ancient Deity.* New Haven: Yale University Press, 2002

Leeuwen, Arend Theodoor, van. *Christianity in World History.* New York: Charles Scribner's Sons, 1964

Levenson, Jon D. *Creation and the Persistence of Evil.* San Francisco: Harper & Row, 1988

———. *Sinai and Zion: An Entry into the Jewish Bible.* Minneapolis: Winston, 1985

———. *The Death and Resurrection of the Beloved Son: The Transformation of Child Sacrifice in Judaism and Christianity.* New Haven: Yale University Press, 1993

———. *The Hebrew Bible, the Old Testament, and Historical Criticism: Jews and Christians in Biblical Studies.* Louisville: Westminster/John Knox. 1993

Levin, Yigal. "Did Pharaoh Sheshonq attack Jerusalem?" *BAR* 38/4, 2012

Lohfink, Norbert. *Theology of the Pentateuch: Themes of the Priestly Narrative and Deuteronomy.* Minneapolis: Fortress, 1994

Longeneker, Richard N. *Galatians.* Dallas: Word, 1990

McClelland, Mac. "To Catch a Warlord." *Mother Jones,* September + October 2011

McGrath, James F. *The Only True God: Early Christian Monotheism in its Jewish Context.* Urbana: University of Illinois Press, 2009

Maier, Johan. "Self-Definition, Prestige, and Status of Priests Toward the End of the Second Temple Period." *Biblical Theology Bulletin,* 23/4, 1993

Malone, Calvin. "A Little Closer Home." *Fellowship,* 7/1–3, 2011

———. *Razor-wire Dharma: A Buddhist Life in Prison.* Somerville MA: Wisdom Publications, 2008

Marshall, Jay W. *Israel and the Book of the Covenant: An Anthropological Approach to Biblical Law.* Atlanta: Scholars Press, 1993

Martin, Troy, "Paul's Argument from Nature for the Veil in 1 Corinthians 11:13–15: A Testicle Instead of a Head Covering." *JBL* 123/1, 2004

Mayes, A. D. H. *Deuteronomy.* Grand Rapids: Eerdmans, 1979

———. *Israel in the Period of the Judges.* Naperville: Allenson, 1974

Mays, James L. *Psalms, a Bible Commentary for Teaching and Preaching.* Louisville: John Knox, 1994

Mendels, Doron. "Why Paul Went West: The Differences Between the Jewish Diasporas." *BAR* 37/1, 2011

Mendenhall, George E. *The Tenth Generation: the Origins of the Biblical Tradition.* Baltimore: Johns Hopkins University Press, 1973

Meyer, Ben F. "Appointed Deed, Appointed Doer: Jesus and the Scriptures." In Bruce D. Chilton and Craig A. Evans, eds. *Authenticating the Activities of Jesus.* Leiden, Boston: Brill, 1999

Miles, Jack. *God: A Biography.* New York: Random House, 1995

Miller, Patrick D. "Man and Woman: Toward a Theological Anthropology." In J. Cheryl Exum and H. G. M. Williamson, eds. *Reading from Right to Left: Essays on the Hebrew Bible in Honour of David J. A. Clines.* London: T & T Clark, 2003

———. *The Religion of Ancient Israel.* Louisville: Westminster/John Knox, 2000

Moor, Johannes C. de. *The Rise of Yahwism: The Roots of Israelite Monotheism.* Leuven: University Press, 1977

Morse, Melvin. *Transformed by the Light: The Powerful Effects of Near Death Experiences on People's Lives.* New York: Villard, 1982

Myers, Ched. *Binding the Strong Man: a Political Reading of Mark's Story of Jesus.* Maryknoll, NY: Orbis, 1990

Nelson, Richard D. *Raising Up a Faithful Priest: Community and Priesthood in Biblical Theology.* Louisville: Westminster/John Knox, 1993

Nelson-Pallmeyer, Jack. *Jesus Against Christianity: Reclaiming the Missing Jesus.* Harrisburg PA: Trinity Press, 2001

Newberg, Andrew and Mark Waldman. *How God Changes Your Brain.* Random House, 2009

———, Eugene d'Aquili, and Vince Rause. *Why God Won't Go Away: Brain Science and the Biology of Belief.* New York: Ballentine, 2001

Nicholson, E. W. *Preaching to the Exiles: A study of the Prose Traditions in the Book of Jeremiah.* Oxford: Basil Blackwell, 1970

Nickelsberg, George. "The Book of Parables or Similitudes," chapters 37–71, "Enoch, First Book of" in *ABD* 2:509-517.

Nielsen, Eduard. *The Ten Commandments in New Perspective: A Traditio-historical Approach.* Naperville: Allenson, 1968

Noth, Martin. *Exodus: A Commentary.* London: SCM, 1962

——. *The Laws in the Pentateuch and other Essays.* Edinburgh: Oliver & Boyd, 1966

Oak Ridge Environmental Peace Alliance. *Reflections for Nonviolent Community, A book of Readings.* PO Box 5743, Oak Ridge, Tennessee, 2010

O'Collins, Gerald. *Salvation for All: God's Other People.* New York: Oxford, 2008

Office of the General Assembly, Presbyterian Church (USA). *Constitution of the Presbyterian Church USA Part I Book of Confessions.* Louisville, 2007

Pedersen, Johs. *Israel: Its life and culture.* Vol. 1-2. London: Oxford, 1926

Pew Forum on Religion and Public Life/Surveys. http://pewforum.org/docs/?DocID=380 Dec 18, 2008

Philippi, Donald L. *Kojiki: Translated with an Introduction and Notes.* Tokyo: University of Tokyo Press, 1968

Pinker, Steven. *The Better Angels of our Nature: Why Violence has Declined.* New York: Viking Penguin, 2011

Plaut, W. Gunther, ed. *The Torah: A Modern Commentary.* Revised Edition. New York: Union for Reform Judaism, 2005

Polley, Max E. *Amos and the Davidic Empire: A Socio-Historical Approach.* New York: Oxford, 1989

Pritchard, James B. ed. *The Ancient Near East Vol. I, An Anthology of Texts and Pictures* Princeton NJ: Princeton University Press, 1958

——. *The Ancient Near East Vol. II, A New Anthology of Texts and Pictures.* Princeton NJ: Princeton University Press, 1975

Propp, William H. C. *Exodus 1–18: A New Translation with Introduction and Commentary.* New York: Doubleday, 1999

Rad, Gerhard von. *Genesis: A Commentary.* London: SCM, 1961

Rainey, Anson. "Where Did the Early Israelites Come From" and "Who Were the Early Israelites?" *BAR* 34/6, 2008

Rehm, Merlin D. "Levites and Priests." In *ABD* 4:297–310

Rendtorff, Rolf. "The Gēr in the Priestly Laws of the Pentateuch." In Mark G. Brett, ed. *Ethnicity and the Bible.* New York, Leiden: Brill, 1996

Ring, Kenneth. *Heading Toward Omega: In Search of the Meaning of the Near-Death Experience.* New York: William Morrow, 1984

Robertson, Edwin. *Dietrich Bonhoeffer's Prison Poems.* Grand Rapids: Zondervan, 1999

Rolston, Holmes, III. *Genes, Genesis, and God: Values and their Origins in Natural and Human History.* Cambridge UK: Cambridge University Press, 1999

Rose, Jacqueline. *The Question of Zion.* Princeton and Oxford: Princeton University Press, 2005

Rowley, H. H. *The Faith of Israel: Aspects of Old Testament Thought.* Philadelphia: Westminster, 1956

Rubenstein, Richard E. *When Jesus Became God: The Epic Fight over Christ's Divinity in the Last Days of Rome.* New York: Harcourt & Brace, 1999

Rusch, William G. *The Trinitarian Controversy.* Philadelphia: Fortress Press, 1980

Sagan, Carl. *The Dragons of Eden: Speculation on the Growth of Human Intelligence.* New York: Random House, 1977

Saggs, H. W. F. *The Encounter with the Divine in Mesopotamia and Israel.* London: Athlone, 1978

Sandars, N. K. *Poems of Heaven and Hell from Ancient Mesopotamia.* Harmondsworth: Penguin, 1971

Sanders, E. P. *Paul and Palestinian Judaism.* Philadelphia: Fortress, 1977

Segal, Alan F. *Paul the Convert: The Apostolate and Apostasy of Saul the Pharisee,* New Haven: Yale University Press, 1990

Schottroff, Luise, and Wolfgang Stegemann. "The Sabbath Was Made for Man: The Interpretation of Mark 2:23–38." In Willy Schottroff and Wolfgang Stegemann. *God of the Lowly: Socio-Historical Interpretation of the Bible.* Maryknoll NY: Orbis, 1984

Bibliography

Seitz, Christopher R. *Isaiah 1–39, A Bible Commentary for Teaching and Preaching*. Louisville: John Knox, 1993

———. *Word without End: The Old Testament as Abiding Theological Witness*. Grand Rapids: Eerdmans, 1998

———. *Zion's Final Destiny: The Development of the Book of Isaiah*. Minneapolis: Fortress, 1991

Shantz, Colleen. *Paul in Ecstasy: The Neurobiology of the Apostle's Life and Thought*. New York: Cambridge, 2009

Shogren, Gary, "Forgiveness in the New Testament; B. Forgiveness by God." In *ABD* 2:835–6

Speiser, E. A. *Genesis: Introduction, Translation, and Notes*. Garden City, NY: Doubleday, 1964)

Staples, Jason A. "What Do the Gentiles Have to Do with 'All Israel'? A Fresh Look at Romans 11:35–37" *JBL* 130/2, 2011

Stegemann, Ekkehard W., and Wolfgang Stegemann. *The Jesus Movement: A Social History of Its First Century*. Translated by O. C. Dean Jr. Minneapolis: Fortress, 1999

Tate, Marvin E. *Psalms 50–100*. Dallas: Word, 1990

Taylor, Arch B. Jr. "Male-Female-Nature-Scripture." *Treatises* (*Ronshū*) No. 26, 1973, Shikoku Christian College, Zentsuji, Japan.

Taylor, Jill Bolte. *My Stroke of Insight: A Brain Scientist's Personal Journey*. New York: Viking, 2006

Taylor, Vincent. *The Gospel According to Mark*. London: Macmillan, 1957

Terrien, Samuel. *The Elusive Presence: Toward a New Biblical Theology*. San Francisco: Harper and Row, 1978

Theissen, Gerd. *Biblical Faith: An Evolutionary Approach*, translated by. John Bowden. Philadelphia: Fortress, 1984

Torrance, Thomas F. *The Mediation of Christ*. Colorado Springs: Helmers and Howard, 1992

Trible, Phyllis. *God and the Rhetoric of Sexuality*. Philadelphia: Fortress, 1978

Voegelin, Eric. *Order and History Vol I: Israel and Revelation*. Baton Rouge: LSU Press, 1956

———. *Order and History Vol II: The World of the Polis*. Baton Rouge: LSU Press, 1957

Waetjen, Herman C. *A Reordering of Power: A Sociopolitical Reading of Mark's Gospel*. Minneapolis: Fortress, 1989

Walters, Stanley D. "The Jacob Narrative." In *ADB* 3:599–608.

Warfield, Benjamin B. *The Plan of Salvation*. Grand Rapids: Eerdmans, 1942

Watts, John D. W. *Isaiah 1–33*. Waco: Word, 1985

———. *Isaiah 34–66*. Waco: Word, 1987

Weber, Thomas. *Gandhi as Disciple and Mentor*. Cambridge UK, Cambridge University Press, 2004

Welch, Adam C. *Prophet and Priest in Old Israel*. Oxford: Basil Blackwell, 1953

Westermann, Claus. *Genesis 1–11: A Commentary*. Minneapolis: Augsburg, 1984

———. *Genesis 12–36: A Commentary*. Minneapolis: Augsburg, 1985

Williamson, H. G. M. *1 and 2 Chronicles*. Grand Rapids: Eerdmans, 1982

Wilson, Robert W. "The Old Testament Genealogies in Recent Research." *JBL* 94, 1975

Wink, Walter. *The Human Being: Jesus and the Enigma of the Son of the Man*. Minneapolis: Fortress, 2002)

———. *The Powers Vol 1, Naming the Powers: The Language of Power in the New Testament*. Philadelphia: Fortress, 1984

———. *The Powers Vol 2, Unmasking the Powers: The Invisible Forces that Determine Human Existence*. Philadelphia: Fortress Press, 1986

———. *The Powers: Vol 3 Engaging the Powers: Discernment and Resistance in a World of Domination*. Minneapolis: Fortress, 1992

Young, T. Cuyler Jr. "Cyrus (Person)." In *ABD* 1:1231–32

Scripture Index

OLD TESTAMENT

Genesis

	8
1	27, 29, 328
1:1	26n12, 33, 84, 357
1:1–2	34, 327
1:1–2:4a	26, 28, 29, 38, 40, 44, 52, 141, 172, 177, 185, 193
1:1–3	34n2
1:1–5	26
1:1–16:16	327
1:1–31	327
1:3	270
1–3	41, 106
1:6–7	178
1:6–8	27n13
1:6–13	27
1:6–30	27
1:11–12	34
1:14–17	27
1–16	73, 74
1:20–25	27
1:21	27
1:26	34, 185, 185n20
1:26–27	73, 327, 333, 337, 349
1:26–28	107
1:27	40, 185n20, 235
1:27–8	19, 41
1:27–28	34
1:28b–2:1	178
1:31	232, 301
2: 21–23	40
2:4b	141
2:4b–3:24	38, 52, 141, 143, 193, 328
2:7	39, 271, 286
2:7, 9, 19, 21–23	328
2:8	143
2:9, 17	143
2:11–12	143
2:15	39, 143
2:15–24	186
2:16–17	39
2:18	39, 40
2:18, 20	40n6
2:18, 21	299
2:19	39, 39n4
2:20	143
2:24	40, 143, 235
2:25	143
3:1	41
3:5–6	42
3:6	143
3:7, 21	42
3:7–13	42
3:12	143
3:15	42
3:19	328
3:22	143
3:22–24	42
3:23	143
3:24	144
4:13	285
4:26	38
5:1	40, 185n20

Scripture Index

Genesis–continued

Reference	Page
5:1–2	19
5:2	27
5:3	185, 185n20
5:24	204, 253
6:2, 4	34
6:17b–18a	188
6:18	43
9:5–6	187
9:5b, 6b	187
9:6a	187
9:8–13	188
9:8–17	43, 69, 101
9:12–17	188
10:15–18	67n10
11:30	65
12:1–3	328
12:1–4a	63
12:2	80
12:2, 7	65
12:6	117
12:6–7	78n4
12:10–20	63
13:14–15	65
13:16	80
13:18	65
14:5	80
14:7–20	69
14:13	65, 88n22, 111
14:14–16	65
14:17–24	78
14:21–24	65
15	68, 69, 93, 188
15:1	66
15:1–5	65
15:1–6	68
15:4	67
15:5	285
15:6	65
15:7	65
15:9–21	66
15:12	66
15:17–18	101
15:18b	67
15:19	67
15:20–21	67
16	68
16:7–14	78
16:11	68
16:13	68
16:15–16	68
17	9, 10, 68, 73, 143, 188
17:1	62, 328
17:1–6	68
17:1–14	101
17:5	80
17:5–7	285
17:7–14	68
17:12	79
17:15–22	68
17:18, 20	80
17:23	80
18:12	178
18:22–33	256
20:1–18	63
20:7a	97
20:8	97
20:12a	98
20:13	98
20:14	98
20:15	98
20:16	98
20:17a	98
21:22–33	64
21:22–34	69, 78
22:1–19	115
22:17	80
22:18	285
23:1–20	69, 111
23:12–18	80
23–24	143
25:1–2	83
25:1–4	68, 80
25:12–18	68n14
25:19–34	73, 74
25:29–34	68
26:3, 24	86
26:12–33	69
26:24	86
26:26–33	64
26:34	80, 111
27:1–28:5	73
27:1–40	68
27:1–46	74
28:1–15	74
28:3	62
28:9	80
28:10–22	79

Scripture Index

28:16–22	74	3:1–2	84
28:18	96	3:4	86n13
29:1–30:43	74	3:6	85, 86n13
31:3	86	3:7–8	85
31:43–54	64	3:8	85n9
32:3–21	78	3:8, 17	67n10
32:22–32	78	3:11	86n13
32:24–30	256	3:11–12	85
33:1–11	78	3:12	86, 88, 134
33:10	256	3:13	85, 120
33:18–20	78, 117, 119, 131	3:13–15	38, 62, 87
34:1–31	79	3:14	88
34:28	89	3:17	85n9
35	68	3:18	88, 89n25
35:1	317	4:5	85
35:1–7	148	4:22	82, 217
35:1–15	79	4:22–23	287n10
35:2	95	4:23	89n25
35:11	62, 285	5:1	89n25
35:14	96	5:3	88n23
36:1–42	80	6:2–3	29, 38, 62, 185n18
37	130	6:2–8	82
38	76	6:5–7	101
39:14, 17	88n22	6:11	89n25
40:15	88n22	7:2	89n25
41:12	88n22	7:16	88n23
41:45, 50	77	8:1, 8, 20	89n25
43:14	62	8:16–19	228
43:32	88n22	9:1, 13	88n23, 89n25
46:2–3	82	10:3	88n23, 89n25
46:3	85	12:31–32	89n25
46:20	77	12:38	79, 89
48:1–22	77	12:43–44	80
48:3	62	12:48	80
48:8–16	77	15:20–21	330
48:19	77, 285, 289	15:22–17:16	88
49:24	148n6	15:24	101
49:25	62	15:29	234
		16:2–3	101
Exodus		16:23–29	97
		17:1–7	101, 220
2:1–3:22	75	18	89
2:1–10	75, 330	18:1	89
2:1–22	82	18:1–27	68
2:15–22	68	18:3–4	85
2:18	82n1	18:4	40n6
2:23–24	82	18:11–12	89
2:24–25	101	18:12–27	92
3:1	82n1	18:13–27	89

Scripture Index

Exodus–continued

Reference	Page
18:16	94
19:1–24:18	91
19:5	95n13
19:5–6	333
19:5–6 NJPS	331
19:8	102
19:16	93n8
19–24	109, 154
20:2	94, 101
20:2–3	94n12
20:3–4	101
20:4	203
20:4a	96
20:5	264n3
20:11	91n3
20:17	91n3
20:18	5, 93n8
20:22–23:19	94n10, 104
20:23–23:19	99
20:23–26	113
20:24	329
20:24–22:16	112
20:24–23:19	75, 110n2, 112
20:24–26	147
21:2	165
21:7–10	165
21:7–11	114
21:20–21	114
22:7–9 H 22:6–8	114
22:9 H 22:8	114
22:10–11 H 22:9–10	114
22:17–23:19	112
22:20	115
22:21	115
22:22–24	115
22:25	116, 246
22:25–27	165
22:26–27	243
22:27	116
22:28 H 27	114
22:29b H 22:28b	115
22:29b–30 H 2:28b–29	115
23:3	116
23:6–8	116
23:9	115
23:10–11	115
23:12	115
23:13	115
23:17	115, 116
23:19	115
23:20	281n10
23:20–21	317
23:23–33	69
23:28	67n10
24:1–8	75
24:3	75
24:3–8	99
24:4	96
24:5	331
24:7	99, 102, 112
24:9–11	99
24:12	94n10
24:15–31:18	102
31:18	94n10
32	96
32:10	102
32:11–14	256
32:12–16	103
32:14	102
32:15	102
32:15–16	94n10
32:16	94n10
32:19	94n10
32:25–29	102
32:31–32	103
32–34	109
32:35	102
33:2	67n10
33:7–11	109
33:18–20	103
33:19	104
33:22	103
34:6	104
34:6–7	103, 104
34:10	104
34:10–26	94n10
34:11	67n10
34:11–26	104
34:14	264n3
34:17–26	94n10
34:27–28	94n10
34:28	94n10, 104
35:4–40:38	109

Leviticus

Reference	Page
	109
13–14	227n19

18:18	161	5:8	203
19:18	213	5:9	264n3
21	329n5	5:15	91n3
24:10–12	89n28	5:21	91n3
25:23	231, 247	5:22	94n10
25:36–37	246	6:4–5	213
25:44–46	114	6:10–14	220
26:11	295	6:15	264n3
		7:1	67n10
		7:1–6	69
		8:3, 5	219

Numbers

1:1–46	110	10:1–5	100n29
1:5	66	10:17	28
1:6	66	12:2–28	113
1:12	66	15:12–17	114
10:29	82n1	18:9–12	151
11:24–29	306	18–13	242
11:26–29	331	18:16	331
12:1–15	331	20:17	67n10
13–14	110	21:22–23	264
14:22–23	101	23:1	308
16:3	330	23:1–6	80n8, 192
16:18–40	330	23:6–7	80
16:36–40	27n13	23:7–8	68
21:29	66n9	23:19–20	246
25	83	24:1–4	158, 235
25:1–13	102, 264	26:12	232
25:1–18	68	26:16–28:68	110
25:11	264n3	28:1–14	106
26	110	28:15–46	106
31	83	28:47–68	239
31:1–12	79	29:4 H 29:3	288
31:13–20	79	29:20	264n3
31–32	110	32	96
34:1–15	110	32:18	96
34:16–29	110	32:31	96
34:16–39	118	32:43	285
		33:2	83
		33:7, 26, 29	40n6
		34:5	204

Deuteronomy

	110
2:1–6	68
4:6	96
4:24	264n3
4:25–26	110
5:1–22	99n27
5:1–33	91
5:6	101
5:7–8	101

Joshua

	110n3
8:30–35	75, 117
9:1	67n10
9:1–27	79
11:3	67n10
11:16–23	118

373

Scripture Index

Joshua–continued

12:7–24	118
12:8	67n10
13:1	118
13:13	118
13–19	76
15:8, 63	76n2
15:63	118
16:10	118
17:11–12	121
18:1–19:51	118, 127
18:28	76n2
19:51	110
19:59	118
22:1–34	134n16
24	78n4
24:1	118
24:1–28	75, 131
24:2, 14	118
24:2–13	119
24:9	264n3
24:11	67n10
24:14–15	119
24:23	95
24:25	119
24:26	96
24:29	119
24:31	75, 119

Judges

	10, 110
1:5–8, 21	118
1:7–8	76n2
1:16	83
1:21	76n2
1:27	118
1:27–35	121
2:6–15	75
2:7	119
2:10b	119
2:11–19	119
2:18	75
2:20–3:6	120
3:2–39	123
3:5	67n10
3:5–6	111
4:1–2	118
4:4	121
4–5	121, 330
4:6–9	121
4:11	82n1, 83
4:11, 17	121
4:15	121
4:18–20	121
5	121
5:3, 5	121
5:4–5	83, 121
5:8b	121
5:11, 13	121
5:14	122
5:17	122
5:20–21	121
6–8	83
6–9	120
6:11	120
6:16	120
6:30–32	120
8	120n6
8:22–23	120
8:27	121
8:33	121
9	120n6
9:1–46	121
11	122
11:1–11	122
11:11	113
11:12–28	122
11:34–40	122
13–16	123
17:1–13	122
17:6	127
17–21	122, 329n6
18:1	122, 127
18:1–31	123
19:1	122, 127
19:1–30	123
19:10–12	76n2
19:23	123
20:6	123
20–21	123
20:26–28	113
21:1–14	123
21:15–24	123
21:19–23	127
21:25	123, 127

Scripture Index

Ruth

1:16–17	79
4:13–22	130

1 Samuel

	110, 127
1:1	128n2
1:3	113
1:7, 24	127
1:17–20	127
2:22	127
3:15	127
4:1–7:2	128
4:10–22	5
6:1–16	132
6:5, 11	186
7:3–13	128
7:12	96
7:14–17	128
7:15–16	113
7:15–18	128
8:1–9	128
8:10–18	146
8:11–18	129
8:19–21	75
8:20	129
9:1–9	330
9–11	129
9:16	129
10:1–14	306
10–11	129
11:1–15	129
12:1–25	129
12:11	120n6
14:47–48	129
14:52	146
15:35	129
16:1–7	146
16:13–14	130
19:12–13	136n18
19:18–24	306
20:5ff	97n21
22:2	131
22:6–8	146
23:6	133

2 Samuel

	110, 127
1:12	129
2:1–4	131
3:2–5	132
3:3	132
3:10	132
5:1–5	130n5
5:3	132
5:5	132
5:6–6:19	132
5:6–9	76n2
5:6–10	132, 161
5:6–12	118
5:7	132
5:11–12	132
5:13–14	132
5:17–25	132
5:18, 22	67
6:1, 5, 15, 19	133
6:1–15	133
6:17–19	132
7:2	133
7:5–7	134, 134n12
7:12–14	168
7:13	134
8:2, 6, 14	131
8:17	133
10:19	131
11:1	129
13	123n9
14:17, 20	143
14:17–24	132
15:24	133
20:24	136, 140
21:1–10	79
22	278n7
23:13	67
24:1–9	136
24:1–17	140
24:18–25	133

1 Kings

	110, 127
1:1–2:35	132
1:1–2:46a	137
2:39	133n11
2:46b–3:1	137

Scripture Index

I Kings–continued

Reference	Page
3:3	143
3:4	79, 133n11
3:9	137, 143
3–10	141
3–11	143
4:6	140
4:20	137
4:25	137
4:31	143
4:33	143
5:1–9:9	138
5:13–18	136, 139
5:14	140
6:12–13	150
6:23–29, 32, 35	144
6:29	143
8:7	91n2
8:13	139
8:54–55	132
9:4–9	150
9:7–9	144
9:10–13	137
9:13	64
9:15–22	136
9:16	118
9:21	137
9:26–28	143
10:2, 10, 11	143
10:22	143
10:23	143
10:26–29	143
11:1	137
11:1–8	150
11:1–25	78n4
11:2	143
11:3–4	143
11:5, 33	138
11:7–8	138
11:11	138
11:12–13	150
11:12–13, 32, 34, 36	142
11:14–22	138n2
11:14–25	140
11:26–40	140
11:32	140
11:32, 34, 36, 38	150
11:43	138
12:1–19	140
12:15, 21–24	140
12:19	140
12:20–14:20	138
12:26–33	148
14:7	145
14:9	148
14:13	145n1
14:21	138
14:23	127n1
14:26	141
14:30	150
15:6–20	150
15:9–13	150
15:11	150n9
15:12	127n1
15:16–24	145
15:22	151
15:30	145n1
16:1–23	146
16:2	145
16:13	148
16:24	147
16:26, 13	145n1
17:1	148
17:1, 14	145n1
17:1–16	229
17:8–24	148, 152
17:17–24	227
18:21	149
18:30–31	113
18:30–40	149
19:1–12	93
19:8	91n2
19:10, 14	113
20:1–43	147
20:30–34	64
21:5–6	114
21:12	113
21:14	113
21:15, 17	113
21:21–23	113
21:22	114
22:1–4	151
22:13	113
22:43	150n9
22:46	127n1
22:53	145n1
32	143
35	143

Scripture Index

2 Kings

	110, 127
2:11	204
3:4–7	151
3:13–17	306
3:26–7	168
4:18–37	227
4:23	97n21
5:1–14	229
5:1–19	153, 344
6:8–23	153, 344
7:11	157
8:9	100n29
8:19	142
9:1–10:27	149
9:1–13	149
9:6	145n1
10:1–31	102
10:15–17	149
10:31	145n1
11:1–20	150
11:8	138
11:18	186
12:2	150n9
14:1–14	151
14:3	150n9
14:8–14	145
14:17–21	151
14:25	145n1
15:2	150n9
15:19–20	157
15:22	177n1
15:34	150n9
16:1–9	168n6
16:1–20	169
16:5–9	151
16:7	168
17:1–4	157
17:1–23	151n10
17:5–6	157
17:7–20	173
17:24–41	190n1
18:3, 5, 8	169
18:3–7	151
18:13	169
18:13–20:19	170
18:29	113
19:1–37	151
19:34	142
19:35–37	169
20:12–19	151
22:10–14	330
22:13	138
22–23	113
23:1–24a	152
23:7	127n1
23:24b–25	152
23:26–27	152
23:28–35	152
24:7	152
24:18–25:21	152
30:1–17	169
31:1–3	169

1 Chronicles

2:55	149
6:33–38	128n2
14:7	120n4
16:1–49	133n11

2 Chronicles

12:2–8	141
36:22–23	183, 189

Ezra

1:1–4	183
1:2–4	189
1:5–11	189
3:1–13	189
4:1–3	192
4:2	190n1
4:2–4	191
5:1–17	191
6:1–22	190
6:3–6	183
7:11–26	183, 191
7:41, 26	191
9:1	67n10
9–10	80, 192
10	238
40:3–4	183

Nehemiah

10:32	214

377

Scripture Index

Nehemiah—continued

13	238
13:3	89n28
13:23–31	80

Job

1:6	34
2:1	34
7:20	107
10:8	107
34:17	28
37:18	27n13
38:7	34
41:28	179

Psalms

2	168, 219, 253
2:7–9	218
7	132
8:4	252
9	132
18	132, 278n7
18:50	285
20:2	40n6
21	132
24:1	292, 301
29	92, 92n6
33	69
33:5b	104
33:20	40n6
33:22	70
44:22	351
44:26	351
45	168
45:6	134
46	132
47	132
48:2b	139
50	132, 134n16, 329n5
56	132
57	132
65:1–3	108
68:7–8	83
70:5	40n6
72	138, 168
72:1–2	138
73	132
74:1	28
74:4–11	28
74:12–17	27n14, 28
74:13–14	34
74:18–23	28
77	132
78	132, 134, 135
78:1–8	135
78:9–10	135
78:9–66	135
78:11–64	135
78:60	128
79:1–5	28
79:6–9	28
79:10–13	28
80:1	147
81:6–13	329
81:10	94
82	132
87	132
89:5–10	34
89:6	34
89:10–11	27n14
89:19	40n6
89:26–27	134
91	132
91:11–12	220
92	132
95:6–11	329
97	132
97:2–5	92
99:1	147
106	132
106:19	91n2
107	132
110	132
111:4	104n6
112:4	104n6
115:4–8	96
115:9–11	40n6
117:1	285
121:1f	40n6
124:8	40n6
130	108
130:3–4	108
132	133
132:2, 5	148n6
132:14	133
134:3	132

135:15–18	96	29:18	228
137	177	30:5	40n6
137:1, 4	28	35:5–6	228
137:8–9	28	36:22	113
139:1–12	107	36–39	170
139:13–18	107	37:5–7	169
139:19–24	108	37:36–38	169
144:5–8	220	39	180
146:5	40n6	40:1–2	180
		40:11	184
Proverbs		40:18	184, 186
		40:19–20	181
8:22–31	316	40:25	184
16:18–19	233	40:27	181
25:21	153n13	40:28–31	181
		40–55	184n16
		40–66	183
Ecclesiastes		41:2	182
1:2	301	41:6–7, 21–24	181
		41:8–9	181
Isaiah		41:9–10	182
		41:21–24	183
	167	41:25	182
1:10–17	166	41:26–29	182
2:2–4	170	42	253
2:11, 17	166	42:1	218
3:16–24	166	42:1–7	182
5:1–7	248	42:7, 18	228
5:1–11	285	42:17	181
5:8	166	42:18–25	181
5:15	166	43:1	181
6:9–10	288	43:2–7	181
7:1–9	168n6	43:3–4	184
7:4, 7	168	43:5–6	332
9:1–7	168	43:8–21	181
9:6	168	43:14–25	183n12
10:5–6	168	43:15	183
10:12	168	43:16–20	183
10:20–23	168	44:6–8	183
10:24–27	168	44:9–20	181
11	253	44:21–22	181
11:1, 10	285	44:23	181
14:13	139	44:28–45:1	182
26:19	228	44:28–45:7	181
27:1	34	45:9–19	181
28:15, 18	169	45:13	182
29:9–10	278	45:14	182
29:14b	278	45:22–23	182
29:17–21	279	45:23	294

Scripture Index

Isaiah–continued

46:1–2	184
46:3–4	184
46:5	184
48:8	184
48:9–11	185
49	253
49:1–6	275
49:15	104
49:23, 26	194
49:24–25	228
49:26	148n6
50:1	162
51:2	162
52:13–53:12	218
52–53	253
53	191
53:7–8	308
54:1–10	162
55	183
56:1–8	193
56:3–8	80
56:7	238
56:8	80n9
60	191, 194
60:1, 3	194
60:12	194
60:16	148n6
60:20–21	194
61:1–2	229
64:1–2	220
64:1a, 2b	278
66	183
66:23	97n21

Jeremiah

1:1, 5	332
1:5	275
2:2–3	158, 172
2:4–8	158
2:9–19	158
2:20–25	158
2:26–37	158
3:1–5	158
3:1–14	236
3:6–1:1	159
3:12–14	159
3:15–18	159
4:19–22	159
7:1–15	171
7:11	238
7:12	128
7:16	163
7:31	115
9:23–24	279
10:23–12:17	163
10:23–25	163
11:1–13	163
11:9–17	163
11:14	163
11:18–23	163
12:7	163
12:14–17	163
14:11	163
16:2	159
18:18–23	163
19:4–6	115
19–29	177n1
22:24	190
23:5	190n3
24	171
25:24	89n28
26:16–19	171
26:17–19	167
27:1–6, 11	171
27:5–7	182, 182n11
28:1–17	171
29:1–14	171
30:7b–8	172
30–33	172
31:2–3	172
31:3	160
31:9	217
31:9b	160
31:9b, 20	172
31:11	172
31:20	160
31:31–34	172
31:32	172
31:33	284
31:33–34	173
31:34	334
32:35	115
33:15	190n3
34:18–20	64
34–44	177n1
44:15–19	177

46–51	172	28:19	144
48:13	66n9	39:25	180
50:27	89n28		

Lamentations

Daniel

3:13	179		196
		2:31–45	196
		7	196, 253, 254n7

Ezekiel

		7:2–8	196
		7:9–14	196
1:1	177	7:13–14	252n2, 253
1:5, 26	179	7:14, 18, 22, 25, 27	253
1:22, 26, 28	178	7:14, 27	254
1:26	255	7:23–27	197
1:28b	270	8:1–25	197n20
2:1	252	8–12	197
2:3–7	178	8:15, 27	253
2:4	179	8:17	253
3:11	179	8:17, 19	197
10:15, 20	178	8:25	197n20
12:14	40n6	9:2	253
16:1–3	161	9:27	195
16:4–8	161	10:2, 7	253
16:9–34	161	10:14	197
16:33–42	161	11:34	40n6
16:35–43a	161	11:35	197
16:43b–52	161	12:4, 9	197
16:53–58	161	12:5	253
16:59–63	161, 180	12:13	197
20:1–9	161		
20:10–17	161		
20:18–26	161	## Hosea	
20:19–32	161		
20:25–26	115	1:2	155
20:43–44	161, 285	1:3	156
20:44	185	1:6, 8–9	156
23	160	1:6, 9	287
23:1–4	160	2:1	156
23:5–49	161	2:2 H 2:4	156
28:1–19	141, 143	2:2–15	156
28:2	143	2:2–20	236
28:3	143	2:7 H 2:9	156
28:4, 13	143	2:8–13 H 2:10–15	156
28:5	143	2:14–15 H 2:16–17	156
28:12b–15a	39	2:14–20	256
28:13	143	2:16–20	217
28:14, 16	144	2:16–20 H 2:18–22	156
28:15	143	2:17	155
28:16	144	2:21–23 H 2:23–25	156
		2:23b	287

Scripture Index

Hosea–continued

3:1	156
3:23	156
4:1–19	155
4–5	21
4:8	257
5:14	21
6:6a	167
8:4–6	166
8:4a	156
8:8	287, 289
8:8, 9b	157
9:15	156
9:30–33	287
10:5–6	166
10:13b–14a	167
10:18–19	156
11:1	217, 287n10
11:1, 8–9	256
11:1–2	157
11:1–10	240
11:5–7	157
11:8	21
11:8–9	157
12:9	94
13:4–6	155
13:8	21
13:9	40n6, 163
13:11	130
13:12	166
14:4	157

Joel

2:28–29 H 3:1–2	331, 332
2:28–32	306
2:30–32a	93
2:32	288
3:1–17 H 4:1–17	194

Amos

1:1–2:6	131
1:2a	164
1:3–2:3	21, 157, 164
2:4–3:2	21
2:4–8	164
2:6–7a	165
2:7b	165
2:8	166
3:1–2	165
3:3	157
3:15	166
4:1	166
4:6–12	165
4:12–13	165
5:11	166
5:21–24	166
6:4–6	166
8:5	97n21
9:1–12	131
9:7–8	165
9:11–12	158, 158n4, 310

Jonah

3:10	104, 256
4:2	104
34:28	104

Micah

2:2	166
3:9–11	167
3:12	167
5:1–5a	172
6:9–16	166

Habakkuk

2:18–20	96
3:3	83

Zephaniah

3:20	194

Haggai

1:1–15	190
2:1–9	190
2:21–23	190

Zechariah

2:6–13	190
2:11	193
3:8	190

Scripture Index

4:6–10	190	6:8	236, 240
6:9–13	190	7:12	345
6:12	190	7:45–52	249
9:9–10	172	8:1–4	227, 231
14:16–19	194	8:5–12	212
41:4b	193	9:8	257, 258
41:24	193	9:9–13	232, 244
43:10–11	193	9:13	167
44:6	193	9:20–22	231
44:24b	193	9:20–23	227
45:6–7, 12	193	9:23–25	227
45:18	193	10:1	251
45:21b	193	10:1–4	232
46:9	193	10:5–6	212n23
		11:2–6	228
		11:5	228
Malachi		11:26	240
1:6–2:9	215	12:1–8	236
4:1–3 H 3:19–21	215	12:7	167
4:4	91n2	12:9–14	236
4:5 H 3:23	215	12:24	222
		12:24–29	228
		12:27	251
		12:43–45	216
NEW TESTAMENT		13:1–9	233
		13:10–15	243
Matthew		13:57	333
		14:3–12	215
	210	15:1–20	232
1:2–17	212	16:13–14	222
1:3–6	130	17:24–27	217
1:18–25	212	18:15–28	212
2:1–12	212n24	19:1–9	236n7
2:16–18	198	19:10	236
2:25	249	19:16–30	247
3:1–6	214	19:23	239
3:2	215	19:30	247
3:7	215	20:1–10	254n8
3:7–10	216	20:1–15	339
3:9	215	20:1–16	247, 248
4:1–11	218	20:13–15	247
4:10	252	20:16	247
5:3–12	241	20:20–28	233
5:23–24	98	20:26–28	234
5:23–28	213n25	21:11	333n17
5:28	99n25	21:23–37	217
5:39–41	242	21:26	215
5:44	240	21:33–46	248, 254n8
5:44–45	153n13, 344	22:1–14	248, 254n8
5:44–45, 48	242		
5:45	240		

383

Scripture Index

Matthew–continued

22:16	249
22:37–40	344
23:1–36	233
23:9–12	233
25:1–46	254
25:14–30	246–247, 254
25:24–25	246
25:29	246
25:31–46	254
25:41, 46	254
26:53	280
26:64	252
28:9	271
28:16–20	212n24
28:17	271

Mark

	210
1:2–6	214
1:4	216
1:5	216
1:6	215
1:9–11	216
1:12–13	217, 222
1:23–26	223, 223n5
1:25	252n1
1:30–31	223
1:40–45	227, 231
2:1–12	256, 290
2:8	257
2:11–12	257
2:13–17	232
2:15	232
2:23–27	236
2:27	97, 237
3:1–6	236
3:4	236
3:5	237
3:6	237
3:13–19	232
3:14–15	251
3:20–21	342
3:20–22	216n8
3:21	222
3:22	222
3:22–27	228
3:22–30	342
3:31–35	342
4:1	222
4:1–9	233
4:10–12	243
4:39	252n1
5:1–20	212, 224, 234
5:25–34	227, 231
5:35–43	227
6:4	222, 333
6:7	251
6:17–29	215
7:1–23	232
7:24–30	212, 224
7:33–35	223
8:27–28	222
8:27–30	251
8:30, 32, 33	252n1
8:31	252
9:38–39	251
9:38–40	342
10:2–9	235
10:5–8	40
10:5–9	235
10:11–12	236
10:23	239
10:35–45	233
10:42b–45	235
10:43–45	234
11:15–19	237
11:17	80n9
11:17–18	238
11:27–33	217
11:32	215
12:1–12	248
12:29–31	213, 344
12:38–40	245
12:40	238
12:41–44	238
13:14	195
14:36	217, 320
14:57	237
14:61–2	252
15:31b–32	278
15:40–41	233
29:13	278
29:14	279
29:15–16	279

Luke

	210, 305
1:1–3	305
1:8–9	214
2:80	214
3:1	201n3
3:1–6	214
3:3	216
3:5–7	219
3:7	215n4
3:7–9	216
3:8	215
3:10–13	215
3:23–38	218
4:1	222
4:1–13	218
4:3	218
4:4	219
4:8	220
4:12	220
4:16–21	333
4:16–30	229
4:18–19	229
4:19	333n17
4:25–27	148n8
4:27	344
4:38–39	223
5:12–16	227, 231
5:27–32	232
6:1–5	236
6:6–11	236
6:12–16	232
6:14	333n17
6:15	232n4
6:20–26	241
6:27	240
6:27–8	242
6:35	236, 240
6:35–36	242
6:43–48	227
7:11–17	227
7:16	333n17
7:18–23	228
7:40	333n17
8:1–3	233
8:4–8	233
8:4–9	233
8:9–10	243
8:26–39	234
8:29–31	216
8:43–48	231
8:49–56	227
9:1–2	251
9:7–9	222
9:17	333n17
9:18–19	222
9:49–50	251
10:17	251
10:21	240
10:25–28	213n25
10:25–37	213, 344
10:33	308
10:38–42	234
11:11–13	240
11:15	222
11:15–22	228
11:19	251
11:20	255
12:54–13:5	344
13:10–17	236
13:16	223n6, 224
13:34	344
13:37	333n17
14:1–6	236
15:1	244
15:1–2	232, 243
17:11–19	212, 227
17:16	308
17:20–21	229
18:1, 6–8	245
18:1–8	245
18:9–14	244–245
18:14a	244
18:24	239
18:26	246
19:11–27	246–247
19:27	247
20:1–8	217
20:6	215
20:9–19	248
20:21	28
20:46–47	245
20:47	238
21:1–4	238
21:5–6, 20	344
22:24–27	233
22:67–69	252
24:13–31	271

Luke–continued

24:19	333n17
24:36–43	355
24:39–43	271

John

	210
1:1–2	317
1:1–5	34n2
1:1–14	316, 333
1:9	19
1:19–23	214
1:29b	19
2:10	248
2:23–3:12	248–249
2:23–25	248
3:1–12	248
3:16–17	19
3:35	318
4:1–42	249
4:9, 39, 40	308
4:42	249
4:43	222
5:19–23, 26	318
5:27	254
6:42	248
7:3–5	222
7:15	233
7:27	248
8:52	248
9:2	257
9:4	248
9:24	248
10:30	258, 318
11:10	248
11:47–53	250
11:50	280
12:32	19
13:30	248
14:9	324
14:28	258, 318
17:3	318
17:20–23	258, 272
17:21–23	318
19:39	249
20:17	259
20:19–22	290
20:19–23	258
20:27	271
21:3	248

Acts

	12, 305–306
1:15–26	306
1:21–22	312
2:1–4	306, 332
2:5–13	306
2:11	332
2:13	332
2:14–21	306
2:14–21, 41	93
2:15–18	332
2:22–41	306
2:42–47	306
2:46	321
3:1	321
3:22–24	333n17
4:13	233
4:23–31	306
4:32–37	306
5:1–11	64n7, 306
6:1	307
6:2–6	307
6:15	307
7:2–8	307
7:8	307
7:9–10	307
7:9–44	307
7:11–14	307
7:44–53	307
7:45	117n2
7:54–60	308
7:58	264, 308
8:1, 3	308
8:2	308
8:4–13	308
8:14–17	332
8:14–18	308
8:27	308
8:34–40	308
8:39–40	308
9:1–20	308
9:11	264
9:19b–25	298
9:37–41	227
9:43	308

10:1–8	308	21:17–36	294, 313		
10:1–11:18	313	21:23–24, 26	321		
10:6, 32	308	22:1–21	308		
10:28, 34–35	309	22:3	264		
10:34	28	26:1–29	308		
10:34–35	342	26:30–32	313		
10:34–48	309	28:30–31	313		
10:44–48	332				
11:1–3	309	**Romans**			
11:4–18	309				
11:19–26	309		263n1, 305		
11:27–29	309	1:7	296, 319		
11:27–30	332	1:16	283		
12:1–25	309	1:18–3:20	283		
13:1	309	1:18–32	283		
13:4–14:28	310	2:4	285		
13:46–47	310	2:7–11	284		
14:8–10	266	2:9–10	283		
15	311, 313	2:11	28, 283, 289		
15:1	310	2:14–15	342		
15:2–11	310	2:18	283		
15:7–11	313	3:22	286		
15:16–17	158, 158n4	3:25	285		
15:20	310	3:29	283		
15:22–25	310	4:1–5	65		
15:36–19:41	312	4:3	285		
15:36–41	311	4:13, 16	80n7		
16:1–3	311n10	4:16–18	285		
16:16–18	266	4:17b	285		
17:16–33	353	4:24	286		
17:22	353	4:24–5	285		
17:23b–29	354	5:3–4	226		
17:25	354	5:6, 10	352		
17:32	355	5:12–21	286		
18:1–3	276	5:14, 18	271		
18:5–11	276	5:15	286		
18:12–17	276	5:18	19, 286, 287		
18:24–19:1	276	5:20	286		
19:12	266	6–7	268		
19:14–20	266	6:12–14	268		
20:4	313	6:16	273		
20:7–10	227	7	269n8		
20:8–10	266	7:7–24	99n25		
20:22–25	313	7:7–25	269		
21:3	234	7:8	269		
21:8	308	7:9–8:2	284		
21:8–9	332	7:10	269		
21:8–13	313	7:12	269		
21:10–11	332	7:14	269		

Scripture Index

Romans–continued

7:15–20a	269
7:20b	269
7:21	268n4
7:24–25	269
7:25–8:2	269
8	269n8, 351
8:2	268n4
8:11	272
8:15	320
8:19–23	301
8:20–21	289
8:29	334
8:29–30	288
8:31b	351
8:35	351
8:36	351
8:37–39	351
9:1–4	287
9:6–13	287
9:11	287
9–11	289, 336, 351
9:16–18	287
9:19–23	287
9:24	287
9:25–26	287
10:1	288
10:12–13	288
10:19–21	288
11:1a, 2a	288
11:8	288
11:12	288
11:13–24	335
11:25	288
11:25b–26a	289
11:26	336
11:32	287, 289, 351
11:32a	19
11:33–36	289
11:35	352
12:1–21	273
12:6–8	332
12:20	153n13
12:21	243
14:5a	293
14:5b–6	294
14:11	19
14:11–12	294
14:14–15	293
14:17	355
15:7–12	285
15:19	312
15:22–33	312
16:1–2	297
16:3	297
16:7	297
16:9	297
16:21	297

1 Corinthians

	263n1, 305
1:1	297
1:2	296
1:3	319
1:10–12	277
1:12	277
1:13	278
1:17–25	278
1:18–3, 4	279
1:18–24	279
1:18–25	277
1:20–21	279
1:25	277
1:26	279
1:26b–31	279
1:27–28	279
2:6, 8	279
2:7	279
2:7–8	280
2:10, 12	279
2:12	279
2:14	279
2:15	279
2:16	279, 297
3:1, 3	279
3:4	279
3:5	296
3:8	296, 296n7
3:9	295, 296
3:16–17	295
3:21–23	297
4:9–13	312
4:16	274
5:1–8	295
5:9–13	276
6:12	292, 295
6:12–13	300n9
6:16	295, 300n10

6:19	300n10
6:19–20	295
7:1	300n9
8:1	292
8:4	292, 293
8:5–6	293, 319
8:16–24	313
9:1	272n14
9:1–2	312
9:1–12	293
9:4–12	274
10:14–22	293
10:20	293
10:23	292
10:26	292
10:31–11:1	293
11:1	274, 292, 299
11:3	299
11:4–16	332
11:7	299, 334
11:8–9	299
11:11–12	299
11:14–15	299
11:25	173
12:1–14:33	300
12:2–3	265
12:8–10	332
12:29	266
13:1–13	274
14:1	274
14:1–5	332
14:1–12	332
14:18	266
14:26	300
14:31–33	300
14:34–35	300
14:37–40	300
14:40	300
15	286, 319
15:8	270, 272n14
15:9–10a	265
15:20–28	359
15:22	20, 271, 286
15:24, 26	281n11
15:24–26	281
15:25–26, 28	319
15:27–28	290
15:28	281, 357
15:35–49	356
15:44	270
15:45	286
15:45–49	271
15:50	355
15:50–57	301
15:51–52	313
16:1–4	312
16:10	297
16:12	297

2 Corinthians

	263n1, 305
1:1	296, 297
1:2–3	319
2:1–17	276
3:6	173
4:4	334
4:5	272
4:6	270
5:11–20	285
5:17–18	301
5:19	20, 108, 285, 291, 352
8–9	312
8:23	297
10:8	272
11:4–5	312
11:8–9, 11–12	41
11:21b–29	312
12:1–10	312
12:2–4	267
12:7	269n7
12:11	312
12:19	272
13:10	272
15:24–28	289

Galatians

	263n1, 305
1:3	319
1:6	266n8
1:11–12, 15–17	312
1:11–24	311
1:13	264, 272
1:13–14	263
1:15–16	275
1:16	268n1, 271
1:16–17	332

Galatians–continued

1:25	283
2:3–4	311
2:3–5	311
2:6	28, 289, 311
2:7–10	311
2:11–14	311
2:13–14	311
2:15	283
2:19	273
2:19–20	268
2:20	272
3:3, 5	266
3:10–14	265
3:14, 18	80n7
3:26–28	298
4:6	320
4:8–9	294
4:10	294
4:13	269n7
5:13–26	348
5:16–26	273
5:24	273

Ephesians

	263n1
1:9–10	20, 163, 282
1:10	17, 33
1:12–16	336
1:20 KJV	18
2:1–10	18
2:11–22	18
6:21	297

Philippians

	263n1, 305
1:1	297
1:2	319
2:5–11	280–281, 319
2:9–11	20
2:10–11	319
2:22	297
2:25	298
3:5–6	263
3:6	264
3:17	274, 292

3:20–21	20, 281
4:2–3	298
4:3	298

Colossians

	263n1
1:1	298
1:5	334
1:15–20	282
1:19–20	20, 163
1:20	81
3:10	334
4:7	298
4:9	298
4:10	298
4:10–11	298
4:12	298

1 Thessalonians

	263n1, 305
1:1, 3	319
1:5	266
1:9–10	284
3:9	284
3:21–5:11	284
3:22	284
3:22–25a	284
4:13–17	301
4:15–17	313
4:16	93n8

2 Thessalonians

	263n1

1 Timothy

1:12–17	265
2:3–4	20
2:5–6	338
2:14	42
4:9–10	338
4:10	20, 70

Titus

2:11	20

Philemon

	263n1, 305
1	298
2	298
3	319
23	298
24	298

Hebrews

1:1–2	333
1:3	333
2:4–17	156
2:17	334
4:8	117n2
4:15–17	334
5:1–6	334
5:13	143
8:1–7	334
8:1–13	173
8:12	334
9:4	100n29
11:8–12	65

James

1:1	313n11
3:10	334

1 Peter

1:1	333
2:5, 9	333

1 John

4:8, 16	357
Jude	
	319
25	320

Revelation

1:5–6	333
5:9–10	333
5:13–14	20
11:19	100n29
12:9, 14–15	41
20:2	41
22:20	320

APOCRYPHA

1 Maccabees

196	
2 Maccabees	196
Wisdom of Solomon	316n7
9:4	316
10:1–11:14	316

Sirach

44:21	285n7

OTHER APOCRYPHA

Thomas	
	210
1 Enoch	
	254, 319
48	253, 253n5
71	253n6
2 Enoch	
	319
Jubilees	
	319
22:14	285n7
32:19	285n7

Author Index

Adamson, Joel Edmund, 104
Alexander, Eben, 50, 356
Allen, Leslie, 179
Anderson, A.A., 134
Aquinas, Thomas, 340
Ashton, John, 216, 266, 267, 268, 270, 283
Avner, Uri, 96

Barker, Margaret, 316–317
Barrett, C. K., 265
Barth, Karl, 325
Barth, Markus, 294
Berry, Wendell, 36n8
Bickerman, Elias, 194
Bonhoeffer, Dietrich, 323–324
Boring, Eugene, 224
Bourguignon, Erika, 205n15
Boyarin, Daniel, 211n20
Brichto, Herbert, 54, 87
Brueggemann, Walter, 57, 134, 187
Buber, Martin, 62–63, 85, 88, 97, 128, 139

Calvin, John, 2, 15, 288
Carman, John B., 3–4
Carroll, James, 335
Castaneda, Carlos, 206
Childs, Brevard, 114
Clark, William, 37n9
Cornfeld, Gaalya, 200, 201
Craffert, Pieter, 204, 205, 216–217, 223, 228, 229, 253, 254, 267, 355
Crane, Henry, 227, 227n18
Cross, Frank M., 66
Crusemann, Frank, 59

d'Aquili, Eugene, 49–50, 318, 348
Davies, James, 225–226
Dearman, Andrew, 166
del Vasto, Joseph Jean Lanza, 340
Descartes, René, 224–225
Donne, John, 36
Durham, John, 99

Einstein, Albert, 50, 341

Fenn, Richard, 198
Flanagan, James F., 130n5
Frankfort, H. and H. W., 51
Fredriksen, Paula, 95, 284, 295, 312
Fry, Douglas P., 345

Galtung, Johan, 341
Gandhi, Mohandas K., 339–342
Garr, Randall, 35
Gelander, Shamai, 133
Gottwald, Norman K., 88, 112
Green, Joel B., 186, 327
Grundstein, Michael, 37n9

Halpern, Baruch, 112
Hanson, Paul D., 196
Haymon, Peter, 315, 316
Henderlite, Rachel, 18–19
Herrmann, Siegfried, 77, 138, 147
Herzog, William R. II, 243, 244
Hollenbach, Paul W., 215
Hopper, Margaret Ruth, 18, 325n30, 351–352
Hulst, A. R., 63
Hurowitz, Victor, 96n16
Huxley, Thomas Henry, 45

Author Index

Irenaeus, 43
Ishida, Ei-ichirō, 23n2, 51, 203

Jacob, Benno, 103

Kim, Seyoon, 290
Kimbangu, Simon, 226, 227, 266n7
King, Martin Luther, Jr., 340
Knoppers, Gary, 130n4

Lampe, G. H. W., 282
Lang, Bernhard, 62n3
Langdon, Stephen, 55
Levenson, Jon D., 35, 100, 154, 327
Luther, Martin, 93, 288

MacLean, Paul, 45
Malone, Calvin, 348–349
McClelland, Mac, 346–347
McGrath, James, 321
Meyer, Ben F., 229–230
Miles, Jack, 87
Miller, Patrick D., 35, 84
Morse, Melvin, 46–47
Myers, Ched, 256

Nash, Ogden, 60
Nelson, Richard, 191
Nelson-Pallmeyer, Jack, 323
Newberg, Andrew, 45, 46, 49–50, 318, 348, 349, 356
Nielsen, Eduard, 97
Noth, Martin, 114

O'Collins, Gerald, 193
Origen of Alexandria, 317

Pederson, Johannes, 64
Philo, 12–13, 34n2, 267, 316, 317, 319
Pinker, Steven, 345–46
Polley, Max, 164
Propp, William H. C., 89
Rainey, Anson, 83
Rendtorff, Rolf, 80
Ring, Kenneth, 47–48, 270, 275
Rolston, Holmes, III, 35–36
Rubenstein, Richard, 336–337
Ruskin, John, 339

Sagan, Carl, 45
Sanders, E. P., 289, 291, 294
Schottroff, Luise, 237
Segal, Alan F., 267

Seitz, Christopher, 87, 170
Shantz, Colleen, 273
Sharp, Gene, 341–342
Smith, Morton, 206
Staples, Jason, 287, 289
Stegemann, Ekkehard and Wolfgang, 237
Stoebe, H. J., 67, 103

Taylor, Jill Bolte, 48, 348
Taylor, Vincent, 217
Theissen, Gerd, 179
Thoreau, Henry David, 340
Tolstoy, Leo, 339
Torrance, Thomas F., 323, 324–325
Tucker, Grayson, 258

von Rad, Gerhard, 327

Waetjen, Herbert C., 251, 255, 334
Waldman, Mark, 349
Warfield, Benjamin B., 15–17, 21, 33, 36, 41, 282, 289
Watts, John D. W., 167–168, 180, 190–191
Weber, Thomas, 339n1
Weizmann, Chaim, 199
Welch, Adam C., 94, 329
Wink, Walter, 25, 178, 237, 242, 255, 256, 257, 269
Woolley, Leonard, 55

www.ingramcontent.com/pod-product-compliance
Lightning Source LLC
Chambersburg PA
CBHW080932020526
44116CB00033B/2135